GLOBAL STUDIES

JAPAN AND THE PACIFIC RIM

THIRD EDITION

STAFF

Ian A. Nielsen   Publisher
Brenda S. Filley   Production Manager
Lisa M. Clyde   Developmental Editor
Charles Vitelli   Designer
Cheryl Nicholas   Permissions Coordinator
Lisa Holmes-Doebrick   Administrative Coordinator
Shawn Callahan   Graphics
Lara M. Johnson   Graphics
Steve Shumaker   Graphics
Laura Levine   Graphics
Libra Ann Cusack   Typesetting Supervisor
Juliana Arbo   Typesetter
Diane Barker   Proofreader

GLOBAL STUDIES

JAPAN AND THE PACIFIC RIM

THIRD EDITION

Dr. Dean W. Collinwood
Weber State University

Dushkin Publishing Group/Brown & Benchmark Publishers
Sluice Dock, Guilford, Connecticut 06437

Japan and the Pacific Rim

OTHER BOOKS IN THE GLOBAL STUDIES SERIES

- Africa
- China
- India and South Asia
- Latin America
- The Middle East
- Russia, the Eurasian Republics, and Central/Eastern Europe
- Western Europe

Library of Congress Cataloging in Publication Data
Main Entry under title: Global Studies: Japan and the Pacific Rim. 3rd ed.
        1. East Asia—History—20th century–. 2. East Asia—Politics and government—20th century–. I. Title: Japan and the Pacific Rim. II. Collinwood, Dean W., *comp.*
ISBN 1–56134–380–3   950   91–71258

Third Edition

Printed in the United States of America

Japan and the Pacific Rim

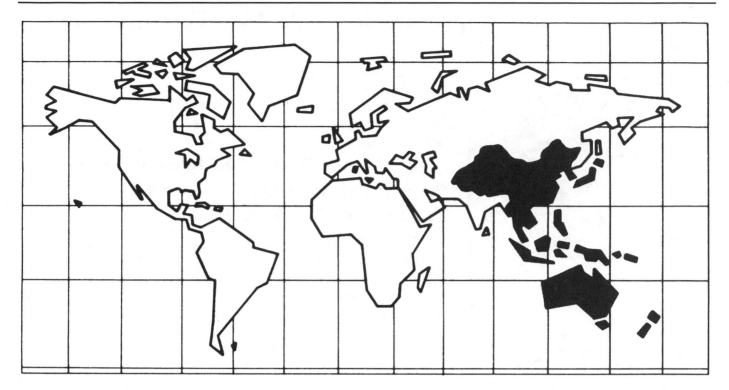

AUTHOR/EDITOR

Dr. Dean W. Collinwood

The author/editor of *Global Studies: Japan and the Pacific Rim* is Director of Asian Studies and Associate Professor of Sociology and Anthropology at Weber State University in Utah. He is also Director of the Utah Asian Studies Consortium and its United States–Japan Industry and Technology Management Training Center. His Ph.D. is from the University of Chicago; his M.Sc., in International Relations, is from the University of London; and his B.A., in Political Science with a minor in Japanese, is from Brigham Young University.

Dr. Collinwood has been a Fulbright Scholar at the University of Tokyo and Tsuda College in Japan and has conducted research in East Asia, South and Southeast Asia, and the Pacific. Under the auspices of the National Endowment for the Humanities and other organizations, he lectures regularly in the United States and other countries on the nature of Asian, especially Japanese, culture. He has authored several books and is currently writing on the growth of individualism in modern Japan.

SERIES CONSULTANT

H. Thomas Collins
PROJECT LINKS
George Washington University

Contents

Global Studies: Japan and the Pacific Rim, Third Edition

Pacific Rim   Page 5

Pacific Islands   Page 13

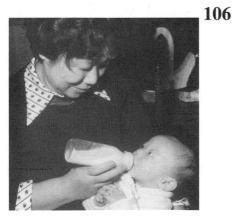

Japan   Page 31

Introduction

THE GLOBAL AGE

As we approach the end of the twentieth century, it is clear that our future will be considerably more international in nature than was ever believed possible in eras past. Each day, print and broadcast journalists make us aware that our world is becoming increasingly smaller and substantially more interdependent.

The energy crisis, world food shortages, nuclear weaponry, and regional conflicts that threaten to involve us all make it clear that the distinctions between domestic and foreign problems are all too often artificial, that many seemingly domestic problems no longer stop at national boundaries. As Rene Dubos, the 1969 Pulitzer Prize recipient, stated: "[I]t becomes obvious that each [of us] has two countries, [our] own and planet Earth." As global interdependence has become a reality, it has become vital for the citizens of this world to develop literacy in global matters.

THE GLOBAL STUDIES SERIES

It is the aim of the Global Studies series to help readers acquire a basic knowledge and understanding of the regions and countries in the world. Each volume provides a foundation of information—geographic, cultural, economic, political, historical, artistic, and religious—that will allow readers to better understand the current and future problems within these countries and regions and to comprehend how events there might affect their own well-being. In short, these volumes attempt to provide the background information necessary to respond to the realities of our global age.

Author/Editor
Each of the volumes in the Global Studies series is crafted under the careful direction of an author/editor—an expert in the area under study. The author/editors teach and conduct research and have traveled extensively through the regions about which they are writing.

In this *Japan and the Pacific Rim* edition, the author/editor has written regional essays on the Pacific Rim and the Pacific Islands, and country reports for each of the countries covered, including a special report on Japan. In addition, he has been instrumental in the selection of the world press articles that appear in this volume.

Contents and Features
The Global Studies volumes are organized to provide concise information and current world press articles on the regions and countries within those areas under study.

Regional Essays
For *Global Studies: Japan and the Pacific Rim, Third Edition,* the author/editor has written narrative essays focusing on the religious, cultural, sociopolitical, and economic differ-

(United Nations/Yutaka Nagata)
The global age is making all countries and all peoples more interdependent.

ences and similarities of the countries and peoples in the region. The purpose of the regional essays is to provide readers with an effective sense of the diversity of the area as well as an understanding of its common cultural and historical backgrounds. Accompanying the essays are maps showing the boundaries of the countries within the region.

Country Reports
Concise reports are written for each of the countries within the region under study. These reports are the heart of each Global Studies volume. *Global Studies: Japan and the Pacific Rim, Third Edition,* contains 20 country reports, including the lengthy report on Japan.

The country reports are composed of five standard elements. Each report contains a small, semidetailed map visually positioning the country among its neighboring states; a detailed summary of statistical information; a current essay providing important historical, geographical, political, cultural, and economic information; a historical timeline, offering a convenient visual survey of a few key historical events; and four graphic indicators, with summary statements about the country in terms of development, freedom, health/welfare, and achievements.

A Note on the Statistical Summaries

The statistical information provided for each country has been drawn from a wide range of sources. (The 10 most frequently referenced are listed on page 240.) Every effort has been made to provide the most current and accurate information available. However, occasionally the information cited by these sources differs to some extent; and, all too often, the most current information available for some countries is dated. Aside from these difficulties, the statistical summary of each country is generally quite complete and up to date. Care should be taken, however, in using these statistics (or, for that matter, any published statistics) in making hard comparisons among countries. We have also provided comparable statistics for Canada and the United States, which follow on the next two pages.

World Press Articles

Within each Global Studies volume is reprinted a number of articles carefully selected by our editorial staff and the author/editor from a broad range of international periodicals and newspapers. The articles have been chosen for currency, interest, and their differing perspectives on the subject countries. There are 32 articles in *Global Studies: Japan and the Pacific Rim, Third Edition.*

The articles section is preceded by an annotated table of contents as well as a topic guide. The annotated table of contents offers a brief summary of each article, while the topic guide indicates the main theme(s) of each article. Thus, readers desiring to focus on articles dealing with a particular theme, say, environment, may refer to the topic guide to find those articles.

Glossary, Bibliography, Index

At the back of each Global Studies volume, readers will find a glossary of terms and abbreviations, which provides a quick reference to the specialized vocabulary of the area under study and to the standard abbreviations (NIC, ASEAN, etc.) used throughout the volume.

Following the glossary is a bibliography, which lists general works, national histories, and current events publications and periodicals that provide regular coverage on Japan and the Pacific Rim.

The index at the end of the volume is an accurate reference to the contents of the volume. Readers seeking specific information and citations should consult this standard index.

Currency and Usefulness

This third edition of *Global Studies: Japan and the Pacific Rim,* like other Global Studies volumes, is intended to provide the most current and useful information available necessary to understand the events that are shaping the cultures of the region today.

We plan to revise this volume on a regular basis. The statistics will be updated, essays rewritten, country reports revised, and articles replaced as new information becomes available. In order to accomplish this task, we will turn to our author/editor, our advisory boards, and—hopefully—to you, the users of this volume. Your comments are more than welcome. If you have an idea that you think will make the volume more useful, an article or bit of information that will make it more current, or a general comment on its organization, content, or features that you would like to share with us, please send it in for serious consideration for the next edition.

(German Information Center/Owen Franken)
Understanding the issues and lifestyles of other countries will help make us literate in global matters.

Canada

GEOGRAPHY

Area in Square Kilometers (Miles):
9,976,140 (3,850,790) (slightly larger than the United States)
Capital (Population): Ottawa (920,000)
Climate: from temperate in south to subarctic and arctic in north

PEOPLE

Population
Total: 28,114,000
Annual Growth Rate: 1.18%
Rural/Urban Population Ratio: 23/77
Ethnic Makeup: 40% British Isles origin; 27% French origin; 20% other European; 1.5% indigenous Indian and Eskimo; 11.5% mixed
Major Languages: both English and French are official

Health
Life Expectancy at Birth: 75 years (male); 82 years (female)
Infant Mortality Rate (Ratio): 7/1,000
Average Caloric Intake: 127% of FAO minimum
Physicians Available (Ratio): 1/449

Religions
46% Roman Catholic; 16% United Church; 10% Anglican; 28% others

Education
Adult Literacy Rate: 97%

COMMUNICATION

Telephones: 18,000,000
Newspapers: 96 in English; 11 in French

TRANSPORTATION

Highways—Kilometers (Miles):
884,272 (549,133)
Railroads—Kilometers (Miles):
146,444 (90,942)
Usable Airfields: 1,142

GOVERNMENT

Type: confederation with parliamentary democracy
Independence Date: July 1, 1867
Head of State: Queen Elizabeth II
Head of Government: Prime Minister Jean Chrétien
Political Parties: Progressive Conservative Party; Liberal Party; New Democratic Party; Reform Party; Bloc Québécois
Suffrage: universal at 18

MILITARY

Number of Armed Forces: 88,000
Military Expenditures (% of Central Government Expenditures): 8.7%
Current Hostilities: none

ECONOMY

Currency ($U.S. Equivalent): 1.39 Canadian dollars = $1
Per Capita Income/GDP: $22,200/$617.7 billion
Inflation Rate: 1.9%
Total Foreign Debt: $435 billion
Natural Resources: petroleum; natural gas; fish; minerals; cement; forestry products; fur
Agriculture: grains; livestock; dairy products; potatoes; hogs; poultry and eggs; tobacco
Industry: oil production and refining; natural-gas development; fish products; wood and paper products; chemicals; transportation equipment

FOREIGN TRADE

Exports: $134 billion
Imports: $125 billion

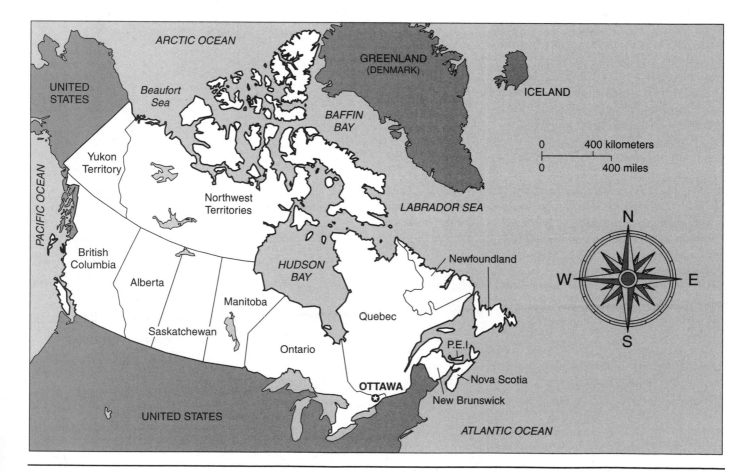

The United States

GEOGRAPHY

Area in Square Kilometers (Miles):
9,578,626 (3,618,770)
Capital (Population): Washington,
D.C. (606,900)
Climate: temperate

PEOPLE

Population
Total: 260,713,600
Annual Growth Rate: .99%
Rural/Urban Population Ratio: 26/74
Ethnic Makeup: 80% white; 12%
black; 6% Hispanic; 2% Asian,
Pacific Islander, American Indian,
Eskimo, and Aleut
Major Languages: predominantly
English; a sizable Spanish-speaking
minority

Health
Life Expectancy at Birth: 73 years
(male); 79 years (female)
Infant Mortality Rate (Ratio):
8.3/1,000
Average Caloric Intake: 138% of
FAO minimum
Physicians Available (Ratio): 1/406

Religions
55% Protestant; 36% Roman
Catholic; 4% Jewish; 5% Muslim
and others

Education
Adult Literacy Rate: 97.9% (official)
(estimates vary widely)

COMMUNICATION

Telephones: 182,558,000
Newspapers: 1,679 dailies;
approximately 63,000,000 circulation

TRANSPORTATION

Highways—Kilometers (Miles):
7,599,250 (4,719,134)
Railroads—Kilometers (Miles):
270,312 (167,974)
Usable Airfields: 12,417

GOVERNMENT

Type: federal republic
Independence Date: July 4, 1776
Head of State: President William
("Bill") Jefferson Clinton
Political Parties: Democratic Party;
Republican Party; others of minor
political significance
Suffrage: universal at 18

MILITARY

Number of Armed Forces: 1,807,177
*Military Expenditures (% of Central
Government Expenditures):* 22.6%
Current Hostilities: none

ECONOMY

Per Capita Income/GDP:
$24,700/$6.38 trillion
Inflation Rate: 3%
Natural Resources: metallic and
nonmetallic minerals; petroleum;
arable land
Agriculture: food grains; feed crops;
oil-bearing crops; livestock; dairy
products
Industry: diversified in both capital-
and consumer-goods industries

FOREIGN TRADE

Exports: $449 billion
Imports: $582 billion

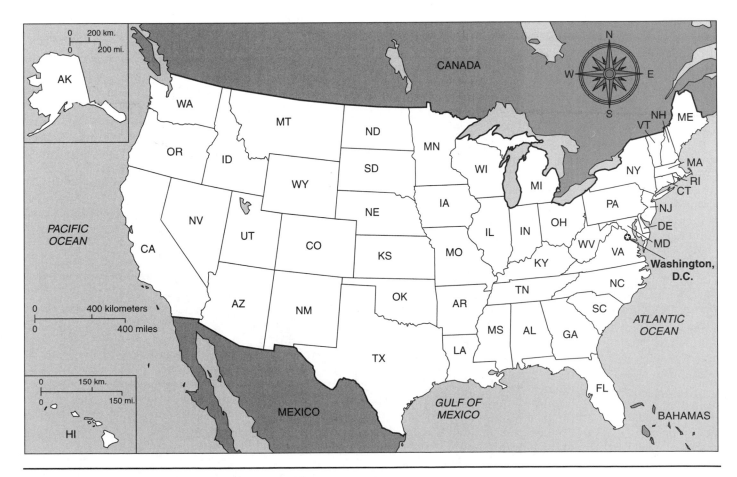

GLOBAL STUDIES

This map is provided to give you a graphic picture of where the countries of the world are located, the relationships they have with their region and neighbors, and their positions relative to the superpowers and power blocs. We have focused on certain areas to illustrate these crowded regions more clearly.

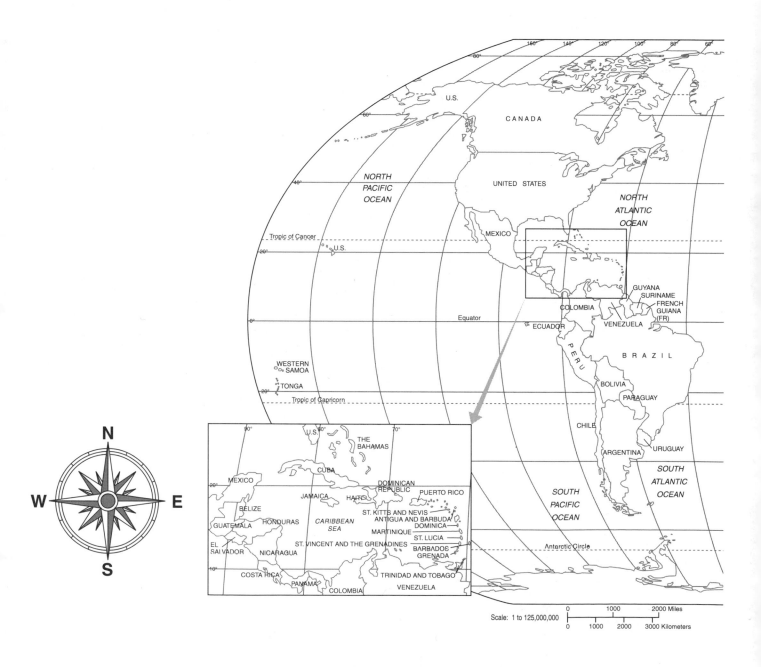

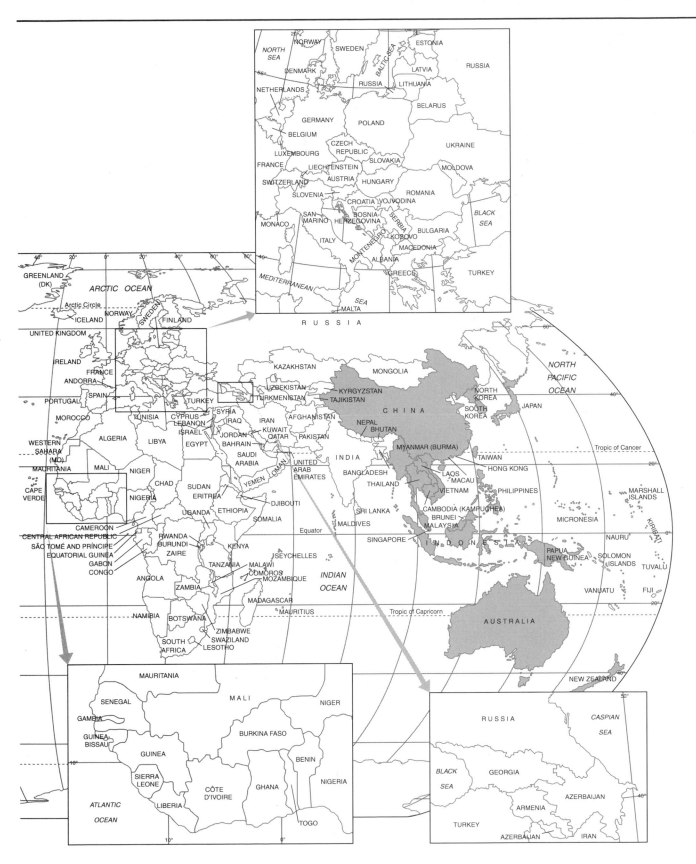

Pacific Rim Map

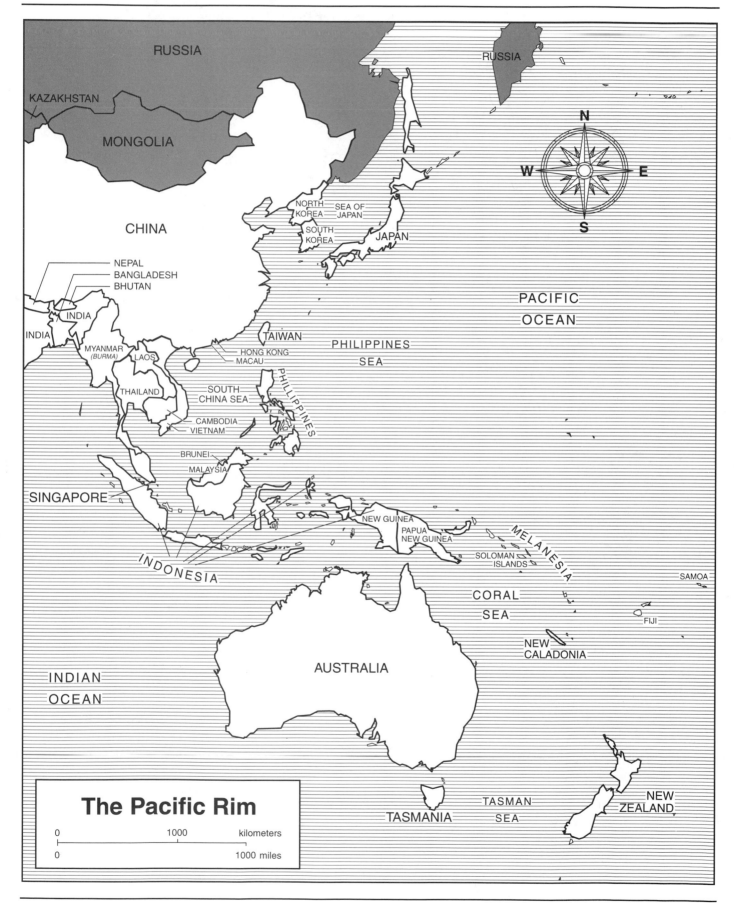

RUSSIA

KAZAKHSTAN

MONGOLIA

CHINA

NEPAL
BANGLADESH
BHUTAN

INDIA

INDIA

MYANMAR
(BURMA)
LAOS

THAILAND

CAMBODIA
VIETNAM

BRUNEI

MALAYSIA

SINGAPORE

INDONESIA

RUSSIA

N
W   E
S

NORTH
KOREA
SOUTH
KOREA

SEA OF
JAPAN

JAPAN

TAIWAN

HONG KONG
MACAU

PHILIPPINES

PHILIPPINES
SEA

SOUTH
CHINA SEA

PACIFIC

OCEAN

NEW GUINEA
PAPUA
NEW GUINEA

SOLOMAN
ISLANDS

MELANESIA

SAMOA

CORAL

SEA

FIJI

NEW
CALADONIA

AUSTRALIA

INDIAN

OCEAN

TASMANIA

TASMAN
SEA

NEW
ZEALAND

The Pacific Rim

0   1000   kilometers

0   1000 miles

The Pacific Rim: Diversity and Interconnection

WHAT IS THE PACIFIC RIM?

The term *Pacific Rim,* as used in this book, refers to 20 countries or administrative units along the Asian side of the Pacific Ocean, plus the numerous islands of the Pacific. Together, they are home to 30 percent of the world's population and produce 20 percent of the world's gross national product (GNP). It is not a simple matter to decide which countries to include in a definition of the Pacific Rim. For instance, if we were thinking geographically, we might include Mexico, Chile, Canada, the United States, Russia, and numerous other countries that border the Pacific Ocean, while eliminating Myanmar (Burma) and Laos, since they are not technically on the rim of the Pacific. But our definition, and hence our selected inclusions, stem from fairly recent developments in economic and geopolitical power that have affected the countries of Asia, Southeast Asia, and the Pacific in such a way that these formerly disparate regions are now being referred to by international corporate and political leaders as a single bloc.

Most people living in the region that we have thus defined do not think of themselves as "Pacific Rimmers." In addition, many social scientists, particularly cultural anthropologists and comparative sociologists, would prefer not to apply a single term to such a culturally, politically, and sociologically diverse region. It is true that many, but certainly not all, of the countries in question have shared similar cultural influences, such as Buddhism and rice cultivation. But commonalities have not prevented the region from fracturing into dozens of societies, often very antagonistic toward one another.

Today, however, something is arising from the region itself that could have the effect of uniting the area in an entirely new way. If current trends continue, the entire Pacific Rim will one day share a common economic system (free market/state capitalism) and some common lifestyle values (materialism and mass consumption). There will also be a common awareness of the value of peaceful interdependence of the various nations to guarantee a steady improvement in the standard of living for all and the capacity of the region to, for the first time in history, supply the basic survival needs of its inhabitants.

What are the powerful forces that are fueling these trends? There are many, including nationalism and global communications. But the one that for the past 2 decades has stood out as a defining force in the region is the yen—the Japanese currency—and its accompanying Japanese business strategy. For more than 20 years, Japanese money has been flowing throughout the Pacific Rim in the form of aid and investment, while Japan's high-tech, export-oriented approach to making money has been facilitating development and helping other regional countries to create their own engines of economic

(UN photo by J. M. Micaud)

In areas of the Pacific Rim such as Vietnam, Laos, and Cambodia, conditions are so grim that thousands of people have elected to leave their homelands and become homeless refugees, trusting that they will find a better place to live. The people pictured above are living at the Hawkings refugee camp in Singapore. In some refugee camps, the living conditions are barely survivable.

WARFARE IN SELECTED PACIFIC RIM COUNTRIES

	Civil Only	Civil/ International	International Only	Religious/ Ethnic	UN Involved	Superpower Involved	Estimated Total Deaths
Myanmar (Burma)	●						6,000 since 1985
Cambodia		●			●	●	2.2 million since 1970
China–Tibet	●						1.2 million since 1956
Indonesia–East Timor		●		●		●	100,000 since 1975
Philippines	●			●		●	35,000 since 1972
Vietnam		●				●	4.5 million (1945–1975)

Adapted from *The Nation* (January 9, 1989), p. 47.

growth in a way that none of them had experienced before. The tenacious Japanese recession of the 1990s has temporarily reduced the intensity of Japanese regional investment, allowing other high-growth countries, such as South Korea, Taiwan, and Hong Kong, to play a relatively larger role in the area. Japan's multibillion-dollar investments, however, will have effects that will be measured in decades, maybe even in centuries. Moreover, the other high-growth countries owe much of their success to the Japanese model, which they have successfully copied.

In the 1960s, when the Japanese economy had completely recovered from the devastation of World War II, the Japanese looked to North America and Europe for markets for their increasingly high-quality products. Japanese business continues to seek out markets and resources globally; but in the 1980s, in response to the movement toward a truly common European economic community as well as in response to free trade agreements among North American countries, Japan began to invest more heavily in countries nearer its own borders. The Japanese hoped to guarantee themselves market and resource access should they find their products frozen out of the emerging European and North American economic blocs. The unintended, but not unwelcome, consequences of this policy were the revitalization of many Asia–Pacific economies and the solidification of lines of communication between governments and private citizens within the region. Recognizing this interconnection has prompted many people to refer to the countries we treat in this book as a single unit, the Pacific Rim.

TROUBLES IN THE RIM

The current preponderance of media images of billionaire Japanese businesspeople and chauffeur-driven Hong Kong Chinese has overshadowed the hard realities of life for most people in the Rim. For the most part, Pacific Rim countries have not met the needs of their peoples. Whether it is the desire of affluent Japanese for larger homes and two-car garages, or of rice farmers in Myanmar for the right to sell their grain for personal profit, or of Chinese students to speak their minds without repression—in these and many other ways, the Pacific Rim has failed its peoples. In Vietnam, Laos, and Cambodia, for example, life is so difficult that thousands of families have risked their lives to leave their homelands. Some have swum across the wide Mekong River on moonless nights to avoid detection by guards, while others have sailed into the South China Sea on creaky and overcrowded boats (hence the name commonly given such refugees: "boat people"), hoping that people of goodwill, rather than marauding pirates, will find them and transport them to a land of safety. Some 20,000 Cambodians currently await repatriation in makeshift refugee camps in Thailand; thousands of ethnic villagers, driven from their homes by the Myanmar Army, await return; and thousands of Vietnamese languish in refugee camps in Hong Kong, the Philippines, Malaysia, Thailand, Singapore, and Japan. A United Nations (UN) repatriation program has sent 42,000 Vietnamese people home, but some 78,000 more are fearful of returning. Almost 14,000 Indochinese refugees reached Japan by boat

(UN photo by Shaw McCutcheon)

The numbers of elderly people in China will triple by the year 2025. Even with the strict enforcement of limiting each family to only one child, China will be faced with the increasing need of caring for retirement-age citizens. This group of elderly men in a village near Chengdu represents just the tip of an enormous problem for the future.

between 1975 and 1994, along with 3,500 Chinese nationals who posed as refugees in hopes of being allowed to live outside China. These examples, and many more not mentioned here, stand as tragic evidence of the social and political instability of many Pacific Rim nations and of the intense ethnic rivalries that divide the people of the Rim.

Warfare

Of all the Rim's troubles, warfare has been the most devastating. Not only have there been wars in which foreign powers like the United States and the former Soviet Union have been involved, but there have been numerous battles between tribes and races and religions. In Japan and China alone, an estimated 15.6 million died as a result of World War II. The chart on the previous page provides a sample of how many people have been killed in selected countries in more recent years.

The potential for serious conflict remains in most regions of the Pacific Rim. Despite intense diplomatic efforts, the outlawed Khmer Rouge continues to wage guerrilla war against the elected government of Cambodia; Japan remains locked in a dispute with Russia over ownership of islands to the north of Hokkaido; Taiwan and China still lay claim to each other's territory, as do the two Koreas; and it was not long ago that Vietnam and China were engaged in battle over their mutual boundary. Of growing concern is the area of the South China Sea. When the likelihood of large oil deposits near the rocks and reefs of the Spratly Islands was announced in the 1970s, China, Taiwan, Vietnam, the Philippines, Malaysia, and Brunei instantly laid claim to the area. By 1974 the Chinese Air Force and Navy were bombing a South Vietnamese settlement on the islands; by 1988 Chinese warships were attacking Vietnamese transport ships in the area. Both China and Vietnam have granted nearby oil-drilling concessions to different U.S. oil companies, so the situation remains tense, especially because China claims sovereignty over almost the entire South China Sea and has been flexing its muscle in the area by stopping, boarding, and sometimes

TYPES OF GOVERNMENTS IN SELECTED PACIFIC RIM COUNTRIES

PARLIAMENTARY DEMOCRACIES
Australia*
Fiji
New Zealand*
Papua New Guinea

CONSTITUTIONAL MONARCHIES
Brunei
Japan
Malaysia
Thailand

REPUBLICS
Indonesia
The Philippines
Singapore
South Korea
Taiwan

SOCIALIST REPUBLICS
China
Laos
Myanmar (Burma)
North Korea
Vietnam

OVERSEAS TERRITORIES/COLONIES
Hong Kong
French Polynesia
Macau
New Caledonia

*Australia and New Zealand have declared their intention of becoming republics by the year 2000.

ECONOMIC DEVELOPMENT IN SELECTED PACIFIC RIM COUNTRIES

Economists have divided the Rim into five zones, based on the level of development, as follows:

DEVELOPED NATIONS
Australia
Japan
New Zealand

NEWLY INDUSTRIALIZING COUNTRIES (NICs)
Hong Kong
Singapore
South Korea
Taiwan

RESOURCE-RICH DEVELOPING ECONOMIES
Brunei
Indonesia
Malaysia
The Philippines
Thailand

COMMAND ECONOMIES*
Cambodia
China
Laos
Myanmar (Burma)
North Korea
Vietnam

LESS DEVELOPED COUNTRIES (LDCs)
Papua New Guinea
Pacific Islands

*China, Vietnam, and, to a lesser degree, North Korea are moving toward free market economies.

confiscating other nations' ships in the area. In addition to these national disputes, ethnic tensions—most Asian nations are composed of hundreds of different ethnic groups with their own languages and religions—are sometimes severe. In Fiji it is the locals vs. the immigrant Indians; in South Asia it is the locals vs. the Chinese or the Muslims vs. the Christians; in China it is the Tibetans and most other ethnic groups vs. the Han Chinese.

With the end of the cold war, many Asian nations have found it necessary to seek new military and political alliances. Forced to withdraw from Vietnam and from its large naval base in the Philippines, the United States has been encouraging its ally Japan to assume a larger military role in the region. However, the thought of Japan rearming itself causes considerable fear among Pacific Rim nations, almost all of which suffered defeat at the hands of the Japanese military only 50 years ago. Nevertheless, Japan has acted to

increase its military preparedness, within the narrow confines of its constitutional prohibition against re-armament, and now has the second-largest military budget in the world (its actual expenses are huge because its economy is so large, but Japan spends only about 1 percent of its budget on defense).

In response, China has also increased its purchases of military equipment (some $2 billion of air and naval purchases from 1992 to 1994), especially from cash-strapped Russia. As a result, whereas the arms industry is in decline elsewhere, it is big business in Asia. Four of the nine largest armies in the world are in the Pacific Rim, and so the tragedy of warfare, which has characterized the region for so many centuries, could continue unless governments manage conflict very carefully and come to understand the need for mutual cooperation.

In some cases mutual cooperation is already replacing animosity. Thailand and Vietnam are engaged in sincere efforts to resolve fishing-rights disputes in the Gulf of Thailand and water-rights disputes on the Mekong River; North and South Korea have agreed to allow some cross-border visitation; and even Taiwan and China have amicably settled issues relating to fisheries, immigration, and hijackings. Yet greed and ethnic and national pride are far too often just below the surface, and when left unchecked, could catalyze a major confrontation.

Overpopulation

Another serious problem is overpopulation. There are well over 2 billion people living in the Pacific Rim. Of those, 1.1 billion are Chinese, and even though China's government has implemented the strictest family-planning policies in world history, the country's annual growth rate is such that more than 1 million inhabitants are added *every month*. This means that more new Chinese are born each year than make up the entire population of Australia. The World Health Organization (WHO) reports, however, that about 217 million people in East Asia use contraceptives today, as compared to only 18 million in 1965. Couples in some countries, including Japan, Taiwan, and South Korea, have been voluntarily limiting family size. Other states, such as China and Singapore, have promoted family planning though government incentives and punishments. The effort is paying off: The United Nations now estimates that the proportion of the global population living in Asia will remain relatively unchanged between now and the year 2025, and China's share will decline. In fact, in some countries, especially Japan, South Korea, and Thailand, single-child families and an aging population are creating problems in their own right (as is discussed later in this section).

Still, so many children have already been born that Pacific Rim governments simply cannot meet their needs. For these new Asians, schools must be built, health facilities provided, houses constructed, and jobs created. This is not an easy challenge for many Rim countries. Moreover, as the population density increases, the quality of life decreases. In crowded New York City, for example, the population is about 1,100 per square mile, and many people, thinking that is too high, have left the city for the suburbs. Yet in Tokyo the density is approximately 2,400 per square mile, and in Manila it is 51,000! Demographers predict that by the year 2000, many of the world's largest cities will be in the Pacific Rim: Shanghai, China, is projected to have 12 million people; Jakarta, Indonesia, will have well over 13 million; Manila, the Philippines, will be home to 11 million; and Bangkok, Thailand, will have nearly 11 million. Migration to the cities will continue despite miserable conditions for many (in some Asian cities, 50 percent of the population live in slum housing). One incredibly rapid-growth country is the Philippines; home to only about 7 million in 1898, when it was acquired by the United States, it is projected to have 130 million people in the year 2020.

Absolute numbers alone do not tell the whole story. In many Rim countries, 40 percent or more of the population are under age 15. Governments must provide schooling and medical care as well as plan for future jobs and housing for all these children. Moreover, as these young people age, they will require increased medical and social care. Some scholars have pointed out that between 1985 and 2025, the numbers of old people will double in Japan, triple in China, and quadruple in Korea. In Japan, where replacement-level fertility was achieved in the 1960s, government officials are already concerned about the ability of the nation to care for the growing number of retirement-age people while paying the higher wages that the increasingly scarce number of younger workers are demanding.

Political Instability

One consequence of the overwhelming problems of population growth, urbanization, and continual military conflict is disillusionment with government.

In many countries of the Pacific Rim, people are challenging the very right of their governments to rule or are demanding a complete change in the political philosophy that undergirds governments. For instance, at least three groups oppose the government of Cambodia because it was installed by the military of Vietnam. In some Rim countries, opposition groups armed with sophisticated weapons donated by foreign nations roam the countryside, capturing towns and military installations. The government of the Philippines has barely survived six coup attempts in less than a decade; elite military dissidents want to impose the old Marcos-style patronage government, while armed rural insurgents want to install a Communist government. Thousands of students have been injured or killed protesting the authoritarian governments of South Korea, China, and Myanmar. Thailand has been beset by numerous military coups, the former British colony of Fiji has recently endured two coups, and half a million residents of Hong Kong have taken to the streets to oppose Britain's decision to turn over the territory to China in 1997. Military takeovers, political assassinations, and repressive policies have been the norm in most of the countries in the region. Millions of people have spent their entire lives under governments they have never agreed with, and unrest is bound to continue because those now alive are showing less and less patience with imposed government.

Part of the reason is that the region is so fractured, between countries and, especially, within countries. In some states dozens of different languages are spoken, people practice very different religions, families trace their roots back to many different racial and ethnic origins, and wealth is distributed so unfairly that some people become well educated and well fed while others nearby remain illiterate and malnourished. Under these conditions it has been difficult for the peoples of the Rim to agree upon the kinds of government that will best serve them; all are afraid that their particular

(UN photo by John Isaac)

Some of the Pacific Rim nations are resource-rich, but development has been curtailed by political instability and a strong traditional culture. This worker is farming as his ancestors did with techniques that have not changed for hundreds of years.

language, religion, ethnic group, and/or social class will be negatively affected by any leader not of their own background.

Identity Confusion

A related problem is that of confusion about personal and national identity. Many nation-states in the Pacific Rim were created in response to Western pressure. Before Western influences came to be felt, many Asians, particularly Southeast Asians, did not identify themselves with a nation but, rather, with a tribe or an ethnic group. National unity has been difficult in many cases, because of the archipelagic nature of some countries or because political boundaries have changed over the years, leaving ethnic groups from adjacent countries inside the neighbor's territory. Years of influence from the colonial era have left many people, especially those in places like Singapore, Hong Kong, and the Pacific islands, unsure as to their roots; are they European or Asian/Pacific, or something else entirely? Indonesia illustrates this problem. People think of it as a Muslim country, as overall its populace is 87

percent Muslim, but in regions like North Sumatra, 30 percent are Protestant; in Bali 94 percent are Hindu; and in East Timor, 49 percent are Catholic and 51 percent are animist. Coups and countercoups rather than peaceful political transitions seem to be the norm because the people have not yet developed a sense of unified nationalism. The Philippines is another example. With 88 different languages spoken, its people spread out over 12 large islands, and a population explosion (the average age is 16), it is a classic case of psychological (and economic and political) fragmentation.

Uneven Economic Development

While the Japanese are wrestling with how to best invest their savings (an average of $45,000 in savings per person, when all banked savings are divided by the population), Laotians and others are worrying about where their next meal will come from. Such disparity illustrates another major problem afflicting the Pacific Rim, namely, uneven economic development.

Many Asians, especially those in the Northeast Asian countries of Japan, Korea, and China, are finding that rapid economic change seems to render the traditions of the past meaningless. For instance, almost all Japanese will state that Japan is a Buddhist country, yet few today claim any actual religious affiliation. Moreover, economic success has produced a growing Japanese interest in maximizing investment returns, with the result that Japan (and, increasingly, South Korea, Taiwan, Singapore, and Hong Kong) is successfully searching out more ways to make money, while resource-poor regions like the Pacific islands lag further behind.

The *developed nations* are characterized by political stability and long-term industrial success. Their per capita income is comparable to those of Canada, Northern Europe, and the United States, and they have achieved a level of economic sustainability. These countries are closely linked to North America economically. Japan, for instance, exports one third of its products to the United States.

The *newly industrializing countries* (NICs) are currently capturing world attention because of their rapid growth. Hong Kong, for example, has exported more manufactured products per year for the past decade than did the former Soviet Union and Central/Eastern Europe combined. Taiwan, famous for cameras and calculators, has had the highest gross national product (GNP) growth in the world for the past 20 years. South Korea is tops in shipbuilding and steel manufacturing and is the tenth-largest trading nation in the world.

The *resource-rich developing nations* have tremendous natural resources but have been held back economically by political and cultural instability and by insufficient capital to develop a sound economy. An example of a country attempting to overcome these drawbacks in Malaysia. Ruled by a coalition government representing nearly a dozen race-based parties, Malaysia is richly endowed with tropical forests and large oil and gas reserves. Developing these resources has taken years (the oil and gas fields began production as recently as 1978) and has required massive infusions of investment monies from Japan and other countries. As of 1994 more than 3,000 companies were doing business in Malaysia, and the country was moving into the ranks of the world's large exporters.

Command economies lag far behind the rest, not only because of the endemic inefficiency of the system but because military dictatorships and continual warfare have sapped the strength of the people. Significant changes in some of these countries are now emerging. China and Vietnam, in particular, are eager to modernize their economies and institute market-based reforms. Historically having directed its trade to North America and Europe, Japan is now finding its Asian/Pacific neighbors—especially the socialist-turning-capitalist ones—to be convenient recipients of its powerful economic and cultural influence.

Many of the *less developed countries* (LDCs) are the small micro-states of the Pacific with limited resources and tiny internal markets. Others, like Papua New Guinea, have only recently achieved political independence and are searching for a proper role in the world economy.

Environmental Destruction and Social Ills

Rapid development promoted by governments and private industries has raised urgent concerns about the loss of pristine forests in such countries as Malaysia and Indonesia. On the Malaysian island of Sarawak, for example, loggers work through the night using floodlights to cut timber to satisfy the demands of international customers, especially the Japanese. The forests there are disappearing at a rate of 3 percent a year. Highway and hydroelectric-dam construction in many countries in Asia has seriously affected the natural environment. While conservationists are raising the alarm about the world's declining green spaces, medical professionals are expressing dismay at the speed at which serious diseases such as AIDS are spreading in Asia. In 1994 the Thai government reported that by 1997, 2.4 million Thais (most of them between the ages of 15 and 44) will be HIV-positive. WHO officials, meeting in Japan in 1994, reported that the epidemic of AIDS is growing faster in Asia and Africa than anywhere else in the world.

GUARDED OPTIMISM

Warfare, overpopulation, political instability, identity confusion, uneven development, and environmental and social ills would seem to be an irresolvable set of problems for the people of the Pacific Rim, but the decade of the 1990s also gives reason for guarded optimism.

Reunification talks between North and South Korea are taking on a new urgency, giving hope that the military tension between the two states will begin to ease. Similarly, the UN peacekeeping effort in Cambodia seems to have paid off; at least there is a legally elected government in place, and most belligerents have put down their arms.

Most heartening of all news is the flood of reports on the growing economic strength of many Pacific Rim countries. Typical is the *World Bank Atlas 1994,* which reports high growth in GNP per capita for most Rim countries: South Korea, 8.5 percent; Hong Kong, 5.6 percent; Indonesia, 4.7 percent; Japan (despite recession), 4 percent; Malaysia, 5.7 percent; Singapore, 5.9 percent; and Thailand, 8.3 percent. By comparison, the U.S. growth rate for the same year was 1.1 percent; the United Kingdom, 1.5 percent; and Canada, 0.3 percent. Other reports on the Rim compare 1990s investment and savings percentages with those of 20 years earlier; in almost every case, there has been a tremendous improvement in the economic capacity of these countries.

The rate of economic growth in the Pacific Rim has indeed been astonishing. In 1987, for example, the rate of real gross domestic product (GDP) growth in the United States was only 3.5 percent over the previous year. By contrast, in Hong Kong, the rate was 13.5 percent; in Taiwan, 12.4 percent; in Thailand, 10.4 percent; and in South Korea, 11.1 percent. In 1992 economic growth throughout Asia averaged 7 percent, as compared to only 4.8 percent for the rest of the world. Countries like China were expected to grow an average of 10 to 12 percent per year throughout the 1990s. The significance of these data is that they reveal a shift in the source of development capital, from North America to Asia. Historically the economies of North America were regarded as the engine behind Pacific Rim growth, and yet today growth in the United States and Canada trails far behind those of the Rim economies. This anomaly can be explained, in part, by the hard work and saving ethic of Pacific Rim peoples and by their external market–oriented development strategies. But hard work and clever strategies without venture capital and foreign aid would not have produced the economic dynamo that the world is now witnessing. This is why Japan's financial contributions to the region, coming in chunks much larger than those of the United States, are so crucial. This is also why we consider that Japan and Japanese investment and aid are central to our definition of the Pacific Rim as an identifiable region. Some subregions are also emerging. There is, of course, the Association of Southeast Asian Nations (ASEAN) trading unit, but the one that is gaining world attention is the region that people are calling "Greater China," consisting of the emerging capitalist enclaves of the People's Republic of China and of Hong Kong and Taiwan. Copying Japanese strategy and aided by a common written language and culture, this region has the potential of exceeding even the U.S. economy in the not-too-distant future. For now, however, Japan remains the major player because it is in a position to lend such large amounts of money to other countries.

Japan has been investing in the Asia/Pacific region for several decades. However, growing protectionism in its traditional markets as well as changes in the value of the yen and

(UN photo by Nichiro Gyogyo)
This Japanese factory ship is a floating cannery that processes the salmon harvested from the Pacific.

the need to find cheaper sources of labor (labor costs are 75 percent less in Singapore and 95 percent less in Indonesia) have raised Japan's level of involvement so high as to give its actions the upper hand in determining the course of development and political stability for the entire region. This heightened level of investment started to gain momentum in the mid-1980s. Between 1984 and 1989, Japan's overseas development assistance to the ASEAN countries amounted to $6.1 billion. In some cases this assistance translated to more than 4 percent of a nation's annual national budget and nearly 1 percent of GDP. Private Japanese investment in ASEAN countries plus Hong Kong, Taiwan, and South Korea was $8.9 billion between 1987 and 1988. In recent years the Japanese government or Japanese business has invested $582 million in an auto-assembly plant in Taiwan, $5 billion in an iron and steel complex in China, $2.3 billion in a bullet-train plan for Malaysia, and $530 million in a tunnel under the harbor in Sydney, Australia. Japan is certainly not the only player in Asian development (Japan has "only" 21 projects underway in Vietnam, for example, as compared to 80 for Hong Kong and 39 for Taiwan), but the volume of Japanese

investment is staggering. In Australia alone, there are now nearly 900 Japanese companies doing business. Throughout Asia Japanese is becoming a major language of business.

Although Japan works very hard at globalizing its markets and its resource suppliers, it has also developed closer ties with its nearby Rim neighbors. In 1991, out of 20 Rim countries, 13 listed Japan as their first- or second-most-important trading partner, and several more put Japan third. Japan receives 42 percent of Indonesia's exports and 26 percent of Australia's; in return, 23 percent of South Korea's imports, 29 percent of Taiwan's, 30 percent of Thailand's, 24 percent of Malaysia's, and 23 percent of Indonesia's come from Japan. Pacific Rim countries are clearly becoming more interdependent, but simultaneously more dependent on Japan, for their economic success.

JAPANESE INFLUENCE, PAST AND PRESENT

This is certainly not the first time in modern history that Japanese influence has swept over Asia and the Pacific. A major thrust began in 1895, when Japan, like the European powers, started to acquire bits and pieces of the region. By 1942 the Japanese were in control of Taiwan, Korea, Manchuria and most of the populated parts of China, and Hong Kong; what are now Vietnam, Laos, and Cambodia; Thailand; Burma (now Myanmar); Malaysia; Indonesia; the Philippines; part of New Guinea; and dozens of Pacific islands. In effect, by the 1940s the Japanese were the dominant force in precisely the area that they influence in the 1990s and which we are calling the Pacific Rim.

The similarities do not end there, for while many Asians of the 1940s were apprehensive about or openly resistant to Japanese rule, many others welcomed the Japanese invaders and even helped them to take over their countries. This was because they believed that Western influence was out of place in Asia and that Asia should be for Asians. They hoped that the Japanese military would rid them of Western rule, and it did: after the war, very few Western powers were able to regain control of their Asian and Pacific colonies.

Today many Asians and Pacific islanders are apprehensive about excessive Japanese financial and industrial influence in their countries, but they welcome Japanese investment anyway because they believe that it is the best and cheapest way to rid their countries of poverty and underdevelopment. So far they are right, for by copying the Japanese model of economic development, and thanks to Japanese trade, foreign aid, and investment, the entire region—some countries excepted—is gaining such a reputation for economic strength that many people believe the next 100 years will be called the "Pacific Century," just as the previous 100 years were called the "American Century." It would not be farfetched to call it the "Japanese Century" and to rename the Pacific Rim the "Yen Bloc," as some observers are already doing. It is important to note, however, that many Rim countries, such as

Taiwan, Hong Kong, and South Korea, are strong challengers to Japan's economic dominance, and that Japan has not felt comfortable about its position as head of the pack, for fear of a backlash. For example, recent complaints against the Japanese military's World War II treatment of civilians in Korea and China have prompted Japan to pledge $1 billion to various Asian countries as a symbolic act of apology.

Why have the Japanese re-created in the 1990s a modern version of the old Greater East Asian Co-Prosperity Sphere of the imperialistic 1940s? We cannot find the answer in the propaganda of wartime Japan—fierce devotion to emperor and nation and belief in the superiority of Asians over all other races are no longer the propellants in the Japanese economic engine. Rather, Japan courts Asia and the Pacific today to acquire resources to sustain its civilization. Japan is about the size of California, but it has 5 times as many people and not nearly as much arable land. Much of Japan is mountainous; many other parts are off-limits because of active volcanoes (one tenth of all the active volcanoes in the world are in Japan), and after 2,000-plus years of intensive and uninterrupted habitation, the natural forests are long since consumed, as are most of the other natural resources—most of which were scarce to begin with.

In short, Japan continues to extract resources from the rest of Asia and the Pacific because it is the same Japan as before—environmentally speaking, that is. Take oil. In the early 1940s, Japan needed oil to keep its industries (as well as its military machine) operating, but the United States wanted to punish Japan for its military expansion in Asia, so it shut off all shipments to Japan of any kind, including oil. That may have seemed politically right to the policymakers of the day, but it did not change Japan's resource environment; Japan still did not have its own oil, and it still needed as much oil as before. So Japan decided to capture a nearby nation that did have natural reserves of oil; in 1941 it attacked Indonesia and obtained by force the oil that it had been denied by trade.

Japan has no more domestic resources now than it did 50 years ago, and yet its needs—for food, minerals, lumber, paper—are greater. Except for fish, you name it, Japan does not have it. A realistic comparison is to imagine trying to feed half the population of the United States from the natural output of the state of Montana. As it happens, however, Japan sits next to the continent of Asia, which is rich in almost all the materials it needs. For lumber there are the forests of Malaysia, for food there are the farms and ranches of New Zealand and Australia, and for oil there are Indonesia and Brunei, the latter of which sells 50 percent of its exports to Japan. A quest for resources is why Japan is flooding its neighbors with Japanese yen, and that, in turn, is creating the interconnected trading bloc of the Pacific Rim.

Catalyst for Development

In addition to the need for resources, Japan has turned to the Pacific Rim in an attempt to offset the anti-Japanese import or protectionist policies of its historic trading partners. Because so many import tariffs are imposed on products sold directly from Japan, Japanese companies find that they can avoid or minimize tariffs if they cooperate on joint ventures in Rim countries and have products shipped from there. The result is that both Japan and its host countries are prospering as never before. Sony Corporation, for example, assembles parts made in both Japan and Singapore to construct video-cassette recorders at its Malaysian factory, for export to North America, Europe, and other Rim countries. Toyota Corporation intends to build its automobile transmissions in the Philippines and its steering-wheel gears in Malaysia, and to build the final product in whichever country intends to buy its cars.

So helpful has Japanese investment (as well as North American and European investment) been in spawning indigenous economic powerhouses that many other Rim countries are now reinvesting in the region. In particular, Hong Kong, Singapore, Taiwan, and South Korea are now in a position to seek cheaper labor markets in Indonesia, Malaysia, the Philippines, and Thailand. In recent years they have invested billions of dollars in the resource- and labor-rich economies of Southeast Asia, increasing living standards and adding to the growing interconnectivity of the region. An example is a Taiwanese company that has built the largest eel-production facility in the world—in Malaysia—and ships its entire product to Korea and Japan.

Eyed as a big consumer as well as a bottomless source of cheap labor is the People's Republic of China. Many Rim countries, such as South Korea, Taiwan, Hong Kong, and Japan, are working hard to increase their trade with China. In 1990 two-way trade between Taiwan and China was more than $4 billion; between Hong Kong and China, it was $50 billion. Japan was especially eager to resume economic aid to China in 1990 after temporarily withholding aid because of the Tiananmen Square massacre. For its part, China is establishing free enterprise zones that will enable it to participate more fully in the regional economy. Already the Bank of China is the second-largest bank in Hong Kong.

Japan and a handful of other economic powerhouses of the Rim are not the only big players in Rim economic development. The United States and Canada remain major investors in the Pacific Rim (in computers and automobiles, for example), and Europe maintains its historical linkages with the region (such as in oil). But there is no question that Japan is the main catalyst for development in the region, and its level of investment is likely to continue for at least the next decade because Japan is awash in investment monies seeking a home. Almost all the top 20 banks in the world are Japanese, and the volume of the Japanese stock market is the biggest in the world. Many of the world's wealthiest business executives are Japanese, and they are eager to find places to invest their capital.

Not everyone is pleased with the way Japan is giving aid or making loans. Particularly in the Pacific Rim, money invested by the Japan International Development Organization (JIDO) is usually connected very closely to the commercial interests of Japanese companies. For instance, commercial loan agreements often require that the recipient of low-interest loans purchase Japanese products.

Nevertheless, it is clear that many countries would be a lot worse off without Japanese aid. JIDO aid around the world in a recent year was $10 billion. Japan is the dominant supplier of foreign aid to the Philippines and a major investor; in Thailand, where U.S. aid recently amounted to $20 million, Japanese aid was close to $100 million. Some of this aid, moreover, gets recycled from one country to another within the Rim—Thailand, for example, receives more aid from Japan than any other country, but it in turn supplies major amounts of aid to other nearby countries. Thus we can see the growing interconnectivity of the region, a reality now recognized formally by the establishment of the Asia Pacific Economic Cooperation Council (APEC).

During the militaristic 1940s, Japanese dominance in the region produced antagonism and resistance, but it also gave subjugated countries new highways, railways, and other infrastructural improvements. Today host countries continue to benefit from infrastructural advances, but they also get quality manufactured products. Once again Asian, Southeast Asian, and South Pacific peoples have begun to talk about Japanese domination. The difference is that this time few seem upset about it; most people no longer believe that Japan has military aspirations against them, and they regard Japanese investment as a first step toward becoming economically strong themselves. Many people are eager to learn the Japanese language; in some cities, such as Seoul, South Korea, Japanese has displaced English as the most valuable business language. Nevertheless, to deter negative criticism arising from its prominent position in the Rim, Japan has increased its gift giving, such that now it has surpassed the United States as the world's most generous donor of foreign aid.

POLITICAL AND CULTURAL CHANGES

Although economic issues are important to an understanding of the Pacific Rim, political and cultural changes are also crucial. The new, noncombative relationship between the United States and the former Soviet bloc means that special-interest groups and governments in the Rim will be less able to rely on the strength and power of those nations to help advance or uphold their positions. Communist North Korea, for instance, can no longer rely on the Soviet bloc for trade and ideological support. North Korea may begin to look for new ideological neighbors or, more significantly, to consider major modifications in its own approach to organizing society.

Similarly, ideological changes are afoot in Myanmar, where the populace is tiring of life under a military dictatorship. The military can no longer look for guaranteed support from the crumbling socialist world.

In the case of Hong Kong, the British government shied away from extreme political issues and agreed to the peaceful annexation in 1997 of a capitalist bastion by a communist nation, China. It is highly unlikely that such a decision would have been made had the issue of Hong Kong's political status arisen during the anti-communist years of the cold war. One must not get the impression, however, that suddenly peace has arrived in the Pacific Rim. But outside support for extreme ideological positions seems to be giving way to a pragmatic search for peaceful solutions. This should have a salutary effect throughout the region.

The growing pragmatism in the political sphere is yielding changes in the cultural sphere. Whereas Chinese formerly looked upon Western dress and music as decadent, most Chinese now openly seek out these cultural commodities and are finding ways to merge these things with the Communist polity under which they live. It is also increasingly clear to most leaders in the Pacific Rim that international mercantilism has allowed at least one regional country, Japan, to rise to the highest ranks of world society, first economically and now culturally and educationally. The fact that one Asian nation has accomplished this fosters hope that others can as well.

Rim leaders also see, however, that Japan achieved its position of prominence only because it was willing to change traditional mores and customs and accept outside modes of thinking and acting. Religion, family life, gender relations, recreation, and many other facets of Japanese life have altered during Japan's rapid rise to the top. Many other Pacific Rim nations—including Thailand, Singapore, and South Korea—seem determined to follow Japan's lead in this regard. Therefore, we are witnessing in certain high-growth Rim economies significant cultural changes: a reduction in family size, a secularization of religious impulses, a desire for more leisure time and better education, and a move toward acquisition rather than "being" as a determinant of one's worth. That is, more and more people are likely to judge others' value by what they own rather than what they believe or do. Buddhist values of self-denial, Shinto values of respect for nature, and Confucian values of family loyalty are giving way slowly to Western-style individualism and the drive for personal comfort and monetary success. Formerly close-knit communities, such as those in American Samoa, are finding themselves struggling with drug abuse and gang-related violence, just as in the metropolitan countries. These changes in political and cultural values are at least as important as economic growth in projecting the future of the Pacific Rim.

The Pacific Islands: Opportunities and Limits

PLENTY OF SPACE, BUT NO ROOM

There are about 30,000 islands in the Pacific Ocean. Most of them are found in the South Pacific and may be classified into three mammoth regions: Micronesia, composed of some 2,000 islands with such names as Palau, Nauru, and Guam; Melanesia, where 200 different languages are spoken on such islands as Fiji and the Solomon Islands; and Polynesia, composed of such islands as Hawaii, Samoa, and Tahiti.

Straddling both sides of the equator, these territories are characterized as much by what is *not* there as by what *is*—that is, between every tiny island lie hundreds and often thousands of miles of open ocean. A case in point is the Cook Islands. Associated with New Zealand, this 15-island group contains only 92 square miles of land but is spread over 714,000 square miles of open sea. So expansive is the space between islands that early explorers from Europe and the Spanish lands of South America often unknowingly bypassed dozens of islands that lay just beyond view in the vastness of the 64 million square miles of the Pacific—the world's largest ocean.

However, once the Europeans found and set foot on the islands, they inaugurated a process that irreversibly changed the history of island life. Their goals in exploring the Pacific were to convert islanders to Christianity and to increase the power and prestige of their homelands (and themselves) by obtaining resources and acquiring territory. They thought of themselves and European civilization as superior to others and often treated the "discovered" peoples with inhumane contempt. An example is the discovery of the Marquesas Islands (from whence some of the Hawaiian people came) by the Peruvian Spaniard Alvaro de Mendana. Mendana landed in the Marquesas in 1595 with some women and children and, significantly, 378 soldiers. Within weeks his entourage had planted 3 Christian crosses, declared the islands to be the possession of the king of Spain, and killed 200 islanders. Historian Ernest S. Dodge describes the inhumanity of the first contacts:

(UN photo by Nagata Jr.)

In the South Pacific area of Micronesia, some 2,000 islands are spread over an ocean area of 3 million square miles. There remain many relics of the diverse cultures found on these islands; these boys are walking between the highly prized stone discs that were used as money on the islands of the Yap District.

THE CASE OF THE DISAPPEARING ISLAND

It wasn't much to begin with, but the way things are going, it won't be anything by the year 2000. Nauru, a tiny 8½-square-mile dot of phosphate dirt in the Pacific, is being gobbled up by the Nauru Phosphate Corporation. Made of bird droppings (guano) mixed with marine sediment, Nauru's high-quality phosphate has a ready market in Australia, New Zealand, Japan, and other Pacific Rim countries, where it is used in industry, medicine, and agriculture.

Many Pacific islanders with few natural resources to sell to the outside world envy the 4,500 Nauruans. The Nauruans pay no taxes, yet the government, thanks to phosphate sales, is able to provide them with free health and dental care, bus transportation, newspapers, and schooling (including higher education if they are willing to leave home temporarily for Australia, with the trip paid for by the government). Rent for government-built homes, supplied with telephones and electricity, costs about $5 a month. Nor do Nauruans have to work particularly hard for a living, since most laborers in the phosphate pits are imported from other islands; most managers and other professionals come from Australia, New Zealand, and England.

Phosphate is Nauru's only export, and yet the country makes so much money from it that, technically speaking, Nauru is the richest country per capita in the world. Unable to spend all the export earnings (even though it owns and operates five Boeing 737s, several hotels on other islands, and the tallest skyscraper in Melbourne, Australia), the government puts lots of the money away in trust accounts for a rainy day.

It all sounds nice, but the rub is that the island is being mined away. Already there is only just a little fringe of green left along the shore where everyone lives, and the government is starting to think about the year 2000 (or sooner) when even the ground under people's homes will be mined and shipped away. Some think that topsoil should be brought in to see if the moonlike surface of the excavated areas can be revitalized. Others think that moving out makes sense—with all its money, the government could just buy another island somewhere and move everyone (an idea that Australia suggested years ago, even before Nauru's independence in 1968). Of course, since the government owns the phosphate company, it could just put a halt to any more mining. But if it does, what would Nauru be to anybody? On the other hand, if it doesn't, will Nauru *be* at all?

The Spaniards opened fire on the surrounding canoes for no reason at all. To prove himself a good marksman one soldier killed both a Marquesan and the child in his arms with one shot as the man desperately swam for safety.... The persistent Marquesans again attempted to be friendly by bringing fruit and water, but again they were shot down when they attempted to take four Spanish water jars. Magnanimously the Spaniards allowed the Marquesans to stand around and watch while mass was celebrated.... When [the islanders] attempted to take two canoe loads of ... coconuts to the ships half the unarmed natives were killed and three of the bodies hung in the rigging in grim warning. The Spaniards were not only killing under orders, they were killing for target practice.

*—Islands and Empires; Western Impact on the
Pacific and East Asia*
(Minneapolis: University of Minnesota Press, 1976), p. 18.

All over the Pacific, islanders were "pacified" through violence or deception inflicted on them by the conquering nations of France, England, Spain, and others. Often rivalries between the European nations were acted out in the Pacific. For example, the Cook Islands, inhabited by a mixture of Polynesian and Maori peoples, were partly controlled by the Protestant Mission of the London Missionary Society until the threat of incursions by French Catholics from Tahiti persuaded the British to declare the islands a protectorate of Britain. New Zealand eventually annexed the islands and controlled them until 1965.

Business interests frequently took precedence over islanders' sovereignty. In Hawaii, for instance, when Queen Liliuokalani proposed to limit the influence of the business community in island governance, a few dozen American business leaders, without the knowledge of the U.S. president or Congress and with the unauthorized help of 160 U.S. Marines, overthrew the Hawaiian monarch, installed Sanford Dole (of Dole Pineapple fame) as president, and petitioned Congress for annexation as a U.S. territory. Whatever the method of acquisition, once the islands were under European or American control, the colonizing nations insisted that the islanders learn Western languages, wear Western clothing, convert to Christianity, and pay homage to faraway rulers whom they had never seen.

This blatant Eurocentrism ignored the obvious: that the islanders already had rich cultural traditions that both predated European culture and constituted substantial accomplishments in technology, the arts, and social structure. Islanders were skilled in the construction of boats suitable for navigation on the high seas and of homes and religious buildings of varied architecture; they had perfected the arts of weaving and cloth-making, tattooing (the word itself is Tahitian), and dancing. Some cultures organized their political affairs much as had early New Englanders, with village meetings to decide issues by consensus, while others had developed strong chieftainships and kingships with an elaborate variety of rituals and taboos (this word is Tongan) associated with the ruling elite. Island trade involving vast distances brought otherwise disparate people together, and although reading and writing was not known on most islands, some evidence of an ancient writing system has been found.

Despite these cultural attributes and a long history of skill in interisland or intertribal warfare, the islanders could not withstand the superior force of European firearms. Within just a few generations, the entire Pacific had been conquered and colonized by Britain, France, Holland, Germany, the United States, and other nations.

CONTEMPORARY GROUPINGS

The Pacific islands today are classified into three racial/cultural groupings. The first, Micronesia, with a population of approximately 352,000 people, contains 7 political entities, 3 of which are politically independent and 4 of which are affiliated with the United States. Guam is perhaps the best known of these islands. Micronesians share much in common genetically and culturally with Asians. The term *Micronesia* refers to the small size of the islands in this group.

The second grouping, Melanesia, with a population of some 5.5 million (if New Guinea is included), contains 6 political entities, 4 of which are independent and 2 of which are affiliated with colonial powers. Perhaps the best known of these islands is Fiji. The term "Melanesia" refers to the dark skin of the inhabitants, who, despite appearances, apparently have no direct ties with Africa.

Polynesia, the third grouping, with a population of 530,000, contains 12 political entities, 3 of which are independent, with the remaining 6 affiliated with colonial powers. *Polynesia* means "many islands," the most prominent of which is probably Hawaii. Most of the cultures in Polynesia have some ancient connections with the Marquesas Islands or Tahiti.

Subtracting the atypically large population of the island of New Guinea leaves about 2.2 million people in the region that we generally think of as the Pacific islands. Although it is possible that some of the islands may have been peopled by or had contact with ancient civilizations of South America, the overwhelming weight of scholarship places the origins of the Pacific islanders in Southeast Asia, Indonesia, and Australia.

Geologically the islands may be categorized into the tall, volcanic islands, which are well endowed with water, flora, and fauna and are suitable for agriculture; and the dry, flat, coral islands, which have fewer resources (but are sometimes rich in phosphate). It also appears that the farther away the island is from the Asian or Australian continental masses, the less varied and plentiful the flora and fauna.

THE PACIFIC COMMUNITY

During the early years of Western contact and colonization, maltreatment of the indigenous peoples and diseases such as measles and influenza greatly reduced their numbers and their cultural strength. Moreover, the carving up of the Pacific by different Western powers superimposed a cultural fragmentation on the region that added to the separateness created by distance. Today, however, improved medicines are allowing the populations of the islands to rebound, and the withdrawal or realignment of European and American political power under the post–World War II United Nations policy of decolonization has permitted the growth of regional organizations.

First among the postwar regional groups was the South Pacific Commission. Established in 1947, when Western powers were still largely in control, many of its functions have since been augmented or superseded by indigenously created organizations such as the South Pacific Forum, which was organized in 1971 and has since spawned numerous other associations, including the South Pacific Regional Trade and Economic Agency and the South Pacific Islands Fisheries Development Agency. These associations handle, through the executive body (the South Pacific Bureau for Economic Cooperation) such issues as relief funds, the environment, fisheries, trade, and regional shipping. These organizations have produced a variety of duty-free agreements among countries and yielded joint decisions about regional transportation and cultural exchanges. As a result, regional art festivals and sports competitions are now a regular feature of island life. And a regional university in New Zealand attracts several thousand island students a year, as do universities in Hawaii.

Some regional associations have been able to deal forcefully with much more powerful countries. For instance, when the regional fisheries association set higher licensing fees for foreign fishing fleets (most fleets are foreign, because island fishermen cannot capitalize such large enterprises), the Japanese protested vehemently. Nevertheless, the association held firm, and many islands terminated their contracts with the Japanese rather than lower their fees. In 1994 the Cook Islands, the Federated States of Micronesia, Fiji, Kiribati, the Marshall Islands, Nauru, Niue, Papua New Guinea, the Solomon Islands, Tonga, Tuvalu, Vanuatu, and Western Samoa signed an agreement with the United States to establish a joint commercial commission to foster private-sector businesses and to open opportunities for trade, investment, and training. Through this agreement the islands hope to increase the attractiveness of their products to the U.S. market.

An increasingly important issue in the Pacific is the testing of nuclear weapons and the disposal of toxic waste. Island leaders, with the occasional support of Australia and the strong support of New Zealand, have spoken out vehemently against the continuation of nuclear testing in the Pacific by the French government (Britain and the United States also tested hydrogen bombs on coral atolls for years but have now stopped) and against the burning of nerve gas stockpiles by the United States on Johnston Atoll. In 1985 the 13 independent or self-governing countries of the South Pacific adopted their first collective agreement on regional security, the South Pacific Nuclear Free Zone Treaty. Encouraged by

New Zealand and Australia, the group declared the Pacific a nuclear-free zone and issued a communique deploring the dumping of nuclear waste in the region. Some island leaders, however, see the storage of nuclear waste as a way of earning income to compensate those who were affected by the nuclear testing on Bikini and Enewetak Islands. The Marshall Islands, for example, are interested in storing nuclear waste on already contaminated islands, although the nearby Federated States of Micronesia, which were observers at the Nuclear Free Zone Treaty talks, oppose the idea and have asked the Marshalls not to proceed.

In 1982 world leaders met in Jamaica to sign into international law the Law of the Sea. This law, developed under the auspices of the United Nations, gave added power to the tiny Pacific island nations because it extended the territory under their exclusive economic control to 12 miles beyond their shores or 200 miles of undersea continental shelf. This put many islands in undisputed control of large deposits of nickel, copper, magnesium, and other valuable metals. The seabed areas away from continents and islands were declared the world's common heritage to be mined by an international company, with profits channeled to developing countries. The United States has negotiated for years to increase the role of industrialized nations in mining the seabed areas; if modifications are made to the treaty, the United States will likely sign the document.

COMING OF AGE?

If the Pacific islands are finding more reason to cooperate economically and politically, they are still individually limited by the heritage of cultural fragmentation left them by their colonial pasts. Western Samoa, for example, was first annexed by Germany in 1900, only to be given to New Zealand after Germany's defeat in World War I. Today the tiny nation of mostly Christian Polynesians, independent since 1962, uses both English and Samoan as official languages and embraces a formal governmental structure copied from Western parliamentary practice. Yet the structure of its hundreds of small villages remains decidedly traditional, with clan chiefs ruling over large extended families, who make their not-particularly-profitable living by farming breadfruit, taro, yams, bananas, and copra.

Political independence also has not been easy for those islands that have embraced it nor for those colonial powers who continue to deny it. Two military coups toppled the elected government of Fiji (a former British colony) in 1987, and anticolonial unrest continues on many of the other, especially French, islands. Concern over economic viability has led most islands to remain in some sort of loose association with their former colonial overseers. After the defeat of Japan in World War II, the Marshall Islands, the Marianas, and the Carolines were assigned by the United Nations to the United States as a trust territory. The French Polynesian islands have

remained overseas departments of France, although in such places as New Caledonia, there has been a growing desire for autonomy, which France has attempted to meet in various ways while still retaining sovereignty. The United Nations decolonization policy has made it possible for most Pacific islands to achieve independence if they wish, but many are so small that true economic independence in the modern world will never be possible.

Indeed, no amount of political realignment can overcome the economic dilemma of most of the islands. Japan, the single largest purchaser of island products, as well as the United States and others, are good markets for the Pacific economies, but exports are primarily of mineral and agricultural products (coffee, tea, cocoa, sugar, tapioca, coconuts, mother-of-pearl) rather than of the more profitable manufactured or value-added items produced by industrial nations. In addition, there will always be the cost of moving products from the vastness of the Pacific to the various mainland markets.

Another problem is that many of the profits from the island's resources do not redound to the benefit of the islanders. Tuna, for example, is an important and profitable fish catch, but most of the profits return to the Taiwanese, Korean, Japanese, and American fleets that ply the Pacific. Similarly, tourism profits largely end up in the hands of the multinational hotel owners. Eighty percent of visitors to the island of Guam since 1982 have been Japanese (over half a million annually)—a potential gold mine for local Guamanians since each Japanese visitor spends more than $2,000 for a visit to Guam. Close inspection of Japanese expenditures, however, reveal that the Japanese tend to purchase their tickets on Japanese airlines and book rooms in Japanese-owned or -managed hotels. Thus, of the $92 million spent in 1992 by Japanese tourists in connection with their Guam vacations, well over 60 percent never made it into the hands of the Guamanians.

The poor economy, especially in the outer islands, has prompted many islanders to move to larger cities (about 1 million islanders now live in the Pacific's larger cities) to find work. Indeed, there is currently a tremendous mixing of all of the islands' peoples. Hawaii, for example, is peopled now with Samoans, Filipinos, and many other islanders; pure Hawaiians are a minority, and despite efforts to preserve the Hawaiian language, it is used less and less. Similarly, Fiji is now populated by more immigrants from India than by native Fijians. New Caledonians are outnumbered by Indonesians, Vietnamese, French, and others. And, of course, whites have long outnumbered the Maoris on New Zealand. Guam is peopled with islanders from all of Micronesia as well as from Samoa and other islands. In addition to interisland migration, many islanders emigrate to Australia, New Zealand, the United States, or other countries and then send money back home to sustain their families. Those remittances are important to the economies of the islands, but the absence of parents

THIS IS LIBERATION?

In 1994 the people of the U.S. Territory of Guam celebrated the 50th anniversary of their liberation by U.S. Marines and Army Infantry from the occupying troops of the Japanese Army. During the 3 years that they controlled the tiny, 30-mile-long island, the Japanese massacred some of the Guamanians and subjected many others to forced labor and internment in concentration camps. Their liberation, therefore, was indeed a cause for celebration. But the United States quickly transformed the island into its military headquarters for the continuing battle against the Japanese. The entire northern part of the island was turned into a base for B-29 bombers, and the Pacific submarine fleet took up residence in the harbor. Admiral Nimitz, commander-in-chief of the Pacific, made Guam his headquarters. By 1946 the U.S. military government in Guam had laid claim to nearly 80 percent of the island, displacing entire villages and hundreds of individual property owners.

In the intervening years, some of the land has been returned and large acreages have been handed over to the local civilian government—which was to have distributed most of it, but has not. The local government still controls about 33 percent of the land, and the U.S. military controls another 33 percent, meaning that only one third of the island is available to the residents for private ownership. Litigation to recover the land has been bitter and costly (more than $40 million in legal expenses since 1975). The controversy has prompted some local residents to demand a different kind of relationship with the United States, one that would allow for more autonomy. It has also spurred the growth of nativist organizations such as the Chamorru Nation, which promotes the Chamorru language (the language of the original Malayo–Polynesian inhabitants and spelled Chamorro by the Spanish) and organizes acts of civil disobedience against both civilian and military authorities.

Guam was first overtaken by Spain in 1565. It has been controlled by the United States since 1898, except for the brief Japanese interlude. Whether the local islanders, who now constitute a fascinating mix of Chamorro, Spanish, Japanese, and American cultures, will be able to gain a larger measure of autonomy after 430 years of colonization by outsiders is difficult to predict, but the ever-present island motto, *Tano Y Chamorro* ("Land of the Chamorros"), certainly spells out the objective of many of those who call Guam home.

---

or children for long periods of time does considerable damage to the social fabric. In a few cases, such as in the Cook Islands and American Samoa, there are more islanders living abroad than remain on the islands. Those who leave often find life abroad quite a shock, for the island culture, altered over the decades by the missionary efforts of Mormons, Methodists, Seventh-day Adventists, and especially the London Missionary Society, is conservative, cautious, and personal. Metropolitan life, by contrast, is considered by some islanders to be wild and impersonal. Some young emigrants respond to the "cold" environment and marginality of big-city life by engaging in deviant behavior themselves, such as selling drugs and joining gangs.

Island society itself, moreover, is not immune from the social problems that plague larger societies. Many islands report an increasing number of crimes and suicides. Young Samoans, for example, are afflicted with many of the same problems—gangs, drugs, and unemployment—as are their U.S. inner-city counterparts. Samoan authorities now report increases in incidences of rape, robbery, and other socially dysfunctional behaviors. In addition, the South Pacific Commission and the World Health Organization are now reporting an alarming increase in AIDS and other sexually transmitted diseases. Out of 22 Pacific island groupings, 13 reported cases of HIV or AIDS as of 1994—a 500 percent increase since 1989.

For decades, and notwithstanding the imposition of foreign ways, islanders have shared a common culture—everyone knows how to raise bananas, coconuts, and yams, how to roast pigs and fish, and how to make breadfruit, tapioca, and poi. But much of island culture has depended on an identity shaped and preserved by isolation from the rest of the world. Whether the essence of island life, and especially the identity of the people, can be maintained in the face of increasing integration into a much larger world remains to be seen.

Japan Map

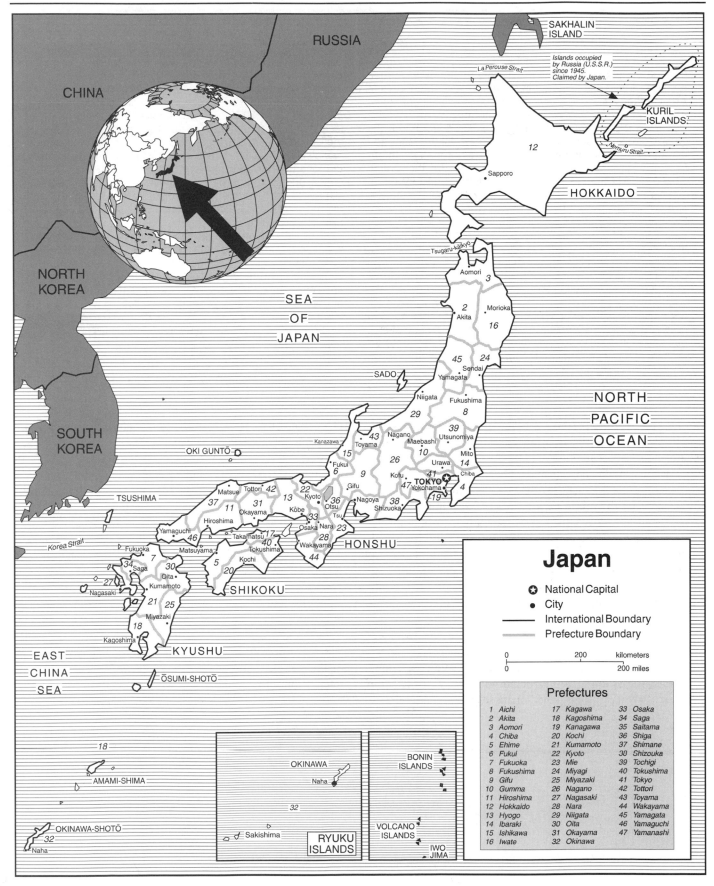

RUSSIA

CHINA

NORTH KOREA

SOUTH KOREA

SAKHALIN ISLAND

La Perouse Strait

Islands occupied by Russia (U.S.S.R.) since 1945. Claimed by Japan.

KURIL ISLANDS

Nemuru Strait

12

Sapporo

HOKKAIDO

Tsugaru-kaikyō

Aomori

3

2
Akita

Morioka

16

SEA

OF

JAPAN

SADO

45

24

Sendai

Yamagata

Niigata

Fukushima

NORTH

PACIFIC

OCEAN

29

8

Kanazawa

43
Toyama

Nagano

Maebashi

Utsunomiya

39

OKI GUNTŌ

15

26

10

Mito

Fukui

Kofu

Urawa

14

6

9

41

Chiba

TOKYO

47 Yokohama

4

TSUSHIMA

Matsue   Tottori

42

22

Gifu

36

Nagoya

38

19

Korea Strait

37   11

31

13

Kyoto

Otsu

Tsu

Shizuoka

Kōbe

33

Okayama

Hiroshima

Osaka Nara

23

Yamaguchi

46

Takamatsu

17

28

HONSHU

Matsuyama

40

Wakayama

Fukuoka

5

Tokushima

44

7

Kochi

34   Saga

30

20

Oita

27

Kumamoto

SHIKOKU

Nagasaki

21   25

Miyazaki

18

Kagoshima

KYUSHU

EAST

CHINA

SEA

ŌSUMI-SHOTŌ

Japan

- ✪ National Capital
- • City
- — International Boundary
- — Prefecture Boundary

0   200   kilometers
0   200 miles

Prefectures

1	Aichi	17	Kagawa	33	Osaka
2	Akita	18	Kagoshima	34	Saga
3	Aomori	19	Kanagawa	35	Saitama
4	Chiba	20	Kochi	36	Shiga
5	Ehime	21	Kumamoto	37	Shimane
6	Fukui	22	Kyoto	38	Shizouka
7	Fukuoka	23	Mie	39	Tochigi
8	Fukushima	24	Miyagi	40	Tokushima
9	Gifu	25	Miyazaki	41	Tokyo
10	Gumma	26	Nagano	42	Tottori
11	Hiroshima	27	Nagasaki	43	Toyama
12	Hokkaido	28	Nara	44	Wakayama
13	Hyogo	29	Niigata	45	Yamagata
14	Ibaraki	30	Oita	46	Yamaguchi
15	Ishikawa	31	Okayama	47	Yamanashi
16	Iwate	32	Okinawa		

18

AMAMI-SHIMA

OKINAWA-SHOTŌ

32

Naha

OKINAWA

Naha

32

Sakishima

RYUKU ISLANDS

BONIN ISLANDS

VOLCANO ISLANDS

IWO JIMA

Japan (Nippon)

GEOGRAPHY

Area in Square Kilometers (Miles):
377,835 (145,882) (slightly smaller
than California)
Capital (Population): Tokyo
(8,300,000)
Climate: tropical in south to cold in north

PEOPLE

Population
Total: 124,712,000
Annual Growth Rate: 0.32%
Rural/Urban Population Ratio: 23/77
Ethnic Makeup: 99.4% Japanese; 0.6%
others (mostly Korean)
Major Language: Japanese

Health
Life Expectancy at Birth: 76 years
(male); 82 years (female)
Infant Mortality Rate (Ratio): 4.3/1,000
Average Caloric Intake: 124% of FAO
minimum
Physicians Available (Ratio): 1/588

Religions
96% Shinto; 76% Buddhist; 13%
Christian and others (most Japanese
observe both Shinto and Buddhist rites,
so the percentages add up to more than
100%)

Education
Adult Literacy Rate: 99%

COMMUNICATION
Telephones: 64,000,000
Newspapers: 124

TRANSPORTATION
Highways—Kilometers (Miles):
1,111,974 (690,536)

Railroads—Kilometers (Miles): 27,327
(16,943)
Usable Airfields: 159

GOVERNMENT

Type: constitutional monarchy
Independence Date: May 3, 1947
(constitutional monarchy established)
Head of State/Government: Emperor
Akihito; Prime Minister Tomiichi
Murayama
Political Parties: Liberal Democratic
Party; Social Democratic Party; New
Frontier Party; New Harbinger Party;
Japan Communist Party; Komeito
Party; others
Suffrage: universal at 20

MILITARY

Number of Armed Forces: 292,600
*Military Expenditures (% of Central
Government Expenditures):* 1% of GNP
Current Hostilities: none

ECONOMY

Currency ($ U.S. Equivalent): 98.56
yen = $1
Per Capita Income/GDP:
$19,800/$2,468 billion
Inflation Rate: 2.1%
Natural Resources: negligible oil and
minerals
Agriculture: rice; sugar beets; vegetables;
fruit; animal products include pork,
poultry, dairy and eggs, fish
Industry: metallurgy; engineering;
electrical and electronics; textiles;
chemicals; automobiles; fishing

FOREIGN TRADE

Exports: $339.7 billion
Imports: $232.7 billion

7–ELEVEN HUSBANDS

The official business day in Japan for most companies is 9:00 A.M. to
5:00 P.M., but most workers would feel disloyal to their companies—or
would not make enough money to live comfortably—if they spent such
a short amount of time at work. Employees often stay at work or
participate in business dinners or other formal socializing until 9 P.M.
or later. The commute home in Tokyo averages about 1½ hours. This
means that workers arrive home at about 11:00 P.M. and leave the next
morning at about 7:00 in order to be to work on time, thus giving rise
to the popular term "7–Eleven husbands." Although most men say that
they would like to spend more (but not much more) time with their
families, 88 percent of wives surveyed said that they prefer spending
their leisure time away from their husbands and feel more relaxed at
home when their husbands are not there.

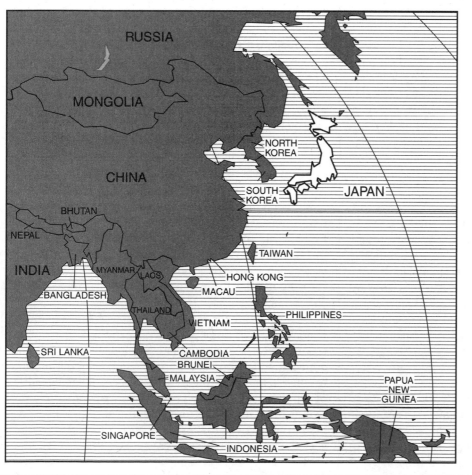

Japan: Driving Force in the Pacific Rim

HISTORICAL BACKGROUND

The Japanese nation is thought to have begun about 250 B.C., when ancestors of today's Japanese people began cultivating rice, casting objects in bronze, and putting together the rudiments of the Shinto religion. However, humans are thought to have inhabited the Japanese islands as early as 20,000 B.C. Some speculate that remnants of these or other early peoples may be the non-Oriental Ainu people (now largely Japanized) who still occupy parts of the northern island of Hokkaido. Asiatic migrants from China and Korea and islanders from the South Pacific occupied the islands between 250 B.C. and A.D. 400, contributing to the population base of modern Japan.

Between A.D. 300 and 710, military aristocrats from some of the powerful clans into which Japanese society was divided established their rule over large parts of the country. Eventually the Yamato clan leaders, claiming divine approval, became the most powerful. Under Yamato rule the Japanese began to import ideas and technology from nearby China, including the Buddhist religion and the Chinese method of writing—which the elite somewhat awkwardly adapted to spoken Japanese, an entirely unrelated language. The Chinese bureaucratic style of government and architecture was also introduced; Japan's first permanent capital was constructed at the city of Nara between the years 710 and 794.

As Chinese influence waned in the period 794–1185, the capital was relocated to Kyoto, with the Fujiwara family wielding real power under the largely symbolic figurehead of the emperor. A warrior class controlled by *shoguns,* or generals, held power at Kamakura between 1185 and 1333 and successfully defended the country from invasion by the Mongols. Buddhism became the religion of the masses, although Shintoism was often embraced simultaneously. Between 1333 and 1568, a very rigid class structure developed, along with a feudalistic economy controlled by *daimyos,* feudal lords who reigned over their own mini-kingdoms.

In 1543 Portuguese sailors landed in Japan, followed 6 years later by the Jesuit missionary Francis Xavier. An active trade with Portugal began, and many Japanese (perhaps half a million), including some feudal lords, converted to Christianity. The Portuguese introduced firearms to the Japanese and perhaps taught them Western-style techniques of building castles with moats and stone walls. Wealthier feudal lords were able to utilize these innovations to defeat weaker rivals, and by 1600 the country was unified under a military bureaucracy, although feudal lords still retained substantial sovereignty over their fiefs. During this time the general Hideyoshi attempted an unsuccessful invasion of nearby Korea.

The Tokugawa Era

In the period between 1600 and 1868, called the Tokugawa Era, the social, political, and economic foundations of modern Japan were put in place. The capital was moved to Tokyo, cities began to grow in size, and a merchant class arose, which was powerful enough to challenge the hegemony of the centuries-old warrior class. Strict rules of dress and behavior for each of the four social classes (samurai, farmer, craftsman, and merchant) were imposed, and the Japanese people learned to discipline themselves to these codes. Western ideas came to be seen as a threat to the established ruling class. The military elite expelled foreigners and put the nation into 2 centuries of extreme isolation from the rest of the world. Christianity was banned, as was most trade with the West. Even Japanese living abroad were forbidden from returning, for fear that they might have been contaminated with foreign ideas.

During the Tokugawa Era, indigenous culture expanded rapidly. Puppet plays and a new form of drama called *kabuki* became popular, as did *haiku* poetry and Japanese pottery and painting. The samurai code, called *bushido,* along with the concept of *giri,* or obligation to one's superiors, suffused Japanese society. Literacy among males rose to about 40 percent, higher than most European countries of the day. Samurai busied themselves with the education of the young, using teaching methods that included strict discipline, hard work, and self-denial.

During the decades of isolation, Japan grew culturally strong but militarily weak. In 1853 a U.S. naval squadron appeared in Tokyo Bay to insist that Japan open up its ports to foreign vessels needing supplies and desiring to trade. Similar requests had been denied in the past, but the sophistication of the U.S. ships and their advanced weaponry convinced the Japanese military rulers that they no longer could keep Japan isolated from the outside.

The Era of Modernization: The Meiji Restoration

Treaties with the United States and other Western nations followed, and the dislocations associated with the opening of the country to the world soon brought discredit to the ruling shoguns. Provincial samurai took control of the government. The emperor, long a figurehead in Kyoto, away from the center of power, was moved to Tokyo in 1868, beginning the period known as the Meiji Restoration.

Although the Meiji leaders came to power with the intention of ousting all the foreigners and returning Japan to its former state of domestic tranquillity, they quickly realized that the nations of the West were determined to defend their newly won access to the ports of Japan. To defeat the foreigners, they reasoned, Japan must first acquire their knowledge and technology.

Thus, beginning in 1868, the Japanese leaders launched a major campaign to modernize the nation. Ambassadors and scholars were sent abroad to learn about Western-style government, education, and warfare. Implementing these ideas resulted in the abolition of the feudal system and the division of Japan into 43 prefectures, or states, and other administrative districts under the direct control of the Tokyo government. Legal codes that established the formal separation of society into social classes were abolished; and Western-style dress, music, and education were embraced. The old samurai

(Japan National Tourist Organization)

The Japanese emperor has long been a figurehead in Japan. In 1926 Hirohito, pictured above, became emperor and ushered in the era named *Showa.* He died on January 7, 1989, having seen Japan through World War II and witnessed its rise to the economic world power it is today. He was succeeded by his son, Akihito, who named his reign *Heisei,* meaning "Achieving Peace."

Islands. Western nations were surprised at Japan's rapid empire-building but did little to stop it.

The Great Depression of the 1930s caused serious hardships in Japan because, being resource-poor yet heavily populated, the country had come to rely on trade to supply its basic needs. Many Japanese advocated the forced annexation of Manchuria as a way of providing needed resources. This was accomplished easily, in 1931. With militarism on the rise, the Japanese nation began moving away from democracy and toward a military dictatorship. Political parties were eventually banned, and opposition leaders were jailed and tortured.

WORLD WAR II AND THE JAPANESE EMPIRE

The battles of World War II in Europe, initially won by Germany, promised to realign substantially the colonial empires of France and other European powers in Asia. The military elite of Japan declared its intention of creating a Greater East Asia Co-Prosperity Sphere—in effect, a Japanese empire created out of the ashes of the European empires in Asia that were now dissolving. In 1941, under the guidance of General Hideki Tojo and with the tacit approval of the emperor, Japan captured the former French colony of Indochina (Vietnam, Laos, and Cambodia), bombed Pearl Harbor in Hawaii, and captured oil-rich Indonesia. These victories were followed by others: Japan captured all of Southeast Asia, including Burma, Thailand, and Malaya, the Philippines, and parts of New Guinea; and expanded its hold in China and in the islands of the South Pacific. Many of these conquered peoples, lured by the Japanese slogan of "Asia for the Asians," were initially supportive of the Japanese, believing that Japan would rid their countries of European colonial rule. It soon became apparent, however, that Japan had no intention of relinquishing control of these territories and would go to brutal lengths to subjugate the local peoples. Japan soon dominated a vast empire, the constituents of which were virtually the same as those making up what we call the Pacific Rim today.

In 1941 the United States launched a counteroffensive against the powerful Japanese military. (American history books refer to this offensive as the Pacific Theater of World War II, but the Japanese call it the *Pacific War.* We use the term *World War II* in this text, for reasons of clarity and consistency.) By 1944 the U.S. troops had ousted the Japanese from most of their conquered lands and were beginning to attack the home islands themselves. Massive firebombing of Tokyo and other cities, combined with the dropping of two atomic bombs on Hiroshima and Nagasaki, convinced the Japanese military rulers that they had no choice but to surrender.

This was the first time in Japanese history that Japan had been conquered, and the Japanese were shocked to hear their emperor, Hirohito—whose voice had never been heard on radio—announce on August 14, 1945, that Japan was defeated. The emperor cited the suffering of the people—almost 2 million Japanese had been killed—devastation of the cities

class turned its attention from warfare to leadership in the government, in schools, and in business. Factories and railroads were constructed, and public education was expanded. By 1900 Japan's literacy rate was 90 percent, the highest in Asia. Parliamentary rule was established along the lines of the government in Prussia, agricultural techniques were imported from the United States, and banking methods were adopted from Britain.

Japan's rapid modernization soon convinced its leaders that the nation was strong enough to begin doing what other advanced nations were doing: acquiring empires. Japan went to war with China, acquiring the Chinese island of Taiwan in 1895. In 1904 Japan attacked Russia and successfully acquired Korea and access to Manchuria (both areas having been in the sphere of influence of Russia). Siding against Germany in World War I, Japan was able to acquire Germany's Pacific empire—the Marshall, Caroline, and Mariana

On December 7, 1941, the Japanese entered World War II by bombing Pearl Harbor, in Hawaii. This photograph, taken from an attacking Japanese plane, shows Pearl Harbor and a line of American battleships about to be attacked.

brought about by the use of a "new and most cruel bomb," and the possibility that without surrender, Japan as a nation might be completely "obliterated." Emperor Hirohito then encouraged his people to look to the future, to keep pace with progress, and to help build world peace by accepting the surrender ("enduring the unendurable and suffering what is insufferable").

This attitude smoothed the way for the American Occupation, led by General Douglas MacArthur. Defeat seemed to inspire the Japanese people to adopt the ways of their more powerful conquerors and to eschew militarism. Under the Occupation forces, the Japanese Constitution was rewritten in a form that mimicked that of the United States. Industry was restructured, labor unions encouraged, land reform accomplished, and the nation as a whole demilitarized. Economic aid from the United States, as well as the prosperity in Japan that was occasioned by the Korean War in 1953, allowed Japanese industry to begin to recover from the devastation of war. The United States returned the governance of Japan back to the Japanese people by treaty in 1951 (although some 60,000 troops still remain in Japan as part of an agreement to defend Japan from foreign attack).

By the late 1960s, the Japanese economy was more than self-sustaining, and the United States was Japan's primary trading partner (it remains so today, with 34 percent of Japanese exports purchased by Americans and 30 percent of

Japanese food imports coming from the United States). Japan's trade with its former Asian empire, however, was minimal, because of lingering resentment against Japan for its wartime brutalities. Even as recently as the late 1970s, anti-Japanese riots and demonstrations occurred upon the visit of the Japanese prime minister to Indonesia.

Nevertheless, between the 1960s and 1990s, Japan experienced an era of unprecedented economic prosperity. Annual economic growth was 3 times as much as in other industrialized nations. Japanese couples voluntarily limited their family size so that each child born could enjoy the best of medical care and social and educational opportunities. The fascination with the West continued, but eventually, rather than "modernization" or "Americanization," the Japanese began to speak of "internationalization," a term that reflects both their capacity for and their actual membership in the world community, politically, culturally, and economically.

The Japanese government as well as private industry began to accelerate the drive for diversified markets and resources in the mid-1980s. This was partly in response to protectionist trends in countries in North America and Europe with which Japan had accumulated huge trade surpluses, but it was also due to changes in Japan's own internal social and economic conditions. Japan's recent resurgence of interest in its neighboring countries and the origin of the bloc of nations we are calling the Pacific Rim can be explained by both external protectionism and internal changes. This time, however, Japanese influence—no longer linked with militarism—is being welcomed by virtually all nations in the region.

DOMESTIC CHANGE

What internal conditions are causing Japan's renewed interest in Asia and the Pacific? One change involves wage structure. For several decades Japanese exports were less expensive than competitors' because Japanese workers were not paid as well as workers in North America and Europe. Today, however, the situation is reversed: Average manufacturing wages in Japan are now higher than those paid to workers in the United States. Schoolteachers, college professors, and many white-collar workers are also better off in Japan. These wage differentials are the result of successful union activity and demographic changes.

Whereas prewar Japanese families—especially those in the rural areas—were large, today's modern household typically consists of a couple and only one or two children. As Japan's low birth rate began to affect the supply of labor, companies were forced to entice workers with higher wages. An example is McDonald's, increasingly popular in Japan as a fast-food

outlet. Whereas young people working at McDonald's outlets in the United States are paid at or slightly above the legal minimum wage of $4.25 an hour, McDonald's employees in Japan are paid as much as $7.10 an hour, simply because there are fewer youths available (many schools prohibit students from working during the school year). The cost of land, homes, food—even Japanese-grown rice—is so much higher in Japan than in most of its neighbor countries that employees in Japan expect high wages (household income in Japan is higher even than in the United States, by about $7,000 per year).

Given conditions like these, Japanese companies find that they cannot be competitive in world markets unless they move their operations to countries like the Philippines or Singapore, where an abundance of laborers keeps wage costs 75 to 95 percent lower than in Japan. Abundant, cheap labor (as well as a desire to avoid import tariffs) is also the reason why so many Japanese companies are being constructed in the economically depressed areas of the U.S. Midwest and South.

Another internal condition that is spurring Japanese interest in the Pacific Rim is a growing public concern for the home environment. Beginning in the 1970s, the Japanese courts handed down several landmark decisions in which Japanese companies were held liable for damages to people caused by chemical and other industrial wastes. Japanese

(United Motor Manufacturing)

As the economy of Japan developed, manufacturing wages rose to a point where Japanese products were less competitive in world markets. In response, Japanese industry began to build manufacturing facilities abroad in partnership with foreign companies. These American workers are busy in a Toyota-General Motors plant in the United States.

industry, realizing that it no longer had a carte blanche to make profits at the expense of the environment, began moving some of its smokestack industries to new locations in Third World countries, just as other industrialized nations had done. This has turned out to be a wise move economically for many companies, as it has put their operations closer to their raw materials. This, in combination with cheaper labor costs, has allowed them to remain globally competitive. It also has been a tremendous benefit to the host countries, although environmental groups in many Rim countries are also now becoming active, and industry in the future may be forced to effect actual improvements in their operations rather than move polluting technologies to "safe" areas.

Attitudes toward work are also changing in Japan. Although the average Japanese worker still works about 6 hours more per week than does the typical North American worker, the new generation of workers—those born and raised since World War II—are not so eager to sacrifice as much for their companies as were their parents. Recent policies have eliminated weekend work in many industries, and sports and other recreational activities are becoming increasingly popular. Given these conditions, Japanese corporate leaders are finding it more cost effective to move operations abroad to countries like South Korea, where labor legislation is weaker and long work hours remain the norm.

MYTH AND REALITY OF THE ECONOMIC MIRACLE

The Japanese economy, like any other economy, must respond to market as well as social and political changes to stay vibrant. It just so happens that for several decades Japan's attempt to keep its economic boom alive has created the conditions that, in turn, are furthering the economies of all the countries in the Asia/Pacific region. If a regional "Yen bloc" (so called because of the dominance of the Japanese currency, the yen) is created in the process, it will simply be the result of Japan doing what it calculates it has to do to remain competitive in the world market.

Outsiders today are often of the impression that whatever Japan does—whether targeting a certain market or reorienting its economy toward regional trade—turns to gold, as if the Japanese possess some secret of success that others do not. But there is no such secret that other nations could not understand or employ themselves. Japanese success in business, education, and other fields is the result of hard work, advance planning, persistence, and outside help.

However, even with those ingredients in place, Japanese enterprises often fall short. In many industries, for example, Japanese workers are less efficient than are workers in other countries. Japan's national railway system was once found to have 277,000 more employees on its payroll than it needed. Investigators revealed that the system was so poorly managed for so many years that it had, by 1988, accumulated a total public debt of $257 billion. Multimillion-dollar train stations

had been built in out-of-the-way towns, for no other reason than that a member of the *Diet* (the Japanese Parliament) happened to live there and had pork-barreled the project. Both government and industry have been plagued by bribery and corruption, as in the Recruit Scandal of the late 1980s, which caused many implicated government leaders, including the prime minister, to resign. Nor is the Japanese economy impervious to global market conditions. Values of stocks traded on the Tokyo Stock Exchange took a serious drop in 1992; investors lost millions of dollars, and many had to declare bankruptcy. Moreover, the tenacious recession that hit Japan in the early 1990s forced Japanese companies to reduce overtime work and slow down expansion plans.

THE 10 COMMANDMENTS OF JAPAN'S ECONOMIC SUCCESS

Still, the success of modern Japan has been phenomenal, and it would be helpful to review in detail some of the bases of that success. We might call these the 10 commandments of Japan's economic success.

1. Some of Japan's entrenched business conglomerates, called *zaibatsu*, were broken up by order of the U.S. Occupation commander after World War II; this allowed competing businesses to get a start. Similarly, the physical infrastruc-

(Sony Corporation of America)
A contributing factor in the modern economic development of Japan was investment from the Agency for International Development. The Sony Corporation is an example of just how successful this assistance could be. These workers are assembling products that will be sold all over the world.

ture—roads, factories—was destroyed during the war. This was a blessing in disguise, for it paved the way for newer equipment and technologies to be put in place quickly.

2. The United States, seeing the need for an economically strong Japan in order to offset the growing attraction of communist ideology in Asia, provided substantial reconstruction aid. For instance, Sony Corporation got started with help from the Agency for International Development (AID)—an organization to which the United States is a major contributor. Mazda Motors got its start by making Jeeps for U.S. forces during the Korean War. Other Rim countries that are now doing well can also thank U.S. generosity: Taiwan received $5.6 billion and South Korea received $13 billion in aid during the period 1945–1978.

3. Japanese industry looked upon government as a facilitator and received useful economic advice as well as political and financial assistance from government planners. (In this regard, it is important to note that many of Japan's civil servants are the best graduates of Japan's colleges and universities.) Also, the advice and help coming from the government were fairly consistent over time, because the same political party, the Liberal Democratic Party, remained in power for almost the entire postwar period.

4. Japanese businesses selected an export-oriented strategy that stressed building market share over immediate profit.

5. Except in certain professions, such as teaching, labor unions in Japan were not as powerful as in Europe and the United States. This is not to suggest that unions were not effective in gaining benefits for workers, but the structure of the union movement—individual company unions rather than industry-wide unions—moderated the demands for improved wages and benefits.

6. Company managers stressed employee teamwork and group spirit and implemented policies such as "lifetime employment" and quality-control circles, which contributed to group morale. In this they were aided by the Japanese tendency to grant to the company some of the same level of loyalty traditionally reserved for families. In certain ways, the gap between workers and management was minimized.

7. Companies benefited from the Japanese ethic of working hard and saving much. For most of Japan's postwar history, workers labored 6 days a week, arriving early and leaving late. The paychecks were carefully managed to include a substantial savings component—generally between 15 and 25 percent. This guaranteed that there were always enough cash reserves for banks to offer company expansion loans at low interest.

8. The government spent relatively little of its tax revenues on social welfare programs or military defense, preferring instead to invest public funds in private industry.

9. A relatively stable family structure (i.e., few divorces and substantial family support for young people, many of whom remained at home until marriage at about age 27), produced employees who were reliable and psychologically stable.

10. The government as well as private individuals invested enormous amounts of money and energy into education, on the assumption that in a resource-poor country, the mental energies of the people would need to be exploited to their fullest.

Some of these conditions for success are now part of immutable history, but some, such as the emphasis on education, are open to change as the conditions of Japanese life change. A relevant example is the practice of lifetime employment. Useful as a management tool when companies were small and *skilled* laborers were difficult to find, it is now giving way to a freer labor market system. In some Japanese industries, as many as 30 percent of new hires quit after 2 years on the job. In other words, the aforementioned conditions for success were relevant to one particular era of Japanese and world history and may not be relevant to other countries or other times. Selecting the right strategy for the right era has perhaps been the single most important condition for Japanese economic success.

CULTURAL CHARACTERISTICS

All these conditions notwithstanding, Japan would never have achieved economic success without its people possessing certain social and psychological characteristics, many of which can be traced to the various religious/ethical philosophies that have suffused Japan's 2,000-year history. Shintoism, Buddhism, Confucianism, Christianity, and other philosophies of living have shaped the modern Japanese mind. This is not to suggest that Japanese are tradition-bound; nothing could be further from the truth, even though many Westerners think "tradition" when they think Japan.

It is more accurate to think of Japanese people as imitative, preventive, pragmatic, obligative, and inquisitive rather than traditional. These characteristics are discussed in this section.

Imitative

The capacity to imitate one's superiors is a strength of the Japanese people; rather than representing an inability to think creatively, it constitutes one reason for Japan's legendary success. It makes sense to the Japanese to copy success, whether it is a successful boss, company in the United States, or educational curriculum in Europe. It is true that imitation can produce conformity, but in Japan's case, it is often conformity based on respect for the superior qualities of someone or something rather than simple, blind mimicry.

Once Japanese people have mastered the skills of their superiors, they believe that they have the moral right to a style of their own. Misunderstandings on this point arise often when East meets West. An American schoolteacher, for example, was sent to Japan to teach Western art to elementary school children. Considering her an expert, the children did their best to copy her work to the smallest detail. Misunderstanding that this was at once a compliment and the first step toward creativity, the teacher removed all of her art samples from the classroom in order to force the students to paint something from their own imaginations. Because the students found this to be a violation of their approach to creativity, they did not perform well, and the teacher left Japan believing that Japanese education teaches conformity and compliance rather than creativity and spontaneity.

There is a lesson to learn from this episode as far as predicting the future role of Japan vis-à-vis the West. After decades of imitating the West, Japanese people are now beginning to feel that they have the skills and the moral right to create styles of their own. We can expect to see, therefore, an explosion of Japanese creativity in the near future. Some observers have noted, for example, that the international fashion industry seems to be gaining more inspiration from designers in Tokyo than from those in Milan, Paris, or New York. And, as of the mid-1980s, the Japanese have annually registered more new patents with the U.S. Patent Office than has any other nation except the United States. The Japanese are also now winning more Nobel prizes.

Preventive

Japanese individuals, families, companies, and the government prefer long-range over short-range planning, and they greatly prefer foreknowledge over postmortem analysis. Assembly-line workers test and retest every product to prevent customers from receiving defective products. Store clerks plug in and check electronic devices in front of a customer to prevent bad merchandise from sullying the good reputation of the store. Insurance companies do a brisk business in Japan, and even though Japanese citizens are covered by the government's national health plan, many people buy additional coverage—for example, cancer insurance—just to be safe.

This concern with prevention trickles down to the smallest details. At train stations, multiple recorded warnings are given of an approaching train to commuters standing on the platform. Parent–teacher associations send teams of mothers around the neighborhood to determine which streets are the safest for the children. They then post signs designating certain roads as "school passage roads" and instruct children to take those routes even if it takes longer to walk to school. The Japanese think that it is better to avoid an accident than to have an emergency team ready when a child is hurt. Whereas Americans say, "If it ain't broke, don't fix it," the Japanese say, "Why wait 'til it breaks to fix it?"

Pragmatic

Rather than pursue a plan because it ideologically fits some preordained philosophy, the Japanese try to be pragmatic on most points. Take drugs as an example. Many nations say that drug abuse is an insurmountable problem that will, at best, be contained but probably never eradicated, because to do so would violate civil liberties. But, as a headline in the *Asahi Evening News* proclaimed a few years ago, "Japan Doesn't Have a Drug Problem and Means to Keep It That Way." Reliable statistics support this claim, but that is not the whole

(Dean Collinwood)

Social problems such as drugs and homelessness are minimal in Japan. Neither the state nor the culture condones the plight of poverty, and there are few places in Japan that could be called a ghetto. Homeless people are a rare, albeit increasing, sight in Japan.

story, because in 1954 Japan had a serious drug problem, with 53,000 drug arrests in one year. At the time the authorities concluded that they had a serious problem on their hands and must do whatever was required to solve the problem. The government passed a series of tough laws restricting the production, use, exchange, and possession of all manner of drugs, and it gave the police the power to arrest all violators. Users were arrested as well as dealers: It was reasoned that if the addicts were not left to buy the drugs, the dealers would be out of business. Their goal at the time was to arrest all addicts, even if it meant that certain liberties were briefly circumscribed. The plan, based on a do-what-it-takes pragmatic approach, worked, and today Japan is the only one of the industrialized countries without a widespread drug problem. In this case, to pragmatism was added the Japanese tendency to work for the common rather than the individual good.

This approach to life is so much a part of the Japanese mind-set that many Japanese cannot understand why the United States and other industrialized nations have so many unresolved social and economic problems. For instance, when it comes to the trade imbalance, it is clear that one of the West's most serious problems is a low savings rate (making money scarce and interest high); another is inferior-quality products. Knowing that these are problems, the Japanese wonder why North Americans and Europeans do not just start saving more and working more carefully. They think, "We did it; why can't you?"

Obligative

The Japanese have a great sense of duty toward those around them. There are thousands of Japanese workers who work late without pay to improve their job skills so that they will not let their fellow workers down. Good deeds done by one generation are remembered and repaid by the next, and lifetime friendships are kept by exchanging appropriate gifts and letters. North Americans and Europeans are often considered untrustworthy friends, because they do not keep up the level of close, personal communications that the Japanese expect of their own friends; nor do these Westerners have as strong a sense of place, station, or position.

Duty to the group is closely linked to respect for superior authority. Every group—indeed, every relationship—is seen as a mixture of people with inferior and superior resources. These differences must be acknowledged, and no one is disparaged for bringing less to the group than someone else. However, equality is assumed when it comes to basic commitment to or effort expended for a task. Slackers are not welcome. Obligation to the group along with respect for superiors motivated Japanese pilots to fly suicide missions during World War II, and it now causes workers to go the extra mile for the good of the company.

Changes in the intensity of commitment, however, are increasingly apparent among modern Japanese. More Japanese than ever before are beginning to feel that their own personal goals are more important than those of their companies or extended families. This is no doubt a result of the Westernization of the culture since the Meiji Restoration, in the late 1800s, and especially of the experiences of the growing number of Japanese—approximately half a million in a given year—who live abroad and then take their newly acquired values back to Japan. (About half of these away Japanese live in North America and Western Europe.)

Inquisitive

The image of dozens of Japanese businesspeople struggling to read a book or newspaper while standing inside a packed commuter train is one not easily forgotten, symbolizing as it does the intense desire among the Japanese for knowledge, especially knowledge of foreign cultures. Nearly 6 million Japanese travel abroad each year (many to pursue higher education), and for those who do not, the government and private radio and television stations provide a continuous stream of programming about everything from Caribbean cuisine to French ballet. The Japanese have a yen for foreign styles of dress, foreign cooking, and foreign languages. The Japanese study languages with great intensity: Every student is required to study English, and many others study Chinese, Greek, Latin, Russian, Arabic, and other languages, with French being the most popular after English.

(Dean Collinwood)

The Japanese are an inquisitive people. Foreign food, dress, languages, and travel are of great interest to the average Japanese. The sign above these travel posters reads "Recommendations for Your Summer Plans."

Observers inside and outside of Japan are beginning to comment that the Japanese are recklessly discarding Japanese culture in favor of foreign ideas and habits, even when they make no sense in the Japanese context. A tremendous intellectual debate, called *Nihonjin-ron*, is now taking place in Japan over the meaning of being Japanese and the Japanese role in the world. There is certainly value in these concerns, but, as was noted previously, the secret about Japanese traditions is that they are not traditional. That is, the Japanese seem to know that in order to succeed, they must learn what they need to know for the era in which they live, even if it means modifying or eliminating the past. This is probably the reason why the Japanese nation has endured for more than 2,000 years, whereas many other empires have long since fallen. In this sense, the Japanese are very forward-looking people and, in their thirst for new modes of thinking and acting, they are, perhaps, revealing their most basic and useful national personality characteristic. Given this attitude toward learning, it should come as no surprise that formal schooling in Japan is a very serious business to the government and to families. It is to that topic that we now turn.

SCHOOLING IN JAPAN

Probably most of the things that the West has heard about Japanese schools are distortions or outright falsehoods. We hear that Japanese children are highly disciplined, for example; yet in reality, Japanese schools at the elementary and junior high levels are rather noisy, unstructured places, with

(Reuters/Bettmann)

Doing well in school is seen by students as fulfilling their obligation to their families. Education is held in high regard and is seen as an important element in achieving a better life; it is supported very strongly by parents.

children racing around the halls during breaks and getting into fights with classmates on the way home. Many readers may be surprised to learn that Japan has a far lower percentage of its college-age population enrolled in higher education than is the case in the United States—35 percent as compared to 50 percent. Moreover, the Japanese government does not require young people to attend high school (they must attend only until age 15), although 94 percent do anyway. Given these and other realities of school life in Japan, how can we explain the consistently high scores of Japanese on international tests and the general agreement that Japanese high school graduates know almost as much as college graduates in the United States?

Structurally, schools in Japan are similar to those in many other countries: there are kindergartens, elementary schools, junior high schools, and high schools. Passage into elementary and junior high is automatic, regardless of student performance level. But admission to high school and college is based on test scores from entrance examinations. Preparing for these examinations occupies the full attention of students in their final year of both junior high and high school, respectively. Both parents and school authorities insist that studying for the tests be the primary focus of a student's life at those times. For instance, members of a junior-high-school soccer

team may be allowed to play on the team only for their first 2 years; during their last year, they are expected to be studying for their high school entrance examinations. School policy reminds students that they are in school to learn and to graduate to the next level, not to play sports. Many students even attend after-hours "cram schools" (*juku*) several nights a week to prepare for the exams.

Time for recreational and other nonschool activities is restricted, because Japanese students attend school 240 days out of the year (as compared to about 180 in U.S. schools), including most Saturday mornings. Summer vacation is only about 6 weeks long, and students often attend school activities during most of the vacation period. Japanese youth are expected to treat schooling as their top priority over part-time jobs (usually prohibited by school policy during the school year, except for the needy), sports, dating, and even family time. Students who do well in school are generally thought to be fulfilling their obligations to the family. The reason for this focus on education is that parents realize that only through education can Japanese youths find their place in society. Joining the army is generally not an option, opportunities for farming are limited because of land scarcity, and most major companies will not hire a new employee who has not graduated from college or a respectable high school. Thus, the

Japanese find it important to focus on education—to do one thing and do it well.

Teachers are held in high regard in Japan, partly because when mass education was introduced, many of the high-status samurai took up teaching to replace their martial activities. In addition, in modern times the Japan Teacher's Union has been active in agitating for higher pay for teachers. As a group, teachers are the highest-paid civil servants in Japan. Public school teachers visit the home of each student each year to merge the authority of the home with that of the school, and they insist that parents (usually mothers) play active supporting roles in the school.

Some Japanese youths dislike the system, and discussions are currently under way among Japanese educators on how to improve the quality of life for students. Occasionally the pressure of taking examinations (called "exam hell") produces such stress that a desperate student will commit suicide rather than try and fail. In recent years the Ministry of Education has worked hard to help students deal with school stress, with the result that Japan's youth suicide rate has dropped dramatically (while the U.S. rate has risen). Despite these and other problems, most Japanese youths enjoy school and value the time they have to be with their friends, whether in class, walking home, or attending cram school. Some of those who fail their college entrance exams continue to study privately, some for many years, and take the exam each year until they pass. Others will travel abroad and enroll in foreign universities that do not have such rigid entrance requirements. Still others will enroll in vocational training schools. But everyone in Japan realizes that education, not money, name, or luck, is the key to success.

Parents whose children are admitted to the prestigious national universities—such as Tokyo, Kyoto, and Waseda Universities—consider that they have much to brag about. Other parents are willing to pay as much as $35,000 on average for 4 years of college at the private (but usually not as prestigious) universities. Once admitted, students find that life slows down a bit. For one thing, parents pay more than 65 percent of the costs, and approximately 3 percent is covered by scholarships. This leaves only about 30 percent to be earned by the students; this usually comes from tutoring high school students who are studying for the entrance exams. Contemporary parents are also willing to pay the cost of a son's or daughter's traveling to and spending a few months in North America or Europe either before college begins or during summer breaks—a practice that is becoming de rigueur for Japanese students, much as taking a "grand tour" of Europe was expected of young, upper-class American women at the turn of the century.

College students may take 15 or 16 courses at a time, but classes usually meet only once or twice a week, and sporadic attendance is the norm. Straight lecturing rather than class discussion is the typical learning format, and there is very little homework beyond studying for the final exam. Students generally do not challenge the professor's statements in class,

but some students develop rather close, avuncular-type relationships with their professors outside of class. Hobbies, sports, and club activities (things the students did not have time to do while in public school) occupy the center of life for many college students. Equally important is the cementing of friendships, which will last a lifetime and be useful in one's career and private life.

THE JAPANESE BUSINESS WORLD

Successful college graduates begin their work careers in April, when most large companies do their hiring. They may have to take an examination to determine how much they know about electronics or stocks and bonds, and they may have to complete a detailed personality profile. Finally, they will have to submit to a very serious interview with company management. During interviews the managers will watch their every move; the applicants will be careful to avoid saying anything that will give them "minus points."

Once hired, individuals are put in training sessions in which they learn the company song and other rituals as well as company policy on numerous matters. They may be housed in company apartments (or may continue to live at home), permitted to use a company car or van, and advised to shop at company grocery stores. Almost never are employees married at this time, and so they are expected to live a rather spartan life for the first few years.

Employees are expected to show considerable deference to their section bosses, even though, on the surface, bosses do not appear to be very different from other employees. Bosses' desks are out in the open, near the employees; they wear the same uniform; they socialize with the employees after work; even in a factory, they are often on the shop floor rather than sequestered away in private offices. Long-term employees often come to see the section leader as an uncle figure (bosses are usually male) who will give them advice about life, be the best man at their weddings, and provide informal marital and family counseling as needed.

Japanese company life can be described as somewhat like a large family rather than a military squad; employees (sometimes called *associates*) often obey their superiors out of genuine respect rather than forced compliance. Moreover, competition between workers is reduced because everyone hired at the same time receives more or less the same pay and most workers receive promotions at about the same time. Only later in one's career are individualistic promotions given.

Employees are expected to work hard, for not only are Japanese companies in competition with foreign businesses, but they also must survive the fiercely competitive business climate at home. Indeed, the Japanese skill in international business was developed at home. There are, for example, some 580 electronics companies and 7,000 textile enterprises competing for customers in Japan. And whereas the United States has only 4 automobile-manufacturing companies, Japan has 9. All these companies entice customers with deep

(Reuters/Bettmann)

In the Japanese business world, employment is taken very seriously and is often seen as a lifelong commitment. These workers have jobs that, in many ways, may be more a part of their lives than are their families.

price cuts or unusual services, hoping to edge out unprepared or weak competitors. Many companies fail. There were once, for instance, almost 40 companies in Japan that manufactured calculators, but today only 6 remain, the rest victims of tough internal Japanese competition.

At about age 27, after 5 years of working and saving money for an apartment, a car, and a honeymoon, the typical Japanese male worker marries. The average bride, about age 25, will have taken private lessons in flower arranging, the tea ceremony, sewing, cooking, and perhaps a musical instrument like the *koto,* the Japanese harp. She probably will not have graduated from college, although she may have attended a specialty college for a while. If she is working, she likely is paid much less than her husband, even if she has an identical position (despite equal-pay laws). She may spend her time in the company preparing and serving tea for clients and employees, dusting the office, running errands, and answering telephones. When she has a baby, she will be expected to quit—although more women are choosing to remain on the job.

Because the wife is expected to serve as the primary caregiver for the children, the husband is expected always to make his time available for the company. He may be asked to work weekends, to stay out late most of the week (about 4 out

of 7 nights), or even to be transferred to another branch in Japan or abroad without his family. This loyalty is rewarded in numerous ways: Unless the company goes bankrupt or the employee is unusually inept, he may be permitted to work for the company until he retires, usually at about age 55 or 60, even if the company no longer really needs his services; he and his wife will be taken on company sightseeing trips; the company will pay most of his health insurance costs (the government pays the rest); and he will have the peace of mind that comes from being surrounded by lifetime friends and workmates. His association with company employees will be his main social outlet, even after retirement; upon his death it will be his former workmates who organize and direct his Buddhist funeral services.

THE FAMILY

The loyalty once given to the traditional Japanese extended family, called the *ie,* has now been transferred to the modern company. This is logical from a historical perspective, since the modern company once began as a family business and was gradually expanded to include more workers, or "siblings." Thus, whereas the family is seen as the backbone of most societies, it might be more accurate to argue that the *kaisha,* or company, is the basis of modern Japanese society. As one Japanese commentator explained, "In the West, the home is the cornerstone of people's lives. In Tokyo, home is just a place to sleep at night. . . . Each family member—husband, wife, and children—has his own community centered outside the home."

Thus, the common image that Westerners hold of the centrality of the family to Japanese culture may be inaccurate. For instance, father absence is epidemic in Japan. It is an unusual father who eats more than one meal a day with his family. He may go shopping or to a park with his family when he has free time from work, but he is more likely to go golfing with a workmate. Schooling occupies the bulk of the children's time, even on weekends. And with fewer children than in earlier generations and with appliance-equipped apartments, many Japanese women rejoin the workforce after their children are self-maintaining.

Japan's divorce rate, while rising, is still considerably lower than in other industrialized nations, a fact that may seem incongruent with the conditions described above. Yet, as explained by one Japanese sociologist, Japanese couples "do not expect much emotional closeness; there is less pressure on us to meet each other's emotional needs. If we become close, that is a nice dividend, but if we do not, it is not a problem because we did not expect it in the first place."

Despite these modifications to the common Western image of the Japanese family, Japanese families do have significant roles to play in society. Support for education is one of the most important. Families, especially mothers, support the schools by being actively involved in the parent–teacher association, by insisting that children be given plenty of homework, and by saving for college so that the money for tuition is available without the college student having to work.

Another important function of the family is mate selection. About half of current Japanese marriages are arranged by the family. Families will ask a go-between (an uncle, a boss, or another trusted person) to compile a list of marriageable candidates. Criteria such as social class, blood type, and occupation are considered. Photos of prospective candidates are presented to the unmarried son or daughter, who has the option to veto any of them or to date those he or she finds acceptable. Young people, however, increasingly select their mates with little or no input from parents.

Finally, families in Japan, even those in which the children are married and living away from home, continue to gather for the purpose of honoring the memory of deceased family members or to enjoy one another's company for New Year's Day, Children's Day, and other celebrations.

WOMEN IN JAPAN

Ancient Confucian values held that women were legally and socially inferior to men. This produced a culture in feudal

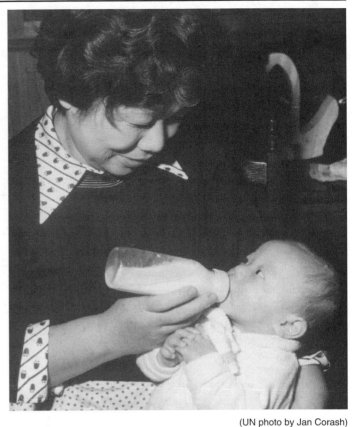

(UN photo by Jan Corash)

In Japan, not unlike in many other parts of the world, economic well-being often requires two incomes. Still, there is strong social pressure on women to stop working once they have a baby. All generations of family members take part in childrearing.

Japan in which the woman was expected to walk several steps behind her husband when in public, to eat meals only after the husband had eaten, to forgo formal education, and to serve the husband and male members of the family whenever possible. A good woman was said to be one who would endure these conditions without complaint. This pronounced gender difference can be seen today in myriad ways, including in the preponderance of males in positions of leadership in business and politics, in the smaller percentage of women college graduates, and in the pay differential between women and men.

Given the Confucian values noted above, one would expect that all top leaders would be males. However, women's roles are also subject to the complexity of both ancient and modern cultures. Between A.D. 592 and 770, for instance, of the 12 reigning emperors, half were women. In rural areas today, women take an active decision-making role in farm associations. In the urban workplace, some women occupy typically pink-collar positions (nurses, clerks, and so on), but many women are also doctors and business executives; 28,000 are company presidents.

Thus, it is clear that within the general framework of gender inequality imposed by Confucian values, Japanese culture, especially at certain times, has been rather lenient in its application of those values. There is still considerable social pressure on women to stop working once they marry, and particularly after they have a baby, but it is clear that many women are resisting that pressure: 1 out of every 3 employees in Japan is female, and nearly 60 percent of the female work force consists of married women. An equal-pay law was enacted in 1989 that makes it illegal to pay women less for doing comparable work (although it may take years for companies to comply fully). And the Ministry of Education has mandated that home economics and shop classes now be required for both boys and girls; that is, both girls and boys will learn to cook and sew as well as construct things out of wood and metal.

In certain respects, Japanese women seem more assertive than women in the West. For example, in a recent national election, a wife challenged her husband for his seat in the House of Representatives (something that has not been done in the United States, where male candidates usually expect their wives to stump for them). Significantly, too, the former head of the Japan Socialist Party was an unmarried woman, Takako Doi. Women have been elected to the powerful Tokyo Metropolitan Council and awarded professorships at prestigious universities such as Tokyo University. And while women continue to be used as sexual objects in pornography and prostitution, certain kinds of demeaning behavior, such as rape and serial killing, are less frequent in Japan than in Western societies. Indeed, Western women visiting Japan often report that they felt free to walk outside alone at night for the first time in their lives. Recent studies show that many Japanese women believe that their lives are easier than those of most Westerners. With their husbands working long hours and their one or two children in school all day, Japanese women find they have more leisure time than Western women. But gender-based social divisions remain apparent throughout Japanese culture, and modern Japanese women have learned to blend these divisions with the realities and opportunities of the contemporary workplace and home.

RELIGION/ETHICS

There are many holidays in Japan, most of which have a religious origin. This fact, as well as the existence of numerous shrines and temples, may leave the impression that Japan is a rather religious country. This is not true, however. Only about 15 percent of the Japanese people claim any active religious affiliation, although many will stop by a shrine

(The Bettmann Archive)

Religion in Japan, while not having a large active affiliation, is still an intricate part of the texture and history of the culture. This temple in Kyoto was founded in the twelfth century.

occasionally to ask for divine help in passing an exam, finding a mate, or recovering from an illness.

Nevertheless, modern Japanese culture sprang from a rich religious heritage. The first influence on Japanese culture came from the animistic Shinto religion, from whence modern Japanese acquired their respect for the beauty of nature. Confucianism brought a respect for hierarchy and education. Taoism stressed introspection, and Buddhism taught the need for good behavior now in order to acquire a better life in the future.

Shinto was selected in the 1930s as the state religion and was used as a divine justification for Japan's military exploits of that era, but most Japanese today will say that Japan is, culturally, a Buddhist nation. Some new Buddhist denominations have attracted thousands of followers. The rudiments of Christianity are also a part of the modern Japanese consciousness, but few Japanese have actually joined Christian churches.

Most Japanese regard morality as springing from within the group rather than pronounced from above. That is, a Japanese person may refrain from stealing so as not to offend the owner of an object or bring shame upon the family, rather than because of a divine prohibition against stealing. Thus we find in Japan a relatively small rate of violent—that is, public—crimes, and a much larger rate of white-collar crimes such as embezzlement, in which offenders believe that they can get away with something without creating a public scandal for their families.

THE GOVERNMENT

The Constitution of postwar Japan became effective in 1947 and firmly established the Japanese people as the ultimate source of sovereignty, with the emperor as the symbol of the nation. The national Parliament, or Diet, is empowered to pass legislation. The Diet is divided into 2 houses: the House of Representatives, with 511 members elected for 4-year terms; and the House of Councillors, with 252 members elected for 6-year terms from each of the 47 prefectures (states) of Japan as well as nationally. The prime minister, assisted by a cabinet, is also the leader of the party with the most seats in the Diet. Prefectures are governed by an elected governor and an assembly, and cities and towns are governed by elected mayors and town councils. The Supreme Court, consisting of a chief judge and 14 other judges, is independent of the legislative branch of government.

Japan's Constitution forbids Japan from engaging in war or from having military capability that would allow it to attack another country. Japan does maintain a well-equipped self-defense force, but it relies on a security treaty with the United States in case of serious aggression against it. In recent years the United States has been encouraging Japan to assume more of the burden of the military security of the Asian region, and Japan has increased its expenditures in absolute terms. But until the Constitution is amended, Japan is not likely to initiate any major upgrading of its military capability. This is in line with the general wishes of the Japanese people, who,

since the devastation of Hiroshima and Nagasaki, have become firmly committed to a pacifist foreign policy. Moreover, Japanese leaders fear that any significant increase in military capability would reignite dormant fears about Japanese intentions within the increasingly vital Pacific Rim area.

This tendency toward not wanting to get involved militarily is reflected in one of Japan's most recent performances on the world stage. The Japanese were slow to play any significant part in supporting military expenditures for the Persian Gulf War, even when the outcome had a direct potential effect on their economy. The Iraqi invasion of Kuwait in August 1990 brought on the wrath of a coalition of countries led by the United States in January 1991, but it generated an initial commitment from Japan of only $2 billion (later increased to $9 billion, still a small fraction of the cost) and no personnel of any kind. This meager support was criticized by some foreign observers, who pointed out that Japan relies heavily on Gulf oil.

In 1992 the Japanese government announced its intention of building its own F-16–type jet fighter planes; and subsequently, amid protests from the public, the Diet voted to send as many as 1,800 Japanese soldiers—the first to go abroad since World War II—to Cambodia to assist in the UN–supervised peacekeeping effort. Countries that had experienced the full force of Japanese domination in the past, such as China and Korea, expressed dismay at these evidences of Japan's modern military capability, but the United States welcomed the moves as an indication of Japan's willingness to share the costs of providing military security to Asia.

The Japanese have formed numerous political parties to represent their views in government. Among these are the Japan Communist Party, the Social Democratic Party, and the New Frontier Party. For nearly 40 years, however, the most powerful party was the Liberal Democratic Party (LDP). Formed in 1955, it guided Japan to its current position of economic strength, but a series of sex and bribery scandals caused it to lose control of the government in 1993. A shaky coalition of eight parties took control for about a year but was replaced by an even more unlikely coalition of the LDP and the Japan Socialists—historic enemies who are unlikely to be able to agree on most policies. With some half a dozen changes in the prime ministership in the early 1990s and further party realignments in 1994, it would be an understatement to say that Japan's government is in flux.

Part of the reason for this instability can be explained by Japan's party faction system. Party politics in Japan has always been a mixture of Western-style democratic practice and feudalistic personal relationships. Japanese parties are really several parties rolled into one. That is, parties are divided into several factions, each comprised of a group of loyal younger members headed by a powerful member of the Diet. The senior member has a duty to pave the way for the younger members politically, but they, in turn, are obligated to support the senior member in votes and in other ways. The

Prepottery, paleolithic culture 20,000 B.C.– 4,500 B.C.	Jomon culture with distinctive pottery 4,500 B.C.– 250 B.C.	Yayoi culture with rice agriculture, Shinto religion, and Japanese language 250 B.C.–A.D. 300	The Yamato period; warrior clans import Chinese culture A.D. 300–700	The Nara period; Chinese-style bureaucratic government at the capital at Nara 710–794	The Heian period; the capital is at Kyoto 794–1185	The Kamakura period; feudalism and shoguns; Buddhism is popularized 1185–1333	The Muromachi period; Western missionaries and traders arrive; feudal lords control their own domains 1333–1568	The Momoyama period; feudal lords become subject to one central leader; attempted invasion of Korea 1568–1600

faction leader's role in gathering financial support for faction members is particularly important, because Diet members are expected by the electorate to be patrons of numerous causes, from charity drives to the opening of a constituent's fast-food business. Because parliamentary salaries are inadequate to the task, outside funds, and thus the faction, are crucial. The size and power of the various factions are often the critical elements in deciding who will assume the office of prime minister and who will occupy which cabinet seats. The role of these intraparty factions is so central to Japanese politics that attempts to ban them have never been successful.

The factional nature of Japanese party politics means that cabinet and other political positions are frequently rotated. This would yield considerable instability in governance were it not for the stabilizing influence of the Japanese bureaucracy. Large and powerful, the career bureaucracy is responsible for drafting more than 80 percent of the bills submitted to the Diet. Many of the bureaucrats are graduates from the finest universities in Japan, particularly Tokyo University, which provides some 80 percent of the senior officials in the more than 20 national ministries. Many of them consider their role in long-range forecasting, drafting legislation, and implementing policies to be superior to that of the elected officials under whom they work. They reason that whereas the politicians are bound to the whims of the people they represent, bureaucrats are committed to the nation of Japan—to, as it were, the *idea* of Japan. Thus, government service is considered a higher calling than are careers in private business, law, or other fields.

In addition to the bureaucracy, Japanese politicians have leaned heavily on big business to support their policies of postwar reconstruction, economic growth, and social reform. Business has accepted heavy taxation so that social welfare programs such as the national health plan are feasible, and they have supported political candidates through substantial financial help. In turn, the government has seen its role as that of facilitating the growth of private industry (some critics claim that the relationship between government and business is so close that Japan is best described not as a nation but as "Japan, Inc."). Consider, for example, the powerful Ministry of International Trade and Industry (MITI). Over the years it has worked closely with business, particularly the Federation of Economic Organizations (Keidanren) to forecast potential market shifts, develop strategies for market control, and generally pave the way for Japanese businesses to succeed in the international marketplace. The close working relationship between big business and the national government is an established fact of life in Japan, and despite criticism from

countries with a more laissez faire approach to business, it will undoubtedly continue into the future, because it has served Japan well.

THE FUTURE

In the postwar years of political stability, the Japanese have accomplished more than anyone, including themselves, thought possible. Japan's literacy rate is 99 percent, 100 percent of Japanese households have telephones, 99 percent have color televisions, and 75 percent own automobiles. Nationalized health care covers every Japanese citizen, and the Japanese have the highest life expectancy in the world. With only half the population of the United States, a land area about the size of Great Britain, and extremely limited natural resources (it has to import 99.6 percent of its oil, 99.8 percent of its iron, and 86.7 percent of its coal), Japan has nevertheless created the second-largest economy in the world. Where does it go from here?

When the Spanish were establishing hegemony over large parts of the globe, they were driven in part by the desire to bring Christianity to the "heathen." The British, for their part, believed that they were taking "civilization" to the savages of the world. China and the former Soviet Union were strongly committed to the ideals of communism, while the United States felt that its mission was that of expanding democracy and capitalism.

What about Japan? For what reason do Japanese businesses buy up hotels in New Zealand and skyscrapers in New York? What role does Japan have to play in the world in addition to spawning economic development? What values will guide and perhaps temper Japan's drive for economic dominance?

These are questions that the Japanese people themselves are attempting to answer; but, finding no ready answers, they are beginning to encounter more and more difficulties with the world around them and within their own society. Animosity over the persistent trade imbalance in Japan's favor continues to grow in Europe and North America as well as in some countries of the Pacific Rim. To deflect these criticisms, Japan has substantially increased its gift-giving to foreign governments, including allocating money for the stabilization or growth of democracy in Central/Eastern Europe and for easing the foreign debt burden of Mexico and other countries.

What Japan has been loathe to do, however, is remove the "structural impediments" that make it difficult for foreign companies to do business in Japan. For example, 50 percent of the automobiles sold in Iceland are Japanese, which means less profit for the American and European manufacturers who

The Tokugawa Era; self-imposed isolation from the West
1600–1868

The Meiji Restoration; modernization; Taiwan and Korea are under Japanese control
1868–1912

The Taisho and Showa periods; militarization leads to war and Japan's defeat
1912–1945

Japan surrenders; the U.S. Occupation imposes major changes in the organization of society
1945

Sovereignty is returned to the Japanese people by treaty
1951

The newly merged Liberal-Democratic Party wins control of the government
1955

Japan passes the threshold of economic self-sustainability
1960s

Student activism; the Nuclear Security Treaty with the United States is challenged
late 1960s

The ruling party is hit by scandals but retains control of the government; Emperor Hirohito dies; Emperor Akihito succeeds
1980s

1990s

Japan reacts to protectionism in major markets by turning its attention to the Pacific Rim

Japan sends troops to maintain peace in Cambodia; Japan remains the second-largest economy in the world

The Liberal Democratic Party loses control of the government after 38 years in power

A devastating earthquake in Kobe kills more than 5,000 people

used to dominate car sales there. Yet because of high tariffs and other regulations, very few American and European cars have been sold in Japan. Beginning in the mid-1980s, Japan began to dismantle many of these trade barriers, and it has been so successful that it now has a lower overall average tariff on nonagricultural products than the United States—its severest critic in this arena.

But Japanese people worry that further opening of their markets may destroy some fundamentals of Japanese life. Rice, for instance, costs much more in Japan than it should, because the Japanese government protects rice farmers with subsidies and limits most rice imports from abroad. The Japanese would prefer to pay less for rice at the supermarket, but they also argue that foreign competition would prove the undoing of many small rice farmers, whose land would then be sold to housing developers. This, in turn, would destroy more of Japan's scarce arable land and weaken the already shaky traditions of the Japanese countryside—the heart of traditional Japanese culture and values.

Today more than 300 foreign firms do business in Japan, and some of them, like Polaroid and Schick, control the Japanese market in their products. Foreign investment in Japan has grown about 16 percent annually since 1980. In the case of the United States, the profit made by American firms doing business in Japan (some 170 of them) in a single year is just about equal to the amount of the trade imbalance between Japan and the United States. Japanese supermarkets are filled with foreign foodstuffs, and the radio and television airwaves are filled with the sounds and sights of Western music and dress. Japanese youth are as likely to eat at McDonald's or Kentucky Fried Chicken outlets as at traditional Japanese restaurants, and many Japanese have never

worn a kimono nor learned to play a Japanese musical instrument. It is clear to many observers that, culturally, Japan already imports much more from the West than the West does from Japan.

Given this overwhelming Westernization of Japan as well as Japan's current capacity to continue imbibing Western culture, even the change-oriented Japanese are beginning to ask where they, as a nation, are going. Will national wealth, as it slowly trickles down to individuals, produce a generation of hedonistic youth who do not appreciate the sacrifices of those before them? Will wealthy Japanese people be satisfied with the small homes and tiny yards that their forebears had to accept? Will there ever be a time when, strapped for resources, the Japanese will once again seek hegemony over other nations? What future role should Japan assume in the international arena, apart from economic development? If these questions remain to be answered, circumstances of international trade have at least provided an answer to the question of Japan's role in the Pacific Rim countries: It is clear that for the next several decades, Japan will continue to shape the pace and nature of economic development, and thus the political environment, of the entire Pacific Rim.

DEVELOPMENT

Japan is now entering a post-smokestack era in which primary industries are being moved abroad, producing a hollowing effect inside Japan and increasing the likelihood of rising unemployment. Nevertheless, prospects for continued growth are excellent.

FREEDOM

Japanese citizens enjoy full civil liberties, and opposition parties and ideologies are seen as natural and useful components of democracy. Certain people, however, such as those of Korean ancestry, have been subject to both social and official discrimination—an issue that is gaining the attention of the Japanese.

HEALTH/WELFARE

The Japanese live longer on average than any other people on earth. Every citizen is provided with inexpensive medical care under a national health care system, but many people still prefer to save substantial portions of their income for health emergencies and old age.

ACHIEVEMENTS

Japan has achieved virtually complete literacy, and although there are poor areas, there are no slums inhabited by a permanent underclass. The gaps between the social classes appear to be less pronounced than in many other societies. The country seems to be entering an era of remarkable educational and technological achievement.

Australia (Commonwealth of Australia)

GEOGRAPHY

Area in Square Kilometers (Miles):
7,686,850 (2,867,896)
Capital (Population): Canberra (310,000)
Climate: generally arid to semiarid;
temperate in the south and east;
tropical in the north

PEOPLE

Population
Total: 17,827,000
Annual Growth Rate: 1.41%
Rural/Urban Population (Ratio): 15/85
Ethnic Makeup: 95% European ancestry;
4% Asian; 1% Aboriginal and others
Major Languages: English;
indigenous languages

Health
Life Expectancy at Birth: 74 years
(male); 81 years (female)
Infant Mortality Rate (Ratio): 7.4/1,000
Average Caloric Intake: 118% of
FAO minimum
Physicians Available (Ratio): 1/438

Religions
26% Anglican; 26% Roman Catholic;
24% other Christian; 24% other or
no affiliation

Education
Adult Literacy Rate: 98%

COMMUNICATION

Telephones: 8,700,000
Newspapers: 143

A LAND OF HEAT AND HARD WORK

Some people immigrate to Australia hoping that the relatively inexpensive land and strong economy will easily provide them with a high standard of living. But in character, many parts of Australia are like the American Wild West of the 1870s: Sweaty and persistent hard work and luck are the only keys to success. For example, cattle ranches in parts of Australia can have as many as 70,000 head of cattle to be cared for over a 5-million-acre spread. Just providing water in the arid climate is a formidable task; dozens of wells must be dug to reach the water table lying far below the earth's surface. Ranchers must also contend with daily temperatures above 100°F and brush fires that destroy hundreds of acres of grassland and roast sheep and cattle alive. In 1994, 155 wildfires destroyed thousands of homes and nearly 2 million acres, including 98 percent of the Royal National Park near Sydney. In the summer (February) of 1993, temperatures in southern and eastern Australia hit 113°F.

TRANSPORTATION

Highways—Kilometers (Miles):
837,872 (51,948)
Railroads—Kilometers (Miles):
40,478 (25,096)
Usable Airfields: 439

GOVERNMENT

Type: federal parliamentary state
Independence Date: January 1, 1901
Head of State/Government: Queen
Elizabeth II, represented by Governor
General William George Hayden;
Prime Minister Paul Keating
Political Parties: Australian Labour
Party; Liberal Party; National Party;
Australian Democratic Party
Suffrage: universal and compulsory
at age 18

MILITARY

Number of Armed Forces: 68,300
*Military Expenditures (% of Central
Government Expenditures):* 2.4%
Current Hostilities: none

ECONOMY

Currency ($ U.S. Equivalent): 1.34
Australian dollars = $1
Per Capita Income/GDP:
$16,700/$293.5 billion
Inflation Rate: 0.8%
Natural Resources: bauxite;
diamonds; coal; copper; iron; oil;
gas; other minerals
Agriculture: beef; wool; mutton;
wheat; barley; sugarcane; fruit
Industry: mining; industrial and
transportation equipment; food processing;
chemicals; steel; motor vehicles

FOREIGN TRADE

Exports: $41.7 billion
Imports: $37.8 billion

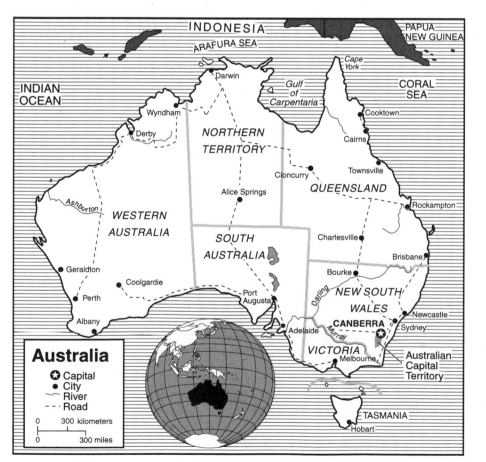

Australia
⊗ Capital
● City
〜 River
- - - Road

0 ___ 300 kilometers
0 ___ 300 miles

THE LAND NO ONE WANTED

Despite its out-of-the-way location, far south of the main trading routes between Europe and Asia, explorers from Portugal, Spain, and the Netherlands began investigating parts of the continent of Australia in the seventeenth century. The French later made some forays along the coast, but it was the British who first found something to do with a land that others had disparaged as useless: They decided to send their prisoners there. The British had long believed that the easiest solution to prison overcrowding was expulsion from Britain. For many years convicts had been sent to the American colonies, but after American independence was declared in 1776, Britain decided to begin sending prisoners to Australia.

Australia seemed like the ideal spot for a penal colony: It was isolated from the centers of civilization; it had some good harbors; and although much of the continent was a flat, dry, riverless desert with only sparse vegetation, the coastal fringes were well suited to human habitation. Indeed, although the British did not know it in the 1700s, they had discovered a huge continent endowed with abundant natural resources. Along the northern coast (just south of Indonesia and New Guinea) was a tropical zone with heavy rainfall and tropical forests. The eastern coast was wooded with valuable pine trees, while the western coast was dotted with eucalyptus and acacia trees. Minerals, especially coal, gold, nickel, petroleum, iron, and bauxite, were plentiful, as were the many species of unique animals: kangaroos, platypus, and koalas, to name a few.

The British chose to build their first penal colony in what is now Sydney. By the 1850s, when the practice of transporting convicts stopped, more than 150,000 prisoners, including hundreds of women, had been sent there and to other colonies. Most of them were illiterate English and Irish from the lower socioeconomic classes. Once they completed their sentences, they were set free to settle on the continent. These individuals, their guards, and gold prospectors constituted the beginning of modern Australian society.

RACE RELATIONS

Convicts certainly did not constitute the beginning of human habitation on the continent, however. Tens of thousands of Aborigines (literally, "first inhabitants") inhabited Australia and the nearby island of Tasmania when Europeans first made contact. Living in scattered tribes and speaking hundreds of entirely unrelated languages, the Aborigines, whose origin is unknown (some scholars see connections to Africa, the Indian subcontinent, and the Melanesian Islands), survived by fishing and nomadic hunting. Succumbing to European diseases, violence, forced removal from their lands, and, finally, neglect, thousands of Aborigines died during the first centuries of contact. Indeed, the entire Tasmanian race (originally 5,000 people) is now extinct.

Most Aborigines eventually adopted European ways, including Christianity. Today they live in the cities or work for cattle and sheep ranchers. Others reside on

(San Diego Convention and Visitors Bureau)

Australia has a number of animals that are, in their native form, unique in the world. The koala is found only in the eastern coastal region, where it feeds very selectively on the leaves of the eucalyptus tree. It is a marsupial, and bears its young every other year. Pictured above is a very rare baby albino koala with its mother.

reserves (tribal reservations) in the central and northern parts of Australia. Modernization has affected even the reservation Aborigines—some have telephones, and some dispersed tribes in the Northern Territories communicate with one another by satellite-linked video conferencing—but in the main, they continue to live as they have always done, organizing their religion around plant or animal sacred symbols, or totems, and initiating youth into adulthood through lengthy and sometimes painful rituals.

Whereas the United States began with 13 founding colonies, Australia started with 6, none of which felt a compelling need to unite into a single nation until the 1880s, when other European powers began taking an interest in settling the continent.

It was not until 1901 that Australians formally separated from Great Britain (while remaining within the British Commonwealth with the Queen of England as head of state). Populated almost entirely by whites from Britain or Europe (people of European descent still constitute about 95 percent of Australia's population), Australia has maintained close cultural and diplomatic links with Britain and the West, at the expense of ties with the geographically closer nations of Asia.

Reaction against Polynesians, Chinese, and other Asian immigrants in the late 1800s produced an official "White Australia" policy, which remained intact until the 1960s and effectively excluded nonwhites from settling in Australia. During the 1960s the government made an effort to

relax these restrictions and to restore land and some measure of self-determination to Aborigines. In the 1990s Aborigines successfully persuaded the federal government to block a dam project on Aboriginal land that would have destroyed sacred sites. The federal government sided with the Aborigines against white developers and local government officials. In 1993, despite some public resistance, the government passed laws protecting the land claims of Aborigines and set up a fund to assist Aborigines with land purchases. Evidence of continued racism can be found, however, in such graffiti painted on walls of highrise buildings as "Go home Japs!" (in this case, the term "Jap," or, alternatively, "wog," refers to any Asian, regardless of nationality).

(Australian Information Service photo)

When Europeans first discovered Australia, they found the continent inhabited by Aborigines, who had survived for millennia by fishing and nomadic hunting. With the Europeans came disease, violence, and neglect. Most Aborigines eventually adapted to the newcomers' customs, but some continue to live in their traditional ways on tribal reservations.

European exploration of the Australian coastline begins **1600s**	British explorers first land in Australia **1688**	The first shipment of English convicts arrives **1788**	The gold rush lures thousands of immigrants **1851**	Australia becomes independent within the British Commonwealth **1901**

ECONOMIC PRESSURES

Despite the prevalence of this sort of attitude, events since World War II have forced Australia to reconsider its position, at least economically, vis-à-vis Asia and Southeast Asia. Australia has never been conquered by a foreign power (not even by Japan during World War II), but the impressive industrial strength of Japan now allows its people to enjoy higher per capita income than that of Australians, and Singapore is not far behind. Moreover, since Australia's economy is based on the export of primary goods (for example, minerals, wheat, beef, and wool) rather than the much more lucrative consumer products manufactured from raw resources, it is likely that Australia will continue to lose ground to the more economically aggressive and heavily populated Asian economies.

This will be a new experience for Australians, whose standard of living has been the highest in the Pacific Rim for decades. Building on a foundation of sheep (imported in the 1830s and now supplying more than a quarter of the world's supply of wool), mining (gold was discovered in 1851), and agriculture (Australia is nearly self-sufficient in food), the country has developed its manufacturing sector such that Australians are able to enjoy a standard of living equal in most respects to that of North Americans.

But as the year 2000 approaches, Australians look warily at the growing tendency to create mammoth trading blocs, such as the North American Free Trade Association, consisting of the United States, Canada, Mexico, and others; the European Union (formerly the European Community), eventually including, perhaps, parts of Central/Eastern Europe; the ASEAN nations of Southeast Asia; and an informal "yen bloc" in Asia, headed by Japan). These blocs might exclude Australian products from preferential trade treatment or eliminate them from certain markets altogether. Beginning in 1983, therefore, the Labour government of then–prime minister Robert Hawke began to establish collaborative trade agreements with Asian countries, a plan that seemed to have the support of the electorate, even though it meant reorienting Australia's foreign policy away from its traditional posture Westward.

Under Labour prime minister Paul Keating, who was returned to office in the 1993 elections, the Asianization plan has intensified. The Japanese prime minister and the governor of Hong Kong have visited Australia in recent years, and Australian leaders have visited South Korea, China, Thailand, Vietnam, and Laos in search of product markets. Australia has even implemented a national plan to have 60 percent of Australian school students studying Japanese and other Asian languages by the year 2010.

Despite such trade initiatives (and a few successes: Japan now buys more beef from Australia than from the United States), the economic threat to Australia remains. Even in the islands of the Pacific, an area that Australia and New Zealand generally have considered their own domain for economic investment and foreign aid, new investments by Asian countries are beginning to winnow Australia's sphere of influence. Moreover, Australia's domestic markets have been so sluggish during the past several years of recession that unemployment in 1992 was more than 10 percent. The government has proposed massive work projects to put people back to work, but opinion polls show that Prime Minister Paul Keating, in office since late 1991, is losing the support of voters.

THE AMERICAN CONNECTION

By any standard, Australia is regarded as a democracy solidly embedded in the traditions of the West. Political power is shared back and forth between the Australian Labour Party and the Liberal-National Country Party coalition, and the Constitution is based on both British parliamentary tradition and the U.S. model. Thus, it has followed that Australia and the United States have built a warm friendship as both political and military allies. A military mutual-assistance agreement, ANZUS (for Australia, New Zealand, and the United States), was concluded after World War II (New Zealand withdrew in 1986). And just as it had sent troops to fight Germany during World Wars I and II, Australia sent troops to fight in the Korean War in 1950 and the Vietnam War in the 1960s—although anti–Vietnam War sentiment in Australia strained relations somewhat with the United States at that time.

Australia also joined the United States and other countries in 1954 in establishing the Southeast Asia Treaty Organization, an Asian counterpart to the North Atlantic Treaty Organization and designed to contain the spread of communism.

In 1991, when the Philippines refused to renew the lease on U.S. military bases there, there was much discussion about transferring U.S. operations to the Cockburn Sound Naval Base in Australia. Singapore was eventually chosen for some of the operations, but the incident reveals the close relationship of the two nations. U.S. military aircraft already land in Australia, and submarines and other naval craft call at Australian ports. The Americans also use Australian territory for surveillance facilities. There is historical precedence for this level of close cooperation: Before the U.S. invasion of the Japanese-controlled Philippines in the 1940s, the United States based its Pacific theater military headquarters in Australia; moreover, Britain's inability to lead the fight against Japan had forced Australia to look to the United States.

A few Australians resent the violation of sovereignty represented by the U.S. bases, but most regard the United States as a solid ally. Indeed, many Australians regard their country as the Southern Hemisphere's version of the United States: both countries have space and vast resources, both were founded as disparate colonies that eventually united and obtained independence from Britain, and both share a common language and a Western cultural heritage. Unlike New Zealand, which has distanced itself from the United States by refusing to allow nuclear-armed ships to enter its ports and has withdrawn from ANZUS, Australia has joined with the United States in attempting to dissuade South Pacific states from declaring the region a nuclear-free zone. Yet it has also maintained good ties with the small and vulnerable societies of the Pacific through its leadership in such regional associations as the South Pacific Commission, the South Pacific Forum, and the ever-more-influential Asia–Pacific Economic Cooperation Group. It has also condemned nuclear bomb testing programs in French-controlled territories.

There is yet another way that Australia is, or would like to be, like the United States: It wants to be a republic. A little

Australia is threatened by Japan during World War II
1940s

Australia proposes the South Pacific Commission
1947

Australia joins New Zealand and the United States in the ANZUS military security agreement
1951

Australia joins the South East Asian Treaty Organization
1954

Relations with the United States are strained over the Vietnam War
1960s

The Australian Labour Party wins for the first time in 23 years; Gough Whitlam is prime minister
1972

After a constitutional crisis, Whitlam is replaced by opposition leader J. M. Fraser
1975

Australia begins to strengthen its economic ties with Asian countries

Depletion of the ozone layer is believed to be responsible for a rapidly rising incidence of skin cancer among Australians
1980s

1990s

The Labour Party is reelected to a sixth term, with Paul Keating returning as prime minister

Australia seeks to become a republic by 2001

less than half the population say that they can see no reason to remain a constitutional monarchy, with the king or queen of England as the head of state. Therefore, in 1993, the prime minister met with Queen Elizabeth II to announce his intention of turning Australia into a republic (within the British Commonwealth) by the year 2001. The queen indicated that she would respect the wishes of the people.

AUSTRALIA AND THE PACIFIC

Australia was not always possessed of good intentions toward the islands around it. For one thing, white Australians thought of themselves as superior to the brown-skinned islanders; and for another, Australia preferred to use the islands' resources for its own economic gain, with little regard for the islanders themselves. At the end of World War I, for example, the phosphate-rich island of Nauru, formerly under German control, was assigned to Australia as a trust territory. Until phosphate mining was turned over to the islanders in 1967, Australian farmers consumed large quantities of phosphate but paid only half the market price. Worse, only a tiny fraction of the proceeds went to the people of Nauru. Similarly, in Papua New Guinea, Australia controlled the island without taking significant steps toward its domestic development until the 1960s, when, under the guidance of the United Nations, it did an about-face and facilitated changes that advanced the successful achievement of independence in 1975.

In addition to forgoing access to cheap resources, Australia was reluctant to relin-

quish control of these islands because it saw them as a shield against possible military attack. It learned this lesson well in World War II. In 1941 Japan, taking advantage of the Western powers' preoccupation with Adolf Hitler, moved quickly to expand its imperial designs in Asia and the Pacific. The Japanese first disabled the U.S. Navy by attacking its warships docked in Pearl Harbor, Hawaii. They then moved on to oust the British in Hong Kong and the Gilbert Islands, and the Americans in Guam and Wake Island. Within 5 months the Japanese had taken control of Burma, Malaya, Borneo, the Philippines, Singapore, and hundreds of tiny Pacific islands, which they used to create an immense defensive perimeter around the home islands of Japan. They also had captured part of New Guinea and were keeping a large force there, which greatly concerned the Australians. Yet fighting was kept away from Australia proper when the Japanese were successfully engaged by Australian and American troops in New Guinea. Other Pacific islands were regained from the Japanese at a tremendous cost in lives and military hardware. Japan's defeat came only when islands close enough to Japan to be attacked by U.S. bomber aircraft were finally captured. Japan surrendered in 1945, but the colonial powers had learned that possession of small islands could have strategic importance. This experience is part of the reason for colonial Europe's reluctance to grant independence to the vast array of islands over which they had exercised control. Australia is now faced with the question of whether or not to grant inde-

pendence to the 4,000 inhabitants of Christmas Island who recently voted to become a self-ruling territory within Australia.

There is no doubt that stressful historical episodes such as World War II drew the English-speaking countries of the South Pacific closer together and closer to the United States. But recent realignments in the world economic system are creating strains. When the United States insists that Japan take steps to ease the billowing U.S.–Japan trade imbalance, Australia sometimes comes out the loser. For instance, both Australia and the United States are producers of coal, and, given the nearly equal distance between those two countries and Japan, it would be logical to expect that Japan would buy coal at about the same price from both countries. In fact, however, Japan pays $7 a ton more for American coal than for Australian coal, a discrepancy directly attributable to Japan's attempt to reduce the trade imbalance with the United States. Resentment against the United States over such matters is likely to grow, and managing such international tensions will no doubt challenge the skills of the leadership of Australia well into the next century.

DEVELOPMENT

Mining of nickel, iron ore, and other metals continues to supply a substantial part of Australia's gross domestic product. In recent years Japan rather than Great Britain has become Australia's primary trading partner. Seven out of 10 of Australia's largest export markets are Asian countries.

FREEDOM

Australia is a parliamentary democracy adhering to the ideals incorporated in English common law. Constitutional guarantees of human rights apply to all of Australia's 17 million citizens. However, social discrimination continues, and despite improvements since the 1960s, the Aborigines remain a neglected part of Australian society.

HEALTH/WELFARE

Like New Zealand, Australia has developed a complex system of social welfare, including government-funded hospital and medical care, maternity payments, and aid to those unemployed, widowed, or aged. Education is the province of the several states. Public education is compulsory. Australia boasts several world-renowned universities.

ACHIEVEMENTS

The vastness and challenge of Australia's interior lands, called "the outback," have inspired a number of Australian writers to create outstanding poetry and fictional novels. In 1973 Patrick White became the first Australian to win a Nobel Prize in Literature. Jill Ker Conway, Thomas Keneally, and Colleen McCullough are other well-known Australian authors.

Brunei (Negara Brunei Darussalam)

GEOGRAPHY

Area in Square Kilometers (Miles):
5,770 (2,228) (slightly larger than
Delaware)
Capital (Population): Bandar Seri
Begawan (51,000)
Climate: tropical

PEOPLE

Population
Total: 277,000
Annual Growth Rate: 2.77%
Rural/Urban Population (Ratio): n/a
Ethnic Makeup: 64% Malay; 20%
Chinese; 16% others
Major Languages: Bahasa Melayu;
English; Chinese; Iban; native dialects

Health
Life Expectancy at Birth: 70 years
(male); 73 years (female)
Infant Mortality Rate (Ratio):
2.5/1,000
Average Caloric Intake: n/a
Physicians Available (Ratio): 1/2,176

Religions
63% Muslim; 15% indigenous
beliefs; 14% Buddhist; 8% Christian

A LITTLE-KNOWN HAVEN

Brunei's capital—and its main center of population—is Bandar Seri
Begawan, previously known as Brunei Town. Located approximately
10 miles from the mouth of the Brunei River, the town boasts pleasant
sightseeing opportunities for travelers, including nearby beaches, the
Hassanal Bolkiah Aquarium, and the Sultan Omar Ali Saifuddin
Mosque, considered one of the most impressive examples of modern
Islamic architecture in Southeast Asia. Visitors to the country are treated
warmly, even when passing through immigration and customs; yet, due
to its healthy reserves of foreign exchange earned from oil and gas
revenues, the government has not actively pursued tourism. The British
influence is palpable (English is one of the two official languages, and
even the city museum is named after Winston Churchill) but wooden
houses built on stilts over the water's edge clearly bespeak Bandar's
Malay heritage.

Education
Adult Literacy Rate: 77%

COMMUNICATION

Telephones: 53,300
Newspapers: 1

TRANSPORTATION

Highways—Kilometers (Miles): 1,090
(676)
Railroads—Kilometers (Miles): 13 (8)
Usable Airfields: 2

GOVERNMENT

Type: Constitutional sultanate
Independence Date: January 1, 1984
Head of State: Sultan and Prime
Minister Paduka Seri Baginda Sultan
Haji Hassanal Bolkiah Mu'izzaddin
Waddaulah
Political Parties: Brunei National
United Party (inactive); Brunei
National Democratic Party (the first
legal party now banned)
Suffrage: none

MILITARY

Number of Armed Forces: 4,250
*Military Expenditures (% of Central
Government Expenditures):* 9%
Current Hostilities: none

ECONOMY

Currency ($ U.S. Equivalent): 1.65
Bruneian dollars = $1
Per Capita Income/GDP: $8,800/$3.5
billion
Inflation Rate: 1.3%
Natural Resources: oil; gas; forest
products
Agriculture: rice; vegetables; arable
crops; fruits
Industry: oil (the prime industry,
employing 7% of population); rubber;
pepper; sawn lumber; gravel; animal
hides

FOREIGN TRADE

Exports: $2.2 billion
Imports: $1.7 billion

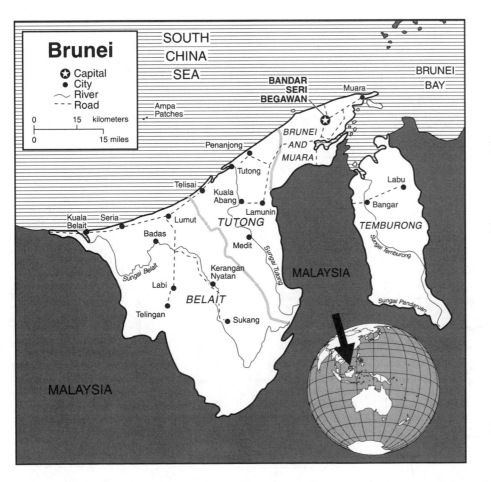

Brunei is first visited by Europeans A.D. 1521	Brunei is known as haven for pirates 1700	Briton James Brooke is given Sarawak as reward for help in a civil war 1800s	The island of Labuan is ceded to Britain 1847	Britain attacks and ends pirate activities in Brunei 1849	The remainder of Brunei becomes a British protectorate 1888	The first Brunei Constitution is promulgated 1959	Brunei rejects confederation with Malaysia 1963	Brunei gains its independence of Britain 1984

1990s

The sultan of Brunei, Hassanal Bolkiah, is said to be the richest person in the world, with assets of $37 billion

Foreign workers are "imported" to ease the labor shortage

A WEALTHY COUNTRY

Home to only 277,000 people, Brunei rarely captures the headlines. But perhaps it should, for despite its tiny size, the country boasts one of the highest living standards in the world. Moreover, the sultan of Brunei, with assets of $37 billion, is considered the richest person in the world. The secret? Oil. First exploited in Brunei in the late 1920s, oil and natural gas today almost entirely support the sultanate's economy, which has an economic growth rate of nearly 7 percent per year. The government's annual income is nearly twice its expenditures, despite the provision of free education and medical care, subsidized food and housing, and the absence of income taxes. Currently Brunei is in the middle of a 5-year plan designed to diversify its economy and lessen its dependence on oil revenues, but some 98 percent of the nation's revenues continues to depend on the sale of oil and natural gas. Japan purchases more than 60 percent of Brunei's exports; the other nations of the Asian Pacific purchase most of the remainder. Brunei's imports come primarily from Asia, especially Japan, and from the United States.

Muslim sultans ruled over the entire island of Borneo and other nearby islands during the sixteenth century. Advantageously located on the northwest coast of the island of Borneo, along the sea lanes of the South China Sea, Brunei was a popular resting spot for traders; and, during the 1700s, it became known as a haven for pirates. In the 1800s the sultan then in power agreed to the kingdom becoming a protectorate of Britain in order to safeguard his domain from being further

whittled away by aggressors bent on empire-building. The Japanese easily overtook Brunei in 1941, when they launched their Southeast Asian offensive in search of oil and gas for their war machine. Today the Japanese Mitsubishi Corporation has a one-third interest in the Brunei gas company.

In the 1960s it was expected that Brunei, which is cut in two and surrounded on three sides by Malaysia, would join the newly proposed Federation of Malaysia; but it refused to do so, preferring to remain under British control. The decision to remain a colony of Britain was made by Sultan Sir Omar Ali Saifuddin. Educated in British Malaya, the sultan retained a strong affection for British culture and frequently visited the British Isles. (Brunei's 1959 Constitution, promulgated during Sir Omar's reign, reflected this attachment: It declared Brunei a self-governing state, with its foreign affairs and defense remaining the responsibility of Britain.)

In 1967 Sir Omar abdicated in favor of his son, who became the 29th ruler in succession. Sultan (and Prime Minister) Hassanal Bolkiah Mu'izzaddin Waddaulah (a shortened version of his name) oversaw Brunei's gaining of independence, in 1984. Not all Bruneians are pleased with the sultan's control over the political process, but opposition voices have been silenced. There are, in effect, no operative political parties in Brunei, and there have been no elections in the country since 1965, despite a constitutional provision for them.

Brunei's largest ethnic group is Malay, accounting for 64 percent of the population. Indians and Chinese constitute sizable minorities, as do indigenous peoples such as Ibans and Dyaks. Despite Brunei's

historic ties with Britain, Europeans make up only a tiny fraction of the population.

Brunei is an Islamic nation with Hindu roots. Islam is the official state religion, and in recent years the sultan has proposed bringing national laws more closely in line with Islamic ideology. Modern Brunei is officially a constitutional monarchy, headed by the sultan, a chief minister, and a Council; in reality, however, the sultan and his family control all aspects of state decision making. The Constitution provides the sultan with supreme executive authority in the state.

In recent years Brunei has been plagued by a chronic labor shortage. The government and Brunei Shell (a consortium owned jointly by the Brunei government and Shell Oil) are the largest employers in the country. They provide generous fringe benefits and high pay. Non-oil private-sector companies with fewer resources find it difficult to recruit in-country and have, therefore, employed many foreign workers. One third of all workers today in Brunei are foreigners. This situation is of considerable concern to the government, which is worried that social tensions between foreigners and residents, as is happening in other countries, may flare up in Brunei.

DEVELOPMENT

Brunei's economy is a mixture of the modern and the ancient: foreign and domestic entrepreneurship, government regulation and welfare statism, and village tradition. Chronic labor shortages are managed by the importation of thousands of foreign workers. Three fourths of Brunei are covered by dense tropical rain forests.

FREEDOM

Although Islam is the official state religion, the government practices religious tolerance. Matters related to Islam are dealt with by Islamic courts; in most respects, however, the legal system in Brunei is derived from the British system. The Constitution provides the sultan with supreme executive authority, which he has used to suppress opposition groups and political parties.

HEALTH/WELFARE

The country's massive oil and natural gas revenues support wide-ranging benefits to the population, such as subsidized food, fuel, and housing, and free medical care and education. This distribution of wealth is reflected in Brunei's generally favorable quality-of-life indicators.

ACHIEVEMENTS

Most of Brunei's college students attend university abroad, but an important project has been the construction of a modern campus accommodating 1,500 to 2,000 students. Since independence the government has tried to strengthen and improve the economic, social, and cultural life of its people.

Cambodia (State of Cambodia)

GEOGRAPHY

Area in Square Kilometers (Miles):
181,040 (69,881) (slightly smaller than Oklahoma)
Capital (Population): Phnom Penh 800,000 (est.)
Climate: tropical

PEOPLE

Population
Total: 9,899,000
Annual Growth Rate: 4.41%
Rural/Urban Population (Ratio): 88/12
Ethnic Makeup: 90% Khmer (Cambodian); 5% Chinese; 5% others
Major Languages: Khmer; French

Health
Life Expectancy at Birth: 48 years (male); 51 years (female)
Infant Mortality Rate (Ratio): 111.5/1,000
Average Caloric Intake: 85% of FAO minimum
Physicians Available (Ratio): 1/27,000

Religions
95% Theravada Buddhist; 5% others

Education
Adult Literacy Rate: 35%

COMMUNICATION

Telephones: 7,315
Newspapers: 16

TRANSPORTATION

Highways—Kilometers (Miles): 13,351 (8,277)
Railroads—Kilometers (Miles): 612 (379)
Usable Airfields: 9

GOVERNMENT

Type: people's republic
Independence Date: November 9, 1949
Head of State/Government: King Norodom Sihanouk; First Premier Prince Norodom Ranariddh, Second Premier Hun Sen
Political Parties: Khmer People's National Liberation Front; National United Front for an Independent, Neutral, Peaceful, and Cooperative Cambodia; Cambodian People's Party
Suffrage: universal at 18

MILITARY

Number of Armed Forces: 56,500
Military Expenditures (% of Central Government Expenditures): n/a
Current Hostilities: border disputes with Vietnam and civil war

ECONOMY

Currency ($ U.S. Equivalent): 2,800 riels = $1
Per Capita Income/GDP: $280/$2.0 billion
Inflation Rate: 250%–300%
Natural Resources: timber; gemstones; iron ore; manganese; phosphates; hydropower potential
Agriculture: rice; rubber; maize; beans; soybeans
Industry: rice processing; fishing; wood and wood products; rubber; cement; gem mining

FOREIGN TRADE

Exports: $59 million
Imports: $170 million

GLIMPSE OF A DICTATOR

In the 1970s most people knew the leaders of ravaged Cambodia only as shadowy men whose names occasionally appeared in the international section of the newspaper. But writer T. D. Allman met several Cambodian leaders. In the following excerpt, he describes Khieu Samphan, the sidekick of the notorious Pol Pot.

While Prince Sihanouk talked and talked [at the 1989 Paris conference to resolve the Cambodian tragedy], another Cambodian smiled and smiled. This was Khieu Samphan, the Khmer Rouge delegate and one of modern history's most notorious killers. The Khmer Rouge leader was chatting amiably in French with some diplomatic ladies who, when he was president of 'Democratic' Kampuchea, would have been tortured to death just for speaking a foreign language.

Excerpted from T. D. Allman, "Sihanouk's Sideshow," *Vanity Fair,* April 1990

Cambodia

⊛ Capital
● City
∿ River
--- Road

0   50 kilometers
0   50 miles

43

A LAND OF TRAGEDY

In Khmer (Cambodian), the word *Kampuchea,* which for a time during the 1980s was the official name of Cambodia, means "country where gold lies at the foothill." But Cambodia is certainly not a land of gold, nor of food, freedom, or stability. Despite a new Constitution, massive United Nations aid, and a formal cease-fire, the horrific effects and the fighting of Cambodia's bloody Civil War continue.

Cambodia was not always a place to be pitied. In fact, at times it was the dominant power of Southeast Asia. Around the fourth century A.D., India, with its pacifist Hindu ideology, began to influence in earnest the original Chinese base of Cambodian civilization. The Indian script came to be used, the name of its capital city was an Indian word, its kings acquired Indian titles, and many of its Khmer people believed in the Hindu religion. The mile-square Hindu temple Angkor Wat, built in the twelfth century, still stands as a symbolic reminder of Indian influence, Khmer ingenuity, and the Khmer Empire's glory.

But the Khmer Empire, which at its height included parts of present-day Myanmar, Thailand, Laos, and Vietnam, was gradually reduced both in size and power until, in the 1800s, it was paying tribute to both Thailand and Vietnam. Continuing threats from these two countries as well as wars and domestic unrest at home led the king of Cambodia to appeal to France for help. France, eager to offset British power in the region, was all too willing to help. A protectorate was established in 1863, and French power grew apace until, in 1887, Cambodia became a part of French Indochina, a conglomerate consisting of the countries of Laos, Vietnam, and Cambodia.

The Japanese temporarily evicted the French in 1945 and, while under Japanese control, Cambodia declared its "independence" from France. Heading the country was the young King Norodom Sihanouk. Controlling rival ideological factions, some of which were pro-West while others were pro-Communist, was difficult for Sihanouk, but he built unity around the idea of permanently expelling the French, who finally left in 1955. King Sihanouk then abdicated his throne in favor of his father so that he could, as premier, personally enmesh himself in political governance. He took the title Prince Sihanouk, by which he is known to most people today, although in 1993 he declared himself, once again, king of Cambodia.

From the beginning Sihanouk's government was bedeviled by border disputes with Thailand and Vietnam and by the in-cursion of Communist Vietnamese soldiers into Cambodia. Sihanouk's ideological allegiances were (and remain) confusing at best; but, to his credit, he was able to keep Cambodia officially out of the Vietnam War, which raged for years (1950–1975) on its border. In 1962 Sihanouk announced that his country would remain neutral in the cold war struggle.

Neutrality, however, was not seen as a virtue by the United States, whose people were becoming more and more eager either to win or to quit the war with North Vietnam. A particularly galling point for the U.S. military was the existence of the so-called Ho Chi Minh Trail, a supply route through the tropical mountain forests of Cambodia. For years North Vietnam had been using the route to supply its military operations in South Vietnam, and Cambodia's neutrality prevented the United States, at least legally, from taking military action against the supply line.

All this changed in 1970, when Sihanouk, out of the country at the time, was evicted from office by his prime minister, General Lon Nol, who was supported by the United States and South Vietnam. Shortly thereafter the United States, now at its peak of involvement in the Vietnam War, began extensive military action in Cambodia. The years of official neutrality came to a bloody end.

THE KILLING FIELDS

Most of these international political intrigues were lost on the bulk of the Cambodian population, only half of whom could read and write, and almost all of whom survived, as their forebears had before them, by cultivating rice along the Mekong River valley. The country had almost always been poor, so villagers had long since learned that, even in the face of war, they could survive by hard work and reliance on extended-family networks. Most farmers probably thought that the war next door would not seriously alter their lives. But they were profoundly wrong, for just as the United States had an interest in having a pro–U.S. government in Cambodia, the North Vietnamese desperately wanted Cambodia to be pro-Communist.

North Vietnam wanted the Cambodian government to be controlled by the Khmer Rouge, a Communist guerrilla army led by Pol Pot, one of a group of former students influenced by the left-wing ideology taught in Paris universities during the 1950s. Winning control in 1975, the Khmer Rouge launched a hellish 3½-year extermination policy, resulting in the deaths of between 1 million and 3 million fellow Cambodians—that is, between one fifth and one third of the entire Cambodian population. The official goal was to eliminate anyone who had been "polluted" by prerevolutionary thinking, but what actually happened was random violence, torture, and murder.

It is difficult to describe the mayhem and despair that engulfed Cambodia during those years. Cities were emptied of people. Teachers and doctors were killed or sent as slaves to work in the rice paddies. Despite the centrality of Buddhism to Cambodian culture (Hinduism having long since been displaced by Buddhist thought), thousands of Buddhist monks were killed or died of starvation as the Khmer Rouge carried out its program of eliminating religion. Some people were killed for no other reason than to terrorize others into submission. Explained Leo Kuper in *International Action Against Genocide* (Report No. 53, 1984, p. 8):

Those who were dissatisfied with the new regime were ... "eradicated," along with their families, by disembowelment, by beating to death with hoes, by hammering nails into the backs of their heads and by other cruel means of economizing on bullets.

Persons associated with the previous regime were special targets for liquidation. In many cases, the executions included wives and children. There were summary executions too of intellectuals, such as doctors, engineers, professors, teachers and students, leaving the country denuded of professional skills.

The Khmer Rouge wanted to alter the society completely. Children were removed from their families, and private ownership of property was eliminated. Money was outlawed. Even the calendar was started over, at year 0. Vietnamese military leader Bui Tin explained just how totalitarian the rulers were:

[In 1979] there was no small piece of soap or handkerchief anywhere. Any person who had tried to use a toothbrush was considered bourgeois and punished. Any person wearing glasses was considered an intellectual who must be punished.

It is estimated that before the Khmer Rouge came to power in 1975, Cambodia had 1,200 engineers, 21,000 teachers, and 500 doctors. After the purges the country was left with only 20 engineers, 3,000 teachers, and 54 doctors.

| France gains control of Cambodia A.D. 1863 | Japanese invasion; King Norodom Sihanouk is installed 1940s | Sihanouk wins Cambodia's independence of France 1953 | General Lon Nol takes power in a U.S.–supported coup 1970 | The Khmer Rouge, under Pol Pot, overthrow the government and begin a reign of terror 1975 | Vietnam invades Cambodia and installs a puppet government 1978 | 1990s |

A kind of bitter relief came in late 1978, when Vietnamese troops (traditionally Cambodia's enemy) invaded Cambodia, drove the Khmer Rouge to the borders of Thailand, and installed a puppet government headed by Hun Sen, a former Khmer Rouge soldier who defected and fled to Vietnam in the 1970s. Although almost everyone was relieved to see the Khmer Rouge pushed out of power, the Vietnamese intervention was almost universally condemned by other nations. This was because the Vietnamese were taking advantage of the chaos in Cambodia to further their aim of creating a federated state of Vietnam, Laos, and Cambodia. Its virtual annexation of Cambodia eliminated Cambodia as a buffer state between Vietnam and Thailand, destabilizing the relations of the region even more.

COALITION GOVERNANCE

The United States and others refused to recognize the Vietnam-installed regime, instead granting recognition to the Coalition Government of Democratic Kampuchea. This entity consisted of three groups: the Communist Khmer Rouge, led by Khieu Samphan and Pol Pot and backed by China; the anti-Communist Khmer People's National Liberation Front, led by former prime minister Son Sann; and the Armee Nationale Sihanoukiste, led by Sihanouk. Although it was doubtful that these former enemies could constitute a workable government for Cambodia, the United Nations granted its Cambodia seat to the coalition and withheld support from the Hun Sen government.

Vietnam had hoped that its capture of Cambodia would be easy and painless. Instead, the Khmer Rouge and others resisted so much that Vietnam had to send in 200,000 troops, of which 25,000 died. Moreover, other countries, including the United States and Japan, strengthened their resolve to isolate Vietnam in terms of international trade and development financing. After 10 years the costs to Vietnam of remaining in Cambodia were so great that Vietnam announced it would pull out its troops.

Soon it became apparent that the Khmer Rouge faction of the coalition was once again gaining control of important parts of the countryside. In late 1991 and early 1992, strenuous diplomatic efforts by United Nations officials and others resulted in a breakthrough. The warring groups agreed to a cease-fire, signed in Paris, that also permitted UN troops to establish a massive peacekeeping force in the country of some 22,000 troops, including Japanese troops—the first Japanese military presence outside Japan since the end of World War II. By 1993 the cost to the United Nations had reached nearly $2 billion.

The Paris agreement called for the release of political prisoners, inspections of prisons, and voter registration for national elections, to be held in 1993. Most importantly, the warring factions, consisting of some 200,000 troops, including 25,000 Khmer Rouge troops, agreed to disarm under UN supervision.

Vietnam withdraws troops from Cambodia; a Paris cease-fire agreement is violated by the Khmer Rouge

1993 elections result in new Constitution, reenthronement of Sihanouk as king, and establishment of dual premiership

Unfortunately, the Khmer Rouge, although a signatory to the agreement, refused to abide by its provisions. With revenues gained from illegal trading in lumber and gems with Thailand, it launched new attacks on villages, trains, and even the UN peacekeepers, and it refused to participate in the elections of 1993, although it had been offered a role in the new government if it would cooperate.

Despite a violent campaign, 90 percent of the people voted in elections that, after some confusion, resulted in a new Constitution, the reenthronement of Sihanouk as king, and the appointment of Sihanouk's son, Prince Norodom Ranariddh of the Royalist Party (FUNCIAPEC) as first premier and Hun Sen of the Cambodian People's Party (CCP) as second premier.

After the elections the new Parliament outlawed the Khmer Rouge and ordered military operations against it. These successful attacks reduced Khmer Rouge control to about 10 percent of the country. Several key Khmer Rouge–controlled towns were recovered.

DEVELOPMENT

In the past China, the United States, and others built roads and industries in Cambodia, but the country remains an impoverished state whose economy rests on fishing and farming. Continual warfare for 2 decades has prevented industrial development.

FREEDOM

Few Cambodians can remember political stability, much less political freedom. Every form of human rights violation has been practiced in Cambodia since even before the arrival of the barbaric Khmer Rouge. Today's Cambodians wish more for food than for freedoms.

HEALTH/WELFARE

Almost all of Cambodia's doctors were killed or died during the Khmer Rouge regime, and warfare disrupted normal agriculture. Thus, disease was rampant, as was malnutrition. The few trained international relief workers in Cambodia are hard-pressed to make a dent in the country's enormous problems.

ACHIEVEMENTS

Despite violence and intimidation, 90% of the Cambodian people voted in the 1993 elections, restoring an elected government, a limited monarchy, and acceding to a new Constitution. The new government has successfully weakened, but not eliminated, the influence of the Khmer Rouge.

China (People's Republic of China)

GEOGRAPHY

Area in Square Kilometers (Miles):
9,572,900 (3,696,100) (slightly larger
than the contiguous United States)
Capital (Population): Beijing
(6,900,000)
Climate: extremely diverse

PEOPLE

Population

Total: 1,177,585,000
Annual Growth Rate: 1.1%
Rural/Urban Population Ratio: 73/27
Ethnic Makeup: 92% Han Chinese;
8% minority groups (the largest being
Chuang, Hui, Uighur, Yi, and Miao)
Major Languages: Standard Chinese
(Putonghua) or Mandarin; Yue
(Cantonese); Wu (Shanghainese);
Minbei (Fuzhou); Minuan (Hokkien-
Taiwanese); Xiang; Gan; Hahka

Health

Life Expectancy at Birth: 67 years
(male); 69 years (female)
Infant Mortality Rate (Ratio):
52.1/1,000
Average Caloric Intake: 104% of
FAO minimum
Physicians Available (Ratio): 1/646

Religions

officially atheist; but Taoism,
Buddhism, Islam, Christianity, ancestor
worship, and animism do exist

Education

Adult Literacy Rate: 73%

COMMUNICATION

Telephones: 11,000,000
Newspapers: 852

THE TEACHINGS OF CONFUCIUS

Confucius (550–478 B.C.) was a Chinese intellectual and minor political figure. He was not a religious leader, nor did he ever claim divinity for himself
or divine inspiration for his ideas. As the feudalism of his era began to collapse,
he proposed that society could best be governed by paternalistic kings who set
good examples. Especially important to a stable society, he taught, were respect
and reverence for one's elders. Within the five key relationships of society
(ruler and subject, husband and wife, father and son, elder brother and younger
brother, and friend and friend), people should always behave with integrity,
propriety, and goodness.

The writings of Confucius—or, rather, the works written about him by his
followers and called the *Analects*—eventually became required knowledge for
anyone in China claiming to be an educated person. However, rival ideas such
as Legalism (a philosophy advocating authoritarian government) were at times
more popular with the elite; at one point 460 scholars were buried alive for
teaching Confucianism. Nevertheless, much of the hierarchical nature of Asian
culture today can be traced to Confucian ideas.

TRANSPORTATION

Highways—Kilometers (Miles):
1,029,000 (639,009)
Railroads—Kilometers (Miles):
64,000 (39,744)
Usable Airfields: 330

GOVERNMENT

Type: one-party Communist state
Independence Date: October 1, 1949
Head of State/Government: President
Jiang Zemin; Premier Li Peng
Political Parties: Chinese Communist
Party; several small and politically
insignificant non-Communist parties
Suffrage: universal at 18

MILITARY

Number of Armed Forces: 12,710,000
on active duty; 8,580,300 in People's
Militia
*Military Expenditures (% of Central
Government Expenditures):* n/a
Current Hostilities: none

ECONOMY

Currency ($ U.S. Equivalent): 8.52
yuan = $1
Per Capita Income/GDP: $370/$413
billion
Inflation Rate: 20% (est.)
Natural Resources: coal; oil;
hydroelectric sites; natural gas; iron
ores; tin; tungsten
Agriculture: food grains; cotton; oil
seeds; pigs; tea
Industry: iron and steel; coal;
machinery; light industry; armaments

FOREIGN TRADE

Exports: $85.0 billion
Imports: $80.6 billion

CHINA

Shakespeare, Columbus, Charlemagne, Julius Caesar, Plato, and Aristotle are names that bespeak historicity to students of Western civilization. But they are all relative newcomers when compared to the great figures of Chinese history. Indeed, China was a thriving culture at least 1,500 years before Plato was born. Therefore, one of the first important characteristics to note about China is its age. In fact, China may be the oldest surviving civilization. There is evidence of human civilization in China as early as 20,000 years ago, at the end of the last Ice Age; a distinctly Chinese culture is distinguishable as early as 2000 B.C. The first documented Chinese dynasty, the Shang, began about 1523 B.C., although legends suggest that an imperial government was in existence much earlier than that. Over the centuries of documented history, the Chinese people have been ruled by a dozen imperial dynasties; have enjoyed hundreds of years of stability and amazing cultural progress; and have endured more hundreds of years of chaos, military mayhem, and hunger. Yet China and the Chinese people remain intact—a strong testament to the tenacity of human culture.

A second major characteristic is that the People's Republic of China (P.R.C.) is very big. It is the third-largest country in the world, accounting for 6.5 percent of the world's landmass. Much of China—about 40 percent—is mountainous; but large, fertile plains have been created by China's numerous rivers, most of which flow toward the Pacific Ocean. China is blessed with substantial reserves of oil, minerals, and many other natural resources. Its large size and geopolitical location—it is bordered by Russia, Kazakhstan, Pakistan, India, Nepal, Bhutan, Myanmar, Laos, Vietnam, North Korea, and Mongolia—have caused the Chinese people over the centuries to think of their land as the Middle Kingdom: that is, the center of world civilization.

However, its unwieldy size has been the undoing of numerous emperors who found it impossible to maintain its borders in the face of outside "barbarians" determined to possess the riches of Chinese civilization. During the Ch'in Dynasty (221–207 B.C.), a 1,500-mile-long, 25-foot-high wall, the so-called Great Wall, was erected along the northern border of China, in the futile hope that invasions from the north could be stopped. Although China's national boundaries are now recognized by international law, recent Chinese governments have found it necessary to "pacify" border areas by settling as many Han Chinese there as possible (for example, in Tibet), to prevent secession by China's numerous ethnic minorities.

A third important characteristic of modern China is its large population. With 1.17 billion people, China is home to about 20 percent of all human beings alive today. About 92 percent of China's people are Han, or ethnic, Chinese; the remaining 8 percent are divided into 56 separate minority groups. Many of these ethnic groups speak mutually unintelligible languages, and although they often appear to be Chinese, they derive from entirely different cultural roots; some are Muslims, some are Buddhists, some are animists. As one moves away from the center of Chinese civilization in the eastern provinces, the influence of the minorities increases. The Chinese government has accepted the

(UN photo/John Issac)

In China today, urban couples are permitted to have only one child, and they can be severely penalized if they dare to have a second, or if they marry before the legal ages of 22 for men and 20 for women.

reality of ethnic influence and has granted a degree of limited autonomy to some provinces with heavy populations of minorities.

China has so many people that it often seems, in historical retrospection, to have treated its people as expendable. For instance, in the Taiping Rebellion of 1851–1865, it is believed that 20 million people died. In the conflict between Communist and Nationalist armies in the 1920s and 1930s, it is estimated that 11 million people lost their lives in a single war-torn province. Over the centuries millions more have died of hunger and malnutrition because for much of its history, China has not been able to feed its people.

In the 1950s Chairman Mao Zedong encouraged couples to have many children, but this policy was reversed in the 1970s, when a formal birth control program was inaugurated. Urban couples today are permitted to have only one child and are penalized if they have more. Penalties include expulsion from the Chinese Communist Party (CCP), dismissal from work, or a 10 percent reduction in pay for up to 14 years after the birth of the second child. The policy is strictly enforced in the cities, but it has had only a marginal impact on overall population growth because some 73 percent of China's people live in rural areas, where they are allowed more children in order to help with the farmwork. In the city of Shanghai, which is expected to have a population of 13.3 million people by the year 2000, authorities have recently removed second-child privileges for farmers living near the city and for such former exceptional cases as children of revolutionary martyrs and workers in the oil industry. Despite these and other restrictions, it is estimated that 15 million to 17 million new Chinese will be born each year until the end of the century.

Over the centuries millions of people have found it necessary or prudent to leave China in search of food, political stability, or economic opportunity. Those who emigrated a thousand or more years ago are now fully assimilated into the cultures of Southeast Asia and elsewhere and identify themselves accordingly. More recent émigrés (in the past 200 years or so), however, constitute visible, often wealthy, minorities in their new host countries, where they have become the backbone of the business community. Ethnic Chinese constitute the majority of the population in Singapore and a sizable minority in Malaysia. Important world figures such as Corazon Aquino, the former president of the Philippines, and Goh Chok Tong, the prime minister of Singapore, are part or full Chinese. The Chinese constituted the

first big wave of the 6.5 million Asian Americans to call the United States home. Thus the influence of China continues to spread far beyond its borders.

Another crucial characteristic of China is its history of imperial and totalitarian rule. Except for a few years in the early part of this century, China has been controlled by imperial decree, military order, and patriarchal privilege. Confucius taught that a person must be as loyal to the government as a son should be to his father. Following Confucius by a generation or two was Shang Yang, of a school of governmental philosophy called Legalism, which advocated unbending force and punishment against wayward subjects. Compassion and pity were not considered qualities of good government.

Mao Zedong, building on this heritage as well as that of the Soviet Union's Joseph Stalin and Vladimir Lenin, exercised strict control over both the public and private lives of the Chinese people. Dissidents were summarily executed (generally people were considered guilty once they were arrested), the press was strictly controlled, and recalcitrants were forced to undergo "reeducation" to correct their thinking. Religion of any kind was suppressed, and churches were turned into warehouses. It is estimated that during the first 3 years of CCP rule, more than 1 million opponents of Mao's regime were executed. During the Cultural Revolution (1966–1976), Mao, who apparently thought that a new mini-revolution in China might restore his eroding stature in the Chinese Communist Party, encouraged young people to report to the authorities anyone suspected of owning books from the West or having contact with Westerners. Even party functionaries were purged if it were believed that their thinking had been corrupted by Western influences.

Historically, authoritarian rule in China has been occasioned, in part, by China's mammoth size; by its unwieldy, mostly illiterate population; and by the ideology of some of its intellectuals. The modern Chinese state has arisen from these same pressures as well as some new ones. It is to these that we now turn.

ORIGINS OF THE MODERN STATE

The Chinese had traded with such non-Asian peoples as the Arabs and Persians for hundreds of years before European contact. But in the 1700s and 1800s, the British and others extracted something new from China in exchange for merchandise from the West: the permission for foreign citizens to live in parts of China without being subject to Chinese author-

ity. Through this process of granting extraterritoriality to foreign powers, China slowly began to lose control of its sovereignty. The age of European expansion was not, of course, the first time in China's long history that its ability to rule itself was challenged; the armies of Kublai Khan successfully captured the Chinese throne in the 1200s, as did the Manchurians in the 1600s. But these outsiders, especially the Manchurians, were willing to rule China on-site and to imbibe as much Chinese culture as they could; eventually they became indistinguishable from the Chinese.

The European powers, on the other hand, preferred to rule China (or, rather, parts of it) from afar as a vassal state, with the proceeds of conquest being drained away from China to enrich the coffers of the European monarchs. Beginning in 1834, when the British forced the Chinese to cede Hong Kong Island, the Western powers began to nibble away at China's sovereignty. Britain, France, and the United States all extracted unequal treaties from the Chinese that gave them privileged access to trade and ports along the eastern coast. By the late 1800s, Russia was in control of much of Manchuria, Germany and France had wrested special economic privileges from the ever-weakening Chinese government, and Portugal controlled Macau. Further affecting the Chinese economy was the loss of many of its former tributary states in Southeast Asia. China lost Vietnam to France, Burma (today, Myanmar) to Britain, and Korea to Japan. During the violent Boxer Rebellion of 1900, the Chinese people showed how frustrated they were with the declining fortunes of their country.

Thus weakened internally and embarrassed internationally, the Manchu rulers of China began to initiate reforms that would strengthen their ability to compete with the Western and Japanese powers. A constitutional monarchy was proposed by the Manchu authorities but was preempted by the republican revolutionary movement of Western-trained Sun Yat-sen. Sun and his armies wanted an end to imperial rule; their dreams were realized in 1912, when Sun's Kuomintang (Nationalist Party, or KMT), took control of the new Republic of China.

Sun's Western approach to government was received with skepticism by many Chinese who distrusted the Western European model and preferred the thinking of Karl Marx and the approach of the Soviet Union. In 1921 Mao Zedong and others organized the Soviet-style Chinese Communist Party (CCP), which grew quickly and began to be seen as an alternative to the

Kuomintang. After Sun's death, in 1925, Chiang Kai-shek assumed control of the Kuomintang and waged a campaign to rid the country of Communist influence. Although Mao and Chiang cooperated when necessary—for example, to resist Japanese incursions into Manchuria—they eventually came to be such bitter enemies that they brought a ruinous civil war to all of China.

Mao derived his support from the rural areas of China, while Chiang depended on the cities. In 1949, facing defeat, Chiang Kai-shek's Nationalists retreated to the island of Taiwan, where, under the name Republic of China (R.O.C.), they continued to insist on their right to rule all of China. The Communists, however, controlled the mainland (and have done so for more than 4 decades) and insisted that Taiwan was just a province of the People's Republic of China. These two antagonists are officially (but not in actuality) still at war. In the 1950s the United States had to intervene to prevent an attack on Taiwan from the mainland.

World opinion initially sided with Taiwan, and it was granted diplomatic recognition by many nations and given the China seat in the United Nations. In the 1970s, however, many nations, including the United States, came to believe that it was dysfunctional to withhold recognition and standing from such a large and powerful nation as the P.R.C. Because both sides insisted that there could not be two Chinas, nor one China and one Taiwan, the UN proceeded to give the China seat to mainland China, and dozens of countries broke off formal diplomatic relations with Taiwan in order to establish a relationship with China.

PROBLEMS OF GOVERNANCE

The China that Mao came to control was a nation with serious economic and social problems. Decades of civil war had disrupted families and wreaked havoc on the economy. Mao believed that the solution to China's ills was to wholeheartedly embrace socialism. Businesses were nationalized, and state planning replaced private initiative. Slowly the economy improved. In 1958, however, Mao decided to enforce the tenets of socialism more vigorously so that China would be able to take an economic "Great Leap Forward." Workers were assigned to huge agricultural communes and were denied the right to grow crops privately. All enterprises came under the strict control of the central government. The result was economic chaos and a dramatic drop in both industrial and agricultural output.

Exacerbating these problems was the growing rift between the P.R.C. and the Soviet Union. China insisted that its brand of communism was truer to the principles of Marx and Lenin and criticized the Soviets for selling out to the West. As relations with (and financial support from) the Soviet Union withered, China found itself increasingly isolated from the world community, a circumstance worsened by serious conflicts with India, Indonesia, and other nations. To gain friends, the P.R.C. provided substantial aid to Communist insurgencies in Vietnam and Laos, thus contributing to the eventual severity of the Vietnam War.

In 1966 Mao found that his power was waning in the face of Communist Party leaders who favored a more moderate approach to internal problems and external relations. To regain lost ground, Mao urged young students called Red Guards to fight against anyone who might have liberal, capitalist, or intellectual leanings. He called it the Great Proletarian Cultural Revolution, but it was an *anti*cultural purge: Books were burned, and educated people were arrested and persecuted. In fact, the entire country remained in a state of domestic chaos for more than a decade.

Soon after Mao died, in 1976, Deng Xiaoping, who had been in and out of Communist Party power several times before, came to occupy the senior position in the CCP. A pragmatist, he was willing to modify or forgo strict socialist ideology if he believed that some other approach

(UN/photo by A. Holcombe)
During Mao Zedong's Great Leap Forward, huge agricultural communes were established, and farmers were denied the right to grow crops privately. The government's strict control of these communes met with chaotic results; there were dramatic drops in agricultural output.

The Shang Dynasty is the first documented Chinese dynasty 1523–1027 B.C.	The Chou Dynasty and the era of Confucius, Laotze, and Mencius 1027–256 B.C.	The Ch'in Dynasty, from which the word *China* is derived 211–207 B.C.	The Han Dynasty 202 B.C.–A.D. 220	The Three Kingdoms period; the Tsin and Sui Dynasties A.D. 220–618	The T'ang Dynasty, during which Confucianism flourished 618–906	The Five Dynasties and Sung Dynasty periods 906–1279	The Yuan Dynasty is founded by Kublai Khan 1260–1368	The Ming Dynasty 1368–1644	The Manchu or Ch'ing Dynasty 1644–1912

would work better. Often pressed by hard-liners to tighten governmental control, he nevertheless was successful in liberalizing the economy and permitting exchanges of scholars with the West. In 1979 he accepted formalization of relations with the United States—an act seen as a signal of China's opening up to the world.

China's opening has been dramatic, not only in terms of its international relations but also internally. During the 1980s the P.R.C. joined the World Bank, the International Monetary Fund, the Asian Development Bank, and other multilateral organizations. It also began to welcome foreign investment of almost any kind and permitted foreign companies to sell their products within China itself. Trade between Taiwan and China (still legally permitted only via a third country) was nearly $6 billion by the early 1990s. And while Hong Kong was investing some $25 billion in China, China was investing $11 billion in Hong Kong. More Chinese firms were permitted to export directly and to keep more of the profits. Special Economic Zones—capitalist enclaves adjacent to Hong Kong and along the coast into which were sent the most educated of the Chinese population—were established to catalyze the internal economy. In coastal cities, especially in south China, construction of apartment complexes, new manufacturing plants, and roads and highways began in earnest. Indeed, the south China area, along with Hong Kong and Taiwan, seemed to be emerging as a mammoth trading bloc—"Greater China"—which economists began to predict would exceed the economy of Japan by the year 2000 and eclipse the economy of the United States by 2012. Stock exchanges opened in Shanghai and Shenzhen. Dramatic changes were implemented even in the inner rural areas. The collectivized farm system imposed by Mao was replaced by a household contract system with hereditary contracts (that is, one step away from actual private land ownership), and free markets replaced most of the system of mandatory agricultural sales to the government. New industries were established in rural villages, and incomes improved such that many families were able to add new rooms onto their homes or to purchase two-story and even three-story homes. Throughout the country a strong spirit of entrepreneurship took hold; and many

people, especially the growing body of educated youth, interpreted economic liberalization as the overture to political democratization. College students, some of whom had studied abroad, pressed the government to crack down on corruption in the Chinese Communist Party and to permit greater freedom of speech and other civil liberties.

In 1989 tens of thousands of college students staged a prodemocracy demonstration in Beijing's Tiananmen Square. The call for democratization received wide international media coverage and soon became an embarrassment to the Chinese leadership, especially when, after several days of continual protest, the students constructed a large statue in the square similar in appearance to the Statue of Liberty in New York Harbor. Some party leaders seemed inclined at least to talk with the students, but hard-liners apparently insisted that the prodemocracy movement be crushed in order that the CCP remain in control of the government. The official policy seemed to be that it would be the Communist Party, and not some prodemocracy movement, that would lead China to capitalism.

The CCP leadership had much to fear; it was, of course, aware of the quickening pace of Communist party power dissolution in the Soviet Union and Central/Eastern Europe, but it was even more concerned about corruption and the breakdown of CCP authority in the rapidly capitalizing rural regions of China, the very areas that had spawned the Communist Party under Mao. Moreover, economic liberalization had spawned inflation, higher prices, and spot shortages, and the general public was disgruntled. Therefore, after several weeks of pained restraint, the authorities moved against the students in what has become known as the Tiananmen Square massacre. Soldiers injured thousands and killed hundreds of students; hundreds more were systematically hunted down and brought to trial for sedition and for spreading counterrevolutionary propaganda.

In the wake of the brutal crackdown, many nations reassessed their relationships with the People's Republic of China. The United States, Japan, and other nations halted or canceled foreign assistance, exchange programs, and special tariff privileges. The people of Hong Kong, who are scheduled to come under P.R.C.

control in 1997, staged massive demonstrations against the Chinese government's brutality. Foreign tourism all but ceased, and foreign investment declined abruptly.

The withdrawal of financial support and investment was particularly troublesome to the Chinese leadership, as it realized that the economy was far behind other nations. Even Taiwan, with a similar heritage and a common history until the 1950s, but having far fewer resources and much less land, had long since eclipsed the mainland in terms of economic prosperity. The Chinese understood that they needed to modernize (although not, they hoped, to Westernize), and they knew that large capital investments from such countries as Japan, Hong Kong, and the United States were crucial to their economic reform program. Moreover, they knew that they could not tolerate a cessation of trade with their new economic partners. By the end of the 1980s, about 13 percent of China's imports came from the United States, 18 percent from Japan, and 25 percent from Hong Kong. Similarly, Japan received 16 percent of China's exports, and Hong Kong received 43 percent.

Fortunately for the Chinese economy, the investment and loan-assistance programs from other countries have now been reinstated in most cases as the repercussions of the events of 1989 wane. China was even able to close a $1.2 billion contract with McDonnell Douglas Corporation to build 40 jetliners, and in 1994 the United States renewed China's most-favored-nation trade status. But the Tiananmen Square incident and the continuing brutality against citizens have convinced many people, both inside and outside China, that the Communist Party has lost, not necessarily its legal, but certainly its moral, authority to govern. Amnesty International reported that more than 1,000 people were executed in China in 1991 alone; world attention has also been drawn to the large number of political prisoners held in *laogai,* or Chinese gulags similar to those in the former Soviet Union.

THE SOCIAL ATMOSPHERE

Many believe that when the aging Communist Party leadership is replaced by younger leaders, China might once again broach the question of democratization and liberalization. In the meantime it is

		Sun Yat-sen's republican revolution ends centuries of imperial rule; the Republic of China is established		Chiang Kai-shek begins a long civil war with the Communists	Mao Zedong's Communist Army defeats Chiang Kai-shek	A disastrous economic reform, the Great Leap Forward, is launched by Mao		Economic and political liberalization begins under Deng Xiaoping; the P.R.C. and Britain agree to return Hong Kong to the Chinese	China expands its relationship with Taiwan; the Tiananmen Square massacre provokes international outrage
Trading rights and Hong Kong Island are granted to Britain **1834**	The Sino-Japanese War **1894–1895**	**1912**	The Chinese Communist Party is organized **1921**	**1926**	**1949**	**1958**	The Cultural Revolution; Mao dies **1966–1976**	**1980s**	●1990s

Crackdowns on dissidents and criminals result in hundreds of arrests and executions; tensions begin to ease

Economists predict that "Greater China's" economy will eventually surpass those of Japan and the United States

evident that the CCP has effected a major change in Chinese society. Historically, the loyalty of the masses of the people was placed in their extended families and in feudal warlords, who, at times of weakened imperial rule, were nearly sovereign in their own provinces. Communist policy has been to encourage the masses to give their loyalty instead to the centrally controlled Communist Party. The size of families has been reduced to the extent that "family" as such has come to play a less important role in the lives of ordinary Chinese.

Historical China was a place of great social and economic inequality between the classes. The wealthy feudal lords and their families and those connected with the imperial court and bureaucracy had access to the finest in educational and cultural opportunities, while around them lived illiterate peasants who often could not feed themselves, let alone pay the often heavy taxes imposed on them by feudal and imperial elites. The masses often found life to be bitter, but they found solace in the teachings of the three main religions of China (often adhered to simultaneously): Confucianism, Taoism, and Buddhism. Islam, animism, and Christianity have also been significant to many people in China.

The Chinese Communist Party under Mao, by legal decree and by indoctrination, attempted to suppress people's reliance on religious values and to reverse the ranking of the classes; the values of hard, manual work and rural simplicity were elevated, while the refinement and education of the urban elites were denigrated. Homes of formerly wealthy capitalists

were taken over by the government and turned into museums, and the opulent life of the capitalists was disparaged. During the Cultural Revolution, high school students who wanted to attend college had first to spend 2 years in manual labor in factories and on farms to help them learn to relate to the peasants and the working class. So much did revolutionary ideology and national fervor take precedence over education that schools and colleges were shut down for several years during the 1960s and 1970s, and the length of compulsory education was reduced.

One would imagine that, after 40 years of communism, the Chinese people would have discarded the values of old China. However, the reverse seems to be true. When the liberalization of the economy began in the late 1970s, many of the former values also came to the fore: the Confucian value of scholarly learning and cultural refinement, the desirability of money, and even Taoist and Buddhist religious values. Religious worship is now permitted in China.

Thousands of Chinese are studying abroad with the goal of returning to China to establish or manage profitable businesses. Indeed, some Chinese, especially those with legitimate access to power, such as ranking Communist Party members, have become extremely wealthy. Along with the privatization of state enterprises has come the unemployment of hundreds of thousands of "redundant" workers (2 million workers lost their jobs in one province in a single year in the early 1990s). Many others have had to settle for lower pay or unsafe work conditions as businesses strive to enter the

world of competitive production. Demonstrations and more than 300 strikes by angry laborers exploded in early 1994. Even those with good jobs were finding it difficult to keep up with inflation, which was running at nearly 20 percent a year. Nevertheless, those with an entrepreneurial spirit were finding ways to make more money than they had ever dreamed possible under an officially communist country. Some former values may help revitalize Chinese life, while others, once suppressed by the Communists, may not be so desirable. For instance, Mao attempted to eradicate prostitution, eliminate the sale of women as brides, and prevent child marriages. Today some of those customs are returning, and gender-based divisions of labor are making their way into the workplace.

Predicting the future is difficult, but it is very unlikely that the economic reform process begun in 1978 will be slowed by political problems. The economy seems to be taking on a life of its own, and once a solid middle class has developed, it is likely that political changes will follow, for that has been the history of the world; and China, despite its size and longevity, cannot realistically expect to bypass the natural history of social change.

DEVELOPMENT

In the early years of Communist control, authorities stressed the value of establishing heavy industry and collectivizing agriculture. More recently China has attempted to reduce its isolation by establishing trading relationships with the United States, Japan, and others and by constructing free enterprise zones. The world's largest dam is currently under construction, despite the objections of environmentalists.

FREEDOM

Until the late 1970s, the Chinese people were controlled by Chinese Communist Party cadres who monitored both public and private behavior. Some economic and social liberalization occurred in the 1980s. However, the 1989 Tiananmen Square massacre reminded Chinese and the world that despite some reforms, China is still very much a dictatorship.

HEALTH/WELFARE

The Communist government has overseen dramatic improvements in the provision of social services for the masses. Life expectancy has increased from 45 years in 1949 to 68 years (overall) today. Diverse forms of health care are available at low cost to the patient. The government has attempted to eradicate such diseases as malaria and tuberculosis.

ACHIEVEMENTS

Chinese culture has, for thousands of years, provided the world with classics in literature, art, pottery, ballet, and other arts. Under communism the arts have been marshaled in the service of ideology and have lost some of their dynamism. Since 1949 literacy has increased dramatically and now stands at 73 percent—the highest in Chinese history.

Hong Kong

GEOGRAPHY

Area in Square Kilometers (Miles):
1,062 (658) (about 1⅓ the size of
New York City)
Capital: Victoria
Climate: subtropical

PEOPLE

Population
Total: 5,553,000
Annual Growth Rate: 0.06%
Rural/Urban Population Ratio: 9/91
Ethnic Makeup: 98% Chinese
(mostly Cantonese); 2% European
and Vietnamese
Major Languages: Cantonese; other
Chinese dialects; English

Health
Life Expectancy at Birth: 77 years
(male); 84 years (female)
Infant Mortality Rate (Ratio): 5.9/1,000
Average Caloric Intake: n/a
Physicians Available (Ratio): 1/1,000

Religions
90% a combination of Buddhism and
Taoism; 10% Christian

Education
Adult Literacy Rate: 77%

HONG KONG'S RESTLESS PEOPLE

As recently as 1989, Chinese student protesters fleeing the political fallout
from the Tiananmen Square massacre in the People's Republic of China
made their way to Hong Kong, where they were smuggled across the border
to safety. Ironically, while these exiles were finding refuge in Hong Kong,
thousands of other people were planning to leave the British colony. Among
them were several hundred Vietnamese refugees, who, induced by a United
Nations repatriation program, were voluntarily returning to Vietnam after
enduring many years in Hong Kong's crowded detention camps. Other de-
partees have included thousands of Hong Kong's well-heeled middle class.
Many have immigrated to England or to British Commonwealth countries
such as Australia and Canada.

Some people are leaving Hong Kong out of fear of China's new prob-
lem-plagued nuclear reactor, built just 30 miles from Hong Kong on Daya
Bay. Most, however, fear life under the Chinese: Hong Kong is scheduled
to revert to Chinese control in 1997.

COMMUNICATION

Telephones: 3,000,000
Newspapers: 69

TRANSPORTATION

Highways—Kilometers (Miles): 1,100
(683)
Railroads—Kilometers (Miles): 35 (22)
Usable Airfields: 2

GOVERNMENT

Type: colonial (British Crown colony)
Independence Date: Chinese sovereignty
to be reestablished on July 1, 1997
Head of State/Government: Queen
Elizabeth II; Governor Chris Patten
(appointed by Britain)
Political Parties: United Democrats
of Hong Kong; Liberal Democratic
Federation; Hong Kong Democratic
Federation; Association for
Democracy and People's Livelihood;
Progressive Hong Kong Society
Suffrage: limited to about 100,000
professionals and electoral college
and functional constituencies

MILITARY

Number of Armed Forces: foreign
relations and defense the responsibility
of British Armed Forces, 12,000 of
whom are stationed in Hong Kong
*Military Expenditures (% of Central
Government Expenditures):* 0.5%
Current Hostilities: none

ECONOMY

Currency ($ U.S. Equivalent): 7.72
Hong Kong dollars = $1
Per Capita Income/GDP:
$14,600/$86 billion
Inflation Rate: 9.4%
Natural Resources: none
Agriculture: vegetables; livestock
(cattle, pigs, poultry); fish
Industry: light—textiles and clothing;
electronics; clocks and watches; toys;
plastic products; metalware; footwear;
heavy—shipbuilding and ship
repairing; aircraft engineering

FOREIGN TRADE

Exports: $118 billion
Imports: $120 billion

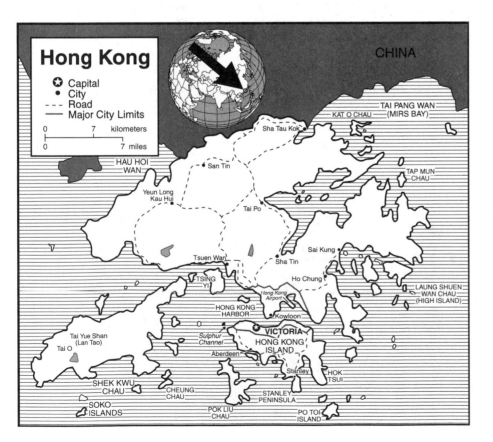

Hong Kong
- ⭐ Capital
- • City
- - - - Road
- —— Major City Limits

0   7 kilometers
0   7 miles

CHINA

HONG KONG'S BEGINNINGS

Opium started it all for Hong Kong. The addictive drug from which such narcotics as morphine, heroin, and codeine are made, opium had become a major source of income for British merchants in the early 1800s. When the Chinese government declared the opium trade illegal and confiscated more than 20,000 large chests of opium that had been on their way for sale to the increasingly addicted residents of Canton, the merchants persuaded the British military to intervene and restore their trading privileges. The British Navy attacked and occupied part of Canton. Three days later the British forced the Chinese to agree to their trading demands, including a demand that they be ceded the tiny island of Hong Kong (meaning "Fragrant Harbor"), where they could pursue their trading and military business without the scrutiny of the Chinese authorities.

Initially the British government was not pleased with the acquisition of Hong Kong; the island had been annexed without the foreknowledge of the authorities in London, and development on the island consisted of nothing more than a small fishing village. Shortly, however, the government found the island's harbor a useful place to resupply ships and to anchor military vessels in the event of further hostilities with the Chinese. The harbor turned out to be one of the finest natural harbors along the coast of China. On August 29, 1842, China reluctantly signed the Treaty of Nanking, which ended the first Opium War and gave Britain ownership of Hong Kong Island "in perpetuity."

Twenty years later a second Opium War caused China to lose more of its territory; Britain acquired permanent lease rights over Kowloon, a tiny part of the mainland facing Hong Kong Island. By 1898 Britain had realized that its miniscule Hong Kong naval base would be too small to defend itself against sustained attack by French or other European navies seeking privileged access to China's markets. The British were also concerned about the scarcity of agricultural land on Hong Kong and Kowloon. In 1898 they persuaded the Chinese to lease them more than 350 square miles of land adjacent to Kowloon. Thus, the colony of Hong Kong consists today of Hong Kong Island (as well as numerous small, uninhabited islands nearby), the Kowloon Peninsula, and the agricultural lands that came to be called the New Territories.

From its inauspicious beginnings, Hong Kong has grown into a dynamic, modern society, wealthier and more densely populated than its promoters would have ever dreamed in their wildest imaginations. Hong Kong is now home to 5.5 million people, nearly 14,000 people per square mile. Most of the New Territories are mountainous or are needed for agriculture, so the bulk of the population is packed into about one tenth of the land space. This gives Hong Kong the dubious honor of being one of the most densely populated human spaces ever created. Millions of people live stacked on top of one another in 30-story-high public tenement buildings. Even Hong Kong's excellent harbor has not escaped the population crunch: Approximately 10 square miles of former harbor have been filled in and now constitute some of the most expensive real estate on earth.

Why are there so many people in Hong Kong? One reason is that after occupation by the British, many Chinese merchants moved their businesses to Hong Kong, under the correct assumption that trade would be given a freer hand there than on the mainland. Eventually Hong Kong became the home of mammoth trading conglomerates. The laborers in these profitable enterprises came to Hong Kong, for

(Photo credit United Nations/J. K. Isaac)

Hong Kong has enormous economic inequalities, with some of the richest people in the world living in close proximity to some of the poorest, a disparity largely caused by the constant influx of refugees. The contrast is illustrated above, with newly arrived Vietnamese shown against a prosperous city backdrop.

the most part, as political refugees from mainland China in the early 1900s. Another wave of immigrants arrived in the 1930s upon the invasion of Manchuria by the Japanese, and yet another influx came after the Communists took over China in 1949. Thus, like Taiwan, Hong Kong became a place of refuge for those in economic or political trouble on the mainland.

Overcrowding plus a favorable climate for doing business have produced extreme social and economic inequalities. Some of the richest people on earth live in Hong Kong, as do some of the most wretchedly poor, notable among whom are recent refugees from China and Southeast Asia (more than 300,000 Vietnamese have sought refuge in Hong Kong since 1975), some of whom have joined the traditionally poor boat peoples living in Aberdeen Harbor. Although they are surrounded by poverty, many of Hong Kong's economic elites have not found it inappropriate to indulge in ostentatious displays of wealth, such as riding in chauffeured, pink Rolls-Royces or wearing full-length mink coats.

Workers are on the job 6 days a week, morning and night, yet the average pay for a worker in industry is only about $4,800 per year. With husband, wife, and older children all working, families can survive; some even make it into the ranks of the fabulously wealthy. Indeed, the desire to make money was the primary reason why Hong Kong was settled in the first place. That fact is not lost on anyone

who lives there today. Noise and air pollution, traffic congestion, and dirty and smelly streets do not deter people from abandoning the countryside in favor of the consumptive lifestyle of the city.

Yet materialism has not wholly effaced the cultural arts and social rituals that are essential to a cohesive society. Indeed, with 98 percent of Hong Kong's residents hailing originally from mainland China, the spiritual beliefs and cultural heritage of China's long history abound. Some residents hang small eight-sided mirrors outside windows to frighten away malicious spirits, while others burn paper money in the streets each August to pacify the wandering spirits of deceased ancestors. Business owners carefully choose certain Chinese characters for the names of their companies or products, which they hope will bring them luck. Even modern skyscrapers are designed, following ancient Chinese customs, so that their main entrances are in balance with the elements of nature.

Buddhist and Taoist beliefs remain central to the lives of many residents. In the back rooms of many shops, for example, are erected small religious shrines; joss sticks burning in front of these shrines are thought to bring good fortune to the proprietors. Elaborate festivals, such as those at New Year's, bring the costumes, art, and dance of thousands of years of Chinese history to the crowded streets of Hong Kong. And, of course, the British

legacy may be found in the cricket matches, ballet troupes, philharmonic orchestras, English-language radio and television broadcasts, and the legal system under which capitalism has flourished.

THE END OF AN ERA

Britain has been in control of this tiny speck of Asia for some 150 years. Except during World War II, when the Japanese occupied Hong Kong for about 4 years, the territory has been governed as a Crown colony of Great Britain, with a governor appointed by the British sovereign. However, Britain's rule will soon come to an end. In 1984 British prime minister Margaret Thatcher and Chinese leader Deng Xiaoping concluded 2 years of acrimonious negotiations over the fate of Hong Kong upon the expiration of the New Territories' lease in 1997. Britain claimed the right to control Hong Kong Island and Kowloon forever—a claim disputed by China, which argued that the treaties granting these lands to Britain had been imposed on them by military force. Hong Kong Island and Kowloon, however, constitute only about 10 percent of the colony; the other 90 percent was to return automatically to China at the expiration of the lease. The various parts of the colony having become fully integrated, it seemed desirable to all parties to keep the colony together as one administrative unit. Moreover, it was felt that Hong Kong Island and Kowloon could not survive alone.

The British government had hoped that the People's Republic of China would agree to the status quo, or that it would at least permit the British to maintain administrative control over the colony should it be returned to China. Many Hong Kong Chinese felt the same way, since they had, after all, fled to Hong Kong to escape the Communist regime in China. For its part, the P.R.C. insisted that the entire colony be returned to its control by 1997. After difficult negotiations Britain agreed to return the entire colony to China as long as China would grant important concessions. Foremost among these were that the capitalist economy and lifestyle, including private-property ownership and basic human rights, would not be changed for 50 years. The P.R.C. agreed to govern Hong Kong as a Special Administrative Region (SAR) within China and to permit British and local Chinese to serve in the administrative apparatus of the territory. The first direct elections for the 60-member Legislative Council were held in September 1991, and the new (and last) British governor, Chris Patten, has

(Photo credit United Nations/S. Jackson)
Hong Kong's freewheeling approach to business and commerce drew millions of people and the possibility of work. This in turn put enormous strains on housing in a geographically limited area. This apartment building in Aberdeen is typical of how the population crunch has been handled.

The British begin to occupy and use Hong Kong Island; the first Opium War
A.D. 1839–1842

The Treaty of Nanking cedes Hong Kong to Britain
1842

The Chinese cede Kowloon and Stonecutter Island to Britain
1856

England gains a 99-year lease on the New Territories
1898

The Boxer Rebellion
1898–1900

Sun Yat-sen overthrows the emperor of China to establish the Republic of China
1911

The Japanese attack Pearl Harbor and take Hong Kong
1941

The Communist victory in China produces massive immigration into Hong Kong
1949

Britain and China agree to the return of Hong Kong to China

Mass demonstrations in Hong Kong against the Tiananmen Square massacre
1980s

1990s

Hong Kong is scheduled to become a Special Administrative Region of China in 1997

made it clear that he intends to extend democratic rule in the colony as much as possible before the 1997 Chinese takeover. China, however, asserts that it should have a say in colony affairs even now.

The Joint Declaration of 1984 was drafted by top governmental leaders, with very little input from the people of Hong Kong. This fact plus fears about what P.R.C. control will mean to the freewheeling lifestyle of Hong Kong's ardent capitalists have caused many residents to pack their bags. Thousands of residents, carrying $10 billion in assets, have resettled in Canada, Bermuda, Australia, the United States, and Britain. It has been reported in the Hong Kong press that as many as one third of the population of Hong Kong would like to emigrate before the mainland Chinese take control in 1997.

Emigration and unease over the future have unsettled, but by no means dampened, Hong Kong's economy. As of 1993 Hong Kong ranked eighth in the world in terms of exports, and seventh in terms of imports (it had been the tenth-largest importer in 1992). Moreover, over the objections of the Chinese government, the outgoing British authorities have embarked on several ambitious infrastructural projects that should allow Hong Kong to continue to grow economically in the future. Chief among these is the airport on Chek Lap Kok Island. At a cost of $21 billion, the badly needed airport is one of the largest construction projects currently under way in the Pacific Rim. Opinion surveys show that despite fears of angering the incoming Chinese government, most Hong Kong residents appear

to support the colony's efforts to improve the economy and to democratize the government by lowering the voting age and allowing direct election rather than appointment of more officials.

These kinds of reports might lead outsiders to conclude that everyone in Hong Kong is unequivocally opposed to the departure of the British. However, although there are large British and American communities in Hong Kong, and although English is the language of government, many residents have little or no contact with the Western aspects of Hong Kong life and feel very little, if any, loyalty to the British Crown. They assert that they are, first and foremost, Chinese, and that as such they can govern themselves without the involvement of any Western power. This, of course, does not amount to a popular endorsement of China's claim to govern Hong Kong, but it does imply that some residents of Hong Kong, if they have to be governed by others, would rather they be Chinese. Moreover, some believe that the Chinese government may actually help rid Hong Kong of financial corruption and allocate more resources to the poor.

The natural links with the P.R.C. have been expanding steadily for years. In addition to a shared language and culture there are in Hong Kong thousands of recent immigrants with strong family ties to the People's Republic. And there are increasingly important commercial ties. Hong Kong has always served as south China's entrepôt to the rest of the world for both commodity and financial exchanges. For instance, for years Taiwan has circumvented its regulations against direct trade

with China by transshipping its exports through Hong Kong. Commercial trucks plying the highways between Hong Kong and the P.R.C. form a bumper-to-bumper wall of commerce between the two regions. Already, 43 percent of Hong Kong's imports comes from China (16 percent from Japan), while 25 percent of its exports goes to China (24 percent to the United States). The P.R.C. realizes that Hong Kong needs to remain more or less as it is—therefore, the transition to Chinese rule may be less jarring to residents than is expected. Most observers believe that even after the transition to Chinese rule, Hong Kong will remain, along with Tokyo, one of the major financial and trading centers of Asia and of the world.

DEVELOPMENT

Hong Kong is one of the financial and trading dynamos of the world. Hong Kong annually exports billions of dollars worth of products. Hong Kong's political future may be uncertain after 1997, but its fine harbor as well as its new $21 billion airport, currently under construction, are sure to continue to fuel its economy.

FREEDOM

Hong Kong has been an appendage to one of the world's foremost democracies for some 150 years. Its residents have enjoyed the civil liberties guaranteed by British law. After 1997 a new Basic Law—currently being implemented with the consent of the Chinese government—will take full effect.

HEALTH/WELFARE

Schooling is free and compulsory in Hong Kong through junior high school. The government has devoted large sums for low-cost housing, aid for refugees, and social services such as adoption. Housing, however, is cramped and inadequate for the population.

ACHIEVEMENTS

Hong Kong has the capacity to hold together a society where the gap between rich and poor is enormous. The boat people have been subjected to discrimination, but most other groups have found social acceptance and opportunities for economic advancement.

Indonesia (Republic of Indonesia)

GEOGRAPHY

Area in Square Kilometers (Miles): 1,919,440 (740,903) (nearly 3 times the size of Texas)
Capital (Population): Jakarta (8,800,000)
Climate: tropical; hot, humid; more moderate in highlands

PEOPLE

Population
Total: 197,233,000
Annual Growth Rate: 1.6%
Rural/Urban Population Ratio: 69/31
Ethnic Makeup: 45% Javanese; 14% Sudanese; 7.5% Madarese, 7.5% coastal Malays, 26% others
Major Languages: Bahasa Indonesian; English; Dutch; Javanese; many others

Health
Life Expectancy at Birth: 58 years (male); 62 years (female)
Infant Mortality Rate (Ratio): 69.6/1,000
Average Caloric Intake: 105% of FAO minimum
Physicians Available (Ratio): 1/7,427

Religions
87% Muslim; 9% Christian; 2% Hindu; 2% Buddhist and others

Education
Adult Literacy Rate: 77%

COMMUNICATION

Telephones: 1,122,100
Newspapers: 252

EXPLOSIVE ISLANDS

Located in an area that geologists call "the belt of fire," Indonesia has more volcanoes per square mile than any other country in the world. Out of 500 volcanoes, 128 are active and 65 more are considered dangerous. An eruption of Krakatau in 1883 killed 35,000 people. Mount Kelud, 390 miles east of Jakarta, erupted in 1990, spewing lava on nearby towns and dumping ash on towns as far as 30 miles away. Kelud has erupted 8 times since 1811, claiming the lives of nearly 6,000 people. Its most recent explosion killed 15, injured 48, and required the evacuation of 4,000 villagers.

TRANSPORTATION

Highways—Kilometers (Miles): 119,500 (74,000)
Railroads—Kilometers (Miles): 6,964 (4,318)
Usable Airfields: 411

GOVERNMENT

Type: republic
Independence Date: August 17, 1945
Head of State: President Suharto
Political Parties: Golkar Party (quasi-official); Indonesia Democracy Party; Muslim United Development Party
Suffrage: universal at age 17 and married persons regardless of age

MILITARY

Number of Armed Forces: 279,000
Military Expenditures (% of Central Government Expenditures): 1.5%
Current Hostilities: none

ECONOMY

Currency ($ U.S. Equivalent): 2,176 Indonesian rupiahs = $1
Per Capita Income/GDP: $680/$133 billion
Inflation Rate: 8%
Natural Resources: oil; minerals; forest products
Agriculture: subsistence food production; rice; cassava; peanuts; rubber; cocoa; coffee; copra; other tropical products
Industry: petroleum; textiles; mining; cement; chemical fertilizer; timber; food; rubber

FOREIGN TRADE

Exports: $29.4 billion
Imports: $24.6 billion

A KALEIDOSCOPIC CULTURE

Present-day Indonesia is a kaleidoscope of some 300 languages and more than 100 ethnic groups. Beginning about 5000 B.C., people of Mongoloid stock settled the islands that today constitute Indonesia in successive waves of migration from China, Thailand, and Vietnam. Animism—the nature-worship religion of these peoples—was altered substantially (but never completely lost) about A.D. 200, when Hindus from India began to settle in the area and wield the dominant cultural influence. Five hundred years later, Buddhist missionaries and settlers began converting Indonesians in a proselytizing effort that produced strong political and religious antagonisms. In the thirteenth century, Muslim traders began the Islamization of the Indonesian people; today 87 percent of the population claim the Muslim faith. Commingling with all these influences were cultural inputs from the islands of Polynesia.

The real roots of the Indonesian people undoubtedly go back much further than any of these historic cultures. In 1891 the fossilized bones of a hominid who used stone tools, camped around a fire, and probably had a well-developed language were found on the island of Java. Named *Pithecanthropus erectus* ("erect ape-man"), these important early human fossils, popularly called Java Man, have been dated at about 750,000 years of age. Fossils similar to Java Man have been found in Europe, Africa, and Asia.

Modern Indonesia was sculpted by the influence of many outside cultures. Portuguese Catholics, eager for Indonesian spices, made contact with Indonesia in the 1500s and left 20,000 converts to Catholicism, many mixed Portuguese–Indonesian communities, and dozens of Portuguese "loan words" in the Indonesian-style Malay language. In the following century, Dutch Protestants established the Dutch East India Company to exploit Indonesia's riches. Eventually the Netherlands was able to gain complete political control; it reluctantly gave it up in the face of insistent Indonesian nationalism only as recently as 1950. Before that, however, the British briefly controlled one of the islands, and the Japanese ruled the country for 3 years during the 1940s.

Indonesians, including then-president Sukarno, initially welcomed the Japanese as helpers in their fight for independence from the Dutch. Everyone believed that the Japanese would leave soon. Instead, the Japanese military forced farmers to give food to the Japanese soldiers, made everyone worship the Japanese emperor, neglected local industrial development in favor of military projects, and took 270,000 young men away from Indonesia to work elsewhere as forced laborers (fewer than 70,000 survived to return home). Military leaders who attempted to revolt against Japanese rule were executed. Finally, in August 1945 the Japanese abandoned their control of Indonesia according to the terms of surrender with the Allied powers.

Consider what all these influences mean for the culture of modern Indonesia. After all, some of the most powerful ideologies ever espoused by humankind—supernaturalism, Islam, Hinduism, Buddhism, Christianity, mercantilism, colonialism, and nationalism—have had an impact on Indonesia. Take music, for example. Unlike Western music, which most people just listen to, Indonesian music, played on drums and gongs reminiscent of Africa and the Polynesian islands, is intended as a somewhat sacred ritual in which all members of a community are expected to participate. The instruments themselves are considered sacred. Dances are often the main element in a religious service whose goal might be a good rice harvest, spirit possession, or exorcism. Familiar musical styles can be heard here and there around the country. In the eastern part of Indonesia, the Nga'dha peoples, who were converted to Christianity in the early 1900s, sing Christian hymns to the accompaniment of bronze pot gongs and drums. On the island of Sumatra, Minang Kabau peoples, who were converted to Islam in the 1500s, use local instruments to accompany Islamic poetry singing. Communal feasts in Hindu Bali, circumcision ceremonies in Muslim Java, and Christian baptisms among the Bataks of Sumatra all represent borrowed cultural traditions. Thus, out of many has come one rich culture.

But the faithful of different religions are not always able to work together in harmony. For example, in the 1960s, when average Indonesians were trying to distance themselves from radical Communists, many decided to join Christian faiths. Threatened by this tilt toward the West and by the secular approach of the government, many fundamentalist Muslims resorted to violence. They burned Christian churches, threatened Catholic and Baptist missionaries, and opposed such projects as the construction of a hospital by Baptists. Indonesia is one of the most predominately Muslim countries in the world, and the hundreds of Islamic socioreligious and political organizations intend to keep it that way.

A LARGE LAND, LARGE DEBTS

Unfortunately, Indonesia's economy is not as richly endowed as its culture. About 75 percent of the population live in rural areas; more than half of the people engage in fishing and small-plot rice and vegetable farming. Forty percent of the gross national product comes from agriculture. The average income per person is only $680 a year (based on gross domestic product), and inflation consumes about 8 percent of that annually. A 1993 law increased the minimum wage in Jakarta to $2.00 *per day*.

Also worrisome is the level of government debt. Indonesia is blessed with large oil reserves (Pertamina is the state-owned oil company) and minerals and timber of every sort (also state-owned), but to extract these natural resources has required massive infusions of capital, most of it borrowed. In fact, Indonesia has borrowed more money than any other country in Asia and must allocate 40 percent of its national budget just to pay the interest on loans. Low oil prices in the 1980s made it difficult for the country to keep up with its debt burden.

To cope with these problems, Indonesia has relaxed government control over foreign investment and banking, and it seems to be on a path toward privatization of other parts of the economy. Still, the gap between the modernized cities and the traditional countryside continues to plague the government.

Indonesia's financial troubles seem puzzling, because in land, natural resources, and population, the country appears quite well-off. Indonesia is the second-largest country in Asia (after China). Were it superimposed on a map of the United States, its 13,677 tropical islands would stretch from California, past New York, and out to Bermuda in the Atlantic Ocean. Oil and hardwoods are plentiful, and the population is large enough to constitute a viable internal consumer market. But transportation and communication are problematic and costly in archipelagic states. Indonesia's national airline, Garuda Indonesia, has launched a $3.6 billion development program that will bring into operation 50 new aircraft stopping at 13 new airports. New seaports are also under construction. But the cost of linking together the 6,000 inhabited islands is a major drain on the economy. Moreover, exploitation of Indonesia's amazing panoply of resources is drawing the ire of more and more people around the world who fear the destruction of the world's ecosystem.

Indonesia's population of 197 million is one of the largest in the world, but 23 percent of adults cannot read or write. Only

Java Man lived here **1.7 million years** B.C.	Buddhism gains the upper hand A.D. **600**	Muslim traders bring Islam to Indonesia A.D. **1200**	The Portuguese begin to trade and settle in Indonesia **1509**	Dutch traders begin to influence Indonesian life **1596**	The Japanese defeat the Dutch **1942**	Indonesian independence from the Netherlands; President Sukarno retreats from democracy and the West **1949–1950**	General Suharto takes control of the government from Sukarno and establishes his New Order, pro-Western government **1966**	Anti-Japanese riots take place in Jakarta **1974**	Indonesia annexes East Timor **1975**

1990s

Economic reforms aim to increase foreign investment and employment opportunities	Oil revenues slump; the rupiah is devalued	Earthquakes kill 2,500 Indonesians in 1992 and injure 1,500 in 1994

about 600 people per 100,000 attend college, as compared to 3,580 in nearby Philippines. Moreover, since almost 70 percent of the population reside on or near the island of Java, on which the capital city, Jakarta, is located, educational and development efforts have concentrated there, at the expense of the communities on outlying islands. Many children in the out-islands never complete the required 6 years of elementary school. Some ethnic groups, on the islands of Irian Jaya (New Guinea) and Kalimantan (Borneo), for example, continue to live isolated in small tribes, much as they did thousands of years ago. By contrast, the modern city of Jakarta, with its classical European-style buildings, is predicted to have a population of more than 13 million by the year 2000. Social problems have been ameliorated somewhat by Indonesia's strong economic growth (an average of 6 percent over the past 20 years), which has reduced the official poverty rate (from 60 percent in 1970 to 15 percent in 1990).

The government is aware that, with 3 million new Indonesians entering the labor force every year and 50 percent of the total population under age 20, serious efforts must be made to increase employment opportunities. For the 1990s the government earmarked millions of dollars to promote the tourism industry, a labor-intensive industry that could bring as many as 2 million visitors to Indonesia per year and provide jobs for many. Hotel construction alone was budgeted at $1.5 billion for 1990–1992. Nevertheless, the most pressing problem was to finish the many projects for which World Bank and

Asian Development Bank loans had already been received.

MODERN POLITICS

Establishing the current political and geographic boundaries of the Republic of Indonesia has been a bloody and protracted task. So fractured is the culture that many people doubt whether there really is a single country that one can call Indonesia. During the first 15 years of independence (1950–1965), there were revolts by Muslims and pro-Dutch groups, indecisive elections, several military coups, battles against U.S.–supported rebels, and serious territorial disputes with Malaysia and the Netherlands. In 1966 nationalistic President Sukarno, who had been a founder of Indonesian independence, lost power to Army General Suharto. (Many Southeast Asians had no family names until influenced by Westerners; Sukarno and Suharto each have used only one name.) Anti-Communist feeling grew during the 1960s, and thousands of suspected members of the Indonesian Communist Party (PKI) and other Communists were killed before the PKI was banned in 1966. In 1975, ignoring the disapproval of the United Nations, President Suharto invaded and annexed East Timor, a Portuguese colony. Although the military presence in East Timor has since been reduced, separatists were beaten and killed by the Indonesian Army as recently as 1991, and in 1993 a separatist leader was sentenced to 20 years in prison.

Suharto's so-called New Order government rules with an iron hand, suppressing student and Muslim dissent and control-

ling the press and the economy. In 1994 Suharto was reelected (in an uncontested election) to his sixth 5-year term, and his Golkar Party continues to hold a solid political majority.

In 1974, upon the visit of the prime minister of Japan, antigovernment and anti-Japanese riots broke out in Jakarta. Many believed that Suharto and the Japanese were in collusion to exploit the Indonesian economy. While the aim may not have been exploitation, it is true that Indonesia and Japan have established very close economic ties. Indonesia sends 42 percent of its exports to Japan and buys 23 percent of its imports from Japan. And Japanese investment money continues to flow into Indonesia, as elsewhere in the Pacific Rim. Japan's Toyota Corporation spent millions of yen in 1993 to purchase stock in Indonesia's PT ASTRA International automobile company. Many of the country's planned tourist-industry expansions are financed by Japanese banks. Other nations, including Taiwan, South Korea, Germany, and the United States, are also heavy investors. Indonesia may try to become a better political neighbor, as the country is feeling the need for more integration into the world economy. It hosted the Asia–Pacific Economic Cooperation meeting in 1994.

DEVELOPMENT

Indonesia continues to be hamstrung by its heavy reliance on foreign loans, a burden inherited from the Sukarno years. Current Indonesian leaders speak of "stabilization" and "economic dynamism." When there are oil stoppages in the Middle East, Indonesia's economy improves. Fifty-five percent of Indonesians are farmers and fishermen.

FREEDOM

Former president Sukarno's Guided Democracy style of government resulted in the suppression of many civil rights and the crushing of left-wing groups, including the Communist Party. Demands for Western-style human rights are frequently heard, but only the army has the power to impose order on the numerous and competing political groups, many imbued with religious fervor.

HEALTH/WELFARE

Indonesia has one of the highest birth rates in the Pacific Rim; 50 percent of the population are under age 20. Many of these children will grow up in poverty, never learning even to read or write their national language, Bahasa Indonesian.

ACHIEVEMENTS

The largely Hindu island of Bali continues to attract tourists from around the world who are fascinated by the beauty of Balinese music and dancing. The dancers' glittering gold costumes and unique choreography epitomize the "Asian-ness" of Indonesia. Despite its heavy debt, Indonesia continues to pay its bills on schedule.

Laos (Lao People's Democratic Republic)

GEOGRAPHY

Area in Square Kilometers (Miles):
236,800 (91,400)
Capital (Population): Vientiane
(377,000)
Climate: tropical monsoon

PEOPLE

Population
Total: 4,569,000
Annual Growth Rate: 2.86%
Rural/Urban Population (Ratio):
81/19
Ethnic Makeup: 50% Lao; 20% tribal
Thai; 15% Phoutheung (Kha); 15%
Meo, Hmong, Yao, and others
Major Languages: Lao; French;
English

Health
Life Expectancy at Birth: 50 years
(male); 53 years (female)
Infant Mortality Rate (Ratio):
104.4/1,000
Average Caloric Intake: 94% of FAO
minimum
Physicians Available (Ratio): 1/6,495

Religions
85% Buddhist; 15% traditional
indigenous and others

Education
Adult Literacy Rate: 84%

WHAT'S FOR DINNER?

When the first entity that could be called the nation of Laos was formed
in the fourteenth century A.D., the country's name was Lang Xang, meaning
"Land of a Million Elephants." One of the founders of Laos was said in
legend to have been sent by God and to have arrived on earth riding on
an elephant. Elephants are still used as beasts of burden in Laos, but other
animals, such as water buffalo, oxen, horses, chickens, and ducks, are more
important to Laotian daily life. Animals are often tied up underneath Laotian
houses, which are built up on stilts. Many animals end up on the dinner
table: Quail, snakes, deer, wild chickens, and fish add protein to the rice-
based Laotian diet. North American cultural sensitivities have been offended
by Laotian Hmong immigrants' culinary preferences; when the Hmong (a
mountain people who were severely persecuted by the Communists and
who subsequently emigrated from Laos en masse) settled in the United
States, city dwellers complained that the Hmong were catching rats in city
parks and cooking them for dinner.

COMMUNICATION

Telephones: 7,400
Newspapers: n/a

TRANSPORTATION

Highways—Kilometers (Miles):
27,527 (17,066)
Railroads—Kilometers (Miles): none
Usable Airfields: 41

GOVERNMENT

Type: Communist state
Independence Date: July 19, 1949
Head of State/Government: President
Nouhak Phoumsavan; Prime Minister
Khamtai Siphandon
Political Parties: Lao People's
Revolutionary Party
Suffrage: universal at 18

MILITARY

Number of Armed Forces: 53,100
*Military Expenditures (% of Central
Government Expenditures):* 3.8%
Current Hostilities: none

ECONOMY

Currency ($ U.S. Equivalent): 710
new kips = $1
Per Capita Income/GDP: $200/$900
million
Inflation Rate: 10%
Natural Resources: timber;
hydropower; gypsum; tin; gold;
gemstones
Agriculture: rice; potatoes;
vegetables; coffee; sugarcane; cotton
Industry: tin mining; timber; electric
power; agricultural processing

FOREIGN TRADE

Exports: $72 million
Imports: $238 million

THE REALITY OF LAOTIAN LIFE

Laos seems a sleepy place. Almost everyone lives in small villages where the only distraction might be the Buddhist temple gong announcing the day. Water buffalo plow quietly through centuries-old rice paddies, while young Buddhist monks in saffron robes make their silent rounds for rice donations. Villagers build their houses on stilts for safety from annual river flooding and top them with thatch or tin. Barefoot children play under the palm trees or wander to the village Buddhist temple for school in the outdoor courtyard. Mothers stay home to weave brightly colored cloth for the family and to prepare meals—on charcoal or wood stoves—of rice, bamboo shoots, pork, duck, and snakes seasoned with hot peppers and ginger.

Below this serene surface, however, Laos is a nation divided. Although the name Laos is taken from the dominant ethnic group, there are actually about 70 ethnic groups in the country. Over the centuries they have battled one another for supremacy, for land, and for tribute money. The constant feuding has weakened the nation and served as an invitation for neighboring countries to annex portions of Laos forcibly or to align themselves with one or another of the Laotian royal families or generals for material gain. China, Burma (today called Myanmar), Vietnam, and especially Thailand—with which Laotian people share many cultural and ethnic similarities—have all been involved militarily in Laos. France, the United States, and the former Soviet Union have also contributed to the tragic military history of the country.

Historically, a cause of unrest was often palace jealousies that led one member of the royal family to fight against a kinsman for dominance. More recently Laos has been seen as a pawn in the battle of the Western powers for access to the rich natural resources of Southeast Asia or as a "domino" that some did and others did not want to fall to communism. Former members of the royal family continue on the opposite sides of many issues.

The results of these struggles have been devastating. Laos is now one of the poorest countries in the world, with the average Laotian earning only $200 a year. There are few industries in the country, so most people survive by subsistence farming—that is, raising just what they need to eat rather than growing food to sell. In fact, some "hill peoples" (about two thirds of the Laotian people live in the mountains) in the long mountain range that separates Laos from Vietnam continue to use the most an-

cient farming technique known, slash-and-burn farming, an unstable method of land use that only allows 3 or 4 years of good crops before the soil is depleted and the farmers must move to new ground.

Even if all Laotian farmers used the most modern techniques and geared their production to cash crops, it would still be difficult to export food (or, for that matter, anything else) because of Laos's woefully inadequate transportation network. There are no railroads, and muddy, unpaved roads make many mountain villages completely inaccessible by car or truck. Moreover, Laos is landlocked. In a region of the world where wealth flows toward those countries with the best ports, having no access to the sea is a serious impediment to economic growth. In addition, for years the economy has been strictly controlled. Foreign investment and trade have not been welcomed, and tourists were not allowed until 1989. But the economy was opening up by the early 1990s, and the government's new Socioeconomic National Development Plan was calling for

foreign investment in all areas and an annual GNP growth rate of 8 percent.

Some economic progress has been made in the past decade. Laos is once again self-sufficient in its staple crop, rice, and electricity generated from dams along the Mekong River is sold to Thailand to earn foreign exchange. Laos imports various commodity items from Thailand, Singapore, Japan, and other countries, and it has received foreign aid from the Asian Development Bank. Exports to Thailand, China, and the United States include teakwood, tin, and various minerals. Laos is also the source of many controlled substances such as opium and heroin, much of which finds its way to Europe and the United States. The Laotian government is now trying to prevent hill peoples from cutting down valuable forests for opium-poppy cultivation.

HISTORY AND POLITICS

The Laotian people, originally migrating from south China through Thailand, set-

(UPI/Bettmann)

Laos is one of the poorest countries in the world. With few industries, most people survive by subsistence farming. These fishermen spend their days catching tiny fish, measuring 2 to 5 inches, that must suffice to feed their families.

The first Laotian nation is established A.D. 1300s | Vietnam annexes most of Laos **1833** | Laos comes under French control **1885** | The Japanese conquer Southeast Asia **1940s** | France grants independence to Laos **1949** | South Vietnamese troops, with U.S. support, invade Laos **1971** | Pathet Lao Communists gain control of the government **1975** | Laos signs military and economic agreements with Vietnam **1977** | The government begins to liberalize some aspects of the economy **1980s** / 1990s

The Pathet Lao government maintains firm control over the country

Laos and Thailand make moves toward improved relations

tled Laos in the thirteenth century A.D, when the area was controlled by the Khmer (Cambodian) Empire. Early Laotian leaders expanded the borders of Laos through warfare with Cambodia, Thailand, Burma, and Vietnam. Internal warfare, however, led to a loss of autonomy in 1833, when Thailand forcibly annexed the country (against the wishes of Vietnam, which also had designs on Laos). In the 1890s France, determined to have a part of the lucrative Asian trade and to hold its own against growing British strength in Southeast Asia, forced Thailand to give up its hold on Laos. Laos, Vietnam, and Cambodia were combined into a new political entity, which the French called Indochina. Between these French possessions and the British possessions of Burma and Malaysia lay Thailand; thus, France, Britain, and Thailand effectively controlled mainland Southeast Asia for several decades.

There were several small uprisings against French power, but these were easily suppressed until the Japanese conquest of Indochina in the 1940s. The Japanese, with their "Asia for Asians" philosophy, convinced the Laotians that European domination was not a given. In 1949 Laos was granted independence, although full French withdrawal did not take place until 1954.

Prior to independence Prince Souphanouvong had organized a Communist guerrilla army, with help from Ho Chi Minh and the Vietnamese Communist Viet Minh. This army called itself the Pathet Lao (meaning "Lao Country"). In 1954 it challenged the authority of the government in Vientiane. Civil war ensued, and by 1961, when a cease-fire was arranged, the Pathet Lao had captured about half of Laos. The So-

viet Union supported the Pathet Lao, whose strength was in the northern half of Laos, while the United States supported a succession of pro-Western but fragile governments in the south. A coalition government consisting of Pathet Lao, pro-Western, and neutralist leaders was installed in 1962, but it collapsed in 1965, when warfare once again broke out.

During the Vietnam War, U.S. and South Vietnamese forces bombed and invaded Laos in an attempt to disrupt the North Vietnamese supply line known as the Ho Chi Minh Trail. Americans flew nearly 600,000 bombing missions over Laos (many of the small cluster bombs remain unexploded in fields and villages and present a continuing danger). Communist battlefield victories in Vietnam encouraged and aided the Pathet Lao Army, which became the dominant voice in a new coalition government established in 1974. The Pathet Lao controlled the government exclusively by 1975. In the same year, the government proclaimed a new Lao People's Democratic Republic. It abolished the 622-year-old monarchy and sent the king and the royal family to a detention center to learn Marxist ideology.

Vietnamese Army support and flight by many of those opposed to the Communist regime have permitted the Pathet Lao to maintain control of the government. The ruling dictatorship is determined to prevent the democratization of Laos: In 1993 several cabinet ministers were jailed for 14 years for trying to establish a multiparty democracy.

The Pathet Lao government was sustained militarily and economically by the Soviet Union and other East bloc nations

for more than 15 years. However, with the end of the cold war and the collapse of the Soviet Union, Laos has had to look elsewhere, including non-Communist countries, for support. The Australian government, continuing its plan to integrate itself more fully into the strong Asian economic market, promised in 1994 to provide Laos with more than $33 million in aid. And in 1992 Laos signed a friendship treaty with Thailand to facilitate trade between these two historic enemies.

Trying to teach communism to a devoutly Buddhist country has not been easy. Popular resistance has caused the government to retract many of the regulations it has tried to impose on the Buddhist church (technically, the *Sangha*, or order of the monks—the Buddhist equivalent of a clerical hierarchy). As long as the Buddhist hierarchy limits its activities to helping the poor, it seems to be able to avoid running afoul of the Communist leadership.

Intellectuals, especially those known to have been functionaries of the French administration, have fled Laos, leaving a leadership vacuum. As many as 300,000 people are thought to have left Laos for refugee camps in Thailand and elsewhere. Many have taken up permanent residence in foreign countries. With a total population of only 4.5 million people, the exodus has imposed a significant drain on Laos's intellectual resources.

DEVELOPMENT

Communist rule after 1975 isolated Laos from world trade and foreign investment. The planned economy has not been able to gain momentum on its own. In 1986 the government loosened restrictions so that government companies could keep a portion of their profits. A goal is to integrate Laos economically with Vietnam and Cambodia.

FREEDOM

Laos is ruled by the political arm of the Pathet Lao Army. Opposition parties and groups as well as opposition newspapers and other media are outlawed. Lack of civil liberties as well as poverty have caused many thousands of people to flee the country.

HEALTH/WELFARE

Laos is typical of the least developed countries in the world. The birth rate is high, but so is infant mortality. Most citizens eat less than an adequate diet. Life expectancy is low, and many Laotians die from illnesses for which medicines are available in other countries. Many doctors fled the country when the Communists came to power.

ACHIEVEMENTS

The original inhabitants of Laos, the Kha, have been looked down upon by the Lao, Thai, and other peoples for centuries. But under the Communist regime, the status of the Kha has been upgraded and discrimination formally proscribed.

Macau

GEOGRAPHY

Area in Square Kilometers (Miles):
16 (6) (about one tenth the size of
Washington, D.C.)
Capital (Population): Macau
(478,000)
Climate: subtropical

PEOPLE

Population
Total: 478,000
Annual Growth Rate: 1.44%
Rural/Urban Population Ratio: 0/100
Ethnic Makeup: 95% Chinese; 3%
Portuguese; 2% others
Major Languages: Portuguese;
Cantonese

Health
Life Expectancy at Birth: 77 years
(male); 82 years (female)
Infant Mortality Rate (Ratio):
5.5/1,000
Average Caloric Intake: n/a
Physicians Available (Ratio): 1/2,470

Religions
46% unaffiliated; 45% Buddhist; 7%;
Roman Catholic; 1% Protestant; 1%
other

Education
Adult Literacy Rate: 90%

COMMUNICATION

Telephones: 55,643
Newspapers: 8

THE LEGEND OF A-MA

Every May the people of Macau celebrate the Feast of A-Ma, a Chinese
goddess after whom the Portuguese named Macau. During the festival
the entire fishing fleet comes to port to honor this patroness of fishermen
and seamen at the temple that bears her name, located at the entrance
of the Inner Harbor.

According to legend, A-Ma was a poor girl looking for a passage to
Canton. She was refused by the wealthy junk owners, but a lowly
fisherman took her aboard. Soon a storm wrecked all the boats but the
one carrying A-Ma. When it landed in Macau, she disappeared, only to
reappear later as a goddess at the spot where the fisherman built her
temple.

TRANSPORTATION

Highways—Kilometers (Miles): 42 (26)
Railroads—Kilometers (Miles): none
Usable Airfields: none

GOVERNMENT

Type: Chinese territory under
Portuguese administration; scheduled
to revert to China in 1999
Independence Date: —
Head of State/Government: President
(of Portugal) Mário Alberto Soares;
Governor Francisco Nabo
Political Parties: Association to
Defend the Interests of Macau;
Macau Democratic Center; Group to
Study the Development of Macau;
Macau Independent Group
Suffrage: universal at 18

MILITARY

Number of Armed Forces: defense is
the responsibility of Portugal
*Military Expenditures (% of Central
Government Expenditures):* n/a
Current Hostilities: none

ECONOMY

Currency ($ U.S. Equivalent): 8.03
patacas = $1
Per Capita Income/GDP: $6,700/$3.1
billion
Inflation Rate: 8.2%
Natural Resources: fish
Agriculture: rice; vegetables
Industry: clothing; textiles; toys;
plastic products; furniture; tourism

FOREIGN TRADE

Exports: $1.8 billion
Imports: $2.0 billion

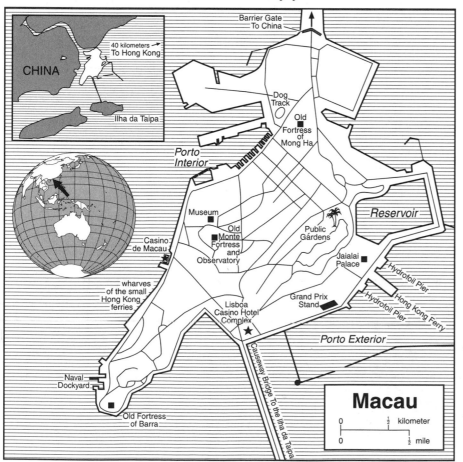

| A Portuguese trading colony is established at Macau A.D. 1557 | Portugal declares sovereignty over Macau 1849 | China signs a treaty recognizing Portuguese sovereignty over Macau 1887 | Immigrants from China flood into the colony 1949 | Pro-Communist riots in Macau 1967 | Portugal begins to loosen direct administrative control over Macau 1970s | Macau becomes a Chinese territory but is still administered by Portugal 1976 | China and Portugal sign an agreement scheduling the return of Macau to Chinese control 1987 |

1990s

50,000 illegal Chinese immigrants seek permanent residency status in Macau

Macau will revert to Chinese control in 1999

MACAU'S HISTORY

Just 17 miles across the Pearl River estuary from British Hong Kong is another speck of foreignness on Chinese soil: the Portuguese territory of Macau (sometimes spelled Macao). The oldest permanent outpost of European culture in the Far East, Macau has the highest population density of any political entity in the world: Although it consists of only about 6 square miles of land, it is home to nearly half a million people, crowded onto the peninsula and two small islands. Some 95 percent of these are Chinese, and Cantonese is universally spoken, although Portuguese is still the official language. Macau's population has varied over the years, depending on conditions within China; during the World War II Japanese occupation of China, for instance, Macau's Chinese population is believed to have doubled, and more refugees streamed in when the Communists took over China in 1949.

Macau was frequented by Portuguese traders as early as 1516, but it was not until 1557 that the Chinese agreed to Portuguese settlement of the land; it did not, however, acknowledge Portuguese sovereignty. Indeed, the Chinese government did not recognize the Portuguese right of "perpetual occupation" until 1887.

In 1987, after 9 months of negotiation, Chinese and Portuguese officials, meeting in Beijing, signed an agreement that will end European control of the first and last colonial outpost in China. The Portuguese will have administered the tiny colony of Macau for close to 450 years; the transfer to Chinese control is scheduled for December 20, 1999.

The agreement is similar to that signed by Britain and China over the fate of Hong Kong. China agreed to allow Macau to maintain its capitalist way of life for 50 years, to permit local elections, and to allow its residents to travel freely without Chinese intervention. Unlike Hong Kong residents, who have staged massive demonstrations against future Chinese rule or have emigrated from the colony, Macau residents—some of whom have been openly pro-Communist—have not seemed bothered by the new arrangements. In fact, plans are under way to bolster the economy in preparation for 1999 by constructing an airport in the territory, and President Mario Soares of Portugal, on an official visit in 1993, indicated that plans for the reversion to China were going smoothly.

Since it was established in the sixteenth century as a trading colony (with interests in oranges, tea, tobacco, and lacquer), Macau has been heavily influenced by Roman Catholic priests of the Dominican and Jesuit orders. Christian churches, interspersed with Buddhist temples, abound. The name of Macau itself reflects its deep and enduring religious roots; the city's official name is "City of the Name of God in China, Macau, There Is None More Loyal." Macau has perhaps the highest density of churches and temples per square mile in the world. Buddhist immigrants from China have reduced the proportion of Christians in the population.

A HEALTHY ECONOMY

Macau's modern economy is a vigorous blend of light industry, fishing, tourism, and gambling. Revenues from the latter two sources are impressive; indeed, they account for 25 percent of gross domestic product. There are five major casinos and many other gambling opportunities in Macau, which, along with the considerable charms of the city itself, attract more than 5 million foreign visitors a year, more than 80 percent of them Hong Kong Chinese with plenty of money to spend. Macau's gambling industry is run by a syndicate of Chinese businesspeople operating under the name Macau Travel & Amusement Company, which won monopoly rights on all licensed gambling in Macau in 1962.

Export earnings derived from light-industry products such as textiles, fireworks, plastics, and electronics are also critical to the colony. Macau's leading export markets are the United States, China, Germany, France, and Hong Kong; ironically, Portugal consumes only about 3 percent of Macau's exports.

As might be expected, the success of the economy has its downside. In Macau's case, the hallmarks of modernization—crowded apartment blocks and bustling traffic—are threatening to eclipse the remnants of the old, serene Portuguese-style seaside town.

DEVELOPMENT

The development of industries related to gambling and tourism (tourists are primarily from Hong Kong) has been very successful. Most of Macau's foods, energy, and fresh water are imported from China; Japan and Hong Kong are the main suppliers of raw materials.

FREEDOM

Under the 1987 agreement, China will acquire full sovereignty over Macau in 1999, but local elections will be permitted, as will the capitalist way of life. The governor is currently appointed by the president of Portugal, while the 17 members of the Legislative Assembly are elected directly by the people of Macau.

HEALTH/WELFARE

Macau has very impressive quality-of-life statistics. It has a low infant mortality rate and very high life expectancy for both males and females. Literacy is 90 percent. In recent years the unemployment rate has been a low 2 percent.

ACHIEVEMENTS

Considering its unfavorable geographical characteristics, such as negligible natural resources and a port so shallow and heavily silted that ocean-going ships must lie offshore, Macau has had stunning economic success. Its annual economic growth rate is approximately 5 percent.

Malaysia

GEOGRAPHY

Area in Square Kilometers (Miles):
329,750 (121,348) (slightly larger
than New Mexico)
Capital (Population): Kuala Lumpur
(1,000,000)
Climate: tropical

PEOPLE

Population
Total: 18,845,000
Annual Growth Rate: 2.32%
Rural/Urban Population Ratio: 62/38
Ethnic Makeup: 59% Malay and
other indigenous; 32% Chinese; 9%
Indian and Pakistani
Major Languages: Peninsular
Malaysia: Bahasa Malaysia, English,
Chinese dialects, Tamil; Sabah:
English, Malay, numerous tribal
dialects, Mandarin and Hakka
dialects; Sarawak: English, Malay,
Mandarin, numerous tribal dialects,
Arabic, others

Health
Life Expectancy at Birth: 66 years
(male); 72 years (female)
Infant Mortality Rate (Ratio):
26.5/1,000
Average Caloric Intake: 117% of
FAO minimum
Physicians Available (Ratio): 1/2,638

Religions
Peninsular Malaysia: Malays nearly
all Muslim, Chinese predominantly
Buddhist, Indians predominantly
Hindu; Saba: 33% Muslim, 17%
Christian, 45% others; Sarawak: 35%
traditional indigenous, 24% Buddhist
and Confucian, 20% Muslim, 16%
Christian, 5% others

Education
Adult Literacy Rate: 78% overall

HAVE YOU DRIVEN A PROTON SAGA LATELY?

Malaysians, once fearful of Japan and its military might, are now welcoming
the Japanese into their industries and businesses. With Japanese money and
Malaysian labor, Malaysia's attempt to industrialize is starting to bear fruit.
A successful example is the $320 million joint venture between the Malay-
sian government-owned Heavy Industries Corporation and Mitsubishi Motor
Corporation of Japan. The venture has produced a Malaysian car called the
Proton Saga, which is being exported to New Zealand, England, Jamaica,
and several countries in Asia. The Proton Saga, which Malaysians are proud
to call their "national car," captured 47 percent of Malaysia's market in its
first year. At full capacity, the company is expected to produce 100,000
cars a year.

COMMUNICATION

Telephones: 1,579,634
Newspapers: n/a

TRANSPORTATION

Highways—Kilometers (Miles):
29,026 (17,996)
Railroads—Kilometers (Miles): 1,801
(1,116)
Usable Airfields: 102

GOVERNMENT

Type: constitutional monarchy
Independence Date: August 31, 1957
Head of State: Prime Minister Datuk
Mahathir bin Mohamad; Paramount
Ruler (King) Azlan Muhibbuddin
Shah ibni Sultan Yusof Izzudin
Political Parties: Peninsular
Malaysia: National Front
Confederation and others; Sabah:
Berjaya Party and others; Sarawak:
coalition Sarawak National Front and
others
Suffrage: universal at 21

MILITARY

Number of Armed Forces: 119,900
Military Expenditures (% of Central

Government Expenditures): 5%
Current Hostilities: dispute over the
Spratly Islands with China, the
Philippines, Taiwan, and Vietnam;
Sabah is claimed by the Philippines

ECONOMY

Currency ($ U.S. Equivalent): 2.62
ringgit = $1
Per Capita Income/GDP:
$2,960/$54.5 billion
Inflation Rate: 4.7%
Natural Resources: oil; natural gas;
bauxite; iron ore; copper; tin; timber; fish
Agriculture: rubber; palm oil; rice;
coconut; pepper; timber
Industry: rubber and palm oil
manufacturing and processing; light
manufacturing; electronics; tin mining
and smelting; logging and processing
timber; petroleum production and
refining; food processing

FOREIGN TRADE

Exports: $39.8 billion
Imports: $34.1 billion

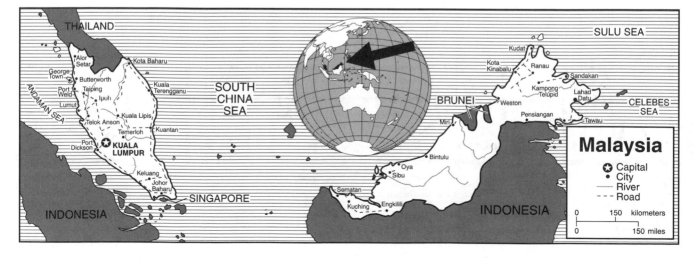

A FRACTURED NATION

About the size of Japan and famous for its production of natural rubber and tin, Malaysia sounds like a true political, economic, and social entity. But Malaysia, although it has all the trappings of a modern nation-state, is one of the most fragmented nations on earth.

Consider its land. West Malaysia, wherein reside 86 percent of the population, is located on the Malay Peninsula between Singapore and Thailand; but East Malaysia, with 60 percent of the land, is located on the island of North Borneo, some 400 miles of ocean away.

Similarly, Malaysia's people are divided along racial, religious, and linguistic lines. Fifty-nine percent of the population of nearly 19 million are Malays and other indigenous peoples, many of whom adhere to the Islamic faith or animist beliefs; 32 percent are Chinese, most of whom are Buddhist, Confucian, or Taoist; and 9 percent are Indians and Pakistanis, some of whom follow the Hindu faith. Bahasa Malaysia is the official language, but English, Arabic, two forms of Chinese, Tamil (from India), and other languages are also spoken. Thus, although the country is called Malaysia (a name adopted only 30 years ago), most people living in Kuala Lumpur, the capital, or in the many villages in the countryside do not think of themselves first and foremost as Malaysians.

Malaysia culture is further fragmented because each ethnic group tends to replicate the architecture, social rituals, and norms of etiquette peculiar to itself. The Chinese, originally imported in the 1800s from south China by the British to work the rubber plantations and tin mines, have become so economically powerful that their cultural influence extends far beyond their actual numbers.

Malaysia's history is equally fragmented. Originally controlled by numerous sultans who gave allegiance to no one or only reluctantly to various more powerful states in surrounding regions, Malaysia first came to Western attention in 1511, when the prosperous city of Malacca, founded on the west coast of the Malaya Peninsula about A.D. 1400, was conquered by the Portuguese. The Dutch took Malacca away from the Portuguese in 1641. The British seized it from the Dutch in 1824 (the British had already acquired an island off the coast and had established the port of Singapore). By 1888 the British were in control of most of the area that is now Malaysia.

However, British hegemony did not mean total control, for each of the many sultanates—the origin of the 13 states that constitute Malaysia today—continued to act more or less independently of the British, engaging in wars with one another and maintaining an administrative apparatus apart from the British. And some groups, such as the Dayaks, an indigenous people living in the jungles of Borneo, remained more or less aloof from the various intrigues of modern state-making and developed little or no identity of themselves as citizens of any modern nation.

It is hardly surprising, then, that Malaysia has had a difficult time emerging as a modern nation. Indeed, it is not likely that there would have been an independent Malaysia had it not been for the Japanese, who defeated the British in Southeast Asia during World War II and promulgated their alluring doctrine of "Asia for Asians."

After the war Malaysian demands for independence from European domination grew more persuasive; Britain attempted in 1946 to meet these demands by proposing a partly autonomous Malay Union. However, ethnic rivalries and power-sensitive sultans created such enormous tension that the plan was scrapped. In an uncharacteristic display of cooperation, some 41 different Malay groups organized the United Malay National Organization (UMNO) to oppose the British plan. In 1948 a new Federation of Malaya was attempted, which granted considerable freedom within a framework of British supervision, allowed sultans to retain power over their own regions, and placed certain restrictions on the power of the Chinese living in the country.

Opposing any agreement short of full independence, a group of Chinese Communists, with Indonesian support, began a guerrilla war against the government and against capitalist ideology. Known as The Emergency, the war lasted more than a decade and involved some 250,000 government troops. Eventually the insurgents withdrew.

The three main ethnic groups—Malayans, represented by UMNO; Chinese, represented by the Malayan Chinese Association, or MCA; and Indians, represented by the Malayan Indian Congress, or MIC—were able to cooperate long enough in 1953 to form a single political party under the leadership of Abdul Rahman. This party demanded and received complete independence for the Federation in 1957, although some areas, such as Brunei, refused to join. Upon independence the Federation of Malaya (not yet called Malaysia), excluding Singapore and the territories on the island of Borneo, became a member of the British Commonwealth of Nations and was admitted to the United Nations. In 1963 a new Federation was proposed that included Singapore and the lands on Borneo. Again, Brunei refused to join. Singapore joined but withdrew in 1965. Thus, what is known as Malaysia acquired its current form in 1966. It is regarded today as a rapidly developing Third World nation that is attempting to govern itself according to democratic principles.

Political troubles stemming from the deep ethnic divisions in the country, however, remain a constant feature of Malaysian life. With 9 of the 13 states controlled by independent sultans, every election is a test of the ability of the National Front (Barisan Nasional), a multiethnic coalition of 11 different parties that has a two-thirds majority in Parliament, to maintain political stability. Particularly troublesome has been the state of Sabah (an area claimed by the Philippines), many of whose residents have wanted independence or, at least, greater autonomy from the federal government. In 1994, however, the National Front was able to gain a slight majority in Sabah elections, indicating the growing confidence that people have in the federal government's economic development policies.

ECONOMIC DEVELOPMENT

The single most important reason why Malaysia has been able to maintain stability has been its steady economic growth. Although it has had to endure the cyclical fluctuations of market demand for its products, the economy has grown at about 5 to 8 percent a year since the 1970s. Malaysia is now the world's 19th top exporter and importer, and the manufacturing sector has been developed to such an extent that it accounts for nearly 70 percent of exports. Malaysia continues to be known for its abundance of raw materials, especially timber (Malaysia produces half of the world's timber exports), tin, and petroleum. Rice, coconut oil, and pepper are also important exports.

This amazing transformation of the economy did not happen accidentally; it has been the result of proactive government planning, directly modeled after Japan's export-oriented strategy and using massive amounts of Japanese investment money. Unlike North Korea or Myanmar, which have resisted integration into the global economy, Malaysia launched a New Economic Policy (NEP) in the 1970s that welcomed foreign direct investment and sought to diversify the economic base. Japan, Taiwan, and the United States invested heavily in Malaysia. So successful has this strategy been that economic growth targets set for the mid-1990s were actually achieved several years early. In 1991 the government replaced NEP with a new plan, now generally called "Vision

The city of Malacca is established; it becomes a center of trade and Islamic conversion
A.D. **1403**

The Portuguese capture Malacca
1511

The Dutch capture Malacca
1641

The British obtain Malacca from the Dutch
1824

Japan captures the Malay Peninsula
1941

The British establish the Federation of Malaya; communist guerrilla war begins, lasting for a decade
1948

The Federation of Malaya achieves independence under Prime Minister Tengku Abdul Rahman
1957

The Federation of Malaysia, including Singapore but not Brunei, is formed
1963

Singapore leaves the Federation of Malaysia
1965

Malaysia attempts to build an industrial base; Mahathir bin Mohamad becomes prime minister
1980s

1990s

The NEP, proclaimed a success, comes to an official end

The NEP is replaced with Vision 2020

2020." Its goal is to bring Malaysia into full "developed nation" status by the year 2020. Sectors targeted for growth include the aerospace industry, biotechnology, microelectronics, and information and energy technology. The government has expanded universities and encouraged the creation of some 170 industrial and research parks, including "Free Zones," where export-oriented businesses are allowed duty-free imports of raw materials.

Despite Malaysia's economic successes, serious social problems remain. These problems stem not from insufficient revenues (until 1990 Malaysia was blessed with an annual budget surplus) but from inequitable distribution. The Malay portion of the population in particular continues to feel economically deprived as compared to the wealthier Chinese and Indian segments. At one time these upper-class households received, on average, 16 times the income of the poorest Malay families. Furthermore, most Malays are farmers, and rural areas have not benefited from Malaysia's economic boom as much as urban areas have.

In the 1960s and 1970s, riots involving thousands of college students were headlined in the Western press as having their basis in ethnicity. This was true to an extent, but the core issue was economic inequality. Included in the economic master plan of the 1970s were plans (similar to affirmative action in the United States) to change the structural barriers that prevented Malays from fully enjoying the benefits of the economic boom. Under the leadership of Prime Minister Mahathir bin Mohamad, plans were developed that would assist Malays until they held a 30 percent interest in Malaysian businesses.

In 1990 the government announced that the figure had already reached an impressive 20 percent. Unfortunately, many Malays have insufficient capital to maintain ownership in businesses, so the government has been called upon to acquire many Malay businesses in order to prevent their being purchased by non-Malays. In addition, the system of preferential treatment for Malays has created a Malay elite, detached from the Malay poor, who now compete with the Chinese and Indian elites; goodwill among races is still difficult to achieve. Nonetheless, social goals have been attained to a greater extent than most observers have thought possible. Educational opportunities for the poor have been increased, farmland development has proceeded on schedule, and the poverty rate has dropped to 17 percent.

THE LEADERSHIP

In a polity so fractured as Malaysia's, one would expect rapid turnover among political elites. But Prime Minister Mahathir, a Malay, has continued to receive the support of the electorate for more than a decade. His primary challenger has been the Chinese Democratic Action Party (DAP), which has reduced Mahathir's majority in Parliament but has not been able to top his political strength. The policies that have sustained Mahathir's reputation as a credible leader include the NEP, with its goals of economic diversification, privatization, and wealth equalization, and his nationalist—but moderate—foreign policy. Malaysia has been an active member of ASEAN and has worked hard to maintain good diplomatic relations with the Western nations, while simultaneously courting Japan and other Pacific Rim nations for foreign investment and export markets (Mahathir's "Look East" policy). Anticipating negative economic consequences from the growing strength of the European Union and from the North American Free Trade Agreement, Mahathir promoted a plan to create an Asian free trade zone that would exclude the United States and other Western nations. Failing in that, he refused to attend the Asia-Pacific Economic Cooperation group meetings that were held in 1993 in the United States and at which more than a dozen regional leaders discussed economic cooperation. Recent rocky relations with Australia and Britain—evidence of Mahathir's intense nationalism—have resulted in Malaysia canceling construction contracts for dams and airports.

Malaysia's success has not been achieved without some questionable practices. The government seems unwilling to regulate economic growth, even though strong voices have been raised against industrialization's deleterious effects on the teak forests and other parts of the environment. Moreover, the blue-collar workers who are the muscle behind Malaysia's success are prohibited from forming labor unions, and outspoken critics have been silenced. Charges of government corruption are becoming more frequent and more strident.

DEVELOPMENT

Malaysia continues to struggle to move its economy away from agriculture. Attempts at industrialization have been successful: Malaysia is the third-largest producer of semiconductors in the world, and manufacturing now accounts for 30% of the gross domestic product.

FREEDOM

Malaysia is attempting to govern according to democratic principles. Ethnic rivalries, however, severely hamper the smooth conduct of government and limit such individual liberties as the right to form labor unions.

HEALTH/WELFARE

City dwellers have ready access to educational, medical, and social opportunities, but the quality of life declines dramatically in the countryside. Malaysia has one of the highest illiteracy rates in the Pacific Rim. Malaysia still spends only a small percentage of its GDP on education.

ACHIEVEMENTS

Malaysia has made impressive economic advancements. The government's New Economic Policy has achieved a measure of wealth redistribution to the poor. Since 1985 the economy has grown at an impressive 5% to 9% annually. Malaysia has also made impressive social and political gains.

Myanmar (Union of Myanmar; also known as Burma)

GEOGRAPHY

Area in Square Kilometers (Miles): 678,500 (261,901) (slightly smaller than Texas)
Capital (Population): Yangon (previously Rangoon) (2,459,000)
Climate: tropical monsoon and equatorial

PEOPLE

Population

Total: 43,456,000
Annual Growth Rate: 1.8%
Rural/Urban Population Ratio: 75/24
Ethnic Makeup: 68% Burman; 9% Shan; 7% Karen; 4% Rakhine; 3% Chinese; 8% Mon, Indian, and others
Major Languages: 60% Burmese; various minority languages

Health

Life Expectancy at Birth: 58 years (male); 62 years (female)
Infant Mortality Rate (Ratio): 65.7/1,000
Average Caloric Intake: 106% of FAO minimum
Physicians Available (Ratio): 1/3,389

Religions

89% Buddhist; 4% Muslim; 4% Christian; 3% animist and others

Education

Adult Literacy Rate: 81%

COMMUNICATION

Telephones: 73,545
Newspapers: 1

TRANSPORTATION

Highways—Kilometers (Miles): 27,000 (16,740)
Railroads—Kilometers (Miles): 3,991 (2,474)
Usable Airfields: 78

GOVERNMENT

Type: military government
Independence Date: January 4, 1948
Head of State: General Than Shwe
Political Parties: National League for Democracy; National Coalition of Union of Burma; National Unity Party; more than 100 others
Suffrage: universal at 18

MILITARY

Number of Armed Forces: 280,000 plus 85,000 paramilitary personnel
Military Expenditures (% of Central Government Expenditures): 40%
Current Hostilities: none

ECONOMY

Currency ($ U.S. Equivalent): 6.09 kyats = $1
Per Capita Income/GDP: $660/$28 billion
Inflation Rate: 50%
Natural Resources: crude oil; timber; tin; antimony; zinc; copper; tungsten; lead; coal; marble; limestone; precious stones; natural gas
Agriculture: teak; rice; corn; oilseed; sugarcane; pulses
Industry: agricultural processing; textiles; footwear; wood and wood products; petroleum refining; copper, tin, tungsten, and iron mining; construction materials; pharmaceuticals; fertilizer

FOREIGN TRADE

Exports: $535.1 million
Imports: $907 million

BUDDHISM

Most people in Myanmar are Buddhists, and the Buddhist hierarchy of priests, called the *Sangha,* has been a powerful opponent of the military dictatorship. This is a rather unusual position for Buddhists, who have generally preferred a passive attitude toward politics and "worldly" issues.

Detachment from the world was the philosophy of Buddhism's founder, Siddhartha Gautama. He was born about 563 B.C. in what is today Nepal. Raised in luxury and expected to follow in his father's footsteps as a ruler and warrior, Gautama instead abandoned his wife, children, and riches to lead the life of a poor wanderer in search of life's meaning. At about age 35, while meditating under a tree, he experienced a spiritual insight that earned him the title of *buddha,* meaning "the awakened" or "enlightened one." From that experience he came to believe that life would continue to be full of pain for everyone unless they renounced their attachment to greed and the other selfish desires of the world.

Myanmar

- ⭐ Capital
- ● City
- ～ River
- --- Road

0   200   kilometers
0   200   miles

THE CONTROLLED SOCIETY

For more than 3 decades, Myanmar (as Burma was renamed in 1989) has been a tightly controlled society. Telephones, radio stations, railroads, and many large companies have been under the direct control of a military junta that has brutalized its opposition and forced many to flee the country. For many years tourists were allowed to stay only 2 weeks (for a while the limit was 24 hours), had to stay at military-approved hotels, and could visit only certain parts of the country. Citizens too were highly restricted: They could not leave their country by car or train to visit nearby countries because all the roads were sealed off by government decree and rail lines terminated at the border. Even Western-style dancing was declared illegal. Until a minor liberalization of the economy was achieved in 1989, all foreign exports—every grain of rice, every peanut, every piece of lumber—though generally owned privately, had to be sold to the government rather than directly to consumers.

Observers attribute this state of affairs to military commanders who overthrew the legitimate government in 1962, but the roots of Myanmar's political and economic dilemma actually go back to 1885, when the British overthrew the Burmese government and declared Burma a colony of Britain. In the 1930s European-educated Burmese college students organized strikes and demonstrations against the British. Seeing that the Japanese Army had successfully toppled other European colonial governments in Asia, the students determined to assist the Japanese during their invasion of the country in 1941. Once the British had been expelled, however, the students organized the Anti-Fasçist People's Freedom League (AFPFL) to oppose Japanese rule.

When the British tried to resume control of Burma after World War II, they found that the Burmese people had given their allegiance to U Aung San, one of the original student leaders. He and the AFPFL insisted that the British grant full independence to Burma, which they reluctantly did in 1948. So determined were the Burmese to remain free of foreign domination that, unlike most former British colonies, they refused to join the British Commonwealth of Nations, an economic association of former British colonies. This was the first of many decisions that would have the effect of isolating Burma from the global economy.

Unlike Japan, with its nearly homogeneous population and single national language, Myanmar is a multiethnic state; in fact, only about 60 percent of the people speak Burmese. The Burman people are genetically related to the Tibetans and the Chinese; the Chin are related to peoples of nearby India; the Shan are related to Thais; and the Mon migrated to Burma from Cambodia. In general, these ethnic groups live in separate political states within Myanmar, i.e., the Kachin State, the Shan State, the Karen State, and so on; and for hundreds of years, they have warred against one another for dominance. Upon the withdrawal of the British in 1948, some ethnic groups, particularly the Kachins, the Karens, and the Shans, embraced the communist ideology of change through violent revolution. Their rebellion against the government in the capital city of Yangon (the new name of Rangoon) had the effect of removing from government control large portions of the country. Headed by U Nu (U Aung San and several of the original government leaders having been assassinated shortly before independence), the government considered its position precarious and determined that to align itself with the Communist forces then ascendant in the People's Republic of China and other parts of Asia would strengthen the hand of the ethnic separatists, whereas to form alliances with the capitalist world would invite a repetition of decades of Western domination. U Nu thus attempted to steer a decidedly neutral course during the cold war era and to be as tolerant as possible of separatist groups within Burma. Burma refused U.S. economic aid, had very little to do with the warfare afflicting Vietnam and the other Southeast Asian countries, and was not eager to join the Southeast Asian Treaty Organization or the Asian Development Bank.

Some factions of Burmese society were not pleased with U Nu's relatively benign treatment of separatist groups. In 1958 a political impasse allowed Ne Win, a military general, to assume temporary control of the country. National elections were held in 1962, and a democratically elected government was installed in power. Shortly thereafter, however, Ne Win staged a military coup. (The military has controlled Burma/Myanmar ever since.) Under Ne Win, competing political parties were banned, the economy was nationalized, and the country's international isolation became even more pronounced.

Years of ethnic conflict, inflexible socialism, and self-imposed isolation have severely damaged economic growth in Myanmar. Despite an abundance of valuable teak and rubber trees in its forests, sizable supplies of minerals in the mountains to the north, onshore oil, rich farmland in the Irrawaddy Delta, and a reasonably well-educated population, in 1987 the United Nations declared Burma one of the least developed countries in the world (it had once been the richest country in Southeast Asia). Debt incurred in the 1970s exacerbated Myanmar's problems, as did the government's fear of foreign investment. Thus, in 1994, Myanmar's per capita income was only $660 a year.

Myanmar's industrial base is still very small; some 70 percent of the population of 42 million make their living by farming (rice is a major export) and by fishing. Only 10 percent of gross domestic product comes from the manufacturing sector (as compared to, for example, approximately 45 percent in wealthy Taiwan). In the absence of a strong economy, black marketeering has increased, as have other forms of illegal economic transactions. It is estimated that 80 percent of the heroin smuggled into New York City comes from the jungles of Myanmar and northern Thailand.

Over the years the Burmese have been advised by economists to open up their country to foreign investment and to develop the private sector of the economy. They have resisted the former idea because of their deep-seated fear of foreign domination. They have similar suspicions of the private sector because it was formerly controlled almost completely by ethnic minorities (the Chinese and Indians). The government has relied on the public sector to counterbalance the power of the ethnic minorities.

Beginning in 1987, however, the government began to admit publicly that the economy was in serious trouble. To counter massive unrest in the country, the military authorities agreed to permit foreign investment from countries such as Malaysia, South Korea, Singapore, and Thailand and to allow trade with China and Thailand. In 1989 the government signed oil exploration agreements with South Korea, the United States, the Netherlands, Australia, and Japan. Both the United States and the former West Germany withdrew foreign aid in 1988, but Japan did not; in 1991 Japan supplied $61 million—more than any other country—in aid to Myanmar.

POLITICAL STALEMATE

Despite these reforms, Myanmar has remained in a state of turmoil. In 1988 thousands of students participated in 6 months of demonstrations to protest the lack of democracy in the country and to demand multiparty elections. General Saw Maung brutally suppressed the demonstrators, imprisoning many students and killing some 3,000 of them. He then took control of the government and reluctantly agreed to multiparty elections. About 170 political parties registered for the elections, which were held in 1990—the first elections in 30 years. Among these were the National Unity Party (a new name for the Burma Socialist Program Party, the only legal party since 1974) and the National League for Democracy, a new party headed by Aung San Suu Kyi, daughter of slain national hero U Aung San.

The campaign was characterized by the same level of military control that had existed in all other aspects of life since the 1960s. Martial law, imposed in 1988, remained in effect; all schools and universities were closed; opposition-party workers were intimidated; and, most significantly, the three most popular opposition leaders were placed under house arrest and barred from campaigning. The United Nations began an investigation of civil rights abuses during the election and, once again, students demonstrated against the military government. Several students even hijacked a Burmese airliner to demand the release of Aung San Suu Kyi, who had been placed under house arrest.

As the votes were tallied, it became apparent that the Burmese people were eager to end military rule; the National League for Democracy won 80 percent of the seats in the National Assembly. But the military junta refused to step down and remains in control of the government. Under General Than Shwe, who replaced General Saw Maung in 1992, the military has organized operations against Karen rebels and has so oppressed Muslims that some 40,000 to 60,000 of them have fled to Bangladesh. Hundreds of students who fled the cities during the 1988 crackdown on student demonstrations have now joined rural guerrilla organizations, such as the Burma Communist Party and the Karen National Union, to continue the fight against the military dictatorship. Among those most vigorously opposed to military rule are Buddhist monks. Five months after the elections, monks in the capital city of Rangoon boycotted the government by refusing to conduct religious rituals for soldiers. Tens of thousands of people joined in the boycott. The government responded by threatening to shut down monasteries in the cities of Yangon and Mandalay.

The military government calls itself the State Law and Order Restoration Council (SLORC) and appears determined to stay in power. SLORC has vowed to keep Aung San Suu Kyi under house arrest. For several years even her husband and children were forbidden to visit her. While under arrest she was

(Photo credit AP Laser-Photo)

In 1990 Myanmar's first elections in 30 years were held; a new opposition party, the National League for Democracy, headed by Aung San Suu Kyi, pictured above, won 80 percent of the seats in the National Assembly. In 1989 the popular opposition leader had been placed under house arrest for trying to topple Myanmar's military government. In 1991 Aung San Suu Kyi was awarded the Nobel Peace Prize; but despite international pressure, she remains in custody in Myanmar at this writing.

awarded the Nobel Peace Prize in 1991, and in 1993 several other Nobelists gathered in nearby Thailand to call for her release—a plea ignored by SLORC. The United Nations has shown its displeasure with the military junta by substantially cutting development funds.

But perhaps the greatest pressure on the dictatorship is from within the country itself; despite brutal suppression, the military seems to be losing control of the people. Both the Kachin and Karen ethnic groups have organized guerrilla movements against the regime; in some cases

Burman people
enter the
Irrawaddy Valley
from China and
Tibet
800 B.C.

The Portuguese
are impressed
with Burmese
wealth
1500s

The First
Anglo-Burmese
War
1824–1826

The Second
Anglo-Burmese
War
1852

The Third
Anglo-Burmese
War results in the
loss of Burmese
sovereignty
1885

The Japanese
invade Burma
1941

Burma gains
independence of
Britain
1948

General Ne Win
takes control of
the government
in a coup
1962

Economic crisis;
the pro-
democracy
movement is
crushed; General
Saw Maung
takes control of
the government
1980s

Burma is
renamed
Myanmar
(though most
people prefer the
name Burma)
1989

1990s

The military
refuses to give up
power; Than Shwe
becomes head of
state

Aung San Suu Kyi
remains under
house arrest in
1995

they have coerced foreign lumber companies to pay them protection money, which they, in turn, use to buy arms against the junta. Opponents of SLORC control one third of Myanmar, especially along its eastern borders with Thailand and China and in the north alongside India. With the economy in shambles, the military appears to be involved with the heroin trade as a way of acquiring needed funds; it reportedly engages in bitter battles with drug lords periodically for control of the trade. To ease economic pressure, the military rulers have ended their monopoly of some businesses and have legalized the black market, making products from China, India, and Thailand available on the street.

Still, for ordinary people, especially those in the countryside, life is anything but pleasant; a 1994 human rights study found that as many as 20,000 women and girls living in Myanmar near the Thai border had been abducted to work as prostitutes in Thailand. For several years SLORC has carried out an ethnic-cleansing policy against villagers who have opposed their rule; thousands of people have been carried off to relocation camps, forced to work as slaves or prostitutes for the soldiers, or simply killed. Some 400,000 members of ethnic groups have fled the country, including 300,000 Arakans who escaped to Bangladesh and 5,000 Karenni, 12,000 Mon, and 50,000 Karens who fled to Thailand. Food shortages plague certain regions of the country, and many young children are forced to serve in the various competing armies rather than acquire an education or enjoy a normal childhood. Despite the lifting of mar-

tial law and some minor liberalization of the economy, including promotion of tourism, it appears that it will be a long time before democracy returns to Myanmar.

THE CULTURE OF BUDDHA

For a brief period in the 1960s, Buddhism was the official state religion of Burma. Although this status was repealed by the government in order to weaken the power of the Buddhist leadership, or Sangha, vis-à-vis the polity, Buddhism, representing the belief system of 89 percent of the population, remains the single most important cultural force in the country. Even the Burmese alphabet is based, in part, on Pali, the sacred language of Buddism. Buddhist monks joined with college students after World War II to pressure the British government to withdraw from Burma, and they have brought continual pressure to bear on the current military junta.

Historically, so powerful has been the Buddhist Sangha in Burma that four major dynasties have fallen because of it. This has not been the result of ideological antagonism between church and state (indeed, Burmese rulers have usually been quite supportive of Buddhism) but, rather, because Buddhism soaks up resources that might otherwise go to the government or to economic development. Believers are willing to give money, land, and other resources to the religion, because they believe that such donations will bring them spiritual merit; the more merit one acquires, the better one's next life will be. Thus, all over Myanmar, but especially in older cities such as Pagan (Bagan), one

can find large, elaborate Buddhist temples, monuments, or monasteries, some of them built by kings and other royals on huge, untaxed parcels of land. These monuments drained resources from the government but brought to the donor unusual amounts of spiritual merit. As Burmese scholar Michael Aung-Thwin explains it, "One built the largest temple because one was spiritually superior, and one was spiritually superior because one built the largest temple."

Today the Buddhist Sangha is at the forefront of the opposition to military rule. Monks have joined college students in peaceful-turned-violent demonstrations against the junta. Other monks have staged spiritual boycotts against the soldiers by refusing to accept merit-bringing alms from them or to perform weddings and funerals. The junta has retaliated by banning some Buddhist groups altogether and purging many others of rebellious leaders. The military regime now seems to be relaxing its intimidation of the Buddhists, has reopened universities, and has invited some foreign investment. Although the Japanese have continued to invest in Burma throughout the military dictatorship, some potential investors from other countries refused to invest in a regime that is so obviously brutal and which gives little evidence of any desire to return the country to democracy.

DEVELOPMENT

Primarily an agricultural nation, Myanmar has a poorly developed industrial sector. Until recently the government forbade foreign investment and severely restricted tourism. In 1989, recognizing that the economy was on the brink of collapse, the government permitted foreign investment and signed contracts with Japan and others for oil exploration.

FREEDOM

Myanmar is a military dictatorship. Until 1989 only the Burma Socialist Program Party was permitted. Other parties, while now legal, are intimidated by the military junta. The democratically elected National League for Democracy has not been permitted to assume office. The government has also restricted the activities of the Buddhist church.

HEALTH/WELFARE

The Myanmar government provides free health care and government pensions to citizens, but the quality and availability are erratic. Malnourishment and preventable diseases are common, and infant mortality is high. Overpopulation is not a problem; Myanmar is one of the most sparsely populated nations in Asia.

ACHIEVEMENTS

Myanmar is known for the beauty of its Buddhist architecture. Pagodas and other Buddhist monuments and temples dot many of the cities, especially Pagan, one of Burma's earliest cities. Politically, it is notable that the country was able to remain free of the warfare that engulfed much of Indochina during the 1960s and 1970s.

New Zealand (Dominion of New Zealand)

GEOGRAPHY

Area in Square Kilometers (Miles):
268,680 (98,874) (about the size of Colorado)
Capital (Population): Wellington (148,000)
Climate: temperate; sharp regional contrasts

PEOPLE

Population

Total: 3,369,000
Annual Growth Rate: 0.61%
Rural/Urban Population (Ratio): 14/76
Ethnic Makeup: 88% European; 9% Maori; 3% Pacific islander
Major Languages: English; Maori

Health

Life Expectancy at Birth: 72 years (male); 80 years (female)
Infant Mortality Rate (Ratio): 10/1,000
Average Caloric Intake: 132% of FAO minimum
Physicians Available (Ratio): 1/359

Religions

81% Christian; 18% unaffiliated; 1% others

Education

Adult Literacy Rate: 99%

COMMUNICATION

Telephones: 2,110,000
Newspapers: 32 dailies

TRANSPORTATION

Highways—Kilometers (Miles): 92,648 (57,441)

Railroads—Kilometers (Miles): 4,716 (2,923)
Usable Airfields: 120

GOVERNMENT

Type: parliamentary democracy
Independence Date: September 26, 1907
Head of State/Government: Chief of State Queen Elizabeth II, represented by Governor General Dame Catherine Tizard; Prime Minister James Bolger
Political Parties: New Zealand Labour Party; National Party; Democratic Party; Socialist Unity Party; New Zealand Liberal Party; Green Party
Suffrage: universal at 18

MILITARY

Number of Armed Forces: 11,300
Military Expenditures (% of Central Government Expenditures): 2%
Current Hostilities: none; disputed territorial claim in Antarctica

ECONOMY

Currency ($ U.S. Equivalent): 1.95 New Zealand dollars = $1
Per Capita Income/GDP: $14,900/$49.8 billion
Inflation Rate: 2.2%
Natural Resources: natural gas; iron ore; sand; coal; timber; hydropower; gold; limestone
Agriculture: wool; meat; dairy products; wheat; barley; potatoes; pulses; fruits; vegetables; fishing
Industry: food processing; wood and paper products; textiles; machinery; transportation equipment; banking; insurance; tourism; mining

FOREIGN TRADE

Exports: $3.65 billion
Imports: $3.99 billion

MAORI PRIDE

The 257,000 Maoris in New Zealand have, for the most part, been assimilated into white ("Pakeha") New Zealand culture. They speak English, worship in Christian churches, and actively participate in land speculation and other commercial activities of the free-enterprise system. Some have intermarried with whites, others with Japanese, and still others with Indians. Yet originally Maoris enjoyed pride of place in their islands. The word *Maori* means "normal," and the 50 or so tribes began using the term only after white contact to distinguish themselves from those who were so obviously different from the Maori norm. Today pride in being uniquely Maori is coming back.

ITS PLACE IN THE WORLD

New Zealand, like Australia, is decidedly an anomaly among Pacific Rim countries. Eighty-eight percent of the population are of British descent, English is the official language, and most people, even many of the original Maori inhabitants, are Christians. Great Britain claimed the beautiful, mountainous islands officially in 1840, after agreeing to respect the property rights of Maoris, most of whom lived on the North Island.

New Zealand, although largely self-governing since 1907 and fully independent as of 1947, has always maintained very close ties with the United Kingdom and is a member of the Commonwealth of Nations. It has, in fact, attempted to re-create British culture—customs, architecture, even vegetation—in the Pacific. So close were the links with England in the 1940s, for example, that England purchased fully 88 percent of New Zealand's exports (mostly agricultural and dairy products), while 60 percent of New Zealand's imports came from England. And believing itself to be very much a part of the British Empire, New Zealand always sided with the Western nations on matters of military defense.

These efforts to maintain a close cultural link with Great Britain do not stem entirely from the common ethnicity of the two nations; they also arise from New Zealand's extreme geographical isolation from the centers of European and North American activity. Even Australia is more than 1,200 miles away. Therefore, New Zealand's policy—until the 1940s—was to encourage the British presence in Asia and the Pacific, by acquiring more lands or building up naval bases, to make it more likely that Britain would be willing and able to defend New Zealand in a time of crisis. New Zealand had involved itself somewhat in the affairs of some nearby islands in the late 1800s and early 1900s, but its purpose was not to provide development assistance or defense. Rather, its aim was to extend the power of the British Empire and put New Zealand in the middle of a mini-empire of its own. To that end, New Zealand annexed the Cook Islands in 1901 and took over German Samoa in 1914. In 1925 it assumed formal control over the atoll group known as the Tokelau Islands.

REGIONAL RELIANCE DEVELOPS

During World War II (or, as the Japanese call it, the Pacific War), Japan's rapid conquest of the Malay Archipelago, its seizure of many Pacific islands, and its plans to attack Australia demonstrated to New Zealanders the futility of relying on the British to guarantee their security. After the war, and for the first time in its history, New Zealand began to pay serious attention to the real needs and ambitions of the peoples nearby rather than to focus on Great Britain. In 1944 and again in 1947, New Zealand joined with Australia and other colonial nations to create regional associations on behalf of the Pacific islands. One of the organizations, the South Pacific Commission, has itself spawned many regional subassociations dealing with trade, education, migration, and cultural and economic development. Although it had neglected the islands that it controlled during its imperial phase, in the

(The Peabody Museum of Salem photo)

Maoris occupied New Zealand long before the European settlers moved there. The Maoris quickly realized that the newcomers were intent on depriving them of their land, but it was not until the 1920s that the government finally regulated these unscrupulous land-grabbing practices. Today the Maoris have created a lifestyle that preserves key parts of their traditional culture while incorporating the skills necessary for survival in the modern world.

Maoris, probably from Tahiti, settle the islands A.D. **1300s**	New Zealand is discovered by Dutch navigator A. J. Tasman **1642**	Captain James Cook explores the islands **1769**	Great Britain declares sovereignty **1840**	A gold rush attracts new immigrants **1865**	New Zealand becomes an almost independent dominion of Great Britain **1907**

early 1900s, New Zealand cooperated fully with the United Nations in the islands' decolonization during the 1960s (although Tokelau, by choice, and the Ross dependency remain under New Zealand's control), while at the same time increasing development assistance. New Zealand's first alliance with Asian nations came in 1954, when it joined the Southeast Asian Treaty Organization.

New Zealand's new international focus certainly did not mean the end of cooperation with its traditional allies, however. In fact, the common threat of the Japanese during World War II strengthened cooperation between Australia and the United States to the extent that, in 1951, New Zealand joined a three-way, regional security agreement known as ANZUS (for Australia, New Zealand, and the United States). Moreover, because the United States was, at war's end, a Pacific/Asian power, any agreement with the United States was likely to bring New Zealand into more, rather than less, contact with Asia and the Pacific. Indeed, New Zealand sent troops to assist in all of the United States' military involvements in Asia: the occupation of Japan in 1945, the Korean War in 1950, and the Vietnam War in the 1960s. And as a member of the British Commonwealth, it sent troops in the 1950s and 1960s to fight Malaysian Communists and Indonesian insurgents.

NEW ZEALAND'S NEW INTERNATIONALISM

Beginning in the 1970s, especially when the Labour Party of Prime Minister Norman Kirk was in power, New Zealand's orientation shifted even more markedly toward its own region. Under Labour, New Zealand defined its sphere of interest and responsibility as the Pacific, where it hoped to be seen as a protector and benefactor of smaller states. Of immediate concern to many island nations was the issue of nuclear testing in the Pacific. Both the United States and France had undertaken tests by exploding nuclear devices on tiny Pacific atolls. In the 1960s the United States ceased these tests, but France continued. New Zealand argued before the United Nations against testing on behalf of the smaller islands, but France still did not stop. Eventually the desire to end test-

ing congealed into the more comprehensive position that the entire Pacific should be declared a nuclear-free zone. Not only testing but also the transport of nuclear weapons through the area would be prohibited under the plan.

New Zealand's Labour government issued a ban on the docking of ships with nuclear weapons in New Zealand, despite the fact that such ships were a part of the ANZUS security agreement. When the National Party regained control of the government in the late 1970s, the nuclear ban was revoked, and the foreign policy of New Zealand tipped again toward its traditional allies. The National government argued that, as a signatory to ANZUS, New Zealand was obligated to open its docks to U.S. nuclear ships. However, under the subsequent Labour government of Prime Minister David Lange, New Zealand once again began to flex its muscles over the nuclear issue. Lange, like his Labour predecessors, was determined to create a foreign policy based on moral rather than legal rationales. In 1985 a U.S. destroyer was denied permission to call at a New Zealand port, even though its presence there was due to joint ANZUS military exercises. Because the United States refused to say whether or not its ship carried nuclear weapons, New Zealand insisted that the ship could not dock. Diplomatic efforts to resolve the standoff were unsuccessful, and in 1986 New Zealand, claiming it was not fearful of foreign attack, formally withdrew from ANZUS.

The issue of superpower use of the Pacific for nuclear weapons testing is still of major concern to the New Zealand government. The nuclear test ban treaty signed by the United States in 1963 has limited U.S. involvement in that regard, but France has continued to test atmospheric weapons, and both the United States and Japan have proposed using uninhabited Pacific atolls to dispose of nuclear waste.

In the early 1990s a new issue came to the fore: nerve gas disposal. With the end of the cold war, the U.S. military proposed disposing of most of its European stockpile of nerve gas on an atoll in the Pacific. The atoll is located within the trust territory granted to the United States at the conclusion of World War II. The plan is to burn the gas safely away from areas of

human habitation, but those islanders living closest (albeit hundreds of miles away) worry that residues from the process could contaminate the air and damage humans, plants, and animals. The religious leaders of Melanesia, Micronesia, and Polynesia have condemned the plan, not only on environmental grounds but also on grounds that outside powers should not be permitted to use the Pacific region without the consent of the inhabitants there—a position with which the Labour government of New Zealand strongly concurs.

ECONOMIC CHALLENGES

The New Zealand government's new foreign policy orientation has caught the attention of observers around the world, but more urgent to New Zealanders themselves is the state of their own economy. Until the 1970s New Zealand had been able to count on a nearly guaranteed export market in the United Kingdom for its dairy and agricultural products. Moreover, cheap local energy supplies as well as inexpensive oil from the Middle East had produced several decades of steady improvement in the standard of living. Whenever the economy showed signs of being sluggish, the government would artificially protect certain industries to ensure full employment.

All of this came to a halt beginning in 1973, when Britain joined the European Community (today called the European Union) and when the Organization of Petroleum Exporting Countries sent the world into its first oil shock. New Zealand actually has the potential of near self-sufficiency in oil, but the easy availability of Middle East oil over the years had prevented the full development of local oil and gas reserves. As for exports, New Zealand had to find new outlets for its agricultural products, which it did by contracting with various countries throughout the Pacific Rim. Currently a third of New Zealand's trade is within the Pacific Rim. In the transition to these new markets, farmers complained that the manufacturing sector—intentionally protected by the government as a way of diversifying New Zealand's reliance on agriculture—was getting unfair favorable treatment. Subsequent changes in government policy to-

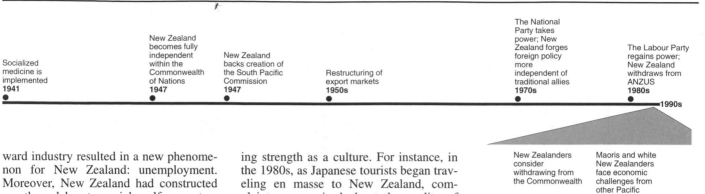

Socialized
medicine is
implemented
1941

New Zealand
becomes fully
independent
within the
Commonwealth
of Nations
1947

New Zealand
backs creation of
the South Pacific
Commission
1947

Restructuring of
export markets
1950s

The National
Party takes
power; New
Zealand forges
foreign policy
more
independent of
traditional allies
1970s

The Labour Party
regains power;
New Zealand
withdraws from
ANZUS
1980s

1990s

New Zealanders
consider
withdrawing from
the Commonwealth

Maoris and white
New Zealanders
face economic
challenges from
other Pacific
Rimmers

ward industry resulted in a new phenomenon for New Zealand: unemployment. Moreover, New Zealand had constructed a rather elaborate social welfare system since World War II, so, regardless of whether economic growth was high or low, social welfare checks still had to be sent. This untenable position has made for a difficult political situation, for when the National Party cut some welfare benefits and social services, it lost the support of many voters; currently the National Party has only a 1-seat majority in Parliament. A 1994 referendum that further democratized the electoral system may add new twists to New Zealand's politics.

In the 1970s New Zealanders, for the first time, began to notice a decline in their standard of living, and 2 decades later the economy is only slightly improved. New Zealand's economic growth rate is the lowest of all Pacific Rim countries (only 2.6 percent per year, as compared to more than 9 percent in Thailand and Singapore); and its per capita income is lower than in Hong Kong, Australia, and Japan. Its inflation rate has dropped in the mid-1990s, however, to an encouragingly low 2.2 percent.

New Zealanders are well aware of Japan's economic strength and its potential for benefiting their own economy through joint ventures, loans, and trade. Yet they also worry that Japanese wealth may constitute a symbol of New Zealand's declin-

ing strength as a culture. For instance, in the 1980s, as Japanese tourists began traveling en masse to New Zealand, complaints were raised about the quality of New Zealand's hotels. Unable to find the funds for a massive upgrading of the hotel industry, New Zealand agreed to allow Japan to build its own hotels; it reasoned that the local construction industry could use an economic boost and that the better hotels would encourage well-heeled Japanese to spend even more tourist dollars in the country. However, they also worried that, with the Japanese owning the hotels, New Zealanders might be relegated to low-level jobs.

Concern about their status vis-à-vis nonwhites had never been much of an issue to Anglo-Saxon New Zealanders; they always simply assumed that nonwhites were inferior. Many settlers of the 1800s believed in the Social Darwinistic philosophy that the Maori and other brown- and black-skinned peoples would gradually succumb to their European "betters." It did not take long for the Maoris to realize that, land guarantees notwithstanding, the whites intended to deprive them of their land and culture. Violent resistance to these intentions occurred in the 1800s, but Maori land holdings continued to be gobbled up, usually deceptively, by white farmers and sheep herders. Government control of these unscrupulous practices was lax until the 1920s. Since that time

many Maoris (whose population has increased to about 260,000) have intentionally sought to create a lifestyle that preserves key parts of traditional culture while incorporating the skills necessary for survival in a white world.

Now, though, Maoris and whites alike feel the social leveling that is the consequence of years of economic stagnation. Moreover, both worry that the superior financial strength of the Japanese and newly industrializing Asian and Southeast Asian peoples may diminish in some way the standing of their own cultures. The Maoris, complaining recently about Japanese net fishing and its damage to their own fishing industry, have a history of accommodation and adjustment to those who would rule over them; but for the whites, submissiveness, even if it is imposed from afar and is largely financial in nature, will be a new and challenging experience.

DEVELOPMENT

Government protection of manufacturing has allowed this sector to grow at the expense of agriculture. Nevertheless, New Zealand continues to export large quantities of dairy products, wool, meat, fruits, and wheat. Full development of the Maui oil and gas deposits could alleviate New Zealand's dependence on foreign oil.

FREEDOM

New Zealand partakes of the democratic heritage of English common law and subscribes to all the human rights protections that other Western nations have endorsed. Maoris, originally deprived of much of their land, are now guaranteed the same legal rights as whites. Social discrimination against Maoris is much milder than with many other colonized peoples.

HEALTH/WELFARE

New Zealand established pensions for the elderly as early as 1898. Child welfare programs were started in 1907, followed by the Social Security Act of 1938, which augmented the earlier benefits and added a minimum wage requirement and a 40-hour work week. A national health program was begun in 1941.

ACHIEVEMENTS

New Zealand is notable for its efforts on behalf of the smaller islands of the Pacific. In addition to advocating a nuclear-free Pacific, New Zealand has promoted interisland trade and has established free trade agreements with Western Samoa, the Cook Islands, and Niue. It provides educational and employment opportunities to Pacific islanders who reside within its borders.

North Korea (Democratic People's Republic of Korea)

GEOGRAPHY

Area in Square Kilometers (Miles): 120,540 (44,358) (slightly smaller than Mississippi)
Capital (Population): P'yongyang (2,694,000)
Climate: temperate

PEOPLE

Population

Total: 22,646,000
Annual Growth Rate: 1.86%
Rural/Urban Population (Ratio): 40/60
Ethnic Makeup: Korean
Major Language: Korean

Health

Life Expectancy at Birth: 66 years (male); 73 years (female)
Infant Mortality Rate (Ratio): 28.6/1,000
Average Caloric Intake: n/a
Physicians Available (Ratio): 1/370

Religions

Buddhism and Confucianism (now almost nonexistent)

Education

Adult Literacy Rate: 99%

FROM WHENCE THE KOREAN NATION?

According to Korean myth, in 2333 B.C. the god Hanul took human form and descended from heaven to Paektusan Mountain, in what is now North Korea. He was a god with three qualities: as a teacher, a king, and a creator. He found tribes of people living on the Korean Peninsula and remained with them for 93 years, teaching them and creating the laws and customs of the Korean people. Eventually he returned to heaven, but his influence was so powerful that until recent times, Korean dates and calendars were reckoned from the year of his arrival. At one time the worship of Hanul was the primary religion of Korea, but that faith was replaced by numerous other religions, especially Buddhism. Under the Communists, the practice of *any* religion has become a rarity.

COMMUNICATION

Telephones: 30,000
Newspapers: 11

TRANSPORTATION

Highways—Kilometers (Miles): 30,000 (18,600)
Railroads—Kilometers (Miles): 4,250

(2,634)
Usable Airfields: 55 (est.)

GOVERNMENT

Type: communist state
Independence Date: September 9, 1948
Head of State/Government: President Kim Jong Il; Premier Kang Song San
Political Parties: Korean Workers' Party (only legal party, but others do exist)
Suffrage: universal at 17

MILITARY

Number of Armed Forces: 700,000
Military Expenditures (% of Central Government Expenditures): 20% (est.)
Current Hostilities: continuing border conflicts with South Korea

ECONOMY

Currency ($ U.S. Equivalent): 2.13 wons = $1
Per Capita Income/GDP: $1,000/$22 billion
Inflation Rate: n/a
Natural Resources: hydroelectric power; oil; iron ore; copper; lead; zinc; coal; uranium; manganese; gold; salt
Agriculture: rice; corn; potatoes; soybeans; pulses; livestock and livestock products; fish
Industry: machinery; military products; electric power; chemicals; mining; metallurgy; textiles; food processing

FOREIGN TRADE

Exports: $1.3 billion
Imports: $1.9 billion

A COUNTRY APART

The area that we now call North Korea has, at different times in Korea's long history, been separated from the South. In the fifth century A.D. the Koguryo Kingdom in the North was distinct from the Shilla, Paekche, and Kaya Kingdoms of the South. Later the Parhae Kingdom in the North remained separate from the expanded Shilla Kingdom in the South. Thus, the division of Korea in 1945 into two unequal parts was not without precedent. Yet this time the very different paths of development that the North and South chose rendered the division more poignant and, to those separated with little hope of reunion, more emotionally painful.

Beginning in 1945 Kim Il-Song, with the strong backing of the Soviet Union, pursued a hard-line communist policy for both the political and economic development of North Korea. The Soviet Union's involvement on the Korean Peninsula arose from its opportunistic entry into the war against Japan, just 8 days before Japan's surrender. Thus, when Japan withdrew from its long colonial rule over Korea, the Soviets were in a position to be one of the occupying armies. Reluctantly, the United States allowed the Soviet Union to move troops into position above the 38th Parallel, a temporary dividing line for the respective occupying forces. It was the Soviet Union's intention to establish a Communist buffer state between itself and the capitalist West, and therefore it moved quickly to establish the area north of the 38th Parallel as a separate political entity. The northern city of P'yongyang was established as the capital.

When United Nations representatives arrived in 1948 to oversee elections and ease the transition from military occupation and years of Japanese rule to an independent Korea, the Soviets would not cooperate. Kim Il-Song took over the reins of power in the North. Separate elections were held in the South, and the beginning of separate political systems got underway. The 38th Parallel came to represent not only the division of the Korean Peninsula but also the boundary between the worlds of capitalism and communism.

THE KOREAN WAR (1950–1953)

Although not pleased with the idea of division, the South, without a strong army, resigned itself to the reality of the moment. In the North a well-trained military, with Soviet and Chinese help, began preparations for a full-scale invasion of the South. The North attacked in June 1950, a year after U.S. troops had vacated the South, and quickly overran most of the Korean Peninsula. The South Korean government requested help from the United Nations, which dispatched personnel from 19 nations, under the command of U.S. general Douglas MacArthur. (A U.S. intervention was ordered on June 27 by President Harry Truman.)

MacArthur's troops advanced against the North's armies and by October were in control of most of the peninsula. However, with massive Chinese help, the North once again moved south. In response, UN troops decided to inflict heavy destruction on the North through the use of jet fighter/bomber planes. Whereas South Korea was primarily agricultural, North Korea was the industrialized sector of the peninsula. Bombing of the North's industrial targets severely damaged the economy, forcing several million North Koreans to flee south to escape both the war and the Communist dictatorship under which they found themselves.

Eventually the UN troops recaptured South Korea's capital, Seoul. Realizing that further fighting would lead to an expanded Asian war, the two sides agreed to cease-fire talks. They signed a truce in 1953 that established a 2.5-mile-wide demilitarized zone (DMZ) for 155 miles across the peninsula and more or less along the former 38th Parallel division. The Korean War took the lives of more than 54,000 American soldiers, 58,000 South Koreans, and 500,000 North Koreans—but when it was over, both sides occupied about the same territory as they had at the beginning. Yet because neither side has ever declared peace, the two countries remain officially in a state of war. Recent agreements have lessened border tensions, but for 4 decades the border between the two Koreas has been one of the most volatile areas in Asia.

Scholars are still debating whether the Korean War should be called the United States' first losing war and whether or not the bloodshed was really necessary. To understand the Korean War, one must remember that in the eyes of the world, it was more than a civil war among different kinds of Koreans. The United Nations, and particularly the United States, saw North Korea's aggression against the South as the first step in the eventual communization of the whole of Asia. Just a few months before North Korea attacked, China had fallen to the Communist forces of Mao Zedong, and Communist guerrilla activity was being reported throughout Southeast Asia. The "Red Scare" frightened many Americans, and witchhunting for suspected Communist sympathizers—a college professor who might have taught about Karl

(UPI/Bettmann photo by Norman Williams)
Pictured above are U.S. Marines with North Koreans captured during the Korean War.

Marx in class or a news reporter who might have praised the educational reforms of a Communist country—became the everyday preoccupation of such groups as the John Birch Society and the supporters of U.S. senator Joseph McCarthy.

In this highly charged atmosphere it was relatively easy for the U.S. military to promote a war whose aim it was to contain communism. Containment rather than defeat of the enemy was the policy of choice, because the West was weary after battling Germany and Japan in World War II. The containment policy also underlay the United States' approach to Vietnam. Practical though it may have been, this policy denied Americans the opportunity of feeling satisfied in victory, since there was to be no victory, just a stalemate. Thus, the roots of the United States' dissatisfaction with the conduct of the Vietnam War actually began in the policies shaping the response to North Korea's offensive in 1950. North Korea was indeed contained, but the communizing impulse of the North remained.

COLLECTIVE CULTURE

With Soviet backing, North Korean leaders moved quickly to repair war damage and establish a communist culture. The school curriculum was rewritten to emphasize nationalism and equality of the social classes. Traditional Korean culture, based on Confucianism, had stressed strict class divisions, but the Communist authorities refused to allow any one class to claim privileges over another (although eventually the families of party leaders came to constitute a new elite). Higher education at the more than 600 colleges and training schools was redirected to technical rather than analytical subjects. Industries were nationalized; farms were collectivized into some 3,000 communes; and the communes were invested with much of the judicial and executive powers that other countries grant to cities, counties, and states. To overcome labor shortages, nearly all women were brought into the labor force, and the economy slowly returned to prewar levels.

Today many young people bypass formal higher education in favor of service in the military, whose combined army, navy, and air personnel number more than 700,000. Although North Korea has not published economic statistics for nearly 30 years, it is estimated that military expenses consume approximately 20 percent of the gross national product.

With China and the former Communist bloc nations constituting natural markets for North Korean products, and with substantial financial aid from both China and the former Soviet Union in the early years, North Korea was able to regain much of its former economic, and especially industrial, strength. Today North Korea successfully mines iron and other minerals and exports such products as cement, fish, and cereals. China has remained North Korea's only reliable ally, and trade between the two countries now exceeds $736 million a year. In one Chinese province, more than two thirds of the people are ethnic Koreans, most of whom take the side of the North in any dispute with the South.

Tensions with the South have remained high since the war. Sporadic violence along the border has left patrolling soldiers dead, and the assassination of former South Korean president Park Chung Hee and attempts on the lives of other members of the South Korean government have been attributed to North Korea, as was the bombing of a Korean Airlines flight in 1987. Both sides have periodically accused each other of attempted sabotage.

The North, seeing in the growing demand for free speech in the South a chance to further its aim of communizing the peninsula, has been angered by the brutal suppression of dissidents by the South Korean authorities. Although the North's argument is bitterly ironic, given its own brutal suppression of human rights, it is nonetheless accurate in its view that the government in the South has been blatantly dictatorial. To suppress opponents, the South Korean government has, among other things, abducted its own students from Europe, abducted opposition leader Kim Dae Jung from Japan, tortured dissidents, and violently silenced demonstrators. All of this is said to be necessary because of the need for unity in the face of the threat from the North, although, as pointed out by scholar Gavan McCormack, the South seems to use the North's threat as an excuse for maintaining a rigid dictatorial system.

In this atmosphere it is not surprising that the formal reunification talks, begun in 1971 with much fanfare, have just recently started to bear fruit. Visits of residents separated by the war were approved in 1985—the first time in 40 years that an opening of the border had even been considered—but real progress came in late 1991, when North Korean premier Yon Hyong Muk and South Korean premier Chung Won Shik signed a nonaggression and reconciliation pact, whose goal was the eventual declaration of a formal peace treaty between the two governments. In 1992 the governments established air, sea, and land links and set up mechanisms for scientific and environmental cooperation. North Korea also signed the nuclear nonproliferation agreement with the International Atomic Energy Agency. This move placated growing concerns about North Korea's rumored development of nuclear weapons and opened the way for investment by such countries as Japan, which had refused to invest until they received assurances on the nuclear question. In 1990, in what many saw as an overture to the United States, North Korea returned the remains of five American soldiers killed during the Korean War.

THE NUCLEAR ISSUE FLARES UP

The goodwill deteriorated quickly in 1993 and 1994, when North Korea refused to allow inspectors from the International Atomic Energy Agency (IAEA) to inspect its nuclear facilities, raising fears in the United States, Japan, and South Korea that the North was developing a nuclear bomb. When pressured to allow inspections, the North responded by threatening to withdraw from the IAEA and expel the inspectors. Tensions mounted, with all parties engaging in military threats and posturing and the United States, South Korea, and Japan (whose shores could be reached in minutes by the North's new ballistic missiles) threatening economic sanctions. Troops in both Koreas were put on high alert. Former U.S. president Jimmy Carter helped to defuse the issue by making a private goodwill visit to Kim Il-Song in P'yongyang, the unexpected result of which was a promise by the North to hold a first-ever summit meeting with the South. Then, in a near-theatrical turn of events, Kim Il-Song, at 5 decades the longest national office-holder in the world, died, apparently of natural causes. The summit was canceled and international diplomacy was frozen while the North Korean government mourned the loss of its "Great Leader" and selected a new one, "Dear Leader" Kim Jong Il, Kim Il-Song's son. Eventually the North agreed to resume talks, a move interpreted as evidence that, for all its bravado, the North wanted to establish closer ties with the West.

THE CHANGING INTERNATIONAL LANDSCAPE

North Korea has good reason to promote better relations with the West, because the world of the 1990s is not the world of the 1950s. In 1989, for instance, several former Soviet bloc countries cut into the North's economic monopoly by welcoming trade initiatives from South Korea; some even established diplomatic rela-

Kim Il-Song
comes to power
1945

The People's
Democratic
Republic of
Korea is created
1948

The Korean War
begins
1950

A truce is
arranged
between North
Korea and UN
troops
1953

A U.S. spy boat,
the *Pueblo*, is
seized by North
Korea
1968

A U.S. spy plane
is shot down over
North Korea
1969

Reunification
talks begin
1971

1990s

A nonaggression
pact is signed
with the South;
North and South
are granted seats
in the UN

Fears of North
Korea's nuclear
weapons
capacity surge

Kim Il-Song dies
and is
succeeded by
his son, Kim
Jong Il

tions. At the same time, the disintegration of the Soviet Union meant that North Korea lost its primary political and military ally. Perhaps most alarming to the North is its declining economy; it was estimated to have dropped 3.7 percent in 1990 and 5.2 percent in 1991. With the South's economy consistently booming and the example of the failed economies of Central/Eastern Europe as a danger signal, the North appears to understand that it must break out of its decades of isolation or lose its ability to govern. Nevertheless, it is not likely that North Koreans will quickly retreat from the communist model of development that they have espoused for so long.

Kim Il-Song, who controlled North Korea for nearly 50 years, promoted the development of heavy industries, the collectivization of agriculture, and strong linkages with the then-Communist bloc. Governing with an iron hand, Kim denied basic civil rights to his people and forbade any tendency of the people to dress or behave like the "decadent" West. He kept tensions high by asserting his intention of communizing the South. His son, Kim Jong Il, who had headed the North Korean military but was barely known outside his country, took over his father's position in 1994—the first dynastic power transfer in the Communist world. How the younger Kim will influence the direction of North Korea is unclear, but the somewhat more liberal authorities at his side know that the recent diplomatic initiatives of the South require a response. The North Korean

government hopes that recent actions will bring it some badly needed international goodwill. But more than good public relations will be needed if North Korea is to prosper in the new, post–cold war climate in which it can no longer rely on the generosity or moral support of the Soviet bloc. When communism was introduced in North Korea in 1945, the government nationalized major companies and steered economic development toward heavy industry. In contrast, the South concentrated on heavy industry to balance its agricultural sector until the late 1970s but then geared the economy toward meeting consumer demand. Thus, the standard of living in the North for the average resident remains far behind that of the South, and unless a broader trading front is opened up, the North will continue to lag behind.

RECENT TRENDS

There is evidence that some liberalization is taking place within North Korea. In 1988 the government drafted a law that allowed foreign companies to establish joint ventures inside North Korea. Tourism is also being promoted as a way of earning foreign currency, and recently the government permitted two small Christian churches to be established. Nevertheless, years of a totally controlled economy in the North and shifting international alliances indicate many difficult years ahead for North Korea. Moreover, the bad blood between North and South would suggest

only the slowest possible reconciliation of the world's most troubled peninsula.

Although political reunification seems to be years away, social changes are becoming evident everywhere as a new generation, unfamiliar with war, comes to adulthood, and as North Koreans are being exposed to outside sources of news and ideas. Now many North Koreans own radios that receive signals from other countries. South Korean stations are now heard in the North, as are news programs from the Voice of America. Modern North Korean history, however, is one of repression and control, first by the Japanese and then by the Kim government, who used the same police surveillance apparatus as did the Japanese during their occupation of the Korean Peninsula. It is not likely, therefore, that a massive push for democracy will be forthcoming soon from a people long accustomed to dictatorship.

DEVELOPMENT

Already more industrialized than South Korea at the time of the Korean War, North Korea built on this foundation with massive assistance from China and the Soviet Union. Heavy industry was emphasized, however, to the detriment of consumer goods. Economic isolation presages slow growth ahead.

FREEDOM

Kim Il-Song's mainline Communist approach meant that the human rights commonplace in the West were never enjoyed by North Koreans. Through suppression of dissidents, a controlled press, and restrictions on travel, the long-time dictator kept North Koreans isolated from the world.

HEALTH/WELFARE

Under the Kim Il-Song government, illiteracy was greatly reduced. North Koreans have access to free medical care, schooling, and old-age pensions. Government housing is available at low cost, but shoppers are often confronted with empty shelves and low-quality goods.

ACHIEVEMENTS

North Korea has developed its resources of aluminum, cement, and iron into solid industries for the production of tools and machinery while developing military superiority over South Korea, despite a population numbering less than half that of South Korea.

Papua New Guinea (Independent State of Papua New Guinea)

GEOGRAPHY

Area in Square Kilometers (Miles):
461,690 (178,612) (slightly larger
than California)
Capital (Population): Port Moresby
(193,000)
Climate: tropical

PEOPLE

Population

Total: 4,100,000
Annual Growth Rate: 2.3%
Rural/Urban Population Ratio: 85/15
Ethnic Makeup: predominantly
Melanesian and Papuan; some
Negrito, Micronesian, and Polynesian
Major Languages: 715 indigenous
languages; English; New Guinea
Pidgin; Motu

Health

Life Expectancy at Birth: 55 years
(male); 57 years (female)
Infant Mortality Rate (Ratio):
64.9/1,000
Average Caloric Intake: 85% of FAO
minimum
Physicians Available (Ratio): 1/11,904

UNREST IN BOUGAINVILLE

In 1988 residents of the Papua New Guinea island of Bougainville, where
many World War II battles were fought, revolted against a large Australian-
owned, open-pit copper mine. The mine was closed, and the rebels, many
of whom were armed with bow and arrows, declared Bougainville an independent nation. The government in Port Moresby, then under Prime Minister Rabbie Namaliu, responded by imposing an economic blockade and
cutting off electricity service to the island. Later battles with government
troops ended in death for many people. New Zealand sponsored peace talks
between the rebels and the government, and a tentative agreement was
reached in August 1990; the government lifted the blockade and restored
electricity. In early 1991, however, violence again erupted, and dozens of
people were killed. In mid-1992 the rebels killed the mediator who had
negotiated a partial settlement. Amnesty International has claimed that both
sides have acted with undue violence. It is estimated that fighting and the
economic blockade have resulted in the deaths of more than 3,000 persons.

Religions

66% Christian; 34% indigenous beliefs

Education

Adult Literacy Rate: 52%

COMMUNICATION

Telephones: 70,000
Newspapers: 1

TRANSPORTATION

Highways—Kilometers (Miles):
19,200 (11,904)
Railroads—Kilometers (Miles): none
Usable Airfields: 457

GOVERNMENT

Type: parliamentary democracy
Independence Date: September 16,
1975
Head of State: Prime Minister Paias
Wingti
Political Parties: Pangu Party; People's
Democratic Movement; People's
Action Party; People's Progress Party;
United Party; Papua Party; National
Party; Melanesian Alliance
Suffrage: universal at 18

MILITARY

Number of Armed Forces: 3,200
*Military Expenditures (% of Central
Government Expenditures):* 1.8%
Current Hostilities: none

ECONOMY

Currency ($ U.S. Equivalent): 1.006
kinas = $1
Per Capita Income/GDP: $850/$3.4
billion
Inflation Rate: 4.5%
Natural Resources: gold; copper;
silver; natural gas; timber; oil potential
Agriculture: coffee; cocoa; coconuts;
palm kernels; tea; rubber; sweet
potatoes; fruit; vegetables; poultry; pork
Industry: copra crushing; palm oil
processing; wood processing and
production; mining; construction; tourism

FOREIGN TRADE

Exports: $1.3 billion
Imports: $1.6 billion

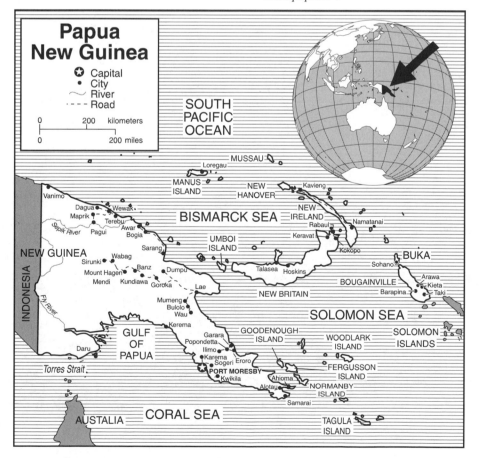

TERRA INCOGNITA

Papua New Guinea is an independent nation and a member of the British Commonwealth. Occupying the eastern half of New Guinea (the second-largest island in the world) and many outlying islands, Papua New Guinea is probably the most overlooked of all the nations in the Pacific Rim.

It was not always overlooked, however. Spain claimed the vast land in the mid-sixteenth century, followed by Britain's East India Company in 1793. The Netherlands laid claim to part of the island in the 1800s and eventually came to control the western half (now known as Irian Jaya, a province of the Republic of Indonesia). In the 1880s German settlers occupied the northeastern part of the island; and in 1884 Britain signed a treaty with Germany, which gave it about half of what is now Papua New Guinea. In 1906 Britain gave its part of the island to Australia. Australia invaded and quickly captured the German area in 1914. Eventually the League of Nations and, later, the United Nations gave the captured area to Australia to administer as a trust territory.

During World War II, the northern part of New Guinea was the scene of bitter fighting between a large Japanese force and Australian and U.S. troops. The Japanese had apparently intended to use New Guinea as a base for the military conquest of Australia. Australia resumed control of the eastern half of the island after Japan's defeat, and it continued to administer Papua New Guinea's affairs until 1975, when it granted independence. The capital is Port Moresby, where, in addition to English, the Motu language and a hybrid language known as New Guinea Pidgin are spoken.

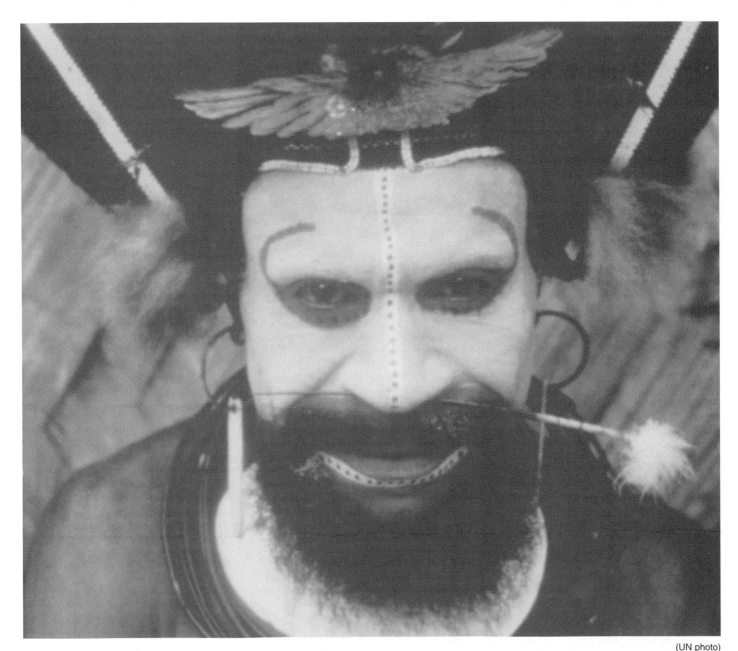

(UN photo)

Despite contact with the modern world because of mining and logging, many of the native peoples of Papua New Guinea have retained their cultures since the Stone Age.

The main island is sighted by Portuguese explorers A.D. **1511**	The Dutch annex the west half of the island **1828**	A British protectorate over part of the eastern half of the island; the Germans control the northeast **1884**	Gold is discovered in Papua New Guinea **1890**	Australia assumes control of the British part of the island **1906**	Australia invades and captures the German-held areas **1914**	Australia is given the former German areas as a trust territory **1920**	Japan captures the northern part of the island; Australia resumes control in 1945 **1940s**	Australia grants independence to Papua New Guinea **1975**	A revolt against the government begins on the island of Bougainville **1988**

1990s

An economic blockade of Bougainville is lifted, but violence continues, claiming 3,000 lives

600 army soldiers storm Parliament, demanding higher pay

Papua New Guinea joins APEC

STONE AGE PEOPLES MEET THE TWENTIETH CENTURY

Early Western explorers found the island's resources difficult to reach. The coastline and some of the interior are swampy and mosquito- and tick-infested, while the high, snow-capped mountainous regions are densely forested and hard to traverse. But perhaps most daunting to early would-be settlers and traders were the local inhabitants. Consisting of hundreds of sometimes warring tribes with totally different languages and customs, the New Guinea populace was determined to prevent outsiders from settling the island. Many adventurers were killed, their heads displayed in villages as victory trophies. The origins of the Papuan people are unknown, but some tribes share common practices with Melanesian islanders. Others appear to be Negritos, and some may be related to the Australian Aborigines. More than 700 languages, often mutually unintelligible, are spoken in Papua New Guinea.

Australians and other Europeans found it beneficial to engage in trade with coastal tribes who supplied them with unique tropical lumbers, such as sandalwood and bamboo, and foodstuffs such as sugarcane, coconut, and nutmeg. Rubber and tobacco were also traded. Tea, which grows well in the highland regions, is an important cash crop. But the resource that was most important for the economic development of Papua New Guinea was gold. It was discovered there in 1890; two major gold rushes occurred, in 1896 and 1926. Prospectors came mostly from Australia and were hated by the local tribes; some prospectors were killed and cannibalized. A large number of airstrips in the otherwise undeveloped interior eventually were built by miners who needed a safe and efficient way to receive supplies. Today copper is more important than gold—copper is, in fact, the largest single earner of export income for Papua New Guinea.

A diplomatic flap between Papua New Guinea and Australia occurred in mid-1992, when Australian environmentalists complained about the environmental damage that a copper and gold mine in Papua New Guinea was causing. They called for its closure. The Papuan government strongly resented the verbal intrusion into its sovereignty and reminded conservationists and the Australian government that it alone would establish environmental standards for companies operating inside its borders. The Papuan government holds a 20 percent interest in the mining company.

The tropical climate that predominates in all areas except the highest mountain peaks produces an impressive variety of plant and animal life. Botanists and other naturalists for years have been attracted to the island for scientific study. Despite extensive contacts with these and other outsiders over the past century, and despite the establishment of schools and a university by the Australian government, some inland mountain tribes continue to live much as they must have done in the Stone Age. Thus the country lures not only miners and naturalists but also anthropologists looking for clues to humankind's early lifestyles. One of the most famous of these was Bronislaw Malinowski, the Polish-born founder of the field of social anthropology who taught at both the University of London and at Yale. In the early 1900s, he spent several years studying the cultural practices of the tribes of Papua New Guinea, particularly those of the Trobriand Islands.

Most of the 4 million Papuans live by subsistence farming. Agriculture for commercial trade is limited by the absence of a good transportation network: Most roads are unpaved, and there is no railway system. Travel on tiny aircraft and helicopters is common, however; New Guinea boasts 457 airstrips, most of them unpaved and dangerously situated in mountain valleys. The harsh conditions of New Guinea life have produced some unique ironies. For instance, Papuans who have never ridden in a car or truck may have flown in a plane dozens of times. Given the differences in socialization of the Papuan peoples and the difficult conditions of life on their island, it will likely be many decades before Papua New Guinea, which joined the Asia-Pacific Economic Cooperation group in 1993, is able to participate fully in the Pacific Rim community.

DEVELOPMENT

Agriculture (especially coffee and copra) is the mainstay of Papua New Guinea's economy. Copper, gold, and silver mining are also important, but large-scale development of other industries is inhibited by rough terrain, illiteracy, and a bewildering array of spoken languages—some 700. There are substantial reserves of untapped oil.

FREEDOM

Papua New Guinea is a member of the British Commonwealth and officially follows the English heritage of law. However, in the country's numerous, isolated small villages, effective control is wielded by village elites with personal charisma; tribal customs take precedence over national law—of which many inhabitants are virtually unaware.

HEALTH/WELFARE

Three quarters of Papua New Guinea's population have no formal education. Daily nutritional intake falls far short of recommended minimums, and tuberculosis and malaria are common diseases.

ACHIEVEMENTS

Papua New Guinea, lying just below the equator, is world-famous for its varied and beautiful flora and fauna, including orchids, birds of paradise, butterflies, and parrots. Dense forests cover 70 percent of the country. Some regions receive as much as 350 inches of rain a year.

Philippines (Republic of the Philippines)

GEOGRAPHY

Area in Square Kilometers (Miles):
300,000 (110,400) (slightly larger
than Arizona)
Capital (Population): Manila
(1,800,000)
Climate: tropical marine

PEOPLE

Population
Total: 68,464,000
Annual Growth Rate: 1.97%
Rural/Urban Population Ratio: 57/43
Ethnic Makeup: 95% Malay; 2%
Chinese; 3% others
Major Languages: Pilipino (based on
Tagalog); English

Health
Life Expectancy at Birth: 63 years
(male); 68 years (female)
Infant Mortality Rate (Ratio): 51.9/1,000
Average Caloric Intake: 92% of FAO
minimum
Physicians Available (Ratio): 1/1,062

Religions
83% Roman Catholic; 9% Protestant;
5% Muslim; 3% Buddhist and others

Education
Adult Literacy Rate: 90%

COMMUNICATION

Telephones: 872,900
Newspapers: 234, of which about 32
are dailies

TRANSPORTATION

Highways—Kilometers (Miles):
157,450 (97,934)

Railroads—Kilometers (Miles): 378
(234)
Usable Airfields: 238

GOVERNMENT

Type: republic
Independence Date: July 4, 1946
Head of State: President Fidel V.
Ramos
Political Parties: PDP-Laban;
Struggle of Philippine Democrats;
Nationalista Party; Liberal Party; the
Philippine Communist Party has
quasi-legal status
Suffrage: universal at 15

MILITARY

Number of Armed Forces: 85,800
*Military Expenditures (% of Central
Government Expenditures):* 1.9%
Current Hostilities: dispute over the
Spratly Islands with China, Malaysia,
Taiwan, and Vietnam; claims the
Malaysian state of Sabah

ECONOMY

Currency ($ U.S. Equivalent): 25.4
Philippine pesos = $1
Per Capita Income/GDP: $860/$54.1
billion
Inflation Rate: 8.9%
Natural Resources: timber; crude oil;
nickel; cobalt; silver; gold; salt; copper
Agriculture: rice; coconut; corn;
sugarcane; bananas; pineapple;
mango; animal products; fish
Industry: food processing; chemicals;
textiles; pharmaceuticals; wood
products; electronics assembly;
petroleum refining; fishing

FOREIGN TRADE

Exports: $9.8 billion
Imports: $14.5 billion

THIS IS ASIA?

The Philippines is a land with close historic ties to the West. Eighty-three percent of Filipinos, as the people of the Philippines are known, are Roman Catholics, and most speak at least some English. Many use English daily in business and government. In fact, English is the language of instruction at school. Moreover, when they discuss their history as a nation, Filipinos will mention Spain, Mexico, the Spanish-American War, the United States, and cooperative Filipino–American attempts to defeat the Japanese in World War II. The country was even named after a European, King Philip II of Spain. If this does not sound like a typical Asian nation, it is because Philippine nationhood essentially began with the arrival of Westerners. That influence continues to dominate the political and cultural life of the country.

Yet the history of the region certainly did not begin with European contact; indeed, there is evidence of human habitation in the area as early as 25,000 B.C.

Beginning about 2,000 B.C., Austronesians, Negritos, Malays, and other tribal peoples settled many of the 7,107 islands that constitute the present-day Philippines. Although engaged to varying degrees in trade with China and Southeast Asia, each of these ethnic groups (nearly 60 distinct groups still exist) lived in relative isolation from one another, speaking different languages, adhering to different religions, and, for good or ill, knowing nothing of the concept of national identity.

Although 5 million ethnic peoples remain marginated from the mainstream, for most islanders the world changed in the mid-1500s, when soldiers and Roman Catholic priests from Spain began conquering and converting the population. Eventually the disparate ethnic groups came to see themselves as one entity, Filipinos, a people whose lives were controlled indirectly by Spain from Mexico—a fact that, unique among Asian countries, linked the Philippines with the Americas. Thus, the process of national-identity formation for Filipinos actually began in Europe.

Some ethnic groups assimilated rather quickly, marrying Spanish soldiers and administrators and acquiring the language and cultural outlook of the West. The descendants of these mestizos (mixed peoples, including local/Chinese mixes) have become the cultural, economic, and political elite of the country. Others, particularly among the Islamic communities on the Philippine island of Mindanao, resisted assimilation right from the start and continue to challenge the authority of Manila. Indeed, the Communist insurgency, reported so often in the news and the focus of attention of former presidents Ferdinand Marcos and Corazon Aquino, is in part an attempt by marginated ethnics and others to regain the cultural independence that their peoples lost some 400 years ago.

As in other Asian countries, the Chinese community has played an important but controversial role in Philippine life. Dominating trade for centuries, the Philippine Chinese have acquired clout (and enemies) that far exceeds their numbers (fewer than 1 million). Former president Aquino was

(United Nations photo by J. M. Micaud)

The Philippines has suffered from the misuse of funds entrusted to the government over the past several decades. The result has been a polarity of wealth, with many citizens living in severe poverty. Slums, such as Tondo in Manila, pictured above, are a common sight in many of the urban areas of the Philippines.

Negritos and others begin settling the islands 25,000 B.C.	Malays arrive in the islands 2,000 B.C.	Chinese, Arabs, and Indians control parts of the economy and land A.D. 400–1400	The islands are named for the Spanish king Philip II 1542	Local resistance to Spanish rule 1890s
●	●	●	●	●

of part-Chinese ancestry, and some of the resistance to her presidency stemmed from her ethnic lineage. The Chinese-Philippine community, in particular, has been the target of ethnic violence—kidnappings and abductions—because their wealth, relative to other Filipino groups, makes them easy prey.

FOREIGN INTEREST

Filipinos occupy a resource-rich, beautiful land. Monsoon clouds dump as much as 200 inches of rain on the fertile, volcanic soil. Rice and corn grow well, as do hemp, coconut, sugarcane, and tobacco. Tuna, sponges, shrimp, and hundreds of other kinds of marine life flourish in the ocean. Part of the country is covered with dense tropical forests yielding bamboo and lumber and serving as habitat to thousands of species of plant and animal life. The northern part of Luzon Island is famous for its terraced rice paddies.

Given this abundance, it is not surprising that several foreign powers have taken a serious interest in the archipelago. The Dutch held military bases in the country in the 1600s, the British briefly controlled Manila in the 1800s, and the Japanese overran the entire country in the 1940s. But it was Spain, in control of most of the country for more than 300 years (1565–1898), that established the cultural base for the modern Philippines. Spain's interest in the islands—its only colony in Asia—was primarily material and secondarily spiritual. It wanted to take part in the lucrative spice trade and fill its galleon ships each year with products from Asia for the benefit of the Spanish Crown. It also wanted (or, at least, Rome wanted) to convert the so-called heathens (that is, nonbelievers) to Christianity. The friars were particularly successful in winning converts to Roman Catholicism because, despite some local resistance, there were no competing Christian denominations in the Philippines and because the Church quickly gained control of the resources of the island, which it used to entice converts. Resisting conversion were the Muslims of the island of Mindanao, a group that continues to remain on the fringe of Philippine society but which signed a cease-fire with the government in 1994 after 20 years of guerrilla warfare. Eventu-

ally a Church-dominated society was established that mirrored in structure—social-class divisions as well as religious and social values—the mother cultures of Spain and Mexico.

Spanish rule in the Philippines came to an inglorious end in 1898, at the end of the Spanish-American War. Spain granted independence to Cuba and ceded the Philippines, Guam, and Puerto Rico to the United States. Filipinos hoping for independence were disappointed to learn that yet another foreign power had assumed control of their lives. Resistance to American rule cost several thousand lives in the early years, but soon Filipinos realized that the U.S. presence was fundamentally different from that of Spain. The United States was interested in trade, and it certainly could see the advantage of having a military presence in Asia, but it viewed its primary role as one of tutelage. American officials believed that the Philippines should be granted independence, but only when the nation was sufficiently schooled in the process of democracy. Unlike Spain, the United States encouraged political parties and attempted to place Filipinos in positions of governmental authority.

Preparations were under way for independence when World War II broke out. The war and the occupation of the country by the Japanese undermined the economy, devastated the capital city of Manila, caused divisions among the political elite, and delayed independence. After Japan's defeat the country was, at last, granted independence, on July 4, 1946. Manuel Roxas, a well-known politician, was elected president. Despite armed opposition from Communist groups, the country, after several elections, seemed to be maintaining a grasp on democracy.

MARCOS AND HIS AFTERMATH

Then, in 1965, Ferdinand E. Marcos, a Philippines senator and former guerrilla fighter with the U.S. armed forces, was elected president. He was reelected in 1969. Rather than addressing the serious problems of agrarian reform and trade, Marcos maintained people's loyalty through an elaborate system of patronage whereby his friends profited from the misuse of government power and money. Opposition to his rule manifested itself in violent

demonstrations and in a growing Communist insurgency. In 1972 Marcos declared martial law, arrested some 30,000 opponents, and shut down newspapers as well as the National Congress. Marcos continued to rule the country by personal proclamation until 1981. He remained in power thereafter, and he and his wife, Imelda, and their extended family and friends increasingly were criticized for corruption. Finally, in 1986, after nearly a quarter-century of Marcos rule, an uprising of thousands of dissatisfied Filipinos overthrew Marcos, who fled to Hawaii. He died there in 1990.

Taking on the formidable job of president was Corazon Aquino, the widow of murdered opposition leader Benigno Aquino. Aquino's People Power revolution had a heady beginning. Many observers believed that at last Filipinos had found a democratic leader around whom they could unite and who would end corruption and put the persistent Communist insurgency to rest. Aquino, however, was immediately beset by overwhelming economic, social, and political problems.

Opportunists and factions of the Filipino military and political elite still loyal to Marcos attempted numerous coups d'état in the years of Aquino's administration. Much of the unrest came from within the military, which had become accustomed to direct involvement in government during Marcos's martial-law era. Some Communist separatists turned in their arms at Aquino's request, but many continued to plot violence against the government. Thus, the sense of security and stability that Filipinos needed in order to attract more substantial foreign investment and to reestablish the habits of democracy continued to elude them.

Nevertheless, the economy showed signs of improvement. Some countries, particularly Japan and the United States and, more recently, Hong Kong, invested heavily in the Philippines, as did half a dozen international organizations. In fact, some groups complained that further investment was unwarranted, because already-allocated funds had not yet been fully utilized. Moreover, misuse of funds entrusted to the government—a serious problem during the Marcos era—continued, despite Aquino's promise to eradicate corruption. A 1987 law, enacted after Corazon Aquino

A treaty ends the Spanish-American War **1898**	The Japanese attack the Philippines **1941**	General Douglas MacArthur makes a triumphant return to Manila **1944**	The United States grants complete independence to the Philippines **1946**	Military-base agreements are signed with the United States **1947**	Ferdinand Marcos is elected president **1965**	Marcos declares martial law **1972**	Martial law is lifted; Corazon Aquino and her People Power movement drive Marcos into exile **1980s**	**1990s**

Marcos dies in exile in Hawaii

The United States withdraws its military bases; Fidel Ramos is elected president

assumed the presidency, limited the president to one term in office. Half a dozen contenders vied for the presidency in 1992, including Imelda Marcos and other relatives of former presidents Marcos and Aquino; U.S. West Point graduate General Fidel Ramos, who had thwarted several coup attempts against Aquino and who thus had her endorsement, won the election. It was the first peaceful transfer of power in more than 25 years (although campaign violence claimed the lives of more than 80 people).

SOCIAL PROBLEMS

The new president inherited the leadership of a country awash in problems. Inflation is nearly 9 percent a year, unemployment is above 11 percent, and foreign debt exceeds $30 billion. The 1991 eruption of Mount Pinatubo caused millions of dollars of damage. The country may overcome these problems eventually, but one seems never to go away: extreme social inequality. As in Malaysia, where ethnic Malays have constituted a seemingly permanent class of poor peasants, Philippine society is fractured by distinct classes. Chinese and mestizos constitute the top of the hierarchy, while Muslims and most country dwellers form the bottom. About half the Filipino population of 68 million make their living in agriculture and fishing; but even in Manila, where the economy is stronger than anywhere else, thousands of residents live in abject poverty as urban squatters. Officially, 55 percent of Filipinos live in poverty. Disparities of wealth are

striking. Worker discontent has been such that the Philippines lost more work days to strikes between 1983 and 1987 than any other Asian country.

Adding to the government's financial woes is the loss of income from the six U.S. military bases that closed in 1991 and 1992. President Ramos wanted the United States to maintain a presence in the country (indeed, U.S. war planes helped Aquino survive a dangerous coup attempt, and Ramos may have sensed the need for similar help in the future), but in 1991 the Philippine Legislature, bowing to nationalist sentiment, refused to renew the land-lease agreements that had been in effect since 1947. Occupying many acres of valuable land and bringing as many as 40,000 Americans at one time into the Philippines, the bases had come to be seen as visible symbols of American colonialism or imperialism. Nevertheless, their closure will severely affect the Philippine economy. Subic Bay Naval Base alone had provided jobs for 32,000 Filipinos on base and, indirectly, to 200,000 more. Moreover, the United States paid nearly $390 million each year to lease the land and another $128 million for base-related expenses. Base-related monies entering the country amounted to 3 percent of the entire Philippines economy. After the base closures, the U.S. Congress cut other aid to the Philippines, from $200 million in 1992 to $48 million in 1993. To counterbalance the losses, the Philippines accepted a $60 million loan from Taiwan to develop 740 acres of the former Subic Bay Naval Base into an industrial park. The International Monetary Fund also loaned

the country $683 million for development purposes.

CULTURE

Philippine culture is a rich amalgam of Asian and European customs. Family life is valued, and few people have to spend their old age in nursing homes. Divorce is frowned upon. Women have traditionally involved themselves in the worlds of politics and business to a greater degree than have women in other Asian countries. Educational opportunities for women are about the same as that for men; literacy in the Philippines is estimated at 90 percent. Unfortunately, many college-educated men and women are unable to find employment befitting their skills. Discontent among these young workers continues to grow, as it does among the many rural and urban poor.

Nevertheless, many Filipinos take a rather relaxed attitude toward work and daily life. They enjoy hours of sports and folk dancing or spend their free time in conversation with neighbors and friends, with whom they construct patron/client relationships. In recent years the growing nationalism has been expressed in the gradual replacement of the English language with Pilipino, a version of the Malay-based Tagalog language.

DEVELOPMENT

The Philippines has more than $30 billion in foreign debt. Payback from development projects has been so slow that about 51 percent of the earnings from all exports has to be spent just to service the debt. The Philippines sells most of its products to the United States, Japan, Hong Kong, Britain, and the Netherlands.

FREEDOM

Marcos's one-man rule meant that both the substance and structure of democracy were ignored. The Philippine Constitution is similar in many ways to that of the United States. President Aquino attempted to adhere to democratic principles; her successor pledged to do the same. The Communist Party was legalized in 1992.

HEALTH/WELFARE

Quality of life varies considerably between the city and the countryside. Except for the numerous urban squatters, city residents generally have better access to health care and education. Most people still do not have access to safe drinking water. The gap between the upper-class elite and the poor is pronounced and growing.

ACHIEVEMENTS

Since the end of the Marcos dictatorship, foreign investment has been increasing in the Philippines. Inflation has eased somewhat. Most significant is the resumption of the peaceful transfer of political power.

Singapore (Republic of Singapore)

GEOGRAPHY

Area in Square Kilometers (Miles):
633 (244) (slightly less than 3½
times the size of Washington, D.C.)
Capital (Population): Singapore
(2,334,400)
Climate: tropical

PEOPLE

Population
Total: 2,826,000
Annual Growth Rate: 1.19%
Rural/Urban Population (Ratio):
almost entirely urban
Ethnic Makeup: 77% Chinese; 15%
Malay; 6% Indian; 2% others
Major Languages: Malay; Mandarin
Chinese; Tamil; English

Health
Life Expectancy at Birth: 73 years
(male); 79 years (female)
Infant Mortality Rate (Ratio):
5.8/1,000
Average Caloric Intake: 134% of
FAO minimum
Physicians Available (Ratio): 1/779

THE PERANAKANS

Most ancestors of the 2.8 million contemporary Singaporeans moved
to the island from various parts of China only about 150 years ago. A
few Singaporeans, however, including former prime minister Lee Kuan
Yew, can trace their origins back to the fifteenth century, when Chinese
traders moved to the Malacca Strait, married local Malay women, and
stayed to create a uniquely blended culture of Chinese and Malay
traditions. Useful to their various European overlords as interpreters,
these people, called Peranakans ("locally born"), became the backbone
of Singapore's upper class.

Religions
42% Buddhist and Taoist; 18%
Christian; 16% Muslim; 5% Hindu;
19% others

Education
Adult Literacy Rate: 88%

COMMUNICATION

Telephones: 1,320,000
Newspapers: 7 dailies

TRANSPORTATION

Highways—Kilometers (Miles): 2,644
(1,642)
Railroads—Kilometers (Miles): 38
(23)
Usable Airfields: 10

GOVERNMENT

Type: republic within the British
Commonwealth
Independence Date: August 9, 1965
Head of State/Government: President
Wee Kim Wee; Prime Minister Goh
Chok Tong
Political Parties: People's Action
Party; Workers' Party; Singapore
Democratic Party; National Solidarity
Party; Barisan Sosialis; Communist
Party (illegal)
Suffrage: universal and compulsory
at 20

MILITARY

Number of Armed Forces: 55,500
*Military Expenditures (% of Central
Government Expenditures):* 4%
Current Hostilities: none

ECONOMY

Currency ($ U.S. Equivalent): 1.47
Singapore dollars = $1
Per Capita Income/GDP:
$16,500/$49.5 billion
Inflation Rate: 2.3%
Natural Resources: fish; deepwater
ports
Agriculture: rubber; copra; fruit;
vegetables
Industry: petroleum refining;
electronics; oil-drilling equipment;
rubber processing and rubber
products; processed food and
beverages; ship repair, financial
services; biotechnology

FOREIGN TRADE

Exports: $61.5 billion
Imports: $66.4 billion

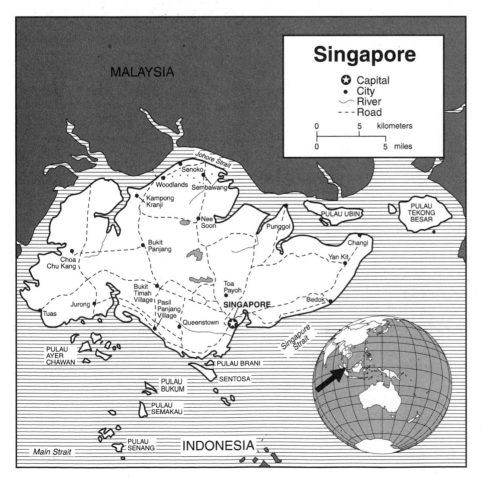

SINGAPORE

North Americans are well-off, it is often said, because they inhabit a huge continent that overflows with natural resources. This explanation for prosperity does not fit even remotely the case of Singapore. The inhabitants of this tiny, flat, humid island, located near the equator off the tip of the Malay Peninsula, must import even their drinking water from another country. With only 244 square miles of land (including 58 mostly uninhabited islets), Singapore is half the size of Hong Kong; however, it has one of the highest per capita incomes ($16,500) in Asia. With more than 11,000 people per square mile, one of the highest population densities in Asia, Singapore might be expected to have the horrific slums that characterize parts of other crowded areas. But unemployment in Singapore is less than 2 percent, inflation is only 2.3 percent, and most of its 2.8 million people own their own homes. Eighty percent of the residences are government-built apartments, but they are spacious by Asian standards and are well-equipped with labor-saving appliances.

Imperialism, geography, and racism help to explain Singapore's unique characteristics. For most of its recorded history, beginning in the thirteenth century A.D., Singapore was controlled variously by the rulers of Thailand, Java, Indonesia, and even India. In the early 1800s the British were determined to wrest control of parts of Southeast Asia from the Dutch and expand their growing empire. Facilitating their imperialistic aims was Sir Stamford Raffles, a Malay-speaking British administrator who not only helped defeat the Dutch in Java but also diminished the power of local elites in order to fortify his position as lieutenant governor.

Arriving in Singapore in 1819, Raffles found it to be a small, neglected settlement with an economy based on fishing. Yet he believed that the island's geographic location endowed it with great potential as a transshipment port. He established policies that facilitated its development just in time to benefit from the British exports of tin, rubber, and timber leaving Malaya. Perhaps most important was his declaration of Singapore as a free port. Skilled Chinese merchants and traders, escaping racist discrimination against them by Malays on the Malay Peninsula, flocked to Singapore, where they prospered in the free trade atmosphere.

In 1924 the British began construction of a naval base on the island, the largest in Southeast Asia, which was nonetheless overcome by the Japanese in 1942. Returning in 1945, the British continued to build Singapore into a major maritime center. Today oil supertankers from Saudi Arabia must exit the Indian Ocean through the Strait of Malacca and skirt Singapore to enter the South China Sea for deliveries to Japan and other Asian nations. Thus, Singapore has found itself in the enviable position of helping to refine and transship millions of barrels of Middle Eastern oil. Singapore's oil-refining capacities have been ranked the world's third largest since 1973.

Singapore is now the second-busiest port in the world (Rotterdam in the Netherlands is number one). It has become the largest shipbuilding and -repair port in the region and a major shipping-related financial center. Singapore's economy has been growing at rates between 6 and 12 percent for the past decade, making it one of the fastest-growing economies in the world. In recent years the government has aggressively sought out investment from non-shipping–related industries in order to diversify the economy. In 1992 Singapore hosted a summit of the Association of Southeast Asian Nations in which a decision was made to create a regional common market by the year 2008. In order to compete with the emerging European and North American trading blocs, it was decided that tariffs on products traded within the ASEAN region would be cut to 5 percent or less.

A UNIQUE CULTURE

Britain maintained an active interest in Singapore throughout its empire period. At its peak there were some 100,000 British military men and their dependents stationed there. The British military remained until 1971. (The U.S. Navy's Seventh Fleet's logistics operations have recently been transferred from the Philippines to Singapore, thereby increasing the number of U.S. military personnel in Singapore to about 300 persons.) Thus, British culture, from the architecture of the buildings, to the leisure of a cricket match, to the prevalence of the English language, is everywhere present in Singapore. Yet because of the heterogeneity of the population (77 percent Chinese, 15 percent Malay, and 6 percent Indian), Singapore accommodates many philosophies and belief systems, including Confucianism, Buddhism, Islam, Hinduism, and Christianity. In recent years the government has attempted to promote the Confucian ethic of hard work and respect for law, as well as the Mandarin Chinese language, in order to develop a greater Asian consciousness among the people. But most

(Reuters/Bettmann photo by Dominic Wong)
Singapore is one of the most affluent nations in Asia. Nevertheless, some of its citizens are mired in poverty. This woman, huddled with her life possessions, ekes out a bare existence in the thriving island state.

Singapore is controlled by several different nearby nations, including Thailand, Java, India, and Indonesia
A.D. 1200–1400

The Japanese capture Singapore
1942

The British return to Singapore
1945

Full elections and self-government; Lee Kuan Yew comes to power
1959

Singapore, now unofficially independent of Britain, briefly joins the Malaysia Federation
1963

Singapore becomes an independent republic
1965

Singapore becomes the second-busiest port in the world and achieves one of the highest per capita incomes in the Pacific Rim
1980s

1990s

Prime Minister Lee steps down; Goh Chok Tong is appointed

The U.S. Navy moves some of its operations from the Philippines to Singapore

Singaporeans seem content to avoid extreme ideology, in favor of pragmatism; they prefer to believe in whatever approach works—that is, whatever allows them to make money and have a higher standard of living.

Yet their great material success has come with a price. The government keeps a firm hand on the people. For example, citizens can be fined as much as $250 for dropping a candy wrapper on the street or for driving without a seat belt. Worse offenses, such as importing chewing gum or selling it, carry fines of $6,000 and $1,200 respectively. Death by hanging is the punishment for murder, drug trafficking, and kidnapping, while lashing is inflicted on attempted murderers, robbers, and rapists. Being struck with a cane is the punishment for crimes such as malicious damage, as an American teenager, in a case that became a brief international cause célèbre in 1994, found out when he allegedly sprayed graffitti on cars in Singapore. Later that year a Dutch businessperson was executed for alleged possession of heroin.

Political dissidents may be arrested, and the press cannot publish whatever it wishes without often generating the government's ire. Government leaders argue that order and hard work are necessities since, being a tiny island, Singapore could easily be overtaken by the envious and more politically unstable countries nearby; with few natural resources, Singapore

must instead develop its people into disciplined, educated workers. Few deny that Singapore is an amazingly clean and efficient city-state, yet in recent years younger residents have begun to wish for a greater voice in government.

The law-and-order tone exists largely because after its separation from Malaysia in 1965, Singapore was controlled by one man and his personal hard-work ethic, Prime Minister Lee Kuan Yew, along with his Political Action Party (PAP). On November 26, 1990, Lee resigned his office. Two days later he was replaced by his chosen successor, Goh Chok Tong. Goh had been the deputy prime minister and was the designated successor-in-waiting since 1984. The transition has been smooth, and the PAP's hold on the government remains intact.

The PAP originally came into prominence in 1959, when the issue of the day was whether Singapore should join the proposed Federation of Malaysia. Singapore joined Malaysia in 1963, but serious differences persuaded Singaporeans to declare independence 2 years later. Lee Kuan Yew, a Cambridge-educated, ardent anti-Communist with old roots in Singapore, gained such strong support as prime minister that not a single opposition party member was elected for more than 20 years. Only one opposition seat exists today. The two main goals of the administration have been to utilize fully Singapore's primary resource—its deep-

water port—and to develop a strong Singaporean identity. The first goal has been achieved in a way that few would have thought possible; the question of national identity, however, continues to be problematic. Creating a Singaporean identity has been difficult because of the heterogeneity of the population, a situation that is likely to increase as foreign workers are imported to fill gaps in the labor supply resulting from a very successful birth control campaign started in the 1960s. Identity formation has also been difficult because of Singapore's recent seesaw history. First Singapore was a colony of Britain, then it became an outpost of the Japanese empire, followed by a return to Britain. Next Malaysia drew Singapore into its fold, and finally, in 1965, Singapore became independent. All these changes transpired within the lifetime of many contemporary Singaporeans, so their confusion regarding identity is understandable. Many still have a sense that their existence as a nation is tenuous, and they look for direction.

DEVELOPMENT

Development of the deepwater Port of Singapore has been so successful that, at any single time, 400 ships are in port. Singapore has also become a base for fleets engaged in offshore oil exploration and a major financial center, "the Switzerland of Southeast Asia."

FREEDOM

Under Prime Minister Lee, Singaporeans had to adjust to a strict regimen of behavior involving both political and personal freedoms. Citizens want more freedoms but realize that law and order have helped produce their high quality of life. Political opposition voices have largely been silenced since 1968, when the Political Action Party captured all the seats in the government.

HEALTH/WELFARE

Eighty percent of Singaporeans live in government-built dwellings. A government-created pension fund, the Central Provident Fund, takes up to one quarter of workers' paychecks; some of this goes into a compulsory savings account that can be used to finance the purchase of a residence. Other forms of social welfare are not condoned. Care of the elderly is the duty of children, not the government.

ACHIEVEMENTS

Housing remains a serious problem for many Asian countries, but virtually every Singaporean has access to adequate housing. Replacing swamplands with industrial parks has helped to lessen Singapore's reliance on its deepwater port. Singapore successfully overcame a Communist challenge in the 1950s to become a solid home for free enterprise in the region.

South Korea (Republic of Korea)

GEOGRAPHY

Area in Square Kilometers (Miles):
98,480 (38,013) (slightly larger than
Indiana)
Capital (Population): Seoul
(9,646,000)
Climate: temperate

PEOPLE

Population
Total: 44,614,000
Annual Growth Rate: 1.05%
Rural/Urban Population (Ratio):
26/74
Ethnic Makeup: homogeneous Korean
Major Language: Korean

Health
Life Expectancy at Birth: 67 years
(male); 73 years (female)
Infant Mortality Rate (Ratio):
23/1,000
Average Caloric Intake: 119% of
FAO minimum
Physicians Available (Ratio): 1/1,066

Religions
49% Christianity; 47% Buddhism;
3% Confucianism; 1% Shamanism
and Chondokyo

WOMEN IN MODERN KOREA

According to the traditions of Confucianism, a woman had three people
whom she was to obey throughout her lifetime: her father until she married;
her husband after marriage; and her son after her husband's death. The
subservience mandated by this ancient custom can still be seen throughout
South Korean society at the interpersonal level, but times are changing in
the public arena. Women may vote in Korea (more than 80 percent cast
votes in presidential elections), and half a dozen women have been appointed to the cabinet at various times since 1948. Fifty-four women have
served in the Legislature, and there are women judges, lawyers, and newspaper editors and reporters. Women account for about 35 percent of the
South Korean work force. Some 21 percent of all civil servants are women,
but there has never yet been a woman president.

Education
Adult Literacy Rate: 96%

COMMUNICATION
Telephones: 13,276,000
Newspapers: 68 dailies

TRANSPORTATION
Highways—Kilometers (Miles):
63,201 (39,248)

Railroads—Kilometers (Miles): 3,019
(1,877)
Usable Airfields: 93

GOVERNMENT
Type: republic
Independence Date: August 15, 1948
Head of State/Government: President
Kim Young-sam; Prime Minister Lee
Yung Duk
Political Parties: Democratic Justice
Party; New Democratic Republican
Party; others
Suffrage: universal at 20

MILITARY
Number of Armed Forces: 750,000
*Military Expenditures (% of Central
Government Expenditures):* 3.6%
Current Hostilities: disputed
Demarcation Line with North Korea;
disputed Liancourt Rocks, claimed by
Japan

ECONOMY
Currency ($ U.S. Equivalent): 792
won = $1
Per Capita Income/GNP:
$6,500/$287 billion
Inflation Rate: 4.5%
Natural Resources: coal; tungsten;
graphite; molybdenum; lead;
hydropower
Agriculture: rice; root crops; barley;
vegetables; fruit; livestock and
livestock products; fish
Industry: textiles; clothing; footwear;
food processing; chemicals; steel;
electronics; automobile production;
shipbuilding

FOREIGN TRADE
Exports: $76.8 billion
Imports: $81.7 billion

EARLY HISTORY

Korea was inhabited for thousands of years by an early people who may or may not have been related to the Ainus of northern Japan, the inhabitants of Sakhalin Island, and the Siberian Eskimos. Distinct from this early civilization are today's Koreans whose ancestors migrated to the Korean Peninsula from Central Asia and, benefiting from close contact with the culture of China, established prosperous kingdoms as early as 1000 B.C. (legends put the date as early as 2333 B.C.).

The era of King Sejong, who ruled Korea from 1418–1450, is notable for its many scientific and humanistic accomplishments. Ruling his subjects according to neo-Confucian thought, Sejong taught improved agricultural methods; published books on astronomy, history, religion, and medicine (the Koreans were the first to invent movable metal type); and was instrumental in the invention of sundials, rain gauges, and various musical instruments. Of singular importance was his invention of *han-qul,* a simplified writing system that even uneducated peasants could easily learn. Before *han-qul,* Koreans used the more complicated Chinese characters to represent sounds in the Korean language.

REGIONAL RELATIONS

For most of its history, Korea remained at least nominally independent of foreign powers. China, however, always wielded tremendous cultural influence and at times politically dominated the Korean Peninsula. Similarly, Japan often cast longing eyes toward Korea but was never able to control affairs successfully there until the beginning of the twentieth century.

Korean influence on Japanese culture was pronounced in the 1400s and 1500s, when, through peaceful trade as well as forced labor, Korean artisans and technicians taught advanced skills in ceramics, textiles, painting, and other arts to the Japanese. (Historically, the Japanese received most of their cultural influence from China via Korea.)

In this century the direction of influence reversed—to the current Japan-to-Korea flow—with the result that the two cultures share numerous qualities. Ironically, cultural closeness has not eradicated emotional distance: Modern Japanese continue to discriminate against Koreans who live in Japan, and Japanese brutality during the years of occupation (1905–1945) remains a frequent topic of conversation among Koreans.

Japan achieved its desire to rule Korea in 1905, when Russia's military, along with its imperialistic designs on Korea, was soundly defeated by the Japanese in the Russo–Japanese War; Korea was granted to Japan as part of the peace settlement. Unlike other expansionist nations, Japan was not content to rule Korea as a colony but, rather, attempted the complete cultural and political annexation of the Korean Peninsula. Koreans had to adopt Japanese names, serve in the Japanese Army, and pay homage to the Japanese emperor. Some 1.3 million Koreans were forcibly sent to Japan to work in coal mines or to serve in the military. The Korean language ceased to be taught in school, and more than 200,000 books on Korean history and culture were burned.

Many Koreans joined clandestine resistance organizations. In 1919 a Declaration of Korean Independence was announced in Seoul by resistance leaders, but the brutally efficient Japanese police and military crushed the movement. They killed thousands of demonstrators, tortured and executed the leaders, and set fire to the homes of those suspected of cooperating with the movement. Despite suppression of this kind throughout the 40 years of Japanese colonial rule, a provisional government

(Reuters/Bettmann photo by Tony Chung)

When Korea was divided, the South Koreans received large amounts of economic and military aid from the United States, which allowed them to follow the Japanese model of development. As the industrial base grew and they focused on specific markets, South Korea became an economic powerhouse. Workers in the Hyundai shipyards are pictured above.

was established by the resistance in 1919, with branches in Korea, China, and Russia. However, a very large police force—1 Japanese for every 40 Koreans—kept resistance in check.

One resistance leader, Syngman Rhee, vigorously promoted the cause of Korean independence to government leaders in the United States and Europe. Rhee, supported by the United States, became the president of South Korea after the defeat of the Japanese in 1945.

Upon the surrender of Japan, the victorious Allied nations decided to divide Korea into two zones of temporary occupation, for the purposes of overseeing the orderly dismantling of Japanese rule and establishing a new Korean government. The United States was to occupy all of Korea south of the 38th Parallel of latitude (a demarcation running east and west across the peninsula, about 150 miles north of the capital city of Seoul), while the Soviet Union was to occupy Korea north of that line. The United States was uneasy about permitting the Soviets to move troops into Korea, as the Soviet Union had entered the war against Japan just 8 days before Japan surrendered and its commitment to the democratic intentions of the Allies was questionable. Nevertheless, it was granted occupation rights.

Later the United Nations attempted to enter the zone occupied by the Soviet Union in order to oversee democratic elections for all of Korea. Denied entry, UN advisers proceeded with elections in the South, which brought Syngman Rhee to the presidency. The North created its own government, with Kim Il-Song at the head. Tensions between the two governments resulted in the elimination of trade and other contacts across the new border. This was difficult for each side, because the Japanese had developed industries in the North while the South had remained primarily agricultural. Each side needed the other's resources; in their absence, considerable civil unrest occurred. Rhee's government responded by suppressing dissent, rigging elections, and using strong-arm tactics on critics. Autocratic rule, not unlike that of the colonial Japanese, has been the norm in South Korea almost ever since, and citizens, particularly university students, have been quick to take to the streets in protest of human rights violations by the various South Korean governments. Equally stern measures were instituted by the Communist government in the North, so that despite nearly a half century of Korean rule, the repressive legacy of the Japanese police state remains.

AN ECONOMIC POWERHOUSE

Upon the establishment of two separate political entities in Korea, the North pursued a communist model of economic restructuring. South Korea, bolstered by massive infusions of economic and military aid from the United States, pursued a decidedly capitalist strategy. The results of this choice have been dramatic. South Korea today is often said to be the fastest-growing economy in the world; by the year 2010, it is expected that per capita income for Koreans will equal that of European economies. About 75 percent of South Korean people live in urban centers, where they have access to good education and jobs. Manufacturing accounts for 30 percent of the gross domestic product. Economic success and recent improvements in the political climate seem to be slowing the rate of outward migration. Some Koreans have even returned home in recent years.

Following the Japanese model, Korean businesspeople work hard to capture market share rather than to gain immediate profit—that is, they are willing to sell their products at or below cost for several years in order to gain the confidence of consumers, even if they make no profit. Once a sizable proportion of consumers buy their product and trust its reliability, the price is raised to a profitable level.

Many South Korean businesses are now investing in other countries, and South Korea is now a creditor rather than a debtor member of the Asian Development Bank—it is now in a position to loan money to other newly industrializing countries rather than to borrow from nations wealthier than itself. Given this kind of economic strength, it is now claimed by some that Japan's towering economic powerhouse could be challenged by a unified Korea and that, therefore, Japan (which is separated from Korea by only 150 miles) is not interested in promoting reunification. The situation is not unlike European countries' concern about the economic strength of the reunified Germany.

SOCIAL PROBLEMS

Economically, South Korea is an impressive showcase for the fruits of capitalism. Politically, however, the country has been wracked with problems. Under presidents Syngman Rhee (1948–1960), Park Chung Hee (1964–1979), and Chun Doo Hwan (1981–1987), South Korean government was so centralized as to constitute a virtual dictatorship. Human rights violations, suppression of workers, and other acts in-

compatible with the tenets of democracies were frequent occurrences. Student uprisings, military revolutions, and political assassinations became more influential than the ballot box in forcing a change of government. President Roh Tae-woo came to power in 1987, in the wake of a mass protest against civil rights abuses and other excesses of the previous government. Students began mass protests against various candidates long before the 1992 elections that brought to office the first civilian president in more than 30 years, Kim Young-sam. Kim was once a dissident himself and was victimized by government policies against free speech; once elected, he promised to make major democratic reforms. The reforms, however, have not been good enough for thousands of striking subway workers, farmers, or students whose demonstrations against low pay, foreign rice imports, or the placement of Patriot missiles in South Korea have had to be broken up by riot police.

A primary focus of the South Korean government's attention at the moment is the several U.S. military bases in South Korea, currently home to 43,500 U.S. troops. The government (and apparently most of the 44.6 million South Korean people), although not always happy with the military presence, believes that the U.S. troops are useful in deterring possible aggression from North Korea. Many university students, however, are offended at the presence of these troops. They claim that the Americans have suppressed the growth of democracy by propping up authoritarian regimes—a claim readily admitted by the United States, which believed during the cold war era that the containment of communism was a higher priority. Strong feelings against U.S. involvement in South Korean affairs have precipitated hundreds of violent demonstrations, sometimes involving as many as 100,000 protesters. The United States' refusal to withdraw its forces from South Korea left an impression with many Koreans that Americans were hardline, cold war ideologues who were unwilling to bend in the face of changing international alignments.

In 1990 U.S. officials announced that, in an effort to reduce U.S. military costs in the post–cold war era, the United States would pull out several thousand of its troops from South Korea and close three of its five air bases. The United States also declared that it expects South Korea to pay more of the cost of the U.S. military presence, in part as a way to reduce the unfavorable trade balance between the two countries. The South Korean government has agreed to build a new U.S. military base about 50 miles south of the

The Yi dynasty begins a 518-year reign over Korea
A.D. **935**

Korea pays tribute to Mongol rulers in China
1637

Korea opens its ports to outside trade
1876

Japan formally annexes Korea at the end of the Russo-Japanese War
1910

Korea is divided into North and South
1945

North Korea invades South Korea; the Korean War begins
1950

Cease-fire agreement; the DMZ is established
1953

President Park Chung Hee is assassinated
1979

Democratization movement; the 1988 Summer Olympic Games are held in Seoul
1980s

1990s

Reunification talks

A nonaggression pact is signed with North Korea; cross-border exhanges begin

President Kim Young-sam and Prime Minister Lee Yung Duk take office

capital city of Seoul, where current operations would be relocated. South Korea would pay all construction costs—estimated at about $1 billion—and the United States would be able to reduce its presence within the Seoul metropolitan area, where many of the anti-U.S. demonstrations take place. Although the bases have been a focus of protest by students, surveys now show that about 90 percent of South Koreans want the U.S. military to remain in the country.

A second issue that has occupied the government for years is the question of reunification with North Korea. The division of the country has left many families unable to communicate with or visit relatives in the North, and the threat of a military incursion from the North has forced South Korea to spend large sums of its national budget on defense. Frequent charges of spying, counterspying, and other forms of subversive activities—not to mention the fact that the two nations have not signed a peace treaty since the Korean War—have kept tensions high. High-profile meetings to discuss reunification have been held for several years, but with little concrete progress, despite a nonagression and reconciliation pact and agreements on cross-border exchanges and other forms of cooperation. The impetus behind improvements in relations appears to be North Korea's loss of solid diplomatic and economic partners, and thus its increasing isolation in the world economy, due to the collapse of the Soviet Union. Some South Koreans have estimated that it will cost $980 billion to reunify with the North.

South Korean government leaders have to face a very active, vocal, and even violent populace when they initiate controversial policies. Among the more vocal groups for democracy and human rights are the various Christian congregations and their Westernized clergy. Other vocal groups include the college students who hold rallies annually to elect student protest leaders and to plan antigovernment demonstrations. In addition to the military-bases question, student protesters are angry at the South Korean government's willingness to open more Korean markets to U.S. products. The students want the United States to apologize for its alleged assistance to the South Korean government in violently suppressing an antigovernment demonstration in 1981 in Kwangju, a southern city that is a frequent locus of antigovernment as well as labor-related demonstrations and strikes. Protesters were particularly angered by then–president Roh Tae-woo's silencing of part of the opposition by convincing two opposition parties to merge with his own to form a large Democratic Liberal Party (DLP), not unlike that of the Liberal Democratic Party (LDP), which governed Japan almost continuously for more than 40 years.

Ironically, demands for changes have increased at precisely the moment that the government has been instituting changes designed to strengthen both the economy and civil rights. Under Roh's administration, for example, trade and diplomatic initiatives were launched with Eastern European nations and with China and the former Soviet Union. Under Kim Young-sam's administration, some 41,000 prison-

ers, including some political prisoners, were granted amnesty, and the powerful business conglomerates called *chaebols* were brought under a tighter rein. Similarly, relaxation of the tight controls on labor union activity gave workers more leverage in negotiating with management. Unfortunately, union activity, exploding after decades of suppression, has produced crippling industrial strikes—as many as 2,400 a year, and the police have been called out to restore order. In fact, since 1980, riot police have fired an average of more than 500 tear-gas shells a day, at a cost to the South Korean government of $51 million.

The sense of unease in South Korea has been tempered by the dynamism of the economy. Economic growth and democratization seem to be high on the agenda, although the latter has been exceptionally difficult to achieve. South Korea recently established unofficial diplomatic ties with Taiwan in order to facilitate freer trade. It then signed an industrial pact with China to merge South Korea's technological know-how with China's inexpensive labor force to build aircraft, automobiles, and even high-definition televisions. Relations with Japan have also improved since Japan's apology for atrocities during World War II and the visit of Kim Young-sam to the Japanese emperor Akihito in Tokyo in 1994.

DEVELOPMENT

The South Korean economy is booming. Construction of new homes and businesses is everywhere evident. Industrial workers have had to bear the brunt of the negative aspects of industrialization: low wages and long hours.

FREEDOM

Suppression of political dissent, manipulation of the electoral process, and restrictions on labor union activity have been features of almost every South Korean government since 1948. Martial law has been frequently invoked, and governments have been overthrown by mass uprisings of the people. Reforms have been enacted under Presidents Roh Tae-woo and Kim Young-sam.

HEALTH/WELFARE

Korean men usually marry at about age 27, women at about 24. In 1960 Korean women, on average, gave birth to 6 children; in 1990 the expected births per woman were 1.6. The average South Korean baby born today can expect to live to be about 70 years old, as compared to 75 for U.S. newborns.

ACHIEVEMENTS

In 1992 Korean students placed first in international math and science tests. South Korea achieved self-sufficiency in agricultural fertilizers in the 1970s and continues to show growth in the production of grains and vegetables. The formerly weak industrial sector is now a strong component of the economy.

Taiwan (Republic of China)

GEOGRAPHY

Area in Square Kilometers (Miles):
36,002 (22,320) (about the size of
West Virginia)
Capital (Population): Taipei (2,720,000)
Climate: subtropical

PEOPLE

Population
Total: 21,092,000
Annual Growth Rate: 1%
Rural/Urban Population Ratio: 25/75
Ethnic Makeup: 84% Taiwanese;
14% Mainlander Chinese; 2%
aborigine
Major Languages: Mandarin Chinese;
Taiwanese and Hakka dialects also
used

Health
Life Expectancy at Birth: 72 years
(male); 78 years (female)
Infant Mortality Rate (Ratio):
5.7/1,000
Average Caloric Intake: n/a
Physicians Available (Ratio): 1/910

Religions
93% mixture of Buddhism,
Confucianism, and Taoism; 4.5%
Christian; 2.5% others

Education
Adult Literacy Rate: 92%

COMMUNICATION
Telephones: 7,800,000
Newspapers: 139

BAMBOO, A SYMBOL OF ASIA

In central Taiwan, near the city of T'aichung, is a 6,000-acre forest research station, located approximately 4,000 feet above sea level. This forest is unique because its trees are mostly bamboo. Bamboo, of which there are some 200 species, is a member of the grass family, but some varieties grow to be more than 150 feet high and 1 foot in diameter. Some species have been known to grow nearly 2 feet a day.

With more than a dozen varieties of bamboo, the Hsitou Bamboo Forest preserves a plant that is now being slowly displaced by plastic and steel but which remains the single most useful building material throughout Asia and Southeast Asia. In Korea and elsewhere, bamboo is used as scaffolding on most construction jobs; in China the small tips of new bamboo shoots are used as food in many dishes; in Japan bamboo is fashioned into fans, flowerpots, water pipes, and a flutelike musical instrument called a *shakuhachi*. Chopsticks, baskets, and even paper are made from bamboo.

TRANSPORTATION

Highways—Kilometers (Miles):
20,041 (12,425)
Railroads—Kilometers (Miles): 4,600
(2,852)
Usable Airfields: 38

GOVERNMENT

Type: multiparty democratic regime
Head of State/Government: President
Lee Teng-hui; Premier Lien Chan
Political Parties: Nationalist Party
(Kuomintang); Democratic
Progressive Party; China Social
Democratic Party; Labour Party
Suffrage: universal over 20

MILITARY

Number of Armed Forces: 400,000
*Military Expenditures (% of Central
Government Expenditures):* 5.4%
Current Hostilities: officially (but not
actually) in a state of war with the
People's Republic of China

ECONOMY

Currency ($ U.S. Equivalent): 26.23
New Taiwan dollars = $1
Per Capita Income/GDP:
$10,566/$209 billion
Inflation Rate: 4.4%
Natural Resources: coal; gold;
copper; sulphur; oil; natural gas
Agriculture: rice; tea; bananas;
pineapples; sugarcane; sweet
potatoes; wheat; soybeans; peanuts
Industry: steel; pig iron; aluminum;
shipbuilding; cement; fertilizer;
paper; cotton; fabrics

FOREIGN TRADE

Exports: $82.4 billion
Imports: $72.1 billion

93

A LAND OF REFUGE

It has been called "beautiful island," "treasure island," and "terraced bay island," but to the people who have settled there, Taiwan (formerly known as Formosa) has come to mean "refuge island."

Typical of the earliest refugees of the island were the Hakka peoples of China, who, tired of persecution on the mainland, fled to Taiwan (and to Borneo) before A.D. 1000. In the seventeenth century, tens of thousands of Ming Chinese soldiers, defeated at the hands of the expanding Manchu army, sought sanctuary in Taiwan. In 1949 a third major wave of immigration to Taiwan brought thousands of Chinese Nationalists, retreating in the face of the victorious Red Chinese armies. Hosting all these newcomers were the original inhabitants of the islands, various Malay-Polynesian-speaking tribes whose descendants live today in mountain villages throughout the island.

Since 1544 other outsiders have shown interest in Taiwan, too: Portugal, Spain, the Netherlands, Britain, and France have all either settled colonies or engaged in trade along the coasts. But the non-Chinese power that has had the most influence is Japan. Japan treated parts of Taiwan as its own for 400 years before it officially acquired the entire island in 1895, at the end of the Sino-Japanese War. From then until 1945, the Japanese ruled Taiwan with the intent of fully integrating it into Japanese culture. The Japanese language was taught in schools, college students were sent to Japan for their education, and the Japanese style of government was implemented. Many Taiwanese resented the harsh discipline imposed, but they also recognized that the Japanese were building a modern, productive society. Indeed, the basic infrastructure of contemporary Taiwan—roads, railways, schools, and so on—was constructed during the Japanese colonial era (1895–1945). Japan still lays claim to the Senkaku Islands, a chain of uninhabited islands, which the Taiwanese say belong to Taiwan.

After Japan's defeat in World War II, Taiwan became the island of refuge of the anti-Communist leader Chiang Kai-shek and his 3 million Kuomintang (KMT, or Nationalist Party) followers, many of whom had been prosperous and well-educated businesspeople and intellectuals in China. These Mandarin-speaking mainland Chinese, called Mainlanders, now constitute about 14 percent of Taiwan's 21 million people.

During the 1950s, Mao Zedong, the leader of the People's Republic of China, planned an invasion of Taiwan. However, Taiwan's leaders succeeded in obtaining military support from the United States to prevent the attack. They also convinced the United States to provide substantial amounts of foreign aid to Taiwan (the U.S. government saw the funds as a way to contain communism) as well as to grant it diplomatic recognition as the only legitimate government for all of China.

Because neither side has been willing to accept the sovereignty of the other, mainland China was denied membership in the United Nations for more than 20 years; Taiwan held the "China seat." World opinion on the "two Chinas" issue began to change in the early 1970s. Many countries believed that a nation as large and powerful as the People's Republic of China should not be kept out of the United Nations nor out of the mainstream of world trade in favor of the much smaller Taiwan. In 1971 the United Nations withdrew its China seat from Taiwan and gave it to the P.R.C. The United States and many other countries wished to establish diplomatic relations with China but were denied that opportunity as long as they granted recognition to Taiwan. In 1979 the United States, preceded by many other nations, switched its diplomatic recognition from Taiwan to China. Foreign-trade offices in Taiwan remained unchanged but embassies were renamed; the U.S. embassy was called the American Institute in Taiwan. As far as official diplomacy with the United States was concerned, Taiwan became a non-nation, but that did not stop the two countries from engaging in very profitable trade, including a controversial U.S. agreement in 1992 to sell $4 billion to $6 billion worth of F-16 fighter jets to Taiwan. Similarly, Taiwan has refused to establish diplomatic ties, yet continues to trade, with nations that recognize the mainland Chinese authorities as a legitimate government. In 1992, for instance, when South Korea established ties with mainland China, Taiwan immediately broke off formal relations with South Korea and suspended direct airline flights. However, Taiwan continued to permit trade in many commodities. Recognizing a potentially strong market in Vietnam, Taiwan also established air links with Vietnam in 1992, links that had been broken since the end of the Vietnam War. In 1993 a Taiwanese company collaborated with the Vietnamese government to construct a $242 million highway in Ho Chi Minh City (formerly Saigon). Only 29 states formally recognize Taiwan today, but Taiwan nevertheless maintains close economic ties with more than 140 countries.

AN ECONOMIC POWERHOUSE

Diplomatic maneuvering has not affected Taiwan's stunning postwar economic growth.

(UN photo by Chen Jr.)

Taiwan has one of the highest population densities in the world, but it has been able to expand its agricultural output rapidly and efficiently through a number of innovative practices. By terracing, using high-yield seeds, and developing adequate irrigation, Taiwanese can grow a succession of crops on the same piece of land throughout the year.

(UN photo by Chen Jr.)

Taiwan is described as an economic miracle. After World War II, it emerged as a tremendous source for labor-intensive industries, such as electronics and clothing. Many Western manufacturers moved their facilities to Taiwan to take advantage of the savings in labor costs.

Like Japan, Taiwan has been described as an economic miracle. In the past 20 years Taiwan has enjoyed more years of double-digit economic growth than any other nation on earth. With electronics leading the pack of exports, about 45 percent of Taiwan's gross domestic product comes from manufacturing. Taiwan has been open to foreign investment and, of course, to foreign trade. However, for many years Taiwan insisted on a policy of no contact and no communication with mainland China. Private enterprises eventually were allowed to trade with China—as long as the products were transshipped through a third country, usually Hong Kong. In 1993 government-owned enterprises such as steel and fertilizer plants were allowed to trade with China, on the same condition. By the early 1990s, Taiwanese trade with China had exceeded $13 billion a year and China had become Taiwan's seventh-largest trading partner. The liberalization of trade between China (especially its southern and coastal provinces), Taiwan, and Hong Kong has made the region, now known as Greater China, an economic dynamo. Economists predict that Greater China will bypass Japan's economy in the near future.

As one of the newly industrializing countries of Asia, Taiwan certainly no longer fits the label "underdeveloped." Taiwan holds large stocks of foreign reserves and carries a trade surplus with the United States (in Taiwan's favor) 4 times greater than Japan's, when counted on a per capita basis. The Taipei stock market has been so successful— sometimes outperforming both Japan and the United States—that a number of workers reportedly have quit their jobs to play the market, thereby exacerbating Taiwan's already serious labor shortage.

Successful Taiwanese companies have begun to invest heavily in other countries where land and labor are plentiful and less expensive. In 1993 the Philippines accepted a $60 million loan from Taiwan to build an industrial park and commercial port at Subic Bay, the former U.S. naval base; and Thailand, Australia, and the United States have also seen inflows of Taiwanese investment monies. By the early 1990s, some 200 Taiwanese companies had invested $1.3 billion in Malaysia alone (Taiwan has now supplanted Japan as the largest outside investor in Malaysia). Investment in mainland China has also increased.

Taiwan's economic success is attributable in part to its educated population, many of whom constituted the cultural and economic elite of China before the Communist revolution. Despite resentment of the mainland immigrants by native-born Taiwanese, everyone, including the lower classes of Taiwan, has benefited from this infusion of talent and capital. Yet the Taiwanese people are beginning to pay a price for their sudden affluence. It is said that Taipei, the capital city of Taiwan (and the sixth most expensive city in the world for foreigners) is awash in money, but it is also awash in air pollution and traffic congestion. Traffic congestion in Taipei is rated near the worst in the world. Concrete high-rises have displaced the lush greenery of the mountains. Many residents spend their earnings on luxury foreign cars and on cigarettes and alcohol, the consumption rate of which has been increasing by about 10 percent a year. Many Chinese traditions—for instance, the roadside restaurant serving noodle soup—are giving way to 7-Elevens selling Coca-Cola and ice cream.

Some Taiwanese despair of ever turning back from the growing materialism; they wish for the revival of traditional Chinese (that is, mostly Confucian) ethics, but they doubt that it will happen. Still, the government, which has been dominated since 1949 by the conservative Mandarin migrants from the mainland, sees to it that Confucian ethics are vigorously taught in school. And there remains in Taiwan more of traditional China than in China itself, because, unlike the Chinese Communists, the Taiwanese authorities have had no reason to attempt an eradication of the values of Buddhism, Taoism, or Confucianism. Nor has grinding poverty—often the most serious threat to the cultural arts—negatively affected literature and the fine arts, as it has in China. Parents, with incense

Portuguese sailors are the first Europeans to visit Taiwan
A.D. 1544

Taiwan becomes part of the Chinese Empire
1700s

The Sino-Japanese War ends; China cedes Taiwan to Japan
1895

Taiwan achieves independence from Japan
1945

Nationalists, under Chiang Kai-shek, retreat to Taiwan
1947-49

A de facto separation of Taiwan from China; Chinese aggression is deterred with U.S. assistance
1950s

China replaces Taiwan in the United Nations
1971

Chiang Kai-shek dies and is succeeded by his son, Chiang Ching-Kuo
1975

The first two-party elections in Taiwan's history are held; 38 years of martial law end
1980s

Chiang Ching-Kuo dies; Lee Teng-hui is the first native-born Taiwanese to be elected president

1990s

Relations with China improve; the United States sells F-16 jets to Taiwan

sticks burning before small religious altars, still emphasize respect for authority, the benefits of harmonious cooperative effort, and the inestimable value of education. Traditional festivals dot each year's calendar, among the most spectacular of which is Taiwan's National Day parade. Marching bands, traditional dancers, and a huge dragon carried by more than 50 young men please the crowds lining the streets of Taipei. Temples are filled with worshipers praying for health and good luck.

But the Taiwanese will need more than luck if they are to escape the consequences of their intensely rapid drive for material comfort. Some people contend that the island of refuge is being destroyed by success. Violent crime, for instance, once hardly known in Taiwan, is now commonplace. Six thousand violent crimes, including rapes, robberies, kidnappings, and murder, were reported in 1989—a 22 percent increase over the previous year. Extortion against wealthy companies and abductions of the children of successful families are causing a wave of fear among the rich.

Furthermore, there are signs that the economy is heading for a slowdown. Labor shortages have forced some companies to operate at only 60 percent of capacity, and low-interest loans are hard to get because the government fears that too many people will simply invest in get-rich stocks instead of in new businesses.

POLITICAL LIBERALIZATION

These disturbing trends notwithstanding, in recent years the Taiwanese people have had much to be grateful for in the political sphere. Until 1986 the government, dominated by the influence of the Chiangs, had permitted only one political party, the Nationalists, and had kept Taiwan under martial law for nearly 4 decades. A marked political liberalization began near the time of Chiang Ching-Kuo's death, in 1987. The first opposition party, the Democratic Progressive Party, was formed, martial law (officially, the "Emergency Decree") was lifted, and the first two-party elections were held in 1986. In 1988, significantly, for the first time a native-born Taiwanese, Lee Teng-hui, was elected to the presidency, and further Taiwanization of the government is anticipated.

Nevertheless, the Taiwanese people, like their counterparts in Singapore, have over the years accustomed themselves to limited civil liberties, because violators have often been silenced by force. It is still against the law for any group to advocate publicly the independence of Taiwan—that is, to advocate international acceptance of Taiwan as a sovereign state, separate and apart from China. When the opposition Democratic Progressive Party (DPP) resolved in 1990 that Taiwan should become an independent country, the ruling Nationalist government immediately outlawed the DPP platform. Recent high-level talks between the Taiwanese government and China on trade and tourism have further complicated the issue. Some believe that such talks will eventually result in Taiwan being annexed by China just as Hong Kong and Macau will be (although from a strictly legalistic viewpoint, Taiwan has just as much right to annex China). Others believe that dialogue will eventually diminish animosity, allowing Taiwan to move toward independence without China's opposition. Opinion is clearly divided. Even some members of the anti-independence Nationalist Party have bolted and formed a new party (the New KMT alliance, or the New Party) to promote closer ties with China. As opposition parties proliferate, the independence issue could become a more urgent topic of political debate. In the meantime contacts with the P.R.C. increase daily; Taiwanese students are now being admitted to China's universities, and Taiwanese residents by the thousands are now visiting relatives on the mainland. Despite complaints from China, Taiwanese government leaders have been courting their counterparts in the Philippines, Thailand, Indonesia, and South Korea. Moreover, President Lee has publicly promoted better relations with the People's Republic (the first president to do so), but China has vowed to invade Taiwan if it should ever declare independence. Under these circumstances, many—probably most—Taiwanese will likely remain content to let the rhetoric of reunification continue while enjoying the reality of de facto independence.

DEVELOPMENT

Taiwan has vigorously promoted export-oriented production, particularly of electronic equipment. In the 1980s manufacturing became the leading sector of the economy, employing more than one third of the work force. Ninety-nine percent of Taiwanese households own color televisions, and other signs of affluence are abundant.

FREEDOM

For nearly 4 decades, Taiwan was under martial law. Opposition parties were not tolerated, and individual liberties were limited. A liberalization of this pattern began in 1986. Taiwan now seems to be on a path toward greater democratization. In 1991, 5,574 prisoners, including many political prisoners, were released in a general amnesty.

HEALTH/WELFARE

Taiwan has one of the highest population densities in the world. About 92 percent of the population can read and write. Education is compulsory to age 15, and the country boasts more than 100 institutions of higher learning. Social programs, however, are less developed than those in Singapore, Japan, and some other Pacific Rim countries.

ACHIEVEMENTS

From a largely agrarian economic base, Taiwan has been able to transform its economy into an export-based dynamo with international influence. Today only 20 percent of the population work in agriculture, and Taiwan ranks among the top 20 exporters in the world.

Thailand (Kingdom of Thailand)

GEOGRAPHY

Area in Square Kilometers (Miles): 514,000 (198,404) (slightly more than twice the size of Wyoming)
Capital (Population): Bangkok (5,833,000)
Climate: tropical

PEOPLE

Population

Total: 58,722,500
Annual Growth Rate: 1.36%
Rural/Urban Population Ratio: 80/20
Ethnic Makeup: 84% Thai; 12% Chinese; 4% Malay and others
Major Languages: Thai; English; dialects; others

Health

Life Expectancy at Birth: 65 years (male); 72 years (female)
Infant Mortality Rate (Ratio): 38.5/1,000
Average Caloric Intake: 105% of FAO minimum
Physicians Available (Ratio): 1/4,227

Religions

94% Buddhist; 4% Muslim; 2% others

MONKS BEFORE MARRIAGE

In some parts of Thailand, a young man who has never served as a Buddhist monk is not considered prime marriage material. Young women may think of him as an "unripe person." To overcome this stigma, many young Thai men shave their heads and accept a temporary ordination into the Buddhist priesthood.

This important rite of passage into adulthood is usually undertaken during the monsoon season, when daily rain prevents extensive labor in the rice paddies. The process is not particularly difficult, and boys spend much of the time chatting and resting. However, recruits are expected to don a saffron robe and go from door to door each morning to beg for rice from the faithful; both the giver and the receiver are said to gain spiritual merit for this deed, and the family of the young monk receive even more spiritual merit for having enrolled their son as a monk. After a few weeks or months, most young men return to their normal lives, with spiritual merit to their names and a heightened chance of marriage.

Education

Adult Literacy Rate: 93%

COMMUNICATION

Telephones: 739,500
Newspapers: 23 dailies in Bangkok

TRANSPORTATION

Highways—Kilometers (Miles): 77,697 (48,328)

Railroads—Kilometers (Miles): 3,940 (2,442)
Usable Airfields: 95

GOVERNMENT

Type: constitutional monarchy
Independence Date: traditional founding date: 1238 (never colonized)
Head of State: King Bhumibol Adulyadej
Political Parties: Democratic Party; Thai Nation Party; National Development Party; New Aspiration Party; Social Action Party; Liberal Democratic Party; Solidarity Party; Mass Party; Thai Citizens' Party; People's Party; People's Force Party
Suffrage: universal at 21

MILITARY

Number of Armed Forces: 283,000
Military Expenditures (% of Central Government Expenditures): 2%
Current Hostilities: boundary dispute with Laos

ECONOMY

Currency ($ U.S. Equivalent): 25.95 baht = $1
Per Capita Income/GDP: $1,800/$103 billion
Inflation Rate: 4.5%
Natural Resources: tin; rubber; natural gas; tungsten; tantalum; timber; lead; fish; gypsum; lignite; fluorite
Agriculture: rice; cassava; rubber; corn; sugarcane; coconuts; soybeans
Industry: tourism; textiles and garments; agricultural processing; beverages; tobacco; cement; electric appliances and components; electronics; furniture; plastics

FOREIGN TRADE

Exports: $32.9 billion
Imports: $41.5 billion

THAILAND'S ANCIENT HERITAGE

The roots of Thai culture extend into the distant past. People were living in Thailand at least as early as the Bronze Age; and by the time Thai people from China (some scholars think from as far away as Mongolia) had established the first Thai dynasty in the Chao Phya Valley, in A.D. 1238, some communities, invariably with a Buddhist temple or monastery at their centers, had been thriving in the area for 600 years. Early Thai culture was greatly influenced by Buddhist monks and traders from India and Sri Lanka (Ceylon).

By the seventeenth century, Thailand's ancient capital, Ayutthaya, boasted a larger population than did London. Ayutthaya was known around the world for its wealth and for the beauty of its architecture, particularly its religious edifices. Attempts by European nations to obtain a share of the wealth were so inordinate that in 1688 the king expelled all foreigners from the country. Later, warfare with Cambodia, Laos, and Malaya yielded tremendous gains in power and territory for Thailand, but it was periodically afflicted by Burma (present-day Myanmar) which briefly conquered Thailand in the 1760s (as it had done in the 1560s). The Burmese were finally defeated in 1780, but the destruction of the capital required the construction of a new city near what is today Bangkok.

Generally speaking, the Thai people have been blessed over the centuries with benevolent kings, many of whom have been open to new ideas from Europe and North America. Gathering around them advisers from many nations, they improved transportation systems, education, and farming while maintaining the central place of Buddhism in Thai society. Occasionally royal support for religion overtook other societal needs, at the expense of the power of the government.

The gravest threat to Thailand came during the era of European colonial expansion. However, although both France and Britain forced Thailand to yield some of its holdings in Southeast Asia, Thailand—which means "Free Land"—was never completely conquered by European powers. Today the country occupies a land area about the size of France.

MODERN POLITICS

Since 1932, when a constitutional monarchy replaced the absolute monarchy, Thailand (formerly known as Siam) has weathered 17 attempted or successful military or political coups d'état (most recently

in 1991). The Constitution has been revoked and replaced numerous times; governments have fallen under votes of no-confidence; students have mounted violent demonstrations against the government; and the military has, at various times, imposed martial law or otherwise curtailed civil liberties.

Clearly, Thai politics are far from stable. Nevertheless, there is a sense of stability in Thailand. Miraculously, its people were spared the direct ravages of the Vietnam War, which raged nearby for 20 years. And despite all the political upheavals, the same royal family has been in control of the Thai throne for 9 generations, although its power has been severely delimited for some 60 years. Furthermore, before the first Constitution was enacted, in 1932, the country had been ruled continuously, for more than 700 years, by often brilliant and progressive kings. At the height of Western imperialism, when France, Britain, Holland, and Portugal were

in control of every country on or near Thailand's borders, Thailand remained free of Western domination, although it was forced, sometimes at gunpoint, to relinquish sizable chunks of its holdings in Cambodia and Laos to France, and holdings in Malaya to Britain. The reasons for this singular state of independence were the diplomatic skill of Thai leaders, Thai willingness to Westernize the government, and the desire of Britain and France to let Thailand remain interposed as a neutral buffer zone between their respective armies in Burma and Indochina.

The current king, Bhumibol Adulyadej, born in the United States and educated in Switzerland, is highly respected as head of state. The king is also the nominal head of the armed forces, and his support is critical to any Thai government. Despite Thailand's structures of democratic government, any administration that has not also received the approval of the military

(Photo credit United Nations/Prince)

Buddhism has been an integral part of the Thai culture. Six hundred years ago, Buddhist monks traveled from India and Ceylon (today Sri Lanka) and built their temples and monasteries throughout Thailand. These newly ordained monks are meditating in the courtyard of a temple in Bangkok.

elites, many of whom hold seats in the Senate, has not prevailed for long. The military has been a rightist force in Thai politics, resisting reforms from the left that might have produced a stronger labor union movement, more freedom of expression (many television and radio stations in Thailand are controlled directly by the military), and less economic distance between the social classes. Military involvement in government increased substantially during the 1960s and 1970s, when a Communist insurgency threatened the government from within and the Vietnam War destabilized the external environment.

Until the February 1991 coup, there had been signs that the military was slowly withdrawing from direct meddling in the government. This may have been because the necessity for a strong military appeared to have lessened with the end of the cold war. In late 1989, for example, the Thai government signed a peace agreement with the Communist Party of Malaya, which had been harassing villagers along the Thai border for more than 40 years. Despite these political/military improvements, Army Commander Suchinda Kraprayoon led a coup against the legally elected government in 1991 and, notwithstanding promises to the contrary, promptly had himself named prime minister. Immediately Thai citizens, tired of the constant instability in govern-

ment occasioned by military meddling, began staging mass demonstrations against Suchinda. The protesters were largely middle-class office workers who used their cellular telephones to communicate from one protest site to another. The demonstrations were the largest in 20 years, and the military responded with violence; nearly 50 people were killed and more than 600 were injured. The public outcry was such that Suchinda was forced to appear on television being lectured by the king; he subsequently resigned. An interim premier dismissed several top military commanders and removed military personnel from the many government departments over which they had come to preside. Elections followed in 1992, and Thailand returned to civilian rule, with the military's influence greatly diminished.

The events of this latest coup show that the increasingly educated and affluent citizens of Thailand wish their country to be a true democracy. Still, unlike some democratic governments that have one dominant political party and one or two smaller opposition parties, party politics in Thailand is characterized by diversity. Indeed, so many parties compete for power that no single party is able to govern without forming coalitions with others. Parties are often founded on the strength of a single charismatic leader rather than on a dis-

tinct political philosophy, a circumstance that makes the entire political setting rather volatile. The Communist Party remains banned. Campaigns to elect the 360-seat Parliament often turn violent; in the most recent election, 10 candidates were killed when their homes were bombed or sprayed with rifle fire, and nearly 50 gunmen-for-hire were arrested or killed by police, who were attempting to protect the candidates of the 11 political parties vying for office.

FOREIGN RELATIONS

Thailand is a member of the United Nations and of the Association of Southeast Asian Nations. Throughout most of its modern history, Thailand has maintained a pro-Western political position. During World War I, Thailand joined with the Allies; and during the Vietnam War, it allowed the United States to stage air attacks on North Vietnam from within its borders, and it served as a major rest and relaxation center for American soldiers. During World War II, Thailand briefly allied itself with Japan but made decided efforts after the war to reestablish its former Western ties.

Thailand's international positions have seemingly been motivated more by practical need than by ideology. During the co-

(UN/photo by Saw Lwin)

Rice is Thailand's most important export and utilizes a majority of the agricultural work force. Today the government is attempting to diversify this reliance on rice, encouraging farmers to grow a wider variety of crops that are not so dependent on world markets and the weather.

Possible horticulture in Thailand 10,000 B.C.	Migrants from China move into what is now Thailand 200 B.C.	The formal beginning of Thailand as a nation A.D. 1200s	King Sukhothai creates the Thai alphabet 1279–1299	Foreigners are expelled from Thailand 1688	Long-time rival Burma attacks Thailand 1760s

lonial era, Thailand linked itself with Britain because it needed to offset the influence of France; during World War II, it joined with Japan in an apparent effort to prevent its country from being devastated by Japanese troops; during the Vietnam War, it supported the United States because the United States seemed to offer Thailand its only hope of not being directly engaged in military conflict in the region.

Thailand now seems to be tilting away from its close ties with the United States and toward a closer relationship with Japan. In the late 1980s, disputes with the United States over import tariffs and international copyright matters cooled the prior warm relationship (the United States has accused Thailand of allowing the manufacture of counterfeit brand-name watches, clothes, computer software, and many other items, including medicines). Moreover, Thailand found in Japan a more ready, willing, and cooperative economic partner than the United States.

During the cold war and especially during the Vietnam War era, the Thai military strenuously resisted the growth of Communist ideology inside Thailand, and the Thai government refused to engage in normal diplomatic relations with the Communist regimes on its borders. Because of military pressure, elected officials refrained from advocating improved relations with the Communist governments. However, in 1988 Prime Minister Prem Tinslanond, a former general in the army who had been in control of the government for 8 years, stepped down from office, and opposition to normalization of relations seemed to mellow. The subsequent prime minister, Chatichai Choonhavan, who was ousted in the 1991 military coup, invited Cambodian leader Hun Sen to visit Thailand; he also made overtures to Vietnam and Laos. Chatichai's goal was to open the way for trade in the region by helping to settle the agonizing Cambodian conflict. He also hoped to bring stability to the region so that the huge refugee camps in Thailand,

the largest in the world, could be dismantled and the refugees repatriated. Managing regional relations will continue to be difficult: Thailand fought a brief border war with Communist Laos in 1988, and refugees from the civil wars in adjacent Cambodia and Myanmar continue to strain relations.

Part of the thrust behind Thailand's diplomatic initiatives is the changing needs of its economy. For decades Thailand saw itself as an agricultural country; indeed, nearly two thirds of the work force remain in agriculture today, with rice as the primary commodity. Rice is Thailand's single most important export and a major source of government revenue. Every morning Thai families sit down on the floor of their homes around bowls of hot and spicy *tom yam goong* soup and a large bowl of rice; holidays and festivals are scheduled to coincide with the various stages of planting and harvesting rice; and, in rural areas, students are dismissed at harvest time so that all members of a family can help in the fields. So central is rice to the diet and the economy of the country that the Thai verb equivalent of "to eat," translated literally, means "to eat rice." Thailand is the fifth-largest exporter of rice in the world.

Unfortunately, Thailand's dependence on rice subjects its economy to the cyclical fluctuations of weather (sometimes the monsoons bring too little moisture) and market demand. Thus, in recent years the government has invested millions of dollars in economic diversification. Not only have farmers been encouraged to grow a wider variety of crops, but tin, lumber, and offshore oil and gas production have also been promoted. Foreign investment in export-oriented manufacturing has been warmly welcomed. Japan in particular benefits from trading with Thailand in food and other commodities, and it sees Thailand as one of the more promising places to relocate smokestack industries. For its part, Thailand seems to prefer Japanese investment over that from the United States, because the Japanese seem more willing to engage in joint ventures and to show patience while enterprises become profitable. Indeed, economic ties with Japan are very strong. For instance, Japan is the largest single investor in Thailand and accounts for 41 percent of foreign direct in-

(Photo credit United Nations/J. M. Micaud)

Industrialization in Thailand has drawn many people to the cities. The resultant overcrowding and strains on job availability have forced people into homelessness. These Thais are living under an elevated highway near Klong Toey Port in Bangkok.

King Rama I ascends the throne, beginning a nine-generation dynasty 1782	King Mongkut builds the first road in Thailand 1868	Coup; constitutional monarchy 1932	The country's name is changed from Siam to Thailand 1939	Thailand joins Japan and declares war on the United States and Britain 1942	Thailand resumes its historical pro-Western stance 1946	Communist insurgency threatens Thailand's stability 1960s–1970s	Student protests usher in democratic reforms 1973

1990s

A military coup attempt is thwarted

Chatichai Choonhavan replaces a former army general as prime minister

Chatichai is deposed in a military coup; mass demonstrations force a return to civilian rule

vestment (Taiwan, Hong Kong, and the United States each account for about 10 percent). Thirty percent of Thai imports come from Japan, and about 16 percent of its exports go to Japan.

Thailand's shift to an export-oriented economy is paying off. The growth rate of Thailand's gross domestic product has averaged about 10 percent a year—one of the highest in the world, and as high, or higher than, all the newly industrializing countries of Asia (Hong Kong, South Korea, Singapore, Taiwan, and China). Furthermore, unlike the Philippines and Indonesia, Thailand has been able to achieve this incredible growth without high inflation; unemployment is about 6 percent.

SOCIAL PROBLEMS

Industrialization in Thailand, as everywhere, draws people to the cities. It is estimated that, by the year 2000, Bangkok will have a population of 10.7 million, making it one of the largest cities in the world. Numerous problems, particularly traffic congestion and overcrowding, already complicate life for Bangkok residents. An international airport that opened in 1987 near Bangkok was so overcrowded just 4 years later that a new one had to be planned, and new harbors had to be constructed south of the city to alleviate congestion in the main port. Demographic projections indicate that there will be a decline in population growth in the future as the birth rate drops and the average Thai household shrinks from the 6 people it was in 1970 to only 3 people by 2015. This will alter the social structure of urban families, especially as increased life expectancy adds older people to the population and forces the country to provide more services for the elderly. Today, however, a majority of Thai people still make their living on farms, where they grow rice, rubber, and corn, or tend chickens and cattle, including the ever-present water buffalo. Thus, it is in the countryside (or "upcountry," as everywhere but Bangkok is called in Thailand) that the traditional culture of Thailand may be found. There one still finds villages of typically fewer than 1,000 inhabitants, with houses built on wooden stilts alongside a canal or around a Buddhist monastery. One also finds, however, unsanitary conditions, higher rates of illiteracy, and lack of access to potable water. Of increasing concern is rapid deforestation, as Thailand's growing population continues to use wood as its primary fuel for cooking and heat. The provision of social services does not meet demand even in the cities, but rural residents are particularly deprived.

Culturally, Thai people are known for their willingness to tolerate (although not necessarily to assimilate) diverse lifestyles and opinions. Buddhist monks, who shave their heads and vow celibacy, do not find it incongruous to beg for rice in districts of Bangkok known for prostitution and wild nightlife. And worshippers seldom object when a noisy, congested highway is built alongside the serenity of an ancient Buddhist temple (although the mammoth scale of the proposed $3.2 billion, 4-level road and railway system in the city and its likely effect on cultural and religious sites when it is completed in the late 1990s prompted the Thai cabinet to order the construction underground; the cabinet had to recant, however, when the Hong Kong firm designing the project announced that it was technically impossible to build it underground).

This relative openness has mitigated ethnic conflict among Thailand's numerous minority groups. The Chinese, for instance, who are often disliked in other Asian countries because of their dominance of the business sectors, are able to live with little or no discrimination in Thailand; indeed, they constitute the backbone of Thailand's new industrial thrust. About 84 percent of the population of 58.7 million are ethnic Thai, 12 percent are Chinese, and 4 percent (mostly in the south) are Malay Muslims and other groups—tribal peoples and Cambodian and Vietnamese refugees.

Ninety-four percent of Thailand's people are Buddhists. Prayers to Buddha (and to the king) are offered in the public schools every day. Many children receive part of their education in Buddhist monasteries, and most males will live the life of a monk for at least a few weeks or months in their youth. Thai Buddhist monks are extremely sensitive to any comments or behavior that seems to insult or denigrate the Buddhist faith.

DEVELOPMENT

Two thirds of Thailand's work force are small-plot or tenant farmers, but the government has energetically promoted economic diversification. Despite high taxes, Thailand has a reputation as a good place for foreign investment. Electronics and other high-tech industries from Japan, the United States, and other countries have been very successful in Thailand.

FREEDOM

Since 1932, when the absolute monarchy was abolished, Thailand has endured numerous military coups and countercoups, most recently in February 1991. Combined with the threat of Communist insurgencies, these have resulted in numerous declarations of martial law, press censorship, and suspensions of civil liberties.

HEALTH/WELFARE

About 2,000 young men and women out of every 100,000 inhabitants attend college (as compared to only 200 per 100,000 in Vietnam). Thailand has devoted substantial sums to the care of refugees from Cambodia and Vietnam. The rate of nonimmigrant population growth has dropped substantially since World War II. AIDS has emerged as a significant problem in Thailand.

ACHIEVEMENTS

Thailand is the only Southeast Asian nation never to have been colonized by a Western power. It was also able to remain detached from direct involvement in the Vietnam War. Unique among Asian cultures, Thailand has a large number of women in business and other professions. Thai dancing is world-famous for its intricacy.

Vietnam (Socialist Republic of Vietnam)

GEOGRAPHY

Area in Square Kilometers (Miles):
329,560 (121,278) (slightly larger
than New Mexico)
Capital (Population): Hanoi (3,100,000)
Climate: tropical

PEOPLE

Population

Total: 71,788,000
Annual Growth Rate: 1.85%
Rural/Urban Population Ratio: 80/20
Ethnic Makeup: 90% Vietnamese; 3%
Chinese; 7% Muong, Thai, Meo, and
other mountain tribes
Major Languages: Vietnamese;
French; Chinese; English; Khmer;
tribal languages

Health

Life Expectancy at Birth: 63 years
(male); 67 years (female)
Infant Mortality Rate (Ratio):
46.4/1,000
Average Caloric Intake: 91% of FAO
minimum
Physicians Available (Ratio): 1/3,096

Religions

Buddhists, Confucians, and Taoists
most numerous; Roman Catholics;
Cao Dai; animists; Muslims; Protestants

Education

Adult Literacy Rate: 88%

COMMUNICATION

Telephones: 179,100
Newspapers: 4 dailies

TRANSPORTATION

Highways—Kilometers (Miles):
approximately 85,000 (52,700)
Railroads—Kilometers (Miles): 3,059
(1,896)
Usable Airfields: 100

VU QUANG: A WILDLIFE PARADISE

Located on 65 acres of forested land near Laos in what was formerly North
Vietnam is the Vu Quang Nature Reserve. Largely unspoiled despite decades
of warfare, the area is proving to be a veritable paradise for natural scientists. Recently, as reported by Associated Press correspondent David Bris-
coe, a team of biologists from the World Wildlife Fund and the Vietnamese
government found 62 kinds of known fish as well as 1 new tortoise species,
2 new species of birds, and a mammal with goatlike horns. The area is also
home to tigers, leopards, and elephants. To protect the park from development (Vu Quang is only a 10-hour drive from Hanoi), the Ministry of Forestry
has banned logging in the area and hopes to expand the boundaries of the
park. Laotian officials have also been asked to declare adjacent land inside
Laos a nature reserve as well. Unique in Southeast Asia, the reserve may add
significant new chapters to humankind's knowledge of the animal kingdom.

GOVERNMENT

Type: communist state
Independence Date: September 2,
1945
Head of State/Government: President
Le Duc Anh; Prime Minister Vo Van
Kiet; head of Communist Party: Do
Muoi
Political Parties: Vietnam
Communist Party
Suffrage: universal at 18

MILITARY

Number of Armed Forces: 940,000
(reductions have been announced)
*Military Expenditures (% of Central
Government Expenditures):* 19.4%
Current Hostilities: boundary
disputes with Cambodia; sporadic
border clashes with China; other
boundary disputes with China,
Malaysia, Taiwan, and the Philippines

ECONOMY

Currency ($ U.S. Equivalent): 10,800
new dong = $1
Per Capita Income/GNP: $230/$16.0
billion
Inflation Rate: 15%–20%
Natural Resources: phosphates; coal;
manganese; bauxite; chromate;
offshore oil deposits; forests
Agriculture: rice; corn; potatoes;
rubber; soybeans; coffee; tea; animal
products; fish
Industry: food processing; textiles;
machine building; mining; cement;
chemical fertilizer; glass; tires; oil;
fishing

FOREIGN TRADE

Exports: $2.3 billion
Imports: $1.9 billion

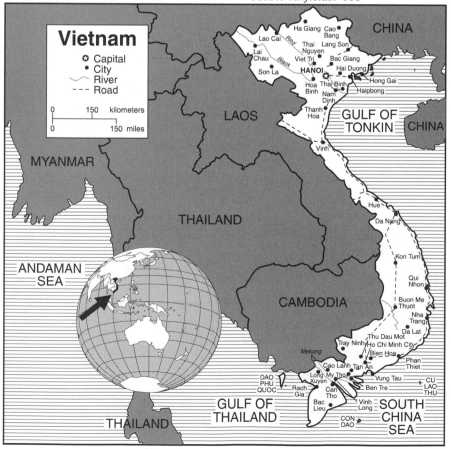

FOREIGNERS IN VIETNAM

Foreign powers have tried to control Vietnam for 2,000 years. Most of that time it has been the Chinese who have had their eye on control—specifically of the food and timber resources of the Red River Valley in northern Vietnam.

Most of the northern Vietnamese were ethnically Chinese themselves, but over the years they had forged a separate identity for themselves and had come to resent Chinese rule. Vietnam was conquered by China as early as 214 B.C. and again in 111 B.C., when the Han Chinese emperor Wu Ti established firm control. For about 1,000 years (until A.D. 939, and sporadically thereafter by the Mongols and other Chinese), the Chinese so thoroughly dominated the region that the Vietnamese people spoke and wrote in Chinese, built their homes like those of the Chinese, and organized their society according to Confucian values. In fact, Vietnam (*viet* means "people" and *nam* is Chinese for "south") is distinct among Southeast Asian nations because it is the only one whose early culture—in the north, at least—was influenced more by China than by India.

The Chinese did not, however, directly control all of what constitutes modern Vietnam. Until the late 1400s, the southern half of the country was a separate kingdom known as Champa and was inhabited by people called Chams, who originally came from Indonesia. For a time Champa was annexed by the north. However, between the northern region called Tonkin and the southern Chams-dominated region was a narrow strip of land occupied by Annamese peoples (a mixture of Chinese, Indonesian, and Indian ethnic groups), who eventually overthrew the Cham rulers and came to dominate the entire southern half of the country. In the 1500s the northern Tonkin region and the southern Annamese region were ruled separately by two Vietnamese family dynasties. In the 1700s military generals took power, unifying the two regions and attempting to annex or control parts of Cambodia and Laos as well.

In 1787 Nguyen-Anh, a general with imperial ambitions, signed a military aid treaty with France. The French had already established Roman Catholic missions in the south, were providing mercenary soldiers for the Vietnamese generals, and were interested in opening up trade along the Red River. The Vietnamese eventually came to resent the increasingly active French involvement in their internal affairs and took steps to curtail French influence. The French, however, impressed by the resources of the Red River Valley in the north and the Mekong River Delta in the south, were in no mood to pull out.

War broke out in 1858, and by 1863 the French had won control of many parts of the country, particularly in the south around the city of Saigon. Between 1884 and 1893, France solidified its gains in Southeast Asia by taking the northern city of Hanoi and the surrounding Tonkin region and by putting Cambodia, Laos, and Vietnam under one administrative unit, which it called *Indochina.*

Ruling Indochina was not easy for the French. For one thing, the region was comprised of hundreds of different ethnic groups, many of whom had been traditional enemies long before the French arrived. Within the borders of Vietnam proper lived Thais, Laotians, Khmers, northern and southern Vietnamese, and mountain peoples whom the French called Montagnards. Most of the people could not read or write—and those who could wrote in Chinese, because the Vietnamese language did not have a writing system until the French created it. Most people were Buddhists and Taoists, but many also followed animist beliefs.

In addition to the social complexity, the French had to contend with a rugged and inhospitable land filled with high mountains and plateaus as well as lowland swamps kept damp by yearly monsoon rains. The French were eager to obtain the abundant rice, rubber, tea, coffee and minerals of Vietnam but found that transporting these commodities to the coast for shipping was extremely difficult.

VIETNAMESE RESISTANCE

France's biggest problem, however, was local resistance. Anti-French sentiment began to solidify in the 1920s; by the 1930s Vietnamese youth were beginning to engage in open resistance. Prominent among these was Nguyen ai Quoc, who founded the Indochinese Communist Party in 1930 as a way of encouraging the Vietnamese people to overthrow the French. He is better known to the world today as Ho Chi Minh, meaning "He Who Shines."

Probably none of the resisters would have succeeded in evicting the French had it not been for Adolf Hitler's overrunning of France in 1940 and Japan's subsequent military occupation of Vietnam. These events convinced many Vietnamese that French power was no longer a threat to independence; the French remained nominally in control of Vietnam, but everyone knew that the Japanese had the real power. In 1941, Ho Chi Minh, having been trained in China by Maoist leaders, organized the League for the Independence of Vietnam, or Viet Minh. Upon the defeat of Japan, in 1945, the Viet Minh assumed that they would take control of the government. France, however, insisted on reestablishing a French government. Within a year the French and the Viet Minh were engaged in intense warfare, which lasted for 8 years.

The Viet Minh initially fought the French with weapons supplied by the United States when that country was helping local peoples to resist the Japanese. Communist China later became the main supplier of assistance to the Viet Minh. This development convinced U.S. leaders that Vietnam under the Viet Minh would very likely become another Communist state. To prevent this occurrence, U.S. president Harry S. Truman decided to back France's efforts to recontrol Indochina (although the United States had originally opposed France's desire to regain its colonial holdings). In 1950 the United States gave $10 million in military aid to the French, an act that began a long, costly, and painful U.S. involvement in Vietnam.

In 1954 the French lost a major battle in the north of Vietnam, at Din Bien Phu, after which they agreed to a settlement with the Viet Minh. The country was to be temporarily divided at the 17th Parallel (a latitude above which the Communist Viet Minh held sway and below which non-Communist Vietnamese had the upper hand), and country-wide elections were to be held in 1956. The elections were never held, however; and under Ho Chi Minh, Hanoi became the capital of North Vietnam, while Ngo Dinh Diem became president of South Vietnam, with its capital in Saigon.

THE UNITED STATES ENTERS THE WAR

Ho Chi Minh viewed the United States as yet another foreign power trying to control the Vietnamese people through its backing of the government in the South. The United States, concerned about the continuing attacks on the south by northern Communists and by southern Communist sympathizers called *Viet Cong,* increased funding and sent military advisers to help prop up the increasingly fragile southern government. By 1963 President John F. Kennedy had sent 12,000 military "advisers" to Vietnam. In 1964 an American destroyer ship was attacked in the Gulf of Tonkin by North Vietnam. The U.S. Congress responded by giving then-president Lyndon Johnson a free hand in ordering U.S. military action against the north; be-

China begins 1,000 years of control or influence over the northern part of Vietnam 214 B.C.	Northern and southern Vietnam are ruled separately by two Vietnamese families A.D. 1500s	Military generals overthrow the ruling families and unite the country 1700s	General Nguyen-Anh signs a military aid treaty with France 1787	After 5 years of war, France acquires its first holdings in Vietnam 1863	France establishes the colony of Indochina 1893	Ho Chi Minh founds the Indochinese Communist Party 1930	The Japanese control Vietnam 1940s	France attempts to regain control Post-1945

fore this time U.S. troops had not been involved in direct combat.

By 1969 some 542,000 American soldiers and nearly 66,000 soldiers from 40 other countries were in battle against North Vietnamese and Viet Cong troops. Despite unprecedented levels of bombing and use of sophisticated electronic weaponry, U.S. and South Vietnamese forces continued to lose ground to the Communists, who used guerrilla tactics and built their successes on latent antiforeign sentiment among the masses as well as extensive Soviet military aid. At the height of the war, as many as 300 U.S. soldiers were being killed per week.

Watching the war on the evening television news, many Americans began to withdraw emotional support. Anti-Vietnam rallies became a daily occurrence on American university campuses, and many people began finding ways to protest U.S. involvement: dodging the draft by fleeing to Canada, burning down ROTC buildings, and publicly challenging the U.S. government to withdraw. President Richard Nixon had once declared that he was not going to be the first president to lose a war, but after his expansion of the bombing into Cambodia to destroy Communist supply lines, and after significant battlefield losses, domestic resistance became so great that an American withdrawal seemed inevitable. The U.S. attempt to Vietnamize the war by training South Vietnamese troops and supplying them with advanced weapons did little to change South Vietnam's sense of having been sold out by the Americans.

Secretary of State Henry Kissinger negotiated a cease-fire settlement with the North in 1973, but most people believed that as soon as the Americans left, the North would resume fighting and would probably take control of the entire country. This indeed happened, and in April 1975, under imminent attack by victorious North Vietnamese soldiers, the last Americans lifted off in helicopters from the grounds of the U.S. Embassy in Saigon, the South Vietnamese government surrendered, and South Vietnam ceased to exist.

The war wreaked devastation on Vietnam. It has been estimated that nearly 2 million people were killed during just the American phase of the war; another 2.5 million were killed during the French era.

Four-and-a-half million people were wounded, and nearly 9 million lost their homes. U.S. casualties included 58,000 soldiers killed and 300,000 wounded.

A CULTURE, NOT JUST A BATTLEFIELD

Because of the Vietnam War, many people think of Vietnam as if it were just a battlefield. But Vietnam is much more than that. It is a rich culture made up of peoples representing diverse aspects of Asian life. In good times Vietnam's dinner tables are supplied with dozens of varieties of fish and the ever-present bowl of rice. Sugarcane and bananas are also favorites. Because about 80 percent of the people live in the countryside, the population as a whole possesses a living library of practical know-how about farming, livestock raising, fishing, and home manufacture. Today only about 214 out of every 100,000 Vietnamese people attend college, but most children attend elementary school and 88 percent of the adult population can read and write.

Literacy was not always so high; much of the credit is due the Communist government, which, for political education reasons, has promoted schooling throughout the country. Another thing that the government has done, of course, is to unify the northern and southern halves of the country. This has not been an easy task, for upon the division of the country in 1954, the North followed a socialist route of economic development, while in the South, capitalism became the norm.

Religious belief in Vietnam is an eclectic affair and reflects the history of the nation; on top of a Confucian and Taoist foundation, created during the centuries of Chinese rule, rests Buddhism (a modern version of which is called Hoa Hao and claims 1 million believers); French Catholicism, which claims about 15 percent of the population; and a syncretist faith called Cao Dai, which claims about 2 million followers. Cao Dai models itself after Catholicism in terms of hierarchy and religious architecture, but it differs in that it accepts many gods—Jesus, Buddha, Mohammed, Lao-Tse, and others—as part of its pantheon. Many Vietnamese pray to their ancestors and ask for blessings at small shrines located inside their homes.

Animism, the worship of spirits believed to live in nature, is also practiced by many of the Montagnards. (About 400 Christianized Montagnards, incidentally, fought the Communists continually since 1975 and have only recently taken refuge outside of Vietnam.)

Freedom of religious worship has been permitted, and church organizational hierarchies have not been declared illegal. In fact, the government, sensing the need to solicit the support of believers (especially the Catholics), has been careful in its treatment of religions and has even avoided collectivizing farms in areas known to have large numbers of the faithful.

THE ECONOMY

When the Communists won the war in 1975 and brought the capitalist South under its jurisdiction, the United States imposed an economic embargo on Vietnam, which most other nations honored and which remained in effect for 19 years, until President Bill Clinton ended it in 1994. As a consequence of the embargo, war damage, and the continuing military involvement of Vietnam in the Cambodian war and against the Chinese along their mutual border, the first decade after the war saw the entire nation fall into a severe economic slump. Whereas Vietnam had once been an exporter of rice, it now had to import rice from abroad. Inflation raged at 250 percent a year, and the government was hard-pressed to cover its debts. Many South Vietnamese were, of course, opposed to Communist rule and attempted to flee on boats—but, contrary to popular opinion, most refugees left Vietnam because they could not get enough to eat, not because they were being persecuted.

Beginning in the mid-1980s, the Vietnamese government began to liberalize the economy. Under a restructuring plan called *doi moi* (similar in meaning to Soviet *perestroika*), the government began to introduce elements of free enterprise into the economy. Moreover, despite the Communist victory, the South remained largely capitalist; today, with wages lower than almost every other country in Asia (about $1 a day; doctors earn about $22 per month and teachers make $15), an infrastructure built by France and the United States, and laborers who can speak at least

| The United States begins to aid France to contain the spread of communism **1950s** | Geneva agreements end 8 years of warfare with the French; Vietnam is divided into North and South **1954** | South Vietnam's regime is overthrown by a military coup **1961** | The United States begins bombing North Vietnam **1965** | Half a million U.S. troops are fighting in Vietnam **1969** | The United States withdraws its troops and signs a cease-fire **1973** | North Vietnamese troops capture Saigon and reunite the country; U.S. embargo begins **1975** | Vietnamese troops capture Cambodia; China invades Vietnam **1979** | Communist Vietnam begins liberalization of the economy **1980s** |

1990s

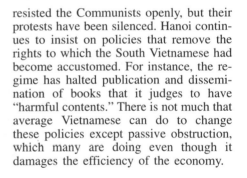

U.S. and Vietnamese officials begin meetings to resolve the Cambodian war

The U.S. economic embargo of Vietnam is lifted

some English or French, foreign nations are finding Vietnam a good place to invest funds. In 1991 alone, Australian, Japanese, French, and other companies spent $3 billion in Vietnam. After the embargo ended, firms poured into Vietnam to do business. By the end of 1994, more than 540 firms, especially from Singapore, Hong Kong, Japan, and France, were doing business in Vietnam, and some 70 other countries had expressed interest. The government's move toward privatization and capitalism, begun in 1986, was so successful that by the early 1990s, nearly 90 percent of the workforce was in the private sector, and loans from the World Bank, the Asian Development Bank, and the International Monetary Fund were flowing in to jumpstart national development.

Perhaps most significant is that the Vietnamese people themselves want to move ahead and put the decades of warfare behind them. Western travelers in Vietnam are treated warmly, and the Vietnamese government has cooperated with the U.S. government's demands for more information about missing U.S. soldiers. In 1994, after a 40-year absence, the United States opened up a diplomatic mission in Hanoi as a first step toward full diplomatic recognition. So eager are the Vietnamese to reestablish economic ties with the West that the Communist authorities have even offered to allow the U.S. Navy to lease its former port at Cam Ranh Bay (the offer has not yet been accepted). Diplomatic

bridge-building between the United States and Vietnam increased in 1990, when a desire to end the agony of the Cambodian conflict created opportunities for the two sides to talk together. Telecommunications were established in 1992, and in the same year, the United States gave $1 million in aid to assist handicapped Vietnamese war veterans.

HEARTS AND MINDS

As one might expect, resistance to the current Vietnamese government comes largely from the South Vietnamese, who, under both French and American tutelage, adopted Western values of capitalism and consumerism. Many South Vietnamese had feared that after the North's victory, South Vietnamese soldiers would be mercilessly killed by the victors; some were in fact killed, but many former government leaders and military officers were instead sent to "reeducation camps," where, combined with hard labor, they were taught the values of socialist thinking. Several hundred such internees remain incarcerated 2 decades after the end of the war. Many of the well-known leaders of the South fled the country when the Communists arrived and now are making new lives for themselves in the United States, Canada, Australia, and other Western countries. Those who have remained—for example, Vietnamese members of the Roman Catholic Church—have occasionally

resisted the Communists openly, but their protests have been silenced. Hanoi continues to insist on policies that remove the rights to which the South Vietnamese had become accustomed. For instance, the regime has halted publication and dissemination of books that it judges to have "harmful contents." There is not much that average Vietnamese can do to change these policies except passive obstruction, which many are doing even though it damages the efficiency of the economy.

DEVELOPMENT

Vietnam is again a major exporter of rice. It also produces cement, fertilizer, steel, and coal. Aid and loans from other Asian nations are helping with the construction of roads and other infrastructure, but the average worker still earns only $230 a year.

FREEDOM

Vietnam is nominally governed by an elected National Assembly. Real power, however, resides in the Communist Party and with those military leaders who helped defeat the U.S. and South Vietnamese armies. Civil rights, such as the right of free speech, are curtailed. Private property rights are limited.

HEALTH/WELFARE

Health care has been nationalized and the government operates a social security system, but the chronically stagnant economy has meant that few Vietnamese receive sufficient health care or have an adequate nutritional intake. The World Health Organization has been involved in disease-abatement programs since reunification of the country in 1975.

ACHIEVEMENTS

Vietnam provides free and compulsory schooling for all children, but the curricular content has been changed in an attempt to eliminate Western influences. New Economic Zones have been created in rural areas to try to lure people away from the major cities of Hanoi, Hue, and Ho Chi Minh City (formerly Saigon).

Articles from the World Press

Annotated Table of Contents for Articles

Topic Guide to Articles

TOPIC AREA	TREATED IN	TOPIC AREA	TREATED IN
Health and Welfare	11. Agricultural Policy from the Ground Up 12. Life in a Box 14. Cambodia: A Heritage of Violence 18. Lure of Chinese Cities Draws Runaway Children 25. Burma: Still the Generals 30. Social Values, Singapore Style	Political Development	1. The Coming Pacific Century? 2. What Is a Pacific Century?
History	1. The Coming Pacific Century? 2. What Is a Pacific Century? 3. Organizing the Rim 4. Protecting Asia from Itself 8. Japan's Asia Card 13. Destination: Down Under 15. Indochina: From Confrontation to Cooperation 20. Chinese Women Soldiers	Political Reform	1. The Coming Pacific Century? 2. What Is a Pacific Century? 9. Japan's Self-Reform 10. Japan's New Orientation
		Political Unrest	4. Protecting Asia from Itself 9. Japan's Self-Reform 10. Japan's New Orientation 14. Cambodia: A Heritage of Violence 19. The New Voices of Dissent 23. Indonesia Is Striving to Prosper 25. Burma: Still the Generals
Hong Kong	21. Hong Kong's New 1997	Politics	4. Protecting Asia from Itself 10. Japan's New Orientation 16. China, the Biggest Dragon of All? 17. China's Second Long March 19. The New Voices of Dissent 23. Indonesia Is Striving to Prosper 27. "Lure" North Korea 31. Taiwan Slowly Creeps Toward Nationhood
Human Rights	14. Cambodia: A Heritage of Violence 18. Lure of Chinese Cities Draws Runaway Children 23. Indonesia Is Striving to Prosper 25. Burma: Still the Generals		
Industrial Development	1. The Coming Pacific Century? 5. Economic Cooperation Zones 6. Building the New Asia 7. A Survey of Japan 15. Indochina: From Confrontation to Cooperation 16. China, the Biggest Dragon of All? 17. China's Second Long March 22. Indonesia on the Move	Social Reform	9. Japan's Self-Reform 12. Life in a Box 15. Indochina: From Confrontation to Cooperation 18. Lure of Chinese Cities Draws Runaway Children 29. The Politics of Economic Chaos 32. Private-Enterprise Communism
Khmer Rouge	14. Cambodia: A Heritage of Violence	Social Unrest	1. The Coming Pacific Century? 4. Protecting Asia from Itself 14. Cambodia: A Heritage of Violence 15. Indochina: From Confrontation to Cooperation 19. The New Voices of Dissent 25. Burma: Still the Generals 28. War in the Pacific
Korean Reunification	27. "Lure" North Korea		
Leisure Time	26. Unforgettable New Zealand		
Minorities	13. Destination: Down Under	Standard of Living	1. The Coming Pacific Century? 3. Organizing the Rim 6. Building the New Asia 12. Life in a Box 24. From Carpet Bombing to Capitalism 29. The Politics of Economic Chaos
Natives	13. Destination: Down Under 18. Lure of Chinese Cities Draws Runaway Children 29. The Politics of Economic Chaos		
Natural Resources	6. Building the New Asia 11. Agricultural Policy from the Ground Up 16. China, the Biggest Dragon of All? 17. China's Second Long March 24. From Carpet Bombing to Capitalism 26. Unforgettable New Zealand 28. War in the Pacific	Taiwan Independence	31. Taiwan Slowly Creeps Toward Nationhood
		Urban Life	12. Life in a Box 18. Lure of Chinese Cities Draws Runaway Children
Nuclear Power	10. Japan's New Orientation 27. "Lure" North Korea	Women	20. Chinese Women Soldiers

Article 1   *Current History,* January 1994

The Coming Pacific Century?

"Americans expect every society—including their own—to become more free and democratic in tandem with economic modernization. Seen from East Asia, the picture is more complex."

Takashi Inoguchi

Takashi Inoguchi is a professor of political science at the University of Tokyo's Institute of Oriental Culture. His most recent books are Japan's Foreign Policy in an Era of Global Change *(London: Pinter, 1993) and* Japan: The Governing of an Economic Superpower *(Tokyo: University of Tokyo Press, 1993).*

In the long process of European capitalism's development, economic dynamism diffused from northern Italy through northern France and the Rhineland to the Low Countries and southeastern England. After World War II, capitalist dynamism spread from the United States to Japan, beginning in the 1950s, and then to other parts of East Asia. It reached South Korea, Taiwan, Hong Kong, and Singapore in the years after the original oil crisis, and transformed them into the "four tigers." Malaysia, Thailand, Indonesia, and the Philippines were next, and dynamism has finally arrived in China, Vietnam, and Russia's Far East. In succession, after the years of American preeminence, Japan in the 1960s, the four tigers in the 1970s, the countries of the Association of Southeast Asian Nations (ASEAN, whose members include Brunei, Indonesia, Malaysia, the Philippines, Singapore, and Thailand) in the 1980s, and now China have led the world in annual economic growth. Japanese economists call it the flying-geese pattern of development.

East Asia has come to be regarded as a region to be reckoned with; a 1993 World Bank report on its accomplishments is entitled *The East Asian Miracle*.[1] Increasingly, other regions are attempting to integrate with it, as evidenced by the high percentage of schoolchildren in Australia and the rest of Oceania who are learning Indonesian, Japanese, and Chinese. The countries of South Asia, for whom Japan is the largest provider of official development assistance, have been looking east to Japan and ASEAN rather than to the Middle East, eastern Africa, and western Europe, as before. The new countries of Central Asia have been seeking far-off friends, including Japan, along with the United States and Turkey.

Most important, the United States has come to believe it will benefit from closer integration with the Pacific, as its latest call for an enhanced Asian Pacific Economic Cooperation (APEC) conference indicates. Rather than competing with East Asia from outside, the United States seems to be moving in the direction of competing with it from within—integrating with it and gradually forming a Pacific free trade area that would essentially combine the present APEC zone and the North American Free Trade Area. As a matter of fact, Mexico was granted full membership in APEC, and Papua New Guinea and Chile observer status at the group's annual meeting in Seattle in November. Aside from these, half a dozen countries, including Vietnam, Russia, and Argentina, have expressed their desire to become observers and the European Community has asked APEC to allow it to take part in the group's discussions.[2] The world is jumping on the bandwagon of East Asian dynamism.

It seems now that the Uruguay Round of world trade talks under the auspices of the General Agreement on Tariffs and Trade will not be successfully concluded by the December 15, 1993, deadline and even if it is, GATT's usefulness as a vehicle for global free trade appears to have declined considerably in recent years. In contrast, the Asian Pacific Economic Cooperation conference's potential usefulness in that role is increasing. APEC, with a total population of 1.9 billion, has a 35 percent share of world trade. And direct investment as well as trade has been a major means of transmitting economic vigor throughout East Asia.

THE FLIP SIDE OF DYNAMISM

Yet dynamism is Janus-faced. It means both energy and uncertainty: an energy that can transform economies, and uncertainty and apprehension about what the results of the transformation will be. Rapid growth means that adjustments occur regularly in the economy, and may even be breathtaking. Capital, labor, and technology must always be ready to move in different directions so as not to bring about comparative disadvantage in the increasingly liberalizing global market; structural adjustments require, among other things, agility and flexibility, and if you are unable to change your relationship with the market you are bound to go down. Such adjustments sometimes leave workers jobless and firms bankrupt.

Rampant unemployment and business failures in times when it is difficult to find new positions or to set up new ventures can create social unrest and perhaps also lead to political turmoil.

If institutional and market infrastructures are relatively well developed, these kinds of problems are not likely so long as the economy keeps growing. But infrastructures in many East Asian countries are not sufficiently developed and economic dislocation could easily occur, even if only temporarily.

Furthermore, in much of East Asia political practices have been less than fully democratic. Many of the region's regimes have pointed to strong national economic performance to shore up their political legitimacy. But once per capita income in a country reaches a certain level, demands for a larger say in the political process tend to increase. Rapid growth creates or makes more self-assertive social groups such as urban youth, a middle class, peasants, or minorities—some of which often begin to call for more radical political democratization than the government is willing to allow. Hence the great need in East Asia to balance the disequilibrium continually created by rapid economic development.

A number of political disturbances in East Asia in the late 1980s and early 1990s are directly related to the unbalancing of society by rapid economic change: the pro-democracy demonstrations in Beijing's Tiananmen Square in 1989; the movement against Indonesia's annexation of East Timor; the four days of confrontations between citizens and troops in Bangkok in May 1992; and even the protests against Myanmar's military regime. These all led to the use of force by authorities and, except in the case of Thailand, to further government repression. On the positive side, in addition to the fall of the military government in Thailand, the democratization of the Philippines and South Korea took place mainly or partly because of popular protests.[3] But whether by moving toward or away from democracy, East Asian regimes seem to have ridden out the upheavals.

Janus-faced East Asia can be portrayed as an extremely prosperous and peaceful swath of the world; looking at Somalia, Bosnia and Herzegovina, Georgia, and Kashmir, one can easily be persuaded that East Asia is relatively tranquil, at least for the time being. Yet it could also be viewed as a dangerous and war-prone region over the longer term.

First, no region-wide security arrangements have been agreed on other than those with the United States, which are largely bilateral. And the United States has vacillated between pursuing supremacy in every major region of the world and focusing its domestic energies on enhancing economic competitiveness. Neither aggressive proposing and disposing nor populist-backed isolationism seems to be welcome in East Asia. Meanwhile, American

policy on North Korea, which makes keeping the global nuclear Non-Proliferation Treaty regime intact a priority seems, inadvertently, to encourage Japan and (to a lesser degree) South Korea to go nuclear—somewhat like the way American insistence on dealing almost exclusively with Russia on the subject of nuclear nonproliferation in the Commonwealth of Independent States encourages Ukraine to hold onto its nuclear weapons.

Developmental momentum alone could create an alarmingly large military establishment in East Asia once anxiety and suspicion come to prevail in the general uncertainty. The hostility the West directed toward China for a couple of years after the Tiananmen Square massacre has led China to rely more on its military power. With the Chinese economy's annual growth rate exceeding 10 percent, adjacent countries cannot help regarding the military buildup in China with some apprehension, especially when the emphasis on long-range air and naval capabilities is perfectly clear.

Another reason for regarding the region as a possible trouble spot is that East Asian states have traditionally been intensely nationalistic toward each other as well as when facing outsiders. Long memories prevent the Japanese and the Russians, who have fought several wars against each other, from coming to terms. The Khmers maintain their vigilance against both the Vietnamese and the Thais. Most Pacific Asians hold Japan's history against it and harbor ambivalent feelings toward Americans. A sense of shared interests and hence community has been much slower to develop than the mutual desire to keep up developmental momentum and maintain the global free trade regime—which in some regions would have overridden all other hindrances much earlier.

JAPAN'S STARRING ROLE

As other East Asian countries ride the bandwagon of regional dynamism while trying to balance the forces tending to unsettle them, Japan's role has been to channel economic energy while shoring up regional stability. Of course Japan is not the only country to make such efforts, but it has been the most consistent and effective in carrying out these two tasks. Japan's channeling of dynamism throughout East Asia has been largely through market forces; its ingenuity lies in the fact that while it is deferential to market forces, it does not hesitate to take advantage of them to add to the region's common stake as well as to satisfy its own national interests.

It is important to stress here, as Winston Lord, the United States assistant secretary of state for East Asian and Pacific affairs, did in the *Far Eastern Economic Review* of last November 11, that "It is the business community that is the driving force behind the region's growth and prosperity." But this does not hinder the Japanese government from helping business do better in East Asia. If an East Asian country receiving development assistance has low per capita national income and if its infrastructure is too primitive to begin building manufacturing bases, Japanese official development aid will employ more grant elements than loans. If income is sufficiently high and infrastructure steadily being enhanced, assistance will involve more loans than grants. Japan's philosophy of development is essentially one of self-reliance; hence Tokyo expects recipients to possess the self-discipline necessary to pay back such loans. Also, the Japanese model emphasizes infrastructure and manufacturing. This thinking has gradually come to be ingrained in Japanese demands and development planning, as well as trade and investment decisions.

But most important, it is market forces, through trade and investment, that help Japan channel dynamism to the rest of East Asia. Thanks to Japan's early industrialization after World War II, the country forged ahead of the remainder of the region in exporting products with greater value added—especially capital goods—thus encouraging the rest to move in the direction of manufacturing-based economies. Japan's exports of capital goods to East Asia caused it to register a chronic trade surplus with the countries of the region that did not export oil, such as South Korea. As wage levels in Japan rose, many Japanese firms based their manufacturing sites throughout East Asia; these constituted direct investments in the region's other countries. At the same time, exporting higher-value-added products—cars, machinery, and electronic products—to the United States meant Japan had chronic trade surpluses there also. To cope with a protectionist surge in the United States as well as wage hikes in Japan, many Japanese businesses invested in America, which has helped channel dynamism to North America as well. Now, with the deep recession in Japan, coupled with the further appreciation of the yen against the dollar, many Japanese manufacturers have located the bulk of their manufacturing and even research and development facilities in East Asia, thus fueling economic growth in countries such as Thailand, Malaysia, and, most recently, China. By 1991 Japan's trade with East Asia surpassed that with North America, and last year's trade surplus with East Asia was likely to top the surplus with North America. This creates simmering resentment against Japan in East Asia, but the overall benefits of riding the bandwagon seem to alleviate or at least mask it.

Transmitting dynamism has its negative consequences. One of these is the growing social and political instability mentioned earlier. The Japanese government has discreetly and yet often effectively helped keep East Asian countries from exploding during particularly rough periods—for example, China after Tiananmen Square. Japan joined its fellow industrial nations in the Group of

Seven in imposing economic sanctions against China in 1989. But sanctions dried up the foreign loans that China had heavily relied on for years, and this weakened the central government and further unsettled the country. Since it was in the best interests of the seven not to destabilize China excessively for too long, Japan persuaded them to lift sanctions in 1991.

When Indonesia suppressed East Timor's independence movement in 1991—killing of as many as 200 protesters by troops—Japan was among the countries that convinced the Indonesian government to release basic information on the suppression and to set up an international forum to discuss the issue of human rights. Needless to say, Tokyo has been criticized, especially in the West, for being too soft on China and Indonesia, even at the expense of its own reputation. But the government seems to believe in change from within more than change by outside intervention. It also places supreme emphasis on regional stability.

More directly furthering stability—though its role here has often been overlooked—Japan has actively aided local firms and governments in training their managers and employees and their bureaucrats. Programs have ranged from setting up a joint cafeteria for workers and managers to skill retooling through a dose of the government models on taxes, banking, budgeting, and planning.

THREE ENDS MAKE A BEGINNING

Whether or not such efforts in potentially contradictory directions—keeping the bandwagon rolling while balancing destabilizing forces, and simultaneously channeling dynamism and shoring up stability—bear fruit can be examined from another angle: setting East Asia in a global context.

As the new millennium approaches, observers are discussing a number of "ends" that might characterize the changing world order. I will use three of these—the end of the cold war, "the end of geography," and "the end of history"—to characterize the transformation that has been penetrating the entire world, and East Asia in particular.[4] The three are usually seen as triumphs: respectively, the victory of the United States over the Soviet Union, the victory of international liberal capitalism, and the victory of liberal democracy. But I view each of them in a different light—one that I believe more accurately captures the dialectics of world order at the century's close.

I see the end of the cold war as a contradiction in international security between current United States military supremacy and America's perception of its inescapable technological and economic decline. By the end of geography I mean the contradiction in the world economy between the globalizing forces of economic activities today and self-encapsulating, inward-looking forces. And by the end of history I mean the contradiction in societies between the liberalizing and the regulating tendencies of political economy.

In other words, the end of the cold war denotes an extremely worrisome situation in which the United States vacillates between a desire for primacy and supremacy on the one hand and isolationism and passivity on the other. The end of geography denotes something no less troubling about competition between economic liberalism and protectionism and between globalism and regionalism. And the end of history has spawned unsettling questions about how societies are organized now that the more than century-long ideological struggle between capitalism and communism and between liberalism and ideological authoritarianism has "ended."

East Asia has been deeply affected by each of these, albeit not yet visibly. The cold war's end has left East Asian states apprehensive about the future of regional security. The region's development is bound to accelerate military buildups in its countries over the longer term, since gross national product and military expenditures tend to go hand in hand. Yet there are no multilateral security arrangements governing East Asia; as previously mentioned, what the region has is largely United States–led bilateral arrangements. The United States, compromising between clashing groups in society, seems to swing between activism in the world and isolationism. The United States plays a leading and sometimes hegemonic role in instituting such arrangements and yet in carrying them out has to mobilize cooperation and compliance from other countries when it itself cannot guarantee an equal return.

East Asian countries, however, seem unable to build their own multilateral security arrangements, in part because of rivalry and mutual suspicion. Looked at from a slightly different angle, the United States role in East Asia has increased in the short term. Only America can restrain the region's steady military buildup, yet America's role, most agree, will shrink over the longer run. East Asian countries endeavor to become self-reliant in the face of threatening military buildups by others and at the same time to construct regional security arrangements; ironically, United States efforts to retain the American military presence in the area and to constrict regional security arrangements tend to undermine East Asian initiatives toward such goals. Grave issues like North Korea's nuclear program and China's rise as a military power must not be handled by the United States alone.

Of the three recent fundamental changes in the world, "the end of geography" has in East Asia had the most profound and perhaps the most long-lasting effects. The momentum in development and the way the region has been growing propels East Asia to seek ever-expanding access to markets around the globe. Given its enormous population, the strong push for development, and the need for energy and food from other regions, East Asia has been forced in a sense to chalk up manufacturing successes in order to export successful manufactures, earn hard currency, and import petroleum products, foodstuffs, and other key commodities for such manufacturing. Needless to say, this is not the only method for acquiring wealth, but it has happened to be the most popular one in East Asia. Thus the more momentum development gains in East Asia, the more likely it is that Europe, North America, or other regions will resort further to protectionism and regionalism.

The efforts under the Maastricht Treaty on European union and the proposed North American Free Trade Agreement (NAFTA) to establish comprehensive systems covering all economic endeavors seem to have lost the drive and enthusiasm of past years. Although they represent the rules for further market liberalization, they are tinged with the colors and flavors of regionalism and protectionism. Lack of progress toward further liberalization of markets could mean different arrangements between the European Community and North America. It seems to this author that the EC would be more likely to slide into regionalism and protectionism of a more malign kind if liberalization lags, and that NAFTA would be less likely to do so if this were the case. Western Europe has not developed its relationship with East Asia as assiduously as North America, and the areas adjacent to it—central and eastern Europe, the Middle East, Africa—have not yet shown the developmental vigor East Asia has. North America has been more varied internally as to growth momentum, but Mexico and some other Latin American economies will register growth powerful enough to lift the continent, especially if they are more closely tied into North American and East Asian economies. Thus protectionism and regionalism would make less sense for North America than they might seem to make for the countries of western Europe.

At any rate, East Asia's dilemma is real. The more single-mindedly it pursues its development strategy, the more trouble it will face down the road when western Europe and North America combined still represent the largest market. Yet East Asia's resort to regionalism of one kind or another is widely believed to send the signal to North America and western Europe that they can go ahead with their scheme of organizing their trade and economic activities through more or less regionally defined norms. As long as East Asia seeks global free market access, and as long as it wants to leave differences in thinking within the region to market forces as well as to more gradually developed schemes of rule making, it does not believe itself fit to develop some codification of trade, investment, and international property that it would then present to the rest of the world as comprehensive. It looks as if the Asian Pacific Economic Cooperation conference will in time encompass both sides of the Pacific, and codification efforts will begin gradually if GATT negotiations continue to fail to further market liberalization as a comprehensive package.

The "end of history" has been no less difficult to handle. The disappearance of European communism does not mean communism is dead in East Asia. Yet the region's remaining Communist regimes—China, Vietnam, North Korea, and Laos—face immense problems coping with popular demands that are now brewing. These will be invigorated as development increases. In the extreme case of China, development has been let loose under the Communist dictatorship, and the resultant dynamism has had destabilizing effects. Since Chinese institutions are not geared to the market, corruption has become a substitute for market forces. In non-Communist East Asian countries as well, governments' suppression of freedom and democracy on the pretext of keeping communism at bay must be redressed steadily in the direction of accommodating more popular demands.

The end of history not only creates problems from within, but also invites difficulties from without. The most important of these are the critical voices raised on issues of human rights, democracy, military development, and the environment. The former two especially are a new kind of challenge to East Asian countries. Americans expect every society—including their own—to become more free and democratic in tandem with economic modernization. Seen from East Asia, the picture is more complex. This region of growing wealth and competitiveness invites jealousy and enmity from beyond its borders, especially from North America, which has been vexed by its own ambivalence about primacy and competitiveness. In the words of Singapore's senior minister, Lee Kwan Yew, if East Asia adopts American-style democracy, chaos will ensue and competitiveness will dip.

As East Asia works to channel its dynamism while maintaining stability, the addition of new forces for disequilibrium is hardly welcome. Two major categories are noteworthy: economic sanctions and humanitarian intervention. Sanctions have been imposed on the occasion of Vietnam's invasion of Cambodia, China's Tiananmen Square crackdown, and Myanmar's suppression of a fledgling democracy movement. Humanitarian intervention has been tried in Somalia, but not yet in any East Asian country. The very idea that foreign countries like the United States or international institutions like the United Nations can intervene on the pretext that demonstrators are being suppressed or human rights otherwise violated is perceived in some quarters of East Asia, where the more traditional notion of state sovereignty has held sway and where Western and Japanese coloni-

alism has hardened the meaning of state sovereignty, as radical or overly Machiavellian. Yet the trend in the world has been to reduce the state's monopoly on action in favor of business, minority groups, citizens movements, and other groups, some of them transnational, and East Asia cannot be the exception.

AMONG THE SCENARIOS

In January 1989 I predicted that a form of the Pax Americana was most likely for the region during the next quarter- to half-century, despite all the foreseeable difficulties. I further said that this might evolve into either bigemony (Japan and the United States acting jointly as global managers) or Pax Consortis (an issue-oriented coalition managing the world), depending on how science and technology, the neutralization of nuclear arsenals, and the region's historical legacy evolved.[5]

This forecast seems to have held up under the test of the global upheaval of 1989–1993. The military supremacy of the United States has been demonstrated by the demise of the Soviet Union and by the Persian Gulf War, in which the United States organized and led the winning coalition. The United States has been able to dilute or discourage the regionalist efforts of two other major parts of the world—namely the Maastricht Treaty and the East Asian Economic Council. And America has been able to bring up agendas of a new kind, turning on humanitarian intervention and human rights and democracy.

Yet recognition that the United States might damage itself severely in the longer run in the attempt to sustain its current strength leads some to propose scenarios for the future based on the direction of United States policy. These include "Back to the Future," which sees the world returning to the war-filled days of the first half of this century; "managed trade," which envisions the world with international economic liberalism substantially reduced; and "The Clash of Civilizations," which confesses to impotence in the face of self-assertion from outside the nostalgically imagined circle of Anglo-Saxon elite. All can be taken as symptoms of American anguish.[6]

Despite these and other inflated anxieties, the military supremacy of the United States, the disappearance of the tyranny of distance, and the predominance of capitalist democracy—albeit in a much more twisted form because of the contradictory forces working against it—seem to be the three major developments carrying us into the new millennium. The question is, how twisted has capitalist democracy become in the different societies that espouse it?

In international security, Euro-American effectiveness seems somewhat on the wane, as can be seen in its failure to prevent wars in the former Yugoslavia and the former Soviet Union from deepening. Whether the Pacific effort as vindicated by the success of the UN mission in Cambodia is the wave of the future is difficult to say. How the United States handles North Korea's determination to become a nuclear state could be a good indicator. In the world economy the possible failure of trade talks under GATT and the steady success of the Asian Pacific Economic Cooperation conference, coupled with the EC's further integration, currently somewhat stalled, would herald the bi-gemony scenario. As Bruce M. Russett points out in his *Grasping the Democratic Peace,* published this year, the way capitalist democracy is organized in each society seems to determine the degree of twisting that takes place. So long as capitalist democracy remains the wave of the future, the Pax Consortis is not ruled out. Democratic peace may not be a perpetually unfulfilled dream.

East Asia enters the new millennium powered by dynamism, the economic and political bases for its societies substantially enhanced, and closer links with North America steadily being forged. The coming century is more likely to be the Pacific Century than the Atlantic Century, let alone the century of the Indian Ocean or of the Eurasian landmass.

NOTES

1. World Bank, *The East Asian Miracle: Economic Growth and Public Policy* (New York: Oxford University Press, 1993). See also Tran Van Tho, *Sangyo hatten to takokuseki kigyo: Ajia Taiheiyo dainamizumu no jissho kenkyu* [Industrial development and multinational firms: A study of the Asian Pacific dynamism] (Tokyo: Toyo keizai shimposha, 1993).
2. "Goodbye GATT, Hello APEC," *Foreign Report* (London), October 28, 1993, pp. 1–2.
3. James William Morley, ed., *Driven by Growth: Political Change in the Asia-Pacific Region* (New York: M. E. Sharpe, 1993).
4. See Richard O'Brien, *Financial Integration: The End of Geography* (London: Pinter, 1992); and Francis Fukuyama, *The End of History and the Last Man* (New York: Basic Books, 1991). George Bush may be credited as the original author of the end of the cold war.
5. "Four Japanese Scenarios for the Future," *International Affairs,* vol. 65, no. 1 (Winter 1988–1989), pp. 15–28.
6. See John Mearsheimer, "Back to the Future," *International Security,* vol. 15, no. 1 (Summer 1990); Clyde V. Prestovitz, Jr., "Beyond Laissez-Faire," *Foreign Policy,* no. 87 (Spring 1992); and Samuel Huntington, "The Clash of Civilizations?" *Foreign Affairs,* vol. 72, no. 3 (Summer 1993).

Article 2

Current History, December 1994

What Is a Pacific Century—and How Will We Know When It Begins?

"The people of the Pacific Rim did not know they inhabited a bustling new sector of the world system until they were told—just as the 'Indians' did not know they were in 'West India' until Europeans informed them. 'Rim' is an American construct, an invention exactly like the steam engine, incorporating the region's peoples 'into a new inventory of the world'; 'Pacific' is itself a Euro-American name, measuring, delineating, and recognizing living space for the people who live there."

Bruce Cumings

Bruce Cumings is John Evans Professor of International History and Politics at Northwestern University, where he directs the Center for International and Comparative Studies. He has also taught at Swarthmore College, the University of Washington, and the University of Chicago. He is the author of The Origins of the Korean War, *two vols. (Princeton:*

Princeton University Press, 1981 and 1990), War and Television *(London: Verso, 1992), and the forthcoming* Korea's Place in the Sun: A Modern History *(New York: Norton, 1995).*

We are now closer to 2000 than to the watershed year of 1989, and closer to the inevitable deluge of fin de siècle premonitions and celebrations. If we pause to remember 1989, it is not just the fall of the Berlin wall, the collapse of Eastern European communism, the end of the cold war, and the quickening crisis of the Soviet Union that come to mind; we may also recall a widespread sense that Japan and Germany were the real victors of the cold war, and that ultimately the United States might very well go the way of the Soviet Union, spending itself into the oblivion of useless military facilities, hollowed-out industries, and technological obsolescence. For many, the American victory in the cold war seemed Pyrrhic, merely a way station between the American Century and the Pacific Century. Somehow, though, the atmosphere has changed, and it isn't clear what caused the alteration—or even how the new atmosphere might be characterized. It could be, however, that the American Century is not yet over.

These days almost any anniversary is enough to provoke outpourings of nostalgia. But a century is something else. A century is worth a celebration, particularly one that closes a millennium. The nineteenth century was a British one, running from Waterloo and the Congress of Vienna to World War I. The twentieth century had no claimant to its first 40 years, no doubt because the breakdown of the balance of power in 1914 was followed by the collapse of the world economy in 1929. Henry Luce, a founding editor of *Time,* waited until 1941 to claim the century for the United States. If Luce seemed like a visionary a decade later when the United States accounted for nearly half the world's industrial production, he looked myopic by 1975 when the Vietnamese won their war and the first murmurings of a Pacific Century were heard with Japan's dramatic advance and "miracle" economies flowering in South Korea and Taiwan. It appeared to have been the shortest "century" ever, a mere 34 years.

Examining the dating, however, may make Americans feel a bit better. Suppose England's century ended in 1914 and America's began in 1941. By the turn of the century the United States was the most productive industrial economy in the world, and by the early 1920s its banks were the effective center of global commerce. But America had a laughably small military, and neither the political will nor the domestic political base for global hegemony. The years from 1914 to 1941 thus constitute a hegemonic interregnum, during which England could no longer lead and the United States was not yet

ready to. Then the German attack on Poland in 1939 changed everything, and Pearl Harbor finally committed the United States to global leadership.

If America's "1815" was 1941, and if the United States is allotted a century as the British were, Americans should only begin to wring their hands and fill themselves with the proper end-of-an-era angst around the year 2040, and they should have nothing better to do than fret about the peccadilloes of the First Family (for lack of a royal family) for a good 75 years after that. Is the American Century an unaccountably short one, overtaken by the dawning Pacific Century, or will the United States get the "normal" run of 100 years?

AN AMERICAN GROWTH INDUSTRY

The 1970s watchword for card-carrying internationalists and executives of multinational corporations was "Pacific Rim," and it was only a short step from there to "Pacific Century." Suddenly there was a hue and cry about a new Pacific era, especially up and down the West Coast (but also in other states with large free trade coalitions) and especially among academics trying to find some way to interest donors in funding Asian or international studies. "Pacific Rim" was a discourse in search of the research funds necessary to prove the thing itself existed, targeted at exporters with Asian markets and importers of Asian products.

Rimspeak is thus a recent phenomenon, a construct of the mid-1970s that revalued East and Southeast Asia as Westerners (mostly Americans) recognized and defined the region in ways that highlighted some parts and excluded others. The central actor was Japan, a newly risen sun among advanced industrial countries—indeed, "Number One" in Harvard sociologist Ezra Vogel's perfectly timed book, *Japan as Number One: Lessons for America,* published in 1979. Organized into the region were the so-called miracle economies in Japan, South Korea, Taiwan, Hong Kong, Malaysia, and Singapore—also termed NICs, or newly industrializing countries. Honorable mention went to Thailand, the Philippines, Indonesia, and post-Mao (but pre-Tiananmen) China. Left out were the remaining communist countries that had not instituted economic reforms and what some have called the "oinks" (old industrialized countries) such as Myanmar and North Korea.

In other words, "Pacific Rim" painted the entire region differently than it had been since 1945. Paint it red, the pundits said from 1949 to 1975. Paint it white, was the post-1975 notion of artistry—or simply blank out the years since 1949 and Mao Zedong's revolution, or 1945 and Ho Chi Minh's Viet Minh resistance. "Pacific Rim" heralded a forgetting, a hoped for amnesia in which the decades-long but ultimately failed American effort to obliterate the Vietnam revolution would enter the realm of Korea, "the forgotten war."

MEASURING THEIR WORLD

The people of the Pacific Rim did not know they inhabited a bustling new sector of the world system until they were told—just as the "Indians" did not know they were in "West India" until Europeans informed them. "Rim" is an American construct, an invention exactly like the steam engine, incorporating the region's peoples "into a new inventory of the world"; "Pacific" is itself a Euro-American name, measuring, delineating, and recognizing living space for the people who live there.[1] That these are Western constructs does not mean the natives think them unimportant, or that they have their own confident definitions; indeed, well-known Rimsters have doors held open for them throughout East Asia.

"Pacific Rim" has a class-based definition of Asia. The Pacific "community" is a capitalist archipelago, based on indigenous labor power and purchasing power—although mainly labor power until recently. It has been the "workshop of the world," using cheap and efficient labor to manufacture exports for other regions with consumer buying power; the vast American market has been and is its mainstay. The archipelago runs through but also divides the Pacific and Asian region. North Korea, for example, remains outside, and China carries this division within itself: vast interior peasant China versus upwardly mobile coastal and urban China. So capitalist classes—obviously—are organized into the archipelago. Peasant Asia (Vietnam, Cambodia, and much of India, Indonesia, and China) is out. Dense, developed, highly differentiated urban nodes are in, the two most important being Tokyo and Los Angeles, but city-states like Hong Kong and Singapore are also critical. China's old treaty ports and new Special Economic Zones such as Shenzhen are in; vast reaches of interior China are on the outside. South Korea is part of it, while the northern part of the peninsula is not. Thus the majority of the populations in Asia are either not included in the Rim or only participate as unskilled or semiskilled laborers. This is a trading network as well, with Chinese and Korean diaspora businesspeople making a Mediterranean of the Pacific Ocean—from Vancouver, Seattle, and Los Angeles through "island China" in East and Southeast Asia, all the way to China itself.

Rimspeak tells us all these things, explicitly or implicitly. But it is also a slippery discourse with a half-life of months or years, depending on the source. It tells us that we are situated in the dynamic present, turning our eyes to a yet more dynamic future where all things are possible—until something like the 1989 Tiananmen bloodletting or even a much lesser affair like the caning of

Michael Fay in Singapore this year demolishes the seemingly incorrigible optimism of the genre, and sends a handful of recent books to the secondhand stores. Wasn't development supposed to lead to democracy? Well then, why is Michael Fay's posterior so tender, and why does Singapore's strict moral code make our "politically correct" police look like pantywaists?

ASIA AND US

Rimspeak still scopes the future, however, and if things aren't as good they should be today, rest assured they will soon become so. But rimspeak can also cloud one's vision on the present: consider this statement beginning a 1991 book by Simon Winchester, *Pacific Rising: The Emergence of a New World Culture* (admittedly one of the genre's more interesting and thoughtful texts): "Rarely indeed is one fortunate in being able to live through times in which a major shift in the world's history can be seen to be taking place. . . . One such event . . . came about when the fifty-odd countries now grouped around the Pacific Ocean seemed to take the torch of leadership from those hitherto grouped around the Atlantic. . . ."

A torch passed to whom? To 50 countries, including the Sultanate of Brunei? Maybe just to the Four (or is it Five?) Tigers? Pundits like Clyde Prestowitz in his book *Trading Places* had already proclaimed Japan the new global hegemon in 1989. But when exactly was the torch passed? Sometime after Japan went catatonic at the hint that it might do something significant about Iraq's 1990 invasion of Kuwait? But was it Japan that put Jean-Bertrand Aristide back in the presidential palace in Haiti, or brokered new peace agreements in the Middle East and Ireland, or intervened again when Iraqi divisions marched toward the Kuwait border this fall? Did Japan even try to deal with the nuclear problem in its own neighborhood, in North Korea?

In fact, of course, it was the United States that influenced all this, a United States that also sees itself in a new Pacific era—but one that it will lead. The day after President Bill Clinton's victory on the North American Free Trade Agreement last November 18, *The New York Times* heralded a fundamental turning point in American foreign policy resulting from a combination of Clinton's emphasis on reviving the domestic economy and new directions in foreign economic policy. But it was not Mexico or Canada that drew the attention. Under the headline "Bright Sun of Trade Rising in the East," *Times* correspondent Thomas Friedman implied that NAFTA was a sideshow compared to the markets, exports, and jobs to be had in connecting up with East Asia. The Clinton administration hoped to fashion the Asia Pacific Economic Cooperation (APEC) forum, 14 of whose 15 heads of state were then meeting in Seattle at the president's invitation, into a battering ram to knock down protected markets and tariffs, opening up "the most lucrative terrain for American exports and American jobs."

Dreams of a rising APEC sun (trade with APEC countries now accounts for 40 percent of all United States trade, and the United States exports $128 billion annually to APEC nations, compared with $102 billion to Europe) meant that, in the words of Secretary of State Warren Christopher, Europe was finding itself in the shade and Washington had to get over its traditional Eurocentric diplomacy. A shift from the Atlantic to the Pacific had been in the works since the mid-1980s, observers said, but a new generation in Washington, unschooled in the Atlanticist verities of the Eastern seaboard and the Council on Foreign Relations, would now make it happen. Or as baby boomer Labor Secretary Robert Reich told Friedman, the United States was moving "away from our European roots" toward greater involvement with Asia and Latin America, "where more and more of our population is coming from."

What we are witnessing is not a transfer of hegemonic power but a glimmer, an emergence (of Japan), that starts imaginations wandering to different futures. Friedrich Nietzsche, in the *Genealogy of Morals,* used the term "emergence" (*entstehung*) to denote "the principle and the singular law of an apparition." Emergence does not mean "the final term of a historical development"; "culminations" are "merely the current episodes in a series of subjugations," and so, "Emergence is thus the entry of forces; it is their eruption, *the leap from the wings to the center stage.* . . . Emergence designates a place of confrontation [emphasis added]." An event (or an emergence) is not a decision, a treaty, a war, but "the reversal of a relationship of forces, the usurpation of power, the appropriation of a vocabulary turned against those who had once used it."

Nietzsche helps us answer the question of where Rimster tropes come from, in helping us understand a peculiar history: Japan is always "emerging." "Pacific Rim" and "Japan as Number One" emerged in what seemed a sudden and mysterious fashion not just in the 1970s but at several points during the past 150 years. Thus we have had "emergence," but not "the reversal of a relationship of forces." Throughout the Pacific industrial era, going back to the mid-nineteenth century, Japan has been a junior actor under Anglo-American hegemony, save for six years or so from 1939 to 1945. And what happened then does not come under the rubric "Pacific Rim Community."

THE HEGEMON WRITES HISTORY

"Pacific Rim" was there from the beginning, soon after Commodore Matthew Perry's "Black Ships" arrived in the ports of Tokugawa Japan in 1853. The high-tech conveyance of that era was the steamship, so much less expensive than the ongoing building of continental railroads that it made of the Pacific a vast plain traders could skate across, toward the putative China market. Their longings also brought American ships to Manila Bay (won from Spain in 1898), seen as the first important colonial way station in the quest for the treasures of the Rim.

Somehow, back then, just as today, Japan was regarded as separate from the rest of the Rim—honorary Westerner, pearl of the Orient, good pupil (or bad pupil: Secretary of State Dean Acheson called it "the West's obstreperous offspring"). "They are Asiatics, it is true, and therefore deficient," declared the *Edinburgh Review* in 1852, "in that principle of development which is the leading characteristic of those ingenious and persevering European races. . . . But amidst Asiatics," the *Review* went on to say, "the Japanese stand supreme."[2]

The steamships sailed toward Asian markets, but also toward a presumed earthly paradise that purportedly housed occult knowledge unavailable to the rational Westerner. That this second theme persists today can be seen in the pages of *The Economist,* where an article on "The Pacific Idea" in the March 16, 1991, edition has as its subtitle, "There is a Better World." The Pacific idea, the article announces, "is important for the mental well-being of the world," because it stands for "belief in the survival of innocence." The accompanying map centers the globe on tropical islands of the central and South Pacific (described in the article as "a village pond for the Seventh Fleet"), unwittingly placing Bikini at the epicenter—an island the United States rendered uninhabitable with H-bomb tests in the 1950s. Meanwhile the article speaks wistfully of Gauguin's women, Melville's lory-lory, and Marlon Brando's Tahiti, and places the burden of exclusion from the Rim on the natives: "the places that people call Eden and Paradise can really become so, if only the Pacific islanders will heave themselves to their feet [translation: get dynamic]."

During the halcyon days of the Anglo-Japanese Alliance (1902–1922), Japan was a model of industrial efficiency for an England in incipient decline. As Phillip Lyttleton Gell remarked in 1904: "I shall turn Japanese for they at least can think, and be reticent! [Witness] their organization, their strategy, their virile qualities, their devotion and self-control. Above all, their national capacity for self-reliance, self-sacrifice, and their silence!"[3]

The British weren't saying such kind things about the Japanese by the 1930s, of course, and Japan's militarists by that time had their eye on a different "Pacific Rim Community," known to history as the "Greater East Asia Co-Prosperity Sphere." Japan emerged in the Western mind not as an enlightened pupil but as a nightmare. Still, Japan's "old" empire in Northeast Asia was, from 1910 to 1931, the empire the United States and Britain wanted it to have. Even when Manchuria was colonized in 1931, Britain and the United States chose to do little about it, other than spout rhetoric about the "open door." The reason for this was that Japan preserved a modified open door in Manchuria until 1941, and encouraged American and British investment—of which there was much more than is generally thought. Two years after the war ended, American planners again urged a modified restoration of Japan's position in Northeast Asia.

Dean Acheson and the State Department's George Kennan masterminded this remaking of Japan in the world system, deciding to position Japan as an engine of the world economy, an American-defined "economic animal" shorn of its prewar military and political clout. Meanwhile the United States kept Japan in a defense dependency and shaped the flow of essential resources to the country, hoping to accumulate a diffuse leverage over all its policies and retain an outer-limit veto on Japan's global orientation. Japan would also need an economic region "to its south," in Kennan's words, and by 1949 Acheson had come up with an elegant rim metaphor to capture this restoration: a "great crescent" from Tokyo to Alexandria linking Japan with island Asia, around Singapore, and through the Indian Ocean to the oil of the Persian Gulf. It was this "crescent" that lay behind Acheson's famed "defense perimeter" speech in January 1950. This redefinition of Japan's role was hammered out as the cold war was emerging, and it deepened as Japan benefited from America's wars to lock in an Asian hinterland in Korea and Vietnam.

During this era, which ran from Presidents Harry Truman through Lyndon Johnson, Japan was a dutiful American partner, and the partner was tickled by Japan's economic success. In the 1960s, however, as America's capacity to unilaterally manage the global system declined, a new duality afflicted the relationship: Japan should do well—but not so well that it hurt American interests. President Richard Nixon was again the agent of change, with his neomercantilist "New Economic Policy" announced on V-J Day in 1971. American thinking about Japan remains firmly within that duality today, reflected by policymakers' inability to do more than oscillate between free trade and protectionism, admiration for Japan's success, and alarm at its prowess.

Japan has been thriving in the hegemonic net for 90 years, but nonetheless "emerges" in the Western mind—leaps from the wings to center stage, in Nietzsche's phrase—at three critical and incommensurable points: at the turn of the century, when it was an industrial marvel (at least in British eyes); during the world depression of the 1930s, when it was an industrial monster (again in British eyes); and in the 1980s, when it was a marvel to American internationalists and a monster to American protectionists. The Four Tigers, Three or Four Tiger Cubs,

and all the other developing Asian nations tread this same path, encouraged to do well, but not so well that they threaten the United States, because in that case the tropes reverse and the Asian states move from miracle to menace, from market-driven dynamo to crypto-fascist upstart. The point is that there has been no fundamental reversal of relationships, no torches have been passed, and no such transition is likely for the near term. Thus the American Century has some time left to run.

In the near term of the next couple of decades I would hazard the guess that the world system will have three nodal points, centered in New York, Tokyo, and Berlin, and a core point of hegemony, headquartered in Washington. New York will have a tendency to connect with Europe, and Los Angeles with East Asia, and Washington will attempt to manage a trilateral condominium among the three nodes, while cooperating with industrial powers of the second rank (France, England, Italy) with annual gross national products of around $1 trillion. In other words, this is the eve not of a regionalization of the world economy but of a period of prolonged North-North cooperation propelled by a historic "peace interest" on the part of internationalist finance and the modal capitalist organization of our era, the transnational corporation.

A LONG WAY FROM COMMUNITY

The Pacific Century is not here yet, and the Pacific Rim is neither a self-contained region nor a community but just a rim—peripheral and semiperipheral societies oriented toward Tokyo and the American market. Consumer purchasing power is still lower than in Western Europe or the United States (though rising rapidly in South Korea, Taiwan, and Singapore), and its lower labor costs still orient the region toward assembly and finishing work using Japanese, American, or Korean technology. It is still a region under dual economic hegemony, held together by a unilateral American security network.

From the mid-1980s, it is true, Japan deepened its influence in Asia, both northeast and southeast. Its direct investment in the region grew sixfold from 1985 to 1991, trade with Taiwan tripled over the same period, and its manufactured imports from the region as a whole more than doubled from 1985 to 1988 (in spite of the pundits who argue that the Japanese economy is basically closed.) The Pacific region inclusive of Northeast Asia, the ASEAN countries, and Australia will, according to current projections, have a combined GNP of $7.2 trillion by the year 2000, surpassing that of the European Union. The number of effective consumers will be about 330 million, as large a market as the EU though not as affluent.

This is grist for the mill of those who detect a developing tendency toward regional economic blocs. But an

Asia Pacific bloc is unlikely short of a major world depression. What is much more likely is a regime of cooperation and free trade linking Europe with the Far East and the Americas, with the three great regional markets underpinning and stabilizing capitalist rivalry in the world system and encouraging interdependence rather than go-it-alone strategies that would be deleterious to all.

The Pacific community, as has been indicated, is really not much of a community. Compared with the European version, East Asia lacks the intense horizontal contact or the expected multilateral institutions. Much has been made of the Asia Pacific Economic Cooperation forum, founded in 1989, but this remains a weak assemblage of 15 countries that do not interact with each other well or often. Malaysia's preferred option of an exclusively Asian regional economic group generates a lot of heat and attention, but it is much less advanced even than APEC. ASEAN is still a loose collection of smaller countries in Southeast Asia. There is no equivalent of the North American Free Trade Agreement, but if something transpires it will most likely be an enlargement of NAFTA to include selected Pacific Rim economies. It is right to say, as Richard K. Betts does in the winter 1993–1994 issue of *International Security*, that the Asian "web of interdependence" is weak.

The main organization connecting the region is still the private business firm. There is nothing like the European Customs Union or the European Parliament or the Conference on Security and Cooperation in Europe, though there was some movement in the latter part of last year toward creating a CSCE-like forum. Travel is no longer restricted for businessmen traversing the region, but it is for ordinary citizens wishing to go from Taiwan or South Korea to China, let alone South Korea to North Korea or vice versa. Even the common cultural background presumed to have been provided by Confucianism does not create ties between, say, Korea and Japan or Japan and China. The lingering animosities of colonialism and war, combined with the dominance of American mass culture, tend to override this heritage.

Apart from the momentum of economic development, it is the United States that drives the countries of the region together (or keeps them apart, as with North and South Korea). We may say it is still the United States that drives the region itself. The ultimate logic of Washington's position resides in Japan being for the United States today what the United States was for Britain in the 1920s: the emergent financial and technological center, but a long way yet from assuming hegemonic responsibilities. As the Persian Gulf War demonstrated in 1991 and other crises have demonstrated since, Japan (and Germany) will be content for some time to let Washington shoulder these responsibilities—why take on an expensive security role when the United States is willing

to, and in the absence of major threats from Russia or anywhere else?

But simply because American hegemony has defined the region since 1945 does not mean it will continue to do so indefinitely. Many American analysts see an impending shift in the balance of power in East Asia, which almost all of them lament—because they are Americans. An ineffable triumphalism affects almost everyone in America, beginning with superficial judgments about how the cold war was won and what it means for an American liberalism now said to be the solution to all problems worldwide. In many ways the cold war ended in East Asia a generation ago (except for Korea), and tendencies already well under way for decades have merely deepened in the 1990s. But that does not guard against American smugness with regard to this region, either.

This is evident in Richard Betts's condescending question, "So should we want China to get rich or not?" and his frank recommendation that Americans continue serving as "voluntary Hessians" for Japan for as long as possible, since the only alternative is for Tokyo to "start spending blood as well as its treasure to support international order," at which time Japan "will justifiably become interested in much more control over that order." Better Americans police the world and let Japan remain what Betts terms "a unidimensional superpower"; otherwise, Betts warns, mixing metaphors, "a truncated End of History in East Asia could be destabilizing rather than pacifying." Stability is equated with a revived American hegemony. The pièce de resistance, though, is Betts's assertion that "a China, Japan, or Russia that grows strong enough to overturn a regional balance of power would necessarily also be a global power that would reestablish bipolarity on the highest level"—so no matter which of the three gained power commensurate with the United States, it would be America's enemy.

Samuel Huntington characteristically tops Betts in claiming that continued American hegemony is not merely in America's interests but also the world's: "no other country can make comparable contributions to international order and stability." Japan, however, is not to be trusted, because it unremittingly pursues "economic warfare" against the rest of the globe and is already dangerously close to hegemonic predominance.[4] Yet Huntington's argument is looking like yesterday's porridge. If in the recent past most American pundits focused on Japan as the rising power—even on "the coming war with Japan"—many now regard China as more threatening. Betts again: "The state most likely over time to disturb equilibrium in the region—and the world—is China." Betts seems to think that if current projections hold up, China will not only soon be rich but will be "the clear hegemonic power in the region."

Has something momentous happened in East Asian security? Is Betts correct in saying that "the [East Asian] balance of power . . . is up for grabs"? Looking solely at defense budgets to gauge changes after the cold war, Japan would seem to be the most menacing state in East Asia, since its spending in this category increased by more than 38 percent between 1990 and 1993. But that figure ignores the trend over the past 25 years, with Japan consistently spending less than 1 percent of GNP on defense, while West Germany hovered at around 3 percent and the United States at around 6 percent; it also ignores Japan's continuing inability to agree on a post-cold war defense strategy. Furthermore, by the same measure "renegade" North Korea is the least menacing state in the region, since its military spending fell more than 58 percent over the same period. The security experts seem able only to come up with arguments justifying more of the same in East Asia, as if evidence counted little and the end of the cold war and collapse of the Soviet bloc were essentially irrelevant to the security of the region.

WHAT IF THEY HAD A PACIFIC CENTURY AND NOBODY SHOWED UP?

We are left, I think, with but one grand event encapsulated by the terms "Pacific Century" and "Pacific Rim," and that is the rise of Japan. Japan is the only true new arrival in the past century among the ranks of the advanced industrial core, given a drastically deindustrialized Russia and a still developing China. (South Korea and Taiwan may soon approach Spain in per capita GNP, but will not go much beyond that in the near term.) Japan is also the only non-Western country there. If it does not wish to be, and cannot right now serve as, the lode-

stone for an autonomous non-Western reorganization of the region, one day it might. If and when that happens, an old soldier and charter Pacific Rimster, General Douglas MacArthur, Japan's benign American emperor, will have been right. In an address in Seattle in 1951, MacArthur opined:

> Our economic frontier now embraces the trade potentialities of Asia itself; for with the gradual rotation of the epicenter of world trade back to the Far East whence it started many centuries ago, the next thousand years will find the main problem the raising of the sub-normal standards of life of its more than a billion people.

It is a classic piece of Rimspeak. In the meantime, enjoy the American Century while it lasts—you've got until 2040.

NOTES

1. See Arif Dirlik, "The Asia-Pacific Idea: Reality and Representation in the Invention of a Regional Structure," Duke University (February 1991); and Bruce Cumings, "Rimspeak; or, The Discourse of the "Pacific Rim," in Arif Dirlik, ed., *What Is in a Rim?* (Boulder, Colo.: Westview Press, 1993), from which this section is drawn.
2. Quoted in Jean-Pierre Lehmann, *The Image of Japan: From Feudal Isolation to World Power*, 1850–1905 (London: Allen and Unwin, 1978), p. 46.
3. Quoted in Colin Holmes and A. H. Ion, "Bushido and the Samurai: Images in British Public Opinion, 1894–1914," *Modern Asian Studies*, vol. 14, no. 2 (1980).
4. Samuel Huntington, "Why International Primacy Matters," *International Security*, vol. 17, no. 4 (Spring 1993).

Article 3
Current History, December 1994

Organizing the Rim: Asia Pacific Regionalism

"Have the extent, speed, and consequences of Asia Pacific economic growth made it . . . 'the most important global development in the second half of the twentieth century'? . . . Karl Marx, Theodore Roosevelt, and Yasuhiro Nakasone are among the many who predicted a Pacific era. Can . . . a German philosopher, an American president, and a Japanese prime minister all be wrong? Yes, they can."

Donald K. Emmerson

Donald K. Emmerson is a visiting professor at the Asia/Pacific Research Center at Stanford University. His latest publication is a chapter in The Pacific Century: Scenarios for Regional Cooperation *(Westport, Conn.: Praeger, 1994), edited by Barbara K. Bundy et al.*

So extensive and rapid has been the growth of the [Asia Pacific] region and so profound its consequences, that it has been described aptly as the most important global development in the second half of the twentieth century.
— Pacific Business Forum (1994)

The [European] Community we have created is not an end in itself . . . [but] only a stage on the way to the organized world of tomorrow.
— Jean Monnet, *Memoires* (1976)

Whether or not we stand on the threshold of a "Pacific Century" depends in part on what that notoriously ambiguous term means. The global significance of the vast, populous, and relatively booming Pacific Rim is already beyond dispute. But the idea of a Pacific era implies more. It suggests that over the coming hundred years, the Asia Pacific will be more significant than any other region. (The name "Asia Pacific" sounds odd in English, but in Asia it is winning out over "Asian Pacific" and "Pacific Asia," which seem to exclude the other non-Asian, Pacific coastal countries of the Americas, and over "Pacific Rim," which does not mention Asia at all.)

Whether the Asia Pacific will become the most important region in the world—important enough to dominate perceptions of an entire century—will depend on the efforts to give shape not only to that region but to others as well, including the "Atlantic Rim" and the corresponding "Europe Atlantic" that could—who knows?—animate a coming "Atlantic Century."

REGIONALISM'S NEW SHAPE

For help in thinking about world regions and how they form, one need look no farther than the bottom row of keys on a touch-tone phone: * O #.

The pound sign (#) symbolizes the great divides that until recently organized global politics. The two vertically slanting lines evoke the cold war face-off of West against East: the North Atlantic Treaty organization versus the Warsaw Pact. The horizontal lines recall the effort by the poor countries of the South to organize against and demand concession from the higher-income North: the nonaligned Movement versus the industrial countries grouped in the Organization for Economic Cooperation and Development (or, alternatively, the Group of 77 versus the Group of 7).* But such diverse and dispersed coalitions cannot be called regions; West, East, South, and North are not the names of neighborhoods.

If the pound sign represents the past, the asterisk (*) offers a future shape in which world regions could intersect—namely, as spokes around the hub of the sole remaining superpower, the United States.

The elements of a possible asterisk-like pattern of United States-centered regionalization in the twenty-first century are in place or are taking shape in the world economy. A North American Free Trade Agreement (NAFTA) already links America to Canada and Mexico.

---

*The Group of 77 actually gathers more than a hundred of the developing countries in the United Nations Conference on Trade and Development, while America, Britain, Canada, France, Germany, Italy, and Japan make up the Group of 7.

And it appears that the Summit of the Americas, which is scheduled to be convened in Miami by President Bill Clinton this December, could endorse the eventual creation of a Hemispheric Free Trade Area. Implementing an HFTA will not be easy. But the "Miami process," as it is being called in Washington, could focus policy attention on the long-term goal of a free trade zone running from Arctic Canada through near-Antarctic Chile.

Like the north-south height of an HFTA, the east-west arms of this still fanciful body are intriguing but problematic. The European Union already forms the potential end of an eastern spoke, but it does not connect to the American hub. Since 1993 former British Prime Minister Margaret Thatcher has sought backing for a North Atlantic Free Trade Area (what might be dubbed a NATLAFTA) that would link Western Europe to the United States in a Euro-American common market. Despite some American support, notably from labor unions feeling a tactical need to propose an alternative to NAFTA, nothing has come of her suggestion. But the goal of Euro-American free trade will not go away. The more economic regions proliferate and consolidate, the more the Atlantic "gap" will seem like unfinished business, especially in the eyes of east coast Americans and west coast Europeans concerned over the growing Asian bias of the American economy. (According to the State Department, Americans now trade nearly two-thirds as much with Asia as they do with Europe.)

A NATLAFTA was to be discussed at the First International Congress on the Atlantic Rim this November in Boston. Among the meeting's sponsors were mayors of cities on both sides of the North Atlantic, including port cities with a lot to gain from their location on this potential eastward arm of an asterisk of United States—centered free-trade regions. American Atlanticists and their European counterparts appear to have coined the term "Atlantic Rim" expressly to offset and copy the popularity of the Pacific Rim. While acknowledging the importance of Asia, congress organizer James Barron has said that "North Americans should not forget the opportunities that lie in an Atlantic community."

Boosters of Pacific trade, meanwhile, are also pressing ahead. Indonesia was scheduled to host a ministerial meeting of the Asia Pacific Economic Cooperation (APEC) forum in Jakarta on November 11 and 12. Three days later President Clinton and 17 other leaders from around the Pacific Rim were to attend the second informal APEC summit in Bogor, West Java. APEC is explicitly pan-Pacific. In Indonesia, Chile was expected to join Canada, Mexico, and the United States as APEC's fourth member from the Western Hemisphere.

Compared with the still unlikely prospect of a trans-Atlantic free trade area, the chances of a trans-Pacific one seem only slightly more realistic. True, in Indonesia the leaders of APEC were scheduled to consider making the year 2020 the deadline for achieving free trade in the Asia Pacific. But even if APEC's leaders agree to set a date for free trade, one can anticipate a lot of foot-dragging in the process of implementation, given the reluctance of the more protected and less productive Asian economies to expose themselves fully to the goods and services of industrial powerhouses such as the United States (ranked as the world's most competitive economy by the World Economic Forum in 1994). The sheer diversity of the Pacific Rim also promises to slow progress toward free trade. So does the opposition of some labor unions and human rights activists in the United States to unconditional commerce with societies such as China and Indonesia, where cheap labor is abundant and democracy scarce.

OTHER REGIONS, OTHER HUBS

Another obstacle to a future world economy in the shape of regional spokes radiating from an American hub is that other countries and regions may aspire to become hubs in their own right. The two main candidates for such a role are Western Europe and Japan.

Western Europe, through initiatives such as the European Bank for Reconstruction and Development, has begun to involve itself in a prospective economic zone reaching eastward into the former Soviet Union. This October the European Commission of the European Union proposed a regional economic and security pact that would incorporate the countries of North Africa and the Middle East. If implemented, the scheme would create a free trade zone of some 800 million people living in as many as 40 countries. EU leaders planned to discuss the idea at their own summit in Essen, Germany, in early December. As if not to be outdone by the possibility that the APEC summit in Indonesia would propose free trade in the Asia Pacific by the year 2020, the European Commission hoped the summit in Germany would aim for free trade around the Mediterranean Rim ten years earlier, in 2010.

The regional trade summitry of this November and December will thus likely highlight the region-organizing initiatives of two powerful would-be hubs: the United States trying to accelerate trade liberalization within APEC and driving in Miami toward hemispheric free commerce, and the EU in Essen seeking its own eastern and southern trade spokes.

But the process of region-formation cannot be reduced to a simple story of large and powerful cores organizing their peripheries. Such an oversimplification is particularly unwarranted in the Asia Pacific, where vast distances, heterogeneous populations, proud nationalisms, booming economies, and a history of conflict since World

War II complicate the ability of the United States to lead the region even if it wanted to. And Japan, the logical alternative core, is still too preoccupied with its bilateral relations with the United States to play the role of regional organizer. Nor does the brutally hub-serving character of Tokyo's earlier device for the region—the Greater East Asia Co-Prosperity Sphere imposed during World War II—inspire confidence in a future asterisk centered on Japan.

Finally, the physical shape of the Pacific Rim makes it hard to organize into an asterisk. On a touch-tone phone, as in regionalization, the asterisk and the zero are opposites. The hub-and-spokes asterisk lacks a rim and magnifies the core. Because all roads lead to Rome, Roman leaders can, in theory, divide and rule bilaterally. But the zero is nothing except a rim. On a map the Pacific-littoral countries are all circumference and no core. In the Asia Pacific the continental United States lacks the physical centrality it enjoys in North America or that Germany has in Europe. Geophysically, every member of the Pacific Rim is peripheral. (The Pacific island microstates south and west of Hawaii are negligible exceptions, economically and politically unimportant and easily bypassed by jet aircraft and satellite links.)

The vast zero that is the Pacific Rim could become a zone of contention between asterisks—one centered on the United States, one stemming from Japan, and perhaps someday a third led by China. So far, however, the region has sent two contrary signals about its future shape. In divided Northeast Asia, where powerful states with legacies of conflict are in close proximity, bilateralism is still the rule. A different situation prevails in Southeast Asia. There six countries with a solid record of cooperation offer a multilateral prototype for the economic and political organization of the larger region. Most of these Southeast Asian states are weaker than their Northeast Asian counterparts. But acting as a group, they have come to exercise far more influence over the shaping of the Pacific Rim than they could have separately.

STRENGTH IN UNITY

In 1967, only 10 years after the Treaty of Rome founded the European Economic Community and more than 20 years before APEC and NAFTA, five developing countries—Indonesia, Malaysia, the Philippines, Singapore, and Thailand—established the Association of Southeast Asian Nations (ASEAN) (Brunei joined in 1984 and in 1994 steps were under way to extend membership to Vietnam within a year or two). ASEAN's record of facilitating peace and cooperation among its members, and thus the economic growth of nearly all of them, has made it the most successful regional organization of developing countries since World War II.

NAFTA and ASEAN differ greatly. The first is a binding contract specifically focused on trade; the second is a general, loose, multifunctional organization. While the text of NAFTA runs to well over 1,000 pages, it took but 16 for Southeast Asian leaders to establish an ASEAN Free Trade Area (AFTA). Yet both arrangements illustrate the interest of smaller countries with much larger neighbors in promoting regions that can help make those huge neighbors more benign and less unpredictable. The behemoths in North America and Southeast Asia are, of course, the United States and Indonesia. (Americans outnumber Canadians and Mexicans combined, as Indonesians do the five other populations inside ASEAN).

NAFTA's forerunner and kernel, the 1988 Canada-United States Free Trade Agreement, resulted more from Canadian than American initiative. NAFTA's own inception owed more to Mexico pressuring America than vice versa. And ASEAN's establishment in 1967 and expansion in 1984 reflected the desire of Malaysia and Singapore on the first occasion and Brunei on the second to make Indonesia promise to foster "good neighbourliness . . . among the countries of the region," and help "ensure their stability and security from external interference in any form or manifestation in order to preserve their national identities," to quote ASEAN's founding document. In the 1960s Indonesian President Sukarno had waged small-scale wars against Malaysia and Singapore and endorsed a rebellion in Brunei.

But if regionalization suits the desire of smaller actors to contain and tame a big neighbor in a framework within which they constitute a majority, it also can serve the wish of that same large neighbor to create for itself a sphere of support. A regional regime organized around one powerful country can take shape, flourish, or atrophy depending on how well it satisfies these two differing and potentially contradictory interests. So far ASEAN has done so and flourished. Another reason for ASEAN's success is that its largest and potentially most threatening member, Indonesia, is also the poorest and thus, economically, the weakest. Singapore, conversely, is rich but also tiny, which makes its wealth less worrisome to its neighbors.

Singapore needs Indonesian land and labor; Indonesia needs Singapore's capital. This is the surface rationale for what might be called the Regionally Industrializing Core (RIC) of investment and trade that has tied the Indonesian province of Riau to neighboring Singapore and Singapore to its own complementary northern neighbor, the Malaysian state of Johore. Singapore's deeper interest in this RIC is to so thoroughly entwine Indonesia and Malaysia in its own economic prosperity, and vice versa, as to preclude in the two larger countries any thought of attacking the smaller one. Farther north a more embryonic RIC would multiply connections between the ports of Medan in Indonesia, Penang in Malaysia, and Phuket in Thailand. In eastern Southeast Asia another such plan would join the economies of Indonesian North Sulawesi, Malaysian Sabah, and Philippine Mindanao.

No one knows quite what to call these new transnational formations. They have been termed "Natural Economic Territories," but many of them are artificial, political, and maritime—driven by governments across water, not land. Were it not for Singaporean policy, the RIC across the Strait of Singapore would not exist. The most common name for such schemes is "growth triangles." But some have more than three sides: the development area proposed for the part of northern Southeast Asia where Myanmar, China, Laos, and Thailand meet is a "growth square." The hypothetical development zone around the Tumen River in Northeast Asia involves five countries, including current or former antagonists such as the two Koreas, whose enmity can be reduced through economic interdependence—or so this RIC's promoters hope.

Comparably, political logic helps to motivate, on the south coast of China, the most successful and dynamic RIC in East Asia. Here Hong Kong (and potentially Taiwan) plays Singapore's role in relation to its own large neighbor, China. Whether China will be constructively enlisted through trade and investment in the security of the small, rich economies on its periphery is, of course, a gamble not a certainty.

Compared with China, Japan too is small and rich. But given its vast size and power compared with Hong Kong, Japan can hardly play the latter's role as a gateway city peacefully energizing its neighbors. Japan is instead a candidate to become a—conceivably the—future hegemon of East Asia. Yet its power has been lopsidedly economic, and that has reduced Asian anxieties about the prospect of Japanese domination. The potential for rearmament that Japan's wealth represents has, however, helped legitimate in Asian eyes a security role for the United States as insurance against that prospect.

SOUTHEAST ASIA AS MODEL

In this complex and multipolar setting ASEAN has been, in relation to Asia Pacific regionalism, reluctant, but at the same time inventive. Its reluctance stems from the fear that APEC could become a field for power projection by the United States. That concern led Malaysian Prime Minister Mahathir Mohamad in 1990 to announce an East Asian Economic Grouping that excluded the United States. But many in ASEAN clearly preferred the larger framework, APEC, where they could benefit from American trade and investment while playing the United States off against Japan and perhaps China.

In response to such criticism, Mahathir reduced his idea to an East Asian Economic Caucus (EAEC) safely inside APEC. But so long as Tokyo remains lukewarm to the concept it will not be realized. On the eve of the November APEC summit in Indonesia, Japan did not want to endanger further its already rocky relations with Washington by seeming to approve a move that could be interpreted as excluding the United States from East Asia.

In September ASEAN sped up the deadline for achieving AFTA from 2008 to 2003, well before the target dates for free trade that APEC or its Euro-Mediterranean counterpart might envisage. A major impetus behind AFTA is to create a large, attractive market better able to compete with other Asian countries, notably China, for foreign investment.

Most innovatively of all, ASEAN has taken the lead in extending Asia Pacific multilateralism into the realm of security, a topic long considered too controversial to handle in anything but bilateral fashion. The first meeting of the ASEAN Regional Forum (ARF) in Bangkok in July 1994 accomplished nothing, but it included such a range of countries at loggerheads—China and Vietnam disputing the South China Sea, Russia and Japan the southern Kurile Islands, to cite two examples—that merely holding the event made it a success. Noteworthy too has been the series of multilateral "workshops" hosted by Indonesia to alleviate jurisdictional tensions over the Spratly Islands.

ASEAN will continue to play an important role in shaping the Asia Pacific. Singapore hosts the secretariats of APEC and the related Pacific Economic Cooperation Council. To mollify ASEAN's fears of being dominated by the United States, Japan, or China, APEC has agreed to hold every other one of its annual meetings in a Southeast Asian member country. Indonesia will host the next gathering of ARF. The existence of the EAEC as an implicit deterrent to American aggressiveness in pushing its free-trade goals too hard will also help to ensure that ASEAN, or at any rate Malaysia, remains a player in the region-forming game.

But the Asia Pacific will not become a fully organized region until Southeast Asia's penchant for multilateralism takes hold in Northeast Asia. It is there that the most intractable interstate disputes lie and there that the potential for interstate violence is highest. China's People's Liberation Army may smash democracy in Hong Kong when that colony reverts to Chinese control in 1997, or invade Taiwan if and when that country's leaders declare its independence from the mainland. Notwithstanding the framework agreement reached in 1994 by Washington with Pyongyang, North Korea could someday threaten the South with nuclear weapons. And because of their failure to resolve their dispute over the southern

Kuriles, Japan and Russia still have not signed a peace treaty ending World War II.

There is no Association of Northeast Asian Nations that could lower these tensions. Compared with Southeast Asia, Northeast Asia is grossly underorganized. Until this imbalance is reduced, Asia Pacific regionalism—in the sense of multilateral action by neighbors to better themselves and become more secure—will remain fragile and incomplete.

BEYOND BILATERALISM

In relation to the weakness of regionalism, United States policy is both part of the solution and part of the problem. While generally supporting ASEAN-based multilateralism, Mahathir's EAEC notably excepted, the United States has approached Northeast Asia bilaterally. Bilateral deals are pursued with Japan on economic access, with North Korea on nuclear fuel, with China on military cooperation or human rights. However effective the results of these negotiations may (or may not) be, they impede the growth of a regional capacity to solve local problems.

For a giant such as the United States, the temptation is great to become the core of an asterisk—the one indispensable hub projecting its influence through bilateral spokes to other countries. But, as was noted, there are two other candidate hubs in the Asia Pacific: Japan and potentially China. Time and economic growth could

someday add Russia to this list. Further raising the stakes of conflict if any one of these countries should seek hegemony is the fact that they face each other, across the Bering and Japan Seas and the Amur and Ussuri Rivers. Such close, tense quarters raise the risks of making asterisks.

Have the extent, speed, and consequences of Asia Pacific economic growth made it, as the Pacific Business Forum believes, "the most important global development in the second half of the twentieth century"? Will the coming hundred years add up to a Pacific Century? Karl Marx, Theodore Roosevelt, and Yasuhiro Nakasone are among the many who predicted a Pacific era. Can Pacific Rim executives, a German philosopher, an American president, and a Japanese prime minister all be wrong?

Yes, they can. Surely the cold war, decolonization, and the collapse of communism are also in the running for "most important global development" of 1950–2000. And while the relative rise of the Pacific is unmistakable, the continuing significance of other regions may make a Global Century the safer prediction for the years beyond 2000. A more immediate question is whether the still fragile institutions and still nationalistic leaders of the Pacific Rim can cultivate the multilateral relations necessary to sustain a prospering "pacific" century of betterment and peace across this vast and crucial part of the world. A reasonable stance at the end of the twentieth century is to hope for such an outcome without believing it to be inevitable.

Article 4   *The World & I*, June 1994

Protecting Asia from Itself

Although given little attention in the West, historical animosities and territorial disputes have resurfaced, fueling local rivalries in the East.

Parris H. Chang

Parris H. Chang is director of the Center for East Asian Studies at Pennsylvania State University

On July 25, 1993, the foreign ministers of 17 Asia-Pacific nations, including the United States, Japan, and six members of ASEAN, the Association of Southeast Asian Nations, met in Singapore and agreed to create a security forum called the Asian Regional Forum (ARF) to keep peace. ARF is a significant step toward establishing a multilateral institution to deal with Asian security matters in the post–Cold War era.

The new era has reduced global military spending by $240 billion, but the proliferation of nuclear, chemical, and biological weapons is now a growing problem for Asia, and arms spending has risen fast.

Although the dangers of military conflict are not clear or imminent, they lie just over the horizon. Conflicts could arise from (1) an imploding former Soviet Union that spurs Beijing's hegemonic ambitions; (2) a possible remilitarized Japan; (3) competitive in-

Regional Security

During the Cold War, the greatest security threats to most Asian states were communist insurgencies and political instability.

Historical suspicions and rivalries between states were kept in check or held in abeyance by superpower confrontation.

The collapse of the Soviet empire has given China the opportunity to become Asia's next great hegemonic power.

Through its arms sales, cash-hungry Russia has enabled China to increase its weapons procurement by 60 percent since 1988.

Security institutions like the Asian Regional Forum are more diplomatic debating clubs than effective tools for ensuring safety.

T. S. Lam / The World & I

A long road ahead: Poverty is one of many problems Asia–Pacific nations must solve if progress is to continue.

traregional rivalries, especially between China and Japan; (4) North Korea's nuclear weapons, which could push Japan to become a nuclear power—a move that would alarm other Asian states; (5) an arms race in Asia; and, above all, (6) a reduction of U.S. presence and military forces in the Asian region.

Due to historical suspicions and rivalries, as well as its size and diversity, the Asia-Pacific area has no equivalent among European institutions like NATO or the Conference on Security and Cooperation in Europe (CSCE). Western Pacific security has been anchored by a credible American military presence, a network of bilateral defense agreements, and security cooperation with the United States.

A consensus has emerged among many scholars and government officials in the region that new arrangements are needed, as the present institutions can no longer cope with all the problems of post-Cold War Asia. ARF is an important beginning toward the creation of an Asia-Pacific collective-security system, providing a mechanism for discussing problems as well as managing potential and actual crises.

This multilateral grouping would supplement rather than replace the valuable bilateral ties established between Washington and its Asian allies. The goals of such a multilateral security system are not to fight adversaries but (1) to engage the nations in the region, including potential rivals, in establishing regional security; and (2) to build mutual trust among Asian states through security cooperation and confidence building.

New-era politics

Far-reaching political and economic changes are taking place in the Asia-Pacific. The same global trends that have transformed Europe are playing out in the region: failure of communism as a political and economic system, movement toward democracy, progress toward global economic integration, and free-market policies. This is not the "end of history," as Francis Fukuyama argued, but the beginning of a new era. The economic dynamism of the Pacific Rim is well recognized as a major engine of global economic growth. A new multilateral institution, the Asia Pacific Economic Cooperation (APEC), has been launched to improve regional economic relationship. Rapid growth is transforming the economic landscape of East Asia.

During the Cold War, the greatest security threats to most Asian states were communist insurgencies and domestic political instability. Historical suspicions and rivalries between states were kept in check or held in abeyance by superpower confrontation. With the end of the Cold War, however, unresolved territorial disputes among Asian states (among them, ownership of the Spratly Islands and potential conflict between Taiwan and China and the two Koreas) and other issues came to the fore. In other words, the strategic landscape in the Asia-Pacific region has been transformed, and there is an acute need for new security structures to defuse tensions and cope with potential crises.

The collapse of the Soviet empire has given China the possibility of becoming Asia's next hegemonic power. There is little doubt that it harbors such an inten-

Taiwanese goods: Taiwan is a world-class economic power worthy of inclusion in the Asia Regional Forum.

tion. With the fastest growing economy in Asia and a population of 1.2 billion, Beijing and its claims on the islands of the South China Sea pose a major threat to the entire region.

Five other countries, namely, Taiwan, the Philippines, Brunei, Vietnam, and Malaysia, also lay claim to portions of the oil-rich islands, but the People's Republic of China (PRC) has adopted an uncompromising position. The Chinese stand also threatens Japan and South Korea, whose trading ships are dependent on peaceful waters in the South China Sea.

The economic crisis in Russia and the other former Soviet republics has negative implications for security throughout the region. Because Russia is desperate for foreign exchange to pay for imports, it is exporting large quantities of arms. Moscow's "bargain-price sale" of conventional weapons has enabled China to increase weapons procurement by 60 percent since 1988. According to President Boris Yeltsin, China bought $1.8 billion worth of Russian arms in 1992 alone.

Yet these purchases pale in comparison to Beijing's intention to acquire technology and production rights from its former adversary. Russian scientists are currently working with their counterparts in China to manufacture advanced weapons and improve defense technology. Over 400 Russian scientists are reportedly based in Beijing working at defense organizations, and more than 2,000 are said to be working throughout China.

> *Problems include piracy, drug trafficking, smuggling of illegal migrants, and the ongoing arms buildup by China, Japan, and several ASEAN nations.*

Russia has reduced its military deployments in Asia and fundamentally redefined its strategic aims in the region. If the United States is also perceived to be reducing its military forces or losing its will to play a leadership role, the PRC would be inclined to fill the power vacuum, fueling new races and tensions in the region.

Collective-security system

What will ARF do? How will it evolve? Will it eventually lead to some kind of collective-security system? What states should be included or excluded? What will be the future functions of the regional-security arrangement?

Scholars and government officials are in general agreement that deep divisions exist among some countries in the region; hence, the ARF can only be a "diplomatic debating club" for now. However, no one rules out the possibility that, in a few years, governments may be willing to set aside their differences and begin to engage in significant confidence-building measures.

In the 1950s and '60s, an organization known as SEATO (the Southeast Asia Treaty Organization), an Asian version of NATO, existed, but it failed because it was largely imposed by the United

States and had no local support. Washington shows little enthusiasm today for a similar institution, unless the ASEAN countries take a strong initiative, which seems highly unlikely.

Likewise, American and Asian officials see no merit in creating an Asian version of the CSCE, because political, geographical, and historical conditions in Asia are vastly different and more complicated. The CSCE, a pact between the western European states and the USSR and eastern European communist countries, was made possible by an important quid pro quo, namely, Western recognition of postwar borders, which the communists wanted, in exchange for communist concessions on human rights. It seems highly questionable whether Asian countries would formally commit themselves to accepting current borders. Territorial disputes are present in the Spratly Islands, Japan's northern territories, Senkaku Shoto, and along the Sino-Russian and Sino-India borders, to cite only a few cases. Moreover, China and ASEAN countries strongly object to U.S. criticism of the human rights conditions in their countries.

On the other hand, the fact that 17 states in the Asia-Pacific region agreed to ARF is quite an achievement. Even though they may not agree on the answers or solutions, they seem to concur on the problems that need to be addressed. These problems include the ongoing arms buildup by China, Japan, and several ASEAN countries and territorial disputes, as well as such new issues as piracy, drug trafficking, smuggling of illegal migrants, proliferation of weapons of mass destruction, North Korean nuclear capability, and any U.S. military withdrawal from Asia that would prompt Japan to rearm and thereby kindle a fierce Sino-Japanese arms race and rivalry.

To promote regional-security dialogues, ARF will hold its first meeting in Bangkok this summer. It is premature to say whether ARF will evolve into a new regional-security institution. In the next three to five years, ARF will serve primarily as a forum for security dialogues allowing member states to debate and exchange views on the actual and potential threat to the region. ARF could function merely as a debating club, or it could become an effective security forum and cooperative-security structure.

Already many ideas that would build trust and confidence are being circulated. ASEAN would like other countries, particularly China, to sign the Treaty of Amity and Cooperation of 1976, which binds the signatories to the principles of peaceful coexistence, peaceful settlement of disputes, mutual respect, and noninterference in each other's internal affairs.

Other ideas include a Russian proposal for a code to govern arms sales so as not to aggravate existing conflicts. Another suggestion is to establish a Center for Regional Security, with a goal of making each country's defense policy clearer through (1) regular white papers on defense policy; (2) invitations to foreign governments to send observers to military exercises; and (3) creation of a regional register of arms transfers and arms holdings.

Because of the potential threat to regional stability, the United States has kept a military presence in East Asia to balance Chinese and North Korean forces.

After a sense of trust has been established, a regional-security system could cover a "no-use of force pledge" on disputed areas and a nonaggression agreement.

Taiwan's role in ARF

ASEAN countries have taken the initiative by viewing ARF as an instrument to defuse potential threats to regional security in the post–Cold War era. Their primary concern is how to contain Beijing's ambitions. Despite Chinese officials' repeated assurances that the PRC has no hegemonic design and intends to settle disputes with its neighbors peacefully, Asian countries remain wary. They are suspicious of Chinese military capabilities, Beijing's claims of sovereignty over Taiwan and the South China Sea, and its threats to use force to resolve these issues. Thus, it is wise to engage China in regional discussions about the concerns of its neighbors and security cooperation.

Likewise, it is imperative that ARF invite Taiwan to take part in its dialogues.

If ARF is to function effectively as a regional-security forum, it should not exclude Taiwan merely because the PRC objects to Taiwan's participation. As Taiwan possesses a garrisoned outpost (Itu Aba Island) in the South China Sea and is a claimant to the disputed territories therein, Taiwan has a legitimate right to take part in regional deliberations on security cooperation.

By any reasonable definition, Taiwan is an independent sovereign state in the international system and should be treated as such. Moreover, Taiwan has maintained extensive economic ties with most states in Asia. In fact, Taiwan has become one of the major sources of foreign capital in Southeast Asia, helping to propel the region's rapid growth. In 1991, Taiwan became the largest investor in Vietnam, Indonesia, and Malaysia. It is the third major investor in Vietnam and the ASEAN countries, after Japan and the United States, with a total investment of over $16 billion as of August 1993.

Taiwan has good reason to fear Chinese invasion and domination. Ever since the Kuomintang government relocated to Taiwan in 1949, the Chinese communists have called for Taiwan's "liberation"; on several occasions, they have attempted force to achieve a goal of so-called national reunification, causing serious international crises. The PRC has consistently asserted that Taiwan is a province of China and that liberation of Taiwan is China's internal affair, in which no other country has the right to interfere. However, Taiwan is by no means China's "domestic" affair: It has maintained strong and extensive external relations over which the PRC has no control.

The PRC has never ruled Taiwan nor exercised any jurisdiction over the island. The claim that Taiwan is a province of the PRC is an illusion of the Chinese communists; it is not based in reality or justified by international law. The government in Taiwan has embarked on a drive to join the United Nations both because Taiwan is an independent state and because the government and people believe Taiwan should take part more actively in world affairs and contribute more to the wellbeing of mankind.

If the PRC persists in its sovereign claim to Taiwan and resorts to saber rattling and intimidation, periodic tensions will inevitably mark Beijing-Taipei relations. Because of the potential Chinese threat to regional peace and stability, the United States has kept a military presence in East Asia to balance the overwhelming military superiority of China and North Korea. American support for Taiwan has manifested itself in maintaining close ties with the Taipei government, including continuous military cooperation under the Taiwan Relations Act.

If ARF is to become an effective security forum and successfully defuse the threats to regional security, it must make

Taiwan a full participant. President Lee Teng-hui of Taiwan has frequently expressed his support for a collective-security system, saying his country is ready to make its contribution. It can be expected that the PRC will object to Taiwan's participation. Previously, the PRC tried to isolate Taiwan, yet Taiwan remains a member of the Asian Develop-

ment Bank and APEC. Beijing has also tried in vain to prevent Taiwan from participating in two major intergovernment regional organizations.

There is an important lesson here: For a multilateral forum, such as ARF, to perform successfully, no one member should be allowed to dictate policy and exclude others from legitimate participation.

Article 5   *The Christian Science Monitor*, December 1, 1993

Economic Cooperation Zones Create New Asian Geometry

Triangles of growth promote trade, limit risks of collapse from instability

Clayton Jones

Staff writer of The Christian Science Monitor

SINGAPORE

In Asia's post–cold-war world, a new geometry of boundaries is taking shape as more nations create markets that defy national borders.

In one corner of Asia is the "southern growth triangle," the name for a new economic zone that cuts across the borders of Singapore, the southern Malaysian state of Johor, and the Riau Islands of Indonesia.

Then there is "Greater China," which includes southern coastal China, Taiwan, and Hong Kong, where hundreds of millions of ethnic Chinese have created the fastest-growing economic area in the world.

Another emerging economic shape is forming around the oval Japan Sea, where the five nations of Russia, China, Japan, and the two Koreas are opening doors to each other that were shut only a few years ago.

Yet another market contour may emerge along the southern Mekong River, which ties together the former adversaries of Thailand, Cambodia, Laos, and Vietnam.

In effect, the "little tiger" economies of Asia (Hong Kong, Singapore, South Korea, and Taiwan) and other would-be tigers are trying to cooperate to make themselves more powerful on world markets.

"There's a new competition in Asia— chasing after scarce capital," says Lee Tsao Yuan, deputy director of the Institute of Policy Studies in Singapore. "Countries are discovering that they must cooperate to make themselves more attractive for foreign investment."

Unlike Europe, Asian nations have little modern experience with open economic borders or joint infrastructure that supports investment. After all, the region is home to four of the remaining five communist-run nations, which are still experimenting with free markets, let alone porous borders or cross-border projects.

But it is just because China, Vietnam, and other closed-market countries are opening up that the map of Asia is being redrawn along the lines of economic strength. The new markets, especially China, are taking much of the foreign investment that in the past might have gone to the six noncommunist countries of the Association of Southeast Asian Nations. ASEAN includes Indonesia, Singapore, Thailand, the Philippines, and Malaysia.

"We are creating growing regions within ASEAN that will focus the attention of foreigners outside ASEAN to the area which can provide competitive and comparative advantages in some cases," says Malaysia's minister of international trade and industry, Seri Rafidah Aziz.

The most common phrase to describe these new sub-regional zones is "growth triangle," which was coined in 1989 by Singapore's then-deputy prime minister, Goh Chok Tong.

"It's a bandwagon," says J. Malcolm Dowling, an economist with the Asian Development Bank (ADB) in Manila. "All the governments are eager to support this trend. Nations are groping for ways to cooperate and take advantage of the fact that they are growing fast."

But he warns, "it may all go into the ocean" if there is not the right "natural" mix of capital, labor, land, and resources. Governments cannot force markets to cooperate, he says.

The Singapore government, however, has been the driving force behind the "southern growth triangle," which gives the small island-nation more "economic space."

Cramped for land and short on cheap labor, Singapore helped to set up agreements and infrastructure to enable its own companies and multinationals to establish factories on nearby islands in Indonesia and across a causeway in southern Malaysia.

For a growth triangle to work, says Dr. Lee, it must have "complementary" factors. Singapore brings managerial capability, finance, transport, and telecommunications, while Johor and Riau offer everything else.

Each morning, for instance, dark-suited Singapore businessmen can be seen taking a ferry to Batam Island, where young women brought from Java work for low wages in industrial parks. The businessmen can quickly pass through immigration checkpoints with a computer "smart card."

"The first and foremost lesson is that growth triangles are primarily an economic, and not political concept," Lee states. "Merely politically motivated growth triangles won't fly."

Two more triangles are in the works within ASEAN. One, tagged the northern triangle, encompasses southern Thailand's Kra Isthmus, northern Malaysia, and the Indonesian island of Sumatra. The area's 26 million people are mainly Muslim but the commercial center, like Singapore, is Penang Island, which is largely Chinese. Leaders of the three countries have endorsed the plan.

An eastern triangle is being planned that would tie together eastern Malaysia, northern Indonesia, and southern Philippines, or the islands of Sulawesi, Borneo, and Mindanao respectively.

Growth triangles offer lower political and economic risks compared with a trading bloc approach, says ADB Vice President William Thomson. "Should anything go wrong, the consequences can be largely restricted to the areas concerned."

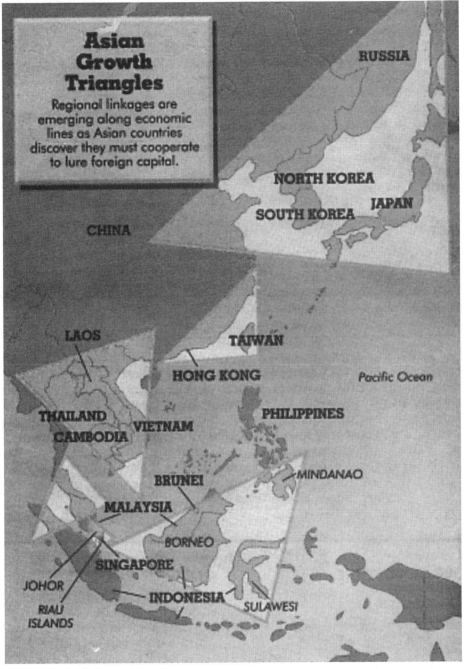

Dave Herring—Staff

Article 6   *Business Week*, November 28, 1994

BUILDING THE NEW ASIA

An infrastructure boom is reshaping the region—
and priming the East to compete in the 21st century

The sleepy rice town of Chonan, 60 miles south of Seoul, has long felt left out of South Korea's dash for modernization. But now, huge machines are eating through the area's steep green hills to make way for a track that will carry Europe's famous *trains à grande vitesse*. The trains, designed by GEC-Alsthom, will link Seoul with Pusan, 270 miles south. Some farmers in Chonan worry that the $13.4 billion project will displace them. But most, such as Kim Wan-Hee, are hoping for a big increase in land values "when people from Seoul move here and build houses."

Along the coastline of China's southern Guangdong province, three huge smokestacks from a power plant built mostly by Hong Kong's Hopewell Holdings Ltd. shoot up from sugar-cane and banana fields. Power lines snake out from the Shajiao plants into the countryside, supplying energy to new factories. Peasants have donned bright clothes and taken jobs in the factories. Many have moved into apartment blocks with TVs and refrigerators. "Having enough power has changed everything for the local people," says station manager Wu Hongbo.

In Bangkok, Tasdanee Milimtasut can't believe how times have changed. The 62-year-old housewife waited seven years for her first telephone line in 1991. Such was the demand for phone lines that she quickly sold it for $2,400, four times what she paid. These days, however, a joint venture between Charoen Pokphand group and Nynex Corp. is trying to fix Bangkok's phone crisis by installing 2 million lines. "Now, they send around trucks offering to install them immediately," Milimtasut exclaims.

A burst of infrastructure building is remaking Asia (see map next page). Rocky islands are being flattened to give birth to airports. Mountains are being knocked down to make room for freeways. And massive reclamation work is shifting shorelines. Earlier this year, the Asian Development Bank estimated that the region would spend $1 trillion by 2000, primarily on energy, telecommunications, and transportation. But now, that estimate is viewed as conservative. Hong Kong's Peregrine group estimates that China, South Korea, Taiwan, Hong Kong, and the five biggest nations of Southeast Asia will require $1.9 trillion (chart, page XX).

"GROWTH MACHINE." This building is already having a vast social and environmental impact. But most Asians are willing—and eager—to pay the price. They see infrastructure as the key competitive battle as the cheap-labor advantage begins to slip away and they push on to reach fully industrialized status. "If you don't offer the infrastructure to make world-class, high-quality products and services, then you're left making shoes with low-cost labor," says Linda Y. C. Lim, a Singaporean who heads the University of Michigan's Southeast Asian Business Program.

Asia's infrastructure is also a crucial battleground for the industrial world's technology and financial giants. Japanese companies lead in winning 27% of the work on Hong Kong's $20.3 billion airport project. Anglo-French GEC-Alsthom sees its victory over Germany's Siemens in Korea as a stepping-stone for other high-speed train deals. Nynex, regarded as slow-footed at home, put itself on the map throughout Asia by scoring the $3 billion alliance with Thailand's CP group. "Asia is our growth machine," says Michael J. Heath, Asia/Pacific managing director for Nynex.

In some ways, the Asians must make the massive infrastructure push just to avoid choking on the growth they have already achieved. With auto use exploding, traffic jams are paralyzing capitals from Beijing to Bangkok. Airports are overwhelmed with long lines of travelers. Energy needs are growing exponentially, and the demand for mobile telephones, faxes, and new television services is taking off.

To be sure, there are boondoggles, white elephants, and mismanagement aplenty. The $11.2 billion Three Gorges Dam hydroelectric project in China, in particular, is a deal skeptics think will never happen because it is too grandiose. Taiwan's $17.1 billion Mass Rapid Transit program has been plagued by mysterious fires and cracks in its support pillars, not to mention corruption and contract disputes. Similarly, Thailand's politics have stalled projects that might ease Bangkok's notorious traffic. **FOREIGN AID.** The fact that some Asians are managing the infrastructure challenge better than others could create competitive gaps among nations once considered on a par with one another. Malaysia, for example, is doing a better job than neighboring Indonesia. It has only 10%

ASIA'S CHANGING FACE

Foreigners are winning leading roles in many of the major infrastructure projects that are under construction or near final approval. But Asians are increasingly building and managing the projects themselves:

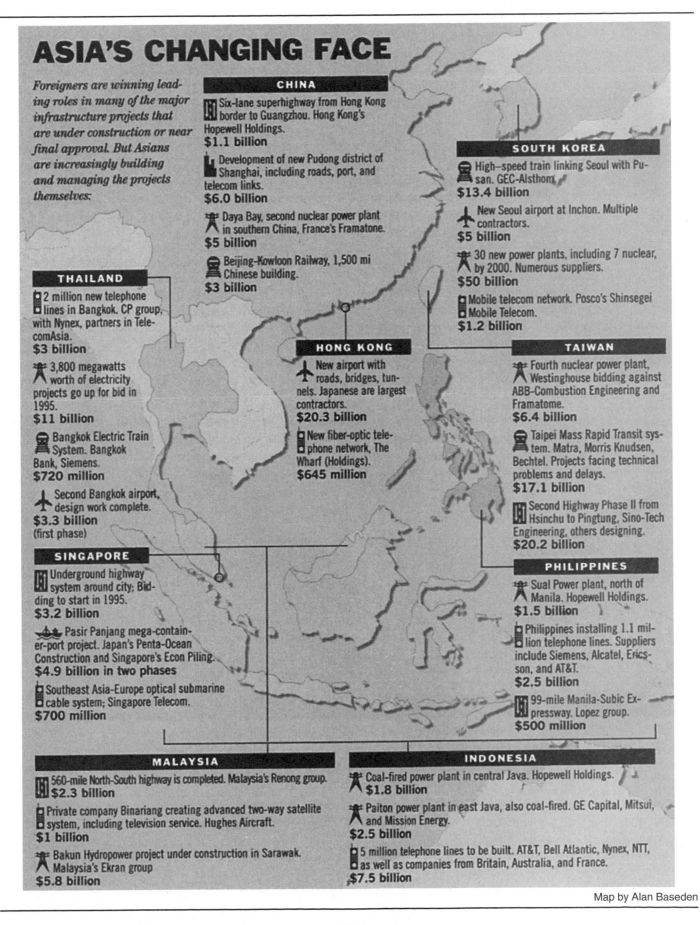

CHINA

Six-lane superhighway from Hong Kong border to Guangzhou. Hong Kong's Hopewell Holdings.
$1.1 billion

Development of new Pudong district of Shanghai, including roads, port, and telecom links.
$6.0 billion

Daya Bay, second nuclear power plant in southern China, France's Framatone.
$5 billion

Beijing-Kowloon Railway, 1,500 mi Chinese building.
$3 billion

SOUTH KOREA

High-speed train linking Seoul with Pusan. GEC-Alsthom
$13.4 billion

New Seoul airport at Inchon. Multiple contractors.
$5 billion

30 new power plants, including 7 nuclear, by 2000. Numerous suppliers.
$50 billion

Mobile telecom network. Posco's Shinsegei Mobile Telecom.
$1.2 billion

THAILAND

2 million new telephone lines in Bangkok. CP group, with Nynex, partners in TelecomAsia.
$3 billion

3,800 megawatts worth of electricity projects go up for bid in 1995.
$11 billion

Bangkok Electric Train System. Bangkok Bank, Siemens.
$720 million

Second Bangkok airport, design work complete.
$3.3 billion
(first phase)

HONG KONG

New airport with roads, bridges, tunnels. Japanese are largest contractors.
$20.3 billion

New fiber-optic telephone network, The Wharf (Holdings).
$645 million

TAIWAN

Fourth nuclear power plant, Westinghouse bidding against ABB-Combustion Engineering and Framatome.
$6.4 billion

Taipei Mass Rapid Transit system. Matra, Morris Knudsen, Bechtel. Projects facing technical problems and delays.
$17.1 billion

Second Highway Phase II from Hsinchu to Pingtung, Sino-Tech Engineering, others designing.
$20.2 billion

SINGAPORE

Underground highway system around city; Bidding to start in 1995.
$3.2 billion

Pasir Panjang mega-container-port project. Japan's Penta-Ocean Construction and Singapore's Econ Piling.
$4.9 billion in two phases

Southeast Asia-Europe optical submarine cable system; Singapore Telecom.
$700 million

PHILIPPINES

Sual Power plant, north of Manila. Hopewell Holdings.
$1.5 billion

Philippines installing 1.1 million telephone lines. Suppliers include Siemens, Alcatel, Ericsson, and AT&T.
$2.5 billion

99-mile Manila-Subic Expressway. Lopez group.
$500 million

MALAYSIA

560-mile North-South highway is completed. Malaysia's Renong group. **$2.3 billion**

Private company Binariang creating advanced two-way satellite system, including television service. Hughes Aircraft. **$1 billion**

Bakun Hydropower project under construction in Sarawak. Malaysia's Ekran group **$5.8 billion**

INDONESIA

Coal-fired power plant in central Java. Hopewell Holdings. **$1.8 billion**

Paiton power plant in east Java, also coal-fired. GE Capital, Mitsui, and Mission Energy. **$2.5 billion**

5 million telephone lines to be built. AT&T, Bell Atlantic, Nynex, NTT, as well as companies from Britain, Australia, and France. **$7.5 billion**

Map by Alan Baseden

of Indonesia's 190 million population, but the quality of the government's decision-making, combined with a competitive private sector, has played a role. In October, Renong, a private company, completed at 560-mile superhighway the length of the Malay peninsula without foreign help. In power, the Ekran group is clearing a site in the heart of Borneo's tropical forest to build a dam and 2,500-megawatt power plant. It will create a lake the size of Singapore.

To catch up, Indonesia is giving foreigners a bigger role. The government has lifted a ban on foreign investment in sensitive areas such as electrical generation, airports, and telecoms. "The Indonesians are realizing that they have to change or they are going to fall way behind," says Cesar C. Zalamea, president of American International Group's Asian investment arm.

Likewise, among the traditional Four Tigers, three of them—Singapore, Hong Kong, and South Korea—seem to be pulling ahead of Taiwan. Taiwan still boasts loads of cash and technology, but it has made such a mess of its infrastructure that it is attracting a shrinking volume of foreign investment. Even its own manufacturers fear that power outages, lack of clean water, and chronic traffic tie-ups will gnaw away at their competitiveness.

One reason Taiwan has failed is that it waited too long. Now, it is faced with the task of doing too much at once. Yet its fractious internal politics don't allow Taipei to relinquish management control of big projects to nonpartisan consortiums or civil authorities. In the case of its ill-fated MRT, Taiwan did hire Bechtel, Morrison Knudsen, France's MATRA, and others—but didn't listen to them. The lesson is that a closed, highly politicized decision-making model isn't good enough.

Among foreign companies, who will reap the biggest rewards from Asia's infrastructure boom? In power, General Electric and Westinghouse Electric are fighting ABB Asea Brown Boveri, Siemens, Hitachi, Mitsubishi Heavy, Toshiba, and others. U.S. competitors also are battling to manage power plants: California's Mission Energy will manage a $2.5 billion coal-fired plant in Java. CMS Energy, the Dearborn-based parent of Michigan's Consumers Power, is managing Philippine power plants. In telecommunications, AT&T, the Baby Bells, Motorola, GTE, GE's information-services unit, and IBM are going head to head with the likes of France's Alcatel Alsthom, Canada's Northern Telecom, Germany's Siemens, and Japan's NEC and Toshiba.

Overall, the Japanese see Asia's infrastructure spending as a major growth engine for themselves. But they don't own the game. Against Japan's construction companies, for example, the Americans enjoy an undeniable lead in advice, design, and project management. Bechtel Corp. and Fluor Corp. are involved in dozens of deals,

but so is a surprisingly deep cross section of small companies. Two examples: Black & Veatch of Kansas City, Mo., a leading designer and building of power plants, and Greiner Engineering Inc. in Dallas, which designs airports. "The U.S. is hugely competitive," says Will Liley, managing director of Peregrine's Asian Infrastructure Fund in Hong Kong.

ALLIANCES. The Americans achieved their advantage in design and management skills partly because Japanese construction companies have been able to rely on rigged bidding in their own market rather than honing their competitive edge worldwide. Similarly, Japanese telecom-equipment makers have been more sheltered than their U.S. rivals. They also are more reluctant to transfer technology. So while the Japanese sold switches, optical cable, and other equipment worth $2.3 billion in 1993, they are not at the cutting edge of forming alliances to help Asians build their telecom systems. "Japan is a little behind Europe and the U.S.," acknowledges Yoshio Utsumi, director-general of international affairs at Japan's Posts & Telecommunications Ministry.

Among Europeans, the French and Germans are mounting a surprisingly aggressive push. To create jobs back home, governments, companies, and financial institutions are teaming up to offer advanced technology at sweetheart prices. Beneath the chaos of Shanghai's cluttered streets, for example, schoolgirls in bright, flowered skirts ride subway cars built by AEG, a unit of Daimler Benz, near Berlin. The $250 million deal was made possible by German government soft loans.

European companies such as Siemens acknowledge that their willingness to give away technology is one advantage over Japanese rivals. "The Japanese have no real interest in helping China become a real economic power by transferring knowhow," says Juergen Oberg, Siemens' executive director for the Far East. "For Germany, it's easier to be best friends in areas far away."

The Europeans also seem guaranteed a seat at Asia's table because of an almost universal desire to use three-way competition among the Europeans, Americans, and Japanese to extract the best deals. "A lot of the countries want to have a U.S. presence, a European presence, and a Japanese presence," says Nynex' Heath. "There's a propensity to carve up the pie."

Where will all the money come from? World Bank funding, European soft loans, and Japanese aid are no longer enough. As a result, Asians are starting to tap private capital from around the world. "The demands simply outstrip available capital," says AIG Chairman Maurice Greenberg, who has launched a $1 billion fund to invest in the high-return equity portion of major deals. Investors such as AIG and Peregrine want guaranteed 20% or higher annual rates of return. That strikes some Asians as too dear. So the big funds haven't yet been able to fully invest.

It's all a question of what price Asia will pay for the money. Asian officials and industrialists argue that coming up with the equity isn't the problem. Their governments are often willing to put up certain amounts of capital, and equipment providers are eager to help finance the sale of their equipment. The need instead is for big flows of money at lower rates.

U.S. investment banks are trying to act as the bridge between Asian needs and Western markets, but they have had limited success. Merrill Lynch, Morgan Stanley, Goldman Sachs, and others are bringing Chinese power plants and Indonesian satellite companies to the New York Stock Exchange. But the Chinese share prices have not done well, partly because investors don't believe the companies will yield high enough profits.

QUESTION MARK. Gradually, however, the terms of the engagement are shifting in Asia's favor. One key is that the Japanese are playing a quiet but important role in making the money flow. Although Japanese banks are not winning high-profile advisory roles or innovating with the latest instruments, they have huge financial muscle. Rather than looking for the big fees that Western investment banks are after, Sanwa Bank Ltd., Industrial Bank of Japan, and others are moving huge amounts of money through plain-vanilla instruments such as project finance and syndicated loans.

Moreover, Asia's own capital markets are evolving with astonishing speed. Thailand's Electricity Generating Co. is raising $180 million in the Bangkok market this fall. Malaysia has been able to fund its highway and power projects in its own currency, the ringgit. Singapore is even exporting capital. So a large percentage of Asia's projects are going to move ahead, whether the West's investors come along or not. All of which helps explain why Hopewell Chief Executive Gordon Wu says: "Money is a commodity. You can buy as much as you want."

Aside from financial capital, the Asians are also developing their human capital—the skills needed to handle such rapid, complex growth. Because so many Asian decision-makers are equipped with MBAs or educations from the best Western universities—and so many are advised by the likes of Bechtel or Morgan Stanley & Co.—it's only a matter of time before they will absorb the management and design skills they need. That's even true in China. "All of us working in China realize we are probably working ourselves out of future opportunities as the Chinese obtain the experience," says Don Hackl, a Chicago architect designing high-rises in Shenzhen.

China is clearly the major question mark. After fast progress in allowing power plants such as Shajiao to be built, decision-makers in Beijing scuttled similar deals because of a perception that foreigners were making excessive profits. These leaders have been able to insist that China not grant foreign investors rates of return above 12% a year, and they've stalled on allowing the spread of the build-operate-transfer (BOT) model that is sweeping Southeast Asia.

"LEAPFROGGING." In telecommunications, however, where decision-making is less centralized, there is huge momentum. China is starting from a primitive position, with only two phone lines per 100 people, but ministries, regions, and municipalities are buying digital switches, fiber-optic cables, and other such gear. Most executives agree China could move from 1950s-level systems to 1990-level systems in the space of only two or three years. "What they are buying and installing is state-of-the-art technology," says Jay Carter, AT&T Network Systems President for Asia/Pacific. "It really is leapfrogging."

The problem is, Chinese decision-making in telecoms is so fragmented that all the gear may not function together smoothly. An advanced digital AT&T system in Guangzhou may not communicate with a slightly different Alcatel system in Tianjin. "If they want a national, homogeneous interoperable system, that will be a challenge," says GE Information Services' Daniel Shih in Tokyo.

But even if the infrastructure push in China is uneven, the raw momentum is unmistakable. In sectors where the center is paralyzed, such as power, provinces are still pushing ahead with smaller power plants that don't require foreign financing. There are even hints in Beijing that the government will soon start allowing greater re-

HOW MUCH ASIA WILL SPEND
According to one estimate, Asia will need $1.9 trillion by 2000

	TRANSPORTATION	POWER	TELECOM	OTHER
		IN BILLIONS OF DOLLARS		
ASEAN	$74.0	$64.1	$21.0	$63.3
CHINA	968.4	54.0	25.2	NA
HONG KONG	23.2	12.8	1.2	29.6
KOREA	132.3	46.2	32.3	145.7
TAIWAN	124.3	28.5	9.6	84.1

DATA: PEREGRINE'S ASIAN INFRASTRUCTURE FUND

HIS DREAM: REVAMP SHANGHAI. THE COST: $100 BILLION

Xu Kuangdi is Shanghai's $100 billion man. As the city's executive vice-mayor, the ex-metallurgy professor heads a committee that approves infrastructure projects in Shanghai and its new development zone, Pudong. Roads, bridges, tunnels, and subways worth $6.2 billion have been built, but that's just a start. Shanghai hopes to spend $50 billion on itself and $50 billion on Pudong by 2000.

Xu's sophistication speaks volumes about the challenge foreign companies face in Asia. Decision makers such as the English-speaking Xu, 57, combine the best expertise of their native lands with that of the West. Hugely ambitious, they have access to world-class advice about how to make multinationals such as General Electric Co. and ABB Asea Brown Boveri (Holding) Ltd. compete fiercely against each other. They also boast outstanding political connections.

IDEA MAN. Xu's most important connection dates to 1989, when he was vice-president of the Shanghai University of Industry. Having spent two years as a technical manager with Saab in Sweden, Xu was a critic of the Shanghai municipality's heavy-handed central planning. His views attracted the attention of reformer Zhu Rongji, who had just become Shanghai's mayor. Over breakfast one morning while both were part of a delegation traveling in Europe, Zhu asked Xu to become director of Shanghai's planning commission.

"I don't believe in planning," Xu recalls saying.

"That's what I need," Zhu replied. "Someone with new ideas."

Xu took the job and by August, 1992, had been named executive vice-mayor. Zhu, now China's vice-premier in Beijing in charge of the whole country's economy, remains one of Xu's biggest supporters. In short, both men are part of the Shanghai-based network of officials managing China's economy.

To cope with Shanghai's infrastructure challenge, Xu has won help from World Bank experts, and he consults with an advisory panel of 23 foreign CEOs, including the heads of American International Group, Bank of Tokyo, Toshiba, and L. M. Ericsson. Xu hopes to harness that expertise to reestablish Shanghai as China's economic center. A student of development around the world, he says he wants to avoid white-elephant projects like Brazil's capital, Brasília, or its huge Itaipu dam. "We must keep the speed of infrastructural growth balanced with overall economic growth," Xu says. "If it's too fast, then you're putting too much money into cement."

It is a task of mind-numbing complexity because the pressure is on to do everything at once. Pudong, located across the Huangpu River, is in effect a 46-square-mile construction site, including export processing and trade zones, technology areas, and a financial district. Throughout the Shanghai area, construction of new highways is forcing massive relocation of residents into high-rise apartment buildings.

CAPITAL QUEST. Xu's biggest headache? How to finance it all. So far, he has tapped the Asian Development Bank for bridges, the World Bank for sewage projects and new roads, and German government cheap loans for $250 million in subway cars supplied by AEG Corp.

But to achieve his ambition will require far greater flows of foreign, private capital—and that's still controversial in China. Xu doesn't have ideological difficulty with the build-operate-transfer model, which guarantees foreigners the profit levels they demand. Beijing, however, is balking these days at allowing foreigners much more than 12% annual profits. Against that backdrop, Xu is negotiating with GE and ABB over two 1,200-megawatt power plants, each costing $2 billion. The "annual return ratio," as Xu delicately puts it, is the key issue. If anyone can cut the best deal with a foreign company while keeping Beijing happy, Xu is the one. That's what it will take to keep Shanghai's infrastructure boom on track.

By William J. Holstein in Shanghai

turns on the big power deals. Other projects are either done or nearing completion: Gordon Wu's six-lane highway cuts through former rice paddies to connect Guangzhou with the Hong Kong border at Shenzhen. A major new rail link between Beijing and Guangdong is nearly complete.

The question is whether China's leaders can make it all happen fast enough. This speed—and quality—of decision-making is a challenge for the entire region. The countries that allow decisions to be made by qualified technocrats rather than corrupt generals or squabbling politicians are making faster progress. So, too, are the countries that find the right formulas to attract the best foreign technology and financing.

The winners from the outside will be those who transfer technology and provide financing at a price the Asians are willing to pay. They won't concentrate on one-shot sales but will become part of long-term alliances. They also will keep pushing into newer technologies, because Asians clearly want to become exporters of infrastructure themselves. Singapore already is exporting telecom expertise. Korean companies are trying to export nuclear-power-plant knowhow and, soon, a rash of new players such as Thailand's CP will be on the move in telecoms.

In short, Asia's infrastructure spending is shaping up as a massive transfer of technology and human capital. The Asian winners will set the stage for the next leg of their spectacular economic emergence—and foreigners who play it cleverly will enhance their global competitive clout. Thus Asia's infrastructure building is about more than pouring concrete. It's about defining who wins—and who falls behind—in the 21st century.

By William J. Holstein in Hong Kong, with bureau reports

Article 7 *The Economist, July 9, 1994*

A SURVEY OF JAPAN
Death of a role model

Foreigners often look for lessons in Japan. But the Japanese have more to learn from the West, writes Sebastian Mallaby

"Japan will disappear," wrote Yukio Mishima, novelist and nationalist; "it will become inorganic, empty, neutral-tinted; it will be wealthy and astute." Some 25 years after this prediction that material success would destroy Japan's traditional values, an opposing suggestion has gained currency: that a superstar economy, admired internationally, might enable Japan to spread those values beyond its shores.

Superstars
GDP growth, annual averages 1960-93

		GDP per head‡, 1992 United States=100
Malaysia*		34.8
South Korea		38.7
Singapore		72.3
Thailand		25.5
Japan		87.2
Canada		85.3
France		83.0
Italy		76.7
United States		100.0
Germany†		89.1
Britain		72.4

Sources: IMF; World Bank *1970-93 †Western ‡Purchasing power parity estimates

Japan's post-war success has seemed to threaten the idea that modernisation means westernisation. The West claimed to have discovered universal laws governing everything from economics to aesthetics; until the second world war most political thought assumed that such laws would push countries towards a common destiny. Because western countries were the most advanced, other countries would come to resemble them as they developed.

This belief in a common destiny still pervades America's foreign policy. Yet the idea that modernisation necessarily means westernisation has attracted plenty of critics. It implies a hierarchy of cultures, so offending egalitarians. It puts white nations at the top, so inflaming racial sensitivities. It claims universality for rich nations' values, so conflicting with the reluctance of a free and tolerant world to pass judgment.

The critics take heart from Japan and its neighbours. East Asia has modernised spectacularly (see chart 1); yet it remains stubbornly different from the West. Westernisation, or at least the stereotyped view of it held in America, puts a high value on individualism; Asians like working in groups. It means tolerance of diverse life-

137

styles; East Asia is disciplinarian and conformist. It means freedom of expression; even East Asian societies with free media lack open debate. It means democratisation; but even democratic East Asian countries have unelected bureaucrats wielding enormous power.

East Asia's success has encouraged the view that, far from meaning westernisation, progress can strengthen easternisation. In the past few years a slew of "declinist" books has appeared in the West, arguing that the eastern system is all but invincible, or that Japan is "trading places" with America in economic league tables. The Clinton administration appears to share this fear, to judge by what it says about Japan's "closed" markets and its own industrial policy (such anxieties prompted America's new $500m programme to boost production of flat-panel screens).

East Asians are joining the chorus. Last year regional leaders issued the Bangkok Declaration on human rights, in which the "Asian Way" (harmonious, disciplined, collectivist) was held up against its western counterpart (chaotic, licentious, anarchic). Lee Kuan Yew, Singapore's elder statesman, says that Asians will valiantly defend order against the corrosive advance of western-style freedom. When Singapore's government caned an American teenager in May, plenty of Americans cheered.

True, Asians have not forgotten Japan's wartime brutality. Yet many still see Japan as the natural champion of their system. Malaysia's prime minister, Mahathir Mohamad, spent some time in Japan before launching his "Look East" campaign in the 1980s. South Korea has modelled its industrial policy on Japan's. In February Zhu Rongji, China's top economic official, spent ten days in Japan studying its economy. The Japanese are currently backing the translation into Chinese of an official history of their industrial policy. Last year they paid for a World Bank report on the East Asian miracle which found that aspects of government intervention were among the reasons for its success.

On these arguments, East Asia's envied success seems to present a challenge to the West that is in some ways stronger (if less antagonistic) than that of communism. Such an idea has become common among proud easterners, as well as those westerners who are critical of the West's own policies. But there are several problems with it.

One is that it depends on a crude and monolithic caricature of the West. "Western" economies themselves range from *dirigiste* France, through paternalist, long-termist Germany to the more genuinely (though still far from completely) free market of the United States; some of their societies are atomised and individualistic, others more group- and family-oriented; they offer, all of them, a moving target for any comparison rather than a fixed model. Moreover the prevailing model of development

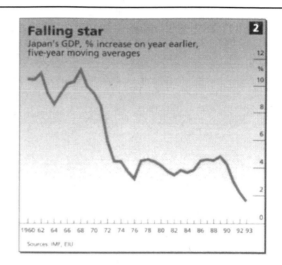

Falling star
Japan's GDP, % increase on year earlier, five-year moving averages

Sources: IMF, EIU

that was widely peddled after 1950 to budding modernisers (almost always with awful results) by western economists encompassed some elements of what many think of as the East Asian model: use trade barriers to force "import substitution", intervene heavily in markets, beat off exploitative foreign multinationals.

Without a western caricature as a comparison, East Asian methods begin to look less exceptional: a different recipe, perhaps, but drawn from a similar list of ingredients. But there is an even bigger objection to the notion of an all-powerful East Asian challenge to the West. For it depends on the vital premise that Japan, the East's first role model, will not grow to resemble the West. And this premise is itself fragile. For reasons that go deeper than Japan's long-drawn-out recent recession, Japan's unwestern features are withering. Just as it seemed poised to become the Oriental role model, Japan may remodel itself instead.

Believers in the East Asian way dispute this. They say that Japan is not about to dump traditions and post-war practices that have brought high growth, low crime and social equality. Yet the model that spawned these achievements is now losing its advantages. Some once-strong features have decayed into weakness. Others were suitable only for an economy that was catching up. This survey argues that Japan is changing; that modernisation is indeed turning out to mean westernisation; and that Japan will grow "neutral-tinted", in Mishima's contemptuous phrase.

One example of a former strength that has become a weakness is the place of hierarchy and social conservatism. These Asian values have encouraged discipline; but they have also stifled new people and ideas. In Japan's post-war years this did not matter, because rapid growth was giving bright youngsters ample chances. But, since the first oil shock of 1973, Japan's rate of growth has slowed (see chart 2). To allow young stars to shine now, Japan needs to soften its traditional belief in hierarchy.

Other aspects of Japan's post-war model have a built-in obsolescence. Japan copied a mass of foreign technologies. But having caught up, it has to switch from copying to originating ideas. Similarly, Japan for years single-mindedly pursued export-led growth. Now its trade surplus is so unpopular—and its currency so strong—that it is having to follow western countries in relying more on domestic consumption to drive the economy forward.

New model politics

It could be that, despite the pressure for change, Japan will continue to cling to its traditions. But its recent political history suggests that this is unlikely. The merger, in 1955, of the country's two biggest political parties to create the Liberal Democratic Party (LDP) produced uninterrupted one-party rule for 38 years. This was at first no bad thing. The LDP provided moderate, pro-business government at a time when the socialist alternative romanticised the Soviet Union. By the 1980s, however, the LDP was choking on its own corruption. In return for bribes, the party handed out public contracts and business licences. Outside firms lost out; competition was inhibited; consumers suffered. Yet the LDP was still not voted out of power, mainly because the electoral laws gave up to three times as much weight to rural votes as to urban ones—and the LDP kept rural voters happy with expensive farm protection.

Plenty of people doubted that Japan would ever shake off the LDP. Last year, however, an LDP government was toppled and replaced by a fractious coalition of reformists, some drawn from its own ranks. In January the new guard pushed through electoral reform, undermining the farm vote. Construction executives who had bankrolled the LDP have been hauled off to prison. And despite the formation in June of a new coalition led by a socialist, Tomiichi Murayama, but dominated by the LDP, the old order shows no sign of reviving.

Reformist ideas are now setting the agenda. Listen, for instance, to Ichiro Ozawa, the ex-LDP man most responsible for unseating the LDP government last year: "We must reform our politics, our economy, our society and our consciousness, to bring them into greater currency with the rest of the world." These are radical words. Yet they provoke surprisingly little dismay among Mr Ozawa's opponents. Kiichi Miyazawa, the prime minister whom Mr Ozawa felled, detests Mr Ozawa's activist foreign policy. But he agrees that Japan should deregulate its economy and encourage individualism. Might this not destroy social strengths like equality and public order? Mr Miyazawa responds to such suggestions by noting that "the Japanese are very practical people", unsentimental about past achievements, ready to adapt.

Reformers are at work inside Japan's bureaucracy too. Japan's mandarins remain notorious for stifling deregulation that would bring them closer to the Anglo-American model. But this is mere foot-dragging. Few bureaucrats now argue that Japan would be better off with no deregulation at all; slowly, liberalisation is proceeding. A 30-something reformist at the Ministry of International Trade and Industry notes that most foot-draggers are older than he is. "And there is one sure thing about generational conflicts: the young guys win."

Shuffled revolutions

There are more reasons for expecting Japan to westernise. Much of Japan's distinctiveness—the power of groups, the lack of vigorous political debate, paternalism, loyalty—reflects a weak individualism. If this were a fixed cultural trait, Japan's distinctiveness might well last. Yet it may instead result from a tangle in the thread of history that is now straightening itself out.

The West, after all, was not always individualistic. In feudal Europe intellectual life consisted mostly of hand-copying manuscripts that spelt out inherited interpretations of God's will; individual reason carried less weight than unreasoning utterances of the Catholic church. Serfs were owned by their masters, who in turn swore allegiance to mightier barons and sovereigns. This intellectual and material bondage faded with the Renaissance. The printing press gave individuals access to a richer variety of ideas. Martin Luther initiated the Reformation by declaring that the individual's interpretation of the Bible mattered more than inherited teaching. Feudal bondage gave way to freer labour markets; eternal pledges of allegiance were replaced by temporary contracts among free men.

Thus in the West individual freedom grew only slowly out of the ashes of a previous feudal order. In Japan feudalism survived into the 19th century. Lords were bound to each other by ties of vassalage; peasants surrendered part of their crops as feudal dues; society was frozen in a caste system. Then, in 1853, American gunboats forced

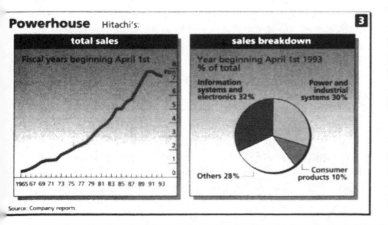

Powerhouse Hitachi's:

total sales

Fiscal years beginning April 1st

1965 67 69 71 73 75 77 79 81 83 85 87 89 91 93

sales breakdown

Year beginning April 1st 1993
% of total

Information systems and electronics 32%

Power and industrial systems 30%

Others 28%

Consumer products 10%

Source: Company reports

Japan to abandon 250 years of isolation. The country's leaders, realising that they would have to modernise to stay independent, responded by organising an industrial revolution in record time. But intellectual revolutions are slower to take hold. So weak individualism lingers on, blending with the bullet trains of Japan's advanced economy.

This mix seems strange to westerners, because their societies modernised in the opposite order to Japan's: the intellectual revolution came before the industrial one. Japan's disordered revolutions have produced a society celebrated as proof that progress can be combined with traditional group harmony. Yet the truth is that Japan's intellectual revolution was delayed, not cancelled. Individualism has been catching up; and with it, the notion of a distinctive Japanese role model is fading.

The long march from harmony

Prosperity, international links and technology are all promoting individualism

In 1910, says a proud museum notice, an engineer at the local mine's repair shop wept tears of happiness: he had become the first person in Japan to build an electric motor. The following year Namihei Odaira founded his own company. He called it Hitachi, after the town.

It was the age of lightning industrialisation. About 100 miles north of Tokyo, crammed between green mountains and the Pacific, Hitachi was a fishing village until the turn of the century, when the Nippon Mining company found copper and gold underground. By 1915 the town boasted Asia's tallest chimney; early sepia photos of the area show poisoned hillsides cleared of undergrowth by the mines' acidic fumes. The Hitachi company built Japan's first electric locomotive in 1924 and its first electric refrigerator in 1932; during the war it made munitions for the imperial army. American bombers flattened its main factory in 1945; but Hitachi soon bounced back. By the 1960s the output of Odaira's electrical company ranged from computers to bullet trains to electron microscopes.

As its technologies and workforce multiplied, Hitachi evolved a distinctive industrial culture. New recruits were lectured on Odaira's reverence for *wa*, or harmony. Managers and workers, all dressed in identical uniforms, all tirelessly punctual, trusted each other like brothers, to the amazement of the strike-prone West. With sales accounting for over 1% of GNP in 1965, Hitachi was a potent sign of Japan's industrial miracle.

Last year the mine chimney collapsed; the remaining stump fumes gently with smoke from burning refuse, and elderly nostalgics are collecting money to erect a monument to its past glory. The mines have closed, leaving Odaira's electrical firm as the pride of the city. Hitachi's sales have risen 20-fold in the past three decades (see chart 3). But, like the chimney, the founder's prized harmony is collapsing. As it yields to the slow advance of individualism, Hitachi is becoming a new kind of a symbol for a new Japan.

In Toshio Iiyama's childhood, harmony owed much to poverty. Mr Iiyama, now Hitachi's mayor, grew up in a company "dormitory", a long terrace of houses with a few communal taps. If mother had to go out, a neighbour looked after him. Father's work down the mine was dangerous, so he and his mates formed pacts with one another: if I die, you will look after my children; if you die, I will be responsible for yours. Material need, more than a cultural inclination towards harmony, led the miners to trust each other like brothers.

The same went for the dormitories of the Hitachi company. Younger workers slept two to a room, and ate all their meals communally in the company cafeteria. Because public facilities were few, everybody went to the bath-house built by the company. In the evenings workers saw the same colleagues in the same company bar. Their wives shopped at the company store and went to the company beautician. The company even provided a wedding hall and funeral parlour.

Toshihiko Kawamura, now a top executive at one of the four Hitachi factories in the city, recalls that in the 1960s workers often spent evenings in their boss's house, drinking his sake, thwacking the mahjong counters on the table. At new year, 50 men would crowd into their boss's house, keeping his wife busy in the kitchen. "Hitachi as one family" ran the personnel managers' slogan.

Turning unJapanese

These days prosperity has dented harmony. Nobody sleeps two to a room in the company dormitory any more. The company bath-house has given way to private bathrooms. Since the 1960s workers have been moving "outside the fence": away from company dormitories to private apartments. Today, 85% of blue-collar workers at Mr Kawamura's factory own their own homes. Dispersed in different suburbs, they call on each other less often. Even by the 1970s, the nightly visits to Mr Kawamura's house were rarer, much to his wife's relief. Nowadays he is visited only at new year; the old bonding sessions have withered into ritual.

Prosperity has also brought more entertainment to Hitachi city: the choice between a French restaurant and a curry house divides one man from the next. Hobbies have grown diverse, says Katsuto Kashiwahara, a manager in a plant making thermal-power equipment. There are cars, drink, bonsai gardening, music bands; before it was only drink. Workers spend more time accompanying wives on shopping trips, and playing with their children: the biological family is displacing the company one. Even Hitachi's president, Tsutomu Kanai, is said to be as happy playing golf with his wife as with his fellow executives.

The mayor's office thinks more leisure is essential to the city's future. In 1991 it built a futuristic civic centre in front of the station. A pink and green robot welcomes visitors to the science museum; a party of schoolchildren mobs a virtual-reality machine that simulates, in turn, a bob-sleigh, a racing car, and a roller-coaster. The centre runs an annual high-school contest for drawings by computer: a girl flies off in a balloon, a witch's castle is visited by a man riding an elephant. Hitachi, goes the message, is no longer a monotonous company town: it is a tapestry of individual creativity.

The company used to provide for all aspects of the workers' lives. Now leisure is an opportunity for individualism, not a prop for workplace harmony. But the old group cohesion depended on more than poverty; there was also a nationalist side to it. In the 1960s the company was managed by methods peculiar to Japan; and it was driven partly by the urge to rebuild the nation after its wartime ignominy. Now both distinctiveness and patriotism are on the wane. Indeed, Hitachi's future success hangs on a dilution of its Japaneseness.

This reflects a built-in obsolescence. Japan's export drive, of which Hitachi was part, produced a trade surplus and a strong yen; to remain competitive, Hitachi has had to shift simple production to cheaper Asian countries. At overseas plants, its traditional harmony has not been reproduced. Far from being brothers, managers and workers come from different countries; far from ex-

uding natural harmony, they communicate awkwardly through a third language, English.

Similarly, Japan once expanded by copying foreign ideas; now it has caught up, so its big firms are rushing to set up research centres in countries with longer traditions of scientific creativity. Since 1989 Hitachi has established seven laboratories abroad. The firm also has research alliances with a string of foreign companies. Altogether Hitachi has 700 Japanese executives posted abroad.

At head office in Tokyo, hardly a trace of nationalism remains. Instead internationalism is rife: a top personnel manager says bluntly, "monoculture firms will not survive." The company runs annual English courses for 1,200 employees, a figure that doubled this year. Every year 50 young managers leave Japan to attend foreign universities; another 50 go to work for foreign subsidiaries.

In 1991 Hitachi set up a department to educate executives in other cultures. This deliberately downplays harmony. In Japan, managers traditionally consult juniors exhaustively before making a decision: abroad, says Takeo Ito, the head of the new department, juniors want firm leadership. Foreign example has encouraged senior managers to seek firmer leadership in Japan, too: hence a new policy to concentrate power in a few hands.

At the factories in Hitachi city, internationalism is spreading too. The tradition of life-time employment once meant that workers and managers would spend their entire careers together; now bright youngsters aspire to foreign postings. Conformist discipline used to be a strength; now workers need to deal more with foreigners. Mr Kawamura, the top executive, speaks English; a computer specialist chats about his holiday in Stratford-upon-Avon; a foreman relishes his business trips to Hitachi's plants in East Asia. One of the engineers at the turbine plant is Malaysian.

Even manufacturing remodels

Prosperity and internationalism widen experience and ideas; inward-looking, homogeneous groups join a more open, diverse culture. There is another force behind the rise of individualism: technology, which is altering work so fast as to undermine the manufacturing part of the Japanese model.

Back in the 1960s, you needed muscles to work at Hitachi, says Kiyoshi Oikawa, the well-travelled foreman; now you need brains. Shop-floor workers tap away on computers while machines do the lifting and lathing; in the turbine factory an unmanned vehicle ferries vast steel parts between computer-controlled machine tools. The lowliest human job remaining is actually quite sophisticated: to oversee and sometimes repair the mechanical proletariat.

More and more of the jobs that remain are white-collar ones, requiring education: designers, computer specialists, international purchasing executives. Naturally enough, the educated workers who do the new jobs are more likely to think for themselves, less likely to conform for the sake of company harmony. Mr Oikawa recalls that, as a young worker, he accepted criticism meekly, seldom asking what he had done wrong. His son, who also works at Hitachi, refuses to apologise unless the boss explains the cause of his displeasure.

Mr Oikawa senior seems unworried by the fading of the old factory culture. In the past it made possible "quality circles"—meetings in which workers suggest efficiency improvements—and these contributed hugely to Hitachi's manufacturing prowess. Now, says Mr Oikawa, quality circles matter less, because human procedures have been so precisely honed that little scope remains for improvement. The next big advances will come in the use of computerised machine tools, not of workers: harmony among the lathes and unmanned ferries has become the new imperative.

Indeed, technology threatens just about every part of Japan's manufacturing model. In the past, shop-floor discipline made possible more rigorous quality checks than in America or Europe; in semi-conductors, for example, it was by reducing the number of defective chips that Hitachi and other Japanese firms came to dominate world markets in the late 1980s. Increasingly, however, quality checks can be done by machines. Good software, not shop-floor perfectionism, will deliver victory.

Harmony between production workers and designers is a waning asset too. In the past, close cooperation between these two groups produced designs that were cheap to manufacture; meanwhile western designers, disdaining the shop-floor, set production workers tasks that were cumbersome and expensive. Now the need for designers to consult makers is fading, because the practicality of most designs can be tested by computer. As computer-aided design grows more sophisticated, Japan's harmonious designer-maker links will decline further in significance.

Computers also undermine the advantage of Japanese firms' much-praised relations with a core group of subcontractors. These links ensure that manufacturers obtain faultless parts at short notice. But now technology offers a new way of securing reliable supplies: manufacturers will soon be sending three-dimensional drawings down modem links to subcontractors. The assiduous purchasing officer, who visits subcontractors to explain what parts are needed and even how they might be made, will soon be redundant.

The electronic Renaissance

Once communication moves on-line, having a core group of subcontractors turns from strength to weakness. It is as quick and easy to send out a parts order to 50 subcontractors as to five; or to Arkansas as to Aichi prefecture. Having placed an order on-line, the purchaser can wait to see which supplier offers to fulfil it most efficiently. By scouring the world for the best deal, technology favours on-line opportunists. The tight family of subcontractors traditional in Japan will become uncompetitive.

Some of these threats to Japan's strengths remain in the future. Recently western companies such as Ford and Motorola have actually been thinning the ranks of their suppliers, and fostering closer relationships with the survivors. But the logic of technology seems likely to reverse this trend. Already, Hitachi has linked its subsidiaries and core subcontractors to a computer network, which it uses to transmit orders for parts. Hitachi is also part of a project called Electronic Data Interchange, which will standardise networks so that big manufacturers can send orders to each other's suppliers.

If this is the future, it could spell the end of the manufacturing part of the Japanese model. Technology may supersede the advantages of harmony between workers and managers, between shop-floor and designers, between big firms and suppliers. Japanese firms such as Hitachi may continue to prosper, but only by de-emphasising the long-term human bonds that have mattered in the past. Creative workers and flexible opportunism towards suppliers might count for more in future.

Such a shift would promote stronger individualism. For technological advance changes people's work, and eventually even their thinking. In the West's Renaissance, breakthroughs such as the printing press expanded the range of potential business partners from which an individual could choose; he became freer, but at the same time less tied to those around him. A new communications revolution is multiplying Hitachi's contacts around the world, diluting its contacts among neighbours: a sort of electronic renaissance.

This survey is indebted to many conversations, articles and books. As well as the sources mentioned in the text, particular thanks are due to "British Factory, Japanese Factory" by Ronald Dore of MIT and Imperial College, London, published in 1973; and to numerous articles by Gary Saxonhouse of the University of Michigan.

Article 8   *The National Interest*, Winter 1994/95

Japan's Asia Card

Ivan P. Hall

Ivan P. Hall, a Japan historian long resident in Tokyo, has also served as an academic consultant for Harvard in East and Southeast Asia and as a USIS cultural officer in Bangladesh and Afghanistan.

Is Japan, having drawn its last drop of cultural strength from the West, about to turn its back and abscond with Asia, adding a new intellectual and ideological dimension to the economic co-prosperity sphere it has so dramatically resurrected? Those in the West who attend to geocultural matters have long predicted the "return" of Japan to its "Asian" roots, and we now find the Japanese themselves proclaiming the "Re-Asianization" of their country.

The old, bifurcated political map drawn in 1955, with both conservative and socialist camps outwardly hitched to foreign lodestars—to American security ties and anti-communism on one hand, and to a U.S.-sponsored "peace" constitution and European Marxism on the other—has been torn to shreds. In its place we may possibly see an implosion of formerly antagonistic ideological forces around a new "consensus" nationalism, and that could easily take as its first task the switching of Japanese national purpose and cultural orientation away from the West toward Asia.

As Japanese enthusiasts for a warmed-over pan-Asianism tug at the tillers of national self-definition and cultural diplomacy, we can at least expect some high swells of touchiness and disdain for the now overtaken West, and a froth of magisterial *vade mecums* for Asians still bobbing in the wake. One can only hope that with the new strength and self-esteem of the other Asian peoples, and Japan's own position in an increasingly transnational post-industrial civilization, Tokyo may eventually find its way to a mode of cultural dialogue that is less fixated on hierarchical power relationships, less dichotomous about East versus West, and more in keeping with its genuinely global needs and responsibilities.

Regrettably, we are now witnessing the latest replay of an unproductive, six-part cycle that it has yet to break out of.

In the opening bars, Tokyo's leaders dissociate themselves from a "backward Asia," seeking to emulate and join the "advanced West;" next, this exercise in impersonation provokes a nationalistic reaction and Western condescension; in the third movement Japan's intellectuals and statesmen then expound the singularity of their country and its divergence from the West, fourth, their Western counterparts avidly concur that, indeed, Japan *is* different; fifth, Japan then turns emotionally and ideologically to a condescending and largely unsolicited "leadership" of Asia and to a resentful anti-Westernism; finally, that runs into a dead end, so it's *da capo*, all over again.

One macro-cycle ran from the forced-march Westernization of the 1870s to the traditionalist counter-thrusts of the 1880s and 1890s and then through a series of perceived rejections by the West in the 1920s—Britain dropping its alliance in 1922, and America slamming the door on Japanese immigration in 1924—to the dalliance with Greater East Asia during the 1930s and World War II. We are today approaching stage five in a micro-cycle of trade liberalization spanning the past quarter century. This cycle began with Tokyo promising Western-style standards but pleading for time. As the United States and Europe began to lose patience and as domestic resistance built up in Japan in the 1970s, Japanese intellectuals built a cottage industry dedicated to the manufacturing of theories of "uniqueness" to justify special treatment for their country. But when European and American revisionist writers of the late 1980s joined this exploration of Japanese dissimilarity, Tokyo cried "Foul!" and complained of Western cultural absolutism. The upshot, from the early part of this decade, has been a Japan turning to the notion of "Asian values"—an expansion of the earlier "uniqueness" gambit—as a common regional shield against further U.S. trade-related pressures.

In a recent Japanese poll, 60 percent thought their country should place equal emphasis on Asia and the West (the United States and Europe), with only 6 percent favoring a tilt toward the West and 28 percent opting for a tilt toward Asia.[1] This nearly two-thirds vote for equidistance, with "Asia First" supporters approaching one third, already represents a major shift away from the Westward-looking postwar orthodoxy. It is also a trend that is likely to continue. Indeed, as Japan's media tout an alleged clash between Asian and Western values—and dwell with some relish on the Clinton administration's failed pressures for human rights in China and numerical targets for Japan trade—cooler heads have had to warn that the security, trade, and environmental challenges in the region can hardly be met without a continued U.S. presence, and that a fairer break on economic access would be the chief incentive for that. Furthermore, over two-thirds of the Japanese between the ages of twenty and forty in the survey judged their country to be "disliked" by other Asians—an implicit admission of the long, steep road ahead.

Old Reflexes . . .

Japan's periods of identification with Asia have typically expressed themselves in grandiose, holistic, pan-Asianist terms—more reminiscent of America's postwar appointment of itself as defender of "Western Civilization" against the Stalinist menace than of the quiet, steady flows that defined our earlier view of cultural relations across the Atlantic.

Japan's recurrent pan-Asianist paradigm, simply expressed, is that of two posts and a lintel. On one side a solidified Asia, much put upon and brimming with resentment; on the other an equally monistic but predatory West; and between the two a cultural gap spanned only by Japan, which towers above the Orient and serves as its cultural spokesman to the Occident. The Japanese sense of draconian alternatives was first honed by the early Meiji Period slogans of "Escape from Asia" (*datsu-A*) and "Joining Europe [the West]" (*nyu-O*)—terms that are still very much in use along with their increasingly fashionable inversions, *datsu-O* and *nyu-A*—while the visual finality of their Chinese ideograms, like red or green traffic lights, further impedes the conceptualization of more nuanced, intermediate choices.

Geographically speaking, although Japan's economic power is now felt throughout the Asian continent, the psychologically intimate "Asia" of the Japanese mind encompasses mainly China, Korea and Southeast Asia, closely fitting the area marked in prewar ideology for the Greater East Asia Co-Prosperity Sphere. Leaving out the "white" nations of Australia and New Zealand (despite strong economic links), as well as the Indian and other peoples of South Asia (despite ancient cultural ties), these boundaries reflect a natural but powerful fellow-Mongolian racial consciousness.

Historically, Japan's past flings with pan-Asianism have been marred by failure to assume a more egalitarian posture toward the rest of Asia, by hyperbolic rejections of the West, and by the sterility of a strictly intra-Japanese monologue. Although certain Japanese liberals over the decades have envisioned the non-exploitative nurturing of an Asian comity of nations, Japanese nationalism has always intruded to provoke its counterpart elsewhere, as the Janus face of worship-the-West and eschew-the-East simply switches its Asian mask from one of rejection to that of imperious orchestration—best expressed today by the "flying geese" development model for which Tokyo, at least, imagines a permanent Japanese lead. Even the selling of the Pacific War and the old Co-Prosperity Sphere as a struggle for the liberation of Asia did not come into play until the severe military setbacks of 1943, having until then been couched in terms of Japan's self-defense and resource needs—the expansion of its own empire.

Japan also finds it difficult to re-enter Asia without denigrating the West, or to celebrate the rise and creativity of its own region without invoking Occidental decline. The inflation of cultural threats is suggested by the odd way in which many Japanese still put the argument in terms of resisting Christianity—a force that has achieved less than 1 percent penetration in Japan and has long been on the defensive in a secularizing West. In his 1976 call for a return to Buddhism, philosopher Takeshi Umehara characterized Christianity as a "blood-stained" religion and its civilization as one of power, assault, and combativeness. Right-wing publicist Hideaki Kase complained to foreign journalists in 1988 of a century's onslaught by Christianity on Japan. And political scientist Yonosuke Nagai in 1994 traced the U.S. containment on communism to the anti-heterodox impulses of Christian theology.[2] What all this hides is probably less concern about Christian religion, in which Japan has very little interest, than vexation with the pressure placed on traditional values by Western rationalism and industrial society; it recalls the yearning of Japan's prewar ideologues for "overcoming modernity."

Pan-Asianist ideology in Japan, short on input or feedback from other Asians, has to date served mainly as an extension of domestic chauvinism. One can hope that the old reflexes will simply prove to be transitional, as the current surge in student, arts and sports exchanges; in two-way travel; in new Asian language electives; and in primetime programming on everything from Tibetan burial customs to train rides in northern Burma gradually transform "Asia" from a mere slogan into a compelling human reality. For the moment, the hype often grates, with its too obvious evidence of pre-arrangement, as in Fuji Television pan-Asian singing contests where young Asians in traditional dress are cheered along in English—the only language they all understand—by a breathless bilingual lady emcee, who then turns to analyze it all for the television in Japanese. More serious conceptual barriers to the real Asia persist in Japan's approach to regional cultural diplomacy, its advocacy of allegedly shared values, and its legacy of wartime bitterness.

... And New Tricks

The old pan-Asianist touch was evident in the cultural policy recommendations for North- and South-East Asia presented at the Second Asia-Pacific Conference in May of 1991, after a year's preparation by a panel of scholars under the aegis of the Treasury and Foreign Ministry. As their sole Western commentator, I was struck by the emphasis on creating a new "organic cultural sphere." This appeal to unity was based on anti-colonialist and anti-white resentment, the old dichotomy of "Eastern spirit" versus "Western technology," the put-downs of Western rationalism and "modernity," the same autistic insensitivity to Japan's neighbors (once again, apparently not consulted), and the presumptuous proposal for an Asian press center in Tokyo to "deliver the ABCs of Asian coverage" to Western journalists. Calls for the construction of imposing pan-Asian cultural centers in capital cities and the staging of flashy events betrayed an expectation that the powerful initiatives by Japan could produce the sort of regional cultural blend that, in other areas of the world, has been the product of centuries of unprogrammed development.[3]

Tokyo's cultural stance in the broader trans-Pacific APEC region emerged with its proposal, just before the November 1993 Seattle summit, for an Asia-Pacific exchanges conference that would help remove an alleged "psychological wall" separating the United States and developing Asian nations. Echoing the government's new theme of American insensitivity was a press cartoon featuring Bill Clinton on a dog sled, whip in hand, stunned as Asia's leaders break out of husky harness to scamper away muttering, "Can you really expect *him* to understand Asia?" American negotiators and opinion leaders should rebut Tokyo's concoction of a mid-Pacific cultural divide as a means of enlisting its entire region against U.S. market-opening pressures and posing as the guardian of Asian economic chastity. Compared to Japan's tightly hoisted drawbridges, lowered only to let the economic samurai out, American political, intellectual, and human ties in the postwar period have spanned the region like a freeway cloverleaf—in immigration, intermarriage, refugees, university ties, and in professional opportunities for Asian artists, scholars, and journalists. Japan should be asked to forge its long overdue Asian links on its own merits and stop trying to gain points by painting the U.S. as a common economic and cultural threat.

The immediate business of Japan's "cultural gap" ploy is to encourage and amplify the recent postulation by certain Asians of a monolithic set of common values under attack by Western cultural absolutism. After fighting in Korea and Vietnam to save Japan and Southeast Asia for democracy and capitalism, what an irony it would be if we now watched the region link arms to reduce American participation under the culturalist rubric that U.S.-style free markets, political liberalism, and individual rights don't really suit their preferences for guided development, "Confucian" paternalism, and group ethics. To the counter-arguments previously advanced in these pages, I should simply like to add two.[4]

On the celebration of Confucian survivals, a distinction needs to be made between the so-called "Little Tradition" of ancient and extraordinarily stable Confucian popular ethics—still alive in education, workplace, and family life—and the "Grand Tradition" of Mandarin-led, theoretically benevolent, bureaucratic government with its rationalization of political autocracy. The late nineteenth- and early twentieth-century Chinese and Japanese reformers who viewed the Confucian legacy of agrarianism, anti-commercialism, xenophobia, bureaucratism and imperial authoritarianism as the greatest obstacle to modernization must be turning in their tombs, along with Japan's Edo-Period Shintoist scholars who reviled the rigid Confucian canons as the bane of Japan's native literary and human sensibilities.

Second, throughout Asian history there has been a broad awareness of the individual as a morally self-directed and responsible entity—in the Brahmin's lonely working out of his individual karma, in the Buddhist's progress toward enlightenment, and in the sort of proto-liberalism which the late Sinologist John King Fairbank noted in the personal integrity and humanistic self-cultivation of the traditional Confucian gentleman-scholar. Indeed, only in warrior-dominated Tokugawa Japan (and some of its modern projections) and in the Maoist attempt to mold a New Man have Asians come anywhere close to creating the sort of self-denying automaton touted by the region's latter-day prophets of political obedience.

The greatest "cultural gap," of course, remains Japan's reluctance to liquidate the emotional residue of its past aggression in Asia and dissolve suspicion among its former victims regarding its true intentions in moving toward armed participation in peacekeeping operations and a permanent Security Council seat. Since their universalistic values are weak, and since justice ultimately comes down to the well-being of the collectivity—be it clique, company, or country—it is especially painful for the Japanese people to admit to any wrongdoing by their nation as a whole.

Asia on Japan

No clear, let alone unified, Asian response to Japan's cultural wooing has emerged to date. Professed attitudes toward Japan depend a great deal on whether one has been talking to consumers and economic planners eager for goods and investment, to politicians still playing the old "aggression card," to an elder generation with bitter memories, or to younger intellectuals looking for new and non-Western self-definitions. The nature of Asian's future links with Japan will in any case depend far less on cultural than on economic, political, and military considerations—including

the nature and extent of America's future commitment to the area.

Since Japan itself has couched the argument in terms of cultural affinity, it is worth recalling the continent's bewildering diversity of traditional civilizations, even leaving out Muslim West Asia. Islam and former colonial influences pull South and Southeast Asia more to the west—toward Mecca and London—than north toward the Confucian orbit, which protrudes southward only into Vietnam and the overseas Chinese communities. Malaysian Muslims and Filipino Catholics have Creator-centered, Western-style religions doctrinally incompatible with this-worldly Confucianism or Japan's group absolutisms. Buddhism, long since extruded from its Indian birthplace by an enduring Hinduism, still supplies in its stricter *Theravada* form the core of social life and national identity in Thailand, Burma, and Sri Lanka, while its broader *Mahayana* version yielded primacy to Confucianism in traditional China (and "ultra-Confucian" Korea) and was heavily infiltrated by Shinto in Japan—where eclectic assimilation has given a unique Japanese twist to every Asian import.

Traditional cultures aside, the region today is differentiated by the politico-cultural divide between communist and non-communist states, by divergent intellectual residues of colonialism, by emotional gradations in anti-Japanese sentiment, by rival conceptions of "Asia," and by dissimilar ties with Japan's primary partner, the United States. Samuel P. Huntington, writing on "The Clash of Civilizations?" (*Foreign Affairs*, Summer 1993), titillated Japanese readers with his sharp East-West fault lines—and his grand cultural zonings, not in fashion since Toynbee—only to upset them with his clear-cut demarcation of their own country from the rest of Asia. Although some even suspected a politically motivated point here, Japan does have a backlog of bilateral business blocking any common cultural approach to Asia.

Proof of the Pudding

Korea (for now, the South) will be the litmus test of Japan's willingness to surmount its past. Nowhere do grudges run deeper than in Japan's cultural sibling—closest in race and language, in corporate and educational ethos, and in a joint intellectual inheritance from China and the West. Unprocessed rage at Japan's colonial attempt to eradicate Korean cultural identity continues to break out—in

the decision to tear down the massive former Japanese capitol building in Seoul, in the barely-lifted ban on performing Japanese popular music, and in the recent vandalizing of a Japanese art exhibit. Christianity, in part a riposte to Japan, now commands a third of the population, and anti-Americanism among certain younger Korean intellectuals does not translate into follow-Japan sentiment. Some pragmatists in Seoul now call for a more normal emotional tie, but Tokyo seems to be counting on its economic leverage rather than an atonement that signifies a genuine change in Japanese attitudes and is psychologically credible to the Koreans.

At the opposite extreme, Malaysia has gratified Japan with its "Look East" economic and educational policies, as has Singapore with its resolutely dichotomizing "school" of West-versus-Rest pundits. At the risk of never being allowed to set foot in Kuala Lumpur or the Lion City again, I suspect that the Japanese—avoiding offense to America by letting others do the talking—have been very much behind Malaysia's proposal for an East Asian Economic Caucus which they would handily dominate; and that Singapore's self-generated harping on incompatible values—with a command of English idiom, Oxford Union oratory, and Western guilt buttons far beyond that of the Japanese—has served Tokyo's policy goals well. Prime Minister Mahathir's startling suggestion that the Japanese stop apologizing about the war reflects, of course, the preferred treatment which ethnic Malays received during the occupation in contrast to the Chinese, as well as the wartime education in Japan of a number of still-active national leaders. In Singapore, where the Chinese suffered horribly, the distaste for human rights probably has less to do with the glint of Japan-harnessed economic growth than with Mr. Lee Kuan Yew's desire to strengthen political ties with China.

Whereas America's intellectual presence in Britain's former possessions has always been peripheral and subject to a certain colonially-transmitted disdain, Japan's newly funded institutes, chairs, book distributions and academic exchanges with the Philippines and Thailand flow into the void of receding, or at best static, U.S. cultural and informational activity resulting from the sharp reduction in former strategic ties. Economic, sentimental, and family links to the United States, wartime memories, and sheer temperamental exuberance will keep Filipinos chary of any heavy-handed Japanese cultural embrace, but in Bangkok—as one Thai professor friend recently put it to me, scrunching his shoulders to make the point—"The American ambassador looks *sooo* small, compared to the Japanese." Thailand, with its parallel history as the only other non-colonized modernizer in Asia, its shared monarchical tradition, and its ancient skill in adjusting to new power balances, is moving self-assuredly toward closer cultural ties with Japan. In an ironic reversal, Vietnam now openly calls for an American economic presence to balance Japan's, and the conceivable role of returning U.S.-based refugees as bridges between the two societies may someday establish the cultural price of Japan's stinginess in turning away so many of the "boat people."

Finally, what of Japan's two giant rivals for the mantle of "Asian" cultural leadership: China and India? Tokyo's concern with China today focuses far more on economic, political, and military tangibles, while the Chinese have hardly shed their traditional view of the Japanese as culturally peripheral—if technologically adept—barbarians, and retain a historical mistrust of Tokyo-sponsored campaigns on behalf of Sino-Japanese "brotherhood" and "friendship." Chinese inclinations toward Confucian magnanimity and Buddhist forgetting cannot erase the reality of millions of lives lost during the war. Japan's obtuseness with this historical fact was inadvertently betrayed by a Tokyo editorial writer who returned from Hong Kong not so long ago amazed by the way the Chinese and British got along with each other in spite of the Opium War of 1842, and puzzling over what was missing in the Japanese approach.

The sleeper in the cultural game may prove to be India, should it shift its political and cultural attention from West to East and vigorously re-enter the cultural zone which it once enriched with its religion, philosophy, and art. Several strengths conceivably could override negative reviews pertaining to its slower economy, caste society, and ethnic quarrels. Indian experience in holding together the world's most diverse nation for nearly half a century—without revolutionary paroxysm or military takeover, and according to Western-derived secular governance—is clearly the *political* miracle of post-war Asia. Indian familiarity with Western intellectual idiom also positions it as the most effective rhetorical bridge, a sort of "Super Singapore" capable of mercilessly twitting the

Occident if it so chooses—and especially America, with which political ties have never been close. More to the point, any *cultural* definition of Asian togetherness will eventually have to go beyond the materialistic appeal of Japanese or Chinese economic performance to something more of the mind and spirit. And as India's preeminent cultural spokesman and pan-Asianist in this century, Rabindranath Tagore, learned during his visits to Japan in 1916 and China in 1924, the "Asias" of the Samurai, Mandarin, and Brahmin are different indeed.[5]

India's philosophical bent for tolerance and inclusion, and its preservation of a medley of traditional cultures as the rest of Asia goes looking for its withered roots, could give it the last laugh in a bargain with the modernization devil that was the reverse of Japan's (leave aside the Maoist ruination of China's heritage). Alarmed precisely by India's political subjugation and its cultural bifurcation into an English-speaking, Westernized elite riding a multitude "mired" in tradition, Japan opted for an integrated but hybrid modern civilization with leaders and masses sharing a twice-thinned mix of extracted Western culture and attenuated Japanese tradition, sustained by a permanent political ideology of external imperilment. The dualistic "both-and" of India's looser amalgam—with its deeper accessing of both Western universalism and time-honored roots—may just possibly have more to say to the coming century than the unsettled tension of Japan's "neither-nor," which crops up repeatedly in its sense of cultural loss, its awkwardness in dealing with the outside world, and its outbreaks of xenophobic nationalism.

Asians today worry less about two Japanese faces than about none, as Tokyo fails to clarify (or deliberately veils) its intentions toward their region. The one face Asians as a group do see is that turned toward their students in Japan, where discrimination in housing, difficulty in making friends, and ceilings on advancement in Japanese companies suggest that Tokyo may be risking an output of one hundred thousand foes rather than fans as it approaches its foreign-student goal for the year 2000. (As for Westerners, who are present mainly as teachers, a 1992 directive from the Ministry of Education pushing for the retirement of all foreign staff over age fifty at national universities, with a ban on new hires over age forty, substantiates the ingrained resistance of the Japanese to any serious foreign involvement in their cultural institutions.)

Sayonara Uncle Sam?

Japan's relationship with the United States is marked by a distancing that expresses itself primarily in a new tone of contempt. Unlike the earlier anti-Americanisms of Japan's political left (which did not rule out an admiration for American ideals or a personal liking for Americans) or of the politico-cultural right (whose paeans to U.S. Cold War policy veiled its gut antipathy), this new virus reflects a pervasively perceived erosion of both American virtue and power. This is partly the result—as some tried to warn—of talking tough to Japan about trade without meaning it, or of actually getting tough without being prepared to handle the emotional backlash. The Japanese, who are quicker than most to bow to *force majeure* and cooperate with perceived moral superiors, are also "peculiarly sensitive to the smell of decay" and quickest to resent abuse from a morally flabby, retreating hegemon.[6]

The abstract, politically connoted term *han-bei* (anti-America) has been superseded by the more personal *ken-bei* (dislike of America) and *bu-bei* (contempt for America)—the character *bu* combining visual nastiness with the scorn which the Japanese ear associates with the lip-voiced sonant "b" (like the Bronx cheer overtones of "boob" or "blubber" in English). Although some of this rests on popular sentiment, one suspects that much of it was originally manufactured and then took on a life of its own. If fabricated, we might infer yet another attempt to frighten Uncle Sam with the specter of anti-Americanism, or, what now seems more likely, a strategy to prepare the Japanese public for an emotional break with America. The break will come if and when Tokyo decides—whether by grand design, or through the inertia of vested interests—that the effort to join the world by genuinely opening up Japan's economy and society is more troublesome than establishing a defensive primacy over its own region. An anesthesia of anti-American grievances may be required to neutralize the considerable residue of familiarity, trust, and even affection for the United States at the grass-roots level, and to numb any anxiety over an untested recoil onto Japan's own technological inferiors.

We are already witnessing a media buildup to the fiftieth anniversary of the atomic bomb next summer, when the Japanese possibly may use the immolation of Hiroshima and Nagasaki as the occasion to finally admit their wartime responsibility one-sidedly towards Asia, position themselves among the victims of the West, and shift the opprobrium to America. Certainly, the unreconstructed "neo-nationalists" are ready to make such an argument, if the comments of Ryutaro Hashimoto, Minister for International Trade and Industry, are representative. He recently declared it a fact that Japan "had no intention of fighting the area's inhabitants. . . . It was not those [Asian] countries Japan chose to fight, but the United States, England, and others." Further, he was "not willing to say we fought a war of aggression in World War II."[7] At the climactic anniversary of the end of World War II, the U.S. will have to look sharp lest it squander the last significant V-J Day to make its own case.

Americans will also have to address Japan's overdrawn sense of victimization, which goes all the way back to Commodore Perry's black ships, and realize that there is little guilt or remorse toward the U.S. with respect to the Pacific conflict. Speaking for the government in August 1991, Deputy Chief Cabinet Secretary Nobuo Ishihara averred that "It will take tens or hundreds of years before the correct judgment is delivered on who is responsible for the [Japan-U.S.] war,"[8] while former Prime Minister Noboru Takeshita is now famous for his private view that historians have yet to pin the blame on Hitler for the tragedy in Europe. Japan's leading Freudian theorist, Takeo Doi, writing of the cultivation of *higaisha ishiki* (victimization consciousness) among his countrymen has even gone so far as to surmise that "The Japanese tend to feel wronged and to dwell on their being imposed upon to the extent that such a state of mind becomes often an important ingredient of their identity."[9]

A typical Japanese docu-drama on the 1937–45 conflict might open with Mitsubishi bombers over China (politely, from a hazy height), proceed to sensational shots of the Pearl Harbor attack, continue with the metal *Niagara* of U.S. Navy offshore shelling (such brute force!), and conclude with the Hiroshima cloud and prostrate crowds sobbing outside the Imperial Palace. I myself once watched a Tokyo University historian

conclude his educational TV account by remarking that the war had indeed been dreadful—but listing up only the Japanese casualties.

Unfortunately, the controversy over the Smithsonian's exhibit of the *Enola Gay*, planned for next summer, shows how close America's amnesiac postwar generation has come to losing its historical perspective on the Pacific War. Congress and the veterans, however, should have insisted less on playing down the sufferings of the Japanese than on playing up the pain inflicted by them, along with Tokyo's expansionist policies leading to the war and the suicidal fanaticism of military leaders willing to prolong it to the last sixth-grader. Indeed, the most effective antidote to the predictable binge of Japanese self-pity next August would be the counter-testimony of a richly visual American documentary film on the recorded behavior of Japan's militarists, fascists, and ultranationalists at home and abroad from 1931 to 1945 to illustrate what the U.S. was fighting against and what it would have faced in any invasion. Let the film be a bit partisan and pro-American for a change—sponsored if need be by the veterans' organizations themselves, funded exclusively from American coffers, and unencumbered by any binational committee fudging up a "balanced" view. The Japanese, after all, have never asked Americans to contribute any balance to their own heavily slanted documentaries and dramas about the war.

On the economic front, the U.S. will either have to fork out the additional political capital required to open markets in Asia, or stop annoying its APEC partners to no good purpose through unilateral pressures and entrust its economic future to the new World Trade Organization—precisely what the Japanese would like to have us do, sealing their triumph at a quarter century of stonewalling. Either way, Washington should never allow itself to be outflanked by the sort of Japanese propaganda that, at the collapse of the Clinton-Hosokawa summit last February, succeeded in portraying the U.S. to the world as the protectionist offender.

American cultural and information officials will have to shed their Cold War shyness about risking any possible offense to the Japanese and engage the economic dynamo of East Asia with all the ardor once lavished on the communist challenge, albeit with a very different tone and message. America's public intellectuals, too, will have to become more involved with the ideas, visions, hopes, and rhetoric of the region if they do not want the coming inter-Asian rapprochements to take on a gratuitously distant and exclusionary tone toward us. At the very least, clearer perceptions and sharpened forensic skills will be required if the U.S. wants to cope constructively with the changing attitudes of the Japanese toward Asia and America, and of Asians toward Japan.

Notes

1. *Asahi Shimbun*, August 23, 1994.
2. Umehara in *Nihon Bunkaron* (On Japanese Culture), (Tokyo: Kodansha International, 1976), pp. 53–54; Kase in a speech to the Foreign Correspondents Club of Japan, September 26, 1988; Nagai as reported in *Asahi Shimbun* evening edition, September 14, 1994.
3. See the report, "Bunka Shakaimen Kenkyu Gurupu Hokoku" (Final Report of the Cultural and Social Study Group), Second Asia-Pacific Conference, FAIR (Foundation for Advanced Information and Research), Tokyo, 1991.
4. See *The National Interest* (Spring 1994) and (Summer 1994).
5. See the superb study by Stephen N. Hay, *Asian Ideas of East and West: Tagore and His Critics in Japan, China and India*, (Cambridge: Harvard University Press, 1970).
6. See pages 38–39 of the prewar German economist Kurt Singer's *Mirror, Sword and Jewel*, (Tokyo: Kodansha International, 1981) which should be required reading for the entire U.S. foreign policy establishment.
7. Reuter, *Asahi Evening News*, October 25, 1994, p. 4.
8. *Japan Times*, August 16, 1991.
9. Takeo Doi, "A Psychiatrist's View on *Zeitgeist*," *Solidarity* (Manila), August 1971, p. 19.

Article 9

New Perspectives Quarterly, Fall 1994

Japan's Self-Reform

Ichiro Ozawa

The maneuverings of Ichiro Ozawa, Japan's contemporary equivalent of Machiavelli, led to the fall from power of the Liberal Democratic Party and has given birth to a new pro-reform party that counts former Prime Ministers Morihiro Hosakawa and Toshiki Kaifu among its members.

Ichiro Ozawa's recent book, A Blueprint for Japan *is considered a reliable guide to the coming political and policy changes in that island nation.*

TOKYO—Today we live in a tripolar world in which the United States is the pivot between Japan and Asia on the Pacific and Europe and Africa on the Atlantic.

Asia and Europe share the same Eurasian continent and in their long history have fought countless wars with each other. Each has its own ethnic and cultural prejudices about the other. The US, however, has not soiled its hands with this kind of history. Despite its enormous power, it is comparatively free of these racial and cultural conflicts. I am thus convinced that today's tripolar relationship, with the US as a bridge between Europe and Asia, is ideal. As such, I strongly hope that Americans will never forget the responsibility that history and geography have imposed on them; that they will avoid being distracted by immediate problems.

However, peace and prosperity cannot be realized just by shoving onto the American people all the burden and all the responsibility. The burden must be shared by the entire world. Japan, in particular, must accept its appropriate share.

Under the Cold War structure, Japan left the responsibility for the development of the free-trade system as well as its prerequisite—maintaining international peace—to the countries of the West led by the US. Nor was this all. Japan's own economic development depended on the fact that the US supplied it with the biggest and freest market in the world—the American market.

For Japan to gain the international community's trust in what is now a new era, we Japanese must change—with our own hands—our politics, our administrative machinery, our economy and our society. In fact, self-reform is the only way in which we can survive among our global neighbors and maintain the peace and prosperity we enjoy today.

In last year's general election, we advocates of reform won the votes to end the Liberal Democrats' (LDP) 48-year monopoly on power, and established a new coalition government led by Morihiro Hosakawa. The new government's first tasks were to change the electoral system and to thoroughly reform the political funding system. In the Uruguay Round talks, the new government also made the politically difficult decision to partially open the rice market.

Unfortunately, the Hosakawa cabinet had to resign after eight months, and its successor, the Hata cabinet, also left office at the end of June. A new coalition government of the Liberal Democrats and the Socialists, with Socialist Party Chairman Tomiichi Murayama as prime minister, has come into being. These two parties have fought each other for nearly half a century, with diametrically opposed concepts and policies.

Even the Japanese, who are very good at differentiating between *tatemae,* one's public facade, and *honne,* one's real feelings, were speechless at this turn of events. No wonder non-Japanese were even more surprised.

Historical Interlude

Geographically, Japan is cut off from the continent by the sea, and ethnically its people are more or less a homogeneous race. They have very little experience of negotiations with foreign countries, or any kind of exchange, friendly or hostile, with others. Within this homogeneous society, the Japanese lived in a mutual relationship of "you scratch my back, I'll scratch yours." As a result, they became isolationist and ignorant of worlds other than their own. Their pattern of thinking tended toward sentimentality rather than reason and logic.

It was US Commodore Perry and his Black Ships who sailed into Tokyo Bay in 1853 and dragged Japan into the international community. Fifteen years later, Japan replaced its feudal system with the structure of a modern state, thus giving the country a fresh start as a member of the international community. That was only 126 years ago.

Subsequently, Japan invited large numbers of European and American engineers, civil servants and scholars, to teach new systems and technology. Under the outstanding leadership of the new government, modernization proceeded apace in all fields—politics, administration, economy and society. Japan carried out its responsibilities under the rules of the international community.

Unfortunately, neither political leadership, nor the policy of emphasizing international cooperation lasted very long. By the mid-1920s, statesmen with broad vision had disappeared from the scene one by one, and no new leaders of equal stature took their place. As a result, Japanese politics took the easy path, the one to which Japan was habituated by years of history—namely, close-mindedness and isolationism. Reacting emotionally to whatever it confronted, instinctively Japan gravitated toward isolationism, taking action after action that lacked awareness of the international consequences. Finally, Japan plunged into a reckless war with the US and its allies.

> *America's post-war policy was designed not to build up Japan, but to make sure it would never be active in international politics.*

Defeated in war, Japan undertook various reforms under the guidance of American occupation policy. But American policy during this period was not designed to build Japan into a responsible member of the international community, but to make sure it would never again be active in international politics, and most certainly not allowed to play a military role of any kind.

Prime Minister Yoshida took advantage of this American policy to keep armaments at a minimum, while devoting the government to economic recovery. He made the economy his top priority. This policy not only suited the closed-mindedness of the Japanese people, it was the most convenient path for Japan to follow. Japan left international politics entirely in American hands, concentrating exclusively on economic growth and the resulting improvement in living standards. The only task of Japanese politics was a fair distribution of wealth created by economic development.

Although Japan's development depended on the world free trade system, it participated in the international community at a minimal cost. It was the Cold War structure that made it possible for Japan to take this course. The US and other Western countries shouldered what would otherwise have been Japan's share of the common burden. Even though the scale of its economy reached a level second only to that of the US, Japan could, until a few years ago, afford to sing the praises of peace and prosperity without ever being pressed to bear any share of the mutual defense burden. What a wonderful paradise, what unbelievable good fortune!

With the end of the Cold War, the US and the European countries no longer have any need to carry Japan's share of the costs of peace. It is perfectly natural for the US and others to strongly demand that Japan play an appropriate role and take up its proper share of this responsibility. It is to establish a structure capable of shouldering these costs that I advocate political, administrative and economic reforms.

But having basked in this comfortable set-up for so many years, many of Japan's political and business leaders wish to continue enjoying the status quo. They have deluded themselves into thinking that it is still viable. I regret having to admit that this is the situation in Japan today.

The real reason for the birth of the coalition between Liberal Democrats and the Socialists lies in these elusive hopes and dreams. Japan never had real liberals or real socialists. The political fault lines in Japan today are elsewhere. On one side stand the forces we represent, asserting that Japan must face squarely a historic moment of change and undertake its own reform, on its own initiative. On the other side are those who say that Japan has no need to change, that it has managed pretty well so far and will continue to do so in the future. The LDP-Socialist coalition government represents this second stream of thought. These are people who do not admit the need for change, who have totally discarded even the facade of past differences over concepts and policies, and who have joined hands in pursuit of naked power. Otherwise, a coalition between the Liberal Democrats and the Socialists is simply unthinkable.

Although this change of government was not based on policy differences, it is significant that the Socialists, the perennial opposition party, became one of the governing parties. Now the Socialists are having to confront problems in a practical manner, as a responsible political party. In the process they are having to change.

If the party follows in the footsteps of Prime Minister Murayama's Diet, answers and clearly changes its basic policies, the senseless and unproductive confrontation over foreign policy and security that divided national opinion for half a century will be dissolved.

One-Country Pacifism Is Over

Japan's very existence depends on being able to trade freely around the world. For us, more than for any other country, a stable prosperous world order is essential. We hold, therefore, that the US–Japan security structure must be the bedrock of Japan's foreign policy, and that at the same time we must participate vigorously in all the various kinds of UN peacekeeping activities, thus fulfilling our responsibility as a member of the international community.

The people of the Murayama government, on the other hand, talk about cooperating with the UN; but they never forget to add one condition: "within the framework of the Japanese constitution." What does "framework" mean in this context? Even in UN peacekeeping operations, not only does direct participation violate Japan's constitution, but even indirect participation is unconstitutional if it has the slightest connection to the use of force. If the UN called for a naval blockade, Japan would even be prevented from supplying fuel and food to American and other ships participating in the blockade, because to do so would be to join the structure of force that a naval blockage represents. Can the nations of the world accept so self-centered a position? The answer has to be no.

Unilateral pacifism is selfish. Nor can we expect it to be viable.

It can be argued that not only Japan's undertaking of peace activities under the UN flag is constitutional; but that it is by our doing so that we will actually fulfill the ideals and spirit of our constitution and its emphasis on internationalism. These views are what we call "international pacifism." Murayama's government is "unilateral," or "one-country pacifism." Such "one-country pacifism" says that it is enough if Japan itself is at peace—this despite the fact that we continue to depend on other countries for almost all our resources and trade. Unilateral pacifism is selfish. Nor can we expect it to be viable. Nevertheless, the fact remains today that most people in Japan do not try to understand this.

Another fundamental difference between the current government and those of us now in the opposition is our approach to deregulation. I do not exaggerate when I say that Japan is a society given to regulation. This is true for a number of historical reasons. Legal and administrative regulations penetrate every sector of our society, every nook and cranny of our lives. We have lived comfortably to the present day in this kind of framework, in part because we have lived almost exclusively among ourselves.

But so uniform a society, governed by regulations, cannot generate the energy for technological innovations or for the development of new industries or other innovations demanded by the present age. It is only by relaxing regulations and making things freer that we can inject the imaginative power and the originality we need into Japan's economy and society. Deregulation is, in other words, something that we must undertake on our own accord, for our own sakes. We must deregulate, not because other nations demand that we do so, but in order that Japan can continue to develop and renew itself. The result of this effort that we make on our own behalf will be a market and a society that are freer and more open to the international world.

A New Party

Our coalition government, led by Prime Minister Hosakawa last January, passed bills for electoral reform and reform of the political funds contribution system. We did so in the belief that this would be the most effective means of achieving overall political reform. There now remain a number of related tasks, including that of drawing up the districts for the new electoral system. There are of course forces in the current LDP–Socialist ruling coalition who want to scuttle these remaining bills and kill political reform altogether. But since the opposition will be putting maximum pressure on the government to complete these tasks, I am confident that all the remaining reform-related bills will pass by the end of this year.

No matter how much the Socialists change their tune in order to maintain this government, I am convinced that they and the LDP will not be able to overcome their many policy differences and come together as a single group.

Therefore, the formation of the present coalition government is no guarantee of future growth, either for the LDP or for the Socialists. In fact, many Japanese think the formation of the LDP–Socialist administration is bound to push back the restructuring of our political world—the fundamental change required in our politics. I believe, however, that the reverse is true and that the turnabout in politics will be hastened, not delayed.

For the opposition, the most pressing task is to unite our several parties and political groupings into a single new party. If we can truly come together as one, we have every possibility of becoming Japan's largest political party, outdoing even the LDP and returning to power without fail in the not-too-distant future. We are now doing everything we can to build one, large new party.

The confusion in Japanese politics probably seems very strange to most of the world. Perhaps it is best to think of it as the birth pains of a nation struggling to be reborn.

Article 10   *The American Enterprise*, May/June 1994

JAPAN'S NEW ORIENTATION

REELING AT HOME
RE-TURNING TO ASIA
RETHINKING ITS U.S. TIES

John H. Makin

John H. Makin is a chief economist at the Caxton Corporation and the director of fiscal policy studies at the American Enterprise Institute.

The sudden resignation on April 8 of Japanese Prime Minister Morihiro Hosokawa just two months after the remarkable televised collapse of U.S.–Japan trade talks at a joint White House press conference featuring President Clinton and Prime Minister Hosokawa may have created the impression that the two events were connected. They were not. The sudden resignation of Japan's fifth prime minister in as many years has far more to do with rapid changes in Japan than it does with any rapid metamorphosis of U.S.–Japan relations.

Prime Minister Hosokawa resigned because his coalition government, having exhausted itself on enacting political reform and a modest tax cut, could not pass a desperately needed budget containing more economic stimulation measures. The corruption charges leveled against Hosokawa by Japan's long-ruling Liberal Democratic Party (LDP), now its opposition party, would not have stuck had he been the head of a workable government.

The Hosokawa resignation marks the beginning of an unusually long election campaign leading up to the first elections for the upper and lower houses of Japan's Parliament under Japan's new election law, which attempts to stem corruption in campaigns while according more representation to urban dwellers. While a new prime minister and a new cabinet will run Japan between now and then, the real interest will be in the battles that try to shape the election either

as a vehicle to accelerate the rapid pace of change in Japan or as a vehicle to preserve the old order.

Japan's accelerating domestic transformation, now underscored by overt political turmoil, is one that many American observers have neglected. They have been preoccupied instead with changes in the U.S.–Japan relationship, especially the nettlesome trade relationship. The turmoil in Japan is not necessarily good news for the United States, particularly if the Clinton administration continues to press Japan on contentious trade issues, but the rapid changes under way in Japan may not be entirely good for Japan either.

Japan may be evolving from a primarily economic global power to a regional economic and geopolitical force in Asia. A decade from now Japan's position in the world may be closer to the one it held in the interwar period, when Japan emerged as a dominant economic and military power in Asia.

Little attention has been given in the United States to Japan's probable need to develop independent nuclear deterrent capability, but this development will surely send powerful signals throughout Asia about the role Japan intends to play there. If Japan cannot depend on a nuclear umbrella from an increasingly contentious United States, it must take steps to avoid leaving itself defenseless in a region that includes a hostile North Korea and a nuclear China. This reality is a corollary to the inevitable dissolution of the abnormal U.S.–Japan relationship of the last 50 years. A major economic power has never remained as dependent for its national security on another nation as Japan has on the United States since 1945.

It is in America's interest to understand the changes in Japan and to consider where they may lead. America

needs to decide on policies toward Japan that are consistent with U.S. goals yet take into account the transformation under way there.

Three major changes in Japan particularly worthy of attention are the collapse of the economy, the emergence of political instability, and the sharp increase in Japanese investment and trade in Asia at the expense of its trade and investment ties with Europe and the Americas.

Japan's Economic Collapse

The collapse of the Japanese economy since 1991, following the collapse a year earlier of its stock market, has been astounding both in its intensity and because of the failure of the rest of the world to notice the severe weakening of an economic powerhouse. As recently as several years ago, experts stated unequivocally that Japan would be the world's greatest economic power in the twenty-first century.

But Japan's economy slowed from 4.8 percent growth in 1990 to 1.3 percent growth in 1992 and virtually zero growth in 1993. The outlook for 1994 is the same, with perhaps a little more weakness than in 1993 because of delays in policy initiatives and increased uncertainty resulting from the aftermath of the Hosokawa resignation. Japan's stock market reached a high of 39,000 early in 1990 but then during the first nine months of that year plunged by 45 percent to below 22,000. For the Japanese, 1991 was a year of denial. Forecasters there joked that a Japanese recession meant 3 percent growth, suggesting that even in recession Japan would grow at a rate more rapid than the 2.5 to 3 percent growth rate considered sustainable for normal industrial economies. As hopes of recovery evaporated during 1991, the stock market, which had struggled back up to 26,000, plunged again to 15,000 by mid-1992. That drop, along with a sharp slowdown in economic growth, convinced even the confident bureaucrats at Japan's Ministry of Finance that some stimulus might be in order. Since then, Japan has announced expansion packages totaling over $360 billion while the economy has continued to languish and the stock market has failed to recover significantly.

> *Particularly worth of attention are the collapse of the economy, the emergence of political instability, and the sharp increase in Japanese investment and trade in Asia.*

Japan's economic problems and perceived need for massive stimulus programs—largely in the form of extra spending on public works but more recently including tax cuts as well—stem from an overcorrection of the economy after excessive stimulus following a 1986 economic slowdown. The 1987–1989 stock market bubble artificially depressed the cost of financing large investments in manufacturing for Japanese companies. When the stock market bubble burst in 1989, after the Bank of Japan began to tighten monetary policy, the cheap funding for investment projects dried up. The annual growth rate of investment in Japan fell from a high of 26 percent in 1988 to a negative 5.2 percent by 1992.

Japan's initial response to the investment collapse was to pretend that it was temporary and would go away. But by the middle of 1992, when economic growth in Japan had become negative, policymakers proposed a 10.2 trillion yen (about $95 billion or 2 percent of GNP) stimulus package aimed largely at increasing spending on public works. Since easy money had caused the bubble, the Bank of Japan vowed to deflate it. But deflation went too far.

The 10.2 trillion yen package became a model for the failure of subsequent stimulus plans. First, the actual increase in net demand in the first package was far less than advertised. Second, the expenditure on Japan's inefficient public works sector was wasteful and hurt its manufacturing sector, causing investment to collapse further. Japanese companies were forced to cut bonuses and press for layoffs. The threat and reality of increased layoffs in Japan's normally stable employment environment made households very nervous, and as a result they increased their savings.

The reduction in investment and the increase in savings in the private sector that accompanied Japan's bungled attempt to stimulate its economy more than offset the stimulus in the public sector. As a result, the economy slowed and Japan's current account surplus rose.

By the spring of 1993 it was clear that Japan's first stimulus package had failed to reinvigorate the economy and reduce the current account surplus. Japan's then-prime minister Miyazawa thereupon proposed a still larger fiscal package of 13.2 trillion yen (about $122 billion or 2.8 percent of GNP). That package was voted upon in June 1993 but was never fully implemented because the Miyazawa government fell that same month. A shaky seven-party coalition headed by Prime Minister Hosokawa took power in August. Since the 13.2 trillion yen stimulus package had been engineered by corrupt politicians in the LDP who sold access to construction projects in return for political contributions, the loss of power by the LDP prevented the full implementation of the stimulus package.

Despite these stimulus attempts, private demand in Japan has been dropping by more than the increase in public demand contained in the stimulus packages. The drop, moreover, has been compounded by the overly restrictive policy of the Bank of Japan.

The failure of Japan's policies to jolt the economy out of a worsening recession, combined with the continued deterioration of U.S.–Japan relations over the contentious trade issue, should have convinced Japan to search for new solutions to its serious economic problems. Japan's new 15 trillion yen (about $140 billion or nearly 3 percent of GNP) stimulus package announced early in 1994 included a 6 trillion yen tax cut that could have given Japanese consumers the means to increase spending. But the tax cut, the equivalent of $1,000 per household, was too little, too late. Japan's

stingy Ministry of Finance has already signaled that in the near future an increase in consumption and social security taxes will more than offset the reduction in income taxes in this year's stimulus package. Beyond that, Japan's households, jittery about job prospects, will save most of their windfall tax cut. Meanwhile the public works portion of the new stimulus package will likely have the same effect as past packages, producing little growth while increasing the current account surplus and elevating trade tensions even further.

> *Japan's desperate economic situation contains alarming parallels with America in the early 1930s after the 1929 stock market crash.*

Against the background of Japan's rather desperate economic situation, which contains alarming parallels with America in the early 1930s after the 1929 stock market crash, especially the continuation of a tight money policy and failed efforts at pump priming, the Clinton administration has chosen to press Japan hard for more trade concessions. Tensions rose significantly after the dramatic failure of trade talks in February, and the outlook is not bright for their relaxation.

Prime Minister Hosokawa apparently believed that he had a trade agreement with the United States when he left Japan on February 10 for his discussions the following day in Washington with President Clinton. However, by the time Hosokawa's plane landed in Washington, American last-minute demands for further Japanese concessions had caused the trade talks to collapse. Prime Minister Hosokawa was placed in the ridiculous position of having flown over 5,000 miles to make a joint appearance with the American president only to announce the collapse of critical U.S.–Japan trade talks. The immediate and surprising result was a further strengthening of the yen. Currency traders reasoned that America's get-tough policy with Japan would include efforts to talk up the yen further, possibly to a level below 100 yen per dollar.

The strengthening of the yen, while it may be temporary, severely exacerbates Japan's economic problems. While it is undoubtedly emotionally satisfying for American trade negotiators to watch their Japanese counterparts experience extreme discomfort over the economic problems caused by a stronger yen, it is not clear that a further weakening of the Japanese economy is in the best interests of the United States. The strong yen tactic being applied by American trade negotiators also suggests that the risk of further economic deterioration in Japan is not being taken seriously by the Clinton trade team.

Political Turmoil

The Hosokawa coalition government came to power in August 1993 with ambitious plans for political reform. Their aim was to change Japan's electoral system—to eliminate the incentives for corruption and to change the representation in the Diet to reflect the increase in Japan's urban population and thus reduce the disproportionate representation of Japan's agricultural sector.

The U.S. tactic of pushing up the yen, further worsening the problems of Japan's manufacturers, while threatening trade reprisals will undoubtedly backfire in the long run.

Unfortunately for the coalition government, it did not recognize that Japan's economy was still weakening after two years of subpar performance and numerous efforts to prop it up with stimulus packages. By the time the government began to grapple with Japan's economic problems, the opposition LDP parties had decided that the best way to unseat Hosokawa would be to block his efforts to stimulate the economy. This stalemate continued until early January 1994 when Hosokawa decided to press

hard for political reform as a necessary precondition to achieving changes in economic policy.

By late January, Hosokawa had barely succeeded in passing a watered-down political reform package that was almost scuttled by the defection of the powerful socialist block. Hosokawa then tried to force through a significant stimulus package only to be stymied by the bureaucrats at the Ministry of Finance, who insisted on consumption tax increases to offset the income tax cut he sought. Forced again to compromise, Hosokawa brought forth a much weakened stimulus package just before the February 10 departure for his meeting with President Clinton.

Hosokawa's many difficulties brought him back to Japan from Washington determined to shape a more stable coalition government. His domestic political problems were so intense and the political outlook in Japan so uncertain that the trade dispute with the United States was well down on the list of problems receiving Hosokawa's attention. Hosokawa's shaky coalition government needed to succeed with deregulation measures to help Japanese consumers, but it was no match for the intransigent bureaucrats bent on maintaining Japan's status quo.

The American perception that a tougher stance on trade negotiations with Japan will bring concessions seems to be predicated on the notion that smooth trade relations with the United States are a major preoccupation of the Japanese government. The U.S. tactic of pushing up the yen, further worsening the problems of Japan's manufacturers, while threatening trade reprisals against Japan may seem savvy, but it will undoubtedly backfire in the long run. Surely Japan can only conclude that redirecting its economic interests to Asia and away from North America and Europe is a better option.

It is indeed true that Japanese markets need opening and that Japanese consumers would be far better off if this took place. It is not clear however that American producers and consumers would be better off. A smaller trade surplus for Japan would mean more spending and less saving in Japan and therefore fewer capital exports from Japan to a low-saving country like the United States. If, as is apparently desired by the Clinton administration and many members of Congress, Japan's trade surplus were to fall to zero over the next several years, American interest rates would have to be higher than they otherwise would be, not because Japan

would sell American treasury securities in retaliation, but simply because the flow of Japanese savings into global capital markets would have to contract, and savers elsewhere in the world would have to be convinced to save more. That requires higher interest rates, which in turn would harm American businesses and consumers.

Japan Refocuses on Asia

Japan has reasons to emphasize its economic and geopolitical future within Asia for reasons beyond those related to its trade difficulties with the United States and Europe. Asian economies, led by the rapidly transforming Chinese economy, are the fastest growing in the world. Rapidly growing, capital-poor economies present very attractive opportunities for capital-rich Japan and its high savers. Beyond that, the relative proximity of the Asian economies and their abundant supply of inexpensive labor make them especially attractive to the Japanese. Capital-rich Japan has a better chance of becoming an Asian superpower than it does of becoming a major global power. During 1992 alone, Japan's investment in Asia rose by 12 percent, a third faster than the increase in its investment in North America.

It is more than likely that Japan will develop its own nuclear weapons over the next decade largely to develop as an Asian economic superpower able to withstand nuclear threats.

Japan will eventually lower its trade surplus with the United States, both by selling less in the United States and, ultimately, by buying less from the United States. Japan is currently America's second-largest trading partner, absorbing over 10 percent of American exports, which amounts to nearly 24 percent of total Japanese imports. Furthermore,

American exports to Japan have been rising rapidly in recent years while the growth of American imports from Japan has slowed.

The American market has been very important to Japanese exporters and will continue to be. But the potential for growth in Japanese exports to the United States is clearly limited by the determination of the American government to insist, as a precondition for such growth, on an even more rapid increase in American exports to Japan. Furthermore, even with Japanese deregulation and the increased competitiveness of American companies, the American appetite for Japanese-manufactured products means that a sharp reduction in America's bilateral trade deficit with Japan is unlikely. To point out that it is also undesirable from the standpoint of American consumers and the many American producers who use Japanese components has unfortunately become irrelevant in the intensely political debate over trade with Japan.

The need for capital in the rapidly growing economies of Asia means that Japanese exports first of machinery and then of consumer goods will be welcomed in economies more able than the American economy to increase their absorption of Japanese production.

Japan's increasing attention to regional development in Asia is part of a broad phenomenon related to the end of the Cold War. Previously Japan and the United States had to settle their trade disputes in order to maintain global security arrangements for the containment of the Soviet Union in Asia. Americans groused about large trade deficits with Japan but ultimately settled for minor trade concessions under pressure from the Pentagon and the State Department not to jeopardize Japan's willingness to serve as "an American aircraft carrier" off the coast of Asia, to use the vivid phrase coined in the mid-1980s by Japan's prime minister Nakasone.

As Japan is forced to lessen its economic ties to the United States, surely it will wish to end its strategic dependence on the United States as well. It is more than likely that Japan will develop its own nuclear weapons over the next decade largely in order to develop as an Asian economic superpower able to withstand nuclear threats from China or renegade nations like North Korea. Japan's evolution as a nuclear power will be largely in a deterrent mode.

Japan's movement toward defensive nuclear capability will likely be enhanced by political developments within Japan that are in turn being forced by the elevation of trade tensions emanating from Washington. Selection of a new Japanese prime minister like Tsutomu Hata from the conservative wing of the coalition government would signal a trend toward leadership that advocates a more independent strategy for insuring Japan's national security. Ultimately, the coalition must be able to govern without the liberal socialist faction that strongly rejects any hint of nuclear capability for Japan. That will require some combination of the coalition government and conservative LDP members. Some conservative LDP members have already left the party.

Japan is in a major transition affecting far more than U.S.–Japan trade relations. America's insistence on trade measures that hurt an already severely weakened Japanese economy sends a clear message to Japan's leaders that their economic and strategic dependence on the United States must be reduced as rapidly as possible. The Japanese government will play for time, taking actions it deems necessary to prevent a complete rupture in U.S.–Japan relations before Japan is ready to emerge as an Asian superpower. This may ultimately prove to be the only way to reduce the trade tensions that have preoccupied American governments in their dealings with Japan since the end of the Cold War. It may also constitute a stable and viable outcome after a 50-year abnormal relationship between Japan and the United States. Nevertheless, the Clinton administration and subsequent American governments should consider seriously whether it is the outcome they desire.

Article 11   *Look Japan, April 1994*

Agricultural Policy From the Ground Up

Japanese voters and consumers face a political and moral dilemma in the wake of the GATT agreement on rice imports. Without protection, the Japanese rice farming industry cannot survive. Now is the time to rethink our values and build a new agricultural policy.

Fumio Egaitsu

Born in 1935, the author graduated from the Faculty of Agriculture at the University of Tokyo. He is now a professor of agricultural economics at his alma mater and is also a member of the Agricultural Policy Council of MAFF. His publications include Japanese Agricultural Policy: Unfair and Unreasonable?

One of the most difficult issues in the agricultural phase of the GATT (General Agreement on Tariffs and Trade) nego-tiations was the issue of imports to the Japanese rice market. Negotiators finally reached a compromise that allowed Japan to delay liberalization for six years, in exchange for granting "minimum access" to its market. The government of Japan has already submitted its total

Country Schedule of Japan

	Out-quota tariff (Rate of tariff imposed on imports over 50,000 tons)		Minimum Access	
	1995	2000	1995	2000
Rice	Grace period		379,000t	758,000t
Wheat	65 yen/kg	55 yen/kg	5,565,000t	5,740,000t
Barley	46 yen/kg	39 yen/kg	1,326,000t	1,369,000t
Skim milk	466 yen/kg + 25%	396 yen/kg + 21.3%	137,000t	137,000t
Butter	1,159 yen/kg + 35%	985 yen/kg + 29.8%	} (Amount of milk used. Figures are for national trade only.)	
Starch	140 yen/kg	119 yen/kg	157,000t	157,000t

Source: MAFF

amount of minimum import quotas based on that promise.

Neither those in favor of, nor those opposed to liberalizing the rice market are likely to be satisfied by this outcome. Those who had wanted the rice market completely liberalized complain that the government needlessly hobbled the process; those opposed say that the government was unable to defend Japanese interests. Either way, they say, the government has come off looking weak and ineffectual. Both sides have a point, but on the whole, the deal is acceptable.

If Japan had its way, free trade would be maintained as a general system, but exceptions would be granted for products that Japan would rather not liberalize because of domestic concerns. Yet one cannot have one's cake and eat it, too. The December 15, 1993 final GATT agreement marks a middle ground. Japan's claim that rice was a "non-trade interest that impinged on national food security and environmental protection" was at least nominally accepted by other nations, and, while the agreement will inflict severe damage domestically, especially on rice producers, it was not the worst case scenario.

Japan is in a weak position in trade negotiations. It has no way to respond when people claim that Japan benefits most from free trade, for indeed, Japan does. Free trade only harms agriculture; in every other industry Japan requires free trade to survive. Moreover, Japan needs agricultural imports. This island country, devoid of both oil and iron ore, is home to 120 million people. What would happen if trade suddenly ground to a halt? Japan has only five million hectares of arable land, not nearly enough to feed the population.

Yet neither the US nor Europe was inclined to understand when we tried to claim that because food security is a "non-trade interest," free trade alone would be unacceptable, however important free trade may be in the abstract.

HOUSE ON SAND

Free trade only harms agriculture, but it is not just farmers or members of the JA (Japan Agricultural cooperatives) who will be in trouble. When food security becomes unstable due to free trade, it affects the food situation of consumers in urban areas, too. If food imports ever stopped, city dwellers would suffer greatly, as happened during and after WWII.

There are other reasons besides food security to be against the complete liberalization of agricultural imports. Some, for instance, are against the idea of trade and market economies and would like to revert to the "good old days"—back in feudal times—when Japan was self-sufficient. If one places absolute value in a stable, sustainable economic and social structure that avoids wasting resources or polluting the environment, then Japan's current economic prosperity is like the proverbial house built on sand. Our GNP of $20,000 per person is a mirage lacking both substance and meaning.

Japan will need to maintain some agricultural capacity and support rural communities in order to provide a rich life for the Japanese of the next century, but rice is not something that we should defend to the death.

Part of the reason the Uruguay Round did not accept Japan's claims in their entirety is that the US and Europe both decided to place more priority on their own national interests than those of Japan. Right now Japan is one of the biggest import countries in the world, but GATT forces Japan to import still more. The US and European countries are export nations, and are not significantly harmed by the agreement. Yet international negotiations are a matter of compromise, of giving in and making deals so that the world's trading system does not grow too out of kilter. In this sense, the agreement was a good one.

The fact remains that Japanese farming and farming communities cannot survive without protection. The table on the next page compares labor productivity and wages (important components of international competitiveness) for rice production in Japan, Thailand, and the US. Japanese rice producers are more productive than their counterparts in Thailand, but as large as that gap is, the gap in wages is even larger. Japanese rice simply cannot compete against Thai rice.

In the not-too-distant future, the wages of Thai farmers will probably rise closer to Japanese levels. However, Thai rice producers have far more room for improvement in their labor productivity. By using just a bit more fertilizer and agrochemicals, they could see vast improvements in their per-hectare yields, which are currently only about half of Japan's. The use of tractors and other farm machinery would also shorten working hours. Even with the higher cost of wages, Thai rice would still be more competitive than Japanese.

Nor can Japanese rice compete with American rice, as US labor productivity is much higher and, thanks to the strong yen, wages are lower. The price of rice is partly determined by its quality, so there is some danger in generalizing, but overall, Japanese rice is about ten times more expensive than that of Thailand and about five times more expensive than that of the US.

In 1993, the Ministry of Agriculture, Forestry and Fisheries (MAFF) published a plan to double labor productivity in rice production over the next ten years. The government will encourage rice farmers to expand their farm size by ten to twenty hectares and to lower their production costs by 40%–50%. Yet even if all goes according to plan, Japanese rice farmers will still be working on farmland only about one-tenth the size of their American counterparts, and their labor productivity will only be about one-fiftieth. If the Japan–US wage gap does not appreciably change, Japanese rice will still be more expensive than American rice.

OUTDATED CONTROLS

Thus Japanese rice farming cannot survive without protection. Whether or not it is worth protection is something for the entire country to decide. Yet if the goal of agricultural policy is to maintain Japanese farming, then its first hurdle will be to develop consensus among the people regarding the need for agricultural protection. This point is crucial because unless it is clearly stated, important policy choices become murky and ambiguous.

MAFF has already provided an answer in the policy paper "Basic Directions of the New Policies for Food, Agriculture, and Rural Areas" released in June 1992, outlining agricultural policies for the next 10 or 20 years: First, remove old regulations which bind domestic agriculture, allow the market mechanism to work, and establish agricultural structures that correspond to the new age. Second, recognize the values inherent in agriculture itself and in rural communities, and provide the necessary protection. Third, maintain domestic production so that the self-sufficiency rate of food does not fall any further.

This vision is a start, but there is further to go. The biggest problem to be overcome is the Food Control Law. The most forceful criticisms of agricultural protection stem from a deeply-rooted suspicion in all layers of society that farmers are overprotected. Even those in favor of providing Japanese agriculture with the protection it needs to survive would be against unnecessary coddling, which would merely sap agriculture of its future vitality.

The primary purpose of the Food Control Law is to cope with shortages. The law is designed to allow government control of all rice distribution to ensure that everyone receives a fair share of the rice supply, which, when the law was created in 1942, was insufficient to meet the demand. However, in the last 20 years, increasing yield and falling per capita consumption has led to excess supply in Japan.

Distribution controls are outdated, and only serve to confine the rice economy within an ancient framework. Yet the law's controls have been in place for so long that the general public can no longer imagine a rice economy without it. People start to worry when they hear that the system might be abolished, but they should not. If the Food Control Law were scrapped, consumers, distributors, and particularly farmers themselves

Comparison of Rice Productivity (1987)

	Japan	Thailand	US
Average planted area per farm (ha)	0.8	5.3	114.0
Unpolished rice yield (t/ha)	5.3	1.5	4.9
Labor hours (hour/ha)	481	600	20
Labor productivity (kg/hour)	11.0	2.5	245.0
Wages ($/hour)	6.91	0.18	5.82
Labor cost per ton ($/t)	627	72	24
Total cost per ton ($/t)	2,158	132	199

Note: Calculations based on data from *Kome Sangyo no Kokusai Hikaku* (international comparison of the rice industry), edited by Tadashi Kamegai and Tadao Hotta.

would welcome the new, liberated environment.

We cannot rely entirely on market mechanisms for staples such as rice. Political intervention is necessary to ensure price stability. However, intervention should not take the form of total, direct control of the rice market, as it does now under the Food Control Law. Rather, minimum, indirect controls should be designed to ensure that the nation has stockpiles of rice, that prices are stable, and that farmers receive income compensation.

The time has also come for us to upgrade our paddy-conversion policy. The current policy was adopted in 1970 as a means of tackling the issue of excess rice production. Since then, the policy has taken different forms, but the basic measure of uniform production quotas oppresses efficient and motivated producers, and is a major impediment to the development of Japan's rice economy. In addition to scrapping the Food Control Law, we should also abolish production quotas.

NEW DIRECTION

Japanese farmers are still enclosed in a web of regulations and protective measures that in many cases date from before WWII. Many have long ago fulfilled their historical mission and are now both irrelevant and unnecessary. The Food Control Law is not the only one to fall into this category, but is the prime symbol of how obsolete and irrational

agricultural policy has become. It is time to rebuild the system from the ground up.

With regard to rice, we can either concern ourselves only with the six-year grace period and how to take measures against the quantities of rice now coming into the market, or we can embark on a more radical course based on a more long-term perspective.

The first option would not require much tinkering with the system. In 1995 Japan will import 380,000 tons of polished rice, gradually increasing the amount to 760,000 tons by the year 2000. The imports could be stored as reserves, or we could reduce the acreage under cultivation in Japan.

Yet we need a long-term direction for fundamental reform, a vision that will take us well beyond the six-year grace period. Obviously, no one knows for certain what will happen when the six years are up; that will be decided in negotiations scheduled to take place in the fifth year. Yet while greater liberalization is likely, it is inconceivable that imports of rice, once begun, will ever be halted. Japanese rice cannot insulate itself from the world any more than Japan can return to isolationism. National borders have become porous, and Japan's uncompetitive rice farmers face almost insurmountable odds.

If we are serious about preserving Japanese rice farming into the next century, then we must be prepared to abandon the fetters of the past and search for new possibilities.

Article 12   *The New York Times*, January 2, 1994

Life in a Box: Japanese Question Fruits of Success

James Sterngold
Special to The New York Times

SAKADO, Japan—As the jammed 7:38 A.M. express train rolled into the station here on a recent chilly morning, and Hiroyuki Ogata waited to be packed aboard for the toughest leg of his nearly two-hour commute into Tokyo, he admitted that he had things pretty good.

Two years ago he was able to buy a home for his family of four, a 600-square-foot apartment in a bland 50-building housing complex criss-crossed by power lines. And since he attended one of the nation's top universities, he stands a good chance of becoming director some day at the food and spice company where he has inched up the ranks for 14 years.

He can afford luxuries like a cram school for his son, and for his daughter lessons on their narrow upright piano, which rests in a corner of the living room, a cozy family gathering place about 10 feet by 12 feet. The deep Japanese recession has had almost no impact on him.

Resigned to the Dream
In fact, if there is such a thing as the Japanese dream, the 36-year-old Mr. Ogata and his family live it. They came to Tokyo from Kamaishi in Japan's northern rust belt—where the primary employer, a steel mill, had long since closed—and sought greater security. Statistically speaking, they live on the comfortable side of typical.

But Mr. Ogata is resigned to his life rather than contented. He aches with a passion that puts creases around his friendly eyes when he describes the one aspect of the Japanese dream that may always elude him: a home that is both roomy and that spares him the salaryman's curse, a long commute.

Such desperately long and cramped commutes are a daily ritual that along with sky-high prices for consumer goods, have come to represent for many Japanese much of what has gone wrong in their society.

Government regulations and tax laws keep housing prices astronomical by encouraging inefficient use of land and discouraging an active market in property. Thus, the only home Mr. Ogata could afford was his apartment in a typical danchi, the sprawling, Government-financed housing blocks that ring Tokyo in ever widening circles as salarymen, as businessmen are called here, move farther out to fulfill their dreams of home ownership. Mr. Ogata's 1,400-unit danchi is one of several near this hamlet in Saitama Prefecture, about 30 miles north of Tokyo.

But despite spending nearly $200,000, he got both a tiny dwelling and a long trip to work every morning. Mr. Ogata's commute, like that of many other train-bound survivalists, is an endurance contest in overheated cars often filled to twice their capacity, where nobody talks and few have enough room to read, even late at night.

Japan is the richest nation on earth by some measures and is a ferocious competitor, but decades of Government policy focused on creating industrial might rather than consumer benefits has left the country with a standard of living that many people, including top politicians, are ashamed of.

Tokyo residents, for instance, enjoy one-eighth the amount of parkland a person as their counterparts in New York. Slightly fewer than half of the nation's homes are hooked up to modern sewerage systems. In many Tokyo suburbs the average size of homes—less than half the average in the United States—is shrinking.

'Cogs in a Wheel'
The Japanese used to bristle when foreigners referred to their homes as rabbit hutches. They scoffed at those who pointed out that consumer prices here were double and triple those elsewhere, and complained that such critics failed to understand their culture. Not anymore.

"People have been relegated to the status of cogs in a wheel," Ichiro Ozawa, the key strategist in the new reform-minded Government, wrote in a recent book. He described Japan as "an ostensibly high-income society with a meager life style."

Some critics have made those claims for years. And politicians have been saying for a decade that they would improve living standards. The last Prime Minister, Kiichi Miyazawa, vowed to make Japan a "life style superpower," for instance, but it was a hollow pledge that some critics now regard as a cruel hoax.

What is new is that even politicians like Mr. Ozawa, who for the last decade was a member of the Liberal Democratic Party, helping formulate and carry out the policies against which he is now objecting, are pushing the commuter's plight to the top of their agendas.

Mr. Ozawa reckoned that the average salaryman spends three and a half years commuting during his career. "The only apt way to describe the situation is to call him a commuter slave of commuter hell," Mr. Ozawa wrote.

A newspaper column this summer by a reporter returning to the trains after vacation began, "The monster is back." A weekly magazine recently claimed to have found the salaryman with the single worst commute in Tokyo—three and a half hours each way.

Pledge by New Premier
Perhaps most important, the rallying cry has taken on a special significance for Prime Minister Morihiro Hosokawa. He ended 38 years of Liberal Democratic Party rule in August and has won widespread support by vowing to put the Mr. Ogatas of Japan first for a change.

But of all the tough issues Mr. Hosokawa confronts, from rooting out political corruption to ending the stubborn recession, delivering relief to consumers and commuters may be the most daunting.

No one expects his term to hang on whether he delivers such relief, but he stormed into office as a conservative populist whose promises of aid for ordinary Japanese rang a surprisingly harmonious chord. People wanted to believe him.

To be sure, the anger among the Japanese salarymen and women condemned to "commuter hell" is more of a slow burn than an outcry. The Mainichi Shimbun, Japan's largest-circulation daily newspaper, observed the sardine-like conditions on Tokyo's trains recently and marveled, "Despite the indignity and physical agony, commuters suffer in silence."

People rarely boil over. The Japanese are taught from their youngest days to accept, if sullenly, those aspects of life considered unpleasant but immutable.

The Mood Is Changing
But the mood has started to change. The end of the cold war, with its implicit calls for self-sacrifice, the fact that increasing numbers of Japanese are observing firsthand how much better people live in other industrial societies and economic data showing how wealthy corporate Japan has become have sobered people up.

Nevertheless, Mr. Ogata, like most salarymen, is skeptical.

"I don't really complain because I'm used to it," he said as he stamped his feet in the cold and prepared for the first leg of his commute, a crowded 20-minute bus ride to the train station. "I know that in itself is a problem, that I think this commute is ordinary. If you ask me if I'd like to sit on the train, of course, I would love to. But this is the best someone like us can hope for."

His 36-year-old wife, Kumiko, is only slightly more sanguine.

"Nobody expects the changes to be big," she said, edging as close to optimistic as most Japanese get. "But little by little something could happen."

A look at the life of Mr. Ogata, head of the accounting section at S & B Foods, and one of his neighbors, 37-year-old Hatsuo Toku, a manager at Sanko Corporation, a Tokyo building maintenance contractor, provides an eye-opening encounter with the life styles four decades of consumer sacrifice has brought the Japanese, and why they now want change.

THE HOME
The Space Is at a Premium

Mr. Toku and Mr. Ogata serve together as officers of the tenants' association at their danchi, and so they have met regularly for more than a year. But a gathering in Mr. Toku's apartment on a recent Sunday afternoon was the first time either had entered the other's home.

That is common in the salaryman's world, since their homes tend to be so small that entertaining—even casual meetings—generally takes place in restaurants or other public places.

Indeed, the Japanese are often self-conscious about their homes. Mr. Toku and his wife, Noriko, who sells insurance, were happy to entertain a visitor in their comfortable yet minuscule living room—offering cups of hot green tea and traditional snacks made of sweet potato, sesame or sweetened bean paste. But they demurred when asked if they would show the rest of their apartment.

The two families have nearly identical homes, except that Mr. Ogata had slid open the doors separating the kitchen from his living room to create a greater sense of space. Everything, of course, is relative, and that extra space, though tidy, was packed with appliances and storage.

Next to the unusually narrow refrigerator was a series of shelves. On one, under the toaster, was a plastic bucket in which the Ogatas' 12-year-old son, Shogo, had placed his baseball mitt.

There was also a tiny coffee maker, a water heater for making tea, an electronic rice cooker—a staple in Japanese kitchens—and a small microwave oven. The gas stove had two burners. In a narrow cabinet with a glass front rested Japanese earthenware tea cups, rice bowls and plates.

The center of activity in both homes was the low table in the living room, where one sits cross-legged on the floor. It is where meals are generally served and where the television, videotape player and stereo are situated, all within arm's reach.

Two desks had been arranged in the bedroom, less than 10 feet by 10 feet, shared by Shogo Ogata and his sister, 8-year-old Wakana. On a shelf over Shogo's stood a stack of manga, thick Japanese comic books, while Wakana's was neatly arranged with some stuffed animals. About a quarter step away, against the opposite wall, were the bunk beds in which they sleep.

The bedroom Mr. Ogata shares with his wife, a full-time housewife, was even smaller, with barely enough room for the futon they roll up into the closet each morning. Mr. Ogata's suits hung from a cord stretched along a wall.

Although many American college dormitories are more spacious, it was all fairly typical for a mid-level Japanese corporate manager. Mr. Ogata would not give his precise income, other than to say it was average, which would prob-

ably put it at the equivalent of about $65,000 a year.

The Tokus said that their combined annual income was closer to $90,000, but that much of Mrs. Toku's pay was used to purchase retirement policies from her insurance company.

Asked if they would prefer a larger home or a home closer to Tokyo, the Ogatas did not hesitate.

"Closer, definitely," said Mr. Ogata.

"I'd say bigger," Mrs. Ogata chimed in.

A BETTER LIFE
Saving Money a Preoccupation

A big part of the problem is the tightly centralized control Government bureaucrats maintain over the economy. Companies need licenses, approvals and informal guidance to do just about anything, so they cluster close to the ministries lined up near the Imperial Palace in central Tokyo.

With power emanating from the center, the best jobs in Japan have migrated steadily toward the capital. That process has transformed Tokyo into the center of a metropolitan region of 30 million people, one-fourth of Japan's population on less than 5 percent of its land.

That is a key reason why, even though the area is traversed by a dense web of train and subway lines, they are often overburdened. It is also why, though Mr. Ogata and Mr. Toku own autos, they would never consider driving to work; the roadways are vast bottlenecks. The Yamanote Line, which rings central Tokyo, often operates at 250 percent capacity in the morning rush hour.

The Tokus, like their neighbors, came to Tokyo seeking a better life. They were raised in a relatively poor area in the far north, Aomori, and said they hold a wistful dream of returning someday.

Nonetheless, they said, they are generally pleased with the upbringing they are giving their two sons, 12-year-old Yohei and 9-year-old Teppei, who both have a passion for sports. Common suburban problems in the United States, like vandalism, truancy, street crime and drug use, are almost unheard of in the danchi.

"I think it's pretty good for kids here," Mrs. Toku said. "They can go out and find all sorts of bugs. They can even find crayfish. But shopping is so difficult. You have to have a car or you can't shop, and I don't have a driver's license."

They admit their home is a bit cramped, but they know it could be worse. Before they moved to their current home the Tokus lived with their first son in an apartment almost half its size.

Saving money on daily necessities is a constant preoccupation. The Tokus said they had taken to a relatively new Japanese pastime, shopping at the large discount stores that are popping up, and that are often filled with imports.

"I don't care if it's made in Japan or not," said Mr. Toku, contradicting arguments long made by Government bureaucrats, that the Japanese always preferred familiar, if more expensive, Japanese-made goods. I just want good value."

Mrs. Ogata belongs to a food co-op, which she said consumes most of their disposable income. She especially complained about recent sharp increases in the price of rice, caused by a Government-induced panic after a poor harvest.

She buys a 22-pound bag each month. The price shot up recently to the equivalent of nearly $63 from $45, and one market limited shoppers to a single 11-pound bag, she said. The cost of education is also high—particularly the cram schools that are essential for a student to gain acceptance to the good high schools necessary to enter elite universi-

ties—so neither family saves much money each month.

Both families take one vacation each year for about a week, visiting their hometowns in the north. They venture out on what is by far the most crowded season for traveling, the Obon holiday in August—a Buddhist festival when people pay respects to their ancestors—but that is the only extended period a salaryman can usually take off.

For the most part, however, life is taken up with commuting and work, subjects they do not particularly enjoy discussing.

THE COMMUTE
No Longer Taking Sacrifices Willingly

"There's no room to read a paper or a magazine," Mr. Ogata said as he jostled against a reporter aboard the train. "I carry a radio sometimes and listen to the news or music. I'm alone. I don't know anyone on the train. Everyone is like that."

Mr. Toku enjoys the advantage of boarding his train at its first stop, so he usually has a seat. Shortly afterward, the

train becomes so full that nobody can move but that does not bother him. He said he sleeps the entire ride.

Evenings provide no letup. When Mr. Ogata joins colleagues for dinner and bouts of drinking twice a week or so, and he comes home after 10 P.M., commuting is a battle. Recently, the 10:53 P.M. express was a weary mass of men in navy blue suits and some students pressed against each other in pained, soporific poses, the air redolent of alcohol and occasional curses when someone struggled on or off.

Mr. Toku follows another salaryman custom when he dines late with colleagues; he stays in Tokyo at a company dormitory meant for those unwilling, unable or too late to take the train.

These sacrifices were taken for granted as the price the Japanese had to pay for their nation to make its way in the world. Slowly, it is dawning on them that they have not reaped the benefits of huge trade surpluses and that their life styles are an unnecessary burden.

As Mr. Ozawa concluded in his book, "What I would like to propose is the emancipation of the individual."

Article 13   *The Rotarian*, January 1993

DESTINATION: DOWN UNDER

David McGonigal

David McGonigal is a free-lance travel writer based in Sydney and the author of 10 books on Australia, including "Fodor's Australia" (five chapters) and "The Insight Guide to Australia."

Australia

Australia is an enigma, a land of contradictions. With 7.5 million square kilometres (2.9 million square miles) of land, it is the world's largest island and its smallest continent. Despite its vast size (roughly the same as the continental U.S.), there are just 18 million Australians.

Most people have a popular image of Australia as the last frontier stretching across the dusty outback, yet most Australians live in large modern cities along the east coast. Australia is one of the last places on earth to become a nation, yet the Aboriginal people have lived here for millennia. It is widely regarded as an

unpolluted, uncrowded paradise—but the British prisoners who founded it considered it to be hell on earth.

There is no single view of Australia. The first Aboriginal people arrived on the northwest coast of the continent over 50,000 years ago. But the British who came to these shores in 1788 regarded Australia as an outpost of England. The Queen of England is still the Queen of Australia.

Since the Second World War, successive waves of immigration have created a culturally rich and diverse country. The first immigrants were from Yugoslavia, Greece, Italy, and Lebanon. Others followed from the Middle East and Asia, including refugees from Vietnam and Cambodia. Chinese, Indians, Malays, and Koreans also arrived in large numbers. The new multiculturalism has resulted in an open-minded society where the rights of minority groups (including the native Aborigines) are being more seriously considered. Even so, 75 percent

of the population is still of Anglo-Celtic descent.

Australia takes its name from "Terra Australis Incognita"—the unknown south land. But in the last few years, more people—especially tourists—have come to know Australia as a refreshingly different land.

New South Wales

Sydney—the country's best-known city—was the site of the first European settlement in 1788. Despite being the nation's largest city (with a population of 3.5 million), it doesn't feel like a big metropolis. Sydney is scattered across waterways and interspersed by swathes of natural bushland, and is considered one of the world's most beautiful harbours. Its honeycombed sandstone bays and coves lead to the glass spires of the city framed by the Opera House and the Harbour Bridge. Yet away from the high rises, long stretches of shoreline look

All Photos Courtesy Australian Tourist Commission

The Pinnacles, fossilized remains of an ancient forest, stand as eerie sentinels in the desert.

much as they did when Captain James Cook arrived in 1770. Sydney also embraces about 60 kilometres (37 miles) of Pacific ocean front: a grand panorama of scalloped headlands linked by golden sandy beaches. In this egalitarian society, no one is allowed to own a beach, so all are open to the public. During the summer, the local radio stations broadcast regular reports of surfing conditions.

Most of Sydney's main attractions are located on or near the harbour. Taronga Park Zoo, overlooking the harbour, is a naturalist's dream, while the Sydney aquarium offers a preview of the neon-colored fish that can be found at the Great Barrier Reef. Darling Harbour is a popular complex of stores and restaurants on the western edge of the city. The Rocks is a maze of tiny shops and restored houses in the shadow of the Bridge; many of the buildings from the early days of the colony are still standing. And, of course, there are the "sails" of the Opera House, which resemble a giant white prehistoric reptile crouched on Bennelong Point.

Sydney's most famous beach, Bondi, is about a 15-minute drive from the city centre. On the way back to town, detour to Watsons Bay and stay for the sunset. You can sit on the beach and watch the sun disappear behind the distant Harbour Bridge. It's the perfect way to put the relationship between the city and the water in perspective: Sydney lives for its harbour.

Water sports are a passion in Australia.

Sailboats dot the waters of Perth, sunny gateway to Western Australia.

Most of the other drawing cards of New South Wales are found along its north coast. Some of the best surf in the world is along the undeveloped beaches between Sydney and Queensland. Port Macquarie is one of the best places to stay along the way: it's big enough to have all the amenities, yet small enough to have hometown hospitality. It also has a large park where you can see cuddly koalas. Several hundred kilometres further north you'll find the decidedly up-market resort town of Byron Bay: here Aussie actor Paul Hogan ("Crocodile Dundee") and his American actress wife maintain a large country home.

The Blue Mountains, only an hour's drive from Sydney are part of the Great Dividing Range: their deeply etched valleys, so close to a major city, are one of the best places to experience the bush that is such an integral part of the Australian self image.

Canberra, located in eastern New South Wales, is the national capital and a separate entity administered by a federal bureau. On a sunny day, Canberra's pastoral calm, placid lake, and manicured lawns resemble the set for the U.S. television series, "Happy Days." Canberra was a carefully planned city of government buildings and gardens created by Chicago architect Daniel Burnham. Over the past 10 years, the population has grown to about 280,000 and the city has taken on a character of its own. It's no longer merely a conglomeration of grand buildings and monuments surrounded by public servants—but a pleasant place to live and a great place to visit.

Canberra has an abundance of attractions. Two of the newest are the National Casino, which opened late in 1992, and the Vietnam War Memorial, dedicated in September 1992 to the many thousands of Australians who served in that war. The new, vaguely Art Deco Parliament House (which cost more than a billion dollars) is a major point of interest. You can also spend several afternoons at the National Gallery, the National Science and Technology Centre, the National Aquarium, the Institute of Sport, the Mint, the National Film and Sound Archive, and the Botanic Gardens.

A space-age addition to Canberra is its observatory, inauspiciously located in the suburb of Dickson. It has a single telescope capable of magnification of up to 800 times, providing an excellent view of the stars of the southern sky.

Queensland

Queensland is Australia's tropical playground. Brisbane, its capital in the southeastern corner, has become much more cosmopolitan in recent years but still has the raw character of a big country town. Down on the coast, however, the high-rise sprawl of the Gold Coast more closely resembles a bonsai version of Miami Beach or Honolulu.

Most visitors to Queensland come to see the Great Barrier Reef, the tropical sun, and the island resorts. All are found further north and the main access points are the Whitsunday airports of Proserpine and Hamilton Island, and Cairns, a bustling city in the far north. Cairns can well claim to be the action centre of Australia: it features every conceivable sport from scuba diving and sailing to mountain hiking and whitewater rafting.

The Great Barrier Reef is an aquatic wonderland. One of the world's largest living ecosystems, the reef is more than 2,000 kilometres (1,200 miles) long. It is made up of some 400 types of coral and is inhabited by over 1,500 species of fish (all wearing their brightest Day Glo).

Of the 500 Barrier Reef islands, only about 20 have resorts. These range from the diving resorts on the coral cays (keys) of Lady Elliot and Heron islands to the sybaritic indulgences of Hayman and Bedarra islands. In fact, most of the Queensland islands aren't islands at all, but sunken mountains fringed by reefs. Only Heron Island and Lady Elliot Island are actually part of the reef. However, the colours and complexities of the corals around resorts like luxurious Orpheus Island are at least the equal of their coral walls. Most resorts offer cruises to the outer reef where the coral shelf drops dramatically to the depths of the Pacific. The best of these trips is from the very upscale marlin-fishing base of Lizard Island, Queensland's most northerly island resort.

Each resort island has its own distinct character. Dunk Island is renowned for its rainforests and beautiful blue butterflies. It was here that E. J. Banfield wrote the escapist classic "Confessions of a Beachcomber." Tiny Daydream Island and Brampton Island are pleasant family resorts; Lindeman Island has now become a Club Med; Fitzroy and Hinchinbrook islands are wilderness experiences. Hamilton sells itself as all things to all people while Great Keppel is trying to shrug off its bop-till-you-drop youth image.

The Whitsunday Islands are justifiably famous as a superb sailing ground. Here you can take to the water in your own hired boat or join an organised cruise by motorised yacht or restored square rigger.

The best time to visit Queensland is between April and October, when the weather is still warm and there is little threat of monsoons or hurricanes.

Unfortunately, many visitors to Queensland never raise their gaze past the high-tide mark and miss the other side of Queensland. The jungle-clad mountains of Lamington National Park near the Gold Coast are known as "the Green behind the Gold." The beautiful forest mountain village of Kuranda behind Cairns is famous for its Tjapukai Aborigine dance troupe. And out west is Longreach, a prosperous outback town where Australia's national airline, Qantas, was first based. The airline's

Wine lovers will enjoy a visit to scenic Hunter Valley in New South Wales, one of Australia's premier wine-producing areas.

name is an acronym of "Queensland and Northern Territory Aerial Service."

South Australia

Adelaide, the capital of South Australia, was the first Australian city to be founded by free settlers. It's one of the best planned and most picturesque cities in Australia. Its rather conservative image is livened by the annual Formula One World Championship race. The Adelaide Grand Prix is the final round of the world championship and is held on a challenging street circuit.

Every two years, the city is also host to the famous Adelaide Festival of the Arts, a three-week program of music, drama, and dance.

The most refined of Australia's casinos is located in the gloriously elegant old Adelaide Railway Station. Hobart, Launceston, Surfers Paradise, Townsville, Darwin, and Perth also have lively casinos.

Head north or south for a few kilometres from Adelaide and you'll be strolling through well-kept vineyards. (South Australia is the nation's driest state.) The Barossa Valley to the northeast is the best-known vineyard area, but to the south lie the up-and-coming Southern Vales wineries. Most Australia wineries welcome guests for tastings.

The German influence in South Australia is evident in place names like Hahndorf and Kaiser Stuhl. Those first Teutonic settlers must have arrived with vine cuttings in their luggage and immediately set out to find the best place to plant them. It worked: South Australia today produces 75 per cent of the nation's wine and 80 percent of its brandy. Australian wines are winning awards around the world and South Australia is leading the way.

Kangaroo Island is only a few kilometres from the coast but a holiday here has some of the aura of a passage on Noah's ark. The profusion and variety of natural life is astounding. On a single day you can spot koalas resting in the trees, hand-feed kangaroos, and observe sea lions sunning themselves on a beach, unperturbed by human proximity.

Western Australia

Western Australia is enormous. It covers two and a half million square kilometres (965,000 square miles), or 3.5 times the area of Texas. But while Texas has a population of 12 million, the total number of West Australians is only 1.5 million, and a million of those live in Perth, a brash, youthful city that grows with every mineral boom.

Closer to Bali, Indonesia, than it is to Sydney (on the other side of the vast Nullarbor Desert), Perth seems quite isolated from the population centres it universally dismisses as the "eastern states." Still, Perth's easygoing character and peaceful location on the banks of the Swan River (where European explorers first saw black swans) causes visitors to contemplate settling here.

The spectacles of Western Australia are on the same grand scale as the land. At the top end of the state, the Kimberley coast has thousands of tropical islands with beautiful beaches—and bays like jewels on a turquoise sea—yet no one lives on them. Indeed, the total population of the Kimberley coast (roughly the size of Japan or California) is just 23,000.

In the 1980s, a national park was created in the Kimberley to protect the maze of beehive-shaped, tiger-striped

Explore the underwater wonders of the Great Barrier Reef.

sandstone mountains known as the Bungle Bungle Range, scattered over 750 square kilometres (290 square miles). They are difficult to reach, and lie at the end of a long and very rough four-wheel-drive track. It's worth a special trip to see what is one of the world's most spectacular natural sights.

At a place called Monkey Mia south of Carnarvon and north of Perth, a group of friendly dolphins regularly come into the shallows to swim with people. They haven't been tamed, they just like to mingle.

The Pinnacles are another dramatic sight. These sand dunes, near the coast at Cervantes, are covered with protruding natural sandstone spires that create a bizarre array of forms. From the sea, early Dutch explorers thought the Pinnacles were a ruined city. In fact, the structures are the result of limestone forming around the roots of ancient dune plants. Seen by moonlight, the pillars, which may stand several metres high, take on grotesque, malignant shapes. Yet during the day, they appear as harmless oddities.

The rest of the state also has its share of superlatives. The southwest boasts the world's largest hardwoods in the giant Jarrah and Kauri forests. The region also produces some of Australia's best wine. Kalgoorlie and the desert goldfields still produce 112,000 Troy ounces (16,537 grams) of gold each year and the architecture of the towns reflects their early glory days.

Northern Territory

Australians regard the Northern Territory as the "frontier." There are only two population centres of note: Darwin in

the north, with 60,000 residents, and Alice Springs in central Australia, with 22,000 hardy souls. Throughout the Territory the Aborigine influence is strong: galleries are full of their vibrant and distinctive art works.

Some Aborigine groups conduct tours that provide insight into their special relationship with the land. Aborigines also own and operate the major national parks.

The Red Centre (central Australia) is unlike any other place on earth. Alice Springs, now a modern service town, is severing the links to its pioneering past. Even so, there are no towns nearby and the desert stretches out in all directions for hundreds of kilometres.

Australia is an ancient land, worn down by eons of erosion. So it's remarkable that the enormous bulk of Ayers Rock, the world's greatest monolith 348 metres (1,143 feet high), stands almost exactly in the centre of the continent. It's a cosmic marker set dead centre in Australia's bull's eye.

Explorer William Gosse who came here in 1873 was certainly impressed. He noted "one immense rock rising abruptly from the plain.... This rock is

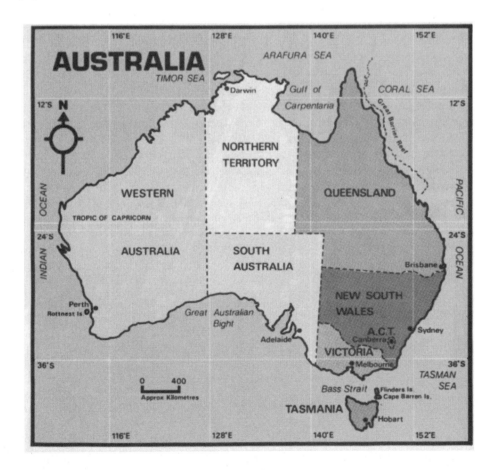

certainly the most wonderful natural feature I have ever seen." Unlike Gosse and generations who followed him, you don't have to rough it these days to visit the Rock. Yulara Resort, some 20 kilometres (12 miles) from the Rock, offers a full range of accommodations and services. Even from here the Rock is clearly visible—no longer as a looming presence but as a focal point on the horizon. It undergoes a remarkable colour shift throughout the day. In a final daily pyrotechnic display, a sunset can turn it to an iridescent red that quickly fades to shades of muted mauve. Finally there's nothing but a vast blackness that blocks out the stars.

The grand feature near the remote northern city of Darwin is Kakadu National Park, where much of the movie "Crocodile Dundee" was filmed. It contains sites of Aboriginal rock art with images drawn thousands of years ago, lush wetlands crowded with crocodiles and colourful birds, and glorious waterfalls plunging over natural escarpments.

Twin Falls, for example, is almost too good to be true. It looks more like an idealised film set than a work of nature. You can only reach it by four-wheel drive vehicle, followed by a walk down to a creek and a swim 300 metres (984 feet) upstream. You emerge from a dark, narrow defile into a sunny paradise. Palm trees shade the sands and a cooling waterfall cascades onto the end of the beach.

The whole of Australia has a lot in common with Twin Falls. Getting there requires a long journey and a high degree of commitment—but the rewards are many for those who take the time to visit Down Under.

Article 14

World Policy Journal, Fall 1994

Cambodia

A Heritage of Violence

Sheri Prasso

Sheri Prasso was Cambodia bureau chief for Agence France-Presse from September 1991 to January 1994. She is currently on leave at Cambridge University.

Visiting Cambodia, one cannot help but be beguiled by its almost-constant sunshine, its tranquilly swaying palm trees, and the overt friendliness of its smiling people, who greet each other and everyone else with the words "Sok s'bai?"—"Are you happy?" Indeed, happiness is one of the most valued aspects of Khmer society.

But Cambodia is a master of façade. It has never been a country at peace. Chroniclers from the very beginning of Khmer civilization have documented a "warrior heritage" of battles with neighbors Siam (Thailand), Annam (Vietnam), and Champa (wiped out by Vietnam in the fifteenth century). Internal divisions have allowed Cambodia's neighbors to take advantage of its instability to divide and conquer the country time and time again. Cambodians are further burdened with a brutal history of fratricide, medieval-style torture, summary justice, banditry, decapitation, and human-liver eating. Cambodians have the capacity to turn from seeming passivity to passionate rage in seconds with little reflection on the consequences.

Every one of these violent practices—including decapitation and the cutting out and ingestion of enemies' internal organs—continues in Cambodia today. While this violence is not unique to the Khmer people—such practices are documented in many other Asian and Middle Eastern societies—Cambodia has few socially acceptable outlets for the release of tension and anger and thus, I believe, finds it more difficult than other countries to reconcile its heritage of violence. Often Khmers blame their most raw, embarrassing foibles on foreigners or foreign "minds" in Khmer bodies, never resolving the reasons behind them or trying to find solutions from within. That this society produced one of the most vicious, despotic dictators of the twentieth century, Pol Pot, the man responsible for the deaths of a million people during his reign from 1975 to 1979, should have come as no surprise to those who know Cambodia's brutal history. That a $1.8 billion U.N. peacekeeping operation from 1992 to 1993 could not rectify the fundamental roots of conflict in Cambodia and that the result is a government wracked by infighting in a country still at war should not hold much surprise either.

Blood Brothers

The government that was elected in U.N.-run elections in May 1993 is anything but stable. As the result of a power-sharing agreement forced by the outcome of the vote, in which neither the former Communists nor the royalists won a governing majority, Cambodia is the only country in the world with two prime ministers—three counting the illegal, unrecognized government recently proclaimed by the Khmer Rouge guerrillas, who were supposed to have laid down their weapons and participated in the elections under the 1991 peace accords that formally ended the civil war. The Khmer Rouge refused to cooperate with U.N. peacekeepers and boycotted the peace process, returning the country to war. Still led by Pol Pot, who is rumored to be seriously ill with heart problems, the estimated force of 5,000 to 20,000 people—spread out "like a leopard's spots," as Cambodians say, in 19 of 21 provinces—has won significant military victories this year.

While the government in Phnom Penh survived a coup attempt in July of this year, it remains threatened from the outside by the Khmer Rouge and from within by its own failings: rampant corruption; inept administrators; a woefully inadequate and undertrained army that rarely receives its wages and secretly sells its ammunition to the enemy; a loose and uneven application of law and order; and destabilizing divisions between its leaders, who put personal interests before national ones in their continuing struggles for power.

The failed putsch was led by Prince Norodom Chakrapong, the half brother of the co-prime minister Prince Norodom Ranariddh, and masterminded by former Communist hard-liners in the Interior Ministry. There has been speculation that the hard-line factions within the government led the men into a trap in order to quell dissent, as well as the theory that the hard-liners were actually attempting to take power from the ruling coalition. Regardless of its motivations, the unrest is an indication of the fragility of the government and yet another example of the deeply rooted disunity and fratricidal tendencies that characterize Cambodian politics.

Prince Chakrapong and Prince Ranariddh, both sons of King Norodom Sihanouk, are sworn enemies. It was Prince Chakrapong who led the secessionist drive against his half brother when the formerly communist Cambodian People's Party (CPP) refused to accept its loss in the May 1993 elections. At that time he had the backing of the CPP, which now makes up half of the coalition but maintains total control over the administration of the country. Whether this year's uprising had outside support is not immediately clear, but the government's announcement that it had arrested 14 Thais in Phnom Penh in connection with the coup plot further highlights Thailand's ambiguous role in Cambodia. Prince Chakrapong fled into exile in Malaysia.

Such behavior among blood relatives has many precedents. In 1970, then Prince Sihanouk was ousted from power in a coup d'état by his cousin, Prince Sirik Matak, and his trusted prime minister, Gen. Lon Nol. During the era Cambodians regard as the glory days of their civilization, the Angkor period in the tenth to fifteenth centuries, a new king on his coronation day would order that all his brothers be mutilated, each losing a finger, nose, or other appendage, to prevent rival bids to the throne. (For Cambodians, a body that is not whole indicates a soul that is incomplete—a belief with devastating social implications for the thousands of land mine victims created every year.) Rivals from other families were decapitated.

Dispassion at Death

Cambodia has a long history of the use of decapitation, both as ritual and as punishment. Khmers of the lowest social status were beheaded to ensure the success of large construction projects during the Angkor period. In the 1960s, Prince Sihanouk's troops decapitated more than a dozen peasants involved in an antigovernment uprising and drove their heads to the capital in the back of a truck to show that the government would tolerate no dissent. When the Khmer Rouge captured the capital in April 1975, they rounded up top military officials and beheaded them on the tennis courts of the downtown sports club where Phnom Penh's elite played.[1] This May, Cambodian government troops decapitated a Khmer Rouge prisoner of war and left his head on display at a military headquarters in northwest Battambang, where Western news photographers spotted it. Soldiers fighting the Khmer Rouge in the province told journalists, with the dispassion of a butcher discussing how to filet a steak, that both sides often cut off their captured foes' heads and, for spite, send them back over enemy lines.

U.N. human rights monitors documented the grisly practices of liver eating and bile ingestion this year by Cambodian government soldiers in Battambang who were kidnapping civilians for ransom and then executing them to eliminate evidence of their misdeeds. One witness told a U.N. official in April that a particular captive in question was "eaten up," meaning that his liver was cut out, grilled, and eaten and his bile consumed. Cambodians have a traditional belief that the liver and bile contain the soul of the individual and that consuming them imbues the killer with the victim's life spirit. Following the Lon Nol coup in 1970, the general's brother was apprehended by a pro-Sihanouk mob in Kompong Cham province; his liver was cut out and eaten in a near-riot scene at a local restaurant. In 1296, Chou Ta-kuan, a Chinese envoy to the court of Angkor, wrote home to Beijing that the court still had a "minister for the collection of bile," although the practice had been officially abolished by that time. This man was charged with dispatching assassins among the population to sneak up on the unsuspecting, slice open their abdomens, and drain their gall bladders. This liquid was presented to the king in a large vat in order to ensure a good harvest. He added that once a Chinese had been forced to contribute to the collection and that his bile had spoiled the vat and thus the harvest. From then on, the Chinese population of Cambodia was left alone. Chou also documented the live burial outside the city gates of people accused of serious crimes and limb amputations of those accused of lesser crimes.

In Cambodia today, prisons are rife with disease, including tuberculosis, scurvy, and beriberi. Although the U.N. peacekeeping operation succeeded in getting the government to abolish the use of shackles to hold prisoners in their cells, barbaric, medieval-like punishments continue. The United Nations in 1993 tried to arrest a prison warden nicknamed the "Battambang barbequer," who allegedly strung up his victims and inflicted third-degree burns on their bodies, including on their genitals, in order to extract confessions. He eluded capture. I have met men kept for nearly two years in solitary confinement, shackled to a wall for 23 hours a day, hours in which they were ravaged by mosquitoes and vermin and bugs crawled over their legs and gnawed at their deadened toes. Another man was forced to soak in his own excrement in a large water vat for 14 days. Still worse, two men I knew, one a dissident and the other a controversial journalist, turned up dead of severe blows to the head in what the police ruled were traffic accidents. Cambodians have a belief similar to the West's "the squeaky wheel gets the grease" axiom, except that the consequences are always expected to be deadly. The fool who sticks out his neck will have his head chopped off, they say.

Anger seems to lurk just below the surface in Cambodia, and is evident in the folk tradition. Folk tales, in which Cambodians allow violent passions to overrule common sense, draw no moral conclusions and end abruptly. They show that violence is part of life, that violence begets more violence, and that cruelty goes unpunished. When I first arrived in 1991, a colleague told me to be acutely aware of clues indicating impatience or anger on the part of Cambodians, because unlike in the West, or even in East Asian cultures, where there are emotional pressure valves to let off tension, a Cambodian "will smile right up to the moment he kills you." This is an exaggeration, but unlike in neighboring Vietnam, where a traffic accident will usually result in a vulgar shouting match as good as one can find anywhere in New York, in Cambodia there is silence and then, if justice isn't done with cash on the spot, revenge. Shouting is frowned upon and anger is swallowed. To raise one's voice in Cambodia is to be called "crazy," and to call someone crazy is to use a provocation equal to the ugliest epithet imaginable in the English language.

So outlets come in other forms: children hurl cats by their tails against walls, a teenage boy empties an AK-47 magazine into a tree, young men kick around a mutt as if it were a soccer ball. By adulthood, the outlets are fewer. The deaths of strangers are met with what appears to be complete dispassion. Cambodians who have just witnessed or even committed murder recount it with sobering detail and without emotion. A Khmer Rouge defector confessed in a shockingly matter-of-fact manner to U.N. peacekeepers that he had helped massacre a score of ethnic Vietnamese men, women, and children in central Kompong Chhnang province in late 1992 under orders from his commander. He did not realize that this was a criminal act until the United Nations placed him in custody, charging him with mass murder. (He later died of a heart ailment in detention.)

Foreigners tell another story with startling repetitiveness, and I have witnessed it myself: at a traffic accident scene, people will gather around, shrug their shoulders, and observe to each other, "Look, the wheels are still spinning," while a victim lies in the road bleeding of a head wound. Again and again, foreigners intervene to administer first aid and take the wounded to a hospital.

The Consequences of Salvation

Expecting foreigners to save the day is a theme repeated over and over in Cambodia. The people were ecstatic when the United Nations arrived in 1992, thinking salvation had come at last. It was an old refrain, however, and one that has had serious consequences for the country's sovereignty. The Khmer Empire at its height encompassed much of mainland Southeast Asia, incorporating the Mekong Delta in southern Vietnam and most of Thailand, including the present-day Thai capital, Bangkok, and the Laotian capital, Vientiane. In order to hold on to power, Cambodian leaders throughout the centuries have appealed to outside powers for help in conquering their internal enemies without realizing, or perhaps without caring, that foreign domination is a double-edged sword: it makes the whole country weaker as it makes one faction strong.

Such a house divided in the face of neighbors Thailand and Vietnam, countries that throughout history have attempted to divide and conquer the Khmer people, has led to an irreparable loss of territory, contributing to the Cambodians' present-day sense of wounded pride and fear of racial extinction. A realistic concern about encroachment by neighbors is one of the key factors motivating Cambodia's foreign and domestic policies today.

Cambodia is a country of tremendous natural resources and, most important to its neighbors, vast empty stretches of arable land. Overpopulated and expansionist, Thailand and Vietnam cannot help but be tempted by Cambodia's ongoing vulnerability, particularly given the historical context: both countries have occupied large portions of Cambodia within the last 50 years. Moscow-backed Vietnam invaded to oust the Chinese-supported Khmer Rouge from power in 1978 and occupied the country for the next decade. U.S. diplomatic recognition of Vietnam and Vietnam's desire to protect its growing trade ties with Asian countries that opposed U.S. involvement in Cambodia—trade crucial to the country's economy following the collapse of the Soviet Union—rule out any immediate expansionist policies; in the long run, however, Vietnamese expansionism is not unlikely. Thailand continues to carry out annual, 12-day military exercises on its border with Cambodia, training against the threat of Vietnamese invasion.

Vietnam is keeping well out of the Cambodian conflict for the moment. Phnom Penh envoys sent to contact their old allies in Hanoi in February in order to buy arms were refused "even a single bullet" by President Le Duc Anh, in what was perhaps a concession to the mistakes of the past but also perhaps an omen for the future.[2] The Thais have no clearer conscience. The Cambodian capital at the magnificent temples of Angkor moved elsewhere after the Siamese sacked it in 1353 and again in 1431. The French colonial government in 1863 granted protection to the Cambodian royal court, threatened with domination from competing Thai and Vietnamese interests, then recovered what are now parts of Cambodia's three northwestern provinces from Thai annexation, once in 1907 and again following the Second World War.

Despite Cambodia's official sovereignty over its northwest provinces, Khmer residents there watch Thai television, buy imported Thai clothing and household goods, and plaster the walls of their wooden homes with posters of Thai pop stars. To say that a Cambodian woman "looks like a Thai" is a compliment. The United Nations fostered this cultural domination by sending 700 Thai soldiers to these northwest provinces, where another Thai group had already been doing road repairs under a bilateral agreement. The commanders of the U.N. Thai contingent opened a Thai restaurant in Battambang and reaped substantial profit during the U.N. presence.

Thailand has every interest in keeping a buffer between itself and Vietnam and then using that buffer to develop its own economic interests: the logging of Cambodia's hardwood forests and mining of its gems through concessions with the Khmer Rouge. The resulting overlap of political and economic interests frequently leads to accusations by Cambodian government officials—backed by U.S. diplomatic pressure—that Thailand is still supporting the Khmer Rouge in the ongoing civil conflict. Without recourse to Thai territory from which to regroup in order to mount new attacks, a recurring event within the last year, the Khmer Rouge would have quickly dissolved into isolated pockets, some of which easily could have succumbed to government forces. In response to a new law passed by the Cambodian National Assembly in July that declared the

Khmer Rouge illegal and their passports invalid, Thailand pledged to stop allowing Khmer Rouge leaders to leave Cambodia through Thai territory.

The government in Bangkok has made such claims about full support for the Phnom Penh government before, only to have been caught red-handed helping the Khmer Rouge. It is important here to distinguish between the military and the civilian parts of the Thai government. Thailand's generals exert enormous power, particularly in business dealings, along the country's borders with Burma, Laos, and Cambodia. Thai diplomats concede that central control over the military fringes is tenuous at best. Foreign correspondents were invited by the Thai Foreign Ministry to the Thai-Cambodian border this year to clarify Thailand's position; they were briefed with a map showing Cambodia as "Democratic Kampuchea," the name of the country when it was under Khmer Rouge rule—to the embarrassment of ministry officials escorting the journalists.

Cambodian officials usually make their allegations against Thailand in the throes of anger and to deflect criticism of their own mismanagement. Most of these charges lack proof, but evidence of Thai support for the Khmer Rouge was uncovered in December 1993 when Thai police (rivals of the Thai military) found 1,500 tons of Chinese-made weapons, enough to defend a small country, stockpiled and guarded by the Cambodian guerrillas inside Thailand. The seizure came during a routine police check as some of the weapons were being transported in rice sacks by a Khmer Rouge driver who admitted he had been ordered to truck the weapons across the border to Pailin. (Pailin is the symbolic Khmer Rouge headquarters in western Cambodia, a pretty town in a Cardamon Mountain valley full of the ruby and sapphire mines that keep the guerrilla operation funded through Thai business concessions. Its capture by the Cambodian army in March and subsequent recapture by the Khmer Rouge in April were the highlights of the 1994 dry season offensive, which ended in May. As a result of their military victories, the Khmer Rouge now hold more territory than during the U.N. peacekeeping operation, most of it along the border with Thailand. The Khmer Rouge have declared their zone a separate country.)

When U.N. peacekeepers were in Cambodia, they documented many Thai infringements of Cambodian sovereignty, all of which were denied by Bangkok. When the Khmer Rouge captured a government-held crossing point into Thailand on Cambodia's northern border in August 1993, the attack was launched "from three to four directions, including the Thai side of the checkpoint," and during the attack U.N. peacekeepers assigned to the checkpoint were "detained in Thai territory by [the Khmer Rouge]," according to the United Nations. (From this same checkpoint I witnessed and photographed the crossing of 140 trucks carrying an average of five logs each in violation of the U.N. moratorium of January 2, 1993, on log exports from Cambodia. The Thai government denied the violation, but the United Nations later named Thailand as the biggest violator of the ban on log exports from Cambodia.) During a government offensive against the Khmer Rouge in the northwest province of Banteay Meanchey in August 1993, "there [was] absolutely no doubt that [Khmer Rouge] forces and civilians . . . were allowed by Thailand to cross the border and seek refuge on its territory."3

Cambodia is not without means to retaliate if Thai support for the Khmer Rouge continues. Only half joking, a senior Cambodian military official told me it would be relatively easy to begin arms shipments to Muslim separatists in southern Thailand or to stir up unrest among the four million ethnic Khmers living in Thailand's Surin province.

The China Hand

It is impossible to understand the destabilizing foreign influences in Cambodia without looking at China as well. For more than 20 years, China supplied arms to Cambodia's Communists. Beijing announced in 1991, just ahead of the signing of the peace accords, that it would supply no more military aid to Cambodia. After all, Chinese diplomats quickly pointed out, it was the fanatics of the Cultural Revolution in China who funded the fanaticism of the Maoists in Cambodia, and it is a new era in both countries. U.S. diplomats say their intelligence has not detected any Chinese arms shipments since 1991. In fact, Prince Ranariddh said in May that when the Cambodian government tried to order Chinese ammunition through a Singapore company the Chinese government blocked the delivery."4

That does not mean China is no longer interested in Cambodia's affairs. Rather, Beijing wants to keep Cambodia as a thorn in the side of Vietnam, its historical nemesis, which contests China's claim to the Spratly Island chain. The less stable Cambodia, the more powerful China.

Beijing—where King Sihanouk has sought refuge and support over the years, maintains a residence, and has undergone treatment for cancer—holds considerable influence over the actions of the monarch. It surely has been at China's insistence that King Sihanouk has pounded the theme of peace talks with the Khmer Rouge rather than advocating a military solution—as most Western observers and diplomats do—that would turn them into a manageable insurgency along the lines of those currently existing in the Philippines or Peru. Including the untrustworthy Khmer Rouge, who have violated every international covenant they have been asked to uphold, in the government could only lead to further

destabilization of the country. While chairing roundtable peace negotiations with the Khmer Rouge earlier this year, King Sihanouk admitted that the Khmer Rouge were only attending as a stalling tactic in their attempt to regain total power over Cambodia. "They are not sincere," he told a group of journalists gathered at his Royal Palace in May. "Even with 100 roundtables there will be no peace. The prospect is very bleak."

The Paths of History

The king, nearly 72 years old and suffering from cancer that has spread to his bone marrow, could have launched his country on a new path of stability and independence following the U.N. operation. Instead, he started again down the same mistaken paths of history by appealing anew for foreign intervention, which could only destabilize the government over which he presides but does not control. Expressing desperation over his inability to bring peace to Cambodia before his death, he made moves to retake the reins of power from the elected prime ministers in what is probably a sincere belief that his rule is the best for the country, and called for help from abroad to "save Cambodia from the yoke of the Khmer Rouge." He cited Australia, France, and the United States, saying he wanted those countries to come in to train and arm royal units under his command.

Washington and Paris have provided limited aid to the Cambodian government, in the form of technical advisers and mine clearers, and have considered stronger forms of lethal assistance, a move publicly opposed by Thailand. The needs are great, particularly in terms of the air power necessary to gain the upper hand against the Khmer Rouge. Of 21 MiG-21 fighter jets donated to the former Phnom Penh regime by the Soviet Union, only two are in flying condition. Australia also considered lethal aid but stated that Cambodia's army is in such disarray that weapons would be wasted without complete retraining of the armed forces.

Cambodia's 100,000-strong military force is unusually top heavy, with 2,000 generals and 10,000 colonels. Rank usually has more to do with political favor or wealth than ability on the battlefield. Half of the ammunition sent to the battlefront at Pailin in March and April this year disappeared from stockpiles and was sold off to the enemy or on the black market, according to Western diplomats. Undisciplined soldiers (as well as Khmer Rouge guerrillas) routinely kidnap people for ransom, exact "tolls" from passing motorists, and rob markets in the cities of Battambang and Siem Reap. The government's loss of Pailin after it had held it for only four weeks was directly attributable to the greedy commanding officers' concentration on collecting loot rather than defending the territory. Nonetheless, the Association of Southeast

Asian Nations (ASEAN) decided in late July that the Cambodian government should receive lethal aid to fight the Khmer Rouge.

Given Cambodia's history, more weapons will not bring a long-term solution. For without the Khmer Rouge threat to rally against, the government would likely turn in on itself in an endless circle of factionalism and division. The true solution must come from within the Khmer society at the behest of fair, unified rulers who have Cambodia's greater interests at heart. But before that can happen there must be the one fundamental change advocated by Thun Saray, a dissident who spent 17 months in prison before founding a local human rights group in 1992. It is his belief that unless every opposing group can trust that the men in power will not persecute them, they will continue the bloody struggle to take power for themselves, for their very survival is at stake. Unless there are basic human rights in Cambodia, there can never be peace.

Notes

1. Elizabeth Becker, When the War Was Over (New York: Simon and Schuster, 1986), p. 84.
2. Nate Thayer and Nayan Chanda, "Things Fall Apart . . . ," Far Eastern Economic Review, May 19, 1994, p. 17.
3. UNTAC Interoffice Memorandum, August 24, 1993.
4. Thayer and Chanda, "Things Fall Apart," p. 17.

Article 15   *The World Today*, August–September 1994

Indochina: from confrontation to cooperation

Martin Gainsborough

Earlier this year, and for the briefest of moments, the international media descended on Laos. The reason: the opening on 8 April of the cross-Mekong river 'friendship' bridge linking Laos with Thailand. The bridge provides landlocked Laos with its first modern road link with the outside world. While the event was of great moment to Laos, it is also of significance for the planned economic development of the whole Mekong river sub-region, incorporating China (notably Yunnan province), Thailand, Vietnam, Laos, Cambodia and Burma. To date, these countries have met on three occasions, most recently in Hanoi on 20–23 April. Each meeting has taken place under the auspices of the Asian Development Bank (ADB), which has been instrumental in bringing them together.

The ADB's starting point is that recent political changes—largely a product of the end of the Cold War—and recent economic changes—the widespread pursuit of market-oriented economic reforms in the region—have created a climate in which coordinated activities in six areas (trade, investment, transportation, energy, water resources and tourism) can take place. Such activity will, the ADB argues, hasten economic development.

At its most ambitious, the Bank talks in terms of the benefits to the private sector of harmonised investment codes, financial reporting systems, foreign exchange and banking regulations. It also envisages such things as the free flow of workers, the exchange of technology, and the 'rational' development of resources.

Infrastructure development is understandably regarded as the crucial first stage. Key projects involve upgrading the road from Ho Chi Minh City to Phnom Penh and on to Bangkok; constructing an East-West corridor from Thailand across Laos to the Vietnamese coast; building a good quality road linking Chiang Rai with Kunming via Burma on the one hand, and via Laos on the other; and upgrading the Kunming-Lashio road.

The ADB aims primarily to build on existing cooperation—not necessarily involving all six countries nor requiring their unanimous approval. The Bank envisages its role as being that of 'catalyst', i.e., facilitating dialogue between the participants and increasing the benefits of a particular project by forging links with related projects in neighbouring countries. It also has a role in providing financial and technical backing where appropriate.[1]

Though the ADB's 'vision' remains a long way from the Indochina of today—one which, despite recent economic reforms, is beset by poverty and economic underdevelopment and which has been paralysed by conflict and political suspicion for much of the last fifty years—there are signs that a climate more conducive to cooperation is emerging.

Differences over Cambodia

This is not to say that there are not still differences of outlook over Cambodia on the part of Vietnam, Thailand and China—the powers whose cooperation is essential if Indochina is to enter a more peaceful era and who have traditionally and most recently played out their rivalries in Cambodia, notably following Vietnam's 1978 invasion. These differences have been particularly apparent between Vietnam and Thailand. During the run-up to the May 1993 UN-supervised elections in Cambodia, Vietnam supported sanctions against the Khmer Rouge following its refusal to disarm, arguing that UN resolutions were not tough enough. The Thai Foreign Ministry, meanwhile, declared that it supported all Cambodian factions equally, which meant taking no unilateral line against the Khmer Rouge. After the formation of Cambodia's FUNCINPEC–Cambodian People's Party (CPP) coalition government in October 1993, Bangkok expressed its support for incorporating the Khmer Rouge into the administration. Hanoi, on the other hand, has expressed its concern if such an eventuality was to come to pass.[2]

Cambodia's request for foreign military assistance, floated by King Norodom Sihanouk in May 1994, has also highlighted differences between Hanoi and Bangkok. Both the Thai government and the army have voiced their opposition. However, Hanoi's Deputy Foreign Minister, Le Mai, while stressing that Vietnam would not itself provide military assistance to Cambodia, has implied that he would have no objections if other countries wished to assist Phnom Penh in its fight against the Khmer Rouge.[3] Accusations of continuing close relations between individuals in the Thai establishment, notably in the army, and the Khmer Rouge, while souring relations between Phnom Penh and Bangkok, are also a thorn in relations between Vietnam and Thailand.

Since the 1991 Cambodia peace agreement, China, meanwhile, has convincingly articulated its commitment to seeing the political process there work. In March 1993, in the approach to the Cambodian elections, the Chinese Prime Minister, Li Peng, said that Beijing neither agreed with actions that violated the Paris Accord nor with methods which would lead to confrontation. Then, in April 1993, when the situation was looking especially precarious, the Chinese Foreign Ministry spokesman, Wu Jianmin, said that China would not support any Cambodian parties in the event of civil war. He also said that China would not put pressure on the Khmer Rouge to disarm. This brought Beijing closer to the Thai Foreign Ministry line and potentially more at loggerheads with Vietnam.

Since the election, however, the Chinese appear to have distanced themselves from the Khmer Rouge.[4] Beijing has expressed its support for the coalition government in Cambodia under the leadership of King Sihanouk, notably during the Cambodian government's visit to Beijing in January 1994. Moreover, in December 1993 China appointed a new Ambassador in Phnom Penh, replacing Fu Xuezhang with Xue Yuee. Fu's tenure suggested a certain ambivalence in Beijing's position, given that he had served in Phnom Penh during the Pol Pot period.[5] Xue, on the other hand, has pledged China's support for reconstruction in Cambodia.

Although Beijing has not publicly expressed an opinion on the provision of foreign military assistance to Cambodia, it is quite likely that—like Thailand—it would oppose it. Li Peng has stressed his hope that Cambodia will be a neutral and non-aligned country. Beijing's stand on integrating the Khmer Rouge into the government is also not clear. However, its support for King Sihanouk suggests that it would share his leanings towards a government of national reconciliation that included the Khmer Rouge. The Chinese President, Jiang Zemin, said in January 1994 that he hoped that the Phnom Penh government would 'further advance the process of national reconciliation'.

Nevertheless, China's position on Cambodia is not identical to Thailand's. During the August–September 1993 visit of the Thai Prime Minister, Chuan Leekpai, to Beijing there was a hint of a veiled warning made by the Chinese to the Thais, advising them to stop meddling in Cambodia.[6] In this, China and Vietnam are in agreement. Hanoi regards the Khmer Rouge as capable of causing serious disruption but not representing a serious threat as long as they are not backed by an external power.[7] A stand against the Khmer Rouge on the part of China, and anything that suggests that the *de facto* Sino-Thai alliance of the 1980s is over, will therefore reassure Hanoi.

The Cold War dividend

There are, however, more fundamental reasons why remaining differences between the countries in Indochina are unlikely to deteriorate into conflict. There is a school of thought which regards the end of the Cold War as making conflict more likely. However, in the case of Indochina, there is reason to believe that the end of the Cold War has diminished the prospect of conflict.[8] Rather than suppressing indigenous conflicts, the superpower 'overlay' heightened the fears of local states. The Vietnamese threat was perceived by China and Thailand as being more serious because of the Soviet–Vietnamese friendship treaty of 1978. In the context of the Sino-Soviet split, China's support for the Khmer Rouge and its attack on northern Vietnam shortly after Vietnam's invasion of Cambodia served a dual purpose. Equally, it was the loss of Soviet support that led Vietnam to a more realistic assessment of its capabilities.[9]

The collapse of European Communist regimes has had a profound impact on Asia's Communist Party leaderships, and also represents a reason why conflict is less likely. Beijing, Hanoi and Vientiane all understand that economic underdevelopment risks a loss of political power. Consequently, they, along with Phnom Penh and Rangoon, are all pursuing some sort of market-oriented reforms. These reforms depend on expanding foreign relations, attracting foreign investment and developing trade. Ensuring a peaceful external environment in which reform can be pursued is therefore crucial.

The transformation that has taken place in Vietnam offers a salient example. A fear frequently expressed by Hanoi is that of being left behind economically in the region. This, above all else, is viewed as the greatest threat to the country's independence and territorial integrity.

There is also a recognition in Hanoi that the invasion of Cambodia turned out to be a very costly error, in that it led to its international isolation and the imposition of economic sanctions, thereby stymieing Vietnam's economic reform programme. Certainly, it is appropriate to see the Cambodia experience as profoundly influencing current Vietnamese foreign policy. Consequently, Hanoi will do its utmost to avoid any action that might result in international sanctions. For example, it will learn to live with attacks on ethnic Vietnamese living in Cambodia, confining itself to diplomatic protest and not allowing itself to be provoked. Moreover, though it will at times feel incensed by the gulf between China's words and actions in the South China Sea—a key unresolved area of dispute between the two countries—it will do all it can to avoid taking action which might cause alarm in the region.

Following the loss of Soviet support and its near economic collapse, Vietnam has come to terms with its relative weakness. It has recognised that the 'special relationship' it once had with Cambodia and Laos is not acceptable, and that relations must be developed along more conventional diplomatic lines. Vietnam's accession to the 1976 Bali Treaty of Amity and Cooperation in July 1992 is an encouraging pointer as to the direction it wishes to take. Comments by the Deputy Prime Minister, Phan Van Khai, in May 1994 suggest that Vietnamese membership of the Association of South East Asian Nations (ASEAN) may happen sooner rather than later.[10]

ASEAN is playing an important role in the economic development of Indochina.[11] Significantly, however, Bangkok's ability to dictate the organisation's policy towards Vietnam as it largely did during the 1980s—if things were to take a turn for the worse—have been reduced, now that the other ASEAN members have their own economic interests in Vietnam.[12]

Neighbours talk—and trade

While there remains a legacy of mistrust and a number of unresolved areas of dispute in dealings between Vietnam and China and Vietnam and Thailand, overall, relations have progressed to a sounder footing in recent years. During the visit of the Vietnamese President, Le Duc Anh, to China in November 1993—the first by a Vietnamese head of state since 1955—the Chinese Foreign Ministry spokesman, Wu Jianmin, said that Sino-Vietnamese relations had swerved between being 'too close' to being 'abnormally hostile', and that they were now seeking a 'normal relationship'. The October 1993 signing of a 'declaration of principles' for solving the territorial dispute, in which the two sides agreed not to take action which would complicate matters, is a step in this direction.

A deepening of Sino-Vietnamese economic relations also suggests that the foundations are being laid for future cooperation along lines envisaged by the ADB. Commercial links no longer exclusively consist of small-scale cross-border trade. In October and November 1993, a number of large Chinese trading companies for the first time opened offices in Hanoi. There has also been discussion of Chinese assistance to Vietnam for the establishment of a chemical fertiliser and a hydroelectric power plant.

With the development of commercial links between adjacent Chinese and Vietnamese provinces, it is worth considering the extent to which a deterioration in Sino-Vietnamese relations at the national level still acts as an impediment to Sino-Vietnamese relations at the cross-border level. In many respects, relations between adjacent Chinese and Vietnamese provinces have a momentum of their own and are not affected by ups and downs over the Spratly Islands.[13]

Despite this, Beijing–Hanoi relations are not easy and are unlikely to be so for some time to come.[14] There is a strong sense in Hanoi that the declaration of principles on the territorial dispute is only this, and that agreement on the ground is a long way off.[15]

Relations between Hanoi and Bangkok have been troubled by a number of issues recently, including overlapping claims in the Gulf of Thailand; fishing disputes, with the frequent detention of fishermen from the other country; and civil aviation rights. Nevertheless, one should not exaggerate the problems. Relations are qualitatively better than a few years ago. Since October 1991, for example, there have been a series of high-level exchanges. In January 1992, the then head of the Thai army, Suchinda Kraprayoon, visited Hanoi, proclaiming that he no longer considered Vietnam a threat. Though one can qualify this statement, in the short term there is an element of truth in it. Also, Thailand and Vietnam are not party to the kind of direct 'face-off', which afflicts China and Vietnam in the South China Sea. In addition, progress towards settling outstanding differences—if at times rather tortuous—has been made. In January, important steps towards resolving the dispute over civil aviation rights were made.

Differences of outlook regarding Cambodia have not soured Thai–Vietnamese relations in a public way recently. Nevertheless, a convincing cessation of Thai links with the Khmer Rouge is important if tensions between Thailand and Vietnam—and Thailand and Cambodia—are genuinely to be eased. Given the long-standing nature of Thai–Khmer Rouge contacts, their evident commercial value and the inability of the Thai government to enforce its writ among 'frontline' military commanders, this may not happen quickly.

Hanoi, however, has hinted at a willingness to take Thai statements at face value. In November 1993, Vietnam's Foreign Minister, Nguyen Manh Cam, while saying that it was up to foreign countries not to create the conditions in which the Khmer Rouge could survive, noted that it was not the Thai government's policy to support them—thus seemingly making a distinction between the Thai army and the government. Moreover, in the longer term, and without the strategic *raison d'être* that sustained Thai–Khmer Rouge contacts during the 1980s, one can well imagine that such associations will decline, particularly if the Khmer Rouge is reduced to a small band of insurgents.[16]

Against the backdrop of gradually improving political relations, economic relations in Indochina are beginning to develop along the lines envisaged by the ADB. One example is the cooperation between Vientiane and Bangkok in which Laos sells hydroelectricity to Thailand. Moreover, the opening of the 'friendship' bridge across the Mekong is unlikely to be the last. Three further crossing points from Thailand into Laos are currently being considered, all with connecting roads across Laos to the Vietnamese coast. The French government is financing a detailed feasibility study.[17]

Although few infrastructure schemes are past the feasibility study stage, a wide range of schemes are under discussion. In July 1993, Cambodia's Foreign Minister, Prince Norodom Sirivudh, offered Laos access to the sea via Cambodian territory. Though it is questionable how economically viable such a route would be for traders, given the distance goods would have to travel, the two sides have set up a joint commission to plan a new road between their respective capitals. In December 1993, a route from Thailand (Mai Sai) to China (Jinghong) via Burma was opened through an area of Burma that had effectively been 'closed off' for the past 50 years.[18] There has also been discussion among Mekong river countries of blasting rapids on sections of the river to make it navigable.

Infrastructure development is likely to happen on a piecemeal basis, gradually interlocking to form an international network. Visiting Vietnam in November 1993, Singapore's Lee Kuan Yew predicted that it would be 10 years before Vietnam had a 'functioning' infrastructure. It is conceivable that infrastructure development in Vietnam will be faster than in other parts of Indochina.

Trade and tourism are also increasing. Links between Laos and China's south-western provinces are expanding. In November 1993, a Laos delegation visited Yunnan province and discussed trade and cooperation in agriculture, hydroelectric power generation, tourism and communications.[19] In November 1993, the third and last border checkpoint between Vietnam and Yunnan province was opened.

Thais are visiting their ancestral homeland of Xishuangbanna in China's Yunnan province in increasing numbers. There are now 14 flights a week between Kunming and Chiang Mai. Opening up the sub-region to trade fits with the Thai government's desire to shift economic activity away from Bangkok to the north and north-east. It has given strong support to the so-called Economic (or Golden) Quadrangle, which focuses on economic cooperation between Thailand, China, Burma and Laos. Thai government visits to China in February, July, and August–September 1993 all included visits to western provinces. Thailand and China have opened consulates in Kunming and Songkhla respectively. According to data published in August 1993, cumulative Thai investment in China is close to $1bn. Thailand is also the largest foreign investor in Laos and Cambodia.

The Mekong Committee, the sub-regional body grouping Vietnam, Thailand, Laos and Cambodia responsible for overseeing developments in the Mekong river basin, is also important in an assessment of relations in Indochina. Its interactions, particularly between Thailand and Vietnam, have not been problem-free. Disagreements have centred on concern among downstream committee members, notably Vietnam and Cambodia, about upstream members' plans to divert upstream water for agricultural and other use.

Nevertheless, progress has been made. In January 1994, Hanoi announced that agreement had been reached on 38 out of 42 articles of a draft accord on managing the water resources, although, according to Hanoi, Thailand has yet to agree on the key principle of 'prior consultation' before using water.

The Committee is an important 'litmus test' of the way in which the Mekong river countries conduct their relations. There is every likelihood that China and Burma will be invited to become members, once the existing Committee develops some ground rules.[20]

Outlook for Indochina

Although there are reasons to be optimistic about Indochina's prospects, the future is not without its risks. A number of factors threaten to slow or undermine the sub-region's advance. Undoubtedly there must be genuine concern that Sino-Vietnamese diplomatic exchanges over disputed claims in the South China Sea might escalate into something more serious. But the greatest threat to a more cooperative era in Indochina lies in the domestic set-up of each Mekong river country. Over the next decade, the majority will undergo a process of generational change. Economic reform is creating new challenges for ruling elites, in terms of the shift from a 'political society' to a 'civil society',[21] reinforced differences between provinces and regions, and unemployment. Although the exact relationship between the type of economic policy pursued and political change is not clear, the lesson from the more economically advanced Asian nations is that sustained, high-level economic growth gradually leads to demands for a more pluralistic political society. In the case of Indochina's Communist Parties, an increased emphasis on the market is resulting in a diminution of some traditional areas of their authority.[22]

The ability of ruling elites to manage the pressures for change smoothly will have important implications for the foreign relations of Indochina's states. Weak governments might well be tempted to appeal to age-old national prejudices. Deep-seated anti-Vietnamese sentiment in Cambodia, which is evident in its media, is restricting the Phnom Penh government's ability to respond to Hanoi's calls that it guarantees the safety of ethnic Vietnamese living in Cambodia.

Political fragility in Cambodia is itself cause for concern. While there are doubts about the durability of the FUNCINPEC–Cambodian People's Party (CPP) coalition, splits within FUNCINPEC itself, and between those with interests in the 'old order' and those seeking to introduce reform, are possibly more serious. The Finance and Economy Minister, Sam Rainsy, who is attempting to bring taxation under central control, has encountered opposition from a 'conservative' alliance comprising both senior FUNCINPEC and CPP politicians, business and the armed forces. Notwithstanding the constitutional limits on the monarch's power, King Sihanouk's ability to 'rein in' the coalition partners is unrivalled. His death would therefore remove a key figure for stability.

Political instability in Cambodia also highlights the danger that economic development will happen unevenly in Indochina. Given Vietnam's much larger population and its more stable political set-up, it is likely that it will absorb a far larger portion of foreign investment than its neighbours. Laos, which in terms of political stability rates higher than Cambodia, nevertheless attracted around 12 times less foreign investment than Vietnam in 1993. Also, infrastructure development is likely to be constrained by the state of lawlessness which afflicts parts of Indochina. Conflict between the Burmese government and the country's ethnic rebel groups is taking place where new roads are scheduled to be built.

The development of commercial relations in Indochina is also limited by the fact that the countries in the sub-region are economic competitors. The modest achievements of ASEAN in the economic sphere—particularly the difficulties encountered in establishing the Asian Free Trade Area (AFTA)—point to the constraints. In Indochina, there is a widespread fear of being swamped by Chinese or Thai goods and the damage this would cause to emerging domestic industries. Vietnam, for example, has raised tariffs and tightened import controls to stem the influx of Chinese goods. Vientiane has delayed a decision on the opening of a second bridge across the Mekong to assess the impact on trade of the first.

As one considers the future course of relations in Indochina, it is worth recalling the path down which ASEAN has come since its establishment in 1967. Formed in the wake of 'confrontation' between Malaysia and Indonesia, there now exists a state of affairs whereby, although ASEAN members are economic competitors and their views differ on certain issues, they would only settle their disputes by diplomatic means. Despite the obstacles, there are signs that Indochina is setting off down a similar path.

NOTES

1. See *Subregional Economic Cooperation*, Asian Development Bank, February 1993; *Second Conference on Subregional Economic Cooperation*, Summary Paper, August 1993; 'River of Promise', *Far Eastern Economic Review*, 16 September 1993.
2. Khmer Rouge admission to the government looks less likely following the repeated failure of round table talks, culminating in the closure of the Khmer Rouge office in Phnom Penh in June 1994 and in the outlawing of the Khmer Rouge in July.
3. *Voice of Vietnam*, External Service, BBC Summary of World Broadcasts, Far East, 2020 B/6, 13 June 1994.
4. See, however, 'Back to War', *Far Eastern Economic Review*, 30 June 1994, p. 12, which quotes Cambodian government sources as saying that their intelligence services have evidence that 'Chinese supplied arms' were received by the Khmer Rouge in March.
5. Ben Kiernan. 'The Cambodian Crisis, 1990–1992: The UN Plan, the Khmer Rouge, and the State of Cambodia', *Bulletin of Concerned Asian Scholars*, No 2, 1992, p. 9.
6. I am grateful to Alan Boyd, correspondent based in Bangkok, for his observation here.

7. Conversation with Assistant Foreign Minister and Director General of Institute for International Relations, Dao Huy Ngoc, in Hanoi, November 1993.

8. For a fuller discussion of both the 'liberal' and 'realist' schools, with leanings towards the latter, see Barry Buzan and Gerald Segal, 'Rethinking East Asian Security', *Survival*, Volume 36, No 2, 1992, pp. 3–21.

9. See Michael C. Williams 'Vietnam at the Crossroads', Royal Institute of International Affairs, 1992, for background on this issue.

10. Deputy Prime Minister Phan Van Khai said that Vietnam would join ASEAN 'at an early stage'. Previously, the official line was that Vietnam would join 'at an appropriate time'.

11. For a discussion of ASEAN's involvement in Vietnam, see M. Gainsborough, 'Vietnam and ASEAN: the Road to Membership?', *The Pacific Review*, No 4/1993.

12. See Surin Maisrikrod, 'Thailand's Policy Dilemmas Towards Indochina', *Southeast Asia*, Vol. 4, No 3, 1992.

13. For a discussion of these issues from the perspective of China, see Gerald Segal, *China Changes Shape*, Adelphi Paper No. 287 (London: Brassey's for the IISS, 1994), especially pp. 34–53.

14. See Martin Gainsborough, 'Vietnam II: a turbulent normalisation with China', *The World Today*, November 1992.

15. A point made by Deputy Foreign Minister Le Mai during conversation in November 1993.

16. It is too early to write the Khmer Rouge off. Towards the end of the dry season fighting in 1994, the Khmer Rouge retook ground previously lost to the government, at one point coming within 20 kilometres of Battambang. However, the guerrillas hold no provincial capitals.

17. The three proposed crossings are between Mukadahan in Thailand's north-east and Savannakhet in Laos, continuing on to the Vietnamese port of Danang; from Nakhon Phanom to the Laotian province of Khammouan, continuing to the Vietnamese coast at Honla; and from Thakkhek in Nakhon Phanom province to roughly due east of Vientiane, continuing to the Vietnamese port of Cua Lo, near Vinh.

18. James Pringle, 'Convoy on road to trade boom', *The Times*, 4 December 1993.

19. At the national level, relations between Beijing and Vientiane are no longer troubled as they were in the 1980s by Laos's close association with Vietnam. In December 1993, China and Laos signed a border demarcation agreement.

20. Confirmed by Deputy Foreign Minister Le Mai in Hanoi, November 1993.

21. *The Daily Telegraph*'s China correspondent, Graham Hutchings, has described this shift with reference to China as follows: 'Political society, the traditional order is built around families, cellular "work units" and the formal apparatus of government control. Collective values predominate.' Meanwhile, 'Civil society, the new order, is characterised by growing differentiation between home, work and leisure; differences in values between generations; the evolution of a "natural" class structure; and demands for more autonomy for the individual'.

22. For assessment of political changes in Vietnam, see Russell Heng Hiang Khng, 'Leadership in Vietnam: Pressure for Reform and Their Limits', *Contemporary Southeast Asia*, Vol. 15, No 1, June 1993.

Article 16   *USA Today*, September 1994

CHINA

The Biggest Dragon of All?

*Bold free-market reforms are leading to economic growth that may outstrip Japan,
Taiwan, and South Korea—the so-called "financial dragons" of the global
economy—by the 21st century.*

Abu Selimuddin

*Dr. Selimuddin is professor of economics,
Berkshire Community College, Pittsfield,
Mass.*

China lost its lead to Europe as the world's most advanced civilization around 1500. Before then, China was the envy of everyone for its science, technology, and productivity. Between 1500 and 1978, as the West grew richer and more powerful, China was ravaged by revolutions, war, famine, tyranny, and anarchy.

Today, though, China is East and Southeast Asia's largest country in terms of natural resources, population, and land. A quarter-century ago, China saw no foreign investment and loans, and had one of the lowest ratios of foreign trade relative to the size of its population and economy. Things have changed radically. Southern China is attracting huge amounts of capital from the U.S., Japan, Taiwan, Hong Kong, and South Korea. As a result, southern China is the world's fastest growing economy and the developing world's largest trading province.

China has built better economic ties with Japan, Taiwan, Hong Kong, and South Korea despite its difficult political relationships with them. For example, China does not recognize Taiwan's government, which continues shopping for arms to assert its independence from the mainland. China also worries about Japanese growing nationalism, militarism, and ambition regarding Taiwan.

Southern China's explosive economic boom began in 1978. Between then and 1991, it averaged nine percent growth in Gross Domestic Product (GDP), nearly double the rate of the Japanese economy and three times that of America. In 1992, when the three leading economies—U.S., Japan, and Germany—were mired in the global slump, China grew at a 12% rate. The mainland's foreign trade reached $165,000,000,000, an 18% gain in exports from the previous year.

Based on its spectacular economic performance, many veteran China-watchers predict that, by 2002, the Chinese economy will be eight times bigger than it was in 1978. At that point, China will have matched the performances of Japan, Taiwan, and South Korea during their fastest quarter-centuries of economic progress. As *The Economist* magazine points out, "If China's economy grows as fast for the next 20 years as it has for the past 14, it will be the biggest economy on earth."

It makes many wonder how an underdeveloped China could push its economic progress so spectacularly after more than a decade of anarchy in the Cultural Revolution. There is no question that Premier Deng Xiaoping's bold free-market reforms in major sectors of the economy—such as farming, manufacturing, trading, and foreign investment—have been critically important to China's dramatic progress.

In farming, for instance, failed communes are being abolished and replaced by family farms as the unit of production. In addition to a dramatic leap of real income in the countryside, this reform increased production of grain, fruits, and poultry enormously.

In manufacturing, the once dominating state-owned firms have shrunk quickly. In 1978, the state-owned firms accounted for nearly 80% of China's industrial output. By 2000, that share is expected to drop to 25%.

China's "open-door policy," by eliminating the central government's monopoly over foreign trade and investment, has been just as significant as its farm and industrial reforms. By 1991, there were 20,000 foreign ventures in China, with a total investment value of $25,000,000,000. In 1992, about 27,000 projects with a total value of more than $30,000,000,000 had been recorded.

China also is widening the door for retailers. It has signed a number of joint ventures with American firms such as Occidental Petroleum, McDonnell Douglas, Xerox, Warner-Lambert, PPG Industries, Babcock & Wilcox, H. J. Heinz, General Bearings, and Hewlett-Packard. Among other big U.S. deals in China are Wing-Merrill's power plants ($2,000,000,000); Arco's natural-gas project ($1,200,000,000); AT&T's telecommunications, semiconductors, mobile phones, and research and development ($1,000,000,000); Boeing's planes ($800,000,000); and Coca-Cola's bottling plants ($150,000,000). Despite its rapidly rising income and an insatiable appetite for foreign goods, China restricts its imports. According to management theorist Peter Druker: "The world is confounded by a Chinese dragon that exports like a capitalist but imports like a communist."

The mainland's economic ties with Japan are growing at a time when U.S. relations with Japan have deteriorated over trade friction and American relations with China have become strained. Japan has become one of China's largest export markets. Trade between China and Japan in 1992 surged 27% from a year earlier to a record $29,000,000,000. The amount was estimated to top

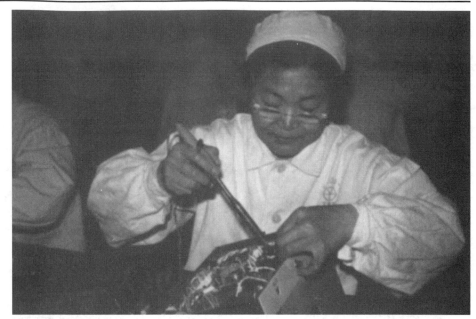

N.Y. Public Library Picture Collection

Transistor factory in Beijing is among those facilities translating technological progress into export gains, pushing China's positive trade balance to record heights.

$30,000,000,000 in 1993, the Japan External Trade Organization indicated. Japan's 1992 exports to China rose 39% to nearly $12,000,000,000; more than half the shipments were machine tools, which soared 62%. Japan's imports from China advanced 19% to nearly $17,000,000,000, mainly farm products and clothing.

Japanese direct foreign investment in China has increased eightfold since 1986, from less than $500,000,000 to more than $4,000,000,000 in southern China. Such a rapid rise in trade and investment can be attributed to lower Chinese labor costs, its recent investment liberalization, including the lifting of bans on imports, and growing confidence in the Chinese economic reforms.

A "greater China" ahead?

There is hardly any doubt that China's economic momentum will be accelerated further if Beijing and Taipei successfully can conclude reunification negotiations before 1997, when the British are scheduled to hand over Hong Kong to mainland China. Regardless of political hurdles, one can envision the emergence of a "greater China" in the 21st century, because growing cross-border investment, trade, tourism, and cultural exchanges are binding mainland China, Hong Kong, and Taiwan together. Hong Kong and Taiwan, for instance, have invested more than $25,000,000,000 in southern China. Moreover, the three

have accumulated $160,000,000,000 in reserves—more than Japan's $71,000,000,000.

Taiwan's indirect trade with China jumped 31% in 1992; exports to China leaped 40%; and Taiwanese are estimated to have invested $3,000,000,000 in China in 1992 alone, roughly double 1991's level. Two factors are pulling them close. First, the rising value of land, labor, and Taiwanese currency is making its labor-intensive manufacturing less competitive in the global marketplace. Second, China, by contrast, has an almost unlimited supply of cheap labor.

Two-thirds of foreign investment in southern China comes from Hong Kong Chinese. In Guangdong Province, for example, more than 25,000 Hong Kong-backed factories employ 3,000,000 Chinese. The mainland has invested roughly $16,000,000,000 in Hong Kong, and the Chinese government raised nearly $1,000,000,000 through a private placement of shares—the largest transaction in the history of Hong Kong's stock exchange.

Moreover, the rising cost of Japanese products has added to the Chinese incentive to import cheaper manufactured goods from South Korea. Indirect trade with Korea was $3,800,000,000 in 1990, and it reached $4,500,000,000 in 1991. South Korean steel and automobile manufacturers are among the businesses setting up joint ventures in China, which has become the third largest market for South Korean cars. Trade offices have opened between South Korea and the Chinese province of Shangdong, across the Yellow Sea.

Chinese who live outside the country are making significant contributions to China's growth. According to sinologist Andrew Brick, "Today, at least 75% of the mainland's roughly 28,000 enterprises are financed by ethnic Chinese who live outside China. Hong Kong and Taiwan account for two-thirds."

Three points are worth noting. First, a well-defined relationship in the family and society called "Confucian tradition" binds the Chinese together against all odds. Some traditional values—such as hard work, honesty, loyalty, obedience to patriarchal authority, and interest in tangible goods—also are mainstays of China's expansion. John Kao of the Harvard Business School calls these "life-raft" values.

Second, China has followed the South Korean and Taiwanese models of economic development, whereby initial economic growth took place under authoritarian rule. Third, the Chinese leaders are nurturing a booming private sector while pumping huge amounts of money into the crumbling state sector. This means China is pushing for an economic system that The Wall Street Journal calls "Socialist Market Economy." For instance, about 10% of government spending, or $7,700,000,000, was used to subsidize unprofitable factories from closing. Another few billion was spent as wage subsidies to compensate workers for prices being decontrolled.

There is no doubt that a combination of the capital, technology, and entrepreneurial genius of the three little dragons—Taiwan, Hong Kong, and South Korea—with China's 1,200,000,000 consumers, cheap labor, and natural resources will have conceivably huge implications for Asia and the global balance of economic power. Hundreds of millions of Chinese are reaping the yield of reform-led long-term economic expansion. For example, between 1978 and 1992, grain consumption of the average Chinese went up 20%; pork consumption, three times; poultry consumption, fourfold. In 1980, each 125 urban families in China averaged less than one color television among them; a decade later, it was more than 100. In 1980, there were approximately six washing machines and one refrigerator for each 140 city households; in 1992, more than 100 and almost 70, respectively. In 1978, about 250,000,000 Chinese were living in poverty. Today, this figure is down to 100,000,000.

Sustaining long-term growth

There are a number of things China should change and reform to sustain a long-term economic growth. First, it will have to maintain internal political peace and social order. This is critically important because China needs to earn the trust of its major foreign investors and trading partners. This means that China in no way can repeat the same mistake as the Tiananmen Square massacre in June, 1989, lest it jeopardize relationships with the U.S.

Second, China continues to gain economically and technologically from its American connection. However, its exploitation of child workers and prisoners, unethical labor practices, consistent violation of copyright laws, and arms proliferation have tarnished its image abroad. Although China has released a large number of prisoners in recent months and is signaling that it may free others, its over-all crackdown against dissent and religion appears to be continuing.

China also is making Washington and other Asian countries worried because it has augmented defense spending by a whopping 50% over two years, and recently announced a 15% hike. To make matters worse, China has gained $18,000,000,000 in trade surplus with the U.S. All these could threaten its most-favored-nation trade status under the Clinton Administration, thus hampering its economic growth. China has to come to grips with the reality that economic modernization calls for an increasing global interdependence and that it must play according to the same rules as the rest of the world.

Third, Japan, one of China's major investors and trading partners, is accusing China of dumping its exports. Consequently, Japan is considering punitive duties on cheap Chinese goods. China hardly can afford to outrage Japan at a time when its relations with the U.S. are strained.

Fourth, despite a literacy rate of almost 70%, its higher education system is one of the most backward. There are barely 2,000,000 university students in China—a painfully low figure, considering that it has 20% of the world's population. The looming shortage of highly skilled professionals—such as engineers, scientists, managers, accountants, physicians, nurses, and teachers—will be another hurdle. Although China has been sending about 50,000 students a year to the U.S. for higher education and training, that hardly will be adequate to meet the surging demand of a growing economy.

Fifth, China has Third World-level railway, road, and health care systems; financial services and institutions; and information and telecommunications. What urgently is needed is more public investment in its woefully inadequate infrastructure. It is interesting to note that China has fewer telephones and consumes less electricity per household than Hong Kong and Thailand. Moreover, Tokyo has more phones than all of China.

It would be a mistake to assume that the mainland's economic boom has reached out and touched all parts of the country equally. Instead, unbalanced growth has created an economic dualism. For example, Guangdong Province, which has a population of 60,000,000 and has maintained a 12% growth rate for the past decade, rapidly is becoming a regional powerhouse. This is the new rich China of entrepreneurs, higher standards of living, booming exports and foreign investment, skyscrapers, luxury hotels, and modern factories. In 1980, its GDP was $13,800,000,000. One decade later, it was $44,500,000,000. The Cantonese of this province are traditionally business-minded and little interested in politics. A vast number of them have migrated to the U.S., Canada, Hong Kong, and other parts of Southeast Asia, where they have made fortunes in business, restaurants, real estate, and semiconductors.

Inland Hunan Province, by contrast, represents the old China that is weighed down by bureaucracy and poverty, shows slow growth in exports, virtually attracts no foreign capital, and has an infrastructure full of mudholed roads, shanties, open sewers, and polluted water. Although this province is proud to have nurtured a famous national leader like Mao Zedong, its people are not good at economic development.

Between these two regions, prosperous Guangdong is attracting thousands of farmers from Hunan to work in its factories. Furthermore, it is sucking out Hunan's natural and capital resources, exporting inflation to Hunan, eating up potential exports, and depriving Hunan of its hard foreign currency. As a result, economic disparity is widening, and Guangdong's success is stirring envy. Economic dualism between the mainland's rich and poor provinces could sow the seeds of tensions and social strife to threaten China's free-market reforms in the years ahead.

Article 17

USA Today, September 1994

China's Second Long March:

The Rise of an Economic Trade Giant

The world's most populous country offers virtually unlimited opportunities for American businessmen—if they understand how the Chinese operate.

Lawrence P. Creedon

Dr. Creedon is managing director, Pacific Rim Trade and Business Consultants, Reston, Va.

The generation that led China on its historic long march and to the establishment of the People's Republic of China in 1949 has all but passed from the scene. Before doing so, however, it set the nation on its second long march. The goal was making China the world's number-one economic power. The direction was set in 1979 by Senior Leader Deng Xiaoping, who initiated economic reforms that have produced enormous results in the most populous country, with a population of over 1,200,000,000. China has quadrupled its Gross Domestic Product; boasts the world's third largest economy, behind the U.S. and Japan; and has become the 11th largest exporting nation. Even with these incredible advances, its economic might continues to be more potentiality than reality.

Doing business in China is not like doing business in the U.S. or in any other country with a market economy. While opening its trade doors to the West, China is not interested in emulating the West as a capitalist market economy. Neither are the Chinese signaling that their state-controlled economy has been all wrong.

During the past 15 years, a middle class has begun to emerge in China. Estimates are that it numbers 40–50,000,000 people, approximately three–four percent of the total population. This middle-class minority constitutes the new rich, and they are more interested in pursuing the "good new life" than in who makes the decisions at the top. Meanwhile, Beijing decision-makers have concluded that national socialist goals can be realized more quickly and fully by adopting China's economy to certain Western-style market forces.

Container port in Xiamen, Fujian Province. Trade in this special economic zone, one of five authorized by Beijing, produces more than $3,000,000,000 in revenue a year.

In contemplating a trade relationship with the Chinese, there are three key issues that American businesses need to understand: What a market economy means to the Chinese, where to trade in China, and the direction for getting started.

The Chinese have come to appreciate that the marketplace is driven by market forces, but, as yet, private enterprise as practiced in the U.S. neither is understood nor available. In China, behind everything lies the state.

Such basic concepts as market research and product or service promotion are not fully understood, appreciated, or practiced, except in rare situations. In part, the reasons for this is a long tradition of decisions being made in Beijing as to what will be produced, regardless of the market forces, along with a reliance on Hong Kong as China's window to the West.

Since 1979, Beijing has allowed limited autonomy and local decision-making for selected industries, as well as in the nation's five special economic zones established in 1980. Nevertheless, strong government control continues to be the official position of Beijing as it moves the country toward a socialist—not a capitalist—economy.

In a 1993 report to the central government, Chinese economists Wang Shaoguang and Hu Angang argued that local governments have too much economic muscle, which, they concluded, is used at the expense of the central government. As reported in the *China Daily*, July 21, 1992, they observed that, "Although many [Chinese] have failed to realize it, economists have already made clear that sustained economic development is impossible without a strong state as its regulator and promoter."

"By their nature unregulated market systems put little or no heed to such strategic areas as basic industries, health and education, scientific and technological research, and the preservation of the environment and natural resources." Their conclusion is clear: "It would cost the country dearly if people believed the market economy cleared them to indulge in tactics like undisciplined speculation in real estate and securities, tax fraud, regional protectionism and bad local tax policies."

To illustrate the point, consider the Chinese approach to the small businessperson or shop owner. Under the present way of doing business, enterprises ultimately are owned and controlled by the state. However, according to the Ministry of Domestic Trade, as the result of initiatives taken within the past 15 years, approximately one-half of China's small state-owned shops have been leased to entrepreneurs. The businesspeople who lease their stores from the government now are in direct competition with the remaining state-owned stores. The lessees have the power to set their own prices, purchase whatever goods they think will sell, and decide on employees' pay.

According to the Ministry, the leasing program has helped bail out state-owned shops from financial difficulties and contributed to increased state revenues and reduced government subsidies. In return for this level of autonomy, the "owners" of the shops pay the government a standard leasing fee.

In Beijing alone, the number of leased shops totals about 4,000 and, according to government figures, account for more than 60% of state-owned stores in the capital. Shanghai has over 5,000 private enterprises, the highest number for China. The official government figures for the nation indicate that there are 18,000,000 entrepreneurs now employing a workforce of 42,000,000. The bottom line is that the American approach to a market economy is not to be confused with the Chinese socialist market economy.

Special Economic Zones

After a lapse of 21 years, trade between the U.S. and China reopened in 1971 with the signing of the Shanghai Communique by Pres. Richard Nixon and Premier Zhou Enlai. For the next few years, the only place where the Western world could deal directly with China was through the Canton Fair (now Guangzhou). In 1972, 20 American trade pioneers attended the fair and quickly were lost among the 21,000 attendees, mostly Chinese expatriots from Hong Kong. In that year, sales to U.S. traders amounted to $5,000,000.

Two decades later, the situation is dramatically different. In 1980, Beijing authorized the establishment of special economic zones (SEZs), and change has been taking place at a rapid rate, with these zones playing a major role. All in the southeast China coastal region, the five SEZs are the cities of Shenzhen, Zhuhai, and Shanton in Guangdong Province, Xiamen in Fujian Province, and Hainan Island.

The SEZs enjoy special privileges and autonomous powers granted by the Beijing government. They have more autonomy in trade matters, receive special tax considerations, and increasingly are active places for international trade.

During the first half of 1993, official Chinese figures indicate that the foreign trade volume in the five SEZs reached a record $12,100,000,000. This represented an increase of 18% over the first six months of 1992.

First among the SEZs is Shenzhen, the zone that rapidly is being recognized as a mini Hong Kong. Guangdong Province, and the city of Shenzhen in particular, is being heralded in China as the flagship of international trade. The province now accounts for more than 20% of Chinese exports. During the first half of 1993, this amounted to over $6,000,000,000. The region currently boasts the highest industrial growth rate in all of China, up 27% since 1991. The other SEZs all posted increases in trade for the first half of 1993: Shantou, $1,900,000,000; Xiamen, $1,600,000,000; Zhuhai, $1,500,000,000; and Hainan, the newest zone, $1,100,000,000.

Xiamen, a coastal city of more than 1,000,000 inhabitants, is situated one hour north of Hong Kong by air, to which it also is connected by overnight ferry. In Xiamen, there are in excess of 200 companies authorized by the government to trade with the outside world, although few of them have any direct contact with potential trading partners in the U.S. In an effort to change that, the province sponsored a trade mission to the American West Coast in the fall of 1993.

Xiamen, like most other Chinese centers for international trade, relies heavily on Hong Kong as its channel for contact with the world. It is not unique in this regard. China long has relied on Hong Kong as its window and passageway to the West. It is estimated that up to 70% of Hong Kong's trade consists of re-exports from China. While China depends heavily on Hong Kong to be its middleman with the West, the five special economic zones increasingly are competing as centers of international trade.

A related matter is the growing trade imbalance issue between America and China. The U.S. includes in its trade imbalance figure with China those products that are channeled through Hong Kong. China does not. As a result, the two countries have very different views of the trade imbalance.

In 1991, the U.S. showed a trade imbalance in excess of $12,700,000,000, while China, including the products channeled through Hong Kong, maintained that it was $1,900,000,000. Nevertheless, the American trade deficit with China is growing at a more rapid rate than it is with Japan.

In addition to the five SEZs, China has established more than a dozen "open cities." These are places that do not enjoy the full status of an SEZ, but have many of the same privileges. As Beijing's grip loosens, it seems reasonable to assume that many of the open cities will become SEZs in practice, if not by designation.

For those interested in opening or expanding trade with China, serious consideration should be given to establishing contact with the trading companies in the SEZs. Their knowledge of American business practices may be limited, but they are anxious to proceed. Most have one or more individuals who can speak English with enough fluency to carry on a business meeting. Still, due to the language barrier and different understandings of a market economy, the going is slow.

The bottom line for each of these government-owned or authorized trading companies is that, if they do not carry their weight in trade agreements, they face extinction as a company. Consequently, they are anxious to do business.

When it comes to trading with China, both now and in the years ahead, there are enormous opportunities for those companies willing to take the appropriate steps. To get started:

• Check the nearest metropolitan telephone directory for listings under China.

• Contact the China Council for the Promotion of International Trade, 4301 Connecticut Ave., N.W., Washington, DC 20008, (202) 244-3244.

• Contact the World Trade Center Association in your area or the World Trade Center Association, One World Trade Center, New York, NY 10048.

- Subscribe to journals focusing on China trade such as *The China Business Review*, 1818 N St., N.W., Washington, DC 20036 or the daily English language newspaper *China Daily*, 15 Mercer St., New York, NY 10013.
- Access computer on-line databases, including DIALOG, Mead Data Central, WilsonLine, NewsNet, WEFA Group, On!, USCBC, and Maxwell Online BRS.
- Make contact with an American agency, export management company, or trade consultant who has personal contacts in China and who can facilitate an introduction to Chinese officials.
- At some point, it will be necessary to make an exploratory, get acquainted trip to one or more of the five special economic zones in China. Any number of organizations can assist in making initial contacts. Among them are the U.S. Department of Commerce, the nearest consulate office of the People's Republic of China, a trade consultant, and the organizations cited above.

To facilitate your trip and assist in arranging appointments, contact the foreign affairs office of the municipal government in China where you wish to visit. These offices have English-speaking staff members and among their duties is rendering assistance to visiting businesspeople.

Napoleon is credited with having made the observation that, when China wakes, it will shake the world. The planet's most populous country has embarked on its self-proclaimed second long march. In doing so, it is well on its way to making Napoleon a prophet. Aggressive American businesspeople might wish to consider getting in the line of march.

Article 18   *The Christian Science Monitor*, May 17, 1994

Lure of Chinese Cities Draws Runaway Children

Sheila Tefft

Staff writer of The Christian Science Monitor

SHANGHAI

Ask Xu Yacheng about his home, and he shrugs and slips into silence.

A wisp of a boy with a green jacket and haunted, downcast eyes, 10-year-old Yacheng whispers that he left his parents, sister, and brother in Yunnan Province three years ago and rode the train to Shanghai because he "just wanted to come here." Along the way, he begged for food and was beaten and abused. Unable to read or write, the boy denies knowing his real name or his home town.

"We can't get anything out of him," says Chen Yunfeng, a counselor at the Shanghai Children's Welfare Institute where the boy—whom institute officials named Yacheng—was sent by police who found him living in the railroad station.

"We keep asking for his exact address, but he can't tell us," says Mr. Chen. "If we knew his address, we would send him back."

As economic reforms pry open Chinese society and strain the fabric of family life, a growing corps of homeless and runaway children roams the streets of China's major cities—a problem unheard of just a decade ago. Children as young as four years old are fleeing problems at home and poverty in the countryside and joining the rural exodus to urban centers, Chinese researchers say.

A 1992 survey of 10,000 children in the city of Shanghai and in the Hunan, Anhui, and Guangdong Provinces, sponsored by the Chinese Civil Affairs Ministry and UNICEF, estimates there are 200,000 homeless children in these areas. Researchers call this estimate conservative.

That number is only a fraction of the 300 million Chinese under the age of 18 and pales in comparison to armies of waifs in other Asian cities, Chinese officials say.

Still, Chinese analysts contend that the ranks of homeless children are burgeoning amid an unprecedented migratory wave of millions of jobless rural laborers seeking work in cities along China's fast-growing eastern seaboard.

Officials worry that thousands of young runaways are turning to crime and fueling juvenile delinquency, which

has more than doubled in the last decade, according to the New China News Agency.

"Compared with other countries, China's problem is not yet that serious," says Tao Zhiliang, a Shanghai civil-affairs official who helped conduct the UNICEF study. "But the crime rate for juvenile delinquents is on the rise with the socialist market economy. If we don't treat this seriously, the homeless children will join the ranks of juvenile delinquents."

Many runaways left home because of natural disasters, mistreatment, or just for fun. "Some just went out for play. This is related to a more open society," says Wang Jiachun of the Shanghai Children's Welfare Institute. "In the past, remote areas were not open. But with the broadcast media, children can learn more about the big cities."

The main impetus driving children to run away is turmoil within families, often broken by divorce, experts say.

Divorce, previously frowned upon and discouraged, is on the increase for the first time in China and is spreading from urban areas to the countryside, social observers say. According to the Civil Affairs Ministry, 909,000 Chinese couples were divorced in 1993, a nearly 300 percent increase from 1990.

"Compared with Western countries, one can still say that the family fabric in China is stable as a whole," says Mr. Tao, the researcher. "In the past, people looked down on divorce. Even though there was no mutual feeling between husband and wife, they would still keep the family together.

"Now, because of the increase in the divorce rate, there are more broken families and disadvantaged children," he continues. "This has given rise to social problems due to inadequate care of the children in a divorce."

The problem of child runaways is particularly acute in Shanghai, a booming port city of 11 million people which is at the forefront of China's monumental economic and social shifts. According to the Wenhui Daily newspaper, Shanghai has absorbed 2.5 million migrants in recent years, 40 percent of whom lack legal rights of residence.

The income gap between rich and poor is at its most stark in Shanghai, where millionaires live not far from those who subsist on $30 a month, according to official Chinese press reports. Divorce has increased tenfold in the last decade. And every year, Shanghai authorities detain and send more than 3,000 homeless children to their families.

For Xu Guokung, a slight child of about 8 or 9 years living at the welfare institute in Shanghai, home is somewhere in Anhui Province, he says.

One day, while playing outside, he says he was lured onto a train by someone who abused him and left him in Shanghai. Before being caught by police, he stayed in the air-conditioned waiting rooms at the city's train station where he begged leftover food from passengers.

Guokung, a name given him at the Shanghai home, says he misses his parents in Anhui although food is often scarce there and his family's house frequently floods. He recalled a time when "the water came in our house, and we watched all our things float away on the water. We had to run away."

Shanghai is building a new detention center for homeless children who cannot be sent home. Although some live at the welfare institute along with the orphans and abandoned children with handicaps, most are kept in a makeshift camp on the outskirts of Shanghai which authorities would not allow journalists to visit.

Social experts say the key to preventing more runaways is educating not just the children, but also their parents.

"Efforts have to be taken to make parents more cultured and educated so they will have a greater sense of responsibility toward the children," says Tao. "Schools should be held responsible for preventing the kids from running away. But mainly it is up to the parents to educate and make the child stay at home."

Article 19　　　　　　　　　　　　　　　　　　　*U.S. News & World Report*, May 30, 1994

The new voices of dissent

Armed with pagers, Chinese dissidents are challenging Beijing

Zhang Lin, 31, once trained to be a nuclear physicist at Qinghua University, the MIT of China. Wang Zhongqiu, 27, studied law at the equally prestigious Beijing University. Now the men are challenging Communist rule through their League for the Protection of Working People of the People's Republic of China, a labor movement organized along the lines of Poland's Solidarity. Zhang dreams of sparking a large-scale industrial action in a major Chinese manufacturing center such as Wuhan or Nanjing, similar to the strike at the Lenin Shipyard in Gdansk that launched Solidarity.

Chinese dissidents may still be like the proverbial ants trying to shake a tree, but nevertheless, Beijing's Communist leaders are rattled. Their round-up in recent weeks of scores of well-known Chinese dissidents probably has less to do with Bill Clinton's crucial most-favored-nation status decision than with growing concern that a new generation of well-educated, high-tech dissidents poses an increasing danger to the existing order.

In response to U.S. pressure, China recently released the two most prominent political prisoners from the 1989 pro-democracy movement, Wang Juntao—who left immediately for medical treatment in the United States—and Chen Ziming. But authorities have haled into police custody other dissidents—including Wei Jingsheng, who is considered the "father" of China's democracy movement, and key members of the Shanghai Human Rights Association. It is activists like Zhang and Wang, however, who worry the government most, because they seek revolution, not reform.

Outside the system. Economic reform has weakened Beijing's grip on traditional levers of control over individuals. State-run workplaces, which could be counted on to clamp down hard on troublemakers, no longer ration housing, grain and incomes, allowing dissidents like Zhang and Wang to operate outside the system. And the information boom that has accompanied economic liberalization has put China's dissidents in closer contact with one another and with supporters in the outside world.

The dissidents also have new, fertile ground in which to sow discontent: Millions of workers in failing state industries have seen their salaries cut or stopped altogether as the government struggles to control a ballooning budget deficit. They are battered by high inflation and are angry over widespread official corruption.

Meeting in a public place that offers easy escape routes should the security forces appear, Zhang and Wang pepper their conversation with references to Poland's Lech Walesa and Czechoslovakia's Vaclav Havel, whose autobiographies they have read in translation. Zhang and Wang claim the league has a network of some 200 activists, concentrated in the provinces of central China. Their mission is to help labor groups with grievances to file formal complaints, form their own trade unions and organize strikes and public demonstrations.

In an earlier era, would-be travelers needed a letter of introduction from their place of work in order to buy train tickets. Now, when dissidents want to travel to the provinces to do their work, they need not even show an identity card; they buy tickets from the black marketeers who loiter in front of stations.

When they are in Beijing, Zhang and Wang and their provincial associates live in safe houses, usually apartments that they or their friends sublet from the registered tenants. Today, Beijing is full of fortune seekers from the provinces; nobody seems to think twice about the two young men with no apparent jobs. Threats and even jail terms do not faze the dissidents. Zhang has been imprisoned five times since 1986.

While many leaders of Poland's labor movement were themselves workers, China's labor organizers are intellectuals—most of them with little work experience—who see labor activism primarily as a means of organizing resistance to the government. Wang says the league is eager to link up with disaffected groups of all stripes, even with traditional secret societies and underworld gangs. "They aren't very popular people," he admits. "But they are very good at publicity work and at damaging the government."

Solidarity sprouted in a country with a planned economy and backward telecommunications. China's dissidents are operating in a society that is modernizing at breakneck speed in every way but politically. They have at their disposal a growing array of advanced technology, and they benefit from the financial backing and strategic advice of mainland Chinese scholars and political exiles who have settled in the United States in the 15 years since Deng Xiaoping began allowing Chinese to exit through his "Open Door" policy for studies in the West.

The defining technology for 1990s Chinese dissidents is the Motorola-brand pager. For activists on the run like Zhang and Wang, the little black box on their belts is a lifeline to other dissidents and foreign journalists that does not betray their whereabouts. Taking no chances, they switch papers every few months, before the authorities can obtain their numbers and set up sting operations against them.

Sophisticated papers flash not just phone numbers but also messages: 32C in the Motorola code book means, "My friend and I cannot come." And 330 means, "I'll wait for you at X place at Y time." Users turn to another set of Motorola codes to specify X and Y. There are codes for the train station and airport, well-known hotels, major Beijing intersections and even bus stops.

Zhang's pager works both in Beijing and in his hometown of Bengbu, in Anhui province. But he will probably swap it soon for a new $100 Motorola pager that he can use in 24 cities across China. The military runs two such nationwide networks; a government ministry runs the third. Anyone can sign up, with no questions asked and no identity documents required.

Dissidents rely on a burgeoning network of public and private telephones that is another product of China's technological revolution. In 1991, China had 15 million telephones. By 1995, with the help of firms such as U.S. telecommunications giant AT&T, it expects to have 36 million, or 3 for every 100 people.

In the past year, public telephones have sprung up all over Beijing, in shops and restaurants and even in unfamiliar public phone booths on street corners. Because China has leap-frogged directly into the age of fiberoptic cables and digital switching, many public phones offer direct-dial domestic and international long-distance service.

In touch. It is the expansion of telephone networks that allows Liu Qing, chairman of the New York-based group Human Rights in China (HRIC), to keep a high profile in the dissident community in China two years after he began living the life of an exile in America. Liu, who spent a decade in prison in China for his role in the 1978–79 Democracy Wall movement, regularly calls activists.

If dissidents and other Chinese with grievances against the government want to call Liu but cannot afford the international tolls, they can now dial a free number, 10810, from any phone in more than 30 Chinese cities to reach a Chinese-speaking AT&T operator in the United States who will place a collect call for them.

Fax machines, computers and copiers are changing the lives of dissidents, but more slowly. Regulations requiring fax machines to be registered are used to stifle dissent. Among the charges against Zhou Guoqiang, a league founder who has been in detention since March, is writing and sending antigovernment articles to Hong Kong "by means of an unauthorized fax machine."

Even with their high-tech advantages, dissidents such as Zhang and Wang still face an uphill battle. Two of the league's five founders are in police custody. A third escaped to America. He called recently to warn Zhang and Wang that they are on a priority list for arrest. And the technology that helps them organize is also their greatest vulnerability: Security forces are growing more adept at eavesdropping on telephone calls, intercepting faxes and monitoring pager messages. Unless they keep one step ahead of the authorities, Zhang and Wang could wind up like the clay Buddha in the Chinese proverb who tries to cross a river on a mission of mercy, but by stepping into the waters dooms himself.

By Susan V. Lawrence in Beijing

Article 20   *Social Education*, February 1994

Chinese Women Soldiers: A History of 5,000 Years

Xiaolin Li

Xiaolin Li served in the navy, air force, and army of China's PLA from October 1969 until June 1987. She retired with the rank of Battalion Commander. Her service experiences included working as a telephone operator, English typist, cadet, interpreter/translator, and staff officer. Xiaolin's interest in the military began as a child, for her father was a general and her mother a lieutenant colonel. Currently, she is a doctoral candidate in sociology at the University of Maryland, where her research is on women in the Chinese military.

Hundreds of wars and uprisings have occurred in China during its more than 5,000 years of history. A dozen major dynasties and a similar number of minor dynasties ended through military actions. One major difference between China and other cultures is that war has never been glorified in China with heroic warriors like Caesar or Napoleon. However, similar to other societies, war in China has been primarily a masculine activity. Only occasionally have Chinese women been recorded as participants.[1] However, women actually appear in Chinese military history as early as Sun Tzu's time (496–453 B.C.), when King Wu's palace concubines were turned into soldiers as a demonstration of the effects of discipline (Military History of China Compilation Group 1986), since Chinese military thinkers believe that it is discipline and training that make good soldiers.

According to a consensus of mainland Chinese scholars, the 5,000 years of Chinese history can be divided into three major periods: the Ancient time period—five thousand years ago to A.D. 1840; the Post Opium War time period—1840 to 1949; and the Modern time period—1949 to present. This article will give an overview of Chinese women in the military during these three periods.

Ancient Period

Nineteen historical women warriors are identified by Li (1992) for the ancient period. All nineteen are either com-

Figure 1

Women Warriors in Ancient China

GENERALS

Name	Dynasty	Dates
Fu, Hao	Shang	16 BC-11 BC
Princess Ping Yang	Sui	?-623 AD*
Liang, Hong Yu	Nan Song	1127-1279 AD
Qin, Liang Yu	Ming	1574-1629 AD*

LEADERS OF UPRISINGS
(Peasant and Nationality)

Name	Dynasty	Dates
Lu, Mu	Xi Han	?-18 AD*
Chen, Shuo Zhen	Tang	?-653 AD*
Yan, Miao Zhen	Nan Song	1127-1279 AD
Tang, Sai Er	Ming	1403-1424 AD*
Wang, Cong Er	Qing	1777-1798 AD*

HEROINES

Name	Dynasty	Dates
Hua, Mu Lan	Han	206 BC-220 AD
Xun, Guan Niang	Jin	265-420 AD
Madame Xi	Sui	581-618 AD
Madame Huan Hua	Tang	618-907 AD
Madame Xu	Yuan	1271-1368 AD
Bi, Zhu	Ming	1368-1644 AD
San Niang Zi	Ming	1368-1644 AD
Shen, Yun Yin	Ming	1368-1644 AD
Madame Wa Shi	Ming	1498-1557 AD*
Ge, Nen Niang	Ming	1368-1644 AD

* Known dates of birth and death. Others are dates of dynasties.

manders of armies or leaders of peasant uprisings. In addition to these historical women soldiers, there are many fictional women warriors and female knights errant[2] (Yu 1978; Jiang 1986; Liu 1981; May 1985). Both in ancient and modern times, numerous literary and artistic works portray these historical and fictional women warriors. Chinese cultural heritage includes legends of women soldiers. No matter how she is educated or where she is located, all Chinese women know the names of such heroines as Mu Lan Hua or Hong Yu Liang.

The first Chinese woman general, Hao Fu,[3] appeared about 3,200 years ago.[4] One oracle inscription carved on animal bones describes her as a commanding marshal of over 13,000 soldiers, who went on a punitive expedition to Qiang Kingdom; on another expedition, a male general, Gao Hou, was under her command.[5] Two other women generals were of minor nationalities: Madame Xi of the Li nationality and Madame Wa Shi of Zhuing nationality, whose victories aided the ruling emperor.[6]

However, the most famous women generals were Liang Yu Qin and Hong Yu Liang. Qin is known for her many victories in both national defense and the suppression of internal uprisings. The last emperor of the Ming Dynasty wrote several poems to praise her.[7] For many years, Liang and her husband Marshal Shi Zhong Han were stationed in border areas. Liang was known for fighting at the side of her husband in many battles. In 1130, her husband's troops engaged the enemy in a major campaign at a place called Gold Mountain [Jin Shan] along the Yang Zi River. Liang beat the battle drum and used flag lights to guide the army. She was not afraid of being killed by the enemies' arrows and stones, and eventually their 8,000 troops defeated the enemy's 10,000. Until today, the story "beat battle drum at Gold Mountain" [Ji Gu Zhan Jin Shan] is still used to mobilize Chinese women for national self defense.

As the first woman leader of a peasant uprising, Mu Lu [Lu's mother] was the only woman who took part in military operations simply because of a personal reason: to bring revenge on a bad county governor who had wrongly executed her son. Another peasant leader, Shuo Zhen Chen, was the first and the only Chinese woman to designate herself the emperor after launching a peasant uprising. Her peasant army occupied most of Jiang Xi province, but in the end she was captured by the official army and executed. Three of the six women uprising leaders, Shuo Zhen Chen, Sai Er Tang, and Cong Er Wang, used religious activities and symbols to mobilize people. Both Tang and Wang relied on a Buddhist religion named "White Lotus," which developed during the Ming and Qing, the last two feudal dynasties. This pattern was also observed among some women warriors' behavior in the Boxer Movement and Tai Ping Tian Guo Movement.

Most famous as defenders of homeland or home city were Mu Lan Hua and Guan Nfang Xun. Hua is the earliest legendary woman warrior in Chinese culture and was recently verified by various scholars as a real woman living during the Han Dynasty (206 B.C.–A.D. 220). She is recorded in a name book compiled at the end of Jin Dynasty around the year A.D. 419 (Huang 1991). Hua's deed inspired the largest number of literary and artistic works about Chinese heroines. These peasant heroines either refused to be promoted after victory or their participation in military operations was comparatively shorter than that of women generals. Most were involved in only one major combat.

All women warriors in Figure 1 are regarded as heroic combatants. Bravery, strong mastery of martial art, and unique leadership are common characteristics of these heroines. Most have little if any military training, but they practiced and mastered martial art since childhood, contrary to the common behavioral expectation for their gender. Observing strict discipline, sharing hardships with soldiers, and having clever tactics are common descriptions of the women warriors' leadership.

Two common patterns of the ancient heroines' participation in military operations are apparent. One is a crisis of group survival in which the country or city is under attack, and which therefore justifies the warfare; second is a key male family member with military commanding status is absent, dead, or disabled or has been involved in the same uprising as the woman warrior. Hua, for example, disguised as a man, joins the army because her father is sick and cannot go to war. Xun, at the age of 13, breaks out of the encirclement to get the relief troops because her father has to remain in command of the defense and her scholarly brothers do not have skills in the martial arts. Princess Ping Yang raises an army and joins her father's uprising to keep her whole family from being executed by the emperor in power. As a governor's concubine, Madam Huan Hua leads the defense of her city because the governor is away. Both Bi and Shen launch counterattacks on the enemies, not only for the defense of their cities but also to get back their fathers' dead bodies. Women leaders of peasant uprisings fight shoulder to shoulder with their male family members. All of the women generals have highly positioned male family members. Given the patriarchal structure and feudal culture of ancient Chinese society, it is understandable that such strong family ties to male relatives are prominent in the women's actions. The only Chinese women warriors who act independently of their families are those who are female knights errant.

Ancient Chinese heroines serve as an everlasting inspiration to Chinese women. The loyalty of the ancient women soldiers is emphasized in both history books and artistic works. These women exhibit either strong loyalty to their families or the emperors or the causes of rebelling peasants. Their nobility is shown through loyalty to the group. The legendary figures in Chinese history and their participation in military operations during crises in group survival encourage similar behavior for Chinese women in modern times.

Post Opium War Time Period, 1840–1949

Chinese women warriors were very active during the eighteen-year Tai Ping Tian Guo Movement (1850–1868), China's largest and longest peasant uprising. Thousands of women officers and soldiers, organized in gender-segregated battalions, engaged in a wide range of military activities, including combat. Similarly, women also participated in the national revolution of 1911, which overthrew the last emperor of the Qing Dynasty. Jin Qiu, the most famous female revolutionary of this period, organized an unsuccessful military uprising in Shaoxin, Zhe Jiang Province, for which she was captured and executed (Bao 1979; Chen 1975).

In the early years of the Chinese communist movement (1927–1935), women again served in large numbers in a wide range of combat and noncombat military roles (Segal, Li, and Segal 1992). About 3,000 women are recorded as participating in the thirteen-month Long March of over 12,500 kilometers in 1934–35 and in over 500 military engagements with the nationalist Guomintang and local warlords, after the Red Army broke through the Nationalist siege of the Jiangxi Soviet base. The 2,000-member Women's Independence Brigade, a logistical unit, carried the machines and equipment necessary for keeping the Red Army supplied. It also includes a 500-person Women's Engineer Battalion, responsible for carrying the hard currency (much of it in precious metal) for the Red Army. Women in the Fourth Front Red Army also carried litter and built roads and bridges. The Women's Independence Brigade engaged in several battles as part of the West Wing Army and suffered with them in a major defeat. Large numbers of women were casualties, and the women captured became the spoils of war for Guomintang soldiers and officers. The 32 women soldiers in the First Front Army who were the wives of such leaders as Mao Ze Dong and Zhou En Lai and the women who served as ministers of the Soviets in various provinces survived the Long March. The Central Work Regiment, which engaged in propaganda work, contained twenty-four women. Fewer than twenty of the women who served in the Second and Sixth Red Army Corps as confidential secretaries, nurses, cooks, and commanders have thus far been identified. One of these women, Zhen Li, was the only woman general to emerge during this period (All-China Women's Federation 1986). Toward the end of the Long March, the gen-

der-segregated units were disbanded, and the remaining women integrated into other units. Smaller numbers of women then served in other military elements of the communist movement during this period. Recently, 149 women who survived the Long March have been identified by researchers.

The period following the Long March from 1935 to 1945 is known as the Yan An and was a time of recuperation and reorganization of the Red Army. In August 1937, the Red Army became the Eighth Route Army of the National Revolution Army and, under an agreement with the Guomintang, formed a united Anti-Japanese Front. It was during this period that women were relegated to support functions. The few women remaining in the Red Army were joined by thousands of young anti-Japanese women in noncombat auxiliary roles of nursing, communications, administration, propaganda, and logistics.

Many received training in political, medical, or art schools at Yan An and participated actively in economic production. This pattern of mobilizing women in auxiliary support roles continues through the Liberation War period (1945–1949), during which the Eighth Route Army officially becomes the People's Liberation Army (PLA). In addition to the women cadres within the PLA, women militia and thousands of women in the Liberated Areas joined in by playing important roles in combat support, pushing wheelbarrows full of gasoline, food, and ammunition into battle areas and carrying wounded soldiers back to the rear. They also supervised and trained prisoners of war. Still other supportive roles included making shoes and building bridges and roads. In Shandong Province, there was an especially heroic example of women's service when hundreds of village women formed a human bridge in icy waters at night for the PLA to cross. Since its early days, women in the Guomindang army have played supportive but minimal roles in the nationalist forces.

Modern Times, 1949–present

After the communist victory in 1949, the PLA became primarily a force for counterinsurgency, for postwar reconstruction of the societal infrastructure, and for the mobilization of the peasantry for land reform. Much of the military cadre was demobilized and assumed civilian administrative positions. In 1951, despite an engagement of Chinese combat troops in the Korean War, 150,000 women cadres (8 percent of the total cadre corps) were assigned to civilian positions. Chinese women soldiers did go to war during the Korean War as cultural workers, nurses, doctors, and telephone operators. These PLA women were ostracized as were most Chinese POWs when they returned home.

In 1955, with the hostilities in Korea over, the postwar Soviet model of military organization which minimized the role of women in the military was implemented and a major demobilization of military women occurred[8] (Jones 1985, 101). As many as 764,000 women (14.5 percent of the total) were assigned to civilian positions (All-China Women's Federation 1986). Since that time, China's military operations have primarily been conflicts over international boundaries,[9] and women have not been in combat roles in any of these conflicts. Only during the last conflict in 1979 did women serve in the combat zone as doctors and nurses, telecommunication personnel, and cultural workers.

Today's Women in the Chinese Military

Today, Chinese women comprise about 4.5 percent of total military personnel in the PLA.[10] Serving in the military enjoys high popularity among young Chinese women because it opens opportunities for education and training, better jobs in the future, possible residence in cities, and higher status in society.[11] Nearly all women soldiers serve in traditional female roles or in military support positions and are concentrated in headquarters, hospitals, research institutions, and communication facilities. There they serve as medical workers, administrative personnel, communications specialists, logistical support staff, political and propaganda workers, scientific researchers, and technicians. There are no women combat pilots and no women in ground combat troops; only recently have women been assigned to military medical ships.[12] Although they are in positions of relative prestige within the military, women do not have equal chances of promotion.

In the 1980s, there was a shift from Soviet to American influence on Chinese military organization. Many policies and new regulations were developed in the process of professionalization. But women remain primarily in the roles that they occupied in the recent past. There are no special policies or regulations regarding women in the military, partially due to the persistent emphasis on equal treatment advocated by the Party. Two changes, however, are worthy of note. First, some previously military noncombat roles filled by women have been made civilian roles. Second, with the reestablishment of ranks within the PLA (a form of stratification that had been regarded previously as unsocialist), women received officer rank, including eight women major generals who immediately became public examples of social equality.

If China follows a pattern observed in western industrialized nations, trends toward gender equality in other spheres of life, such as civilian work and family life, may lead eventually to the widening of opportunities in the military where national legislation prohibiting gender discrimination in employment has removed gender-based exclusions from military assignments (Stanley and Segal 1988). But these changes have occurred in a climate of declining numbers of men eligible for military service (while the armed forces remained large) and cultural values fostering gender role changes. Judging from historical precedent in China and other nations, it is unlikely that women will be incorporated into the Chinese armed forces in large numbers or with greatly expanded roles until they have achieved greater equality in other areas of life and/or there is a national crisis which creates a shortage of men qualified for military service.

Notes

1. Six of them were officially designated as generals; another six women warriors were leaders of peasant uprisings. Only 5 percent were women combatants, who were without official rank but who had their deeds recorded in history books.
2. They were "women social bandits" (May 1985, 185), who single-handedly tried to correct wrongs in society by use of stealth, cunning, and violence.
3. All Chinese names in this article are ordered according to Western style, which puts last name at the end. The surname goes with a title, e.g., Madame Xi.
4. Among inscriptions on bones or tortoise shells which have been verified as carved in middle and late Shang dynasty (16th to 11th century B.C.). Hao Fu's name has been found over 250 times. Most of these oracle inscriptions expressed King Ding Wu's concern about Hao Fu's well-being and health. Hao Fu is the first documented at this time, but additional discoveries may reveal women generals and soldiers at earlier times as archeological work is continuing in the ancient tombs.
5. Inscriptions not only recorded how many places she had conquered, but also her various strategies and tactics. In addition to over 600 jade wares and 7,000 sea shell currency discovered in her tomb in 1976, there were two bronze hatchets, which were symbols of her status as a military commander and her ruling power in that period (Chen 1991). After Hao Fu's death, her husband, King Ding Wu, continued practicing divination and offering sacrifices to her, asking her spirit in heaven to guide the army and to guarantee victory for his kingdom.
6. Madame Xi was promoted to general because of her assistance to the Emperor of Sui (A.D. 581–618) in suppressing several uprisings that occurred in her time. Madame Wa Shi led troops to cross several thousand li (Chinese miles) for the defense of Shanghai in March 1555, and rescued a Marshal of the Ming Dynasty from the enemy's ambush. She also had a big victory at a place near Su Zhou, Zhe Jiang province. where the name of the place was changed to "Victory Port" to memorialize her.

7. Her promotion to general was after her husband's miserable death in jail caused by a court eunuch's slander.

8. Despite negative reactions from veteran women soldiers (a small proportion of whom were able to stay in the military because of familial or personal contacts or because as women professionals their skills were needed), as part of the process of transforming the PLA from an irregular revolutionary army to a conventional military force, 764,000 women cadres (14.5 percent of the total cadre force) were assigned to civilian positions (All-China Women's Federation 1986).

9. These international conflicts are: the Sino-India boundary conflict in 1962; the Sino-Soviet boundary conflict in 1969; the South China Sea conflict with Vietnam in 1974; and the Sino-Vietnam boundary conflict in 1979.

10. A source stated that 136,000 women worked in the PLA at the end of 1987. Among them, 104,000 were officers (76.5 percent of the total military women), and 32,000 were enlisted women (23.5 percent). In proportion to the total number of the 46,876,000 female staff and workers (not including female labor in rural areas) at the end of 1986, military women only account for 0.3 percent of the total female employees. But compared with the total of 8.7 million women officials in the country, women officers account for 11.95 percent.

11. Talented girls have more chances to be recognized and recruited by the military. Through the military cultural troops and military art college, girls as young as twelve years old start their prolonged training within the military to become future artists with military rank. It is also the case for military athletes. The military women's volleyball team and basketball team are the best teams in China and have produced several cohorts of players for the national teams.

12. From 1951 to 1987, the Chinese Air Force trained 208 women pilots of five cohorts; 55 of the first cohort graduated in 1952. At present, 37 women of the sixth cohort are being trained in Northeast China. None of them has been assigned to combat, although a few of them have become test pilots.

References

All-China Women's Federation. *Study Materials for the History of the Women's Movement.* Beijing, 1986.

Bao, Jia Lin, ed. *Collected Works on the History of Chinese Women.* Tai Pei: Mu Tong Publisher, 1979.

Chen, Dong Yuan. *A History of Chinese Women's Life.* Tai Pei: Shang Wu Publisher, 1975.

Chen, Ming Fu. *Zhong Guo Li Dai Nu Bing [Women Warriors in Chinese History].* Beijing: Chinese Women Publisher, 1991.

Gu Jin Zhong *Wai Nu Min Ren Ci Dian [Dictionary of Famous Women in the World: From History to Contemporary],* compiled by College of Chinese Women Administrative Cadres. Beijing: China Broadcasting and Television Publisher, 1989.

Huang, Can Zhang. "Hua Mu Lan's Last Name is not Hua." *People's Daily Abroad,* April 10, 1991.

Jiang, Tao, et al., eds. *Zhong Guo Chuan Qi [Chinese Legend],* Vol. 15.22 Lie Nu Zhuan [Women Biography]. Taipei: Zhuang Yan Publisher, 1986.

Jones, Ellen. *Red Army and Society: A Sociology of the Soviet Military.* Boston: Allen and Unwin Inc., 1985.

Li, Xiaolin, "Patterns of Chinese Women's Participation in Military Operations in Ancient Times." Presented at the Section on the Sociology of Peace and War, 87th Annual Meeting, American Sociology Association, Pittsburgh, Pennsylvania, August 1992.

____. "Chinese Women in the People's Liberation Army: Professionals or Quasi-Professionals?" *Armed Forces and Society* 20, no. 1 (Winter 1993).

Lie Nu Zhuan [Women Biography], compiled by Guo Xue Stuey Group. Taipei: Han Xue Publisher, 1984.

Liu, Hsiang. *Cong Lie Nu Zhuan Kan Gu Dai Zhong Guo Fu Nu De Di Wei [Women's Status in Ancient China Through the Study of Women Biography],* 1981.

Lu, Yin Quan. "How many women identified are there in The Twenty Four Histories?" *People's Daily Abroad,* April 10, 1991.

Mao, Ze Dong. "Report of an Investigation into the Peasant Movement in Hunan." Beijing: Foreign Languages Press, 1953.

May, Louise Anne. "Worthy Warriors and Unruly Amazons: Sino-Western Historical Accounts and Imaginative Images of Women in Battle." Unpublished Ph.D. dissertation, the University of British Columbia, Canada, 1985.

Military History of China Compilation Group. *Wu Jin Oi Shu Zhu Yi.* Beijing: PLA Publisher, 1986.

Segal, Mady W., Xiaolin Li, and David R. Segal. "The Role of Women in the Chinese People's Liberation Army." In *Armed Forces in the USSR and the People's Republic of China,* edited by Eberhard Sandschneider and Jurgen Kuhlmann. Munich: Forum International, 1992.

Stanley, Sandra Carson, and Mady Wechsler Segal. Military Women in NATO: An Update." *Armed Forces and Society* 14 (1988): 559–585.

Xue, Weiwei, ed. *Dictionary of Chinese Famous Women.* San Xi People's Publisher, 1988.

Yu, Zhenbang. *Zhong Guo Li Dai Ming Nu Lie Zhuan [Biographies of Famous Women in Chinese History].* Taipei: Lian Ya Publishers, 1978.

Article 21   *World Press Review,* July 1994

Hong Kong's New 1997 Jitters

Ever since the Sino-British deal returning Hong Kong to Chinese rule in 1997, the territory's residents have veered from fear of the future to euphoria over Hong Kong's seemingly endless boom. These days, plunging markets and a sharp show of China's repressive side have renewed the territory's jitters, reports the "Sydney Morning Herald." From London, however, the "Financial Times" sees an odd new calm in relations between Beijing and Hong Kong—and speculates on the reasons.

The Sydney Morning Herald

Ask Hong Kongers, "Will you still be here after 1997?" and the response is often laughter. Everybody knows that July, 1997, is simply the date on which Hong Kong gets access to the world's biggest property market—China. Hong Kong is the best place in the world to make money, and the flood of expatriates pouring into Hong Kong proves 1997 is nothing to fear. But recently, some people have stopped laughing. They are taking the 1997 question and all the fear of China it implies very seriously. Several surveys have found that people are again getting anxious about how China will run Hong Kong after it takes over.

Social commentators say this sudden loss of confidence in Hong Kong's future has more to do with the slump in the territory's stock market than anything else. The property market, which had risen so rapidly over the past year that Hong Kong now has the highest retail and office rents in the world, is also suffering. Prices, which were so high that $7.25 billion worth of property changed hands in March alone, dropped by 15 percent in just two weeks in April. Some investors are now convinced the bubble is about to burst and are looking for overseas markets to invest in.

But there is more to the nervousness than concern about the falling stock and property markets. The arrest, secret trial, and 12-year sentence imposed on Xi Yang, a Chinese-born, Hong Kong-based reporter for *Ming Pao,* the most respected of Hong Kong's Chinese-language newspapers, has rattled Hong Kong residents. Xi was arrested in China last year and put on trial months later for "stealing state secrets"—reporting that interest-rate rises were being considered by the People's Bank of China. In March, he was secretly tried in Beijing and sentenced to 12 years in prison.

It is widely believed that the crimes with which Xi was officially charged are not the ones for which the Chinese are really punishing him. Xi made the mistake of breaking some of the most important stories in China last year. Among the most sensitive was his report that the illness that kept Chinese Prime Minister Li Peng out of public view was not a cold, as officially reported, but a much more politically threatening heart attack. Following Xi's sentence, thousands of Hong Kongers took to the streets to demonstrate against his imprisonment. It was one of the biggest demonstrations in recent years and reminded onlookers of the million-strong demonstrations that took place in Hong Kong after the Tiananmen Square massacre in 1989.

The general atmosphere of concern about politics and human rights in Hong Kong after 1997 has prompted a rash of amalgamations and new parties. the United Democrats of Hong Kong, a party formed to demand democracy in Hong Kong, and Meeting Point, a smaller like-minded party, recently announced they were amalgamating to form the Democratic Party. The merger is said to have caused consternation in Beijing. But Beijing must have drawn some comfort from the formation of the Hong Kong Progressive Alliance, a new party made up of businessmen and professionals with strong China ties.

In the 1995 elections, these parties, along with a few set up last year, will be fighting over the handful of directly elected seats available under Hong Kong's electoral laws. Chris Patten, Hong Kong's controversial governor, has raised the number of directly elected seats from 21 to 30, but that is still very few for a city of 6 million. [In fact, Hong Kong has enjoyed very little democracy under British rule, and Beijing regards Patten's democratic reforms as outrageous attempts to change the terms of a deal already made.] Perhaps the Chinese leadership, while publicly scathing about Britain's rule of Hong Kong, is privately quite grateful for the rigid, punitive laws it will inherit from the British colonial rulers.

While the administration of Hong Kong wants to put a workable transition administration in place before 1997, it has been stymied by a policy of sending all changes to Beijing for discussion. A Hong Kong university law lecturer says those documents rarely come back. "They just sit on desks gathering dust," he said. "Meanwhile, nothing gets done here."

—Margaret Harris, "Sydney Morning Herald" (centrist).

Cooling-Off Period

Financial Times

A kind of calm has returned to politics in Hong Kong. The question is whether this is because the eye of the storm is passing over the colony or because the storm has run its course. What is clear is that ever since the breakdown in Sino-British cooperation on Hong Kong's political development—especially since February, when the colony's legislative council (Legco) passed the first stage of Chris Patten's democracy legislation—both sides have moved to take the heat out of the issue. China has scaled back its attack on the governor and his pro-democracy supporters in Legco. For his part, Patten has drawn back from his promised high-profile political campaign and watched Legco review his second reform bill with cool detachment.

Beijing now appears prepared to settle some outstanding issues relating to Hong Kong's economic development. Prospects have brightened for a resolution this year to the dispute over financing Hong Kong's multi-billion-dollar airport and railway. There are also indications that China will permit its surrogates in Hong Kong to contest elections under the terms of the Patten provisions.

The better atmosphere, however, may be no more than inaction born of distraction. A less optimistic interpretation of current events is that China's leaders have their hands full with more pressing matters, such as getting control of the economy and jockeying to secure a place in the post-Deng Xiaoping leadership of the country.

Patten's aides are quietly confident that his second reform bill—which seeks to broaden the democratic franchise for the Legco elections to be held in autumn, 1995—will get through relatively unscathed, if only because the bill is too difficult to amend substantially. On balance, they are probably correct. But the prevailing view among middle-of-the-road Legco members was summed up by one of them recently: "Ironically, the hard-liners in Beijing and Chris Patten are on the same side. He wants his bill to go through, and so do they, so they can tear it up in 1997." If the bill were watered down, the Legco member said, "it would be more difficult for China to tear it up."

China, however, is keeping its powder dry. Amid much fanfare and saber rattling, it launched a "preliminary work committee" (PWC) last year on the administration of Hong Kong. As a precaution against failure in talks with Britain, one of the committee's first task was to draw up specifications for elections to be held in the second half of 1997. However, according to one member of the PWC, the committee is unlikely to come up with recommendations that are set in concrete. "There is a long time between now and 1997; much can happen, and we want to retain flexibility," he says.

Such an attitude casts an interesting light on China's threat to disband the Legco elected in 1995 upon its resumption of sovereignty in mid-1997. It suggests that Beijing may want to assess the outcome of the elections before it makes any firm decision.

—Simon Holberton, "Financial Times" (centrist), London.

Article 22   *Fortune*, September 20, 1993

INDONESIA ON THE MOVE

With a growing middle class, plentiful workers, vast petroleum and mineral resources, and political stability, it's Asia's next big growth market.

Louis Kraar

In a listless world economy, nothing excites global managers more than big emerging countries like India and China. Add another: Indonesia. Want consumers? Nearly 200 million, including a growing middle class. Production workers? All you can use at hourly wages below those of South China. Raw materials? Indonesia is the world's largest exporter of liquefied natural gas, the biggest tin producer; and a major supplier of wood products. Political stability? A former army general who in the Javanese tradition bears the single name of Suharto has kept the lid on for 25 years—though at 71 he has, like most strongmen, designated no heir apparent.

The country is huge—3,000 miles from tip to steaming tip—and disparate. In cities, business suits abound, while in Irian Jaya, the easternmost province, well-dressed men wear little more than leather penis sheaths. In Borneo there are still reports—but no recent sightings—of headhunters. Though the population is concentrated on a few islands, especially Sumatra (more than 1,000 miles long) Java (the most populous), and Bali (a once unspoiled island whose beaches are now lined with high-rise hotels), the country sprawls over 13,000 islands spread along the equator. If the map of Indonesia were superimposed on that of the U.S. it would reach from New York to San Francisco and from Chicago to south of New Orleans. Compared with Europe, it would start in Dublin and end up in the Urals, way beyond Moscow.

Jakarta is a capital city of charm and inefficiency, embodying both the country's great promise and its enormous problems. Its financial district is nearly as imposing as Singapore's. But work inside the soaring buildings comes to a stop during the city's frequent power failures. Phoning anyone can take hours. Finding bureaucrats at work is a challenge; their day officially ends at 3 P.M., when many rush off to second jobs to stretch their meager salaries. The roads are jammed with shiny cars—and with beggars and ragged children peddling cigarettes, candy, and newspapers. With a population of 8.2 million, nearly three times that of Singapore, the city has the sprawl and the stark contrasts between rich and poor of Bangkok or Calcutta. Jakarta smells of sweat, clove-flavored cigarettes called *kretek*, and the fetid canals that lace the city. Yet everyone always smiles.

The rewards to investors have been exceptional. Mobil's Indonesian oil and gas production last year earned an estimated $370 million, 25% of the U.S. corporation's *total* profits. American companies, which have put $4 billion into Indonesia, get a far better than average return on investment—nearly 48% in 1991, the latest year covered by U.S. Commerce Department surveys. No wonder General Electric is leading a consortium to invest nearly $2 billion in the country's first private electric power station. Goodyear's most cost-effective tire factory in the whole world is in Indonesia. President Edward J. Higham says, "This is an excellent place to do business."

If you can handle a tricky web of Third World risks. Companies must deal with a bloated bureaucracy, corruption, and a complex society where business depends heavily on personal relationships. Says a high U.S. executive there: "We must stay away from politics and payoffs, which sometimes means losing business." The most aggressive local business powers include several of President Suharto's children. The government assigned AT&T, among others, a member of the First Family as its joint venture partner. General Motors is teamed up with Suharto's half brother.

The first step toward business success is understanding the people. Inward-looking, very polite, and soft-spoken, they live in a world of their own. Most claim to be Muslim (the country has the world's largest Islamic population: 160 million), but they exhibit none of the fanaticism of Islamic fundamentalists in the Mideast. Mysticism remains a potent force. Ancient myths provide models for behavior and are kept alive in popular Javanese *wayang,* or shadowplay performances, which employ wooden puppets and can last seven to eight hours at a stretch.

Avoiding confrontation is so essential to the culture that Indonesians veil their feelings in amiable ambiguity. In offices and factories, maintaining harmony is far more important than getting something done quickly and efficiently. The lengthy prelude to accomplishing anything is making friends. Moreover, all decisions are made at the top level by a boss always respectfully called *bapak,* literally "father." For the whole nation, Suharto is the big daddy, and no Western investor or manager should forget that.

Since taking command of a bankrupt country in 1967, the Suharto regime has expanded the economy an average of nearly 7% a year, putting it among the ten fastest-growing in the world, reports the World Bank. Per capita income has climbed from a miserable $50 a year to a middling $730. That's roughly on par with Egypt but only half the level of Thailand. By the end of the decade Suharto, with the help of a team of economic advisers popularly known as the "Berkeley mafia" because many studied at the University of California, hopes to raise the average income to $1,000 annually. At that point, millions of Indonesians will be able to trade up from bicycles to motorcycles and cars. The government also needs to find some way to create 2.3 million jobs a year for new entrants into the labor market.

Indonesia's only hope for that is enticing private investors, especially since the country has some $85 billion in foreign debt. Until recently most foreign capital went into developing energy and mineral resources. Now Indonesia is becoming a center for export manufacturing. Companies from Japan, South Korea, and Taiwan, plus a few from the U.S., are producing garments, sports shoes, and radios for the world. Mattel finds Indonesia, where its factory workers get $50 a month, a good place for making Barbie dolls and plans to do one-third of its worldwide production there by 1995.

Actively seeking foreign investment is a new experience for the government, which has become worried about a sudden falloff. Jakarta expects foreign companies to sign contracts for projects totaling $6 billion to $7 billion this year, down from $10.3 billion in 1992, and little more than half the dollar value of government-approved investments ever materializes because companies strangle in red tape.

Investors are deterred by a potent strain of economic nationalism and the tyranny of bureaucracy. Every potential investor must get a letter of approval signed by President Suharto—which takes about nine months. And that is only the start of a paper chase for up to a dozen other permits, which usually require paying off working-level bureaucrats. Selling most products to the government demands a local agent, a system that breeds corrupt practices and, remarks a U.S. corporate executive, "creates an elite that makes millions."

While supposedly embracing market forces, the government is sinking untold billions into inefficient state enterprises, including the largest steel mill and the only aircraft factory in Southeast Asia. A nationalistic breed of presidential advisers, who call themselves "technologists," maintains that Indonesia can leap into high-tech export industries. To do so, they want government subsidies and tariff protection.

Equally worrisome to international creditors is the festering Indonesian equivalent of the U.S. savings and loan disaster. Government-owned banks, which control about half of domestic lending, tend to make loans on the basis of political influence rather than creditworthiness. The result is a mountain of nonperforming loans (using strict accounting standards) that probably totals some $10 billion, more than the net worth of all the state banks together.

All those troubling trends raise a crucial question: Is Indonesia a great business opportunity or a quagmire? It depends on how well companies grasp the peculiarities of a country where managing the risks can deliver handsome returns. Despite the obvious land mines, Indonesia is too big a prospect for most companies to ignore.

General Electric, for example, is expanding. Ram K. Sharma, who heads GE's Indonesian operations, started 14 years ago with a filing cabinet in his Jakarta hotel room. GE now sells around $400 million a year of power-generating equipment, aircraft engines, locomotives, and plastics. GE has begun investing in Indonesian businesses including an auto finance firm and a plant to assemble medical equipment, and is considering taking a stake in a local light bulb maker. In addition, the company has formed a venture with Mission Energy of the U.S., the Japanese trading company Mitsui, and an Indonesian coal-mining company to build a $1.8 billion plant that would sell electric power to the state utility. Indonesia's investment board has approved the plan, but the government is still haggling over price.

An acute shortage of phone lines makes Indonesia a choice market for AT&T, but not an easy one. AT&T Network Systems has invested $25 million in a new plant 18 miles east of Jakarta to assemble the company's flagship 5ESS digital switching system for phone exchanges. The factory employs about 125, mostly bolting together components from the U.S. and Europe. The plant exists only because Indonesia made it a condition for giving AT&T a $100 million contract, the first of many orders that the U.S. company expects.

Still, AT&T had to jump through other incredible hoops to sell telephone switches, long the monopoly of a state-owned manufacturer. In 1989 the government agreed to open bids to other companies. NEC of Japan looked like the sure winner; but George Bush appealed to Suharto for fair play. Ultimately both AT&T and NEC got big orders—provided that they set up joint ventures with Indonesians. AT&T's partner, assigned by the Indonesian government, is Citra Telekomunikasi, a newcomer to the telephone industry. Citra is controlled by a daughter of President Suharto's, Mrs. Siti Hardijanti Rukmana, whose nickname is Tutut. Her brother Bambang is NEC's government-assigned partner. (According to another Javanese custom, children usually take names different from their father's.)

With the collapse of oil prices in the early 1980s, Indonesia finally began to open up the highly protected, state-controlled economy it had built with petroleum revenues. Liberalization is a word that sounds leftist to the conservative Suharto, so his regime calls it "deregulation and debureaucratization." Whatever you call it, the process has weaned Indonesia from dependence on energy sales, now 31% of export revenues, vs. 56% in 1986. Jakarta acted just in time to capture a mass transfer of labor-intensive industries from Japan and other Asian countries seeking sites with lower wages. Indonesian textile workers make only $2.50 a day, about 10% of what South Koreans get and well below the $4 daily wage in booming South China.

Keeping Indonesia on the right economic track depends, above all, on President Suharto. Says Christianto Wibisono, an outspoken U.S.-educated economist who runs a local version of Standard & Poor's: "The weakness of our system unfortunately lies in its strongest asset, the strongman figure of Suharto." He's like the founder of a big corporation. Adds Wibisono: "No one dares challenge or dispute his decisions." The result has been stability, but what happens after Suharto?

Indonesia needs to spruce up its welcome mat for investors—or risk losing them to China, Vietnam, and other Asian suitors. A good start would be paying bureaucrats a living wage and finally ending a promiscuous system of bribes. Says the senior U.S. executive in Jakarta: "The triple-A companies won't go through all that crap. Indonesia must have a process that is transparent, and now it's far from transparent." The best way for Indonesia to attract more job-creating corporations is by simply getting the government off their backs.

Article 23   *The Wall Street Journal*, October 11, 1994

Asian Paradox

Indonesia Is Striving to Prosper in Freedom But Is Still Repressive

*Suharto Regime Talks Up Openness, Closes Down Dissenting Publications
Higher Wages, Labor Strife*

Marcus W. Brauchli

Staff Reporter of The Wall Street Journal

JAKARTA, Indonesia—A tragedy is playing in a darkened theater here. At center stage is a circle of red earth, a symbolic grave. As ceiling fans stir sweet clove-cigarette smoke, an actress in brown sackcloth bemoans life: "Only death is freedom."

The avant-garde performance is a bleak allegory based on the true story of Marisinah, a 24-year-old watch-factory worker who thought she deserved more than a dollar a day and was murdered last year for organizing a strike to get it. Her name—like many Indonesians she has only one—is now synonymous with oppression in this authoritarian land.

Yet there is a shaft of hope in the gloom. Despite political sensitivities, tonight's production is being performed in a government-owned culture center at the heart of the capital. There are no police here, no soldiers, no goons—just 200 or so middle-class theater goers who paid five times Marisinah's daily wage to hear an antiestablishment play on a steamy Friday night.

Call it the Indonesian paradox: The world's fourth most-populous country remains a tight autocracy under President Suharto; soldiers and the rich still hold sway. Dissenters like Marisinah sometimes get crushed. Yet Indonesia also is an emerging Asian dynamo, with the nucleus of a consumer class and considerable craving for openness and frank reflection.

As the country heads down the runway toward economic takeoff, its regime is straining to cope with that contradiction and define the future. "If you want to speed up your takeoff, you increase the angle of attack," says B. J. Habibie, the minister of research and technology and a close friend of President Suharto. "But if you go too fast, you will stall."

So there is a certain ambivalence about change. Clampdowns on labor activists seem at odds with government campaigns to increase wages and benefits. Once-taboo subjects like the festering insurgency in East Timor can be discussed under a new "openness," but three popular journals have just been banned. Free-market economic reforms are the order of the day, yet bribes and connections are still the preferred way to get things done in business.

But after a half-century of independence and nearly three decades of Mr. Suharto's autocratic rule, Indonesia, like it or not, is in the throes of change. What will emerge in the near term, many hope, is a strong but tolerant government that is more responsive to the needs of a better informed and richer society. Then eventually, the nation might follow the path of South Korea and Taiwan, former military dictatorships that have evolved into middle-class dominated democracies.

"We believe that you have to go not through a revolution, because a revolution is expensive and unpredictable, but through an evolution," says Mr. Habibie. "But an evolution is too long. We have to accelerate it."

How Jakarta goes about that is being watched closely. Indonesia is Southeast Asia's giant, a strategically situated country of nearly 190 million, mainly Muslims. Its fast-growing, export-oriented economy makes it an important player in international forums such as the 18-nation Asia Pacific Economic Cooperation group, which will hold its summit here in November. Already, other countries, particularly the U.S., pressure Jakarta on such issues as labor rights and press freedom.

Looming over everything—sometimes from giant billboards along major roads—is President Suharto. At the age of 73, the silver-haired Mr. Suharto is in his sixth five-year term. Many expect him to retire when his current term ends in 1998, if not sooner. He recently suffered from kidney stones. Rumors are rife that he is seriously ill—though his friends deny it—and that certain members of Indonesia's powerful military want him to step aside.

True or not, such talk feeds Indonesia's appetite for change. President Suharto himself raised many people's expectations by rousing the country's economy. Once dependent on oil and gas exports for two-thirds of foreign-exchange earnings, Indonesia is now a base for textile, shoe and other manufacturing exports. Peasants are leaving farms to work in factories. Average annual incomes have spurted to $650 a person—twice what they were a decade ago—as gross national product has expanded at an average clip of 6.8%. Half of all homes have electricity, up from 6%

when Mr. Suharto became president in 1967. Towns are turning into cities, and shopping malls are sprouting.

Yet the man responsible for the ascendant middle class, Mr. Suharto, still paints himself as a cautious agent of change. On the eve of Indonesia's 49th Independence Day in August, the president warned against "defending outdated values or preserving the status quo." But while he promised new ideas, he also cautioned that "we must strongly reject and avoid those which are unsuitable to our identity and the essence of nationalism."

Such mixed signals make Indonesia an "as if" society, one critic says. "It's as if there were freedom of association, as if there were freedom of the press, as if there were freedom of thought," he says. "The problem is that many people act as if it were true. And it's not."

Maybe not entirely. Members of the country's House of Representatives now challenge ministers with once-unthinkable assertiveness: They demand to know why one of President Suharto's ministers spent two months abroad and complain that the number of presidential decrees since independence outnumbers laws by a ratio of about 10 to 1. The legal system, too, is opening up: Lawsuits against government agencies are proliferating, and one non-governmental group has named President Suharto in a complaint.

Yet Indonesians say they never forget that there is a balance between openness and control. "It's like flying a kite," says James T. Riady, vice chairman of Lippo Ltd., a powerful, Chinese family-run business empire that is flourishing in banking, real estate and even manufacturing. "Sometimes you let the string loose, sometimes you pull it tight. Otherwise, the whole thing comes down."

Stress on Stability

The watchword is always stability. Mr. Suharto and his generation have feared chaos since the mid-1960s, when a leftward lurch triggered bloodshed that left hundreds of thousands dead. Many of the dead were ethnic Chinese, who control much of the Indonesian economy and are resented by some other Indonesians. The violence ended only after a group of officers led by Mr. Suharto, a former guerrilla fighter, eased his popular albeit mercurial predecessor, Sukarno, from the presidency and imposed military rule. In 1967, Gen. Suharto became president and to this day the military retains a voice in nearly

all government affairs. "Our dual function will last forever and ever," Armed Forces Chief of Staff Lt. Gen. H. B. L. Mantiri said in early October.

That view still imposes clear limits to government tolerance even today. One of those was reached earlier this year, when labor unrest exploded into riots in the former Dutch trading city of Medan in north Sumatra, 900 miles from Jakarta. The protests began when factory owners, mainly Chinese, didn't pay traditional one-month bonuses at the Muslim-Hari Raya holiday. Many workers weren't getting the minimum daily wage of $1.50, either, and weren't happy about it.

In the sparse, crowded rooms where factory workers in Medan's outskirts live, it is easy to understand why. Workers live in plywood-walled, tin-roofed dormitory rooms in a muddy area near the factories. In one room, four young women who work at canneries and shrimp factories sleep side by side on a wooden platform, their belongings hanging in plastic bags from nails on the wall. The women fear recriminations if they complain and won't give their names, though one blurts out: "We don't have any hope if we stay."

In March and April, they joined 30,000 or so other workers to protest conditions. A mass demonstration turned violent when local officials refused to meet workers. Egged on by provocateurs—officials and human-rights groups agree on that but disagree about exactly who they were—workers broke windows and destroyed cars. There were overtones of racism against the Chinese, who own most factories but account for only about a third of the local population. One Chinese factory owner was killed.

Crackdown in Medan

Alarmed by parallels to the nation-wracking violence of the 1960s, the regime responded with a military crackdown in Medan, arresting dozens of workers. Over loud complaints, including public objections from the U.S.—which grants Indonesia certain trade benefits on the basis of its labor record—the leader of the independent Indonesian Workers' Welfare Union was arrested. Though he was 1,300 miles away in central Java at the time of the protests, he is now being tried under heavy security in Medan on charges of inciting riot. The man accused, 41-year-old Muchtar Pakpahan, faces a prison sentence of up to six years. Labor activists complain that the government is us-

ing the Medan riots to justify crushing his union, which isn't officially recognized.

Not so, government officials say. The demands of the Medan workers are in accord with the government's desire to raise standards of living and to reduce income inequality. After all, three quarters of Indonesia's work force of 83 million are between the ages of 15 and 34, and if incomes aren't rising, the resulting political pressures could be destabilizing. That may explain why, in the months since the Medan riots, the government has stepped in to raise minimum wages and, as of Sept. 16, require that all companies pay out a one-month bonus each year. "We want the people to know that the government will stand up for them," says an official in Jakarta.

Beset 'Nationalist'

Yet that message is muddied by government actions. "Why do they harass us?" asks Alamsyah Hamdani, the director of the Indonesian Legal Aid Society's Medan office, which is defending Mr. Pakpahan and other labor activists. He can't bring more than five people together for a meeting without violating a law against unlicensed assembly and risking arrest by the armed men who keep him under constant surveillance.

Such bullying strikes Mr. Hamdani as self-defeating for a government that seeks legitimacy with the people. He considers himself a nationalist. On a wall of his dining room is a photograph of former President Sukarno with John F. Kennedy. Next to it is a portrait of his own father-in-law, the former regional commander of the same military that now has him under surveillance.

The government seems out of touch. A clear sign of that came in June, when editors of three of the country's most popular publications were abruptly ordered to the Information Ministry for a chat. There, to their astonishment, they were told they were being shut down.

The move stunned and disappointed many Indonesians. "What is the harm of knowledge?" asks Dewi Juita Purba, a 26-year-old hotel clerk. "We are not children. We can judge for ourselves."

That was the credo of the biggest of the closed magazines, Tempo. With a circulation of 190,000, Tempo was the pulse of the incipient middle class—just ask the advertisers who packed the 100-page-plus magazine with ads. The magazine ran blunt stories about sensitive subjects like the business interests of President Suharto's family—in autos, shipping and banking—and even East Timor, a former Portuguese colony where the military's handling of a nationalist insurrection has provoked international charges of human-rights abuses.

Raw Nerve

"We were very issue-oriented," says Fikri Jufri, Tempo's animated deputy chief editor. "It seemed there was some real openness." There was, that is, until the press focused on an issue close to Mr. Suharto's heart—a controversial purchase—arranged by Mr. Suharto's protege, Research and Technology Minister Habibie—of 39 former East Germany Navy ships. The purchase had been opposed by some in the military, and coverage touched a nerve.

"We are not going to pay the price because some newspapers want to have freedom without having appropriate balanced responsibility," says Mr. Habibie. "The price is too high."

The shutdown chilled discourse in Indonesia. Although one new tabloid briefly surfaced, it quickly ceased publication. But Tempo journalists want to set up a new magazine. Mock-ups of a publication called Opini hang on Tempo's office bulletin boards alongside news stories of Tempo's closure and memos

on severance pay. "If you have a strong middle class who think openness is needed, not for dramatic reasons but for necessity, it will happen," Mr. Fikri says. "It's bottom-up, not just granted from above."

The growing economy is expanding that crucial middle class. Lippo Group, the family-run empire of Mr. Riady, is now building big Jakarta suburbs, with multiple-story housing, backyards and private schools. Department-store sales are healthy and houses in the big cities have satellite dishes. General Motors Corp. just put $110 million into revamping an assembly line here to make Opel passenger cars for a booming auto market. Foreign investment hit $19.86 billion in the first nine months of this year, almost double the $10.3 billion inflow for all of 1993.

Guided by Technocrats

Those developments are possible only because the government long ago decided to create a high degree of economic liberalization and equity. President Suharto has relied heavily on the guidance of technocrats—many trained in the U.S.—to steer the economy, and the country's fiscal policies generally get plaudits from the World Bank. Import barriers are being lowered

gradually. The government in June removed many restrictions on foreign investment.

There are still some distortions. A few big companies rely on connections, often to the immediate family of President Suharto, in expanding their businesses. One of the companies to propose setting up a new weekly magazine after Tempo was closed down was backed by Bob Hasan, a friend of Mr. Suharto. Yet even the practice of using connections to do business has come under public attack. A scandal erupted this year when the state-owned Indonesian Development Bank discovered it had lost $449 million through bad loans to a politically connected businessman, Eddy Tansil. Mr. Tansil was sentenced to 17 years in prison, but one of his business partners—Tommy Suharto, youngest son of the president—was never publicly questioned.

Erratic progress is progress nonetheless, and it pleases businessmen who see markets emerging in a changing nation. "Indonesia moves three steps forward, one step back, one step sideways," says Leonard L. Brownfield, president of PT General Motors Buana Indonesia, the GM venture. "But it's a country in transition. And it will be more democratic tomorrow than it is today. Just sit back and watch it happen."

Article 24   *The Christian Science Monitor*, November 10, 1993

From Carpet Bombing to Capitalism in Laos

Once key to US strategy in Southeast Asia, this forgotten Communist land is opening its doors—with deliberate caution

Clayton Jones

Staff writer of The Christian Science Monitor

VIENTIANE, LAOS

On the main avenue of this Southeast Asian capital, once regarded as so strategic that it had the largest United States Embassy in the world, goats and cattle roam freely, unbothered by the few motorcycles and even fewer cars.

But the slow pace in Vientiane, a town of only 125,000 on the Mekong River, is deceptive. Underneath lies a deliberate design by the Communist leaders of Laos to avoid pushing their country pell-mell into the 20th century. "We can't open the door too far," says Sannya Aphay, vice governor of the National Tourism Authority. "But we don't want to close ourselves off and remain poor."

Even though the Communist Party has shed many of its Stalinist ways and embraced free markets since 1986, it has decided recently to try an unusual experiment in economic restraint, or what it calls "the Lao way."

Its leaders, who once suffered American carpet-bombing in jungle hideouts, want to prevent the social and environmental ills of rapid growth that they see in neighboring Thailand, Vietnam, and China.

New investment projects are carefully scrutinized and often delayed, even though this former French colony remains one of the world's poorest nations, with an average annual income of less than $250 per person.

As a result, Laos has retained much of its forest cover and has built few dams on its plentiful rivers. Vientiane remains virtually free of pollution, crime, drugs, AIDS, and large-scale corruption. Unlike Thailand, tourists are allowed to enter Laos only in small numbers.

Perhaps the best example of measured development is Laos's reluctance to seek a second bridge across the wide Mekong to Thailand. The first bridge, called Mitraphap (friendship), will open next April near Vientiane and the Thai town of Nong Khai. "They want to wait one or two years to see what kind of people, goods, and ideas come over from Thailand," says Australian Ambassador Michael Mann, whose country built and paid for the new bridge.

At present, Laos plans to block motorcycles and bicycles from using the bridge. In fact, only about 1,300 vehicles are expected to cross daily, even by 1995.

The unhurried pace of progress, however, has not always been deliberate. Laos suffers the same bureaucratic inertia as any third-world nation, perhaps with less corruption.

Communist takeover

After 1975, when the Hanoi-backed Pathet (land) Lao guerrillas took power from the monarchy in a bloodless Communist coup, private property was confiscated,

'THE LAO WILL ALWAYS BE LAO': A Buddhist monk sections bamboo to make baskets. Buddhism remains as influential as Communism in Laos.

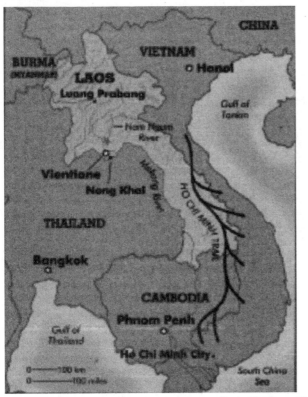

Dave Herring—Staff

farmers collectivized, and some 30,000 to 40,000 people were sent to prison-like "re-education camps." Another 343,000 Laotians, mainly from the Hmong tribe, fled to Thailand. The country was renamed the Lao People's Democratic Republic.

Most of these steps have been reversed as Communist measures lost favor here and party leaders joined with comrades in Vietnam to move toward "market Leninism"—a one-party state with little command over the private economy.

In Vientiane, dozens of private shops sprung up overnight. Big banks from Thailand moved in. The town even sported a cellular phone system. The starting gate was opened for Laos to become another "little Asian tiger." But its leaders have since pulled in the reins.

The ruling Lao People's Revolutionary Party decided to give the country a constitution only in 1991. It also took the hammer and sickle off the national flag. In the party motto, the word "prosperity" has replaced "socialism." A propaganda bookstore in Vientiane with books on Lenin appears closed, but not completely shuttered.

"Laos is not on the way to communism," claims government spokesman Vanhevan Vongvichet, "We are on the way to democracy."

Last year, however, the party sentenced three top officials to 14 years in prison for "antigovernment activities," or advocating a multiparty system. The US claims Laos holds six political prisoners, down from hundreds

in the 1970s. "Being Communist is still the claim of legitimacy by the government," says a Western diplomat.

After longtime leader Kaysone Phomvihan died last year, he was replaced by a shy, former military officer named Gen. Khamtay Siphandon, who rules over a 66,000-member party. He has yet to make noticeable change.

In downtown Vientiane, the party's revolutionary museum showing heroic deeds against the former US enemy today appears unkempt and is closed most of the time. Just down the street, an office of the International Monetary Fund has opened up to dispense capitalist advice to former guerrillas.

The drag on development is the fact that about two-thirds of the estimated 4.4 million Laotians are semi-nomadic peasants who practice slash-and-burn agriculture in a land-locked, hilly nation the size of Oregon with very few roads. Ambassador Mann recounts a recent helicopter trip to a remote village of 8,000 Laotians—none of whom had ever seen a non-Asian before.

Female illiteracy and infant mortality are among the highest in the world, and of all the many small experiments being conducted by international aid groups to find ways to uplift Laotian villages, not one has spread across the country, says Ameerah Haq-Perera, United Nations Development Programme representative in Vientiane. "Laos is practicing preventative development," she says, "and is trying to learn from the errors of its neighbors. Someday, it may be ahead in social cohesion and environmental protection."

The go-slow approach was not adopted at first in 1986 when Laos opened its door. But when foreign investment did not flood in, the older party leaders decided to tighten the reins of development. They also began to worry about being overwhelmed by Laos's bigger and more powerful neighbors: China, Vietnam, Thailand, and Burma. An estimated 40,000 Vietnamese émigés, for instance, were sent home from Laos last year.

What little foreign investment did come, mainly in textiles, also ran into bottlenecks. When it comes to boosting trade and tourism, "we will be sticking to the protection of the environment and human resource development simultaneously," says Phao Bounnaphol, head of the prime minister's staff.

Debating change

Within the party, a lively debate continues over how much change to allow. "The old party guys are conservative, but the younger ones say that Laos must adjust to cope with inevitable changes coming its way," Mann says. The debate may be influenced by Laos's widespread Buddhist faith, a religion that teaches one to look inward during hard times and to avoid extremes.

Reverence for Monarchy Lives on in Sacred Capital of the Kings

LUANG PRABANG, LAOS

Over Luang Prabang hangs a morning haze as heavy as its history.

The haze veils the green jungle hills, the chocolate waters of the Mekong River, and Buddhist temples, whose gold steeples reach skyward in this sacred home of the former Laotian kings.

As has happened every dawn since Luang Prabang's founding in the 14th century, monks in saffron robes walk barefoot through the streets in an act of humility, carrying lacquered bowls to receive offerings from the faithful.

The old people in Luang Prabang, a name that means "royal holy image," refuse to forget the last king who ruled Laos. They are like Russians who refuse to forget the last Czar, or Cambodians who wished for Prince Norodom Sihanouk to be their monarch again. The Lao king was protector of both the people and Buddhism.

Many of the king's former servants can still be found in this isolated town, some 140 miles north of the new capital, Vientiane.

The king's chief artist, Thit Khamtane, makes a meager living selling wood carvings of Buddha. He helps to maintain the palace, having carved some of its most beautiful artworks.

It is even possible to bump into some of the king's relatives. His granddaughter, Chio (princess) Tiene, runs the Villa de la Princesse Hotel, which opened recently in a French colonial house once owned by the former queen.

LAOS'S GOLDEN DOOR: The entrance to the royal palace is a testament to Buddha and the elegance of Laos's former kings: the Communists sent the last king 'to the north.'

Tourism, especially the kind of sex tourism found in Bangkok, worries almost every Lao leader. "There will be many negative effects on our culture," says Mr. Sannya. "Now people are living an easy and peaceful life, and they are happy with this."

But cultural or economic influence from Thailand or the West does not worry Foreign Vice-Minister Phongsavath Boupha. "The Lao take pride in themselves, so we're not too worried," he says. "The Lao will always be Lao."

Laos has yet to make a transition from a subsistence economy to a commodity-based economy, says Dr. Sonephet Inthavong, deputy minister for planning. "We

can't absorb all the assistance given to us." Much of the commerce in Laos is still by barter, not cash.

The estimated economic growth this year may reach 6 percent, not high enough to keep pace with rapid population growth. But in a bold step, Laos signed an agreement with Thailand in June to build several hydroelectric dams by the year 2000 and export the electricity to Thailand. The export revenues could make it easier for the Communist Party to direct development.

The loss of economic help from the former Soviet empire has not greatly changed Laos' direction, even though it lost 25 percent of its export markets and 58

If people in Luang Prabang talk about the king at all, they do so in whispers. Their memories of him are crisp, but their reminiscences are as veiled as the dawn haze.

In 1977, the last king, Savang Vatthana, went "to the north," as the Laotians say. The Communist rulers, who took over Laos in 1975, sent the king, along with thousands of others, to "re-education camps" (prisons) in the northern province of Sam Neua.

To their credit, the Communists did not kill the king outright. He had a relative in the party. But he was too powerful a symbol among the 4 million Laotians to let him become a potential rallying point for dissent.

"He was a good man and protected the people," says an elderly rice farmer, Xieng Eanh. The educated elite, however, say the monarchy failed to modernize the country the way those in neighboring Thailand and Cambodia did. "His family was too decadent," says merchant Chanthone Thattanakham.

Not until 1991 did the Laotian people learn that the king had died, perhaps 10 years earlier. Crown Prince Vongsavang may have died as well, although his wife still lives in Luang Prabang, and is still greeted with bows and honorifics.

The most haunting presence of the king is his palace, which has been kept pretty much the same as the day he left it. Just why the Communists did so is unclear.

Laotians can enter the palace only with permission, which is rare, while the foreign tourists allowed into Laos can take a tour.

Next to a giant throne chamber in the 1904 French-designed building is a room full of foreign gifts to the king, including moon fragments from Richard Nixon and a silver desk set from John Kennedy. A 12-foot painting of the king shows him wearing green silk, holding a gold sheath and flanked by a throne and a statue of Buddha.

The king's and queen's separate bedrooms and their shared bathroom are sparse but elegant. Two safes keep the three gold crowns of previous kings, while a valuable gold Buddha statue has been put in a state vault. But there are many rich touches, such as a gold betel-nut box, the royal palanquin, and a set of French china.

The French, who colonized Laos, paid dearly to defend the monarch and Luang Prabang from Vietnamese Communist guerrillas. In 1954, the French military took a stand not far from Luang Prabang, at Dien Bien Phu on the Laos-Vietnam border, where Ho Chi Minh's jungle fighters defeated them in a historic battle.

During its war in Indochina, the US dropped more bombs on tiny, landlocked Laos than it did on Germany during World War II. Many of the bombs were intended to protect Luang Prabang.

But by the end of the war, the monarchy was no more. In this ancient, quaint town, it survives only in a haze of memory.

On the banks of the Mekong, the monarch's former chef, Phanh Khoumlavong, now sells hot chilies from a wooden table. She remembers the king as a kind man who loved French food and read Proust. And she still cries for him.

—C.J.

percent of its import sources. Much of that has been made up by increased foreign aid, mainly from Sweden, Japan, and Australia.

In a historic irony, the US is now the largest investor in Laos, after once waging war in Indochina from Vientiane. Most of the investment is in oil and minerals.

Remnants of the US war are everywhere. The landscape is pocked with bomb craters. Parachutes from downed US jets serve as awnings for restaurants. Shell casings are used as opium pipes. Motorcyclists wear US Army helmets.

Laos was once so important to Washington that Dwight Eisenhower told John Kennedy in a presidential-transition talk that this country was "the key to the entire area of Southeast Asia." Laos was the key domino in the domino theory, and was a take-off point for much US bombing of Vietnam between 1964 and 1973.

Today, this least-known of Communist nations is nearly forgotten in Asia's political landscape. And to some degree, its leaders, who live in the big, suburban-style houses left by the Americans, prefer it that way.

Article 25　　　　　　　　　　　　　*Freedom Review*, November–December 1994

Imprisoned Conscience

Burma: Still the Generals

Thomas R. Lansner

Thomas R. Lansner, a contributing editor to Freedom Review, *is an international affairs writer and consultant.*

Sixty-two months after being detained under house arrest, Burma's democracy leader and Nobel Peace Prize winner Aung San Suu Kyi appeared on television screens in Burma in mid-September, in apparent good health and chatting with the leaders of the military junta that still keeps her imprisoned.

Reports from Burma's capital, Rangoon, say the meeting has generated huge excitement and hopeful anticipation in Burma. But that it signifies a genuine step away from the brutal dictatorship under which the Burmese people today suffer is uncertain. The meeting took place on the opening day of the United Nations' General Assembly in New York, surely no coincidence. The General Assembly is considering toughening the resolution it adopted last year demanding democratic reform and respect for human rights in Burma. Cautious—or perhaps cynical—observers assay the junta's move as no more than an effort to defuse international pressure against them. Perhaps the coterie of generals who run Burma—the State Law and Order Restoration Council—has garnered greater public relations skills since naming themselves the "SLORC" in 1988.

There is little argument—except from the SLORC—that basic human rights and fundamental democratic freedoms have long been denied Burma's peoples. Yet international policies toward Burma are now the focus of sharp debate. Can a policy of strict isolation, perhaps including an arms embargo or even trade sanctions, force the SLORC to change? Or will a policy of "constructive engagement," opening Burma's economy to the world, prove a more powerful incentive to reform?

Day of the generals: 11,000 and counting

The military junta now in power has effectively ruled Burma in one guise or other since a 1962 coup. The generals' "Burmese Way to Socialism" was paved with xenophobia and repression, and led the resource-rich country's forty million people to increasing poverty. Massive pro-democracy demonstrations in 1988 were quelled only by machine guns; thousands of protesters died. Despite the unmistakable public disdain for military rule, the SLORC conducted multiparty elections in May 1990. For reasons still difficult to fathom, the generals allowed a free vote and honest tabulation of ballots. Perhaps to their surprise only, the opposition National League for Democracy (NLD) and its de facto leader, Aung San Suu Kyi, won a landslide victory over a military-backed party.

Losing the election was one thing; turning over power quite another. Suu Kyi was already under house arrest. A severe crackdown against NLD leaders and activists followed. Reports of severe torture leaked from prisons and military camps, and continue to be heard today. Ruthless military campaigns against ethnic minority peoples along Burma's frontiers intensified. Severe censorship of all forms of free expression remain in force. The duly elected NLD representatives were never allowed to take office and form a government. Instead, the SLORC has convened a little credible "National Convention" it says will draw up a new constitution in preparation for fresh elections. It is also developing a proto-political party, the Union Solidarity Development Association, which may be its vehicle in new—and surely more closely controlled—elections.

Old junta; new tricks?

Could the junta's mid-September meeting with Aung San Suu Kyi be a breakthrough? The regime's often crude and bombastic propaganda attacks against the democratic opposition have toned down. Newly available consumer goods and some public works projects are making the capital, Rangoon, look like it is finally pulling out of the 1940s. But the country sorely needs a massive inflow of international funds to jump-start its moribund economy, money that will not come without an improved image. But so far, glimmerings of democratic reform remain mostly rhetorical. Even as a pair of

---

*A note on names: In 1989, the SLORC junta decreed Burma's official name to be changed to Myanmar. This action has been rejected by the elected Burmese government, now in exile, and so is not used in this text.

top generals met Suu Kyi over a flower-decorated table, hundreds of NLD politicians and supporters are still imprisoned, languishing in cruel conditions in Burma's jails. As recently as July and August, several NLD supporters were arrested. Among them is writer San San Nwe, sentenced to ten years' imprisonment. (*See box.*) One of her crimes, according to the SLORC news agency, was offering "one-sided, opposite views" to foreign journalists.

The AIDS epidemic is promoted by the trafficking of Burmese women and girls to brothels in Thailand, often with the connivance of both Burmese and Thai security officials.

The SLORC has made some progress in quieting conflict along Burma's borders, reaching cease-fires with several ethnic armies. However, fierce fighting continues in other areas. Since 1990, the SLORC has received massive shipments of weapons, mostly from China, to prosecute these wars. Horrific accounts of military brutality against civilians continue to filter from the battle zones. Thousands of people continue to be abducted and forced into virtual slavery as army porters under combat conditions. Many do not survive. Hundreds of thousands of Burmese have escaped only by fleeing to Thailand, China, India and Bangladesh.

While continuing political repression and military action, the SLORC also faces increasing social scourges partly of its own making—the interrelated rise in heroin addiction and AIDS. The AIDS epidemic is promoted by the trafficking of Burmese women and girls to brothels in Thailand, often with the connivance of both Burmese and Thai security officials. The virus is spread by contaminated needles among Burma's growing population of heroin addicts. The country is now the world's largest single grower of opium and producer of heroin in the world. Two-thirds of the heroin reaching the U.S. originates from Burma. Yet sufficient quantities remain in Burma to cause a disastrous and growing level in its domestic addiction.

There are credible reports of Burmese military involvement in drug trafficking. The level of this participation

PSsssssB. . . . . Pass the Ink

Burma is one of the world's most censored societies. Writer San San Nwe and journalist Slein Hla Oo are the latest of many Burmese writers, poets, journalists and editors to be sent to prison by Burma's military dictatorship. On 6 October, they were sentenced to ten and seven years' imprisonment, respectively, for "spreading information injurious to the state." According to the Slorc news agency, San San Nwe had also been arrested for offering "one-sided, opposite views" to foreign journalists.

Official censorship performed by the regime's "Press Scrutiny Board" (PSB) is heavy-handed, severe and often crude. Offending reports are torn from publications or obliterated under black ink. Prohibitions include: "anything detrimental to the ideology of the state . . . any incorrect ideas and opinions that do not accord with the times; any descriptions that, though factually correct, are unsuitable because of the time or circumstance of their writing . . ." In Burma, in the time of the generals, now thirty-two years and counting, such restrictions cut a very broad swath, indeed.

While seeking to pretty up the look of Burma's print media—better paper, new typesetting—the SLORC is keeping an iron grip on the writer's voice. PEN's Writers in Prison Project believes at least fifteen Burmese writers remain in prison. The number could be higher. Poet Maung Thwaka died in prison in 1991. In August 1993, writers Aung Khin Sint and Ma Thida each received twenty-year sentences for supporting the National League for Democracy.

Yet there are plenty of publications. The SLORC's daily *New Light of Myanmar* leaves most Burmese cursing the darkness. Sports and romance magazines are safely diverting, though more daring writers sometimes manage a subtle political subtext. And of course publishing is a business. The U.S. Embassy in Rangoon recently reported that the SLORC is seeking bids to supply newsprint. Any companies responding should also be prepared to provide extra ink.

FR

Recent reports on Burma

Index on Censorship (July–August 1994)

Burma: Human Lives for Natural Resources, Oil & Natural Gas (Southeast Asian Information Network, Chiang Mai, Thailand, June 1994)

Myanmar: Human Rights Developments July to December 1993 (Amnesty International, January 1994)

Inked Over, Ripped Out, by Anna J. Allot (PEN American Center, New York, September 1993)

A Modern Form of Slavery: Trafficking of Burmese Women and Girls into Brothels in Thailand (Asia Watch Women's Rights Project, December 1993)

Paradise Lost: The Suppression of Environmental Rights and Freedom of Expression in Burma. Martin Smith, Article 19, London, September 1994.

is unclear, but even the U.S. government has identified the SLORC as at least a tacit partner in the heroin trade. According to congressional testimony offered by Deputy Assistant Secretary of State for East Asia and Pacific Affairs Thomas Hubbard in June, "The SLORC undertakes few narcotics law related enforcement measures and has reached political accommodations with a number of ethnic insurgent groups which permit them to continue opium production and trafficking in return for ceasing hostilities against the central government." This is true of the groups most closely cooperating with the SLORC; other ethnic forces, it should be noted, have taken strong stands against heroin trafficking.

The litany of abuses outlined above easily answers why the SLORC has earned its status as a "pariah regime." How the world chooses to deal with the junta is a more difficult question.

Dialogue: concessions or collusion?

To date, no serious international action has been taken against the SLORC. There is no arms embargo. There are no economic sanctions. Burma retains its U.N. seat and carries on normal diplomatic and trade relations with most nations. The most significant reaction has been a suspension of international aid. The SLORC has been enticed with "carrots" (renewed IMF and World Bank loans and bilateral development aid) to encourage change, but never threatened with the "stick" of sanctions or embargoes.

Members of the Association of Southeast Asian Nations (ASEAN) and Japan argue that "constructive engagement" of increased dialogue and trade will draw the SLORC toward reform. And trade and investment is growing, including by American companies. The Los Angeles-based oil giant UNOCAL signed an agreement in September to help construct a billion dollar gas pipeline to Thailand. Reports from Burma indicate forced labor is being used on this project, as well as railway extensions and other infrastructure schemes.

Profit, at whatever price, clearly motivates ASEAN, Japanese and Western companies to greater involvement in Burma. For many Asian governments, geopolitical considerations are also compelling. Most are highly concerned over China's ever-growing political, economic and military influence in Burma, with its access to the Indian Ocean. Some argue that they must strengthen their own ties to the SLORC to fend off Chinese expansion.

Yet the counter-argument is clear: as long as the SLORC remains in power, relying on military repression to control its own citizens, Burma will be heavily dependent on China. An elected Burmese government open to the world, with full trade, aid and diplomatic ties, would neither solicit nor desire such strong links to China.

Pressure for "critical dialogue"

The U.S. has resisted resumption of international aid to Burma suspended after the SLORC's takeover and the mass killing of 1988. America's relations with the SLORC remain cool, with no U.S. ambassador in Rangoon. And the U.S., until now, has correctly abstained from aiding the SLORC in narcotics suppression programs of highly dubious value. Pressure is building from some former Western supporters of this policy of official isolation, particularly Australia, to open up a "critical dialogue" with the SLORC. Trade will open Burma and spur formation of a Burmese middle class, some analysts argue, and following examples seen in Korea, Taiwan and Thailand, inevitably lead to greater pressures for democratization. They point further to American "de-linking" of human rights and other issues in China as rationale for a similar policy in Burma.

The Australian initiative could produce positive results, but not unless significant benchmarks for reform in Burma are established and adhered to before the world community offers the SLORC the slightest reward. Only sustained international pressure has brought the SLORC to the point of even talking to Aung San Suu Kyi. Slackening will only encourage hard-line elements. The SLORC's hopes for legitimizing their hold on power in the world arena are today pinned on such "constructive engagement" or "critical dialogue." The example of their Chinese ally's success at liberalizing markets while maintaining political repression must seem enticing. And if opening to foreign commercial interests also gains political lobbies in Western capitals, as China's dictatorship has so happily learned, so much the better. If the SLORC sees the world accepting them before they have made any real concessions, they will believe nothing more than cosmetic change is necessary.

The U.N. General Assembly is now debating how best to press SLORC to give up power and allow democratic government in Burma. A special envoy may be appointed to travel to Burma to encourage a political solution. It is certain that no comprehensive settlement can be achieved overnight. The deeply entrenched generals will necessarily retain some role during transition to democracy. But the U.S. government should maintain its strong stand—and convince other countries to agree—that the SLORC must accept the requirements of existing U.N. resolutions, including freeing political prisoners and respect for basic human rights, before normal international relations with Burma are resumed.

Despite the generals' efforts to present a finer face to the world, the grim truths of their rule remain: Aung San Suu Kyi and thousands of other political activists detained; democracy, after a free and fair election, denied; the Burmese army brutal occupiers in their own land; complicity in heroin trafficking that brings suffering to millions in Burma and America. Change in these realities must be the first measures of reform in Burma, and should inform U.S. and international policy toward the SLORC.

Can a policy of strict isolation, perhaps including an arms embargo or even trade sanctions, force the SLORC to change? Or will a policy of "constructive engagement," opening Burma's economy to the world, prove a more powerful incentive to reform?

Article 26

The Rotarian, January 1993

Unforgettable

New Zealand

Here you can experience nature at its best.

Michael Gebicki

Michael Gebicki is a travel writer and photographer based in Sydney. He is a major contributor to Fodor's 1993 guides to Australia and New Zealand. His most recent book, "Going Overseas," is a guide for first-time travelers.

Travelling in New Zealand is a journey through time as well as distance. The landscape, the country towns, the drivers who nod and wave on the back roads, and even the local grocer, come from a cleaner, greener, friendlier past. But while nostalgia is a strong suit in the New Zealand deck, its trump card is spectacular scenery. In an area about the size of Colorado, U.S.A.,—or just slightly larger than Great Britain—Mother Nature has assembled active volcanoes, subtropical rain forests, geysers, some of the finest trout streams on earth, fiords, palmy beaches, glaciers, and some two dozen mountain peaks that soar to more than 3,047 metres (10,000 feet).

New Zealand is divided into two main islands, North Island, where most of the country's 3.3 million people live, and South Island. The country has scenic spectaculars from top to bottom, but while the North Island often resembles a pristine golf course, the South Island is the postcard side of the country—wild, majestic, and exhilarating. If you travel to New Zealand to experience nature in an exuberant mood, your itinerary should definitely include the South Island.

Remember too that the seasons in New Zealand are the reverse of those in the northern hemisphere. If you arrive in May (before or after the Melbourne convention), you can expect chilly weather and snow-covered mountains.

A one-week tour will allow you to take in the main attractions of both the North and South islands, but New Zealand is an experience to be savored, not rushed. Take a hike through the moss-draped beech forests of Fiordland National Park; board a jet boat and whiz into Dart River Valley; fish, raft, and breathe some of the freshest air on earth. Even if the adventures sound a little intrepid, the sheer beauty of the landscape will lend new vitality to muscles and lungs.

Experiencing New Zealand's natural wonders is relatively easy. The country has a well-developed infrastructure of hotels, tour operators, and air and road transportation. If you prefer to travel independently, you will find a choice of self-drive vacations. Even if you are not used to driving on the left side of the road, you should have no difficulty adapting to local conditions. Apart from the main cities, traffic is light, roads are generally good, and most hazards are of the four-footed variety.

Accommodation options include hotels, motels, guest houses (bed-and-breakfast facilities), and luxurious sporting lodges—a New Zealand specialty. These lodges combine good food, glamorous surroundings, and the very best that nature can provide in the way of scenery, usually with a trout stream gurgling somewhere in the background. The best known is Huka Lodge, close to the North Island's Lake Taupo.

You can't describe the sights of New Zealand without mentioning its most numerous residents—sheep. With a population of about 70 million, the fleecy, four-footed creatures outnumber their human counterparts by more than 20 to one. Despite a blossoming tourism industry, sheep are still the country's biggest source of foreign currency, and no rural scene is complete without one somewhere in the picture.

The gateway to New Zealand is Auckland, on the North Island. Auckland is the only city in the country large enough to have a traffic problem—although one that most international cities would be happy with—and your first impressions will probably be those of calm, cleanliness, and a fertility that extends into the heart of the city.

The drive into town from the airport will take you past the tall cones of extinct volcanoes, where grass as green and smooth as a billiard table is cropped by four-footed lawn-mowers (sheep). Along the way, you will probably pass knots of cyclists and joggers. Aucklanders, like all New Zealanders ("Kiwis"), are addicted to the great outdoors. It is estimated that there are about 70,000 powerboats and sailing craft anchored in the Greater Auckland area, or about one for every four households. Within a one-hour drive of the city center are 102 beaches. The 10-kilometre (6.5 mile) Round-the-Bays race attracts 80,000 runners annually, making it one of the largest "fun runs" on earth.

If you arrive in Auckland at the end of a long trans-Pacific flight and time is limited, the best introduction to the city is a cruise aboard the commuter ferry that crosses the harbour to Devonport. You can soak up the atmosphere of this historic harbourside suburb during a leisurely stroll.

Most visitors find themselves in Wellington, the nation's capital, more by necessity than by choice. Perched at the southern tip of the North Island, the city is the jumping-off point for the ferry that crosses Cook Strait to the South Island. In their rush to the South Island, many leave Wellington without a second glance, yet those who stay for even a single day will discover a sociable city of real charm, small enough to be easily explored on foot yet large enough to cater to cultured tastes.

The city of 354,000 sits in a glorious location on the western shores of Port Nicholson, squeezed against the sea by peaks that rear up almost 914 metres (3,000 feet). Behind the city, suburbs of quaint timber houses spill down precipitous slopes. Wellington's most famous characteristic is wind, caused by the blustery westerlies that are funneled through Cook Strait, the 18-kilometre (11-mile) channel that separates North Island from South Island. Frequently, the streets are roped so that pedestrians can haul themselves hand over hand in the face of a gale.

The best view of the city is from the Kelburn Cable Car, which makes a short, sharp climb from Cable Car Lane, off Lambton Quay to Kelburn, at the height of the city. Sit on the left side of the car for the best scenery on the six-minute journey.

The North Island's main attraction is the city of Rotorua, which sits smack on top of the most violent segment of the Taupo Volcanic Zone. Rotorua is one of the most extraordinary sights in the country. Flower beds steam, rings tarnish, cars corrode, and the rotten-egg smell of hydrogen sulfide hangs in the air. Even the local golf course has its own mud pools, where a lost ball stays lost forever.

The most complete tour of Rotorua's steaming wonders is the one-day Waimangu Round Trip, which includes bus transportation to several violent thermal areas, a launch trip across two lakes, and a tour of a village that was buried a century ago by a volcanic eruption. The trip ends with an invigorating dip in the thermal pools in Rotorua.

Rotorua is also the trout-fishing capital of New Zealand, and considering that the species was introduced to the country from California little more than a century ago, the explosion in New Zealand's trout population has been phenomenal. The average summer rainbow trout taken from Lake Tarawera, near Rotoma, weighs 2.3 kilograms (five pounds), and many fishing guides guarantee that no angler will come home empty-handed.

Rotorua has a large community of Maoris, the original inhabitants of New Zealand, who trace their ancestry back to the great Polynesian migration of the 14th century. Maori culture is stamped indelibly on the town, although for most visitors, their most intimate contact with that culture will be a hangi, a traditional feast cooked in an earth oven.

To the west of Rotorua are the Waitomo Caves, where the bed of an ancient sea has been spectacularly eroded into a surreal landscape of limestone formations and deep fissures, many still unexplored. Only two caves are open to the public for guided tours, the Aranui and the Waitomo, or Glow-worm cave. The Waitomo Cave takes its name from the Maori words *wai* (water) and *tomo* (cave)—since the Waitomo River vanishes into a hillside.

Visitors can take a boat ride through the cave to see the eerie lights of the Glow-worm Grotto. The glow-worm is the larva of a type of gnat, which lives on the roof of caves and snares its prey by dangling filaments of tiny sticky beads. A single glow-worm produces far less light than any firefly, but massed in great numbers, the effect rivals the most splendid star-filled sky at night.

Anyone with time to spare on the North Island should consider a tour of the Coromandel Peninsula, a wild, craggy promontory barbed with volcanic peaks and circled by beaches that are tinted pink with crushed sea shells. A two-day tour from Auckland would allow for a leisurely circuit of the peninsula, reveling in some of the North Island's most inspiring countryside.

Most South Island journeys begin and end at Christchurch, a city that could have been transported from southern England. The city's heart is dominated by church spires, its main streets are named Durham, Gloucester, and Hereford, and the serene Avon River bubbles between banks lined with willows and oaks. Most of the major sights can be seen in a half-day stroll along the river and through the museums, art galleries, and gardens that lie to the west of the city center. If you're looking for souvenirs, the Galleria inside the for-

mer university buildings on Worcester Boulevard has some of the finest arts and crafts shops in the country under one roof.

The second largest city on the South Island is Dunedin, located on the southeast coast. It is one of the unexpected treasures of New Zealand—a harbour city of steep streets and flamboyant Victorian architecture that was built on the vast profits of the New Zealand gold rush. Founded in 1848 by settlers of the Free Church of Scotland (a breakaway group from the Presbyterian Church), Dunedin has the only kilt shop in the country. Dunedin's most compelling attraction may be a colony of royal albatrosses—birds with 3.3-metre (11-foot) wingspans. The colony, just east of the city at Taiaroa Head, is the only place on earth where these majestic sea birds can be seen with relative ease. Access to the colony is strictly controlled and visitors must book in advance.

The southwest corner of the South Island is occupied by two giant national parks, Fiordland and Mount Aspiring, a majestic wilderness of mountains, ice, and beech forests, where glaciers have carved deep notches in the coast. The scenic climax of this area—and perhaps of the whole country—is Milford Sound. Hemmed in by walls of rock that rise almost sheer from the water, the 16-kilometre (10-mile long) inlet was created by a succession of glaciers. Its dominant feature is the 1,694-metre (5,560-foot) pinnacle of Mitre Peak, which is capped with snow for all but the warmest months of the year. Opposite the peak, Bowen Falls tumbles 158 metres (520 feet) before exploding into the sea.

The mountains and beech forests of Fiordland form the backdrop for some of the country's most sensational hiking trails, including the famous Milford Track, a four-day spectacular billed as "the finest walk in the world." The Milford Track can be hiked independently or with a guided party. Any moderately robust person can walk the Milford on a guided tour. While the Milford Track gets the lion's share of publicity, other walks in the vicinity including the Routeburn, the Kepler, and the Hollyford Valley tracks offer a similar combination of scenery and exercise.

To the north of Fiordland, the mountain peaks of the Southern Alps rise to form a chain along the west coast, reaching a climax at Mount Cook National Park. The park includes all the country's highest mountains, the tallest of which is Mount Cook itself at 3,762 metres (12,349 feet). The visitor base for the park is Mount Cook Village, site of the Hermitage Hotel, which has a dramatic mountain view. A network of walking trails unwinds from the village but the best way to get an idea of the grandeur of the Southern Alps is aboard a scenic flight. Flights touch down on the Tasman Glacier. During the winter, ski planes drop skiers on the glacier at a height of 3,047 metres (10,000 feet). Then they ski down the glacier through a fantastic landscape of ice and snow. With a guide, this run is suitable even for intermediate skiers.

Those with a real thirst for adventure can quench it at Queenstown, New Zealand's sporting capital for outdoor activities such as skiing, white-water rafting, horseback riding, parapenting (sailing off a mountain), and the ever popular bungy jumping. Leaping off the Kawarau Bridge and plunging 43 metres (141 feet) with only rubber cords attached to your ankles can be your worst nightmare—or your most uplifting experience.

Many New Zealand adventures demand energy, but one of the greatest adventure trips in the country is the journey aboard the Tranz Alpine Express, which requires nothing more strenuous than sitting for five hours and watching the scenic wonders unfold, with an occasional interruption for tea and scones. The Tranz Alpine is a passenger train that crosses the Southern Alps daily between Christchurch and Greymouth, winding through beech forests, glacial valleys, and mountains that are dusted with snow for most of the year.

Whether your adventures are soft or hard, by the end of your New Zealand journey you'll feel like a different person. The mountain peaks, fresh air, and untainted water will have worked a minor miracle and you'll be refreshed, revitalized, and apple-cheeked—although perhaps a little short of breath.

Article 27   *Foreign Policy*, Winter 1994–95

"LURE" NORTH KOREA

Moon Young (Michael) Park

Moon Young (Michael) Park works as special aide to the defense attaché, embassy of the Republic of Korea, in Washington. The views expressed here are solely the author's and do not reflect the South Korean government's views.

On October 17, 1994, American and North Korean negotiators in Geneva reached an accord that seemed to be a major breakthrough in the 16 month-long negotiation over the alleged North Korean nuclear weapons bid. Coming after an excruciatingly difficult negotiation process and against the backdrop of Kim Il Sung's death and the inception of a new regime in Pyongyang, this accord may convince many that the North Korean nuclear challenge has finally been contained. But the international community has often been disappointed in the past. The world was elated when North Korea signed the Nuclear Non-proliferation Treaty, only to be shocked when it subsequently announced it would withdraw. It was hopeful when both South and North Korea reached an understanding to denuclearize the peninsula, only to be alarmed when it learned that Pyongyang was continuing its nuclear weapons program. The latest breakthrough is much more promising than the earlier developments, but the new accord will take years to fulfill. There will be many bumps along the road, and North Korea may again become intractable. It is imperative that we ready ourselves psychologically and politically for the journey.

In the past, the international community has not been well prepared to deal with North Korean obstinacy. It has repeatedly misjudged North Korean goals, South Korean interests, and Japanese reactions. Over the long run, it needs a totally new approach—one that avoids coercion or appeasement. The world must, through economic incentives, continue to "lure" North Korea toward a nonnuclear status.

Regrettably, the international community has failed to understand that the reason North Korea has repeatedly returned to a strategy of intractability is that the outside world has demonstrated unmistakably to Pyongyang that it fears the North's nuclear development as a *threat*. The preoccupation with North Korean nuclear acquisition as a threat has itself been an obstacle to reaching an accommodation. That is not to say that North Korea should be allowed to acquire nuclear weapons, but that by thinking of North Korea's nuclear ambitions as a threat the international community has failed and will fail to devise effective policies to solve the nuclear question per se and has neglected the related, but overriding, question of Korean unification.

To bolster the claim that North Korea poses a nuclear threat, some analysts and commentators have argued that North Korea will sell nuclear weapons technology to other rogue regimes. Yet what is missing from their presentation is recognition of the existing danger that rogue states will buy nuclear weapons technology from Russia, Ukraine, or other former Soviet republics. That present danger will continue to be greater than any potential one from North Korea.

Furthermore, some fear a nuclear North Korea on the grounds that it might use its nuclear weapons in an attempt to unify the country by force, or to impose its own terms on unification talks with South Korea. Others have suggested that North Korea's atomic armament could trigger a nuclear arms race in northeast Asia, with Seoul and Tokyo also choosing to go nuclear. Convincing though those worries may sound at first, they reflect a serious misunderstanding of nuclear military operations and of the history and politics of Northeast Asia.

Pyongyang cannot use nuclear weapons in a war against the South because it would backfire and be suicidal. It would contaminate the peninsula, thereby preventing North Korea from conducting its own conventional military operations. It would be as if the North dropped the bomb on its own head. We should not deceive ourselves by regarding the North Koreans as so stupid as to perform suicidal acts. Despite the label of "irrational" we assign to the North Koreans, their "irrational" acts have been very rational from their point of view—well-calculated, measured moves to achieve the regime's strategic objectives. Any political, military, or quasi-military acts thus far have served their strategic objectives of strengthening, prolonging, and enhancing their grip on power. Moreover, if North Korea were to use nuclear weapons in a war at all, it is clear that it would in turn be the victim of massive American retaliation, which would bring an end to the Pyongyang regime and to the habitability and productivity of the Korean peninsula for many years to come.

A Well-Prepared South

Those who assert that a nuclear North Korea would attack the South in order to unify the peninsula fail to understand the differences between the 1950–53 Korean War and the current situation. In 1950, the North attacked the South because it believed, first, that it could achieve strategic, operational, and tactical surprise and, therefore, promote a quick victory, allegedly unifying the country in three weeks; second, that it had the backing of both the Soviet Union and China; and finally, that the United States would not intervene, because it had declared several times that South Korea was not a vital U.S. interest or within its defense perimeter.

None of those factors apply now. The North knows that the South and the United States are watching each and every step its military takes; it knows too that these allies are no longer so gullible as to fall into the North's propagandistic trap and let their guard down as they did during the months leading up to June 25, 1950. In a war, the North might achieve some tactical surprises initially, but those successes would not be significant enough to lead to overall strategic or operational advantages. Nor will the North have the support from the Soviet Union or China it would need in a war. The Soviet Union that installed Kim Il Sung is long gone, and Russia

is more a friend to the South than it is to the North. Russia is contemplating a kind of military alliance with South Korea. China has made it clear, publicly and privately, to the North Koreans that it does not want the North to resort to hostilities; China wants disputes on the peninsula to be resolved peacefully. Finally, if the North attacked the South, Washington would certainly intervene and respond decisively to destroy the Pyongyang regime.

Because North Korea cannot use nuclear weapons in a war and because South Korea is covered by the American nuclear umbrella, the South has no reason to go nuclear. Its acquisition of nuclear weapons would not strengthen its military or political position, but rather weaken it. Becoming a nuclear weapon state would compromise its cooperation with the United States, which is key to solving the North Korean nuclear challenge. Seoul's going nuclear would also give Pyongyang more excuse to go (or stay) nuclear. In short, South Korea need not respond to North Korean nuclear weapons with nuclear weapons of its own. At the same time, South Korea can demonstrate its resolve and strength by maintaining its current legitimate conventional deterrent postures.

Nor would there be reason for Japan to go nuclear if North Korea were to gain nuclear weapons. War does not break out simply because one country has a nuclear weapon, but rather because political relations between the countries break down. Of course, in that case the country possessing nuclear bombs can make the other think twice about the steps it takes. However, despite the frequent tug of war between Pyongyang and Tokyo over various issues, there is no political reason for North Korea to attack Japan. Korea has never invaded Japan in its thousands of years of history, and today invasion remains unthinkable. It is true that the longer-range North Korean missiles may be able to reach Japan, and China for that matter, but a cooler-headed assessment indicates that it is less a reflection of political intent to attack Japan or China than an outcome of North Korea's advances in weapons technology. The North Koreans are sufficiently rational and calculating strategists to understand that raining missiles on Japan would only bring about their own destruction.

The fear that North Korean nuclearization will lead to Japan's is based on emotion in another way: It exaggerates the antagonism between North Korea and Japan. Although the Soviet Union fielded a massive nuclear force, Japan never went nuclear. The Soviet Union was (or Russia today is) more an enemy of Japan than is North Korea. The Soviet Union, and earlier Russia, fought Japan vigorously in the Russo-Japanese War of 1904–5 and at the end of World War II. Furthermore, significant territorial disputes persist between Russia and Japan over the Northern Territories seized by the USSR in World War

II. Still, Japan has never sought nuclear weapons. Ultimately, the reason for Japanese restraint has been that Japan is protected by the U.S. nuclear umbrella. Even if North Korea were to go nuclear, Japan would still be shielded by the U.S. umbrella. Unless that changes, even North Korea's going nuclear will not cause Japan to follow suit.

The world must, through economic incentives, continue to "lure" North Korea toward a nonnuclear status.

Despite the intense media and political attention, North Korea's possible nuclear capability is not a "threat," but a paper tiger. North Korea has worked toward a nuclear capability primarily because that capability is its sole source of diplomatic power: It elevates North Korea to the status of a sort of superpower—enabling it to play games with the big powers, reap the attention and respect it wants, and negotiate for what it needs. Even with the new agreement, North Korea probably will continue to take advantage of the psychological pressure that nuclear weapons generate, dangling the prospective dangers over America's head. Yet by and large those are dangers that the United States has subjected itself to because of its single-minded pursuit of nuclear nonproliferation, ignoring Korea's geohistorical context.

Given that North Korea's actual use of nuclear weapons is out of the question, the international community should take its nuclear development not as a threat but rather as a bluff. We should not allow the communists in Pyongyang to continue manipulating us. The regime will fall sooner or later, despite its nuclear capability; having the bomb will not save it, as was amply demonstrated by the collapse of the Soviet Union.

Given Pyongyang's apparent intentions, coercion or appeasement by the outside world will not do much to force the North to give up its nuclear design. Instead, the world must continue the process attempted in the new agreement to "lure" North Korea into giving up its weapons. We should not address North Korea's nuclear efforts in a direct manner, but rather indirectly.

Luring is a pragmatic, functional concept, not an ideological one like coercion or appeasement The tools of luring are, not surprisingly, economic. Whether hardlin-

ers or moderate reformists rule in Pyongyang, their biggest enemy is their wretched economy, not the outside world. There are many signs that their economy may bring about the destruction of the country and an end to the regime. The North is seeking help from the outside world, including the United States and Japan, to improve its economy.

The big powers and South Korea should now concentrate on luring the North into an alliance of sorts to improve its economy. They can show the North Koreans that they refuse to be either their enemy or their appeaser, but that they can become a functional problem-solver for the North's economic plight. One example of how such pragmatism can reign are the ties between China and South Korea; they have established a functional problem-solving relationship on the economic front, setting aside their legacy of the brutal fighting in the Korean War and sharp ideological differences ever since. China and South Korea are neither friends nor enemies. The same sort of relationship can be worked out between the outside world and North Korea.

The indirect approach can be more effective in solving the nuclear question both in the short and long term. Nuclear bombs are useless in attacking North Korea's biggest enemy, its economy, and the nuclear effort even aggravates Pyongyang's economic crisis by draining away human and technological resources. The outside world has, in effect, proposed to North Korea that it is willing to buy its nuclear bombs in exchange for assistance on North Korea's economy. For both sides it will create a win-win situation that could end the nuclear question while promoting North Korea's economic development. Such a tradeoff will eventually be conducive to Korean unification. That approach will no doubt be costly in monetary terms, but its cost is marginal compared to the human lives and wealth that would be destroyed if war—or the objective of nuclear nonproliferation—were to return to the Korean peninsula. Nonproliferation purists should remember that the ultimate aim of nonproliferation is peace and stability. As long as we maintain peace now, anything is possible; time is on our side.

Buying North Korea's nuclear capability also eases the prospect that North Korea will sell bombs to rogue groups. If North Korea wants to sell nuclear technology, it is because it needs money, not because it wants to support rogue ideologies. Therefore, because the whole international community would benefit from ending the North Korean nuclear bid, it should participate in providing assistance to North Korea. The United States, South Korea, Japan, China, and Russia should not bear the entire burden.

There is a precedent for exchanging a country's nuclear capability for economic aid. It is Ukraine. With the breakup of the Soviet Union and the end of the Cold War, Ukraine became a nuclear power. Yet the international community did not try to prevent Ukraine from keeping nuclear weapons by sanctions or threats of war. It instead worked out a formula by which Ukraine is turning over its nuclear arsenal to Russia in return for economic aid. The "Ukraine Formula" offers us a good example of luring. As a functional, and not an ideological, solution, it is more workable in North Korea than is confrontation or appeasement. If the United States believes it is wise for the international community to spend billions of dollars to help former enemies, Ukraine and Russia, with nuclear disarmament and economic development in the belief that their stability and democracy are vital for the United States and the whole world, then it and other countries can do the same with North Korea. They will help solve the North Korean question and promote Korean unification at the same time.

Nonproliferation through Unification

There are two reasons why luring is better than coercion or appeasement. First, both coercion and appeasement work in favor of the hardliners in Pyongyang. Coercion will be used by its hard-line leadership as a pretext to mobilize North Koreans in their cause, portraying the foreign powers as an enemy intent upon destroying North Korea. Conversely, appeasement will be used by the hardliners as a pretext to maintain stubborn positions in order to exact more of what North Korea wants from the outside world.

Second, the cold reality is that because nuclear potential is North Korea's sole source of diplomatic power, the nuclear question will not be completely solved before Korean unification—despite the recent breakthrough. It will remain a problem as long as North Korea exists. In fact, the key to solving the North Korean nuclear issue is in the minds of the North Koreans themselves. Unless we promote changes in North Koreans' rigid minds, there will be no genuine solution to the nuclear quagmire. The only way to change their minds is to cause them to see things from different viewpoints—to cause them to abandon their parochial, myopic vision. It will, of course, take a long time, but patience is a better option than military clashes that will kill hundreds of thousands of innocent people on both sides. Time is on our side.

We should be patient enough to establish extensive economic relationships with North Korea. The new wealth will produce cracks in the old, rigid North Korean thinking as new, younger leaders—concerned with economic progress and compassion for their people—surface within the Pyongyang regime. If the death of Kim Il Sung taught us anything, it is that we were wise not to have struck at North Korea precipitously.

When talk of war in Washington was loud, South Koreans resented the ignorance of American analysts and policymakers about their concerns. Their lives and wealth would have been destroyed by a headlong rush into military action. The country South Koreans have built up working night and day over four decades since the Korean War would have been demolished. Quite simply, war was not an option, and South Koreans questioned why it would be considered as such just when trade between North and South Korea seemed to be offering an opening to a better relationship. Indeed, even as rhetoric over the nuclear controversy raged, trade between the North and the South maintained its tenacious life.

Strange as it may seem to Americans fixated single-mindedly on nonproliferation, the best solution remains to snub North Korea's nuclear bid—to refuse to show Pyongyang that its nuclear attempt was viewed as a threat—and then to begin developing extensive economic relationships with North Korea. Providing North Korea with assistance to obtain light-water reactors and establishing liaison offices between Seoul and Pyongyang and between Pyongyang and Washington can be good first steps in this strategy of luring North Korea into the world community. Cultural exchanges, visits by the new North Korean leadership to the United States designed to open the minds of North Koreans, and even summit meetings between Pyongyang and Seoul and among Pyongyang, Seoul, and Washington, perhaps even talks similar to the Camp David Mideast talks, can follow as part of such an effort.

If the economic approach proves successful, it will enhance the chances for Korean unification by peaceful means and under democratic rule because time is on the side of democracy. And if Korean unification is thus achieved, the nuclear question can be resolved with the democratic government of a single Korea transferring the nuclear leftovers to the United States, fulfilling its non-nuclear declarations.

Article 28   *The Christian Science Monitor,* July 20, 1994

War in the Pacific: Legacy of a Copper Mine

Bougainvilleans have fought six years to save their land and environment and seek independence from Papua New Guinea

Catherine Foster

Staff writer of The Christian Science Monitor

SYDNEY

A war festers in the southern Pacific. It is the first in this ocean basin since World War II, and, at six years, has lasted longer.

The conflict on the small island of Bougainville involves traditional landowners, rebellious islanders, the remote governing authority of Papua New Guinea (PNG), and Australia, a former colonial power. At the center lies a theme echoed in many parts of the world: an indigenous people's struggle against economic exploitation by global industrial interests.

It is also about independence. The Bougainvilleans want to be united again with the Solomon Islands, with which they are culturally and racially allied. Ripples of this desire for independence are spreading. Other small islands around PNG, and one section of the PNG mainland, are talking about uniting to form an independent federation of Melanesian states.

The war began six years ago when the Bougainville Revolutionary Army (BRA)—made up of various island landowners and their supporters—succeeded in forcing the shutdown of a tremendously profitable copper mine owned by an Australian mining interest. In retaliation, the PNG Defense Forces (PNGDF) threw a blockade around the island. But this has not prevented a handful of BRA boat captains from running the blockade to bring in supplies from the Solomon Islands.

The conflict raises difficult questions for Australia, which from 1919 until 1975 had control over PNG. Now its largest aid donor, Australia, is inadvertently funding this war at a time when it is trying to integrate itself into the economically vibrant Asia-Pacific region. Peace talks have begun, but have shown little sign of success.

Wars over the Solomon Islands tend to be dramatic. Fifty years ago, in the climax of a bitter campaign over the Solomons, Allied forces shot down the plane carrying Admiral Yamamoto Isoroku, commander-in-chief of the Imperial Japanese Navy and architect of the attack on Pearl Harbor, over Bougainville. His body was recovered sitting upright against a tree, his left hand still clutching his Samurai sword, according to Japanese accounts.

The remnants of that war have found a new use: The BRA, armed at first with crossbows and axes, has fashioned homemade guns using ammunition salvaged from World War II wrecks.

When the Panguna mine was first proposed in the 1960s, many Bougainvilleans were distrustful of it. The mine was operated by Bougainville Copper Ltd., a subsidiary of Conzinc Riotinto Australia, whose largest shareholder is the enormous London-based RTZ Corp. Roads, port facilities, power generators, the town of Arawa, and workers' housing were built, along with health, educational, and sporting facilities.

Many traditional landowners, however, felt they were being insufficiently compensated by the mining company.

Staff

They also had grave concerns over increasing environmental damage. Francis Ona, now the leader of the BRA, walked out of a meeting in 1988 at which an environmental impact report, commissioned by the PNG government, was released. He called the report a whitewash.

The BRA initially tried various forms of civil disobedience. But when negotiations failed, it turned to sabotage. Riots broke out in the northern part of the island. The mine closed May 17, 1989, and Mr. Ona declared an independent Republic of Bougainville. A month later, the PNG government announced a state of emergency, and in July, helicopters arrived from the Australian government.

Official reports say 2,000 people have died in the war itself, and many others from a lack of medical care. In what has been called the St. Valentine's Day massacre of February 1990, the bodies of five people were dropped off at sea from an Australia-donated helicopter flown by the PNGDF.

An Amnesty International report last November said both sides have committed human rights abuses. It found that the PNGDF had been murdering and torturing suspected opponents. But BRA members reportedly have committed serious abuses, too, including summary executions, torture, and rape. The report said that although the PNG government had claimed to have investigated alleged violations by its troops and punished those responsible, official findings have never been made public. There has been little evidence of judicial or disciplinary proceedings against soldiers suspected of human rights abuses.

This puts Australia in an awkward position. It has given substantial amounts of aid to PNG since its independence. In 1993–94, PNG will receive an estimated $249.3 million in aid, one-quarter of Australia's total foreign-aid bill. Only last year strings were attached to the aid.

An Australian congressional delegation traveled to PNG recently to assess the situation. Its report, released June 8, said that Australia should allocate $7.3 million over the next several years specifically for health and education projects in Bougainville—if the peace process continues. This would be a substantial increase over the $3.6 million earmarked for the island since 1991. The Australian delegation concluded that a military solution is not possible.

There are signs that both sides are tiring of the war. Talks between high-level officials of the PNG government and the BRA took place on the Solomon Islands in June, but were cut off by the government.

PNG Foreign Minister Sir Julius Chan announced in June that he was trying to get other small Pacific island nations to help form a Pacific peacekeeping force to calm things down and start a cease-fire process.

In a related development, the South Pacific Forum meeting in Brisbane on Aug. 1 will for the first time have Bougainville on its agenda. This move was prompted by PNG's wish to discuss the formation of a peacekeeping force.

"The situation in PNG-Bougainville does give us more cause for optimism than we've had for some time," says Australian Foreign Minister Gareth Evans.

Political developments just ahead could open new lines of communication. The Solomon Islands' government is up for a vote of confidence soon. If Solomon Mamaloni, a former prime minister sympathetic to the plight of Bougainvilleans, is elected, it is felt that supply lines to Bougainville might be expanded. And in PNG, the government of Prime Minister Paias Wingti also faces a vote of confidence in the next few weeks. There is tension between him and Foreign Minister Chan, who more strongly supports peace talks.

Article 29

Multinational Monitor, January/February 1994

The Politics of Economic Chaos in the Philippines

Robert Weissman

MANILA—Philippine President Fidel Ramos fears the future may be slipping away.

The gap between the booming economies of the Asian tigers (Taiwan, South Korea, Hong Kong and Singapore) and the emerging tigers (Malaysia, Thailand), and the Philippines is huge and growing. While the 1991 Philippine per capita gross national product was $730, the per capita GNP in Thailand was $1,570 and $6,330 in South Korea. These countries grew rapidly in the 1980s, but the Philippine economy constricted; the Philippines' average growth rate from 1980 to 1991 was negative 1.2 percent, while Thailand achieved a 5.9 percent annual growth rate and South Korea 8.7 percent. And the disparity shows no sign of narrowing; all of its regional competitors registered significantly higher growth rates in 1993 than the Philippines' estimated rate of approximately 1 percent. Even nearby competitor Indonesia is preparing to pass the Philippines in per capita income.

Signs of the economic chaos besetting the Philippines are apparent to even the most casual observer in Manila.

Poor families, mostly immigrants from the countryside, have established squatter communities throughout the Philippine capital. Virtually every Manila neighborhood is now dotted with shanties; the only exceptions are the most exclusive, guarded enclaves, which stand as a testament to the country's extreme concentration of wealth. In neighborhoods with names like Forbes Park and Bel Air, streets are blocked and guarded, the mansions within accessible only to residents and authorized visitors.

Thousands of Filipinos support themselves by sifting through huge garbage dumps in Manila, pulling scrap metal and other items for recycling or reuse out of people's trash. The scene is repeated in other big Philippine cities, though on

©Robert Weissman

Dumpsite community outside of Baguio City.

a smaller scale. Dump-site residents are among the poorest of the huge numbers of Filipinos living below the poverty line. The government's official statistics show 40 percent of the nation's 66 million citizens living in poverty, but the actual percentage is undoubtedly far higher.

At crowded intersections all over the city, vendors rush to cars and buses caught in Manila's paralyzing traffic, offering to sell cigarettes, gum, candy, newspapers or trinkets. The cigarettes are sold individually, not by the pack, to accommodate the tiny budgets of most Filipinos. Some of the vendors are

©Robert Weissman

Sifting trash outside of Baguio City.

adults, but many are children, 10 or 11 years old. An estimated two-thirds of Philippine children work.

Taxi drivers explain to foreign passengers that their dream is to improve their English so they can get a job abroad. People throughout the city—even those with steady jobs—echo the sentiment. They have given up hope of succeeding economically in their own country; instead, women aspire to work as foreign domestics, and men hope for shipping or construction jobs with foreign companies.

Ear-shattering noise plagues the streets in office districts of downtown Manila, the result of small, private electricity generators operated by individual stores and office buildings during the city's daily brownouts. For more than a year, the energy shortage on the main island of Luzon has caused daily brownouts lasting 4 to 12 hours. The resulting loss to industrial and commercial output has been immense; the difficulties imposed on individuals in the form of lost wages, wasted time—much of it literally spent in the dark—and discomfort are incalculable.

Despite his worries and the economic and social misery so pervasive in Manila—and equally apparent in the desperately poor countryside—Ramos is optimistic about the future. He expects to go down in history as the man who transformed the Philippines from an economic basket case to an economic powerhouse similar to the Asian tigers.

Ramos' vision

Ramos's plan for economic rejuvenation, known as the Philippines 2000 program, aims to have the country join the NIC (newly industrializing country) family by the year 2000. Its ambitious outlines are contained in the Philippine Medium-Term Development Plan (MTDP) for the years 1993–1998. Ramos says the MTDP "embodies the vision of a nation empowered, its human resources stretched to optimal capacity, and its industries, products and services of world-class standard."

The MTDP is a comprehensive plan covering all aspects of the Philippine economy. Plan policy goals range from deregulating the financial sector and removing investment restrictions on foreign banks to improving scholastic physical education programs.

The plan establishes formidable targets. By 1998, it calls for: achieving a growth rate of 10 percent; lowering the number of families in poverty by 10 percent; increasing the national investment rate by one-half; and more than doubling the annual rate of export growth to a level of 27.1 percent.

The soaring rhetoric of the plan offers something for everyone. The MTDP promises free market disciples, for example, that the Philippines will "reduce government intervention in the production, marketing and processing of agricultural inputs and outputs," and "discard traditional trade and industrial policies that dispense protection to domestic industries." At the same time, it assures environmentalists that the government will "play its role as custodian of the environment for future unborn generations and give the attention needed to rehabilitating and preserving the country's environmental stock."

The central prongs of the MTDP, however, are much narrower than the plan's rhetorical aspirations. Attracting foreign investment—in manufacturing, in resource-extractive industries such as mining and logging and in the energy sector—is the key element of plan. New foreign and domestic investment in the manufacturing sector will be directed into 15 Regional Industrial Centers (RICs). Geographically dispersed throughout the country, the RICs will function as expanded export processing zones, offering tax breaks and other government incentives and sound infrastructure support (telephone, roads, ports, etc.). The other, complimentary emphases of the plan are to orient both the manufacturing and agricultural sectors toward exports, and to increase government investment in infrastructure.

While Ramos touts Philippines 2000 as representing a bold, new start for the Philippines, grassroots critics of the plan label it nothing more than failed, free-market, foreign-investment-reliant policies presented in new packaging. As Ramos begins to put the program into place, opposition to Philippines 2000 is intensifying among a wide variety of popular sectors.

Militarized "development"

Throughout the Philippines, land and labor conflicts are emerging in areas newly scheduled for "development" under the MTDP, and are continuing and intensifying in areas where the MTDP proposes building on existing projects and developments. With all social conflict in the Philippines taking place against the backdrop of the government's war against the two-decade-long rebel insurgency of the leftist New People's Army (NPA), opposition to Philippines 2000 projects often evokes a violent response from the military.

The Regional Industrial Centers are quickly establishing themselves as a focal point for the battles engendered by the Philippines 2000 program. The Calabarzon RIC, which will build on the economic processing zones, industrial estates and industrial parks established under Marcos and Aquino, is illustrative.

The announcement of plans to create an RIC in Calabarzon—an area combining pieces of five provinces south of Manila—led to rampant land speculation and the expulsion of poor farmers from their land, says Rafael Mariano, former acting chair of the peasant association KMP. Large landowners successfully circumvented the land reform program by converting their lands from agricultural to industrial purposes; the landowners got even richer, and the tenant farmers who had previously worked these lands were evicted.

Labor abuses in the factories established in Calabarzon have been rife, according to Norma Binas, assistant secretary of the KMU labor center's international department. The provincial governments in these areas are stridently anti-union; the governor of Cavite province, Juanito Remulla, has even pledged to enforce a "no union, no strike" policy. (The U.S. Department of Commerce, in a Philippines "Investment Climate Summary," notes that Cavite "enjoy[s] a reputation for being actively 'pro-business,' and has reaped the rewards of new investments.") Companies already operating in the Calabarzon economic zones—mostly Japanese, Taiwanese, South Korean, Hong Kong or Singaporean garment and light manufacturers—aggressively deny their employees' right to organize and commonly abuse their workers, particularly women, who are frequently sexually harassed. The KMU reports that employers routinely fire workers engaged in union organizing activity, and carefully question potential employees about their attitudes toward unions in an attempt to screen out any union sympathizers. Armed guards—from the local police, special economic zone police, a special Calabarzon-wide police force or private security forces—stand at the gates of the economic zones, preventing organizers from entering and intimidating the workers within.

The entire Calabarzon region itself has in fact been militarized, according to Reynaldo Quindara, deputy secretary general for internal affairs of the Ecumenical Movement for Justice and Peace. He says that the government has deployed large number of troops both to protect foreign and domestic invest-

ments from sabotage by the NPA and to discourage independent civilian activists from challenging Philippines 2000 projects and developments.

Generally, Quindara says, the RICs and Philippines 2000 projects are becoming a magnet for mass troop deployments, with many new or ongoing military operations being carried out in close proximity to areas planned to be used for RICs, agrarian export projects connected to the MTDP or development projects tied to the MTDP. Examples include military action in Agusan del Sur in Northern Mindanao, targeted to develop tree and palm oil plantations, and in Western Mindanao, where the government is encouraging resort development and growing vegetables for export. In the Philippines, large-scale deployments like those in Calabarzon, Agusan del Sur and Western Mindanao are often accompanied by widespread harassment of civilians, as well as arbitrary arrests, torture and extrajudicial killings.

MTDP-related violence has also wracked the island of Cebu, the other province which the U.S. Department of Commerce denotes as having a pro-business reputation. At least four peasants were killed on Cebu in the first six months of 1993, apparently because of their efforts to prevent landlords from taking advantage of the opportunities offered by Ramos's Philippines 2000 plan by converting agricultural land into residential and tourist properties. In the case of scenic Cebu, Ramos's commitment to expanding tourism provides a special incentive for such conversion. There is suspicion that two of the murdered peasants were killed by thugs employed by a real estate company, a third by a city councillor associated with a local vigilante group and the fourth by unknown assailants.

Philippines 2000 and indigenous communities

Indigenous peoples' communities are likely to be particularly affected by the large infrastructure projects and major resource-extractive activities proposed in Ramos's economic plan.

The conflict over the Chico Dam, a massive hydroelectric project called off in the mid-1980s, may well be a prototype of the disputes likely to proliferate with the pursuit of the MTDP. The giant hydro project would have dammed the Chico River and displaced thousands of indigenous people in the mountainous five-province Cordillera region in Northern Luzon. Local opposition was intense, and included large demonstrations, civil disobedience (such as lying in front of bulldozers) and a world-famous event at which protesting women bared their chests to shame soldiers in a civilian face-off with the military—as well as armed resistance in collaboration with the NPA. The unprecedented local resistance, combined with international opposition from environmentalists and solidarity organizations, eventually led the World Bank, which had sponsored the project, to call it off. But leaders of the anti-dam struggle were killed during the conflict, and the military committed widespread human rights violations against the mobilized villages.

The Cordillera has remained a hotbed of opposition to the government since the Chico Dam struggle, supporting both civilian and guerrilla resistance movements. Consequently, the region has been a prime target of the military's counterinsurgency program. With new unrest expected as a result of the MTDP, military action against Cordillera civilians is not likely to end any time soon.

The government is now planning a series of 17 so-called mini-dams for the Cordillera region as part of the MTDP. While "mini" connotes the idea of low-impact and sustainability, Dr. Contancio Claver, executive director of the Community Health

Concerns for Kalinga-Apayao, a community health center serving residents of the Cordillera, points out that the rivers which the government has proposed damming are substantial rivers with significant currents. "It is hard to imagine how there can be 'mini-dams' in relatively large rivers," he says. Local residents and outside environmentalists alike fear the new dams will still be large, even if they are not as huge as the originally proposed Chico Dam, and will displace hundreds or thousands of local indigenous people.

For the time being, says Claver, "the people are suspicious but have not yet made up their minds to totally oppose" the dam projects. However, if their fears about the size of the dams are realized, massive resistance is almost guaranteed, and the government's response may well be to further militarize the

region and intensify its repression of the indigenous population.

The root problem in the Cordillera, says Father Eddie Balicao of the Office for Cordillera Peoples' Concerns, is longstanding "laws which have made the Cordillera a resource base for exploitation without even considering what the Cordillera people think." Development projects undertaken as part of the MTDP are likely to exacerbate this enduring problem.

Pushing past the ecological limits

Despite its rhetorical promises to the contrary, the Philippines 2000 program is likely to further devastate the country's already battered environment. As they have in other initiatives over the last several decades, government and private invest-

Economic Shocks

OLONGAPO, PHILIPPINES—The last few years have been viciously cruel to the people of central Luzon. They have had to absorb not only the economic recession that has struck the whole country, but the twin blows of the eruption of Mt. Pinatubo and the closing of the economic centerpieces of the region, the U.S.-operated Clark Air Field and Subic Bay Naval Base.

Food or free trade zones

The desperation of the region's situation is apparent at the foot of Mt. Pinatubo, within the confines of the fence encircling what used to be the U.S. military outpost at Clark. Of the thousands of families who had their homes destroyed by the Pinatubo blast, hundreds now live at Clark, many of them in overcrowded, leaky tents.

"Food is our number one problem here," says one leader of the resettlement community. "We get some from non-governmental organizations, but we often eat only a couple meals a day, and the kids often go hungry." He adds, "Sickness is a major problem because of the tight living conditions," poor sanitation and difficulty in acquiring medicine. The refugees have little money, since virtually all of them are unemployed.

The refugees are demanding that they be allowed to establish permanent dwellings on the base, and that they be allowed to grow crops on its extensive open fields. The government opposes the idea; it wants to turn Clark into a free trade zone or an international airport, and government officials believe having a poor community in close proximity is not likely to be appreciated either by foreign investors or visitors.

Unfortunately for residents of the area, the Pinatubo problem is an ongoing one. The rainy reason causes massive mud and volcanic ash flows that are expected to continue for years. A government project to build a

20-kilometer-long dike has run behind schedule, resulting in the burial of still more communities during the past rainy season.

A baseless economy

The closure of Clark and Subic has hit the region as hard as the Pinatubo eruption.

In September 1991, three months after Mount Pinatubo erupted, the Philippine Senate, in a rare display of independent nationalism, voted not to renew the U.S. bases agreement. The U.S. Air Force withdrew from Clarke in 1991 and the Navy completed its pull-out from Subic in November 1992.

Progressive forces in the Philippines had long demanded the withdrawal of the U.S. forces, but no one was ready for a sudden pullout. The closure threw 70,000 base workers out of work, according to Manuel Torres, chair of the Workers' Alliance of Region III, a Central Luzon labor alliance affiliated with the KMU labor center. Twenty-two thousand of these workers were direct employees on the bases; the rest worked as subcontractors, domestics for U.S. soldiers or in similar positions. Today, Torres reports, the region's unemployment rate stands at 18 percent.

The thousands of sex workers who had served U.S. soldiers at the bases were particularly hard hit by the closings. Ten thousand women worked in 300 to 500 bars when the bases were open, says Pearly Bulawan of the Buklod Center, a community center serving women sex workers. Now there are only 1,000 sex workers, catering primarily to Taiwanese, Japanese and Filipino tourists.

Buklod conducts a variety of skills training and livelihood programs, to teach and provide work for sex

ment in infrastructure projects and resource-extractive activities are likely to have severe environmental effects. The mini-dams and other energy projects may submerge large land areas and create dangerous local pollution problems; and if the government decides to press ahead with opening the Bataan nuclear power plant, the country will be burdened with an immense environmental and public health hazard. New or expanded mining projects are likely to pollute rivers and thousands of people's water supplies with waste-rock and treatment chemicals; the timber industry is likely to continue overlogging of the country's fast-diminishing forests; foreign and domestic fishing companies are likely to overharvest local fisheries.

However, the most significant ecological damage may stem from the increasing inequity of the country's land distribution scheme. The Ramos administration is exhibiting virtually no political will to push through a land reform program. (The KMP's Mariano says that "while the Aquino administration made many empty promises, the Ramos government just sides with the big landlords.") Many landowners are eagerly converting their land to non-agricultural uses or export crop production in order to take advantage of the opportunities posed by the MTDP, and increasing numbers of poor farmers are becoming landless. These displaced rural people have few options but to encroach on forests and other marginal public lands.

Recent Philippine history demonstrates how harmful the ecological consequences of rural displacement can be. Rural uprootedness and increasing landlessness were the proximate causes of the worst environmental effects of the structural adjustment program implemented in the 1980s at the behest of the World Bank and International Monetary Fund, according

---

workers who want to opt out of the business or who can no longer support themselves, but the organization's small soapmaking and dressmaking projects are hardly enough to meet the needs of most of the unemployed women.

The post-bases transition has been particularly difficult for the generally poorly educated and low-skilled unemployed sex workers, the majority of whom came from the provinces in search of a means to make money. A large number have returned to their homes in the countryside, where jobs are scarce and where many, as former prostitutes, will be stigmatized. Others have moved to Manila, seeking sex work or jobs as domestics. Some of the women have remained in the region, working as laundresses or in odd jobs.

A lost opportunity

Much of the tragedy which has befallen Central Luzon could have been averted. The volcano eruption could not have been prevented, but a more efficient handling of the dike-building would have saved many communities, and a more humane assistance package could have been offered to volcano refugees. More significantly, if the U.S. withdrawal from the bases had not been so sudden, and had the government put in place a sound conversion plan, the economic shock of the closure would have been mostly alleviated.

Economic conversion of the bases was a viable option, contends Torres. "The Americans were just overseers; it was Filipinos who were operating the [civilian side] of the base," he says. "All the work was done by Philippine personnel."

Torres points to the example of ship building, an area in which Philippine workers had accumulated important skills. "All that we needed to do was change customers, from the U.S. military to commercial buyers," he says. "That would have spawned so many local industries" and enabled the country to build up a deep-sea fishing industry and otherwise take advantage of the surrounding sea.

But the Philippine authorities, under the leadership of Richard Gordon, head of the Subic Bay Metropolitan Authority, have a different vision—one that calls for integrating the bases into the Ramos administration's Philippines 2000 program. To much international acclaim, Gordon is pressing ahead with plans to convert Subic into a free trade port; plans for Clark remain uncertain.

Many local residents are pinning their hopes on Gordon's project. Bonje, who works in one of the remaining clubs in Olongapo, near Subic, says she hopes that unemployed former sex workers will be able to find work as employees of the new Subic businesses, and maybe even given preferred hiring status. The Philippine experience with free trade zones, however, suggests that the Subic free port—even if it succeeds in attracting foreign investment—will not do much to improve the lives of workers or nearby communities.

Torres sees Gordon's plans as a tragically lost opportunity to pursue a development path different than the one represented by the free trade zones. Proposals for developing self-reliant Philippine industry and harnessing the talents of the former base workers are of little relevance in the context of Gordon's efforts. Torres says, "All those conversion ideas are now difficult even to suggest because of the whole framework of Ramos's Philippines 2000 and the foreign-oriented scheme of Gordon."

—Robert Weissman and Stephanie Donne

to a recent World Resources Institute study. As unemployment rose, the study found, "only the marginal resources in the public domain—forest lands, mangroves and fisheries—remained available to a rapidly growing pool of landless workers." Many unemployed and landless people in the countryside migrated, not on the traditional path to Manila, but from lowland to upland rural and coastal areas—from the lowlands of Central Luzon to the mountain provinces of the Cordillera and from the lowlands of the central Philippine islands to the uplands of the southern island of Mindanao. As these workers "migrated to the open access resources of the uplands and coastal areas, deforestation, soil erosion, the destruction of coastal habitats and the depletion of fisheries increased," the World Resources Institute report concluded.

A blurry vision

Perhaps the worst indictment of the Philippines 2000 program is that despite its social and environmental costs, it is not likely to deliver the benefits which it is designed to produce. Critics denounce the program as unrealistic and based on a misreading of the success of the East Asian tigers, and they say it fails to grapple seriously with the central Philippine political and economic problem—the highly stratified distribution of land.

The first problem identified by critics is that the MTDP aims too high and stretches too far. They say that it really is no more than an arbitrary and exhortory political wish list. One financial analyst comments that the MTDP "is more of a declaration of intent than a plan as such." A plan, he says, would imply the imposition of a concrete schedule, detailed policies to achieve specified goals and a means to finance agreed-upon programs.

Many elements of the MTDP reflect the personal interests of Ramos and the imperatives of Philippine politics rather than sound economic planning, confirms Maria Rina Rosales, a senior economic development specialist with the Philippine National Economic Development Agency (NEDA). For example, says Rosales, NEDA economists recognized the goal of achieving a 10 percent growth rate by 1998 as being wholly unrealistic—but it was included in the MTDP because Ramos insisted on setting a target of double digit growth. The country has already failed to meet the 1993 goal of a 4.5 percent growth rate, indicating that there is little chance of achieving the MTDP's overall goal of a five-year 7.5 percent growth rate. Similarly, Rosales says, NEDA economists acknowledge that the goal of establishing a RIC in each region of the country is unrealistic, but it was included to avoid criticisms from excepted regions.

More generally, there is virtually no chance of the government achieving its goal of turning the Philippines into a NIC by 2000. As Filomeno Sta. Ana, secretary general of the Manila-based Freedom From Debt Coalition, notes, "The NIC goal of the Ramos administration has no long-term vision." He explains, "fulfilling the vision of NIC is not an overnight affair. A giant leap towards industrialization begins with many small steps. . . . And the whole process spans decades, involving a complex but coherent and comprehensive set of measures for reform and transformation."

A second major criticism is that the MTDP's emphasis on recycled policies of export-oriented industrialization and foreign investment is not likely to help the economy escape from the rut in which it lies. In 1979, Ferdinand Marcos said, "Industrialization for exports—this is what we in government . . . proclaim and I think by and large we accept this as the fundamental thrust of our national economy today. There is a natural and necessary correlation between our new industrialization program and our export expansion program which stands at the forefront of our national economic goals today. Marcos' words could have been spoken by Ramos in 1993. There is very little substantive difference between Marcos' export processing zones and Ramos's regional industrial centers, except perhaps that Ramos is promising companies bigger tax breaks and subsidies. What failed under Marcos is not likely to succeed under Ramos.

A third criticism voiced by economists like Sta. Ana is that Ramos is making a crucial error in his attempt to mimic the

Staying the Course

From the perspective of the international financial community, the Philippine economy is already on the right track. They applaud the Aquino government's decision to honor the country's foreign debt; the Foreign Investments Act of 1991, which permits up to 100 percent ownership of companies engaged in all but a few sectors, as well as in firms exporting at least 60 percent of production; and government steps taken in 1992 to liberalize the exchange rate. "The government has already done a serious job" of undertaking reforms, says one international financial analyst. He points to the country's build-up of foreign exchange reserves over the last two years and its recent rapid export-earning growth (11 percent in 1992 and 15 percent in 1993) as signs of the country's upswing.

The financial community is concerned that the government has operated without a formal agreement with the International Monetary Fund since April 1993, a condition which prevents the government from obtaining new foreign loans and forces it to pay in full interest and principal on maturing obligations. However, analysts note with satisfaction, the single issue preventing consummation of a new IMF standing agreement is the government's chronic budget deficit—not the basic structure of the economy.

An economic turnaround driven by foreign investment will slowly come to the Philippines is the position of financial analysts. Building credibility with foreign investors will take time; the Philippines should maintain its present course and stay patient.

Patience, however, is not a viable option for Fidel Ramos.

—R.W.

success of the Asian tigers. In the early stages of industrialization, the tigers did not open their economies to foreign investment and trade and pursue an export-oriented strategy, Sta. Ana notes. Instead, they devoted attention to building up their internal markets; they protected domestic producers; and they limited foreign investment.

A fourth point of contention is the bankruptcy of the notion of "competitiveness" which underlies Ramos's foreign-investment-dependent, export-oriented strategy. As an Asian country with a poorly developed infrastructure and little history of domestically controlled high-tech production, the Philippines has little to offer foreign investors besides low wages, a point conceded by NEDA economist Rosales. But the Philippines is not especially well positioned to compete on the basis of low wages; the country's four-dollar-a-day minimum wage rate is not low enough to compete with Vietnam, China or Indonesia, countries where wages range as low as a dollar a day or less.

"Can we compete with China in the export market?" asks Sta. Ana. "Their labor is much cheaper than ours. The distorted logic, of course, is for us to cheapen our labor further. And that is not the way."

A final—and probably the most important—criticism of the MTDP is that it fails to deal seriously with the country's overriding political and economic problem: land reform. In 1988, according to Department of Agrarian Reform statistics reported by researcher James Putzel, 3,235 land owners (about .2 percent of a total of more than 1.5 million), owned almost one-quarter of the agricultural land in the Philippines, and land ownership is becoming increasingly concentrated.

"Unless the problem of landlessness is addressed first, a 'NIC-hood' development strategy could not only fail but lead to economic disaster," says the KMP's Mariano, noting the dangers of pushing more farmers off the land without providing any jobs for them to fill.

The refusal to confront the powerful agrarian elite and force through a genuine land reform may be sufficient to doom Ramos's Philippines 2000 program to failure, even on its own terms. The achievement of a relatively egalitarian land distribution regime has been a prerequisite to the successes of the Asian tigers. "Study of the industrial transformation of previously agrarian economies—from Japan to the NICs—shows that agrarian reform plays a key role in breaking down the social base, releasing the energies of the peasantry and opening up the possibility for transformation from a feudal to industrial economy," says Satur Ocampo, spokesperson for the National Democratic Front, the political wing of the rebel New People's Army.

Ocampo and others emphasize that land reforms in the Asian tigers helped jumpstart the domestic market by creating a significant market of rural consumers for both agricultural inputs and some consumer goods; reduced the pressure on the rural poor to migrate to the cities by giving them a base to support themselves; and helped equalize labor market conditions in the manufacturing sector by strengthening the bargaining position of workers for whom the option of returning to the countryside became more viable.

Who benefits?

For the last few decades, "Development for whom?" has been the virtual mantra of Filipino activists as they confront one development scheme after another. At first hearing, their question sounds like a demand that the costs and benefits of development be widely and fairly distributed. It is that, but it is a more profound challenge as well.

Sustainable development activists—whether they come out of the labor, environmental, indigenous rights or underground movement—are challenging conventional top-down, foreign-dependent economic development models as inherently unable to improve the well-being of most Filipinos. In the context of recent Philippine experience, "Development for whom?" is an incisive critique of development programs that promise to benefit the elite while hurting the majority and, on balance, worsening the country's economic, environmental and social conditions.

Relentless in their efforts, these activists continue to pose their troubling question, now about Ramos's Philippines 2000 program—and their answer remains disturbing. As Ocampo succinctly says, the Philippines 2000 program is another in a long line of government programs that "fail to consider a lot of factors. It is always the people who are left suffering the consequences of neglect and skewed priorities."

Article 30   *Current History*, December 1994

Social Values, Singapore Style

The city-state Singapore has become an economic powerhouse under a democratically elected government dominated by one party that exercises a high degree of social control. Prime Minister Goh Chok Tong expounds on what he considers the secret of Singapore's success in "Moral Values: The Foundation of a Vibrant State," an address at a National Day rally this August 21.

Four years ago, I could not have predicted that we would do so well. Last year's growth of 9.9 percent was extraordinary. Its momentum has carried over to this year. We grew by 10.5 percent for the first half of this year. Even if the economy slows down in the second half, we should still end the year with more than 9 percent growth, which means civil servants will get a special bonus.

Our strong economic performance translated into higher wages and better schools, housing, and health care. Everyone has benefited, not just big businessmen, the graduates and professionals, but also small businessmen, workers, stall-owners, and taxi drivers.

Singaporeans living in Housing and Development Board [HDB] flats have seen big improvements in their standard of living. They own more luxury items like hi-fi sets, air conditioners, microwave ovens, and personal computers. Thirty-seven thousand HDB homes have maids, including 4,000 three-roomer households. Each year nearly half the HDB families have some members who go abroad for holidays.

Compare yourself with your counterparts in other countries and see how well you have done. If you are a technician or a teacher, compare yourself with technicians or teachers elsewhere. If you are a taxi driver, compare yourself with taxi drivers in Thailand, Taiwan, London, or anywhere else in the world. How many of them own their homes? How many of them own shares? You are ahead of them.

How far ahead? Singaporeans now have one of the highest per capita incomes in the world. The World Bank ranks us eighteenth among 230 countries. We are ahead of Hong Kong and New Zealand, and just behind Australia.

It will not be easy to repeat the 8.1 percent annual growth of the last five years. But I am optimistic. . . . The region is booming. We are seeing the greatest transformation in human history since the Industrial Revolution of the eighteenth century.

Family and Moral Values

I am reasonably confident that things will go well for the next five to ten years. At home, sound economic policies are in place. In the region things look calm but of course, one can never predict international relations. For success to continue, correct economic policies alone are not enough. Equally important are the noneconomic factors—a sense of community and nationhood, a disciplined and hard-working people, strong moral values, and family ties. The type of society we are determines how we perform. It is not simply materialism and pursuit of individual rewards which drive Singapore forward. More important, it is the sense of idealism and service, born out of a feeling of social solidarity and national identification. Without these crucial factors, we cannot be a happy or dynamic society.

These noneconomic factors translate into the political values the society has. Some of the political values we have are already ingrained and are good for our development. For example, society's rejection of corrupt practices and demand for a clean government and civil service. This is a basic expectation and it is a good political value. The more we enshrine this value, the more we ensure that crooked people do not assume responsible positions to make decisions affecting our lives. Only with a set of political and social values grounded on sound moral principles can a country develop progressively and win the respect of other nations.

Singaporeans have the right values to progress. Our Asian culture puts group interests above those of the individual. We have strong family and extended family ties. The generation of those over 40 has shared the hardships of the 1950s, 1960s, and 1970s caused by communists and communalists, and the uncertainties after separation from Malaysia when our survival was at stake. These experiences have tempered this older generation.

But societies change. They change with affluence, with technology, with politics. Sometimes changes are for the better, but sometimes changes make a society lose its vitality, its solidarity, make a people soft and [lead to] decline.

Singaporeans today enjoy full employment and high economic growth, and low divorce, illegitimacy, and crime rates. You may think decline is unimaginable. But societies can go wrong quickly. The United States and British societies have changed profoundly in the last 30 years. Up to the early 1960s they were disciplined, conservative, with the family very much the pillar of their societies.

Since then, both the United States and Britain have seen a sharp rise in broken families, teenage mothers, illegitimate children, juvenile delinquency, vandalism, and violent crime. In Britain, one in three children is born to an unmarried mother. The same is true in the United States. A recent BBC program asked viewers to choose from a list of finalists the model British family. They chose a pretty divorcée, her boyfriend, and her five-year-old daughter by a previous marriage. The boyfriend did not even live with the divorcée. He came over only on weekends. This "family" won by an overwhelming majority. *The Times* of London, which reported this story, said that the BBC viewers chose them not just because they looked attractive but because they easily identified themselves with them.

This is a profound change in the British family structure. Many families have no man at the head of the household. The woman raises her children without him. The man is, as the *London Sunday Times* puts it, "a nonessential extra."

Some American and British thinkers are deeply concerned with this change in the moral fabric. *U.S. News and World Report* recently carried a series of articles entitled "America's New Crusade" on the loss of values in the United States. Twenty-five years ago the United States was swept by the hippie movement, the "flower power" people who smoked pot, promoted free love, believed in "doing their own thing," and opposed the Vietnam War. Today, one article says:

Many Americans feel mired in a deep cultural recession and are struggling to escape by restoring old-fashioned values to a central place in their lives. It is Woodstock turned on its head 25 years later, a counterrevolution that esteems prayer over pot,

self-discipline over self-indulgence, family love over free love.

At the core of this pessimism is an increasingly frantic fear among Americans that the country is suffering a moral and spiritual decline.

It also quoted President Bill Clinton: "Our problems are beyond government's reach. They are rooted in the loss of values."

Singapore society is also changing. Singaporeans are more preoccupied with materialism and individual rewards. Divorce rates are rising slightly. There are some single parents, and some increases in drug addiction and juvenile delinquency.

Recently the *Straits Times* carried an advertisement showing a boy saying: "Come on, Dad. If you can play golf five times a week, I can have Sustagen once a day." I found the language, the way the boy speaks, most objectionable. Why put an American boy's way of speaking to a father into a Singaporean boy's mouth? Do your children really speak to you like that these days? These advertisements will encourage children to be insolent to their parents. Many American children call their fathers by their first names, and treat them with casual familiarity. We must not unthinkingly drift into attitudes and manners which undermine the traditional politeness and deference Asian children have for their parents and elders. It will destroy the way our children have grown up, respectful and polite to their elders.

Lesson 1: Do not indulge yourselves and your family, especially young children and teenagers.

As Singaporeans become more affluent, parents have increasingly indulged their children's whims and fancies. One small sign of this is the growing number of obese children in schools. Between 1980 and 1993, the obesity rate for primary school students went up threefold. I see this in kindergarten students in Marine Parade. There are more chubby children today than in the 1970s. Affluent parents who had poor childhoods want to spoil their children.

The schools are tackling the problem, but too many parents are not cooperating. They think chubby children are cute, because in the old days only wealthy people had chubby children. They do not know that doctors have found that fat cells in children make for a lifetime of problems.

In America, indulgent upbringing of children has brought sorry consequences. If you slap your child for unruly behavior, you risk going to jail. At a grocery store in the state of Georgia, a 9-year-old boy picked on his sister and was rude to the mother. The mother slapped him. A police officer saw red marks on the boy's face and asked if he had been slapped before. "I get smacked when I am bad," the boy said. The mother was hand-cuffed and hauled to jail for child abuse. She was released on S$33,000 bail. The charges were later dropped, not because the police felt they were wrong, but because they feared they could not prove to the court that the mother's slapping had caused excessive pain to her son.

British justice also seems to have gone liberal and soft. One teenager committed burglary and other offenses. To reform him, the judge sent him on an 80-day holiday to Africa: Egypt, Kenya, Tanzania, Malawi, Zambia, and Zimbabwe. I suppose this trip was meant to open his eyes to conditions in poorer countries. The safari cost British taxpayers £7,000 (US$16,100). Within a week of returning from this all-expenses-paid trip, the "Safari Boy," as he was dubbed by the press, went on a burglary spree. He was convicted. The sentence? A six-month stay in a young offenders institution, where the treatment is gentle.

The American and British peoples are fed up with rising crime rates, and want to get tough on crime. This is why Michael Fay's vandalism aroused such interest. Opinion polls showed that the American and British public supported the Singapore government's stand on the caning by large margins. But the liberal establishment, especially in the media, campaigned hysterically against the caning, not least because they felt that the ground in their own countries was shifting against them.

Compare the attitudes of Michael Fay's parents and the parents of Shiu Chi Ho [a youth arrested along with Fay for vandalism]. Fay's parents were outraged instead of being ashamed. They went on radio, television, [and] talk shows, blaming everyone but themselves. Shiu's parents showed pain, avoided publicity, and considered leaving Singapore because of a sense of shame. On the other hand, Michael Fay, back in America, got drunk, and when his father protested, he tackled the father and wrestled him to the ground. I cannot imagine a Chinese son, or any other Asian son, physically tackling his father. But that may happen when sons call their fathers by their first names and treat them as equals. Familiarity can breed contempt.

In Confucian society, a child who goes wrong knows he has brought shame upon the whole family. In America, he may win instant stardom, like Tonya Harding, the ice skater who tried to fix her rival. The difference is stark between what traditional Asians demand of their children and what many Americans now allow theirs to become.

William Bennett, who was President [Ronald] Reagan's secretary of education, wrote an article in the *Asian Wall Street Journal* [March 16, 1993] titled "Quantifying America's Decline." From 1960 to 1990, the United States GDP grew by nearly 300 percent, welfare spending by 600 percent, and the education budget by 225 percent. During the same period, violent crime increased by 560 percent, illegitimate births and divorces by 400 percent. The only thing which went down was student performance: the [average] Scholastic Aptitude Test score dropped by 80 points.

What went wrong? People demand their rights, without balancing them with responsibilities and a sense of social obligation. As Mr. Bennett puts it: "American society now places less value than before on what it owes to others as a matter of moral obligation; less value on sacrifice as a moral good; less value on social conformity and respectability; and less value on correctness and restraint in matters of physical pleasure and sexuality."

This is the result of a me-first-and-society-last attitude to life.

Because we uphold tried and tested traditional values and inculcate them in our young, we are a different society. For instance, the *Straits Times* recently printed a letter from Naresh K. Sinha, a visiting professor at Nanyang Technological University from McMaster University in Ontario, Canada. It was an unsolicited compliment to standards of morality in Singapore. Two days before Mr. Sinha was due to leave Singapore, he went to a CPF [Central Provident Fund, a combination of Social Security, Medicare, and Individual Retirement Account for workers in Singapore] branch office to withdraw his Medisave contributions. To his horror, he discovered he had lost his passport. He panicked and made several phone calls. Meanwhile someone had found his passport and handed it to the police. The police called his office to ask him to go down to the police station and claim it. Mr. Sinha wrote:

There are two amazing facts about this incident. The first is that someone took it immediately to the police station. The second is the efficiency with which the police were able to locate where I worked and inform me that they had my passport. . . . This could be possible only because of the tough law enforcement in Singapore, coupled with the fact that the political leaders here have promulgated a strict code of ethics and morality.

Mr. Sinha lamented that during the last 33 years of his stay in North America, he had seen a steady decline in moral standards, followed by increasing crime and falling standards in education in both Canada and the United States.

I know Mr. Sinha's experience is just one example and there are others who lose their things and never get them back. But I cited Mr. Sinha's letter not to make us proud of ourselves or, worse still, smug. It is to highlight and hold up as examples the good deeds when they are done. In the same vein, I am pleased to see our newspapers, television, and police give prominence to Singaporeans who do honest deeds. Society must hold up these examples so that we can all emulate them and retain our strict code of ethics and morality.

Lesson 2: Compassion can be misguided.

We deal severely with criminals and antisocial elements. We have a reason: we have seen that in such cases, to be kind to the individual offender is to be cruel to the whole society and to him.

When Michael Fay was caned for vandalism, the United States media accused us of being barbaric. We know from experience that strict punishment deters criminals. In particular, it deters those who have been punished from repeating the offense. One United States television crew who was here covering the Michael Fay case interviewed a man who had been caned for participating in a gang rape. He told them that the caning was so painful that he would never commit the crime again. In other words, the punishment worked. . . .

Welfare is the other area where misguided government compassion has led to disastrous results. The biggest welfare program in America is Aid to Families with Dependent Children [AFDC]. Under this program, women who are poor, unmarried, and have children receive welfare checks so long as they remain single and jobless. Result? The women don't get married and they don't get a job. For if they do, they will lose the benefits. So they produce more illegitimate babies.

Before 1960, one in twenty Americans was born out of wedlock. Now it is one in three. Among black Americans, two out of three births are illegitimate. Having babies without getting married is becoming the way of life for many Americans.

The AFDC program costs the United States taxpayers US$34 billion a year, enough to support our armed forces for 11 years!

Our compassion must never remove that spur that makes people work and pay for themselves. Nor should we undermine self-control, discipline, and responsibility.

Singapore is still a conservative society. Few children are born out of wedlock—one in a hundred. . . . I was dismayed that Sumiko Tan, a *Straits Times* journalist whom I know to be a serious-minded young lady, could publicly reveal that she had once entertained the thought of having a child out of wedlock. Japan, despite its wealth, is still conservative, with only one child in a hundred born out of wedlock. Japanese women feel ashamed to have illegitimate children, and quite rightly so.

Lesson 3: Defend and strengthen family values.

One of our shared values is the family as the basic building block of society. Through the family we transmit values, nurture our young, build self-esteem, and provide mutual support. Schools can teach ethics, Confucian studies, or religious knowledge, but school teachers cannot replace parents or grandparents as the principal models for their children.

Many three-generation Singapore families live together. But this is giving way to single nuclear families. Even so, Singaporeans try to buy HDB flats near their parents so grandparents [can] help out with the grandchildren. Married children still have regular dinners or lunches with their parents.

But we have educated all our women and given them a difficult double role as homemaker and co-breadwinner. If the grandparents look after the children, the kids are not at risk. But they will be at risk if left entirely to the maids, or worse, grow up by themselves in front of televisions.

Furthermore, as we go regional, more families will have fathers who are frequently away, and mothers will have to bear the full burden of caring for the children and aged parents. We must help families to stay together, and encourage wives and young children to follow the fathers abroad, to China, Vietnam, India, or Indonesia.

Women's groups have pressed the government to change the Civil Service rule on medical benefits for family members of female officers. The cabinet has discussed this several times and is reluctant to do so. Changing the rule will alter the balance of responsibility between man and woman in the family. Asian society has always held the man responsible for the child he has fathered. He is the primary provider, not his wife. If a woman has a husband, the husband must be responsible for supporting his children, including meeting their medical costs. If she is an unmarried mother, her children will not be entitled to civil service medical benefits. But if she is widowed or her husband is incapacitated and she is the sole breadwinner, an exception is made and the government extends medical benefits to eligible children. If the boyfriend's child, or the woman's husband, can depend on the woman for medical benefits, [the] Singapore man will become a nonessential extra as in Britain.

I am not saying that woman is inferior to man and must play a subservient role. I believe women should have equal opportunities and men should help out at home, looking after babies, cleaning the house, and washing dishes. But we must hold the man responsible for the child he has fathered, otherwise we will change for the worse a very basic sanction of Asian society. We do not accept unmarried single-parent families.

See what has happened in the United States, the UK, and New Zealand in the last 20 years after their governments took the responsibility of looking after unmarried or divorced mothers and their fatherless children. The number of single-mother families skyrocketed out of control.

America, Britain, and several West European governments have taken over the economic and social functions of the family, and so make [the] family unnecessary and superfluous. Marriage to raise a family is now an extra, an optional extra, like optional extras when buying a car. As the pope observed, two lesbians, a dog, and a cat now form a family.

America's and Britain's social troubles, a growing underclass which is violence prone, uneducated, drug-taking, sexually promiscuous, is the direct result of their family units becoming redundant or nonfunctional. Some 20 to 25 percent of American and British children go to school not to study but to fight and make mischief. Teachers cannot control them. In America, many students carry guns to school and have shoot-outs.

The basic error was for governments to believe that they could stand in place of father and even mother. So they have an underclass which grows up unnurtured by mother or father, no family love and support, no role models, no moral instructions. It started with the best of intentions—compassion for the less fortunate. It ended in the dismantling of their family and the creation of troublesome, uncontrollable youngsters who in turn will become parents without forming proper families.

That is why our Small Families Improvement Scheme insists on the family staying intact. When the family breaks up, the payment stops. I know this is harsh, but it is right. We must never end up with our own version of Aid to Families with Dependent Children. . . .

Government's Role to Support the Family

We intend to reinforce the strength of the family. The government will channel rights, and benefits and privileges, through the head of the family so that he can enforce the obligations and responsibilities of family members. We will frame legislation and administrative rules towards this objective. We already give tax rebates for support of parents and children. Children are allowed to top up their parents' CPF. Medisave can be used for parents, siblings, and the extended family. We encourage and will give support to such cross-generational transfers in the family and the extended family.

The government supports Walter Woon's Bill on the Maintenance of Parents. Parents who brought up their children should in turn be cared for by them. They should have legal recourse to seek financial support from their children as a last resort.

Edusave accounts are now in the name of students. We will amend the Edusave Act so that the accounts are jointly held by the students and parents, either the father or mother. The children are too young to have their apron strings cut. Joint accounts will underline and reinforce the family bond.

The government will introduce a new CPF housing grant scheme to help children buy HDB flats near their parents. We will remit a grant of $30,000 into the CPF account of households who purchase, as their first HDB flat, a resale flat in the New Town where their parents live. The $30,000 grant is to be used strictly as a capital payment to reduce the loan principal. The same conditions will apply as for first-time buyers of HDB flats—income eligibility, a five-year minimum period of occupation before resale or reapplication for another flat, and a premium or levy to be paid when they next buy a flat from HDB.

HDB currently allows unmarried mothers to buy HDB flats direct as well as on the resale market. One thousand unmarried mothers have done so. This rule implicitly accepts unmarried motherhood as a respectable part of our society. This is wrong. By removing the stigma, we may encourage more women to have children without getting married. After discovering this slip-up in our rules, we have decided no longer to allow unmarried mothers to buy HDB flats direct from the HDB. They have to buy them from the resale market.

Lessons from Taiwan

Now, let me turn to a related subject. The Western media prescribe Western-style democracy and press freedom for all countries, regardless of their different histories, culture, traditions, and social evolution. They praise countries which follow their prescriptions: a freewheeling democracy designed to produce alternating parties in government, and a press that treats the government party as an overlord to be gunned down and the opposition party as the underdog to root for. So the Western media praise Taiwan and South Korea but criticize Singapore because we do not heed their advice. We are the "authoritarian," "dictatorial" "PAP [People's Action Party] regime," "strait-laced" and "repressive."

The Economist in a recent report on Taiwan said: "The interests of Taiwan are more likely to be served . . . by the evolution of a system of pluralism which enables bad governments to be voted out and good governments to be voted in. . . .

"Taiwan will then look just like any other independent democratic country, and have the same moral claims on the rest of the free world."

The Economist argued that Taiwan should become more "pluralistic" and "democratic," even though it acknowledged that Taiwan was "a society where votes are bought and free elections have proved to be very expensive." The *Asian Wall Street Journal* reported that the Taiwanese government is cracking down on election vote-buying, and in March indicted "436 politicians, including 341 of 858 councillors voted into office early in the year." In the Taoyuan county assembly, out of 60 councillors, 30 have been convicted of corruption and are appealing, 24 more are on trial, and 2 have been acquitted. That means only 4 out of 60 had no charges against them.

In the same issue of the *Asian Wall Street Journal*, an American academic, James Robinson, noted that in the forthcoming elections for mayor of Taipei, the Kuomintang candidate has "a budget of some US$20 million—in the league of a United States presidential campaign." Yet Robinson goes on to say: "The Taiwanese themselves marvel at how far their country has come in ten years, reforming itself and making its democratic processes durable. This polity has room to become more democratic, especially in privatization of television and radio and reform of campaign financing, but the democratic core is firm."

Now, let me quote the Taiwanese themselves. They have a serious magazine called *Commonwealth*. Ten years ago, [*Commonwealth*] sent a team here to produce a special edition on Singapore. Five years ago, it sent another team, and this year, a third team. Its editors and journalists have studied us closely over a period of 10 years.

The publisher and chief editor, Diane Ying, in her article "What Makes a Beautiful Dream Come True," says:

> In ten years, Singapore has faced the reality coolly and soberly, sparing no effort in addressing its problems . . .
>
> [On the other hand,] in ten years, loss of social discipline, confusion of values, rampant gangsterism and drug addiction, a crisis of national identity, poor leadership, and weakening of government power and public trust in Taiwan have left Taiwan further and further behind Singapore.
>
> Taiwan has lost its goal and efficiency after lifting martial law: environmental pollution, backwardness of public construction, and worsening social order. . .
>
> Most Taiwanese share the dream of having a clean environment, gracious living, a safe and stable society, and a clean and efficient government. What they want is social equality and rule of law, *not greater freedom and democracy.*

These are the words from Taiwan's leading intellectual magazine.

The Taiwanese have good reasons for going democratic, American style. Taiwan's leaders know too well that this is a very complex and delicate operation. But to survive they need the support of the United States media and Congress. Moreover, if Taiwan is democratic and China is totalitarian, then the West may support Taiwan if China uses force for reunification.

Western liberals, foreign media, and human rights groups also want Singapore to be like their societies, and some Singaporeans mindlessly dance to their tune. See what happened to President [Mikhail] Gorbachev because he was beguiled by their praise. Deng Xiaoping received their condemnation. But look at China today, and see what has happened to the Soviet Union. It's gone. Imploded! We must think for ourselves and decide what is good for Singapore, what will make Singapore stable and successful. Above all else, stay away from policies which have brought a plague of social and economic problems to the United States and Britain.

Let me end by quoting from a *U.S. News and World Report* editorial, "Where Have Our Values Gone?" which eloquently describes what it calls America's "moral and spiritual decline":

> Social dysfunction haunts the land: crime and drug abuse, the breakup of the family, the slump in academic performance, the disfigurement of public places by druggies, thugs and exhibitionists.
>
> We certainly seem to have lost the balance between societal rights and individual freedoms. There are daily confrontations with almost everyone in authority: . . . children against parents, mothers against matrimony, fathers against child support. . . .
>
> Gone are the habits America once admired: industriousness, thrift, self-discipline, commitment.
>
> The combined effect of these sicknesses, rooted in phony doctrines of liberalism, has been to tax the nation's optimism and sap its confidence in the future.

America was not like this in 1966 when I was there as a student. In one generation, it has changed. Is it for the better or for the worse? That's for Americans to decide. But for me, a Singaporean, it is a change I would not want for my children and my grandchildren. Will Singapore, another generation from now, be like the United States today? This is not an idle question. Popular culture, television, rock music, the buy-now-pay-later advertisements, conspicuous consumption, the desire for more material goods, all combine to erode the traditional virtues of hard work, thrift, personal responsibility, and family togetherness.

Our institutions and basic policies are in place to sustain high economic growth. But if we lose our traditional values, our family strength and our social cohesion, we will lose our vibrancy and decline. This is the intangible factor in the success of East Asian economies, especially the NIEs [Newly Industrialized Economies] and Japan.

We have a built-in set of traditional values that have made our families strong. These values are tried and tested, have held us together, and propelled us forward. We must keep them as the bedrock values of our society for the next century. With no physical resources but with proper values, we have made the grade. To continue to succeed, we have to uphold these values which bond the family and unite our nation.

Article 31

The Wall Street Journal, October 3, 1994

Asian Games

Taiwan Slowly Creeps Toward Nationhood, to China's Annoyance

*Islanders Are Losing Interest in Reunification, Moving Ahead With Democracy
Diplomatic Trouble for U.S.*

Marcus W. Brauchli and Jeremy Mark

Staff Reporters of The Wall Street Journal

TAIPEI, Taiwan—A dawn mist cloaked eastern China's scenic Qiandao Lake when the charred pleasure boat was found. In its hold was a gruesome cargo: 32 bodies, including those of 24 Taiwanese tourists, robbed of their valuables.

The March 31 incident stunned Taiwan. The murders were horrible, but more shocking to many here was the aftermath: Chinese authorities tried to cover them up, refusing to return remains for autopsies, harassing Taiwanese relatives and journalists who came to China, and executing three men for the crime after a brief, poorly documented trial.

"It was barbaric," says Tien Hungmao, a University of Wisconsin professor who heads a research institute in Taipei. For the first time since civil war severed this island from the mainland in 1949, many Taiwanese saw China not as their once and future motherland but as a remote and alien culture. Polls since the killings show that the vast majority

now oppose reunification with China—and that support for full independence of Taiwan has reached an all-time high of 27%.

Collision Course

Wary of China and emboldened by prosperity, Taiwan is creeping toward nationhood. The shift is still subtle, but the implications are enormous: As prospects for a German-style merger recede, Taipei risks a collision with Beijing and its insistence on reunifying, by force if need be. For other nations, the challenge is to accommodate this Asian dynamo's emerging ambition for an international identity without provoking the giant next door.

That makes for a delicate minuet. Taiwan already has the attributes of a prosperous country: 21 million people, the world's 14th-largest trading economy and $90 billion in foreign-exchange reserves—more cash on hand than any other government except Japan's. Taiwan also is turning into a democracy. By 1996, it will have elections for all public offices, including the presidency.

Yet Taiwan is stuck in geopolitical limbo. Its constitution is that of the "Re-

public of China," but only 29 aid-hungry countries still forgo relations with the 1.2 billion people of China to maintain ties with Taiwan. Last month, only a handful of governments stood up for Taiwan at the United Nations in its bid to rejoin the organization, which it quit in 1972 when China joined.

A Diplomatic Problem

To other countries, Taiwan remains a diplomatic problem. Washington, its closest friend, has just revamped the awkward rules governing their "unofficial" relationship for the first time since recognizing Beijing in 1979. The Clinton administration will allow Taiwan's representative office in Washington, long called the Coordination Council for North American Affairs, to use the name Taipei—but not Taiwan. U.S. and Taiwanese officials can meet more freely, though not at the State Department.

The U.S. intends to keep Taiwan at arm's length to avoid harming relations with China, which last month warned of "chaos" if the U.S. lends support to Taiwanese independence. Assistant Secretary of State Winston Lord told a Senate panel Washington would continue to maintain a "balance" in relations with Beijing and Taipei. It is a balance that is sometimes peculiar: Diplomats assigned to Taiwan must officially "resign" when they move to Taipei and "rejoin" the State Department when their tours end.

"The U.S. policy is illogical," says a senior Western observer in Taipei. But because it maintains access to both sides, "It works."

Who's in First?

Perhaps, but will it continue to? The answer will become clearer soon, as Taipei vies with China in the global credibility sweepstakes. Both Taipei and Beijing are racing to become founding members of the World Trade Organization, the successor to the General Agreement on Tariffs and Trade. Trade experts say China is unlikely to qualify for entry by the WTO's launch next year; Taiwan is far closer to meeting the market-opening criteria. GATT members have agreed that China should enter the WTO first, but nothing is certain. "Would other GATT members be willing to block a qualified applicant from joining because of political pressure from Beijing?" a foreign observer in Taiwan asks.

China hopes so. It does what it can to keep Taiwan from gaining global legs. It wants Taiwan's international telephone dialing code changed from 886 to 86, the same as China's. When President Clinton hosted the Asia Pacific Economic Cooperation summit in Seattle last year, Chinese President Jiang Zemin agreed to attend only if Taiwan President Lee Teng-hui wasn't invited. Mr. Lee won't be asked to this year's meeting in Indonesia, either.

Although Beijing fears that each Taiwanese bid for diplomatic breathing room leads toward independence, President Lee himself says China is mistaken. "The ultimate goal of the Republic of China is unification," the 71-year-old head of state says in an interview. "But until conditions [in China] become more mature, we won't talk. If the Chinese Communists continue to behave like they do, then the people of Taiwan will be apprehensive." He adds that it isn't likely Taiwan and China can reunify until China is "free and democratic and the people of the mainland enjoy prosperity."

Japan knows how nettlesome an ambitious Taiwan can be. The international organizing committee for this month's Asian Games in Hiroshima startled Tokyo recently by inviting President Lee to attend the opening ceremony. President Lee, Japanese-educated and longing to visit Japan, set off alarms in Beijing when he accepted. It took pressure from both China and Japan to get the organizers to rescind the invitation. But Tokyo, perhaps mindful of the nearly $25 billion a year in Japanese exports to Taiwan, still said Taiwan's vice premier could attend. And China, despite loud rhetoric against Tokyo, said it would participate in the games.

"This is really a very confused era, when a lot of things are in a state of flux," notes Taiwan's Justice Minister, Ma Ying-jeou. "Our relations with the mainland are uncertain and our international relations are uncertain."

Taiwan's economic stature is not. Some of its high-tech companies, such as computer maker Acer Inc. and chip maker United Microelectronics Corp., are world leaders. Many of its officials have studied in the U.S. or Japan, as about 40,000 Taiwanese do yearly. Taipei is a modern, traffic-shackled capital that has more in common with Tokyo than with developing China, where per capita income is a tenth of Taiwan's $11,000 a year.

Ordinary Taiwanese are increasingly aware of the gap between their cozy, cable-TV-wired island and the vast, nominally Communist realm across the water. Anne Chang, a 38-year-old teacher whose parents were born on the mainland, was stunned by what she saw on a trip to her father's ancestral village in northern China. Her relatives had an eight-month-old baby who had never been bathed.

"Our opportunities have been greater than theirs because we are free," Ms. Chang says. She wants to keep those opportunities, even if doing so requires abandoning reunification. Her parents also have revised their dreams; they now want to be buried in Taiwan, not in the family plot in China.

Slowly Shedding Ties

Taiwanese have been shedding their ties to China for years. Over 90% of them were born here. "I'd always considered myself Chinese because that's what I was taught," says Tsai Fu-hai, a 46-year-old fish farmer. "But I was born in Taiwan, not China. How could I have been so stupid? I'm Taiwanese."

That realization has become a potent political force. Shao Tza-lin, a fiery opposition-party activist, says Taiwan must be prepared for a "bloody revolution" to ensure nationhood. Tsai Shih-yuan, a more cautious opposition leader, says: "If a politician advocates reunification with China, he is doomed. The people want an independent Taiwan."

So, up to a point, do Taiwan's leaders. In July, the government issued a historic white paper aimed at ending two decades of tightening diplomatic isolation and staking out carefully circumscribed independence. Its officials, sensitive to public opinion, say they want Taiwan acknowledged as a "sovereign political entity" that can join international organizations. Some even muse about a formal name change, saying such a move doesn't preclude future unification and might facilitate it, if China achieves the economic and political development that would make unification logical. But, in what once would have been heresy, some officials hint that that day may never come.

"We didn't work 40 years to be a colony," declares Su Chi, 45-year-old vice chairman of the cabinet-level Mainland Affairs Council. He says he considers China's claim to Taiwan "ridiculous."

Political Reforms

Such open talk, especially by senior government officials, reflects a new political reality in this once-authoritarian state. Political reforms were set in motion in the late 1980s by Chiang Ching-kuo, the son of the late dictator Chiang Kai-shek. But the country was under marital law until 1987, and it was President Lee—a Taiwanese native who has never set foot on the mainland—who energized the reforms after the younger Chiang died in 1988.

And only in 1991 did President Lee renounce the claim to sovereignty over China. For decades, Taiwanese had no choice but to accept that they were part of China and deny their own cultural heritage. All opposition to the official dogma was crushed; children were punished just for speaking Taiwanese in school.

The memories of that period, which President Lee has called "the sorrow of the Taiwanese," have been permitted to surface openly only in recent years. Tsai Hsin-yi, a 77-year-old eel farmer in the southern port of Putai, recalls friends disappearing after speaking out for independence early in Chiang Kai-shek's China-obsessed rule.

Today, nonchalance has replaced paranoia. At an army outpost near Putai, where battle-worn soldiers once scanned the sea for Communist Chinese invaders, Taiwanese draftees placidly guard commercial oyster beds and try to stay out of the sun. A pimply 21-year-old serving two years of national service sees no threat from China: "I don't think they'll ever come."

Taiwan now focuses on domestic politics. When Taipei shut unlicensed opposition radio stations in August, hundreds of Taipei taxi drivers and other loyal listeners rioted, throwing bricks and destroying cars before police rushed in with batons. "You see?" yelled Pastor William J.K. Lo, a 53-year-old Presbyterian standing defiantly under a plume of black smoke. "They still oppress us."

But while the mainland is still led by a single party dominated by octogenarians, Taiwan is experimenting with a new and raucous political system. It goes far beyond the film clips, often shown on U.S. TV news, of brawls in the legislature. Most elected politicians are Taiwanese, and office holders who are the children of mainland exiles are learning the local dialect and proclaiming their local roots.

The new pluralism has breathed life into Taiwan's craving for an independent identity just as Taiwan and

China have developed a complex web of contacts. While Taiwanese focus on the possibility of a Chinese invasion, the real assault has been in the other direction: Taiwanese companies have invested at least $15 billion in mainland factories, real estate and karaoke bars. Taiwanese tourists have spent billions of dollars in China, and the government warns of the danger of economic dependence on the mainland.

But to many Taiwanese, all this contact makes Taiwan and China seem even farther apart. Talks that began in 1993 over fishing disputes, plane hijackings and other issues—far from being a prologue to unification—underscore differences.

"Maybe we haven't understood until now that our ideology isn't the same, the thinking isn't the same," says David Tzeng, a 43-year-old owner of an acrylic factory in Tainan. He first visited China in 1989, when pro-democracy protesters were gathering in Beijing. "It was incredibly exciting," he recalls. After the crackdown, he slowly grew more disillusioned. In four subsequent visits to the

mainland, he invested $180,000 to open a restaurant in the eastern city of Hangzhou, then closed it because of harassment by Chinese officials and local gangsters. "Now I have no feeling for China," he says.

Even some veterans of China's civil war who came over to Taiwan as peasant soldiers half a century ago are losing their emotional links. Many married Taiwanese and watched their children grow up as part of the "Taiwan Miracle." They have visited the impoverished villages they left behind and learned that they are usually valued back home for little more than the money they bring. Some men who long nurtured the hope of returning to China as liberators are rethinking their ideas.

"I've been back to China, and I was saddened by what I saw," says Chen Hsiu-jen, a 66-year-old retiree who was drafted into Chiang Kai-shek's army when just 15. "Now, I think we are already independent. Just maybe we shouldn't say it openly and make Beijing angry."

Article 32

Society, January/February 1995

Private-Enterprise Communism

Dwight R. Lee

Dwight R. Lee is Bernard B. and Eugenia A. Ramsey Professor of Economics and Private Enterprise at the University of Georgia.

I recently went to Ho Chi Minh City, Vietnam, to lecture on the virtues of the private-enterprise system to an audience whose political allegiance is supposedly to communism. The reception to my comments was enthusiastic. Most Vietnamese want to live in a private-enterprise economy so they can enjoy the products that most poor people in the United States take for granted. But I was in Vietnam to learn as well as lecture. The most surprising thing I learned, given my uncompromising advocacy of private enterprise, was an appreciation for the political domination of Vietnam by the Communist Party and for the advantages the United States would realize from lifting its embargo against the Vietnamese economy.

I want to point out quickly that in addition to favoring private enterprise I also favor multiparty political democracy. But no matter where you want to go, you always have to start from where you are. And the fact is that political democracy does not exist in Vietnam. Opposing parties are not tolerated, and public criticism of the Communist Party is risky business, so the important question is, What is the best policy for moving Vietnam from its current autocratic regime to an open and democratic political process?

In considering this question one should recognize that while Vietnam's Communist government is hostile to those who want to practice political pluralism, it is increasingly tolerant of those who want to practice private enterprise. As Murray Hiebert noted recently in his *Vietnam Notebook,* "People seem free to do almost anything as long as they do not challenge the communists' hold on power." In response to looming economic collapse by a decade of socialist planning, the Vietnamese Communists began implementing private-enterprise reforms in 1986. The official political rhetoric is still Marxist-Leninist, but the economic reality is increasingly Adam Smith and Milton Friedman.

For many people, particularly those Americans with loved ones still missing in action (MIA) from the Vietnam War, the type of economy Vietnam is moving toward may seem secondary to the fact that Vietnam's political regime remains closed, undemocratic, and insensitive to our concern over basic human rights, as well as less than forthright about their knowledge of the remains or whereabouts of any American MIAs who might still be alive and held against their will. But the fastest path to an open and democratic government in Vietnam—and information about American MIAs—is the one that gives priority to private enterprise rather than political democracy.

Poor people are more interested in being able to purchase reliable products in the marketplace than in being able to vote for unreliable politicians at the polls. According to Hiebert, "Vietnamese young people seem to pay surprisingly little attention to politics. Students in several colleges in Ho Chi Minh City and Hanoi have organised some small protests in recent years. But they were not demanding more democracy but better living conditions." In countries like Vietnam, political democracy may be a luxury that takes root far more securely in a prosperous economy than in an impoverished one. For this reason, the surest means to democracy in Vietnam, oddly enough, seems to be the Communist Party. The Vietnamese Communists are intent on promoting free-market reform. This reform is the only path to prosperity for the Vietnamese people, and probably the quickest path to a Vietnamese government that is democratic at home and forthright in its dealings with the rest of the world.

Private-Enterprise "Communists"

The argument that communism in Vietnam can provide the quickest path to democracy depends crucially on the proposition that Communists can promote the prosperity that comes only from private enterprise. This proposition would have been ridiculed a few years ago. But the dramatic changes in the world's political and economic landscape in recent years suggest that the best hope Vietnam has for a vibrant private-enterprise economy lies in its current autocratic Communist regime.

The most dramatic change arises from the fact that socialist ideology is no longer powerful enough to blind Communist Party politicians to the most important economic lesson of our time: Market economies far outperform socialist economies at generating economic

progress. No longer is it possible for socialist autocrats to keep their populations unaware of how destitute they are in comparison to those in capitalist economies. And if maintaining political power requires embracing socialism in name but private enterprise in practice, few Communist Party leaders have shown reluctance to do so. Socialist autocrats are autocrats first and socialists last. China's powerful Communist patriarch Deng Xiaoping defended his "socialist" market reforms with the comment that he didn't care what a cat is called as long as it catches mice.

Certainly the Communist leaders in Vietnam have elevated economic growth to top priority, even at the ideological cost of becoming private-enterprise "Communists." Vietnam's economy has a long way to go before it is a full-fledged private-enterprise system, but the movement toward the market is unmistakable. Since 1986, when the Vietnamese Communists began implementing their economic restructuring (known as *doi moi*), Hanoi has abolished most trade restrictions, decontrolled export and import prices, allowed market forces to play a larger role in determining the foreign-exchange rate, and taken steps toward privatizing production activity.

Communist leaders may have the motivation to implement free-market reforms, but are they capable of doing so? Private enterprise has traditionally been associated with political democracy. It is natural to question whether economic freedom is compatible with political autocracy. But another dramatic change in the political and economic landscape has been the emergence of rapidly growing free-market economies under autocratic political regimes. These economically successful regimes (concentrated in but not limited to Asia) provide evidence that economic lift-off through free-market reform can be facilitated by autocratic political rule.

Socialist autocrats are autocrats first and socialists last.

The evidence from Asia supports the view that autocratic rule is the most reliable route to free-market prosperity in economically emerging countries. According to a recent survey by *The Economist*, "anyone who hopes East Asian-style government intervention will help an economy should also hope that the government is not a democracy." The market-based economies of Taiwan, South Korea, Singapore, and Hongkong developed successfully under political regimes that were hardly democratic or much concerned with human rights. It is important to note, however, that limited movement to democratic practices has in many instances accompanied or followed the growth unleashed by private enterprise.

The idea that authoritarianism is a precursor to private-enterprise prosperity is foreign to the American experience. The U.S. economy developed under political democracy to become the most productive in the world by the early years of this century. Democracy was undeniably the precursor to the private-enterprise economy of the United States—indeed, the U.S. Constitution contains important protections of private property and market processes. But the democracy under which the U.S. economy developed was crucially different from the democracy we have today or from the democracies that would result from outside pressure on Third-World Asian countries.

Until the second decade of this century (except during wartime) the budget of the U.S. federal government amounted to only about 3 percent of the economy's total output. The U.S. economy developed under a democracy in which the opportunities to obtain wealth through political influence were far more limited than they are today. The best way to improve one's condition was by creating new wealth through market activity rather than by capturing existing wealth through political activity. However, when government controls as large a share of economic output as do most governments today, the political freedom that comes with democracy is easily exploited by well-organized interest groups to increase their share of the economic pie with policies that retard economic growth. Because the United States was fortunate enough to grow rich under a limited government, it can afford the special-interest excesses that thrive in the political freedom of a large democratic government. Third-World economies cannot. According to the same survey by The Economist, "These days you hear top advisers to China's 'Communist' government say, 'We must be careful to avoid the sort of generous social-welfare programmes that have led to such high unemployment in Europe.'"

Economic predation by special interests that have no concern for their negative effect on the general economy is not limited to democracies, and no reasonable person prefers a special-interest tyranny to a special-interest democracy. But those autocratic regimes in Asia experiencing such impressive economic growth have done better than present-day democracies at subordinating political entitlement-seeking to promoting general economic productivity. Once a special-interest program is implemented in a Western democracy it is far more likely to be expanded than exterminated, no matter how much cost it imposes on the economy. The cost of the program is so widely spread that no one group has the motivation

to politically oppose it. When groups take political action in democracies, they do so to fight for special-interest privileges that benefit them, not to fight against the special-interest privileges that benefit others. Although no one would argue that autocratic regimes are immune to special-interest influence, an autocratic regime is in a better position to benefit from the overall productivity of the economy than is any one special-interest group. When special-interest influence leads to programs and policies that noticeably hamper economic performance, the autocratic regime has the motivation, as well as the power, to ruthlessly root out such programs and policies.

India is a good example of a country that has attempted to develop its economy under a large democratic government. India's democracy has permitted a host of politically influential groups to use state control over the economy to obtain advantages that are beneficial from the perspective of each group but ruinous from the perspective of general economic performance. The result is a country with impressive economic potential being left behind by its less democratic neighbors to the east. Contrasting India's situation with that of China, The Economist recently stated that "Indians explained that they were doomed by democracy: whereas China's government could degree radical reform . . . , India was condemned to stagnation by the niceties of electoral politics."

There can be no debate as to the economic success of autocratic regimes in Asia (not to mention examples in South America, such as Chile). Whether the market reforms of the Vietnamese Communists will be another economic success story remains uncertain. But so far the evidence is encouraging. Since the Vietnamese Communists began their policy of free-market reforms in 1986, economic growth has averaged an impressive 7 percent per year, and the inflation rate has declined from 700 percent in 1986 to less than 10 percent at the end of 1993. More recently Vietnam's exports have started to increase rapidly. In 1992 Vietnamese exports were approximately 24 percent larger than in the previous year; Vietnam is now the world's third largest exporter of rice, and it is becoming a significant exporter of petroleum. Even before the U.S embargo was lifted foreign investment was pouring into Vietnam, attracted by abundant natural resources, diligent workers, and 71 million consumers.

From Autocracy to Democracy

There are those who will remain unimpressed with the economic progress of Vietnam as long as its government remains autocratic, Communist or otherwise. For many, the economic progress that comes from private enterprise is secondary to the political ideal of democracy. In their view, the United States should have continued the economic embargo against Vietnam to force its government to begin relinquishing its one-party control.

There are two problems with the "democracy-first" argument for the continuation of the economic embargo of Vietnam. The first is that the U.S. attempt to harm the Vietnamese economy with an embargo became less effective. Businesses in the other major industrialized countries have long been trading with and investing in Vietnam, and a host of U.S. products were being sold there, but not by the U.S. firms that produced them. According to Timothy Karr, in October 1993 Vietnam's First Deputy Prime Minister, Phan Van Khai, told a gathering of American business leaders in New York City that "American goods are widely consumed in Vietnam, but the sellers are not American companies." The accuracy of Phan's statement was clearly apparent to me during my visit to Ho Chi Minh City in November 1993. I had no trouble buying Coca Colas, and if I had wanted to enjoy my Coke with a Marlboro or Winston cigarette, they were also readily available, as were such other U.S. products as Kodak film and IBM and Apple computers.

This does not mean that the U.S. embargo had no effect on the Vietnamese economy. More investment would have flowed into Vietnam and its economy would have developed somewhat faster if the embargo had been lifted earlier. But a plausible argument can be made that the biggest losers from the embargo were the American businesses denied direct access to a large and expanding market.

The second, and more important, problem with the "democracy-first" argument for continuing the embargo is that it put the cart before the horse. To the extent that the embargo hampered the Vietnamese economy, it also hampered the most effective force for political democracy. The surest way to promote democracy in Vietnam is by facilitating its move to private enterprise. Even those who have long been sympathetic to the ideals of socialism recognize the necessity of private-enterprise capitalism for a viable democracy. The economist Robert Heilbroner, who is still hopeful that some form of humane socialism lies in our future, observed recently in his *21st Century Capitalism* that

> no noncapitalist country has attained the levels of political, civil, religious, and intellectual freedom found in all advanced capitalisms. To make the case differently, the state of explicit political liberty we loosely call "democracy" has so far appeared only in nations in which capitalism is the mode of economic organization.

Why is an economy based on private-enterprise capitalism the only type consistent with political freedom and democracy? Consider that the private-enterprise economy is a system of discipline and accountability that makes it possible for people to tolerate the freedom of others. Market prices, which are based on private property and free exchange, communicate information to all market participants on the values others place on goods and services and motivates the appropriate response to this information. Each supplier responds to the concerns of consumers by expanding output when those consumers communicate, through market prices, that the additional output is worth more than alternative products that otherwise could have been produced. Each consumer responds to the concerns of other consumers by purchasing more of a product only when he or she values the additional consumption more than other consumers communicate, through market prices, that it is worth to them.

Given the accountability imposed by markets, we can be confident that others will exercise their freedom in ways that consider our interests as well as theirs. There is no need, or sympathy, for the extensive political micro-managing of our behavior that ultimately requires an autocratic government. Market incentives provide not only a substitute but a superior substitute for the detailed controls of an autocratic government as a means of establishing a harmonious and productive social order.

Freedom to pollute is a freedom that is not tolerated.

To illustrate the connection between market accountability and tolerance for freedom, consider the problem of environmental pollution. Environmental problems arise because important resources such as our airsheds and waterways are owned communally, rather than privately, and therefore are not allocated through market exchange. When the owners of a firm, for example, are deciding how much waste to discharge into the environment, they face no market price that reflects how much cost is imposed on others by the resulting pollution. Without such prices, when people use the environment as a waste-sink they lack both the information and the motivation to consider the concerns of others. So freedom to pollute is a freedom that is not tolerated, at least not in countries wealthy enough to afford the luxury of environmental quality. The American public, for example, has been sympathetic to a proliferation of government controls and regulations restricting our freedom to pollute the environment. These restrictions would not be needed or tolerated if we had the advantage of functioning markets in environmental quality, which would do a far better job protecting the environment than detailed government regulations.

Only by expanding the range of activities disciplined by private property and market exchange can we expand our tolerance for freedom. There is no mystery in the fact that in countries where there is little reliance on private property and market exchange, autocratic governments suppress basic freedoms and ignore human rights. It is possible to have an autocratic government in a country that relies on private enterprise, but, as Heilbroner points out, democratic governments do not take root in the absence of a free-enterprise economy.

Furthermore, it is probably not possible for an autocratic government to long survive the pressures for freedom that are unleashed in a free-market economy. People who are enjoying freedom in the marketplace soon find it difficult to tolerate the denial of freedom in the political arena. As private enterprise increases the general level of material well-being, people shift their attention to concerns that are of little interest to the impoverished. One of these concerns is political democracy. (According to the aforementioned survey in *The Economist*, "As Asian countries move towards rich-world income levels, their appetite for multi-party politics seems to grow.")

The ability of private-enterprise freedom and prosperity to erode autocratic political power is certainly evident in Asia. Few would classify Taiwan and South Korea as ideal democracies, but it should not be overlooked how far they have moved toward democracy in a short time. As recently as the early 1980s, the populations of both countries were subject to a rather unforgiving martial law. The people of China, Singapore, and Vietnam are still denied political freedom, but personal freedom has expanded significantly in these countries as their economies have been liberalized. The political risks to the remaining Asian autocrats of trying to turn back the free-market reforms are greater than continuing forward, but these autocrats are well aware of the strong tendency for an expansion in economic freedom to be followed by popular demands for more political freedom. Lee Kwan Yew, the former prime minister of Singapore, told the Communist leaders of Vietnam on a recent visit to their country that there would be a political price for liberalizing the Vietnamese economy.

No one is predicting that the Vietnamese Communist Party is about to fall or to voluntarily relinquish its po-

litical power, but there is no denying that the free market is beginning to undermine that power. According to Murray Hiebert, Hanoi Bureau Chief for the *Far Eastern Economic Review*, "Economic reforms are gradually eroding the [Vietnam Communist) party's power. By abandoning farm cooperatives, encouraging private enterprise, and relaxing its restrictions on artists and writers, the party has weakened its grip over Vietnamese society." Hiebert quotes one party official who complained that "the party faces serious ideological erosion. . . . The party bosses in the countryside are trying to accumulate land and the sons of the bosses are running private companies. The party has lost its heroic past."

As private enterprise erodes the power of the Vietnamese Communists, the movement is sure to be toward multiparty democracy.

Promoting Political Democracy

The temptation is to argue that the United States should have dropped its embargo of Vietnam earlier to take advantage of the lucrative market and investment opportunities being snapped up by other countries. This argument is a compelling one from a strictly economic perspective, but it would have had little appeal to those concerned with what they see as the more noble objective of promoting an open and democratic regime in Vietnam. The more compelling reason for dropping the embargo is that no other policy would do as much to promote political democracy in Vietnam.

The United States could have continued the attempt to pressure Vietnam to liberalize its political process with the economic embargo, but the Vietnamese Communists are notoriously tenacious in their resistance to external pressures for political reform. The most effective way for the United States to promote democracy in Vietnam is by taking advantage of the fact that the Communist regime in Vietnam is intent on promoting free-market prosperity. Opening up Vietnam to U.S. trade and investment will assist the Vietnamese Communists to achieve a vibrant private-enterprise economy that can only erode their political power from within.

Vietnamese communism has withstood the destructive assault of French and U.S. military power. What Vietnamese communism cannot long survive is the freedom and prosperity of private enterprise.

Credits

Glossary of Terms and Abbreviations

Animism   The belief that all objects, including plants, animals, rocks, and other matter, contain spirits. This belief figures prominently in early Japanese religious thought and in the various indigenous religions of the South Pacific.

Anti-Fascist People's Freedom League (AFPFL)   An anti-Japanese resistance movement organized by Burmese students and intellectuals.

ANZUS   The name of a joint military-security agreement originally among Australia, New Zealand, and the United States. New Zealand is no longer a member.

Asia Pacific Economic Cooperation Council (APEC)   Organized in 1989, this body is becoming increasingly visible as a major forum for plans about regional economic cooperation and growth in the Pacific Rim.

Asian Development Bank (ADB)   With contributions from industrialized nations, the ADB provides loans to Pacific Rim countries in order to foster economic development.

Association of Southeast Asian Nations (ASEAN)   Established in 1967 to promote economic cooperation among the countries of Indonesia, Malaysia, the Philippines, Singapore, Thailand, and Brunei.

British Commonwealth of Nations   A voluntary association of nations formerly included in the British Empire. Officials meet regularly in member countries to discuss issues of common economic, military, and political concern.

Buddhism   A religious and ethical philosophy of life that originated in India in the fifth and sixth centuries B.C., partly in reaction to the caste system. Buddhism holds that people's souls are endlessly reborn and that one's standing with each rebirth depends on one's behavior in the previous life.

Burma Socialist Program Party (BSPP)   The only political party allowed to exist in Burma (now called Myanmar) between 1974 and 1989. It was renamed the National Unity Party in 1989.

Capitalism   An economic system in which productive property is owned by individuals or corporations, rather than by the government, and the proceeds of which belong to the owner rather than to the workers or the state.

Chaebol   A Korean term for a large business conglomerate. Similar to the Japanese *keiretsu.*

Chinese Communist Party (CCP)   Founded in 1921 by Mao Zedong and others, the CCP became the ruling party of the People's Republic of China in 1949 upon the defeat of the Nationalist Party and the army of Chiang Kai-shek.

Cold War   The intense rivalry, short of direct "hot-war" military conflict, between the Soviet Union and the United States which continued from the end of World War II until approximately 1990.

Communism   An economic system in which land and businesses are owned collectively by everyone in the society rather than by individuals. Modern communism is founded on the teachings of the German intellectuals Marx and Engels.

Confucianism   A system of ethical guidelines for managing one's personal relationships with others and with the state. Confucianism stresses filial piety and obligation to one's superiors. It is based on the teachings of the Chinese intellectuals Confucius and Mencius.

Cultural Revolution   A period between 1966 and 1976 in China when, urged on by Mao, students attempted to revive a revolutionary spirit in China. Intellectuals and even Chinese Communist Party leaders who were not zealously communist were violently attacked or purged from office.

Demilitarized Zone (DMZ)   A heavily guarded border zone separating North and South Korea.

European Union (EU)   An umbrella organization of numerous Western European nations working toward the establishment of a single economic and political European entity. Formerly known as the European Community (EC).

Extraterritoriality   The practice whereby the home country exercises jurisdiction over its diplomats and other citizens living in a foreign country, effectively freeing them from the authority of the host government.

Feudalism   A social and economic system of premodern Europe, Japan, China, and other countries, characterized by a strict division of the populace into social classes, an agricultural economy, and governance by lords controlling vast parcels of land and the people thereon.

Greater East Asia Co-Prosperity Sphere   The Japanese description of the empire they created in the 1940s by military conquest.

Gross Domestic Product (GDP)   A statistic describing the entire output of goods and services produced by a country in a year, less income earned on foreign investments.

Hinduism   A 5,000-year-old religion of India that advocates a social caste system but anticipates the eventual merging of all individuals into one universal world soul.

Indochina   The name of the colony in Southeast Asia controlled by France and consisting of the countries of Laos, Cambodia, and Vietnam. The colony ceased to exist after 1954, but the term still is often applied to the region.

International Monetary Fund (IMF)   An agency of the United Nations whose goal it is to promote freer world trade by assisting nations in economic development.

Islam   The religion founded by Mohammed and codified in the *Koran.* Believers, called Muslims, submit to

Allah (Arabic for God) and venerate his name in daily prayer.

Keiretsu   A Japanese word for a large business conglomerate.

Khmer Rouge   The communist guerrilla army, led by Pol Pot, that controlled Cambodia in the 1970s and continues to attempt to overthrow the UN-sanctioned government.

Kuomintang   The National People's Party (Nationalists), which, under Chiang Kai-shek, governed China until Mao Zedong's revolution in 1949; it continues to dominate politics in Taiwan.

Laogai   A Mandarin Chinese word for a prison or concentration camp where political prisoners are kept. It is similar in concept to the Russian word *gulag.*

Liberal Democratic Party (LDP)   The conservative party that ruled Japan almost continuously between 1955 and 1993 and oversaw Japan's rapid economic development.

Martial Law   The law applied to a territory by military authorities in a time of emergency when regular civilian authorities are unable to maintain order. Under martial law, residents are usually restricted in their movement and in their exercise of such rights as freedom of speech and of the press.

Meiji Restoration   The restoration of the Japanese emperor to his throne in 1868. The period is important as the beginning of the modern era in Japan and the opening of Japan to the West after centuries of isolation.

Monsoons   Winds that bring exceptionally heavy rainfall to parts of Southeast Asia and elsewhere. Monsoon rains are essential to the production of rice.

National League for Democracy   An opposition party in Myanmar that was elected to head the government in 1990 but that has since been forbidden by the current military leaders to take office.

New Economic Policy (NEP)   An economic plan advanced in the 1970s to restructure the Malaysian economy and foster industrialization and ethnic equality.

Newly Industrializing Country (NIC)   A designation for those countries of the developing world, particularly Taiwan, South Korea, and other Asian nations, whose economies have undergone rapid growth; sometimes also referred to as newly industrialized countries.

Non-Aligned Movement   A loose association of mostly non-Western developing nations, many of which had been colonies of Western powers but during the cold war chose to remain detached from either the U.S. or Soviet bloc. Initially Indonesia and India, among others, were enthusiastic promoters of the movement.

Opium Wars   Conflicts between Britain and China in 1839–1842 and 1856–1866 in which England used China's destruction of opium shipments and other issues as a pretext to attack China and force the government to sign trade agreements.

Pacific War   The name frequently used by the Japanese to refer to that portion of World War II in which they were involved and which took place in Asia and the Pacific.

Shintoism   An ancient indigenous religion of Japan that stressed the role of *kami,* or supernatural gods, in the lives of people. For a time during the 1930s, Shinto was the state religion of Japan and the emperor was honored as its high priest.

Siddhartha Gautama   The name of the man who came to be called the Buddha.

Smokestack Industries   Heavy industries such as steel mills that are basic to an economy but produce objectionable levels of air, water, or land pollution.

Socialism   An economic system in which productive property is owned by the government as are the proceeds from the productive labor. Most socialist systems today are actually mixed economies in which individuals as well as the government own property.

South Pacific Forum   An organization established by Australia and other South Pacific nations to provide a forum for discussion of common problems and opportunities in the region.

Southeast Asia Treaty Organization (SEATO)   A collective-defense treaty signed by the United States and several European and Southeast Asian nations. It was dissolved in 1977.

Subsistence Farming   Farming that meets the immediate needs of the farming family but that does not yield a surplus sufficient for export.

Taoism   An ancient religion of China inspired by Lao-tze that stresses the need for mystical contemplation to free one from the desires and sensations of the materialistic and physical world.

Tiananmen Square Massacre   The violent suppression by the Chinese Army of a prodemocracy movement that had been organized in Beijing by thousands of Chinese students in 1989 and that had become an international embarrassment to the Chinese regime.

United Nations (UN)   An international organization established immediately after World War II to replace the League of Nations. The organization includes most of the countries of the world and works for international understanding and world peace.

World Health Organization (WHO)   Established in 1948 as an advisory and technical-assistance organization to improve the health of peoples around the world.

Bibliography

GENERAL WORKS

Wm. Theodore de Bary, *East Asian Civilizations: A Dialogue in Five Stages* (Cambridge: Harvard University Press, 1988).
The development of philosophical and religious thought in China, Korea, Japan, and other regions of East Asia.

Mark Borthwick, *Pacific Century: The Emergence of Modern Pacific Asia* (Boulder: Westview Press, 1992).
Timely overview of the history, foreign relations, and domestic politics of East Asia. A companion text to a PBS telecourse.

Commission on U.S.–Japan Relations for the Twenty-First Century, *Preparing for a Pacific Century: Exploring the Potential for Pacific Basin Cooperation* (Washington, DC, November 1991).
Transcription of an international conference on the Pacific with commentary by representatives from the United States, Malaysia, Japan, Thailand, Indonesia, and others.

Robert L. Downen and Bruce J. Dickson, eds., *The Emerging Pacific Community* (Boulder: Westview Press, 1984).
Proceedings of a 1983 conference on the Pacific Rim.

John E. Endicott and William P. Heaton, *The Politics of East Asia: China, Japan, Korea* (Boulder: Westview Press, 1978).
Treatment of the political ideology undergirding the modern states of China, Japan, and Korea.

Hans Hoefer and Geoffrey Eu, eds., *East Asia* (New York: Prentice Hall, 1988).
A travel guide that contains useful historical sketches as well as anecdotes about contemporary life in Hong Kong, Indonesia, Japan, South Korea, Malaysia, Myanmar, the Philippines, Singapore, Taiwan, and Thailand.

Charles E. Morrison, *Japan, the United States and a Changing Southeast Asia* (New York: University Press of America, 1985).
A review of the work of the Asia Society regarding the new roles of Japan and the United States in Southeast Asia.

Seiji Naya and Stephen Browne, eds., *Development Challenges in Asia and the Pacific in the 1990s* (Honolulu: East-West Center, 1991).
A collection of speeches made at a 1990 Symposium on Cooperation in Asia and the Pacific. The articles cover development issues in East, Southeast, and South Asia and the Pacific.

Eric D. Ramstetter, *Foreign Direct Investment in Developing Economies in Asia and the Pacific in the 1990s: Prospects and Policy Issues* (Honolulu: East-West Center, n.d.).
A report on FDI in Asia and the Pacific with useful statistics.

Michael P. Smith, ed., *Pacific Rim Cities in the World Economy* (New Brunswick: Transaction Books, 1989).
The growing role of selected Pacific Rim cities in the world economy.

Colin E. Tweddell and Linda Amy Kimball, *Introduction to the Peoples and Cultures of Asia* (Englewood Cliffs: Prentice Hall, 1985).
A useful introduction to the many ethnic groups and socioreligious ideologies that make up the fabric of modern Asia.

Donald E. Weatherbee, ed., *Southeast Asia Divided* (Boulder: Westview Press, 1985).
Reprints of papers delivered at the 1984 International Studies Association meeting as well as copies of documents of note for the Southeast Asian region.

NATIONAL HISTORIES AND ANALYSES

Australia

Roderick Cameron, *Australia: History and Horizons* (New York: Columbia University Press, 1971).
A review of Australian history during the 1800s. Intended for the general reader, it is liberally illustrated.

W. J. Hudson, ed., *Australia in World Affairs* (Sydney: George Allen & Unwin, 1980).
Australia's foreign relations since 1945.

David Alistair Kemp, *Society and Electoral Behaviour in Australia: A Study of Three Decades* (St. Lucia: University of Queensland Press, 1978).
Elections, political parties, and social problems in Australia since 1945.

John Gladstone Steele, *Aboriginal Pathways in Southeast Queensland and the Richmond River* (St. Lucia: University of Queensland Press, 1984).
A description of Aboriginal culture in Australia.

Andrew C. Theophanous, *Australia Democracy in Crisis: A Radical Approach to Australian Politics* (Melbourne: Oxford University Press, 1980).
The role of capitalism and the maintenance of democracy in Australia.

Brunei

Nicholas Tarling, *Britain, the Brookes, and Brunei* (Kuala Lumpur: Oxford University Press, 1971).
A history of the Sultanate of Brunei and its neighbors.

Cambodia

David P. Chandler, *A History of Cambodia* (Boulder: Westview Press, 1983).
A short history of Cambodia.

Craig Etcheson, *The Rise and Demise of Democratic Kampuchea* (Boulder: Westview Press, 1984).
A history of the rise of the Communist government in Cambodia.

William Shawcross, *The Quality of Mercy: Cambodia, Holocaust, and Modern Conscience; with a report from Ethiopia* (New York: Simon & Schuster, 1985).
A report on political atrocities, relief programs, and refugees in Cambodia and Ethiopia.

China

Frederick H. Chaffee et al., eds., *Area Handbook for Republic of China* (Washington, DC: United States Government, 1982).
A careful treatment of all spheres of modern Chinese life, from population, to education, to governance.

David S. G. Goodman, ed., *Groups and Politics in the People's Republic of China* (Armonk: M. E. Sharpe, 1984).
Special-interest groups and the Chinese government, 1949–1976, are explored.

A. James Gregor, *The China Connection: U.S. Policy and the People's Republic of China* (Stanford: Hoover Institution Press, 1986).
Foreign relations of China and the United States.

Alfred Kuo-liang Ho, *Developing the Economy of the People's Republic of China* (New York: Praeger, 1982).
A discussion of the economic conditions and policies in China beginning in 1949.

D. Gale Johnson, *Progress of Economic Reform in the People's Republic of China* (Washington, DC: American Enterprise Institute, 1982).
Economic policy in China since 1949.

Suzanne Ogden, *China's Unresolved Issues: Politics, Development and Culture* (Englewood Cliffs: Prentice Hall, 1992).
A complete review of economic and cultural issues in modern China.

Hong Kong

Ambrose Y. C. King and Rance P. L. Lee, eds., *Social Life and Development in Hong Kong* (Hong Kong: Chinese University Press, 1981).
Essays on the nature of modern Hong Kong society.

Lennox A. Mills, *British Rule in Eastern Asia: A Study of Contemporary Government and Economic Development in British Malaya and Hong Kong* (New York: Russell & Russell, 1970).
A description of Britain's administrative practices in Hong Kong and the former British Malaya.

A. J. Youngson, ed., *China and Hong Kong: The Economic Nexus* (Hong Kong: Oxford University Press, 1983).
A description of the close economic relationship between China and Hong Kong.

Indonesia

Frederica M. Bunge, *Indonesia: A Country Study* (Washington, DC: United States Government, 1983).
An excellent review of the outlines of Indonesian history and culture, including politics and national security.

Audrey R. Kahin, ed., *Regional Dynamics of the Indonesian Revolution: Unity from Diversity* (Honolulu: University of Hawaii Press, 1985).
A history of Indonesia since the end of World War II, with separate chapters on selected islands.

Hamish McConald, *Suharto's Indonesia* (Australia: The Dominion Press, 1980).
The story of the rise of Suharto and the manner in which he controlled the political and military life of the country beginning in 1965.

M. C. Richlefs, *A History of Modern Indonesia c. 1300 to the Present* (Bloomington: Indiana University Press, 1981).
A detailed review of Indonesian history, especially the early colonization era and the creation of a united Indonesian state.

Japan

Marjorie Wall Bingham and Susan Hill Gross, *Women in Japan* (Minnesota: Glenhurst Publications, Inc., 1987).
A historical review of Japanese women's roles in Japan.

Ray F. Downs, ed., *Japan Yesterday and Today* (Toronto: Bantam, 1970).

A good source for abstracts of important documents, speeches, and commentary related to Japanese history.

Benjamin Duke, *The Japanese School: Lessons for Industrial America* (New York: Praeger, 1986).

A description of the nature of modern Japanese schooling.

Tadashi Fukutake, *Japanese Rural Society* (Ithaca: Cornell University Press, 1967).

A sociological study of the Japanese countryside.

Tetsuya Kataoka and Ramon H. Myers, *Defending an Economic Superpower: Reassessing the U.S.–Japan Security Alliance* (Boulder: Westview Press, 1989).

The security alliance is evaluated in light of Japan's economic strength and changes in the international alignment of military, political, and economic power.

Solomon B. Levine and Koji Taira, eds., "Japan's External Economic Relations: Japanese Perspectives," special issue of *The Annals of the American Academy of Political and Social Science,* January 1991.

An excellent overview of the origin and future of Japan's economic relations with the rest of the world, especially Asia.

Chie Nakane, *Japanese Society* (Berkeley: University of California Press, 1970).

A classic study of modern Japanese society by a Japanese sociologist.

Nippon Steel Corporation, *Nippon: The Land and Its People* (Japan: Gakuseisha Publishing Co., 1984).

An overview of modern Japan in both English and Japanese.

J. A. A. Stockwin, *Japan: Divided Politics in a Growth Economy* (New York: W. W. Norton & Co., 1975).

An Australian political scientist's description of the workings of Japanese politics.

Ezra F. Vogel, *Japan as Number One: Lessons for America* (Tokyo: Charles E. Tuttle Co., 1979).

A challenge to the United States to catch up to Japanese education and commerce.

___, *Japan's New Middle Class* (Berkeley: University of California Press, 1963).

One of the best studies of the nature of life among the middle classes in Japan.

North and South Korea

Korean Overseas Information Service, *A Handbook of Korea* (Seoul: Seoul International Publishing House, 1987).

A description of modern South Korea, including social welfare, foreign relations, and culture. The early history of the entire Korean Peninsula is also discussed.

___, *Korean Arts and Culture* (Seoul: Seoul International Publishing House, 1986).

A beautifully illustrated introduction to the rich cultural life of modern South Korea.

___, *Korean History* (Seoul: Seoul International Publishing House, 1986).

A brief, beautifully illustrated review of Korean culture and history.

Callus A. MacDonald, *Korea: The War Before Vietnam* (New York: The Free Press, 1986).

A detailed account of the military events in Korea between 1950 and 1953, including a careful analysis of the United States' decision to send troops to the peninsula.

Laos

Arthur J. Dommen, *Laos: Keystone of Indochina* (Boulder: Westview Press, 1985).

A short history and review of current events in Laos.

Martin Stuart-Fox, ed., *Contemporary Laos: Studies in the Politics and Society of the Lao People's Democratic Republic* (St. Lucia: University of Queensland Press, 1982).

Events in Laos since 1975.

Macau

Charles Ralph Boxer, *The Portuguese Seaborne Empire, 1415–1825* (New York: A. A. Knopf, 1969).

A history of Portugal's colonies, including Macau.

W. G. Clarence-Smith, *The Third Portuguese Empire, 1825– 1975* (Manchester: Manchester University Press, 1985).

A history of Portugal's colonies, including Macau.

Malaysia

Richard Clutterbuck, *Conflict and Violence in Singapore and Malaysia, 1945–1983* (Boulder: Westview Press, 1985).

The communist challenge to the stability of Singapore and Malaysia in the early years of their independence from Great Britain.

Harry Miller, *A Short History of Malaysia* (New York: Frederick A. Praeger, 1965).

A history of Malaysia, from its earliest beginnings until the creation of the modern state in 1963.

R. S. Milne, *Malaysia: Tradition, Modernity, and Islam* (Boulder: Westview Press, 1986).
A general overview of the nature of modern Malaysian society.

Myanmar (Burma)

Michael Aung-Thwin, *Pagan: The Origins of Modern Burma* (Honolulu: University of Hawaii Press, 1985).
A treatment of the religious and political ideology of the Burmese people and the effect of ideology on the economy and politics of the modern state.

David I. Steinberg, *Burma, a Socialist Nation of Southeast Asia* (Boulder: Westview Press, 1982).
A description of how socialism has been meshed with traditional Burmese life.

New Zealand

Roderic Alley, ed., *New Zealand and the Pacific* (Boulder: Westview Press, 1984).
Focus on New Zealand's economic and foreign policy as well as excellent treatment of issues affecting the islands of the South Pacific.

Joan Metge, *The Maoris of New Zealand Rautahi* (London: Routledge & Kegan Paul Ltd., 1976).
An introduction to Maori life before and after European contact.

W. H. Oliver with B. R. Williams, eds., *The Oxford History of New Zealand* (Wellington: Oxford University Press, 1981).
The story of the early settlement of New Zealand by Polynesians and its subsequent colonization by Europeans; detailed coverage of events until the end of World War II, with less in-depth treatment thereafter.

Papua New Guinea

Timothy P. Bayliss-Smith and Richard G. Feachem, eds., *Subsistence and Survival: Rural Ecology in the Pacific* (London: Academic Press, 1977).
Environmental conditions in Papua New Guinea and Melanesia.

Robert J. Gordon and Mervyn J. Meggitt, *Law and Order in the New Guinea Highlands: Encounters with Enga* (Hanover: University Press of New England, 1985).
Tribal law and warfare in Papua New Guinea.

Kenneth E. Read, *Return to the High Valley: Coming Full Circle* (Berkeley: University of California Press, 1986).
An anthropological study of life in Papua New Guinea.

The Philippines

Frederica M. Bunge, ed., *Philippines: A Country Study* (Washington, DC: United States Government, 1984).
Description and analysis of the economic, security, political, and social systems of the Philippines, including maps, statistical charts, and reproduction of important documents. An extensive bibliography is included.

David Joel Steinberg, *The Philippines: A Singular and A Plural Place* (Boulder: Westview Press, 1982).
An excellent overview of the history, politics, and culture of contemporary Philippines. It includes an extensive annotated bibliography.

Singapore

Robert E. Gamer, *The Politics of Urban Development in Singapore* (Ithaca: Cornell University Press, 1972).
A discussion of Singapore's efforts at urban renewal and city planning.

Hafiz Mirza, *Multinationals and the Growth of the Singapore Economy* (New York: St. Martin's Press, 1986).
Foreign companies and their impact on modern Singapore.

Garry Rodan, *The Political Economy of Singapore's Industrialization: National State and International Capital* (New York: St. Martin's Press, 1989).
An analysis of the sources of Singapore's amazing rise in economic productivity.

South Pacific

C. Beeby and N. Fyfe, "The South Pacific Nuclear Free Zone Treaty," Victoria University of Wellington *Law Review,* Vol. 17, No. 1, pp. 33–51 (February 1987).
A good review of nuclear issues in the Pacific.

Ernest S. Dodge, *Islands and Empires: Western Impact on the Pacific and East Asia* (Minneapolis: University of Minnesota Press, 1976).
Early European explorers' impact on the social values and economic fortunes of the peoples of the South Pacific.

William S. Livingston and Wm. Roger Louis, eds., *Australia, New Zealand, and the Pacific Islands Since the First World War* (Austin: University of Texas Press, 1979).

An assessment of significant historical and political developments in Australia, New Zealand, and the Pacific Islands since 1917.

Taiwan

Philip S. Cox, ed., *United States–Taiwan Relations and Western Pacific Security: A Study in Pacific Security Problems* (Washington, DC: American Foreign Policy Institute, 1984).
Issues affecting the security of the Pacific region around Taiwan.

Yu-ming Shaw, *Beyond the Economic Miracle: Reflections on the Republic of China on Taiwan, Mainland China and Sino-American Relations* (Taipei: Kwang Hwa Publishing Co., 1989).
Economic conditions and government economic policy in Taiwan and the People's Republic of China, from the early 1970s to the present.

Mary Sheridan and Janet W. Salaff, eds., *Lives: Chinese Working Women* (Bloomington: Indiana University Press, 1984).
Case studies of working-class women in Hong Kong, Taiwan, and China.

Taiwan: An Isle of Abundance and Beauty (Department of Information, Taiwan Provincial Government, Republic of China, n.d.).
A beautifully prepared summary of all aspects of modern Taiwan. It is written in both English and Chinese.

Richard W. Wilson, Amy Auerbacher Wilson, Sidney L. Greenblatt, eds., *Value Change in Chinese Society* (New York: Praeger, 1979).
Changes in popular culture in Taiwan and China.

Thailand

Ganganath Jha, *Foreign Policy of Thailand* (New Delhi: Radiant Publishers, 1979).
Thailand's political relations with its immediate neighbors and the world.

Ross Prizzia, *Thailand in Transition: The Role of Oppositional Forces* (Honolulu: University of Hawaii Press, 1985).
Government management of political opposition in Thailand.

B. J. Terwiel, *A History of Modern Thailand, 1767–1942* (St. Lucia: University of Queensland Press, 1983).
The history of Thailand during the crucial years of European colonization in Southeast Asia.

David K. Wyatt, *Thailand: A Short History* (New Haven: Yale University Press, 1984).
A history of Thailand from its beginnings to the present.

Vietnam

Ronald J. Cima, ed., *Vietnam: A Country Study* (Washington, DC: United States Government, 1989).
An overview of modern Vietnam, with emphasis on the origins, values, and lifestyles of the Vietnamese people.

John Pimlott, ed., *Vietnam: The History and the Tactics* (New York: Crescent Books, 1982).
A pictorial history of the Vietnam War, including a review of the events leading up to it.

Andrew J. Rotter, *The Path to Vietnam: Origins of the American Commitment to Southeast Asia* (Ithaca: Cornell University Press, 1987).
A discussion of the events and the thinking of key political leaders that catapulted the United States into the Vietnam War.

D. R. SarDeSai, *Vietnam, The Struggle for National Identity* (Boulder: Westview Press, 1992).
A good treatment of ethnicity in Vietnam and a national history up to the current involvement in Cambodia.

PERIODICALS AND CURRENT EVENTS

The Annals of the American Academy of Political and Social Science
c/o Sage Publications, Inc.
2455 Teller Rd.
Newbury Park, CA 91320
Selected issues focus on the Pacific Rim; there is an extensive book-review section. Special issues are as follows:
"The Pacific Region: Challenges to Policy and Theory" (September 1989).
"China's Foreign Relations" (January 1992).
"Japan's External Economic Relations: Japanese Perspectives" (January 1991).

The Asian Wall Street Journal, Dow Jones & Company, Inc.
A daily business newspaper focusing on Asian markets.

Canada and Hong Kong Update
Joint Centre for Asia Pacific Studies
Suite 270, York Lanes
York University

4700 Keele St.
North York, Ontario M3J 1P3, Canada
A source of information about Hong Kong emigration.

Current History: A World Affairs Journal
Focuses on one country or region in each issue; the emphasis is on international and domestic politics.

The Economist
25 St. James's St.
London, England
A newsmagazine with insightful commentary on international issues affecting the Pacific Rim.

Indochina Interchange
Suite 1801
220 West 42nd St.
New York, NY 10036
A publication of the U.S.–Indochina Reconciliation Project. An excellent source of information about assistance programs for Laos, Cambodia, and Vietnam.

The Japan Foundation Newsletter
The Japan Foundation
Park Building
3-6 Kioi-cho
Chiyoda-ku
Tokyo 102, Japan
A quarterly with research reports, book reviews, and announcements of interest to Japan specialists.

Japan Quarterly
Asahi Shimbun
5-3-2 Tsukiji
Chuo-ku
Tokyo 104, Japan
A quarterly journal, in English, covering political, cultural, and sociological aspects of modern Japanese life.

The Japan Times
The Japan Times Ltd.
C.P.O. Box 144
Tokyo 100-91, Japan
Excellent coverage, in English, of news reported in the Japanese press.

The Journal of Asian Studies
Association for Asian Studies
1 Lane Hall
University of Michigan
Ann Arbor, MI 48109
Formerly *The Far Eastern Quarterly;* scholarly articles on Asia, South Asia, and Southeast Asia.

Journal of Southeast Asian Studies
Singapore University Press
Singapore
Formerly the *Journal of Southeast Asian History;* scholarly articles on all aspects of modern Southeast Asia.

Korea Economic Report
Yoido
P.O. Box 963
Seoul 150-609
South Korea
An economic magazine for people doing business in Korea.

The Korea Herald
2-12, 3-ga Hoehyon-dong
Chung-gu
Seoul, South Korea
World news coverage, in English, with focus on events affecting the Korean Peninsula.

The Korea Times
The Korea Times Hankook Ilbo
Seoul, South Korea
Coverage of world news, with emphasis on events affecting Asia and the Korean Peninsula.

Malaysia Industrial Digest
Malaysian Industrial Development Authority (MIDA)
6th Floor
Industrial Promotion Division
Wisma Damansara, Jalan Semantan
50490 Kuala Kumpur, Malaysia
A source of statistics on manufacturing in Malaysia; of interest to those wishing to become more knowledgeable in the business and industry of the Pacific Rim.

News from Japan
Embassy of Japan
Japan–U.S. News and Communication
Suite 520
900 17th St., NW
Washington, DC 20006
A twice-monthly newsletter with news briefs from the Embassy of Japan on issues affecting Japan–U.S. relations.

Newsweek
444 Madison Ave.
New York, NY 10022
A weekly magazine with news and commentary on national and world events.

The New York Times
229 West 43rd St.
New York, NY 10036

A daily newspaper with excellent coverage of world events.

Pacific Affairs

The University of British Columbia

Vancouver, BC V6T 1W5

Canada

An international journal on Asia and the Pacific, including reviews of recent books about the region.

South China Morning Post

Tong Chong Street

Hong Kong

Daily coverage of world news, with emphasis on Hong Kong, China, Taiwan, and other Asian countries.

Time

Time-Life Building

Rockefeller Center

New York, NY 10020

A weekly newsmagazine with news and commentary on national and world events.

U.S. News & World Report

2400 N St. NW

Washington, DC 20037

A weekly newsmagazine with news and commentary on national and world events.

The World & I: A Chronicle of our Changing Era

2800 New York Ave., NE

Washington, DC 20002

A monthly review of current events plus excellent articles on various regions of the world.

Sources for Statistical Reports

U.S. State Department, *Background Notes* (1994).

C.I.A. *World Factbook* (1994).

World Bank, *World Bank Atlas* (1994).

World Bank, *World Development Report* (1994).

UN *Population and Vital Statistics Report* (January 1995).

World Statistics in Brief (1994).

Statistical Yearbook (1994).

The Statesman's Yearbook (1994–1995).

Population Reference Bureau, *World Population Data Sheet* (1994).

World Almanac (1995).

Demographic Yearbook (1994).

Index